Archaeology

Archaeology

David Hurst Thomas
The American Museum of Natural History

Illustrations by Dennis O'Brien

Holt, Rinehart and Winston

New York
Chicago
San Francisco
Dallas
Montreal
Toronto
London
Sydney

I wrote much of the manuscript for this book while directing excavations at Gatecliff Shelter and on St. Catherines Island. The finished product is sincerely dedicated to some very special friends and colleagues who both encouraged and tolerated me during those trying and sometimes moody months.

You are appreciated.

ACKNOWLEDGMENT is gratefully made to the following to include illustrations in the book: *p. 69:* copyright © 1969 by the University of Texas Press; *p. 76:* adapted with permission of the Macmillan Company, Inc., and copyright © 1967 by William A. McDonald; *p. 127:* the American Anthropological Association; *p. 184:* copyright © 1966 by the American Association for the Advancement of Science; *p. 240:* copyright © 1972 by Annual Reviews, Inc.; *pp. 267, 348, 349, 353:* the Society for American Archaeology; *p. 331:* copyright © 1972 by the University of Texas Press; *pp. 367, 368, 370:* copyright © 1972 by the American Association for the Advancement of Science.

The table on pp. 204–5 is reprinted with permission from R. M. Clark, "A calibration curve for radioactive dates," *Antiquity,* 49, 251–66.

Library of Congress Cataloging in Publication Data

Thomas, David Hurst.
   Archaeology.

   Bibliography: p. 471.
   Includes index.
   1. Archaeology. I. Title.
CC165.T48   930'.1   78-27568
ISBN 0-03-019926-3

Preface

In each human heart are a tiger, a pig, an ass and
a nightingale. Diversity of character is due to
their unequal activity.

Ambrose Bierce

The objective of most archaeology textbooks is to provide an encyclopedic
view of the subject, and authors generally accomplish that objective in an
impersonal, erudite style. This mode of presentation is fine, often enlightening,
and certainly a matter of individual taste and style.

But I can't do it that way. Little about archaeology is impersonal to me, and
my biases are reflected here. In the Prologue, for example, I tell the tale of how
Gatecliff Shelter was discovered, indulging in personal narrative to convey
something of what archaeology really *feels* like. Despite what some may tell you,
archaeology is more than concepts, theory, methods, and typology. Archaeology
is also dust and discouragement. But above all, archaeology is—or should be—
fun. Throughout these pages, I keep the discussion on as personal a level as
seems appropriate. I write more or less as I speak because archaeological

literature has had a tendency to become polluted with the dry and stuffy, and I don't like that.

So it is that this text unavoidably reflects my own personality. In the first chapter, for instance, I describe the history and development of American archaeology. Because individual archaeologists can often be as instructive as the archaeology itself, the history of American archaeology is presented in terms of seven well-known archaeologists. The selections are once again personal, reflecting my own mind-set and experience. Other archaeologists would doubtless choose other people who represent different outlooks. This is what I mean about this being a largely personal book.

You will also note that the text is liberally sprinkled with quotes, once again a matter of personal taste. The hope is to lighten the tone and to inject (somebody else's) humor now and again.

> **I quote others only the better to express myself.**
> *Michel de Montaigne*

The scope of the book can be defined in a single phrase: contemporary American archaeology. The term *contemporary* poses few problems—I mean right now, the late 1970s. By *American,* I refer to the brand of archaeology currently taught and practiced at major universities and museums within the Americas. In this sense, "American archaeology" is promulgated throughout the world, since scholars always reflect their educational background, regardless of where they ply their trade.

The term *archaeology* is meant in the broad sense. What I say in these pages should be relevant to all of modern archaeology, whether prehistoric or historic, traditional or radical, domestic or foreign. Certain concepts apply throughout the discipline. But as I warned earlier, this is not an encyclopedia, and I have been selective in my treatment. Much of the presentation proceeds in terms of prehistoric North American archaeology. I rely rather heavily, for instance, on my own work in the Great Basin and on St. Catherines Island; these data are simply most familiar to me. But the text is certainly not restricted to North American archaeology; in it you will find examples from Mesoamerica, South America, Europe, Africa, and Asia.

I feel perfectly free to interject my own views on the condition of contemporary theory and practice in archaeology. I firmly believe that archaeology can, and should, be a science—that is, archaeological inquiry should proceed according to canons of established scientific methods. Chapter 2 provides the framework of what science *is* and how such procedures are applied to specific archaeological problems. But to me, the philosophy of science is not a particularly rarified and abstract issue; I see science as standard operating procedure used every day by practicing archaeologists. To illustrate the scientific method I present Heinrich Schliemann's search for Homer's Troy as an extended case study. Schliemann is, I am well aware, an unorthodox choice for illustrating the workings of scientific archaeology. Wasn't he after all a pothunting treasure seeker and a first-rate scoundrel? Schliemann's archaeology has, to be sure, its unsavory aspects, but it remains true that he employed the fundamentals of scientific inquiry in his search for Troy (even though he didn't realize it).

> **S**cience is nothing but developed perception,
> integrated intent, common sense rounded out
> and minutely articulated.
> *George Santayana*

Archaeology's overall framework is also largely a matter of personal preference and opinion. I have attempted to tell the story of contemporary archaeology, as practiced by those trained in the Americas. These pages attempt to cut through the tangle of archaeological theory to expose a single, consistent research strategy. American archaeology has recently emerged from a theoretical revolution of sorts, and many colleagues can unfortunately see only conceptual anomie on the archaeological horizon. If we have the *new archaeologists,* the thinking goes, then we must also have the opposing traditional archaeologists. Throw in the conservation archaeologists, astroarchaeologists, and the cognitive archaeologists for good measure and what do we have? An archaeological mess! Many seem to feel that there is no consistency within modern archaeological thinking.

This perspective is dead wrong. There is indeed a single theoretical framework that overarches American archaeology, and this is why this book is written the way it is. As I see it, archaeology is characterized by three hierarchical goals: construct cultural chronologies, reconstruct past lifeways, and understand cultural processes. Part One explains this framework in some detail, correlating it with major trends in anthropological thinking. The next three parts amplify these objectives. As a prelude to this discussion, let me make a couple of points explicit at the start.

One hot spot is the *new archaeology.* Is this a textbook on the new archaeology?

The answer is no. As I explain in Chapter 1, the new archaeology is a historical rather than an evolutionary episode—a movement that began in the late 1950s and lasted little more than a decade. The new archaeologists have contributed some important ideas to contemporary archaeological theory, but much in American archaeology evolved prior to and wholly independent of the new archaeological movement. This book integrates both.

A related point: no matter how influential individual personalities may seem, the present state of archaeological theory would not be radically different had the major figures in the new archaeology pursued careers in different fields.

For the most part, archaeological theory evolves independently of the identities of individual archaeologists. I reject the Great Man Theory of History, and Chapter 1 explains why. The new archaeology is a historical entity, firmly rooted in time and space. I have not written a history book; I have written a book which attempts to cope with current archaeological thought in the Americas. To be sure, the new archaeologists of the 1960s made key contributions to the status of that thinking. So did Thomas Jefferson in 1787. The new archaeology makes fascinating history, but I am more concerned with the evolution and status of contemporary archaeological theory and practice. This is why the term *new archaeology* does not appear in this book after Chapter 1—that's a promise.

You will also find that these pages contain a rather heavy dose of anthropology, more than is customary in an introductory archaeology textbook. I say this as a warning, not an apology. One simply cannot understand the trends and directions of contemporary archaeology without a solid grounding in the specifics of contemporary anthropology. The practical archaeologist needs to understand the major questions in modern anthropology before attempting to provide answers to these questions. Current anthropology is a mixed bag, lumping together a number of different mainstreams of thought. Some of these anthropological mainstreams are downright critical for the development of contemporary archaeology; other mainstreams remain practically irrelevant.

I firmly believe in the old adage that "archaeology is anthropology or it is nothing." But archaeology is not all kinds of anthropology, and we must understand how major anthropological strategies operate before we can place archaeology in its proper anthropological perspective. I stress anthropological theory to a much greater degree than do most writers of archaeological textbooks for this reason.

Despite the personal flavor of these pages, no book is completed by a single pair of hands. Many people have helped me, and it could not have been otherwise. I close this preface with some appropriate words of thanks.

The overall presentation was vastly improved by a carefully selected group of colleagues and friends who reviewed the entire manuscript—sometimes several drafts. My sincerest thanks go to Mark Leone, Christopher Peebles, William Rathje, J. Jefferson Reid, Thomas Riley, Payson Sheets, Patty Jo Watson, and especially William Haviland. Each contributed trenchant suggestions for the improvement of substance, style, and format. And I, like most other authors, was often too opinionated and pig-headed to follow the reviewer's advice. Although the finished product remains my own, I gratefully acknowledge the help of these people for improving the ideas and sharpening the focus.

Several others read and commented on specific sections of the manuscript, including Jane Buikstra, Phil DeVita, William G. Davis, Robert Carneiro, Jeffrey Dean, James Hill, Gregory Johnson, Alexander Marshack, Michael Schiffer, W. W. Taylor, and Joe Ben Wheat. Once again, all of their suggestions were not heeded, and I alone am responsible for shortcomings.

I am especially proud of the artwork illustrating this volume, which is the contribution of Dennis O'Brien. In addition to providing his artistic talent,

Dennis has pitched in variously as archaeological crew chief, topographer, trailblazer, long-haul trucker, and friend. I also acknowledge the assistance of Nicholas Amorosi, who prepared the original illustrations that appear as Figures 7-2, 7-3, and 7-6.

A special measure of gratitude is reserved for Jane Epstein, who prepared the index and much of the glossary; in addition, she functioned as copy editor, bibliographer, emissary, and general midwife for the manuscript. One could hardly dream of more competent assistance, even if Jane has occasional lapses in recalling the alphabet. Several others in The American Museum of Natural History deserve thanks, including Lauren Archibald, Susan Bierwirth, Joan Buttner, Lisa Reed, Margot Dembo, Barbara Krasner, Deborah Mayer, Debra Peter, Nazarie Romain, and Lisa Sherman.

Thanks are also due to the crew at Holt, Rinehart and Winston, especially Andy Askin, who initiated the project, and David Boynton, who inherited the manuscript in midstream. I am also grateful to Herman Makler for his numerous courtesies and insights along the way.

D. H. T.
St. Catherines Island, Georgia
November, 1978

Contents

2 What Is Science?   62

3 What Is Anthropology?   95

7 Sorting Cultural Things in Time   212

part **three**

Archaeology's Intermediate Objective: Reconstruct Extinct Lifeways   237

8 How People Get Their Groceries: Reconstructing Subsistence Practices   242

Why People Live Where They Live: Reconstructing Settlement Patterns 271

How People Relate to One Another: Reconstructing Social Organization 317

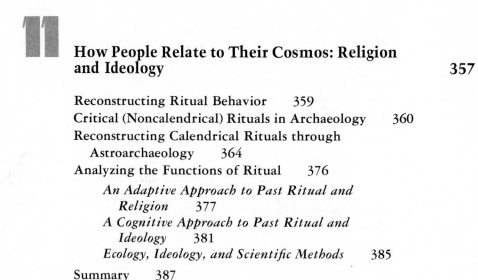

Prologue

Prehistoric, *adj.*   Belonging to an early period
and a museum.

Ambrose Bierce

This book considers some theory, some methods, and some of the working
concepts that make up today's archaeology. But all too frequently, theoretical-
methodological-conceptual discussions are too abstract, at times divorcing themselves from fact altogether; left to their own devices, theory-method concepts
can readily range too far afield. So we will keep this discussion more firmly
grounded, more down to earth.

We must consider archaeological theory-method concepts, to be sure, but
only in the context of archaeological objects. Many of the objects I discuss are
from Gatecliff Shelter, an archaeological site in the American Desert West.

Gatecliff is presented from time to time as a case study, as a collection of archaeological objects that were recovered together. But what is important here is not Gatecliff Shelter or even the archaeological objects it contained. What is important about Gatecliff is what modern archaeologists can learn from the site and its objects. Modern **archaeology**[1] is an exciting field because so much can be learned about ourselves, our humanity, and our past. But we can learn these things only by studying the objects of the past from a variety of perspectives. That is the theme of this book. You will hear it again and again.

Archaeologists do not excavate **data**; archaeologists excavate objects. Data arise only from observations made upon the objects. Each observation answers a question: How old is the site? Who were the people? What language did they speak? Was the ancient climate the same as that of today? Why did they choose to live in this particular cave? Why did they paint on the walls? Where did they go? Each question requires somewhat different observations, giving rise to different data. These observations can and are made on exactly the same objects.

The hallmark of today's archaeology is this: Objects of the past can (and should) be viewed from more than a single perspective. Each perspective answers a different question. Some people think the questions are so different that archaeologists must split themselves into major schools: the processual school vs. the normative school of archaeology; the experimental school vs. the ethnoarchaeologists; the functionalists vs. the cultural evolutionists; the theoretical archaeologists vs. the dirt archaeologists; the new archaeologists vs. the traditional archaeologists. People who think this are wrong.

I accept only one dichotomy in modern archaeology: good vs. bad archaeology. All archaeologists do not conduct the same quality of research. Some are good; others are bad. Either they can answer the questions they ask, or they cannot.

If you can do it, it ain't bragging.
D. Meredith

More than anything else, today's archaeology is flexible. The same objects are used for different purposes. Once one understands the threads of continuity that bind together today's archaeology there need be no contradictions. Gatecliff Shelter will be a recurring point of reference in this book because we can use these objects to illustrate differing perspectives on the past. Sometimes we ask questions about time; we also consider **cultural ecology**; we may ask about religion and prehistoric **social organization**; we might even compare the **prehistoric** Desert West of Nevada to the Australian desert. The objects remain the same; it is the theoretical perspective that changes.

But before we dissect the inner workings of today's archaeology, let me briefly introduce our site, Gatecliff Shelter.

How do archaeologists find their sites? How do they know where to dig? There are as many answers as there are archaeologists. Some sites have been known for centuries, "discovered" by the earliest explorers such as Coronado, de Soto, Pizarro, and Cortez. Other sites are known through oral and written traditions. The site of Tula in northern Mexico was finally identified as the prehistoric Toltec capital by tracing and testing Aztec traditions. Sites are sometimes discovered in large-scale systematic surveys in which entire valleys are scanned for refuse of prehistoric habitation. But probably the majority of archaeological sites known today have been found by accident. Hard work and luck also help.

My experiences at Gatecliff Shelter are probably typical of contemporary archaeologists working in the Americas. While a graduate student at the Davis campus of the University of California, I supported my doctoral fieldwork by conducting archaeological field schools. We offered green, untrained students the opportunity to work in the Reese River Valley in central Nevada. We made a trade. The students paid for the summer's research through their enrollment fees. They also supplied the physical labor. In return, I taught them what I could about archaeological fieldwork. The trade seemed fair; I made progress in my doctoral research, while they received training and credits toward graduation.

Twenty-three students participated in the first summer at Reese River. We spent the summer conducting a regional random sample as part of the field school sponsored by the University of Nevada. We wanted to see whether the cultural ecology of prehistoric Reese River Indians was similar to that of the historic **Shoshoni**. The modern Shoshoni no longer practice their hunting-gathering lifeway. Most have taken up ranching or farming. Because we could no longer observe the actual ecology in action we did the next best thing. We programmed a computer to reconstruct prehistoric Great Basin cultural ecology. We marshaled all the data we could about the ecology of wild plants and animals and put the information into a computer. We then programmed our records of how the Shoshoni collected these wild plants and hunted the animals. The computer proceeded to construct imaginary mathematical archaeological sites. The computer told us that if the weather was just so, if the plants responded in a certain way to this weather, if the Shoshoni gathered certain plants and killed certain animals, then their archaeological sites should look like this. That is, because there were no Shoshoni who still practiced the old ways, we asked a computer to simulate the extinct Shoshoni cultural ecology and then to translate these findings into things that archaeologists could recover.

Thus the computer gave us some hypotheses to test. We then took to the field, collecting **artifacts** to test these theories. This is where the twenty-three University of Nevada students came in. We spent six weeks climbing 12,000-foot mountains and walking arid sagebrush flats looking for archaeological sites. We wanted to see if the computer had actually been able to predict where we would find archaeological sites. Could computers really "predict the past"?[2] It was hot, dry, dusty work, and by the end of August we had located over a hundred prehistoric archaeological sites. Our fieldwork was completed for the year, and I wanted to thank the students for their efforts.

Expending the last dollars of our food budget, I hosted the crew for steak dinners in Austin, Nevada. It was our last night in camp, and even though the dusty trek to Austin took over an hour, the drive seemed worth it. We relaxed, ate our steaks, and relived our summer's work in the desert.

Austin is a small Nevada mining town, boasting fewer than 250 permanent residents. When 25 grubby archaeologists come to town for steaks and beer, the word gets around fast. Our waitress asked who was in charge, and after somebody pointed me out, she told me about her husband, Gale Peer. Mr. Peer is a mining geologist who has prospected the western mountains for forty years. There are few places he has not been. So when I met Mr. Peer, I asked him about the archaeological sites in the area. We were particularly interested in finding a cave or rockshelter in order to check our Reese River findings against a **stratified** cultural sequence. Mr. Peer replied that, yes, he had seen such a cave over in Monitor Valley, several miles east of Austin. He had not been there

Gatecliff Shelter as it appeared when first discovered in 1970.

in years, but the details stood out clearly in his mind. "You take the main dirt road south in Monitor Valley, then turn west, up one of the side canyons. I don't remember which one. As you drive along, oh, let's see, maybe ten or fifteen mile, there's a large black chert cliff. It goes straight up. A thousand feet or so. At the bottom of the cliff is a cave. Sometime, a long time ago, the Indians painted the inside of the cave. There are pictures of people and animals, plus a lot of writing I don't understand. Then the top of the shelter caved in. Maybe in an earthquake. There's not much of the cave left. Drive out there when you get a chance. I'd like to know what's in that cave."

I asked Mr. Peer to draw me a map, which he did on his business card. He could show me exactly where the cave was relative to the canyon, but he was not sure which canyon. We talked for a while longer, then I thanked him for the tip. Many archaeologists find their sites in just this manner, and I hoped that Mr. Peer's advice was as good as his memory seemed to be. Maybe this was the deep cave site I'd been looking for. But of course I had heard of a dozen similar caves, all of which proved uninteresting when investigated.

That was the last night of the field season. We finished our steaks, drained the last beer, and headed for our tents. Camp was broken the next day and we returned to civilization. The students went home; I continued my graduate studies at the university. But throughout that academic year I kept thinking about Mr. Peer's cave. Sometimes I wanted to drop everything to explore Monitor Valley. But pressing schoolwork kept me from breaking away, even for a weekend. And besides, the mountains of Monitor Valley tower to 11,000 feet, and the fall snows often last until late spring. Even if I knew where it was, the cave would be snowed in until at least April. So I toiled away at the computer center, sometimes thinking of an imaginary cave somewhere in the remote Nevada desert.

Finally the next summer arrived. Once again I took college students to help me at Reese River, this time supported by the University of California. Before the field school started, my wife, Trudy, and I drove to central Nevada, looking for a new campsite, and hoping to find the cave Mr. Peer had mentioned almost a year before. We knew the cave must be in a canyon—if we only knew which canyon. We had fifteen canyons to choose from.

So we started looking. Beginning at the southern end of Monitor Valley, we drove up and down each side canyon, working our way slowly northward. The roads were so primitive that we might examine only a single canyon all day. And the weather was no ally. Although it was June, we were snowed into our campsite for three days. When the sun came out, the snow melted and washed out the roads. At times it took all our concentration to remember why we were there.

But we were haunted by a cave. Mr. Peer seemed too good a geologist and observer of nature simply to imagine a shelter covered with prehistoric paintings. We kept looking. Each canyon seemed to have promise. We would see something, stop the truck, scramble up the hillside. But each "cave" turned out to be a shadow, an abandoned mine shaft, or just a jumble of rocks. The cave with rock art eluded us.

After almost a week of this we came upon Mill Canyon. It had no greater potential than the previous ten canyons we had searched. It was just the next on the list. The road was worse than most, however, so we had to inch across a narrow hogback down into the rocky canyon. Even in four-wheel drive our truck slid badly downhill, and the road was so steep that it seemed barely glued to the mountainside. Finally, as we started up the flat canyon bottom, we saw a large black cliff looming around the bend. The cliff face was riddled with small caves and rock shelters. I commented that, if we were in Arizona, each of those caves would be walled with Pueblo masonry and connected by wooden ladders. But this was Nevada, and we knew that the ancestors of the Shoshoni never built such structures. And sure enough, the caves were empty save for the occasional coyote scat, owl pellet, or packrat nest. The cliff is almost a half mile long, and we became discouraged as we moved up the canyon, scanning each of the small alcoves for **pictographs**. There was only one last section to examine, where the black cliff face disappears beneath the **alluvial** bottomland of Mill Canyon. We saw a dark shadow near the bottom, but a dozen similar shadows were just that. Shadows.

It was not until we reached the mouth of the cave that we saw the paintings. There they were, just as Mr. Peer had told us almost a year before: small human figures, painted in red and yellow. In another corner were cryptic designs of white and black. And, yes, the roof had caved in long ago. Half the cave floor was buried beneath tons of chert. A couple of boulders were the size of the truck we had just driven up the canyon.

Archaeologists react to discovery in different ways. Trudy ran back to the truck for the cameras to photograph the cave art. Pictographs are her specialty. Being more inclined to dirt and rocks, I scoured the floor of the shelter, looking for artifacts, animal bones, pieces of basketry. Anything. But no matter how hard I looked, I found nothing remotely suggesting that prehistoric people had lived in the small shelter. Of course there was the rock art, but pictograph caves are sometimes ceremonial, with no habitation remains at all.

Our excavation equipment was packed in the truck, so we decided to first have lunch, then dig a small test in the floor of the cave. Old World archaeologists call such exploratory excavations **sondages**; I always liked the ring of that word. What class! In Nevada, we just call them test pits. We set out a small square, 50 centimeters on a side, and I scraped away the rocks and rat dung with my trowel, noting only a few small pieces of rabbit bone. Scooping everything into buckets, I carried them outside where Trudy screened the dusty soil. Standard procedure.

We dug for most of the afternoon, stopping only after I could no longer reach the bottom of the test pit. Ours was a pretty meager haul. Several pieces of broken bone, a few of which were charred by fire. We found about a dozen stone **flakes**, probably the debris from manufacturing skinning knives or arrowheads. At least we knew that one prehistoric **flintknapper** had paused in the small cave to ply his craft. But this was not particularly startling. The **rock art** had already told of sporadic visits to the cave. We were looking for something more.

Across the sagebrush campfire that night we evaluated our find. The rock art was pleasing. Only two similar sites were known in the central Great Basin. Our photographs could be studied and results compared with sites known elsewhere. The stones and bones from our test pit were suggestive, but the small cave did not seem to be the deep shelter we hoped for. The **midden** seemed only two or three feet deep, and the **strata** were probably mixed. Indians often dug pits for storage, cleared areas for sleeping, and scooped out hearths for fires. Some caves are so jumbled they look as though a rototiller had churned the artifacts. The results of our test pit were equivocal.

We traveled to Reese River the next day, to be joined by the forty-two students enrolled in the summer field course. About a month was spent on my doctoral fieldwork at Reese River. Once I was sure we would finish that project I dispatched a small crew to excavate in Monitor Valley. By that time we had

Early excavation at Gatecliff, showing the method of test trenching.

heard of two or three other caves, so I assigned a few students to test these. If they had the time, they were to return to the Mill Canyon site and sink a larger test unit. A 50-centimeter square is hardly an adequate sample of an archaeological site.

To keep abreast of the progress in both valleys, I commuted. Spend three days in Reese River, drive four hours to Monitor Valley and spend three days there. Then return to Reese River. The Monitor Valley excavations were ahead of schedule, so I asked one of the young crew chiefs, Brian Hatoff, to take a couple of people and work the Mill Canyon cave. When I returned the next week, they had finished their test units, and they laid out the findings for me.

They had excavated a full meter-square test unit, digging down about two meters. The site was much deeper than I had thought. They had to stop because the excavators could no longer climb out of the square hole. Their notes described four broken arrowheads, hundreds of bone fragments including a bighorn sheep skull, several bifacially chipped stone knives, dozens of flakes, a grinding stone, and three small, enigmatic flat rocks with faint scratchings on them. We were encouraged, but had run out of time. The summer was over. The Mill Canyon site was added to our list of "possibles" for excavation during the next field season.

Hatoff's field notes refer to the "Mill Canyon site." Discussing the find with a friend from the U.S. Geological Survey, I learned that the spectacular black cliff was called the "Gatecliff formation." Marshall Kay, a well-known Columbia University geologist, had worked in Mill Canyon several years before, studying the chert and dolomite outcrops. Kay coined the term "Gatecliff" to describe the way in which the chert cliff constricted the canyon into a bottleneck or "gate." I liked this name better than "Mill Canyon Shelter." One of archaeology's minor thrills is to get to name one's discoveries. We recorded the site in the archives of the Nevada State Museum: 26 Ny301.[3] The site now had a name and number.

Gatecliff Shelter came to occupy several years of my life. The archaeological deposits are not two or three feet deep, as I had initially thought. Gatecliff is forty feet deep, apparently the deepest rockshelter in the Americas. The strata are not mixed as I first feared. The site had been periodically inundated by flash floods. The surging water laid down thick layers of mud, forming an impenetrable cap of rock-hard silt. This flooding occurred at least a dozen times, stratifying the deposits into horizontal "floors." Gatecliff had what textbooks describe as "layer-cake stratigraphy." The shelter had been occupied for much more than the last few centuries, as I had thought at first. Gatecliff was old, at least 8,000 years old, as **radiocarbon** tests later established. Prehistoric pollen spoke of the past environments in Monitor Valley. Two large "bone beds" covered the floors of the shelter some six hundred years ago.

The American Museum of Natural History sent five large field expeditions to Gatecliff Shelter. Over 200 people helped excavate the site. In addition to helping finance the fieldwork, the National Geographic Society prepared an

Gatecliff Shelter after four years of excavation. Excavators are exposing a campsite that was occupied about 1500 B.C. (*courtesy of the National Geographic Society*).

One of the deep stratigraphic sections at Gatecliff. The excavators are mapping the sidewalls in strata deposited roughly 8000 years ago. They are standing about 35 feet below the original ground level (*courtesy of the National Geographic Society*).

Artist's rendition of Gatecliff Shelter, after seven years of excavation.

Excavating the basal strata at Gatecliff Shelter using the bucket brigade method (*courtesy of the National Geographic Society*).

educational film about the site. They also wrote a book about our excavations at Gatecliff.[4] The *New York Times* wrote about Gatecliff. So did *The New Yorker* magazine. Then there was television and radio. Even a United States congressman became involved in the struggle to preserve the site. Gatecliff was on the map.

WHAT EXACTLY IS GATECLIFF SHELTER?

Gatecliff is antlers, **anvilstones**, arrowheads, **atlatls**, **awls**, baskets beads, **bifaces**, blankets, blanks, bones, bows, **burins**, **caches**, **cairns**, ceramics, charcoal, chisels, choppers, **coprolites**, **cores**, **crescents**, **denticulates**, dice, digging sticks, drills, effigies, **endscrapers**, and **eoliths**.

Gatecliff is also feathers, feces, **fetishes**, firehearths, flakers, flints, foreshafts, **gastroliths**, gouges, **gravers**, grinding stones, **Haliotis**, hammerstones, hearths, heirlooms, **hematite**, horncores, incised slates, insects, jars, jasper, jewelry, jugs, knives, knots, lances, living floors, manos, manuports, mats, **metates**, **microblades**, **mortars**, needles, nets, **nocks**, nuts, obsidian, **ocher**, Olivella, **ollas**, ornaments, paint palettes, pendants, pestles, **phytoliths**, pictographs, pine nuts, pipes, pollen, potsherds, **projectile points**, **Promontory pegs**, quartz crystals, **quids**, rabbit robes, rattles, reeds, rock art, ropes, **roughouts**, **scapula saws**, scrapers, seeds, **shaft straighteners**, shaman's bundles, sherds, **sidescrapers**, sinew, silt, snail shells, snares, soil, **spokeshaves**, stones, strata, tablets, **talismans**, talus, teeth, thongs, tools, twine, turquoise, **ungulates**, **unifaces**, utilized flakes, **varves**, vessels, **warps**, **wefts**, **whetstones**, **wickerwork**, **xerophytes**, yarn, and **zoomorphs**.

Gatecliff is a collection of archaeological objects. The cultural objects are made of chipped or ground stone, of bone, plant fibers, tanned hides, shells, and turquoise. Archaeologists have a name for such objects: **artifacts**. Archaeological sites contain other objects not made by man. These objects relate to the natural environment, and archaeologists term such objects as **ecofacts**. Prehistoric pollen grains are ecofacts; so are food bones and piñon pine hulls.

Gatecliff Shelter is a collection of archaeological objects, but it is more than that. We see collections of archaeological objects in virtually every small-town saloon in the West. Sometimes the collection is just a bunch of arrowheads in a cigar box. More aesthetically minded collectors arrange their arrowheads in decorative plaques. I have seen large pictures constructed as mosaics of brightly colored arrowheads. Sometimes the pictures are of Indian chiefs, with turquoise beads for eyes.

These frames are full of prehistoric artifacts, but the saloons are not prehistoric archaeological sites.[5] The reason for this is simple: the artifacts are isolates, objects displayed without context. When we dug the dust off Gatecliff we found prehistoric implements and ecofacts where they were discarded by their makers. The artifacts were **in situ**—in place. The artifacts had context.

So as an archaeological site, Gatecliff Shelter had two important attributes:

1. Gatecliff contained objects of the past.
2. The objects of the past are found in their prehistoric context.

This is all that matters in archaeology: objects and contexts. All else is secondary.

> **N**ow I understand everything.
> *Saul Bellow*

NOTES

1. Words set in boldface type are defined in the Glossary at the end of the text.

2. This fieldwork has been discussed in a short book entitled *Predicting the Past* (Thomas 1974, Chapter 5).

3. "26" means Nevada (because it places number 26 in alphabetical order of the 48 continental states); "Ny" is the abbreviation for Nye County; and the shelter was the 301st site located in Nye County. This numbering system is used throughout the United States.

4. The National Geographic film is entitled "Gatecliff: An American Indian Rock Shelter"; Gatecliff is also discussed in *Clues to America's Past,* published by the National Geographic Society in 1976.

5. The saloons are, of course, archaeological sites relating to the midtwentieth century.

part **one**

Anthropology, Science, and Archaeology

The principle of culture already gives
anthropology a viewpoint of enormous range,
a center for coordination of most phenomena
that relate to man. And we anthropologists
feel that this is only a beginning.
Alfred L. Kroeber

Archaeological objects vary. So do archaeological contexts. Deciphering the meaning of the
objects and the nature of the context is the business of archaeology. Archaeologists use
many techniques for studying objects and their contexts. In fact, archaeology has so many
complex techniques that it is physically impossible for any one person to know and
understand all of them. No matter how hard an archaeologist studies he can never learn

everything there is to know about archaeological theory and technique. New techniques appear each year, and with each advance in archaeology individual archaeologists become relatively less knowledgeable in their own field. Archaeologists are learning more and more about less and less.

Archaeological field techniques are becoming so rapidly refined that many of us now regret portions of our own fieldwork. We threw too much away. In 1923, archaeologists did not save charcoal. Why should they? Who knew that in 1949 a physicist named **Libby** would perfect a method of dating solid lumps of charcoal? Archaeologists did not take pollen samples before the 1930s because nobody had thought of reconstructing past environments from prehistoric pollen grains. Animal bones which once would have been discarded are now meticulously studied to determine butchering patterns, seasonality, and even the sex-age characteristics of the prehistoric animal populations. Soil from archaeological sites is a gold mine of information: seeds can be obtained by **flotation**, pH tests tell us about the intensity of prehistoric habitation, **pedological structure** tells us about the nature of deposition on archaeological sites. Some archaeologists are literally afraid to throw away anything; entire sites are sometimes brought back to the university or museum and actually "excavated" in the laboratory.

Archaeologists are proud of their microscopic techniques. No clue from the past is too minor to escape scrutiny. But there is a danger in such procedures, and that danger is myopia—losing sight of the forest for the trees.

This book will not look at archaeology through a microscope. We are going to use a macroscope, which is the opposite of a microscope. Instead of magnifying details, the macroscope merges details in search of overall patterns. Instead of magnifying the minutiae of archaeology, we will look for total patterning.

We will walk away from detail. We will keep walking away until we can see the whole picture. Modern archaeology consists of hundreds, even thousands, of tiny pieces. Some archaeologists think the pieces are so varied they no longer fit into one picture. Some people see two or three very different pictures, scenes that conflict and do not articulate smoothly anymore. People who think this are wrong. The shreds and patches of good archaeology still fit together. There is still a single picture, but we must stand back a long distance before we can visualize it.

That is one problem: fitting together the diversified techniques, concepts, and strategies of archaeology into a meaningful whole.

There is a second problem: What does this framework tell us? Can it stand alone, or does it somehow tie into yet a larger whole?

Part One will consider these questions: What are archaeologists? What are scientists? What are anthropologists? When each question has been answered, we will be in a position to assess what contemporary archaeologists are up to. Then we will find out how they do it.

1

What Are Archaeologists?

Emphasis in archaeology is gradually shifting . . .
from things to what things mean.
Alfred V. Kidder

This book attempts to explain two things: what American archaeologists are trying to do, and how they do it.

If these objectives seem to you to be simple, even obvious, you are dead wrong. American archaeology has been a house divided against itself. A great deal of emotion has been vented and copious ink spilled regarding a phenomenon known as the **new archaeology**. Some archaeologists praise it to the skies; others wholly reject it. I cannot begin my story of American archaeology without taking an explicit stand on recent events in the field. What is the *new archaeology*, and is it new or not?

The answer to this question, of course, lies in an examination of the past. To what other direction could an archaeologist turn? This initial chapter examines how contemporary archaeology came to be. Once the history has been briefly considered, I will set out my interpretation of what the new archaeology means, and how it relates to the overall discipline of American archaeology.

> The only thing that is new is the history we don't know.
>> *Harry S. Truman*

THE EVOLUTION OF WORLD ARCHAEOLOGY

> History! Read it and weep!
>> *Kurt Vonnegut Jr.*

Historians often ascribe the honor of "first archaeologist" to **Nabonidus** (555–538 B.C.), the last king of the neo-Babylonian Empire.[1] A sincerely pious man, Nabonidus's zealous worship of his gods compelled him to rebuild the ruined temples of ancient Babylon and to search among their foundations for the inscriptions of the earlier kings. For this reason, Nabonidus is known to modern historians as more an antiquary than an administrator. In fact, we are indebted to the research of his scribes and the excavations of his subjects for much of our modern picture of the Babylonian Empire. While it stretches a point to call Nabonidus an "archaeologist" in the modern sense of the term, he is an important figure because he examined the actual physical residues of antiquity to answer questions about the past. This is a simple step, but one that contrasts sharply with the beliefs of his contemporaries, who regarded tradition, legend, and myth as the only clues to the past.

Unfortunately, archaeology's family tree also has an unsavory branch, because, in truth, the looters and grave robbers of antiquity also contributed to the archaeological legacy. Unlike Nabonidus, untold generations of mercenaries were attracted by the promise of easy riches through the looting of tombs.

The early twentieth-century Egyptologists often found, to their dismay, that they had been "beaten to the punch" by looters and vandals. Sometimes the corpses were barely cold before the grave goods were purloined. H. E. Winlock, who was director of an expedition to Dier el Bahri, sponsored by New York's Metropolitan Museum, found episode after episode in which the ancient Egyptians had rifled the graves of their own rulers. When the Twenty-first Dynasty (ca. 1090 B.C.) mummies of Hent-Towy and Nesit-Iset were discovered, for instance, Winlock and his associates thought they were perfectly intact. But closer examination revealed that the mummies must have been unwrapped prior to interment and the valuable metal pectoral hawks and finger rings stolen. This deceit could only have been the work of the very undertakers commissioned to prepare the mummies for the hereafter (Winlock 1942:110–114). The pilfering of Egypt's royal tombs has continued for millennia, and, in fact, much of the popular appeal of contemporary Egyptology is the matching of modern wits with the ancient architects of the tombs, who tried every trick imaginable to outfox looters, both ancient and contemporary.

Despite their contributions in other fields, the classical Greeks did little to further the aims of modern anthropological archaeology (see Phillips 1964). As we will see in Chapter 3, the essence of the anthropological world view is the premise that to understand ourselves we must first understand others. As John Rowe (1965:2) has pointed out, "The ancient Greeks for the most part held that the way to understand ourselves is to study ourselves, while what others do is irrelevant." Socrates, for instance, was concerned primarily with his own thoughts and those of his contemporaries; he showed marked disdain for the languages and customs of "barbarians" (by which he meant all non-Greeks). The Romans, of course, traced their intellectual ancestry to the heroes of Greek legend; they imitated Greek protocol; and they shared in the pervasive Greek **ethnocentrism**. The **ethnographic** discussions of Herodotus and Tacitus stand virtually alone in their concern with non-Greek and non-Roman customs and values.

The legacy of pre-Renaissance writings did little to foster the development of either archaeological or anthropological inquiry. The Renaissance changed all of this. It has been suggested that the major contribution of the Renaissance—particularly in Italy—was the distinction between the present and the past (Rowe 1965:8). The classical Greeks and Romans recognized only the most remote past, which they reified in myth and legend. And because the Europeans of the Middle Ages also failed to distinguish between themselves and the ancients, it fell to Renaissance scholars to point up the differences between classical and medieval times.

Petrarch (1304–1374) is considered to be the first humanist, and perhaps the most influential individual of the early Renaissance. Not only a poet and linguist, Petrarch also provided strong impetus for archaeological research. The remote past for Petrarch was an ideal of perfection, and he looked to antiquity for moral philosophy. But in order to imitate classical antiquity, one must first study it. In a real sense, Petrarch's humanism led to a rediscovery of the past. Petrarch's influence can best be seen in the work of his close friend Boccaccio, who wrote extensive essays on classical mythology, and also in Giovanni Dondi, who is generally credited with the first systematic observations on archaeological monuments.

But it remained for **Ciriaco** (1391–ca. 1449) to establish the modern discipline of archaeology. After translating the Latin inscription on the triumphal arch of Trajan at Ancona, he was inspired to devote the remainder of his life to studying ancient monuments, copying inscriptions, and in general promoting the study of the past. His travels ranged from Syria to Egypt, throughout the islands of the Aegean, and finally to Athens. When asked his business, Ciriaco is said to have replied, "Restoring the dead to life," which is still a pretty fair statement of the business of archaeology (see Rowe 1965:10).

The scholars of the Italian Renaissance treated antiquity as a world apart, remote yet accessible through literature and ruins. These people became sensitized to the need for studying cultural differences, a spirit that accounts in large measure for the European explorations of Africa and the Atlantic. One such scholar, Peter the Martyr, considered the European discovery of America to be the most profound event of his lifetime, and while never visiting the New World, he chronicled the discoveries of Columbus and others for his European contemporaries.

The **antiquarian** spirit was also alive and well among the British. In fact, a group of eminent British historians and students of the classics formed an antiquarian society as early as 1572 (Daniel 1950:18). The emphasis of this and later societies was to record and preserve the national treasures, rather than to indiscriminately acquire curios and **objets d'art**. Of course many private collectors were still concerned only with filling their curio cabinets, but the thrust of British antiquarianism turned to mapping, recording, and preserving the archaeological ruins. By the late eighteenth century a healthy interest in classical antiquities became an important part of the "cultivation of taste" among the European leisured classes.

Archaeological research to this point had been largely in the humanistic tradition of Petrarch, concerned primarily with clarifying the picture of the classical civilizations. This information was readily digested by the eighteenth- and early nineteenth-century mind because it was in basic agreement with prevalent religious teachings. The Bible had, after all, discussed the classical cultures in some detail.

But a problem arose with the discovery of very crude stone tools among the ancient gravels of England and continental Europe. In 1836 or 1837, **Jacques Boucher de Perthes**, a controller of customs at Abbéville, began to find axe-heads in the ancient gravels of Somme. Along with those tools, he also found the bones of mammals now extinct.

Figure 1–1
Stone tools similar to those found by Boucher de Perthes in the river gravels of France (*courtesy of The American Museum of Natural History*).

The implication to Boucher de Perthes was obvious: "In spite of their imperfection, these rude stones prove the existence of [very ancient] man as surely as a whole Louvre would have done" (see Oakley 1964:94). But few contemporaries believed him, in part because of Christian scruples. Theological scholars had studied the problem of man's creation in marvelous detail, and they simply refused to allow sufficient time for the coexistence of man and animals of extinct form. In the early nineteenth century the prevalent opinion was that man had been on earth roughly six thousand years. Paley's *Natural Theology* (1802) explained the matter something like this: the earth was created according to a splendid design, not unlike a fine watch; God was the ultimate watchmaker, and he had deliberately placed man on his earth watch about 4000 B.C. Actually, this chronology had been suggested before, when, in 1642, **Dr. John Lightfoot**, master of St. Catharine's College and vice-chancellor of the University of Cambridge, published a treatise with the delightful title, *A Few and New Observations on the Book of Genesis, the most of them certain, the rest probable, all harmless, and rarely heard of before.* Lightfoot's later, slightly refined chronology concluded that "heaven and earth, centre and circumference, were created all together in the same instant and clouds full of water . . . this took place and man was created by the Trinity on October 23, 4004 B.C. at nine o'clock in the morning." Glyn Daniel (1962:19) has irreverently suggested that the vice-chancellor showed a certain understandable prejudice for the beginning of an academic term, and the beginning of an academic morning.

By this reckoning, of course, there was simply not enough time to allow for the presence of very ancient man. Therefore—almost by definition—Boucher de Perthes must be incorrect; his rude implements must be something other than the works of man. Some suggested that the "tools" were really meteorites, or perhaps they had been produced by lightning or by elves or fairies. One seventeenth-century scholar suggested that chipped flints were "generated in the sky by a fulgurous exhalation conglobed in a cloud by the circumposed humour" (see Daniel 1962:39).

Customs officials, however, are not known for their timidity, and Boucher de Perthes refused to admit defeat. More finds were made in the gravel pits of St. Acheul in France, and across the Channel similar discoveries occurred in southern England. The issue was finally resolved when British paleontologist Hugh Falconer visited Abbéville to examine the disputed evidence for himself. A procession of esteemed scholars followed Falconer's lead, and in 1859 a paper was presented to the Royal Society of London supporting the claims of de Perthes. In no time, several influential natural scientists proclaimed their support.

Thus the year 1859 proved to be a turning point in the history of human thought: not only had the antiquity and evolution of man been accepted by many, but Charles Darwin published his influential *On the Origin of Species,* which suggested the process by which that change had occurred.

The floodgates now open, British archaeology followed two rather divergent courses. One direction became involved with the problems of geological time and the in situ evolution of man and nature. Many scholars, of course, following in the tradition of Petrarch, continued their course of classical studies, focusing particularly on ancient Greece and Rome. This philosophical split continues into modern times, and the education of an Old World **prehistorian** differs greatly from that of a **classical archaeologist** (see Taylor 1948).

The European discovery of the Americas opened yet another option for prehistoric studies. Rather early in the game it became abundantly clear that American archaeology would never rival the European finds in sheer antiquity. The **New World** was indeed *new*. Beginning with Columbus's triumphant return to Europe in 1493, men of letters faced multiple vexing issues. When did people first arrive in the New World? Where had these migrants come from, and how did they get there? How could regions such as the Valley of Mexico and Peru boast fantastic riches, while many other areas such as the American West seemed so relatively impoverished and even primitive?

A great deal of confusion and speculation immediately arose. There was, for instance, the "Lost Tribe of Israel" scenario, which pointed up alleged American Indian–Semitic similarities (see Stewart 1973:60–63 and Silverberg 1968, Chapter 2). The fabled Island of Atlantis was seriously proposed by some as the ancestral homeland of the American Indians. The voyaging Egyptians, and even the Vikings were cited as hypothetical proto-Americans. The mystery thickened as more archaeological ruins were discovered. How, for instance, is one to explain the thousands of earthen mounds that dot the North American landscape east of the Mississippi? Prevalent racist theories often suggested that the ancestors of the American Indians were somehow incapable of constructing such monuments, and much debate during the eighteenth and nineteenth centuries centered about the mythic Mound Builders, who had somehow vanished before the arrival of Columbus (see Silverberg 1968).

Gradually, however, investigators came to realize the significant continuities that existed between the unknown prehistoric past and the extant Native American Indian population. As knowledge progressed, the differences between European and American archaeology became more apparent. While the Europeans wrestled with their ancient flints—with few apparent modern correlates—American scholars came to realize that the living American Indian was a valuable intellectual clue for interpreting the remains of the past. In the crass terms of the time, the American Indian was a "living fossil," a relic of times past.

Nearly from the outset, New World archaeology was inextricably wed to the study of living American Indians. That is, while Old World archaeologists began from baselines of geological time or classical antiquity, American scholars turned to the anthropology of Native America. Not only was American Indian ethnology a significant domain of study as such, but it would also provide clues for unraveling the peopling of the New World.

Another point should be made here. When the Europeans studied the archaeology of Europe, they were digging up their own ancestors (Balts, Slavs, Huns, etc). In the New World, Euro-Americans were digging up somebody else's ancestors (Native Americans). This difference goes a long way in explaining some of the racist theories prevalent in nineteenth-century American archaeology. This difference also explains why the European governments enacted antiquity legislation decades before North American governments did so (see Chapter 4).

MAINSTREAMS IN AMERICAN ARCHAEOLOGY

If you want to get across an idea, wrap it up in a person.
Ralph Bunche

As detailed in the Preface, the purpose of this book is to provide a synthesis of how contemporary archaeology is practiced in the Americas. The last section provided the foundation with a whirlwind consideration of the European precursors to American archaeology. A number of excellent discussions of the history of American archaeology have been written, and I recommend Taylor (1948, Chapter 1), Braidwood (1959), Haag (1959), Griffin (1959), Willey (1968), Schwartz (1968), Fitting (1973), Gorenstein (1977), and especially Willey and Sabloff (1974).

As we turn to the Americas, I will change modes of exposition. Rather than write a blow-by-blow narrative of the history of American archaeology, I have elected to reduce history to biography. What follows is a tale of American archaeology as told through the careers of seven of our "forefathers."[2]

The history of American archaeology—in fact all history—is the commingling of tradition and change. We begin with the more traditional figures, who illustrate how archaeology was practiced during their lifetime. This section is evolutionary. Later we will discuss two people who rocked the boat of traditional archaeology; that section is revolutionary. Both aspects are necessary ingredients of progress.

But first a warning: the seven "forefathers" were arbitrarily selected by me. Each person is taken to represent the tenor of his time, and it is certainly true that other authors would probably choose different people. But so long as you understand that my selections were made arbitrarily—and largely for effect—I will make no apologies. Each person represents a critical stage in the growth of American archaeology, and the career of each has a message to tell.

High time it is, that the younger generation stops sneering at its predecessors.
Carleton S. Coon

Thomas Jefferson (1743–1826)

The European Renaissance began in the fourteenth century and lasted well into the 1700s. In addition to providing historians with a convenient division between medieval and modern times, the Renaissance produced a breed of scholars known for their detailed grasp of a fantastic range of topics. Aptly known as *Renaissance men,* these cultivated gentlemen embodied the essence of intellectual and artistic excellence of their time.

Thomas Jefferson was one such Renaissance man. Although in a chronological sense Jefferson postdates the Renaissance period, his accomplishments are so varied that he surely must rank among the best of Renaissance-type scholars. Not only did the author of the Declaration of Independence later become the third president of the United States; he was also described by a contemporary as "an expert musician (the violin being his favorite instrument), a good dancer, a dashing rider, and proficient in all manly exercises." Jefferson was an avid player of chess (avoiding cards), a fearless and accomplished horseman, and a connoisseur of fine French cooking.

When not designing his famous home—Monticello—Jefferson was maintaining an impressive correspondence with friends and colleagues. In fact, it has been estimated that Jefferson wrote some 18,000 letters throughout his lifetime. Jefferson founded the University of Virginia, and his personal library ultimately formed the nucleus for the Library of Congress.

One further achievement marked the career of Jefferson. Willey and Sabloff (1974:38) have called Jefferson the "father of American archaeology," and Sir Mortimer Wheeler (1954:58) has labeled Jefferson's work "the first scientific excavation in the history of archaeology." Jefferson was a leading intellectual force of his time, and his curiosity about American Indian origins tells us a great deal about the initial character of American archaeology.

Jefferson's education was typical of the eighteenth-century colonial rich.

ANCIENT AMERICAN BATTLE-MOUND.

Figure 1-2
Thomas Jefferson and a highly imaginative artist's conception of an "ancient battle-mound" (*courtesy of The American Museum of Natural History*).

Born the son of a wealthy tobacco planter, Jefferson formally studied a broad spectrum embracing the arts, science, and literature. Young Jefferson specialized in law, and quickly decided to enter politics. By the age of 26 he had been elected to Virginia's House of Burgesses.

Yet Jefferson maintained a deep interest in the American Indian tribes of the colonies. Fascinated by Indian lore since boyhood, and trained as he was in classical linguistics, Jefferson argued that the American Indian languages held valuable clues to their origins. Jefferson personally collected linguistic data from more than forty tribes and wrote a long treatise on the subject. Unfortunately, Jefferson's linguistic data were never published, and the manuscript appears to have been lost somewhere between Washington and Monticello in 1809.

Reasoning largely from his linguistic studies, Jefferson sensed an Asiatic origin for American Indians. Jefferson, unlike his contemporaries, was not content to restrict his speculation to armchair theorizing. Always the man of action, he tested his notions on some hard data.

Jefferson's contribution to American archaeology was discussed in the only book he ever published. The project began in 1780, when Jefferson (then governor of Virginia) received a questionnaire from the French government requesting information on his state. The French, attempting to acquaint themselves with the newly formed United States of America, sent similar inquiries to leading figures in other states. The request came at an opportune time for Jefferson, as he was commencing a self-imposed exile from politics. Jefferson labored in great detail on his questionnaire, eventually producing a lengthy treatise covering such diverse topics as topography, geography, economics, zoology, botany, geology, politics, and, of course, American Indians. The manuscript was revised and enlarged from time to time, and was ultimately published in a limited French edition in 1784 and in a widespread American edition in 1787.

Notes on the State of Virginia was structured as a series of replies to queries, the chapter headings reading "Query I," Query II," and so forth. "Query XI" dealt with the aborigines of Virginia. He listed and described the various Virginian tribes, discussed their histories since the settlement of Jamestown in 1607, and included a census of Virginia's current Indian population. His main concern was to discuss the origins of Virginia's Indians, and this discussion precipitated a consideration of the archaeological evidence.

The origin of American Indians had been a compelling topic of speculation since the time of Columbus, and probably even before. Hundreds of prehistoric Indian mounds dotted the landscape east of the Mississippi River, and theories arose by the score to explain the monuments. The Spanish explorer de Soto correctly surmised that the mounds served as foundations for priestly temples, but his astute observation was lost in a flood of fanciful reconstruction. While some scholars theorized that the American Indians had a biblical origin—perhaps descendants of the Ten Lost Tribes of Israel—others suggested a Mexican origin for the ancient monument builders. The prevalent racist atti-

Thomas Jefferson Describing His Excavation of a Burial Mound in Virginia (1787)

I know of no such thing existing as an Indian monument: for I would not honour with that name arrow points, stone hatchets, stone pipes, and half-shapen images. Of labour on the large scale, I think there is no remain as respectable as would be a common ditch for the draining of lands: unless indeed it be the Barrows, of which many are to be found all over this country. . . . There being one of these in my neighbourhood, I wished to satisfy myself whether any, and which of these opinions were just. For this purpose I determined to open and examine it thoroughly. It was situated on the low grounds of the Rivanna, about two miles above its principal fork, and opposite to some hills, on which had been an Indian town. It was of a spheroidical form, of about 40 feet diameter at the base, and had been of about twelve feet altitude, though now reduced by the plough to seven and a half, having been under cultivation about a dozen years. Before this it was covered with trees of twelve inches diameter, and round the base was an excavation of five feet depth and width, from whence the earth had been taken of which the hillock was formed. I first dug superficially in several parts of it, and came to collections of human bones, at different depths, from six inches to three feet below the surface. These were lying in the utmost confusion, some vertical, some oblique, some horizontal, and directed to every point of the compass, entangled, and held together in clusters by the earth. Bones of the most distant parts were found together, as, for instance, the small bones of the foot in the hollow of a scull, many sculls would sometimes be in contact, lying on the face, on the side, on the back, top or bottom, so as, on the whole, to give the idea of bones emptied promiscuously from a bag or basket, and covered over with earth,

tudes of late eighteenth-century America fostered the conception of the mythical **Mound Builder People,** who had constructed the impressive monuments throughout the Americas, then vanished. Sometime in the remote past, these Mound Builders must have undergone a profound degenerative process, rendering them smaller and less intelligent than modern Europeans.

This was the issue that Jefferson confronted in his *Notes on the State of Virginia.* To Jefferson, the problem of American Indian origins required a dual strategy: to learn as much as feasible about contemporary Indian culture, and also to examine the prehistoric remains. He argued emphatically that contemporary American Indians were in no way mentally or physically inferior to the white races and rejected all current racist doctrines explaining their origins. Jefferson reasoned that American Indians were wholly capable of constructing the prehistoric monuments of the United States.

Then Jefferson took a most important step in the story of American archaeology. Shovel firmly in hand, he proceeded to excavate a burial mound located on his property. Today, such a step seems quite logical, but few of Jefferson's contemporaries would think of resorting to bones, stones, and dirt to answer intellectual issues. Contemporary eighteenth-century scholars preferred without any attention to their order. . . . I proceeded then to make a perpendicular cut through the body of the barrow, that I might examine its internal structure. This passed about three feet from its center, was opened to the former surface of the earth, and was wide enough for a man to walk through and examine its sides. At the bottom, that is, on the level of the circumjacent plain, I found bones; above these a few stones, brought from a cliff a quarter of a mile off, and from the river one-eighth of a mile off; then a large interval of earth, then a stratum of bones, and so on. At one end of the section were four strata of bones plainly distinguishable; at the other, three; the strata in one part not ranging with those in another. The bones nearest the surface were least decayed. No holes were discovered in any of them as if made with bullets, arrows, or other weapons. I conjectured that in this barrow might have been a thousand skeletons. Every one will readily seize the circumstances above related, which militate against the opinion, that it covered the bones only of persons fallen in battle; and against the tradition also, which would make it the common sepulchre of a town, in which the bodies were placed upright, and touching each other. Appearances certainly indicate that it has derived both origin and growth from the accustomary collection of bones, and deposition of them together; that the first collection had been deposited on the common surface of the earth, a few stones put over it, and then a covering of earth, that the second had been laid on this, had covered more or less of it in proportion to the number of bones, and was then also covered with earth; and so on. The following are the particular circumstances which give it this aspect. 1. The number of bones. 2. Their confused position. 3. Their being in different strata. 4. The strata in one part have no correspondence with those in another. 5. The difference in the time of inhumation. 6. The existence of infant bones among them.

to rummage through libraries and archives rather than to dirty their hands with the hard facts from the past.

Jefferson's account is written in the rather flowery style of his time (see insert), but note his very acceptable manner of reporting the finds. First he presents his data—location, size, method of excavation, stratigraphy, condition of the bones, artifacts—then he describes his conclusions: *Why* did prehistoric peoples bury their dead in mounds? He first noted the absence of traumatic wounds, such as those made by bullets or arrows, and also observed the interment of children, thereby rejecting the common notion that the bones were those of soldiers who had fallen in battle. Similarly, the scattered and disjointed nature of the bones militated against the notion of a "common sepulchre of a town," in which Jefferson expected the skeletons to be arranged in more orderly fashion. The stratigraphy indicated to Jefferson that the mound represented several distinct burial episodes, each burial group being covered with rocks and earth. Jefferson surmised, quite correctly, that the burials were due to repeated use of a mortuary area, and he saw no reason to doubt that the mound had been constructed by the ancestors of the Indian races encountered by the colonists. To Jefferson, the mythical race of Mound Builders was just that—a myth.

Today, nearly two hundred years after Jefferson's excavations, archaeologists would modify few of his well-reasoned conclusions, but neither Jefferson's conclusions nor the objects he unearthed are of major importance. Jefferson's legacy to American archaeology is the fact that he dug at all. By his simple excavation, Jefferson elevated the study of America's past from a speculative, armchair pastime to an **empirical** science. Jefferson, as a well-educated colonial gentleman of letters, realized the fundamental importance of exposing one's speculation to a barrage of facts. The "facts" in this case lay buried in the earth, and that is precisely where Jefferson conducted his inquiry.

Jefferson also introduced the foremost methodological tool of archaeology: **stratigraphy.** He noted that several distinct strata were embodied in the sidewalls of his excavation and correctly inferred a complex sequence of mound construction. Moreover, his finds were recorded in meticulous detail and ultimately published for scrutiny by interested scholars.

We must also note the overall orientation that Jefferson introduced. Unlike his contemporaries, Jefferson did not dig to obtain bones and artifacts for his mantel. Jefferson excavated to answer a specific, well-formulated problem. He collected his data in as systematic a manner as possible, then proceeded to draw carefully reasoned inferences from his fieldwork.

> **It's not what you find,
> it's what you find out.**
> *David Hurst Thomas*

C. B. Moore (1852–1936)

Clarence B. Moore came of a wealthy family of Philadelphia socialites. He received his B.A. degree from Harvard in 1873. Then, at the age of 24, he traveled across South America, over the Andes, and down the Amazon. His father died shortly thereafter, leaving Moore sufficient income for life. For the next several years, Moore followed the socialite circuit, traveling throughout Europe and going on safaris in exotic Africa.

By 1892, Moore had begun to find the life of a wealthy socialite boring, and he cast about for a more meaningful pursuit. As a man of leisure, unconcerned with earning a living, he felt wholly free to follow his whims and fancy.

Thus at age 40, C. B. Moore progressed from gentleman socialite to gentleman archaeologist. He purchased a specially equipped flat-bottomed steamboat, which he christened the *Gopher*. Moore's plan was to explore the waterways of the American Southeast, excavating the major archaeological sites he encountered. Moore was especially interested in the hundreds of burial and temple mounds that dotted the southeastern landscape, and he was assisted in his studies by Dr. Milo G. Miller, secretary, co-worker, physician, and friend.

From the outset, Moore's pattern of research was firmly established, and his archaeological campaigns were models of organization and efficiency.

Figure 1–3
C. B. Moore, upon graduation from
Harvard University in 1873 (*courtesy of
Harvard University and Robert Neuman*).

Aboard the *Gopher,* Moore and Miller conducted preliminary investigations so that likely sites could be located and arrangements could be contracted with landowners. With excavation to begin in the spring, Moore hired and supervised the workmen and kept the field notes. When human skeletons were located, Dr. Miller would examine the bones in the field to determine sex, age, probable cause of death, and to note any unusual pathologies. The summers were spent cleaning, repairing, photographing, and studying the collection. Moore meticulously prepared his excavation reports for publication in the fall and distributed the unusual artifacts to institutions such as the Peabody Museum at Harvard, the Smithsonian, and The American Museum of Natural History in New York City. The remaining collections were returned to the Philadelphia Academy of Natural Sciences, which published many of Moore's scientific volumes. The subsequent winter was spent initiating another campaign of archaeological fieldwork.

Moore's first investigations concentrated on the shell middens and the sand burial mounds sprinkled along the Gulf Coast of Florida. Gradually, year after year, Moore worked his way northward to Florida's eastern shore and ultimately to the Sea Islands of coastal Georgia and South Carolina. In 1899, Moore returned to the Gulf Coast, traveled up the Alabama River, and examined the coast of northwest Florida. Moore excavated literally dozens of sites in each expedition.

Finally, in 1905, Moore paused on the Black Warrior River, Alabama, to excavate intensively the ruins appropriately known as Moundville (Moore 1905, 1907). Working with several trained assistants and a crew numbering ten to fifteen, Moore explored the large temple mounds to examine the nature of human burials and to unearth spectacular pieces of pre-Columbian art. In 1905, when Moore found a copper fishhook, ceremonial axes, and ornaments, he concluded that the mounds must have been used as dwelling places for royalty because they possessed the choicer objects, and chiefs were evidently buried beneath their residences. The 1906 expedition located objects of sheet copper and copper-coated wood from the flat country surrounding the mounds. The copper artifacts were apparently modeled after implements of stone, pottery, and shell, carrying motifs such as the open hand, the eye, the swastika, forms of the cross, and birds' heads. (Modern archaeologists recognize these artifacts as part of the so-called **Southern Cult**, which was widespread in the Southeast after about A.D.1200) Moore ultimately concluded that Moundville was once a major regional religious center, and he rejected his earlier notion that the mounds had been chiefly residences. They were simply too big. Moore presumed from the varied art forms that the ancient dwellers at Moundville were worshippers of the sun, and the motifs such as the plumed serpent and eagle suggested to him strong ties with contemporary Mexican civilizations. (Modern studies as Moundville are discussed in Chapter 10.)

Following his Moundville excavations, Moore continued his sojourns throughout Arkansas, Mississippi, Louisiana, Kentucky, and Tennessee. One of C. B. Moore's major contributions to archaeology is his work at Poverty Point, Louisiana (Moore 1913). The highly unusual series of concentric earthworks was briefly described by Samuel Lockett in a Smithsonian Institution report in 1872. Moore piloted the *Gopher* up the Bayou Macon in 1912–1913 and spent the winter carefully mapping and describing the unique mounds. Poverty Point was later excavated by The American Museum of Natural History archaeologist James Ford, who described Moore's earlier work as "really quite adequate in so far as can be determined from observation made on the ground. His map . . . is quite good, if the meager instrument work on which it was based is considered . . . if air photographs were not now available, it probably would be unnecessary to amend Moore's description" (Ford and Webb 1956:14). Archaeologists can ask no higher praise from later generations.

By 1916, Moore concluded that the *Gopher* had explored every southeastern river then navigable by steamer. In fact, once a sandbar was removed in northern Florida, and Moore promptly piloted the *Gopher* up the newly navigable Chocktawatchee River. He had truly exhausted the resources available for riverboat archaeology. In his twenty-five years as explorer and excavator, Moore had catalogued an impressive array of archaeological sites. Of course, archaeological techniques have improved markedly since Moore's times, and many contemporary archaeologists wish Moore had been somewhat less thorough: he left so little for the rest of us. Nevertheless, Clarence B. Moore contributed mightily to the progress of American archaeology, both in the intensive nature of his research and the rapid and fairly complete publication of his findings. Over the years, Moore published twenty-one large volumes and several articles describing his fieldwork. Even today, these volumes are valuable references to archaeologists working on the mortuary complex of the prehistoric American Southeast.

Nels Nelson (1875–1964)

The career of Nels Nelson stands in marked contrast to that of C. B. Moore. Whereas Moore was the scion of a wealthy family, Nelson was born on a poor farm in Jutland, Denmark. The eldest of many children, Nelson (born Nels Nielson) was a farmhand first, a student only in his spare time; he later claimed that as a youngster he went to school "just enough to read the catechism." Nevertheless, he stumbled onto the James Fenimore Cooper novels while still quite young and became fascinated with the lore of American Indians. Several of his relatives had already emigrated to America, and in 1892 Nelson's aunt in Minnesota sent him a steerage ticket to New York.

When young Nels arrived in New York harbor, he was caught up in the gigantic wave of European immigration to America. He later recalled that as his ship entered the Narrows he flung his old clothes out the porthole and vowed to start his young life afresh. His initial experiences in America, however, differed little from his life in Denmark, as the Danish colony in Minnesota closely guarded its European heritage. Nelson, determined to become truly Americanized, left his Danish relatives and hired himself out to a farmer near Marshall, Minnesota. Nelson began the American first grade at the age of 17 and graduated from high school at the age of 21.

About this time, a family passed through Minnesota returning to California. They sang the praises of the West "as only Californians can" and invited Nels to go along. Nelson obtained free transportation west by tending stock in a livestock railroad car. In California, after a number of odd jobs (including driving a six-mule team and butchering hogs), he saved sufficient money to enroll in Stanford University. While at Stanford, Nelson studied philosophy by day and took odd jobs at night to pay his expenses. After following his professor across the bay to Berkeley, Nelson finally tired of his philosophical endeavors. Nelson later claimed that his philosophy professor himself admitted reading Kant twenty-six times without being able to achieve anything beyond a frank bewilderment. Nelson concluded that the problems of the universe had confounded greater minds than his, and he gradually abandoned his philosophical studies.

Quite by accident, a friend of Nelson's invited him to attend an archaeological dig in Ukiah, north of San Francisco. Apparently he experienced something of a *déjà vu,* recalling the Indian lore he had first experienced in the pages of James Fenimore Cooper. Nelson was permanently smitten by archaeology, and he immediately enrolled in all the archaeological courses available at Berkeley, finally securing a position at the Museum of Anthropology.

Nelson's M.A. thesis was an archaeological survey of the shell middens surrounding San Francisco Bay (Nelson 1909). According to his pedometer, Nelson walked more than 3,000 miles in the course of his survey and located 425 shell mounds. His report discussed the location of the sites relative to available natural resources, listed the animal bones found in the shell heaps, and considered the ecological adaptation implied by such a bayside lifeway. The increasing crush of urbanism has today destroyed all but a handful of these sites, and Nelson's report map, originally published in 1909, remains an invaluable source to modern archaeologists interested in central California prehistory.

Yet, while he pursued his graduate education and was employed as curator assistant at the Museum of Anthropology, Nelson was forced to keep a nighttime job as a janitor and office boy "doing everything from dusting the president's desk to picking up the money that was left scattered about the tellers' booths after a busy day." American archaeology in the early 1900s remained largely an avocation of the rich, a career poorly suited to the resources of immigrant scholars.

All of this changed for Nelson in 1912. At this time, The American Museum of Natural History in New York was launching an archaeological campaign in Arizona and New Mexico, and Nelson was imported to oversee this important research. As we will discuss in detail in Chapter 5, Nelson's stratigraphic excavations in New Mexico provided a major breakthrough in archaeological technique. In addition to his work in the Southwest, Nelson conducted excavations in the caves of Kentucky and Missouri, and in the shell mounds of Florida during his first few years at the American Museum.

In 1925, Nelson accompanied an expedition to Central Asia. While traveling through the Gobi desert, Nelson later admitted that he forestalled menacing Mongols by pretending to be a magician, able to remove his (artificial) eye and put it back again. The Central Asiatic Expedition took Nelson throughout mainland China, culminating in a 400-mile trip up the Yangtze River in a Chinese junk. Nelson's fieldwork also continued throughout North America and Europe until his eventual retirement in 1943.

In many ways the career of Nels Nelson typifies the state of American archaeology during the first quarter of the twentieth century. Although Nelson received infinitely better archaeological training than predecessors such as C. B. Moore, he still learned largely by firsthand experience. The archaeology of 1906

Figure 1–4
Nels Nelson (*courtesy of The American*
***Museum of Natural History*).**

was in the pioneer stage, and no matter where Nelson turned, whether it was the shell mounds of San Francisco Bay, the pueblos of New Mexico, or the caves of the Yangtze River in China, he was the first archaeologist on the scene. In large measure, his duty was to record what he saw, conduct preliminary excavation, and state some tentative inferences to be tested and embellished by later investigators.

Nelson is best remembered for his contributions to stratigraphic technique. Nelson's 1912 excavations in the Galisteo Basin of New Mexico are generally acknowledged as the first major stratigraphic archaeology in the Americas (Spier 1931; Woodbury 1960; Willey and Sabloff 1974:89–94). At that time, the cultural chronology of the American Southwest was utterly unknown, and Nelson's carefully controlled excavations and meticulous analysis of the pottery recovered provided the first solid chronological framework. The details of Nelson's Galisteo excavations are discussed in Chapter 5; Nelson's advances both in field technique and subsequent analysis made stratigraphic excavation the indispensable approach of the future.

Nelson also typified the new breed of early twentieth-century museum-based archaeologists. Tracing his own fascination with archaeology back to an exhibit of prehistoric tools at the Omaha Exposition in 1898, Nelson strongly believed that the message of archaeology should be brought across to the public in the form of books, popular magazine articles, and, most of all, interpretive displays of archaeological materials.

A. V. Kidder (1885–1963)

Although born in Michigan, the life and career of A. V. Kidder revolved about the academic community of Cambridge, Massachussets. Kidder's father, a mining engineer, saw to it that young Alfred received the best education available. First enrolled in a private school in Cambridge, Kidder was then sent to the prestigious La Villa, in Ouchy, Switzerland, after which he enrolled at Harvard to pursue the premed program. During his junior year Kidder finally admitted he would rather be an archaeologist than a doctor. This decision was determined in part by difficulties with the chemistry curriculum required as part of the premed program, but it also reflected Kidder's strong boyhood interest in archaeology. Writing a few years before his death, Kidder fondly recalled his father's private library, which contained complete sets of the Smithsonian, National Museum, and Bureau of Ethnology annual reports as well as Catlin's famous *North American Indians.* As a junior, Kidder was able to join an archaeological expedition to the still largely unexplored regions of northeastern Arizona. Working under Edgar Hewett of the University of Utah, Kidder mapped ruins at Mesa Verde and also assisted in excavations at Puye, on the Pajarito Plateau in New Mexico. The Southwestern experience sealed his fate; Kidder returned to Harvard, enrolled in the anthropology program, and received his Ph.D. in 1914. He was awarded the sixth American Ph.D. specializing in archaeology, and the first with a focus on North America.

Kidder's dissertation was a detailed examination of Southwestern ceramics and their value in reconstructing cultural history. The work constituted a major breakthrough in Southwestern archaeology. Stressing the use of scientific methods, Kidder showed archaeologists how to unravel the meaning of archaeology's most perplexing prehistoric remains, the lowly potsherd. His presentation urged the accurate description of ceramic decoration and demonstrated how these details could be used to assess relationships among the various prehistoric groups. He argued that only through controlled excavation and analysis could inferences be drawn about such anthropological subjects as **acculturation**, social organizations, and prehistoric religious customs.

In 1915, the department of archaeology at the Philips Academy in Andover, Massachusetts, embarked on a multi-year project, and they were looking for an archaeological site large enough and of sufficient scientific importance to warrant such research. Largely because of his anthropological training, Kidder seemed to represent a new breed of archaeologists, and he was selected to direct the excavations.

Kidder decided to work at Pecos Pueblo, a massive ruin located 25 miles southwest of Santa Fe, New Mexico. Coronado had explored the Pecos ruins in 1540, and Pecos was known from a detailed report on the ruins published by **Adolph Bandelier** in 1881. More recently, Hewett had made a brief study of the seventeen survivors who still lived at the Pueblo of Jemez. Kidder was impressed by the great diversity of potsherds scattered about the ruins, and felt certain Pecos contained sufficiently stratified debris to span several centuries. Kidder excavated at Pecos for ten summers, and ultimately published fifteen short technical reports and five major monographs on his findings.

Kidder's excavations at Pecos were important for a number of reasons. Kidder was the first American archaeologist to test Nelson's stratigraphic method on a large scale, thereby establishing the basic chronology of Southwestern prehistory. Kidder not only focused on pottery, but also examined the range of artifacts and architecture available at Pecos. Working without the benefit of either radiocarbon dating or a tree-ring chronology, Kidder's intensive artifact analysis established the bare framework of Southwestern prehistory, which remains intact today. Kidder's work at Pecos so stimulated the field of Southwestern archaeology that archaeologists found it difficult to keep up with

Figure 1–5
A. V. Kidder directing field operations at Pecos Pueblo in 1920 (*courtesy of the National Geographic Society and Gordon Ekholm*).

Kidder on the Pan-Scientific Approach to Archaeology

Archaeologists are often portrayed in the media as latter-day hermits who forage off into the wilderness to conquer the secrets of the past. In fact, contemporary archaeologists never work alone. Archaeological sites contain information too diverse, too varied for any single scholar to analyze. Teamwork is a requirement of all modern archaeology, but the team approach to archaeology is hardly new. Kidder fully anticipated modern trends with his "pan-scientific" approach at Chichén Itzá, Yucatán, in the 1920s.

In this investigation the archaeologist would supply the prehistoric background, the historian would work on the documentary record of the Conquest, the Colonial and the Mexican periods; the sociologist would consider the structure of modern life. At the same time studies would be made upon the botany, zoology, and climate of the region; and upon the agriculture, economic system, and health conditions of the urban and rural, European mixed and native populations. It seems probable that there would result definite conclusions of far-reaching interest, that there would be developed new methods applicable to many problems of race and culture contacts, and that there would be gained by the individuals taking part in the work a first-hand acquaintance with the aims of allied disciplines which would be of great value to themselves, and through them to far larger groups of research workers. (Kidder 1928:753)

current finds made by their colleagues. In 1927, Kidder sponsored a convention at which the major southwestern archaeologists were invited to exchange information, and to establish a set of uniform terminology. Kidder's **Pecos Conference** has been called the major archaeological event of the 1920s, and reflected the need to share information and attempt a preliminary synthesis of the state of southwestern archaeology. The Pecos Conference continues today and remains the social and intellectual focal point of Southwestern archaeology.

In a way, the Pecos Conference signaled the end of Kidder's first career and the beginning of a second. Shortly thereafter, the Carnegie Institution of Washington created the Division of Historical Research and appointed Kidder as its director. Taking many of his southwestern field associates with him, Kidder launched an aggressive program on the archaeology of the Maya of Middle America. In a vein similar to the Pecos Conference, Kidder convened a conference at Chichén Itzá in Yucatán to take stock of Mayan research and to plan research for the future.

Kidder set forth his master plan of Mayan research and directed the Carnegie's efforts for the next twenty years. Relegating himself to the role of administrator, Kidder amassed a staff of qualified scientists with the broadest possible scope of interest. Kidder argued that a true understanding of Maya culture would require a broad-based plan of action, involving many interrelated areas of research. This plan is a landmark in archaeological research, stressing as it did the importance of enriching the narrow archaeological research with a wide range of anthropological and allied disciplines. Under Kidder's direction, the Carnegie program supported the research of ethnographers, geographers, physical anthropologists, geologists, meteorologists, and of course, archaeologists. Kidder, for instance, demonstrated the effectiveness of aerial reconnaissance by convincing Charles Lindbergh, already an international figure, to participate in the Mayan research. Early in 1929, Lindbergh flew Kidder throughout British Honduras, Yucatán, and the Petén. Not only were new ruins discovered, but the Lindbergh flights also provided ecological information previously unavailable, such as the boundaries of various types of vegetation. Today, the interdisciplinary approach to archaeology is a fact of life, but when proposed by Kidder in the 1920s, the prevailing attitude still reflected the one man–one site mentality.

Beyond his substantive Maya and Southwestern studies, Kidder's primary contribution to archaeology was the wedding of archaeological technique with anthropological objectives. Kidder repeated time and time again that archaeology is "that branch of anthropology which deals with prehistoric peoples," and this doctrine has become firmly embedded in today's American archaeology.[3] Although archaeologists must immerse themselves in the minutiae of potsherd detail and architectural specifics, the ultimate objective of archaeology remains the statement of anthropological universals about mankind. To Kidder, the archaeologist was merely the "mouldier variety of anthropologist."

Although largely occupied with bureaucratic details for the remainder of his life, Kidder still found time to conduct his own archaeological research at the important site of Kamanaljuyu, in Guatemala, and in 1958 he published the final volume on his earlier excavations at Pecos. Kidder died at the age of 78, and it has been suggested that he was more responsible than anyone for transforming archaeology from "antiquarianism to a systematic discipline" (Willey 1967).

James A. Ford (1911–1968)

James A. Ford, the final archaeologist to be considered in this brief historical sketch, was born in Water Valley, Mississippi, and his major interests centered on the archaeology of the southeastern United States. Ford became active as an "archaeologist" at the age of 16, when he was hired by the Mississippi Department of Archives and History. The director of the department was a southern historian of the old school, and Ford was set to work digging up "Indian relics" from various mounds throughout the state. Today, such relic collecting would be considered little better than (illegal) pot hunting. But even as a teenager, Ford's innate sense of order led him to devise rough attempts at controlling the excavations and keeping field notes. Ford eventually studied anthropology at the University of Michigan and belatedly received his Ph.D. from Columbia University in 1946. While Ford attended Columbia, Nels

Figure 1–6
James A. Ford, surveying the site of Boca Escondida, north of the city of Veracruz
(*courtesy of Junius Bird*).

Nelson retired from the Department of Anthropology at The American Museum of Natural History and Ford was hired as assistant curator of North American archaeology.

Ford came of age during the Great Depression and was part of an archaeological generation literally trained on the job. The Roosevelt administration quickly realized that jobs must be created to alleviate the economic conditions, and crews of workmen were commonly assigned tasks including building roads, bridges, and general heavy construction. One obvious make-work project was archaeology, and literally hundreds of unemployed men were set to work excavating major archaeological sites. This program was, of course, a major boost to American archaeology. Data from the WPA excavations poured in at a record rate and, in fact, the results of the 1930s excavations are still being published (e.g., Wauchope 1966).

These massive gangs of workmen needed close supervision, and an entire generation of archaeologists received their training as WPA supervisors. James Ford was one of these archaeologists, working with federal relief–supported crews in Louisiana and Georgia. Following the Depression, Ford moved on to a number of major archaeological projects in Alaska, Peru, and Mexico, but Southeastern archaeology remained his first love.

Mention was made earlier that Ford had conducted a detailed study of Poverty Point, Louisiana, a site explored forty years earlier by C. B. Moore. Ford's work at Poverty Point is fairly typical of mid-1950s archaeology. After completing his mapping and reconnaissance (based in large part on Moore's previous work), Ford conducted a series of stratigraphic excavations to determine the history of the site. His overall objective was to determine what the

Poverty Point site represented in human terms. Ford's goals went far beyond those of, say, C. B. Moore, who collected largely to find outstanding examples of artwork. Ford speculated on what Poverty Point must have looked like when freshly constructed. He estimated that roughly 530,000 cubic yards of earth had been used in construction (some thirty-five times the volume of the pyramid of Cheops in Egypt). Ford continually asked, What does archaeology tell us about the people? He estimated, for instance, that over three million man-hours of labor were involved in the construction of just one of the Poverty Point mounds. He reasoned that a population of several thousand people must have been involved to have created such massive earthworks, and he further postulated that the community must have had a fairly rigid and stratified form of political organization. Furthermore, the splendid geometrical arrangement of the town and the ceremonial precinct suggested the central control by full-time architects and project directors. To Ford, Poverty Point represented a great deal more than a fossilized ceremonial center, and he attempted to re-create the social and political networks responsible for this massive project. In this regard he typified the anthropological concerns of mid-century American archaeology.

The unprecedented rate of data accumulation in the 1930s created a crisis of sorts among American archaeologists: What is to be done with all these data? Ford and his contemporaries were beset by problems of synthesis and classification, and with the pressing necessity to establish regional sequences of culture chronology. Unlike Nelson, Kidder, and the others working in the American Southwest, Ford did not have access to deep refuse heaps; Southeastern sites tend to be shallow, often short-term occupations. To create temporal order from these materials Ford relied on an integrated procedure of surface collection and classification. In a sense, Ford returned to the work of **Sir Flinders Petrie**, an Egyptologist who began working in 1881. While excavating predynastic graves at Diospolis Parva, Petrie devised a system of sequentially ordering stages of pottery development, thereby dating his grave assemblages. As modified by Ford and others, the technique of sequence ordering is known as **seriation**. Chapter 7 discusses the seriation principle in some detail, but the central idea is simple: by assuming that cultural styles (fads) will tend to change gradually, we can chart the relative popularity of pottery decoration through time. A given pottery style is introduced at one specific locality, its popularity spreads throughout a region, then that type is gradually replaced by a subsequent style. While sometimes overly simplistic, Ford's seriational technique did indeed create the fundamental arrangement still in use throughout the American Southeast.

Ford then synthesized his ceramic chronologies into patterns of regional history. When C. B. Moore was excavating the hundreds of prehistoric mounds throughout the Southeast, he lacked a method of adequately dating his finds. Using seriation along with other methods, Ford helped bring temporal order to Southeastern archaeology, and he rapidly moved to synthesize these sequences. Ford proposed the basic division between the earlier **Burial Mound Period**

James Ford on the Goals of Archaeology

The study of archaeology has changed considerably from a rather esthetic beginning as an activity devoted to collecting curios and guarding them in cabinets to be admired for their rarity, beauty, or simple wonder. Students are no longer satisfied with the delights of the collector and are now primarily interested in reconstructing culture history. In recent years methods and techniques have progressed rapidly, and there are indications which suggest that some phases of the study may develop into a truly scientific concern with general principles. This trend seems to be due more to the kinds of evidence that past human history offers than to any planned development. For centuries the perspective of the study of history was narrowed to a listing of battles, kings, political situations, and escapades of great men, an activity which is analogous to collecting curios and arranging them in cabinets. Such collections are fascinating to those who have developed a taste for them, but they contribute little towards the discovery of processes which are always the foremost interest of a science. The evidence that survives in archaeological situations has made it impossible to study prehistory in terms of individual men, or even in terms of man as an acculturated animal. When the archaeologist progresses beyond the single specimen he is studying the phenomena of culture. . . .

I join a number of contemporaries in believing that archaeology is moving in the direction of its establishment as a more important segment of the developing science of culture than it has been in the past. This does not mean that such objectives as discovering chronological sequences and more complete and vivid historical reconstructions will be abandoned; rather these present aims will become necessary steps in the process of arriving at the new goal. (Ford 1952:317–318)

and the later **Temple Mound Period**, which remains in use today (see Chapter 10). Toward the end of his career, Ford attempted to tie the historical developments of the Southeast cultures to happenings in Central and South America. While many contemporary archaeologists are critical of Ford's sweeping generalizations, Gordon Willey (1969:67) has predicted that "a good part of what he [had] advanced will one day be accepted."

TRENDS IN AMERICAN ARCHAEOLOGY

There is properly no history, only biography.
Ralph Waldo Emerson

The biographies of these five archaeologists provide us with a feeling for American archaeology's past. Thomas Jefferson obviously approached his archaeology in a drastically different manner from, say, James Ford. Subsequent chapters will discuss in some detail the major contributions of each, such as Nelson's stratigraphic method, Kidder's southwestern classification, and Ford's thoughts on classification and seriation of artifacts.

But specifics aside, each individual can be classed among the very best of his contemporaries. These careers form an interesting and important continuum. American archaeology has evolved significantly over two centuries, and some important trends are evident.

Perhaps the most striking difference is in the character of the individual scholar. Thomas Jefferson was a prominent world figure, born to the best family and educated as a true colonial gentleman. In the beginning, American archaeology was the pastime of the genteel rich. Even at the beginning of this century, archaeologists were still men of breeding. C. B. Moore, for instance, personally purchased the *Gopher* and privately financed his own fieldwork. Not until the time of immigrant Nels Nelson could the working class hope to penetrate the archaeological establishment.

Concurrently, archaeology arose as a professional scientific discipline. C. B. Moore was among the first generation of professional full-time archaeologists. As practicing professionals, archaeologists from Moore's time and later became affiliated with major museums and universities. This institutional support was necessary not only to foster professionalism and public funding, but also to provide nonprivate repositories for the valuable archaeological artifacts recovered. The twentieth-century American archaeologist is not a collector of personal treasure; all finds become part of the public domain, available for exhibit and study.

We also note of these five archaeologists a progression toward specialization. Thomas Jefferson's interest in archaeology was conditioned by the nagging problem of American Indian origins. So little American archaeology was known at the time that it was possible for a single scholar to control all of the relevant data. Although Jefferson excavated a Virginian burial mound, his interest and speculations embraced the entire New World.

Even in the late nineteenth century, archaeological information was so rapidly accumulating that no single scholar could hope to control all the data relating to American archaeology. C. B. Moore, for instance, became the leading authority on Southeastern archaeology, but he was relatively ignorant about finds being made by his archaeological contemporaries in Peru, Central America, and even the American Southwest. Nels Nelson traveled throughout Asia and Europe in order to keep up with archaeological developments. But to do so Nelson was forced to cease excavating early in the 1930s. A. V. Kidder pursued two careers—Southwestern and Maya archaeology. But by the 1950s, archaeologists such as Ford were forced to specialize even more closely in specific localities within cultural areas. Today, it is rare to find archaeologists with experience in more than a couple of specialized fields.

Probably the most important trend is the nature of the training that archaeologists now receive. Jefferson was a Renaissance man, broadly educated in science, literature, and the arts. His archaeological experience was wholly self-taught and largely a matter of common sense. Moore, although Harvard educated, was untrained in archaeology; his fieldwork, once again, was based on personal trial-and-error method. Nelson and Kidder were among the first professionally trained American archaeologists. Their education was broadly anthropological in nature, and each studied under the best archaeologists of the time. From Nelson's time on, American archaeologists were almost without exception well trained in anthropology.[4]

In *A History of American Archaeology,* Willey and Sabloff (1974) have characterized archaeology's major periods of growth, and the archaeologists discussed above illustrate these trends. Thomas Jefferson belongs to the "speculative period" which began with Columbus's voyage in 1492. The concern of the time was largely to explain the origin of American Indians, and, with the exception of Jefferson's rather sophisticated work, archaeology remained the pastime of the leisured armchair set. The subsequent "classificatory-descriptive period" ran from about 1840 to 1914 and can be characterized by the work of C. B. Moore. Archaeological research flourished during this period, with intensive exploration and excavation throughout the Americas. The stratigraphic excavations of Nels Nelson in New Mexico and simultaneously by Manuel Gamio in the Valley of Mexico ushered in the next major period, which largely emphasized problems of **cultural chronology**. In a sense, Nelson began the period and Kidder represented its culmination. In addition to Nelson's "stratigraphic revolution," the technique of seriation (Chapter 7) was established at the time, as was the refinement of artifact typology and ceramic classification. The goals of the period pointed toward a real synthesis, such as attempted by Kidder for the Maya and the cultures of the American Southwest.

As chronological problems became less acute, archaeologists such as James Ford took their anthropological training to heart and began to eclipse matters of chronology in order to explicate cultural contexts and functions. Although Ford made major contributions to the refinement of regional chronologies, he also participated in programs designed to delimit the overall settlement patterns and to attempt to reconstruct prehistoric social environments. Such was the state of American archaeology at midcentury.

REVOLUTION: ARCHAEOLOGY'S ANGRY YOUNG MEN

> Talent is what you possess; genius is what possesses you.
>
> *Malcolm Cowley*

The last section chronicled the progress of traditional American archaeology. A succession of hardworking, intelligent people such as Moore, Kidder, and Ford represent the mainstream archaeological thinking of their day. The methods and theories of American archaeology evolved along a steady, unbroken course. Individual archaeologists came and went, each contributing something, each lending a few of his own ideas to the cumulative body of archaeological thought. This is mainstream American archaeology.

But archaeology also grew by revolution. A succession of "angry young men" challenged traditional archaeological thinking, urging rapid change and immediate results; two of them have been particularly influential in shaping modern thought in American archaeology, and we will examine their angry words in the contexts of the more traditional thought discussed in the last section.

> **E**very man without passions has within him no
> principle of action, nor motive to act.
> *Claude Helvétius*

W. W. Taylor (1913–)

W. W. Taylor was educated at Yale and Harvard. After completing his doctoral dissertation late in 1942, Taylor promptly enlisted and subsequently spent the next couple of years overseas, as he put it, "not a little incommunicado" (1948:7). Taylor found upon returning to the States that his former professors had arranged a Rockefeller Foundation fellowship, which ultimately allowed him to expand his dissertation for publication.

A Study of Archeology, published in 1948 as a Memoir of the American Anthropological Association, was a bombshell.[5] Received with alarm and consternation throughout the archaeological community, *A Study of Archeology* was

Figure 1–7
Walter W. Taylor during his survey of Coahuilla, Mexico, in 1937 (*courtesy of Walter W. Taylor*).

no less than an overt call for revolution. The bourgeois archaeologists—the fat cats—were bombasted, assailed, and berated by this wet-behind-the-ears newcomer. Few liked Taylor's book, but everybody read it.

Taylor's dissertation set out first to diagnose the ills of pre-1940s archaeology and then to propose drastic remedial action. In the first part of his work Taylor launched an attack on the leading figures in American archaeology. This attack was all the more plucky because Taylor was himself a mere novice; he had published little and had not yet established his credentials as an archaeologist, much less a critic. Undaunted, Taylor sighted in on the archaeological establishment and let them have it between the eyes.

A Study of Archeology included an assault on A. V. Kidder, among others. Taylor considered Kidder to be "the most influential exponent of archeology in the Western hemisphere" (1948:44); and for precisely this reason, Kidder became fair game. What offended Taylor most was Kidder's alleged two-faced attitude: Kidder said one thing, yet did another. Kidder repeatedly asserted that he was an anthropologist who had specialized in archaeology; Kidder's advanced degree was in anthropology; Kidder had taught anthropology; Kidder headed the Carnegie Institution's fine team of anthropologists; Kidder considered himself to be an anthropologist. Taking this as a baseline, Taylor then closely analyzed Kidder's actual contributions to determine how well Kidder's deeds conformed to his own anthropological objectives.

Taylor boldly concluded that there was no conformity. He could find in Kidder's research no cultural synthesis, no picture of life at any site, no consideration of cultural processes, no derivation of cultural laws, no cultural anthropology at all. These are heady criticisms: here was a young archaeologist, barely out of graduate school, attacking the major archaeologist of the decade. And not only did Taylor accuse Kidder of practicing bad archaeology, Taylor also accused Kidder of not practicing what he preached.

These were serious charges, considered by most archaeologists of the time to be blasphemous. Taylor supported his reasoning with a detailed dissection of Kidder's published works. Kidder's research at Pecos, New Mexico, and elsewhere in the American Southwest was called full of "apparent contradictions," merely "description . . . for its own sake." Kidder was scored for failing to present detailed artifact proveniences, for concentrating on very specialized aspects of the archaeological record, for ignoring fragmentary specimens, and for failing to go behind the objects to generate more culturally relevant data. In fact, Taylor said that Kidder was incapable of preparing a decent site report, much less of writing the anthropology of the prehistoric Southwest.

These criticisms were devastating, but Taylor was just warming up. He next focused on Kidder's famous research projects on the archaeology of the Maya. As chairman of the Division of Historical Research for the Carnegie Institution, Kidder possessed unrivaled power to direct and dictate the direction of Mayan research. Once again, Taylor accused Kidder of failing to live up to his own goals. Data were generated for their own sake: "We have descriptions of

Maya artifacts, of Maya buildings, of Maya epigraphy, together with comparative data designed to determine their derivation or inspiration . . . but we have no discussion of the place of all these objects within Maya culture, or even within the culture of any one site or part of one site" (Taylor 1948:48). To Taylor, these goals are antiquarian, not anthropological. And not only did Kidder botch his own research, but as the powerful chairman of the Division of Historical Research of the Carnegie Institution, Kidder misdirected the research of literally dozens of archaeologists who worked under his aegis. Taylor, in 1948, was indeed archaeology's angriest young man, and his eloquent tirade could hardly have been more damning.

Taylor spent page after page chronicling Kidder's failure to consider problems of an anthropological nature. Granting that Kidder had begun his research with anthropology in mind, Taylor concluded that somewhere along the line Kidder had been led astray. Commenting that "the road to Hell and the field of Maya archeology are paved with good intentions," Taylor concluded that the Carnegie Institution, under Kidder's direction, "has sought and found the hierarchical, the grandiose. It has neglected the common, the everyday." Kidder had been blinded by the "pomp and circumstance" of Classic Maya archaeology, and he forgot the mundane world of real people altogether.

Taylor was, in effect, attacking the "comparative" or "taxonomic" approach to archaeology. Kidder—and several other luminaries—were accused of classification and description for its own sake. They said they were anthropologists, but they did not do anthropology. While careful not to deny the initial usefulness of a comparative strategy, Taylor urged archaeologists to get on with the proper business of anthropology: finding out something about people. Chronology, to Taylor, serves only as a stepping stone, a foundation for more anthropologically relevant studies of human behavior and cultural dynamics.

> **W**hen you began with much pomp and show,
> Why is the end so little and so low?
> *W. Roscommon*

W. W. Taylor proposed what he called the **conjunctive approach** to archaeology. By conjunctive, Taylor emphasized the interconnection of archaeological objects with their cultural contexts. Emphasis was squarely on study within particular cultural entities, whereas the comparative studies emphasized relationship outside and between archaeological sites. Taylor attacked Kidder's Mayan research on this basis: Kidder, you're too concerned with comparing things—temples, glyphs, fancy potsherds—between sites; you've failed to explain what goes on within any single Maya site. To Taylor, Kidder was concerned only with skimming off the spectacular and the grandiose. A conjunctive approach would study a single Maya center, with the objective of writing as complete an ethnography as possible of the Maya people who once lived there. In effect, Taylor urged archaeologists to leave the temple steps and look for the garbage dumps. Messy business, this conjunctive archaeology, but Taylor argued that this is the only way for archaeologists to achieve their anthropological goals.

Taylor proposed a number of specific improvements designed to implement a conjunctive approach to archaeology. Archaeologists should quantify their results (trait lists are rarely useful); they should test hypotheses and progressively refine their interpretations (too often initial observations were taken as gospel); they should excavate less extensively and more intensively (too many sites were just "tested" then compared to other faraway "tests" with no effort to find patterning within sites); they should save and closely study food remains (the bones, seed hulls, and garbage heaps were too often shoveled out); they should involve more specialists in the analysis of finds (zoological, botanical, and petrographic identifications were too often made in the field and never adequately verified); and they should write more detailed site reports (too often only the spectacular finds were illustrated and exact proveniences disregarded).

In reading over Taylor's proposals some thirty-five years after they were written, I am struck by how mundane, almost pedestrian, they now seem. Where is the revolution? Archaeologists do quantify their results, they do test hypotheses, they do excavate intensively, they do save food remains, they do involve specialists in analysis, and they do write detailed site reports.

But the fact is that archaeologists did not do these things routinely in 1940, and this is what Taylor was shouting about. Taylor's recommendations of 1948 contain very few surprises for today's student, and this fact alone is a measure of how much archaeological theory and method have improved since Taylor wrote *A Study of Archeology.*

How, one might ask, did young Taylor get away with all of this? In one sense, he did not get away with it at all. Richard Woodbury reviewed Taylor's book in *American Antiquity,* the most prominent archaeological journal in the Americas. Writing in 1954, Woodbury noted that Taylor's book had rarely been discussed in print.

> It is in verbal, and generally informal, comments that archaeologists have been most out-spoken concerning *A Study of Archeology,* and it is my impression that such comments have been preponderantly disapproving and rarely favorable. Some comments have been in the nature of outraged resentment that such "disagreeable" things should have been said in print . . . others, and perhaps especially those more nearly Taylor's contemporaries, have expressed disappointment that the soundness of some of his comments should be completely vitiated by association with such highly opinioned views, and the whole decked out in grandiose language. (Woodbury 1954:292)

Woodbury went on to score Taylor on many counts, for "crusading for a cause" and exhibiting a "patronizing attitude." Although *A Study of Archeology* was never reviewed in *American Anthropologist*—which itself tells us something— Taylor was roundly criticized in a letter to the editor by Robert Burgh (1950).

Taylor had an unfortunate habit of illustrating the "good" archaeology with examples from his own unpublished field studies in the American Southwest and Coahuila, Mexico. Archaeologist Paul Martin's reaction was fairly typical:

> I think Taylor's ideas would have been far more favorably received and more widely accepted if he had first put out an archaeological report embodying his ideas. . . . To me a concrete example is more easily grasped than an abstraction or a theory; and we who teach could then point to the applications of his principles. I still await with pleasure Taylor's publications of his archaeological work in Mexico. (1954:571)

Today, some thirty-five years after publication of *A Study of Archeology,* much of Taylor's field studies remain unpublished, unavailable for scrutiny by other archaeologists, who ask him: "When will you publish your work on Coahuila? You attacked Kidder for saying one thing, yet doing another. If your ideas are so great, why didn't you ever publish the archaeology to back them up?" Taylor recently responded, rather lamely, to these charges, suggesting that he "provided enough pertinent material for critics to chew on for quite a spell . . . I cannot see that my default explains or condones the lack, in the literature of American archeology, of any objective, thorough, critique of *A Study of Archeology"* (Taylor 1972:30). American archaeologists since the time of Thomas Jefferson have acknowledged the necessity, in fact the obligation, to publish their own findings. Taylor's critique suffered because of his failure to do so.

A principle is never useful of living or vital until it
is embodied in an action.
Manly Hall

Lewis R. Binford (1930–   )

Taylor had the aims but not the tools.
Lewis R. Binford

Archaeology's second angry young man is Lewis R. Binford. After a period of military service, Binford enrolled in 1954 at the University of North Carolina. He wanted to become an ethnographer. By the time Binford moved on for graduate work at the University of Michigan he was a confirmed archaeologist.

As a young professional, Binford was a man on the move—literally. He first taught a year at Michigan, then moved on to the University of Chicago, then to the University of California at Santa Barbara, then down the Coast to UCLA, finally out to the University of New Mexico in Albuquerque.

Binford came into contact with the brightest of the upcoming generation of archaeologists in his professional travels, and we will discuss many of them in the later pages of this book. The mid-1960s was a hectic time for archaeology. A great deal of alienation and confrontation was taking place nationwide, and archaeology was imbedded in the academic trends of the times. This revolutionary spirit was due in part to the generally disquieting attitude that permeated university campuses during the Vietnam war era. Things must change—not just war and poverty and racism and oppression, but also the academic structure itself. Scholarship must become relevant; the older ideas must give way to newer thoughts. Such was the social climate in which Binford operated. I am convinced that without the revolutionary spirit and social upheaval of the mid-1960s Binford's archaeology would have taken a much different, somewhat more benign form.

But Binford was a man with a message. A dramatic lecturer, he rapidly took on the role of messiah, and his students became the disciples, spreading the word throughout the land. The Binfordians preached a gospel with great appeal in the 1960s. Archaeology does have relevance; archaeology should transcend potsherds to issues of cultural evolution, human ecology, and social organization; archaeology should take full advantage of modern technology such as computers; archaeology should become more scientific, practicing rigid logic and more sophisticated, quantitative methods of analysis; archaeology should be concerned with the few remaining preindustrial peoples in order to observe the operation of disappearing cultural adaptations. As Binford's movement gained momentum, nothing was considered sacred in the traditionalist paradigm of archaeology. As Binford himself characterized these early years, he and his colleagues were "full of energy and going in all directions at once" (Binford 1972:125).

Binford and his students—and their students—became the agents of change in American archaeology during the 1960s. The phrase *new archaeology* has become associated with their brand of investigating the past. The battle plan for the new archaeology was set forth in a seminal series of articles that Binford wrote throughout the 1960s and early 1970s. Binford's first major paper was entitled "Archaeology as Anthropology" (Binford 1962). In it, Binford squarely confronted the question of why archaeology has made so few contributions to general anthropological theory. His answer was that the material culture of the past had been treated in only cursory fashion. Too much attention had been lavished on artifacts of shared behavior, as traits that "blend," "influence," and "stimulate" one another.

Somewhat later (1965), Binford ridiculed this approach as the *aquatic view of culture:* "Interpretive literature abounds in phrases such as 'cultural stream' and in references to the 'flowing' of new cultural elements into a region. Culture is viewed as a vast flowing stream with minor variations in ideational norms" (1965:205). Echoing Taylor, Binford proposed that artifacts be examined in terms of their cultural contexts. Some tools (**technomic artifacts**) function primarily to cope with the physical environment, and variability is explicable largely in ecological terms. Other (**sociotechnic**) artifacts function primarily in the social subsystem and a third kind of artifact (**ideotechnic**) reflects most clearly the mental, cognitive component of culture.

W. W. Taylor on the New Archaeology

I like to think that this turmoil [the new archaeology], insofar as it represents an active dissatisfaction with traditionalism and a questing for more productive research design, is, at least in part and however belatedly, a result of the ideas and exhortations of *A Study of Archeology* (Taylor 1948). As I see them now, the basic tenets of the conjunctive approach, as explicitly set forth in that monograph, can be particularized as follows:

1. Since archaeology in the United States has long been considered a subdiscipline of anthropology, the subject of archaeological inquiry is the nature and workings of culture—with the corollary that it is interested in the "nature of culture" in all its particularistic, partitive variability, as well as in its "workings" or processes relative to some more generalized, holistic concept of culture.

2. Like cultural anthropology, archaeology is an historical discipline, but one whose empirical data fall within only four categories: chemico-physical specifications, provenience, quantity, and relationships or "affinities" (Taylor 1948:111f.) and whose recourse to inference must therefore be proportionately great—with the corollary that its conclusions are not provable but are in the nature of ever closer approximations to some finitely unknowable reality, i.e., working hypotheses which must be tested and refined by specifically programmed investigations.

3. Culture is integrated, or "systemic" as modern jargon has it, to such an extent that cultural manifestations cannot be truly depicted or understood apart from their contexts—with the corollary that construction of cultural context is an absolute requisite for anthropological archaeology (or archaeological anthropology).

4. Cultural context consists not merely of material objects, singly or in categories, but includes relationships between and among cultural and noncultural phenomena, which relationships or "conjunctives" serve to connect the meaning as well as the construction of archaeological contexts.

5. One of the most efficient and productive ways of utilizing these conjunctives is by multiple categorizations based upon the many inherent characteristics and relationships which each archaeological datum has.

6. The concrete, empirical findings of archaeology can be manipulated and interpreted to provide evidence of cultural behavior, of the nonmaterial results of cultural behavior, and of culture itself—with the corollary that this evidence, specifically and explicitly argued, may be used to enrich the cultural contexts and to support subsequent and consequent studies of culture itself and of cultural process.

If these tenets sound familiar to contemporary archaeologists, especially to those of the "new" or "processual" school, it does not surprise me at all. Much of the "new archaeology" is operating with a conceptual scheme which is virtually identical, in its basic ideas, with that anticipated in *A Study of Archeology*. What does surprise me, however, is that it has taken the many years since 1948 for that conceptual scheme to take hold! Perhaps it is as one colleague predicted: that *A Study of Archeology* would not be widely accepted until a new generation of archaeologists had come along without so much subjective and emotional involvement in the then status quo. Perhaps the popularly held view that my criticism of Americanist archaeology was a polemic aroused such partisan and defensive animosity that the message of the rest of the volume was lost. Perhaps it is somehow indicative that, only a few months ago on the latest of not a few similar occasions, I heard a colleague pay formal, public tribute to the influence upon him of *A Study of Archeology*, only to discover that his most recent theoretical publication cites the monograph only once, a parenthetical page reference, but does quote at considerable length more recent works by other authors as the sources of some of the most basic and distinctive ideas of *A Study of Archeology*.

Perhaps there have been academic-pedagogic-generational reasons for the lag: the older generation taking umbrage but maintaining a dignified silence and largely ignoring my insurgency, at least in public and in print; the next generation (that of my peers) in some cases taking up the cudgels which their mentors and idols had declined to wield, in others tempering their own traditional viewpoint to accept some of my ideas and consequently being more tolerant of their own students' attitudes and actions; and the third, the present generation, once removed from the traditional archaeologists and with more permissive instructors, accepting the insurgency to varying degrees and in varying segments of their archaeological theory. (Taylor 1972:28–29)

Critical here is the notion of the **cultural system**. Following Leslie White (see Chapter 3), Binford argued that archaeologists must view cultures as the nonbiological mechanism for relating the human organism to its physical and social environments. In other words, the same artifact can take on different archaeological significance depending on which questions are asked by the archaeologist.

Along this line, Binford emphasized the importance of explicit scientific methods. Archaeologists cannot function as passive receptors, waiting for the artifacts to speak up. Archaeologists must pose pointed questions (**hypotheses**) of the archaeological record; these hypotheses are then to be tested on the remains of the past. Binford argued, for instance, that preindustrial peoples can function as *analogues* for archaeological inquiry (1967). The analogues serve as the basis for hypotheses, which are then tested on the archaeological record.

If, as Binford argued, archaeologists should be more scientific and use more logical forms of reasoning, then archaeological field procedures must also be refined to provide higher-quality data. Binford argued that because archaeologists always deal with samples, they should collect their data in such a way as to make the samples more representative of the populations from which they were drawn. Binford urged archaeologists to expand their horizons from the individual site to the regional scale (Binford 1964), so that the entire cultural system could be analyzed. And these regional samples must be executed using research designs based on the principles of probability sampling. Random sampling is commonplace in other social sciences, and Binford urged archaeologists to apply these techniques to their own specific research problems.

The hardest thing to learn in life is which bridge
to cross and which to burn.
                                        David Russell

Binford's methodological contributions were then gradually supplemented by major projects designed to show how the approach fosters an understanding of the processes of culture. Complex statistical techniques were applied to a variety of subjects, from the nature of Mousterian (some 50,000 years old) campsites to the patterning of African Acheulian (hundreds of thousands of years old) assemblages. These studies are important because they embroiled Binford in actual, substantive debates. Not only did he advocate different goals and new methods, but he related to field archaeologists through substantive issues. He argued about specifics. He presented a long discussion of the nature of post-**Pleistocene** human adaptations (1968a), and he conducted fieldwork among the Nunamiut Eskimo (Binford and Chasko 1976; Binford 1978) and the Navajo (Binford and Bertram 1977).

The contributions of Binford and his students will be discussed several times throughout this text. For now, we are concerned with the role of Binford as one of archaeology's angry young men.

In true Taylor-like fashion, Binford assailed archaeology's stellar figures and accused them of holding back the discipline. And yet the reception was

Figure 1–8
Lewis R. Binford inspecting an abandoned aborigines' camp near MacDonald Downs Homestead, Australia. The melons scattered about are of a type formerly cultivated when the site was occupied by Alyawara-speaking aborigines (*courtesy of James F. O'Connell*).

really quite different. Why was response to Taylor so muffled, while Binford is now hailed as "the father of the new archaeology"? Why was Binford's work so rapidly discussed throughout the world, while *A Study of Archeology* languished on the shelf for nearly two decades?

A partial answer lies in their plans of attack. Taylor was always the loner, a pup yipping at the heels of archaeology. By contrast, Binford moved into the heart of the archaeological establishment, teaching at the Universities of Michigan, Chicago, California (Los Angeles and Santa Barbara), and New Mexico within a decade. Binford's influence was rapidly spread across an entire archaeological generation, while Taylor's influence remained covert and rarely acknowledged.

Binford had numbers on his side. While Taylor still attempts to defend the lack of application of the "conjunctive method" (e.g., Taylor 1972), the new archaeologists can point to achievements of Binford's dozens of students and cohorts.

Another major factor is that the field of anthropology had itself changed in two decades. The anthropology of Taylor's time was a rather restricted discipline. Theoretical programs such as cultural ecology and human ecology were still treated with skepticism, and the prevailing feeling was generally one of particularism: culture was too complex to be explained by far-reaching theories. In fact, Taylor's own professor at Harvard, Clyde Kluckhohn, had badly scored his anthropological colleagues for narrow-mindedness. Change was hard to come by in the 1940s.

By contrast, the 1960s were a time of profound change. The archaeological-academic establishment had opened up. Postwar enrollments had expanded the campuses so that hundreds of new jobs became available for archaeologists. Contemporary issues such as racial, sexual, and age discrimination forced changes in the hiring practices on campus. No longer could jobs be controlled as part of the "good old-boy" network. Archaeology had grown so much as a profession that by the 1960s plenty of room was available for mavericks, freethinkers, and nonconformists.

Everything changed in the 1960s: popular music, hair length, dress codes, degree requirements, to say nothing of the pervasive social and economic upheavals across the nation. As discussed in Chapter 3, the 1960s were also a time of great change within anthropology. Theorizing was once more acceptable: anthropology witnessed a **"nomothetic"** revival. Moreover, many anthropologists themselves woke up to the relevance of archaeological research in the overall study of mankind. One anthropologist, Marvin Harris, urged his colleagues to reject the unnecessary conditions they had previously placed on the archaeological subdiscipline: archaeological units are every bit as real and acceptable as those used by ethnographers (Harris 1968b; also see Chapter 3). Archaeologists gained a new respectability as anthropologists in the 1960s. This changed attitude was both the cause and the result of Binfordian archaeology.

But perhaps the most important factor in Binford's success was timing.

The Difference between History and Evolution

Are major events in history to be explained as the actions of the genius, or are geniuses the result of the forces of history? This topic has been a major concern of psychologists, historians, and sociologists. Anthropologists, too, have argued the point. Here is what Leslie White, a premier anthropologist, had to say about the role of the genius in history.

Culture does not grow or change at uniform rates; there are periods of intense activity and periods of stagnation and even retrogression. A culture may exhibit little change or progress over a long period and then suddenly burst forth with vigorous activity and growth. An invention or discovery such as metallurgy, agriculture, the domestication of animals, the keystone arch, the alphabet, microscope, steam engine, etc., may inaugurate an era of rapid change and progress.

But are not inventions the work of genius? The answer is of course "yes," if by genius you mean someone who makes a significant discovery or invention. But . . . to appeal to "genius" to explain the invention or discovery is an empty redundancy since genius is here defined in terms of the event, and the appeal to exceptionally great native endowment is unwarranted or at least misleading.

. . . An invention or discovery is a synthesis of already existing cultural elements, or the assimilation of a new element into a cultural system. . . . Just as the discoveries of Pasteur would have been impossible in the time of Charlemagne, so was agriculture impossible in the days of Cro-Magnon. Every invention and discovery is but a synthesis of the cultural accumulation of the past with the experience of the present.

Two significant conclusions can now be drawn: (1) No invention or discovery can take place until the accumulation of culture has provided the elements—the materials and ideas—necessary for the synthesis, and, (2) when the requisite materials have been made available by the process of cultural growth or diffusion, and given normal conditions of cultural interaction, the invention or discovery is bound to take place.

. . . The significance of the Great Man in history has been obscured by a failure to distinguish between history and evolution . . . [history] is characterized by change and is therefore unpredictable to a high degree: no one, for example, could have predicted that Booth would kill Lincoln—or whether or not his pistol would have missed fire when he pulled the trigger. [Evolution] however is determinative: prediction is possible to a high degree. In the decomposition of a radioactive substance one stage determines the next and the course and rate of change can be predicted. In short, we can predict the course of evolution but not of history.

The significance of the distinction between history and evolution and its relevance to the Great Man in history is brought out nicely in the debate between Kroeber and Sapir on the "superorganic." Kroeber argues that had Darwin died in infancy the advance and course of development of biological theory would have been much the same as it has been. Sapir counters by asking if the administration of law in New Orleans would have been the same today had it not been for Napoleon. Both disputants are wholly justified in their claims. Unfortunately, however, they are talking about two different things. One is dealing with a deterministic developmental process, the other with the fortuitous course of history. In the evolutionary process, the individual is, as Kroeber maintains and as the phenomena of multiple and simultaneous but independent discoveries and inventions clearly demonstrate, relatively insignificant. But, in the succession of chance occurrences that is history, the individual may be enormously significant. But it does not follow at all that he is therefore a "genius" or a person of exceptional ability. The goose who saved Rome was more significant historically than many an emperor who ruled it. (White 1949:201, 203, 204–205, 229–230)

Although Taylor's efforts in the 1940s were superficially abortive, they had a great, though covert, effect on archaeology. Many archaeologists were put off by Taylor's needlessly dogmatic and wordy appraisal of his contemporaries. Few actually questioned his aims, but, also, few appreciated his methods. The archaeology of the 1950s was in large measure a reaction to Taylor's suggestions, although he was rarely credited. Taylor in a real sense paved the way for Binford, who freely acknowledges the influence of *A Study of Archeology* on his own thinking: "I have frequently avoided citing Walter Taylor in my writings except in a positive way because his work was inspiring to me. Clearly I disagree with many of his arguments, yet in print I have avoided these issues on more than one occasion" (Binford 1972:541). Taylor is best viewed as the harbinger of significant change; Binford was the architect of that change.

Binford and his students set off a revolution which quickly spread throughout the archaeological community. A 1970s generation of new graduate students and young professionals was greeted with the admonition: Are you a new archaeologist, an old archaeologist, or what? Make up your mind!

> Today, if you are not confused, you are just not thinking clearly.
>
> *Irene Peter*

THE STATE OF CONTEMPORARY ARCHAEOLOGY

> People make their own history; however, they make it not of their own free will or under circumstances they have chosen themselves, but under circumstances directly encountered, given and transmitted from the past.
>
> *Karl Marx*

The development of American archaeology has been discussed in terms of some individual archaeologists because I think it is more interesting to deal with real people—their quirks, their idiosyncracies, their motivations. Biographical history makes a better story, and that is why I wrote Chapter 1 in this fashion.

But there is a danger in this approach, the danger of overemphasizing the role of the individual. I do not believe in the Great Man theory of history. We must distinguish between history and evolution (see inset).

History is a sequence of time-specific events, and people like Thomas Jefferson and Lewis Binford dramatically conditioned the history of American archaeology, which would not be the same without them.

But let us be certain to distinguish the history of archaeology from the **evolution** of archaeological thought. The evolution of important ideas is independent of the individuals who proposed them. Somebody had to go out and excavate the first archaeological site in America, and history tells us that that person was Thomas Jefferson. But had Jefferson died in childhood, nineteenth-century archaeology would have followed roughly the same course. Similarly, stratigraphic methods would have been adopted in America without Nels Nelson, and so would seriation without James Ford.

> **T**here is one thing stronger than all the armies in the world: and that is an idea whose time has come.
>
> *Victor Hugo*

This also applies to today's archaeology, although the distinction is harder to make because we are so much closer to the events. The new archaeology was an important event in the history of American archaeology. We must restrict the phrase new archaeology to an event-specific, historical usage. New archaeologists are specific scholars who made specific proposals, and these proposals made a great impact on the specific history of American archaeology between about 1960 and 1975.

New archaeology was an important historical entity, as was the Whig party or the Emancipation Proclamation. But these events only signified more far-reaching trends of the time.

There is no new archaeology in the sense of evolution. There is only contemporary archaeology. Note, for example, how few modern archaeologists even want to be called new (see inset). The condition of contemporary archaeology evolved from a number of inputs, some of them from the new archaeologists; but many of the contributions came from elsewhere. We must recognize that the thrust of American archaeology today would be almost identical even had Lewis Binford and his students opted for careers in, say, pharmacy.

Struggles twixt new and old make interesting history indeed, but this is not a history book. This book is about the methods, the techniques, the assumptions and the goals of contemporary archaeology. In this sense, we will be concerned more with newer solutions to older problems.

> **W**hen you get there, there isn't any there there.
>
> *Gertrude Stein*

The New Archaeology: What's in a Phrase?

> **N**ew archaeology . . . that precious and prissy phrase.
>
> *Glyn Daniel*

Scientists in general have the annoying habit of throwing the word *new* around indiscriminately. In recent years, we have been treated to the new systematics (Huxley 1940), the new biology (Birdsell 1972:534–535), and, somewhat closer to home, the new ethnography (Sturtevant 1964:99–101) and the new physical anthropology (Washburn 1951; Birdsell 1972).

So it comes as small surprise that we now have a new archaeology. Although the term is most commonly associated with Lewis Binford and his followers, the actual phrase predates the Binford era. In 1917, Wissler referred to his colleagues using stratigraphic excavation techniques as "the new archaeologists" (Wissler 1917). In 1954, Richard Woodbury discussed a "new archaeology," as did Haag somewhat later (1959). But the modern usage stems primarily from an article by Joseph Caldwell, published in *Science* in 1959, entitled "The New American Archaeology."

The term really caught on in the late 1960s and throughout the 1970s. One can hardly scratch the recent archaeological literature without being ambushed by the new: "Koster Site: The New Archaeology in Action" (Struever and Carlson 1977); "Working with the 'New Paradigm'" (Whallon 1974a); "The 'new archaeology' of the 1960s" (R. Watson 1972). BBC Science correspondent David Wilson (1974) even wrote a book entitled (what else?) *The New Archaeology.*

The term new archaeology is a troublesome one, used by many and agreed upon by few. To find out what American archaeologists really think about the term, I conducted an informal poll of the 640 archaeologists listed in the 1977 Guide to Graduate Departments, published by the American Anthropological Association. If there is a new archaeology, then surely these people must know about it.

My question was simple: are you a new archaeologist, a traditional archaeologist, or what? I encouraged people to express their opinion on the subject.

The response was so rapid and heavy that it was apparent that my little questionnaire had struck a nerve: archaeologists really are bothered by the term new archaeology. I received a total of 226 responses (35.3%), which surprised me.

The responses ranged from the enthusiastic to the irate. I was told that this was "probably the silliest questionnaire I have ever received," and my inquiry was called "foolish" and "a particularly loathsome example of simplistic reductionism." One very senior archaeologist berated me for not providing return postage, admitting that "the 13 cents almost prevented my reply." One colleague wrote simply: "Just leave me alone and let me do my own research!"

Other respondents praised me for "conducting relevant research," and I was urged to make the findings available to the archaeological community. One person suggested that "it's about time archaeologists took a good (anthropological) look at themselves."

The actual counts went like this:

Prefer to be called a *new archaeologist*	21.7 percent
Prefer to be called a *traditional archaeologist*	19.9 percent
Prefer to be called *something else*	58.4 percent

I found these results fascinating because they seem to mirror perfectly the split I had already noticed in contemporary archaeology.

Note that on the one hand nearly 40 percent of the archaeologists responding felt relatively comfortable with the new-traditional dichotomy within archaeology. Roughly one archaeologist in five wanted to be considered new, and about one in five wanted to be called traditional.

But the remaining 60 percent were wholly dissatisfied with the labels, and they could not comfortably characterize themselves as new or traditional. This 60 percent thought the categories were "outdated," "misleading," "oversimplified," "a crock of shit," or simply "dumb." While many expressed sympathy for the objectives of the new and the traditional in archaeology, they objected to their separation: "You can't do one without the other."

A number of original self-characterizations were offered, including these: alienated archaeologist, anthropological archaeologist, archaeoethnobotanist, behavioral archaeologist, closet traditionalist, cognitive archaeologist, competent archaeologist, conscientious archaeologist, confused archaeologist, contemporary archaeologist, current archaeologist, diachronic anthropologist, ecological archaeologist, ethnoarchaeologist, general archaeologist, *good* archaeologist, historical anthropologist, hybrid new-old archaeologist, middle-of-the-road archaeologist, modern archaeologist, new antiquarian, new fogey, new-traditional archaeologist, nonconformist, oddball archaeologist, omnivorous archaeologist, paleoenvironmentalist, paradigmatic archaeologist, pragmatic, prehistorian, real archaeologist, renegade archaeologist, salvage archaeologist, scrounge archaeologist, skeptical archaeologist, superannuated, synthetic archaeologist, transitional archaeologist, *working* archaeologist!, and zooarchaeologist.

As I compiled these answers, it became clearer than ever that archaeologists have at least as much trouble analyzing their own culture as they do the cultures of others.

It seems obvious that is is premature to write about the new archaeology in definitive terms. The position adopted here—and discussed fully in the text—is that the new archaeology is really a term describing an important development within the history of American archaeology. The new archaeology began in the early 1960s with the work of Lewis Binford. Today, much of the new archaeological program has been adopted by mainstream archaeology. Those people who still call themselves new archaeologists would seem to be reaffirming that they like what Lewis Binford said. I like what he said too, but I also like much that the traditionalists said. I conclude that too few archaeologists consider themselves new to justify using the term. I therefore relegate the new archaeology to historical contexts, describing it as the movement within archaeology that began about 1960 and ended in the mid-1970s. The rest of the book deals with contemporary archaeology.

SUMMARY

The origins of archaeology can be traced to Nabonidus, a sixth century B.C. Babylonian king, who turned to the physical residues of antiquity to answer relevant questions about the past. From that time to the present, archaeologists have continued, as Ciriaco put it in the thirteenth century, *to restore the dead to life.* The archaeology of the New World has been inextricably wed to the study of native American Indians, who provided endless clues for those attempting to understand America's remote past. The study of American archaeology can be traced through the work of scholars such as Thomas Jefferson and C. B. Moore who, though lacking formal anthropological training, applied the sound principles of scientific research to problems of America's prehistory. No longer the pastime of the genteel rich, twentieth-century American archaeology has become a specialized discipline, requiring intensive training not only in techniques of excavation but also in ethnology, classification, geology and even the philosophy of science. The gradual evolution of American archaeological thought has been stimulated by a few revolutionary archaeologists, most notably W. W. Taylor in the 1940s and Lewis R. Binford in the 1960s. Archaeology's "angry young men" urged their colleagues to stick by their anthropological guns, to attempt to define the processes operative behind the specifics of the archaeological record. The status of contemporary archaeology has been conditioned by both evolutionary and revolutionary thought to such an extent that only a single brand of anthropological archaeology exists today. The following chapters define the methods and goals of contemporary archaeology.

NOTES

1. The purist might argue with the statement that Nabonidus was the first archaeologist. When the famous Sphinx of Gizeh was excavated, a small inscribed slab was found between the paws. The slab related a tale of how Thutmose IV (ca. 1425–1417 B.C.) had once fallen asleep at the foot of the Sphinx and had a dream. Thutmose dreamt that he would receive the kingship if he would first clear away the sand dunes which had encroached onto the Sphinx. Thutmose dutifully did so and later became Pharaoh. Cleator (1976:20) suggests that this episode entitles Thutmose IV to be labeled the first archaeologist because "not only was an ancient site carefully excavated, but an account of the undertaking was subsequently published—two important requisites of archaeological activity in the field." Taylor (1948) also makes the claim that the Irish were collecting antiquities as early as 700 B.C.

2. As my colleague J. Jefferson Reid has pointed out, the selection of *forefathers* seems to preclude *foremothers,* or even the mention of females in the field. This is not a conscious decision on my part, but rather the explicit recognition that American archaeology prior to 1960 was in fact a male-dominated field. Women were excluded from American archaeology for decades, and history will necessarily reflect this. Hence my use of

forefathers. But this unfortunate situation is rapidly changing, a fact that is obvious from my later discussion of what is happening in contemporary archaeology. In fact, a glimpse at my bibliography will be sufficient to underscore the fact that many of the best contemporary American archaeologists also happen to be female.

3. Today, there is a prevalent feeling that archaeology should even include the study of contemporary people (see Chapters 3 and 12).

4. I must mention here that the classical archaeologist receives an education that is more humanistic than anthropological, with major emphasis on philology and art history.

5. *A Study of Archeology* was republished by Southern Illinois Press in 1964.

What Is Science?

The real purpose of scientific method is to make sure Nature hasn't misled you into thinking you know something you don't actually know.
Robert Pirsig

The year was 9268 B.C. The man was trying to make a **Clovis** spearpoint. He crouched on a flat spot at the foot of the chalk cliffs, near Rattlesnake Buttes in northeastern Colorado. "Coughing twice, rubbing his fingertips on his chest, he lifted the heavy rock and studied it for the last time." His tools had been purposefully selected. The hammerstone was ovoid and of a grainy texture: "It was the possession he prized most in his life." Carefully flaking through the cortex, he struck flake after flake, until the core was exhausted. "He dropped his hammerstone, threw back his head and winked at his helper: 'Good, eh.'" Then he reached for his boomerang-shaped soft hammer, fashioned of antler. Gradually, the amorphous flake was "roughed out" into the unmistakable shape of a spearpoint. Taking the elk antler, he pressure-flaked the edges, fashioning "a scimitar-sharp edge around the entire point." Finally, he used his chest-crutch to force off a flake running half the length of the point. The **fluting** complete, the craftsman stood back and admired his finished Clovis point.

Once the point had been mounted on a sturdy wooden shaft, the craftsman summoned his friends to ambush a mammoth at the neighborhood waterhole. "The mammoth took one faltering step and dropped dead. Not once in a hundred times could a hunter reach a vital point with his spear; usually death was a long-drawn process of jabs in the side and chasing and bleeding, requiring two or three days. But this was a lucky blow, and the men howled with delight."

SCIENCE IS SCIENCING

That was how novelist James Michener described incidents in the life of Clovis man in his best-seller *Centennial* (1974). Using the medium of his craft—language—Michener created a slice of American life 11,000 years ago. The Clovis spearpoint, to Michener, is not an inanimate artifact made of gray-brown stone. The Clovis point is "the finest work of art ever produced in the Centennial region . . . a prime fact of our intellectual history." The Clovis craftsman was not a brow-ridged, apelike knuckle dragger; he was "indistinguishable from other men who would occupy this land ten thousand years later . . . he had considerable powers of thought, could plan ahead, could devise tactics for hunting . . . he did not take himself too seriously." This description is imaginative to be sure, but probably not too far from the mark. While not facts, Michener's inferences are credible, given what we now understand about the archaeology of the prehistoric Clovis culture. As an artist, James Michener grappled with a segment of human experience and attempted to render it intelligible to others. Through his art, Michener attempts to assist modern man in adjusting himself to his environment by understanding his human past.

Like James Michener, artists are characterized by what they do: they attempt to confront human reality, then explain it to others by illustration. Generalities are illustrated by specifics, universals by particulars. Michener wanted to explain what it was like to be a Clovis hunter; he did so by considering one particular hunter in 9268 B.C. at Rattlesnake Buttes, Colorado.

As strange as it might seem, modern scientists share Michener's ultimate objective, to render the human experience intelligible. But scientists approach this goal from the opposite direction. To a scientist, particulars are important only for what they can tell about the universal. In a scientific mode, Michener's mammoth, the Clovis point, and the prehistoric flintknapper are relevant only for what they can tell us about the Clovis culture in general.

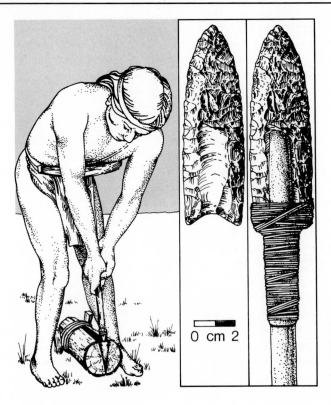

0 cm 2

Figure 2–1
Flintknapper
manufacturing a Clovis
point; the finished
products appear at
right.

So science is an attempt to abstract universals from particulars. But, you might object, so is religion. What distinguishes science from religion is the scientist's commitment to explaining things in naturalistic terms without recourse to supernatural beings and forces. The methods of science and religion also differ. The next section deals with the methods of science in some detail. For now, it is sufficient to use the word **science** to denote the search for the universal in nature, using the established scientific method of inquiry.

A scientist is one who does science. The title of this section, taken from Leslie White's *Science of Culture* (1949), tells it all: science is sciencing. Scientists are not people who wear white lab coats or have offices in science buildings or subscribe to *Science* magazine. The scientist is one who uses the scientific method to abstract universals from a world of particulars. It is that simple.

Art and science thus grasp a common
experience, or reality, by opposite but
inseparable poles.
Leslie White

THE LAWS OF SCIENCE: PREDICTING THE PAST

> **S**cientists are Peeping Toms at the keyhole of eternity.
>
> *Arthur Koestler*

Science *is* what science *does*. That is what we have decided. Scientists systematically search for universals in nature, and these universals are called **laws**. But if archaeology is a science—and it is—then what are the laws of archaeology? And how would we recognize a law if we stumbled upon it?

To begin with, the word "law" is itself ambiguous because, in a legal sense, laws are structures that can be (and are) broken. "Legal" laws are formal prohibitions of acts that people are prone to commit anyway, and can be expected to continue to commit, if on a reduced scale. Many cities have laws prohibiting jaywalking. The mere fact that such a law exists suggests the possibility of someone, somewhere, actually crossing the street illegally. Why else would we need the law?

By contrast, the ultimate laws of science are inviolable. Laws in nature are statements of what has been, what is, and—we have every reason to think— what will be. A scientific law is no more or less than a complete statement of what actually happens. As scientific laws become more completely understood, the better they describe actual phenomena. To imply that a law of this sort could somehow be violated is absurd. One cannot disobey what actually happens. As John Kemeny (1959:38) has suggested, the laws of nature do not prescribe, they describe.

This is somewhat tricky, however, because the actual laws (or better, lawlike generalizations) in science are modified or rejected all the time by scientists. This is because we so imperfectly understand the laws we are after. So while the ultimate laws of nature are inviolable, many of the lawlike generalizations being discussed by scientists are only poor approximations of these ultimate laws. And, of course, the worse the approximation, the less effective is the lawlike statement.

Scientific laws are of interest not just because they describe the past and present, but because they also describe the future. That is, laws predict events that have not yet occurred. Newton's law of gravity, for example, not only tells us about the behavior of apples that have fallen and apples that are falling, but also about all future apples that will fall.

Archaeology, of course, deals largely with past events, so the question arises as to precisely what the archaeologist wishes to predict. Haven't all archaeological events already taken place? Is there such a thing as *predicting the past?* As the title of this section suggests, archaeologists *can* (and do) predict the events of the past. Binford (1968b:271) has reminded us that although the archaeological record is comprised of past events, the knowledge of this record is a contemporary phenomenon. The **Folsom** culture discussed today is not the same Folsom culture discovered in New Mexico in 1926, even though we generalize from some of the same artifacts and features. Science as practiced in archaeology predicts events of the past, but these events are new in the sense that they are new to us. Predicting and verifying that a massive drought occurred in 1530 B.C. is no less a scientific achievement than predicting that such an event will occur sometime in the future.

Although all sciences desire to formulate laws of nature, each specific science deals with its own theoretical structures and subject matter. The laws of physics deal primarily with motion, those of chemistry involve molecular reactions, those of social science relate to actions and reactions of *Homo sapiens*. The laws of archaeology are likewise colored by conditions unique to the study of the past. These characteristics can best be understood through an illustrative sample.

Two threads seem to run through the history of anthropology: Darwin's theory of natural selection, and theories regarding the progressive evolution of culture. While modern biology and physical anthropology have provided ample support for Darwinism, the cultural evolutionists have lagged far behind. Even today, there are still anthropologists who rebel at the very notion that evolution can be described in lawlike fashion. This disagreement is partially terminological, since people often use the same words for different ideas. We owe much to Marshall Sahlins and Elman Service for their lucid clarification of this semantic issue. They suggest that cultural evolution is most profitably viewed as a "double-faceted phenomenon."

> Any given system—a species, a culture or an individual—improves its chances for survival, progresses in the efficiency of energy capture, by increasing its adaptive specialization. This is **specific evolution**. The obverse is directional advance or progress stage by stage, measured in absolute terms rather than by criteria relative to the degree of adaptation to particular environments . . . a man is higher than an armadillo . . . this is **general evolution**." (Sahlins and Service 1960:94–95)

The primary distinction is one between *cultures* and *culture*. Specific cultures adapt to their unique cultural-environmental setting, sometimes evolving toward increasing specialization, at other times remaining relatively stable for thousands of years. Culture, on the other hand—the worldwide, nonbiological knowledge of lifeway—is frequently moving from heterogeneity toward homogeneity, as more technologically advanced groups expand over the world at the expense of the less powerful cultures.

With these two types of evolution in mind, we can examine an anthropological law, which Sahlins and Service term the **law of evolutionary potential**:

> The more specialized and adapted a form in a given evolutionary stage, the smaller its potential for passing to the next stage. Another way of putting it . . . is: Specific evolutionary progress is inversely related to general evolutionary potential. (1960:97)

Sahlins and Service tell us that the group with the more generalized adaptation has the greater evolutionary potential (potential for change) than the group with a highly specific adaptation. The archaeological record abounds with examples of this law, often in the guise of the "northern barbarian" invasion. Mexican prehistory is replete with cases of raiders from the north—Chichimecs—who time after time overwhelmed the established state. Moving from their homeland on the primitive frontiers of northern Mexico, the **Toltecs** moved south to found Tula, the city-state that ruled after the fall of classic **Teotihuacán**. Tula later suffered the same fate as Teotihuacán, namely destruction at the hands of another semibarbaric tribal group. A similar case could be made for the relationship of ancient Rome to Greece, and the rise of modern China. These cases have a common denominator in that, all else being equal, rapid evolutionary progress occurs among the have-nots, not among the establishment. Agriculture, for example, did not arise, as we shall see (in Chapter 13), among the hunter-gatherer groups in ecologically favored areas, but rather in areas of stress and competition. Plant domestication appeared initially among those who were not deeply mired in some stable, yet conservative, productive network.

The law of evolutionary potential—and this is true of any cultural law—is neither purely anthroplogical nor purely archaeological: it is a mixture of both. As archaeological data are progressively incorporated into general anthropological theory, rigid lines will continue to blur, and such laws will become an amalgam—archaeological-anthropological laws. Generalizations stated in law-like fashion will also usually be probabilistic in nature. The Sahlins-Service law is one of *potential,* not strict determinism. Archaeological laws cannot be expected to be exact, since such statements are often about incompletely understood phenomena. That is, we are only dealing with successive approximations to the laws of nature, and we can only hope that such predictions will be correct most of the time until we can specify more and more closely the conditions under which the phenomena will always occur. Additionally, all real-world experiments, especially in the archaeological world, are subject to errors in observation and interpretation. Although we have a powerful method for handling errors—the theory of statistics and probability—we can never be 100 percent sure of our facts. Thus, although an experiment may confirm a theory, we can never be absolutely positive that this outcome is not an error. Since the laws of nature are always incompletely known and experiments are always subject to error, archaeological-anthropological laws must be statistical, often couched in mediating terms such as "potential," "most likely outcome," "will usually," and "most frequently." We assume that the phenomena are not uncertain, but that it is the statement of the laws that must be uncertain.

Stated another way, laws in archaeology are timeless and spaceless generalizations regarding how cultural processes work. Archaeology is a science because archaeologists use scientific methods in the attempt to define cultural laws. Laws should thus be considered the ultimate goal of all archaeologists, and the final part of this book deals with such archaeological laws in detail. At this point, let us forego considering what laws actually are in order to see how those laws are found. How does one begin with particulars and end in generalities?

> **A**ristotle could have avoided the mistake of thinking that women have fewer teeth than men by the simple device of asking Mrs. Aristotle to open her mouth.
>
> *Bertrand Russell*

HOW SCIENCE EXPLAINS THINGS: THE SCIENTIFIC CYCLE

> **W**hen you've hit a really tough one, tried everything, racked your brain and nothing works, and you know that this time Nature has really decided to be difficult, you say, "Okay, Nature, that's the end of the *nice* guy."
>
> *Robert Pirsig*

It seems odd, but science in archaeology is better done than discussed. Archaeologists, it seems, have been doing pretty fair science, but only recently have they begun discussing their science in any detail (e.g. Fritz and Plog 1970; Watson, LeBlanc, and Redman 1971; Salmon 1975; Schiffer 1976; South 1977). Consider, for example, how scientific methods were employed in the search for the origins of plant domestication in the Americas. In 1948, Herbert Dick (then a graduate student at Harvard) excavated a site in southwestern New Mexico named **Bat Cave**. In addition to producing the typical examples of material culture from that area—projectile points, pottery vessels, shell beads, basketry, sandals, and so forth—Bat Cave yielded a very primitive form of corn. Radiocarbon tests indicated that these stubby little corncobs were between 4,000 and 5,000 years old, making them the oldest and most primitive corn in the world. Later the same year, another archaeologist, **Richard "Scotty" MacNeish**, discovered similar specimens in the caves of Tamaulipas, not far below the Mexican border. In the next few years, other northern Mexican excavations failed to recover any corn older than about 3000 B.C. In searching for older evidence of plant domestication, Scotty MacNeish traveled far to the south, into Guatemala and Honduras. Although he found no ancient corncobs, corn pollen was located in strata also dating about 3000 B.C.

With these data to work with, MacNeish paused to plan his next move. Since corn was no older than 3000 B.C. in both North America and far to the south of Mexico City, Scotty reasoned that if any older corn exists it should be found somewhere between the two areas tested—in southern Mexico. Additionally, intensive genetic studies conducted by MacNeish's colleague, Paul Mangelsdorf, indicated that corn had probably been domesticated from a highland grass. At this point, MacNeish decided that the best place to look for early domestication was in the uplands of southern Mexico.

In order to test this speculative theory, MacNeish made specific predictions to be tested in the field. Studying maps of southern Mexico, he narrowed his search to a couple of prime targets. The first area examined was Oaxaca, which was investigated and then rejected: no early corn was to be found there. Then MacNeish moved to his second choice, the Tehuacan Valley of Puebla State, Mexico. Because corncobs can be expected to survive only in deposits protected from moisture, search was limited to dry caves. After personally examining thirty-eight such caves, MacNeish test excavated Coxcatlan Cave, which produced six tiny corncobs more primitive than any ever discovered (see Chapter 10). Subsequent radiocarbon tests placed their antiquity at about 5,600 years, a full 500 years older than other corn. These findings supported MacNeish's theory about the origins of corn in Mexico and also help us to understand the overall processes of man's relationships to domesticated plants and animals (for a more complete discussion of MacNeish's research, see MacNeish 1964, 1978).

Figure 2–2
Initial excavations at Coxcatlan Cave in the Tehuacan Valley, Mexico (*after MacNeish 1967, figure 188; courtesy of Richard S. MacNeish and the University of Texas Press*).

The work of Scotty MacNeish illustrates the three essential components of scientific methods as they have been applied to archaeology:

1. Establish the hypothesis.
2. Determine the test implications of the hypothesis.
3. Test these implications by further observation.

Although MacNeish did not use these terms, he did follow the procedures rather closely. In fact, it has been a characteristic of archaeological research for over a century that archaeologists seem to practice rather careful scientific methods. It has been only in the last couple of decades that archaeologists have decided to talk about these methods in any detail (see Salmon 1976).

The first step is hypothesis formation. A **hypothesis** is a statement that somehow goes beyond the barest description of known facts. As an analogy, consider the known facts to be points drawn on a graph. Hypothesis formation is the process of drawing a single line to describe these points. In all cases, there are infinite hypotheses (lines) which could be drawn to account for the facts (the data points). The initial task of the scientist is to examine a number of the possible theories and then select the most likely—that is, the most probable—for actual testing (see Salmon 1976:378–380). On the graph, the most credible line is that which would pass through each of the points, regardless of how many curves were required in the line. If the points tended to fall in linear fashion, then a straight line would be the simplest hypothesis to describe the known data.

Hypotheses are generated through the process of **induction**. An inductive argument is one in which the conclusions contain more information than the premises (Salmon 1976). The premises in this case are the facts as known; the resulting hypothesis not only accounts for these known facts but also predicts properties of unobserved phenomena. There are no rules for induction any more than there are rules for obtaining good ideas. Some hypotheses are derived by enumeration of the data, isolating common features, then generalizing to unobserved data that are induced to have these common properties. In other cases, archaeologists turn to **analogies**, well-understood situations which seem to have relevance to poorly understood cases. But equally common is the bald application of good sense. Yes, insight, imagination, past experience, and guesswork all have a place in science. It does not matter where or how one derives the hypothesis. What matters is how well the hypothesis accounts for unobserved phenomena.

Of course it is entirely possible that several hypotheses will apply to the same data, just as several lines could be drawn to describe the points of a graph. The method of *multiple working hypotheses* has long been recognized in science (Chamberlin 1890). In practice, scientists generally work their way systematically through the various working hypotheses, testing them one at a time. One common scientific rule of thumb has been that the simpler hypothesis will tend to be correct. One generally commences with the simplest hypothesis to see how well it holds up under some new data. If the hypothesis fails the test, then the next, least-complicated hypothesis is tested, and so on.

Consider once again the MacNeish hypothesis of domestication. He began his research with a careful assessment of the known facts—the finds at Bat Cave and Tamaulipas, the reconnaissance in Guatemala and Honduras, and the available genetic information. These were, in a sense, his points to be accounted for. MacNeish doubtless could have come up with any number of hypotheses to explain these facts: corn could have been domesticated simultaneously all over **Mesoamerica** at 3000 B.C.; corn was domesticated independently in both the north and the south at the same time (3000 B.C.); corn was not domesticated in Mesoamerica at all, but rather traded from somewhere else, such as South America or even Mesopotamia. These are just a few of the large number of possible hypotheses that could be cited to explain the archaeological facts. By choosing the hypothesis he did, MacNeish selected the simplest of the available possibilities. But regardless of which hypothesis is initially selected, none can be accepted until it has been successfully tested by further observation. Mere induction does not lead to scientific acceptance.

The next step in the scientific method is to translate the hypotheses into testable form. A hypothesis can never be tested directly because hypotheses are general statements, and one can test only specifics. As Kemeny puts it, "The key to the verification of hypotheses is that you never verify them. What you verify are the logical consequences" (1959:96). In the classical **hypothetico-deductive** procedure, one uses deductive reasoning to find these logical outcomes.

A **deductive argument** is one in which the conclusions must be true, given that the premises are true. These deductive arguments generally take the form of "if . . . then" statements: *if* the hypothesis is true, *then* we would expect to observe the following logical outcomes. Bridging the gap from *if* to *then* is a tricky step. In the "hard" sciences, these **bridging arguments** derive directly from known mathematical or physical properties. In astronomy, for instance, the position of "unknown" stars can be predicted using a long chain of mathematical arguments grounded in Newtonian physics. The classic deductive method requires one to begin with an untested hypothesis and convert the generalities into specific predictions, based on bridging arguments of established mathematical and/or physical theory.

But how is this done in archaeology? Where is the well-established body of theory which allows us to convert abstract hypotheses into observable predictions? When MacNeish translated his general hypothesis into testable propositions, he actually was assuming several bridging arguments, although they were not explicit. Experience told MacNeish that corncobs will preserve for millennia in an arid cave atmosphere, but will decompose when exposed to moisture. So one should look in the dry cave, not the alluvial riverbanks. This is a bridging argument. Similarly, geneticists had suggested that maize had probably been domesticated as a highland grass, so MacNeish confined his search to the highlands. Here is another bridging argument, based this time on genetic theory.

The fact is that archaeology is almost bereft of explicit theory. The bridging arguments necessary for determining the logical outcomes of hypotheses are generally only seat-of-the-pants statements, and archaeological inference is hampered by this lack of precision (Schiffer 1976, Binford 1977). The development of this "middle-range theory" is a major focus of modern archaeological research, and we will spend an entire chapter discussing these developments (Chapter 12).[1]

The final operation in the scientific cycle is the actual testing of the implications. In the MacNeish example, this testing involved further archaeological reconnaissance in archaeologically unknown regions of southern Mexico, thereby generating new data. This new information was then analyzed, and MacNeish's hypothesis would have been rejected had the predictions not been verified. The Tehuacan case, in fact, confirmed MacNeish's hypothesis, so the proposition was elevated to the status of a lawlike generalization. Of course, a single experiment can never completely validate any hypothesis, and more intensive investigations are always necessary to increase the credibility. MacNeish's work at Tehuacan now stands as new data, ready for synthesis into a more inclusive hypothesis, which must again be tested in similar fashion. Scientific progress thus consists of the progressive pyramiding of verified hypotheses into a hierarchy of more generalized laws.

Figure 2–3 diagrams how the scientific cycle works. Cycle I begins in the

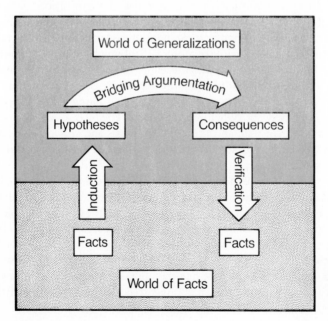

Figure 2–3
The scientific cycle
(*after Kemeny 1959:86;*
courtesy of Van
Nostrand Reinhold
Company).

world of facts. Through the process of induction, these facts are analyzed and hypotheses created in order to account for what is already known. But because the hypotheses are general, they cannot be tested against further facts and they must be translated into logical outcomes by use of relevant bridging arguments. The final step involves a return to the world of facts through the process of verification.

The scientific cycle begins and ends with facts. But these new facts themselves will suggest new hypotheses, and, once again, the process of induction will lead from the world of facts to the world of abstraction, thereby initiating a new cycle of investigation. You should realize that, as a method, science implies a continuing upward spiral in knowledge. The next section examines in detail how this scientific method was applied over a century ago to locate the lost city of Troy.

> **F**acts are stupid until brought into connection with some general law.
>
> *Louis Agassiz*

CASE STUDY: HEINRICH SCHLIEMANN AND THE NEW SIEGE OF TROY

> **H**istory is a cyclic poem written by Time upon the memories of man.
>
> *Percy Bysshe Shelley*

In 1875, **Heinrich Schliemann** captured the imagination of the world by announcing that he had discovered the fabled city Troy in Homer's *Iliad*. Dispelling two millennia of doubt, Schliemann announced in firm tones that not only had Homer been a marvelous epic poet—which everyone already knew— but also that Homer was a reliably accurate historian of the Trojan war. Schliemann's claim has since been subjected to a century of scientific scrutiny, and most contemporary archaeologists believe that he was correct. Schliemann really did find ancient Troy.

And yet Heinrich Schliemann remains an enigma in archaeology. When he began excavating at Troy, he had never conducted an excavation. Biographers and psychologists have seen a strong element of neurotic compulsion in Schliemann's work at Troy, an almost feverish drive to vindicate Homer's *Iliad*. Largely self-taught and lacking academic support, Schliemann organized and completely financed his own expeditions. The Turkish officials who administered his excavations considered him to be a crook and a scoundrel. Greek officials distrusted him, and nineteenth-century academics throughout the world accused him of shoddy scholarship. Frank Calvert, American vice-consul at the Dardanelles, who owned much of Troy, accused Schliemann of fakery and denied him further access to the site.

Figure 2-4
Heinrich Schliemann as a prosperous
young merchant in St. Petersburg, where
he accumulated his fortune as a trader in
commodities (*courtesy of Mrs. Gray***
Johnson Poole).**

In his brief yet colorful career, Schliemann earned an amazing variety of epithets: egotist, hypochondriac, megalomaniac, dilettante, gold seeker, privateer, and treasure hunter of the lowest order.

But Schliemann earned one other title: father of modern archaeology. Despite his mercurial manner and a compulsion to overstate his theories, Schliemann's historic work at Troy truly established scientific standards for thousands of modern archaeological excavations. I recommend that anyone interested in the works and life of Heinrich Schliemann read *The Greek Treasure* (1975) by Irving Stone or *Memoirs of Heinrich Schliemann* (1977) by Leo Deuel (also see McDonald 1967).

This section examines the Trojan excavations in some detail, because they so well illustrate how scientific methods actually work in archaeology. There is a tendency among modern archaeologists to think of scientific methods as somehow new or even revolutionary in archaeology. People who think this are wrong. It is true that archaeologists are becoming increasingly explicit and skillful in the use of scientific explanation, but the basics of this method have been with us for a long while. In fact, we can see every element of proper scientific investigation in Schliemann's Trojan excavation of the 1870s.

Troy: Historical Fact or Poetic Fancy?

The problem goes back to **Homer**, who by general consent has been rated as the world's first and greatest poet. Homer seems to have been born shortly before 850 B.C., although some would place this date as early as the tenth and eleventh centuries B.C. While many of the works traditionally ascribed to Homer have been lost, those that remain include the two famous epics, the *Iliad* and the *Odyssey,* some thirty hymns, and some scattered short pieces. The problem is this: was Homer a real person or a composite of several anonymous epic poets? We will never know.

At least we know that there was a real **Trojan war**. It occurred during the twelfth century B.C., when Troy was a wealthy regional capital. Troy was located just east of the Aegean Sea near the Dardanelles, facing the tiny island of Tenedos. The Trojan horizon was bounded on one side by Samothráke, a high snow-capped peak from which—according to Homer—Poseidon watched the epic siege of Troy. So magnificent were the towers and walls of the citadel that Greek tradition ascribed their construction directly to the hands of Poseidon and Apollo. On the summit of the Acropolis stood the palace of King Priam, and nearby were those of Hector and Paris. A single road led from the Trojan plain through the Scaean Gate into the heart of Troy.

It was on this broad plain that the legendary war took place. The Greeks invaded Troy to recover Helen, wife of Spartan King Menelaus. It seems that Paris, son of King Priam, had carried Helen off to Troy. It happened like this: Peleus and Thetis were getting married, and Eris—the only god not invited to the ceremony—was angry, so she flung a golden apple among the wedding guests. On the apple was inscribed "For the Fairest". This of course caused a furor among the vain Greeks. The goddesses finally referred the decision as to which of them was truly fairest to young Paris. He decided in favor of Aphrodite, thereby securing Helen for his own. In so doing, however, he also secured the enduring wrath of the slighted Greek goddesses. It was then that Agamemnon pledged to avenge the Trojan insult. He first assembled the greatest Greek heroes—Achilles, Patroclus, the two Ajaxes, Nestor, Odysseus, and Diomedes—then sailed to Troy with 100,000 men in 1,186 ships. The siege began when the Trojans refused to return Helen. Tradition tells us that the Greeks held Troy under siege for ten years. We all know how the siege was finally broken by Greek treachery. The Greeks retreated, leaving only a giant wooden horse, which the seemingly victorious Trojans hauled inside their walled city. Unfortunately for the Trojans, the wooden horse contained Greek soldiers who, once inside the walls, proceeded to sack and burn Troy.

> **S**o it goes.
> *Kurt Vonnegut Jr.*

Homer's *Iliad* tells the story of the siege, and stands as a landmark in classic literature. Speculation regarding the whereabouts of the Trojan fortress raged for two millennia. Ancient Greek tradition dictated that the ruin at **Hissarlik** was the actual site of Troy. The classical Greeks believed that, following the sack of Troy, Hissarlik had been periodically reoccupied. All traces of Troy were presumed buried beneath thick layers of later debris.

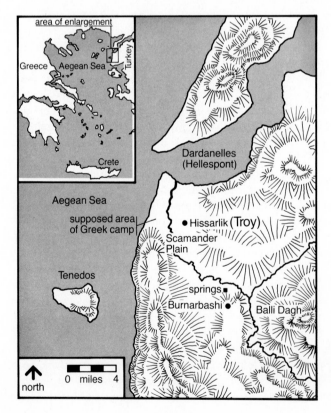

Figure 2–5
Map showing the location of Hissarlik (*after MacDonald 1967; courtesy of The Macmillan Company*).

This prevailing theory was questioned by the Greek historian Demetrios, who was born about 190 B.C. Homer had described Troy's setting in some detail:

> As often as [Agamemnon] looked towards the Trojan plain [from the Greek camp], he wondered at the many fires which were burning before [Troy], the sound of flutes and pipes, and the tumult of men. (10.10–13)[2]

The ruin at Hissarlik fronted a large plain, to be sure, but Demetrios argued that this plain had actually been a bay during Trojan times. According to Demetrios, the modern Scamander Plain fronting Hissarlik (Figure 2–5) was created by a successive buildup of post-Trojan alluvial (flood) deposition. Only recently had this large bay become so badly silted in that it became a low, rolling plain. Demetrios thought it impossible for the Greeks to have landed on the Aegean shore and then to have crossed the Scamander Plain to do battle at Hissarlik. The modern shore had been immersed in Trojan times.

Demetrios saw a second problem with Hissarlik. In book 22 of the *Iliad,* Homer described the final day of fighting at Troy. The Greeks had Troy under siege, and the Trojan warriors were forced to remain behind the locked walls of the city. Hector, son of the Trojan leader Priam, remained outside to meet the feared Greek warrior Achilles.

> Thus [Hector] pondered, remaining; but near him came Achilles, like unto the helmet-shaking warrior, Mars, brandishing upon his right shoulder the dreadful Pelian ash; but the brass shone around, like unto the splendor either of a flaming fire, or of the rising sun. (22. 132–136)

But for all his good intentions and bravery, Hector finally fled before the awesome Achilles:

> Then, as tremor seized Hector, he perceived him, nor could he remain there any longer, but he left the gates behind him, and fled affrighted . . . Hector fled in terror under the wall of the Trojans, and moved his fleet limbs. . . . A brave man, indeed, fled before, but a much braver swiftly pursued him. (22. 132–159)

The Trojans watched helplessly as Achilles chased Hector about their besieged capital.

> And as when prize-winning solid-hoofed steeds run very swiftly round the course, and a great reward is proposed . . . *so they thrice made the circuit of the city of* [*Troy*]: and all the Gods beheld. (22. 162–167)

Face to face, they crossed swords. "There noble Achilles, eager, drove into him with the spear and the point went quite through his tender neck" (22. 326–328). When finally Hector succumbed, the Greeks ran forth and "admired the stature and wondrous form of Hector; nor did any stand by without inflecting a wound" (22. 370–371). Achilles then

> perforated the tendons of both his feet behind, from the heel to the instep, and fastened them in leather thongs, and bound him from the chariot; but left his head to be trailed behind. Then ascending his chariot, and taking up the spendid armour, he lashed [the horses] to go on, and they, not unwillingly, flew. But the dust arose from them while trailing along, and [Hector's] azure locks around approached [the ground], and his entire head, once graceful, lay in the dust. (22. 395–404)

Thus ended noble Hector, dragged into the sunset of the Trojan plain, head bobbing from the chariot of Achilles. Thus also ends the *Iliad.*

As a staunch Greek historian, Demetrios refused to believe that Homer would have fabricated such a critical moment. Particularly crucial is the assertion that Achilles pursued Hector thrice about the city of Troy. Demetrios apparently traveled to Hissarlik and personally judged the topography to be unsuitable for such a chase. Demetrios thus rejected Hissarlik as ancient Troy on two grounds: Achilles could not have chased Hector around Hissarlik three times, and the modern Plain of Scamander had been a deep-water bay during Trojan times. Demetrios's conclusion was endorsed two centuries later by the influential Greek historian Strabo.

With the Hissarlik ruins in disrepute, Greek scholars began to question the historical accuracy of any of Homer's epics. Is the *Iliad* fact or poetic fiction? Through the next fifteen centuries following Demetrios's evaluation, the weight of opinion among Greek scholars shifted toward the notion that Troy was merely a convenient myth, created for poetic effect and wholly lacking in historical reality. F. A. Wolf compared the *Iliad* to the German *Niebelungenlied,* which could be dissected into shorter lays, each celebrating the deeds of individual heroes, and each composed by a different poet. Achilles, for instance, was compared to Siegfried, each having ultimate origins in mythological personages, each once worshipped as divine. Skepticism regarding Homer grew to such proportions in the eighteenth and early nineteenth centuries that few scholars accepted the reality of Troy, the Trojan war, and even Homer.

By the middle of the nineteenth century, those few enthusiasts who still believed in Troy as a real city were divided as to the precise location. Most distinguished scholars and travelers of the day—those, that is, who still believed in Troy at all—favored a small ruin on the summit of Balli Dagh, near the town of **Burnarbashi** (Figure 2–5). Although the ruins at Burnarbashi were far from spectacular, these scholars felt that Homer had, through poetic license, transformed a nondescript mountain community into the royal city of Troy. The palaces of Priam and Hector, the magnificent Scaean Gate, and the fabled Trojan wealth were considered to be creations of a superb poet; the true facts of Troy seemed considerably less impressive.

The Burnarbashi theory gained considerable support in 1802 when the

French scholar Le Chevalier discovered two freshwater springs near the base of the Burnarbashi ruins. Homer had written:

> Under the wall along the public way . . . two springs of the eddying Scamander rise. The one, indeed, flows with tepid water, and a steam arises from it around, as of burning fire; whilst the other flows forth in the summer time, like unto hail, or cold snow, or ice from water. There, at them, are the wide, handsome stone basins, where the wives and fair daughters of the Trojans used to wash their splendid garments formerly in time of peace, before the sons of the Greeks arrived. (22. 146–155)

Le Chevalier reported that both hot and cold springs issue forth near the base of the ruins at Burnarbashi. Because no springs were known near Hissarlik, many influential nineteenth-century scholars—Moltke, Welcker, Kiepert, and Curtius—announced their support of Burnarbashi as the true site of Homer's Troy.

Such was the situation when Heinrich Schliemann first tackled the problem of locating Troy. As a boy, Schliemann's father had read to him of the Trojan war, and the ancient heroes instantly captivated Schliemann's mind. As soon as possible, Schliemann taught himself ancient Greek, so that he might read Homer in the original. The more he read, the more he became convinced that Troy, the Trojan war, and the battles chronicled by Homer were true in every detail. But what became of Troy? Surely it was too magnificent, too monumental simply to have disappeared.

So in 1860 Schliemann began his serious work to find Troy, and in his search we can trace the development of scientific methods of archaeology. As we recount the excavations of Schliemann, let us do so in the idiom of modern science. It is not that Schliemann framed his own work in these terms—for surely he did not—but rather to emphasize the steps he actually took, which follow modern scientific procedures almost to the letter.

Heinrich Schliemann and the Scientific Cycle

As discussed earlier, the scientific cycle begins with hypothesis formation, inducing a general statement to account for specific facts. Remember that science has no rules for induction, any more than there can be rules for deriving good ideas. Induction is the province of the genius, of the creative mind. In the case of Troy, the inductive process evolved over two thousand years and involved hundreds of minds. Three hypotheses were available in the mid-nineteenth century:

Hypothesis A: Burnarbashi is the actual ruin of Troy.

Hypothesis B: Hissarlik is the actual ruin of Troy.

Hypothesis C: There is no actual site of Troy (that is, the *Iliad* is poetic fiction).

Keep in mind here that the scientific method is not designed to prove anything; scientific testing only eliminates untenable hypotheses.

Both hypotheses A and B are testable outright. The physical sites of Burnarbashi and Hissarlik can be physically examined and scrutinized for the Trojan ruins. The third hypothesis—that Troy never existed—is untestable. No quantity of observations can be made to verify or disprove this theory. Hypothesis C becomes feasible only after all the alternatives have been rejected on the basis of the data at hand. More will be said about this point later.

The second step of the scientific cycle requires that one derive explicit and testable outcomes from each alternative hypothesis. Such outcomes are commonly stated as "if . . . then" statements.

If Burnarbashi is the true site of Troy, *then* we should find. . . . This statement is then followed by a lengthy list of logical outcomes, the test implications that can be verified or rejected on the basis of independent physical evidence.

If Hissarlik is the true site of Troy, *then* we should find. . . . In this case, we have multiple working hypotheses. The first hypothesis (Burnarbashi) has precisely the same logical outcomes as the second hypothesis (Hissarlik), because all the hypotheses derive from a single source, Homer's *Iliad.* The site that conforms to these outcomes should be the actual location of Troy. If neither site conforms, then hypothesis C becomes more tenable; maybe Troy is poetic fiction after all.

Schliemann worked out the test implications for ancient Troy in great detail, in all cases documenting the implications with passages from the *Iliad.* While not exhaustive, the following set of eight implications adequately summarizes Schliemann's expectations for ancient Troy:

I. *Troy was a large, wealthy city.* Schliemann particularly expected to find this wealth in the form of precious metals. (This is why he was so often accused of treasure hunting.)

II. *Troy should have ample evidence of magnificent ruined temples and other public architecture.* "But when now [Hector] had arrived at the very beautiful dwelling of Priam, built with well-polished porticoes; but in it were fifty chambers of polished marble, built near one another, where lay the sons of Priam with their lawful wives" (6. 244–248). "The most skilful artificers in fruitful Troy . . . made for him a chamber, a dwelling-room, and a hall, in the lofty citadel, near the palaces of Priam and Hector" (6. 316–318).

III. *The Trojan citadel must be surrounded by great fortification walls.* Homer wrote that so wonderful were these walls that their construction was ascribed to no mortal hand, but rather to the deities Neptune and Apollo. "Neptune, the earth-shaker, thus began to speak: . . . The fame of [Troy] will certainly be wherever light is diffused: but they will forget that [wall] which I and Phoebus Apollo, toiling, built round the city" (7. 445–455).

IV. *Achilles must have been able to chase Hector thrice around the city* (22. 163–167).

V. *Troy had two springs—one hot, one cold—located near the former Scaean Gate, the only exit from the city.*

VI. *Troy was located near the Aegean Sea.* In book 7, Homer wrote that each night after the battle the Trojans returned to Troy, the Greeks to their seaside camp. Messengers were said to be able to leave the city at sunset, travel to the Greek ships, and easily return before sunrise.

VII. *Troy was erected on a long plain, site of the former Trojan battlefield.* Nearby was the island of Tenedos, and the plain itself was bounded by Mt. Samothráke and Mt. Ida. "Cloud-compelling Jove indeed first begat Dardanus. And he build Dardania, for sacred [Troy], the city of the articulate-speaking men, was not as yet build on the plain, and they still dwelt at the foot of the many-rilled Ida" (20. 215–218). "King Neptune . . . sat aloft upon the highest summit of the woody Thracian Samos, admiring the [Trojan] war and the battle. Far from thence all Ida was visible, and the city of Priam [Troy] was visible, and the ships of the Greeks" (13. 10–14).

VIII. *The Scamander River (and tributaries) must flow between Troy and the Aegean coast.* "But when [Hera and Athena] reached Troy, and the two flowing rivers, where Simois and Scamander unite their streams . . ." (5. 773–775). Several additional passages indicate that the Scamander, chief river of the area, flows from its origin on Mt. Ida between Troy and the Greek camp.

The final step in the scientific cycle involves verification—bringing new evidence to bear upon the test implications. The objective here is not to prove one hypothesis correct, but rather to render the competing hypotheses untenable.

In the case of Troy, independent data must come from physical evidence. Homeric poetry provides the source of the hypotheses, not the data against which to test these ideas. The Homeric evidence rests largely upon two criteria: (a) the actual ruins of the Trojan citadel (Implications I–III), and (b) the precise topographic setting surrounding the ruins (Implications IV–VIII).

Schliemann first journeyed to Turkey in 1868 to examine firsthand the various ruins and to inspect the Trojan landscape. He traveled to the village of Burnarbashi and climbed the high hill of Balli Dagh, where so many scholars placed the ancient ruins of Troy. He also visited Hissarlik, a 100-foot-high ruin rising above the Scamander Plain. From the outset, he agreed with the ancient Greeks, feeling strongly that Hissarlik was indeed the site of the Trojan ruin. To him, it just seemed right. These gut-level feelings arose not from hard scientific evidence at all, but rather from an intuitive, initial grasp of the situation. The gift of insight is granted only for the best of field-workers of any generation. Such insights cannot be taught.

Schliemann was not, of course, the first to travel to the Scamander Plain in search of Troy. Other scholars had even carried their worn copies of Homer throughout Turkey in search of clues from the landscape. Remember that Le Chevalier had sixty-five years earlier found the springs of Burnarbashi, evidence that at the time tipped the balance against Hissarlik.

What set Schliemann apart from earlier travelers is that he insisted on more intensive study than merely touring the countryside. Schliemann traveled to Turkey to locate the actual, physical remains of Troy. He was out to locate Homer's Scaean Gate, to exhume the palace of Priam, to stand where Achilles had slain Hector. Schliemann was enamored with Trojan lore, and Homer's descriptions were insufficient. Schliemann wanted to stand on these historic spots and possess the actual swords and pottery (and gold) that had been Homeric Troy.

Was he not a romantic? Of course. But the step-by-step, methodological, and logical procedures that Schliemann followed set him far above his contemporaries and established modern canons of scientific excavation.

Most mid-nineteenth-century scholars considered it sufficient to read the ancient sources, to ponder the critical passages, perhaps even to travel to the region to nurture a feel for the land. Then they were free to pontificate one theory or another. In more contemporary terms, academic investigation of the mid-nineteenth century considered hypothesis testing—induction, bridging argumentation, and verification—to be a haphazard procedure at best, and one most generally ignored.

What is notable about Schliemann is his insistence upon verification. Not only did he plan to walk over ancient ruins but he also intended systematically to excavate these ruins. He would catalogue all finds according to stratum; he would accurately draw and map the temple ruins as they were unearthed. Photographers would document his excavations to provide evidence for a skeptical world.

Schliemann must be considered the progenitor of modern archaeological methods because of his hard-headed appreciation of real data. He lifted research of the past from speculative fancy to the realm of solid fact. Schliemann felt one could not—and should not—argue theories without moving into the field to locate the physical proof.

Schliemann turned his initial fieldwork toward Burnarbashi. Although he personally favored Hissarlik—or perhaps because of this feeling—he felt obliged to dispose of the Burnarbashi theory first. After studying and mapping the mountainous landscape, Schliemann conducted limited excavations at Burnarbashi in both 1868 and 1871. These results were published by Schliemann in *Troy and Its Remains* (1875). We can best summarize these excavations by considering the eight test implications point by point.

Troy must have been a large, complex citadel, exhibiting great wealth (Implication I), temple ruins and public architecture (Implication II), surrounded by massive fortification walls (Implications III and IV). Schliemann's excavations at Burnarbashi, coupled with earlier test probes by Hahn in 1864, showed Burnarbashi to be lacking on all counts. The excavations revealed only the simple remains of a small circuit wall. The occupational debris was quite thin, indicating only a short-term occupation, probably by just a few inhabitants. And the chronology was wrong. The bulk of the remains dated from 400–500 B.C., at least six hundred years too late for ancient Troy. These excavation data strongly hint that Burnarbashi was no more than a small, short-term fortress, and such fortifications are common throughout this region. To Schliemann's mind, no stretch of the imagination could escalate the paltry ruins of Burnarbashi into the Trojan palaces and temples chronicled by Homer.

Then Schliemann turned to Implication V, the springs found in 1802:

> [Burnarbashi] had been almost universally considered to be the site of the Homeric [Troy]; the springs at the bottom of that village having been regarded as the two springs mentioned by Homer, one of which sent forth warm, the other cold water. But, instead of two springs, I found thirty-four . . . moreover, I found in all the springs a uniform temperature of . . . 62.6° Fahrenheit. (Schliemann 1875:68–70)

So much for Le Chevalier's hot and cold running water. Furthermore, these numerous springs were over half an hour's travel from the hilly fortress at Burnarbashi. They could not be seen from the citadel. Schliemann thought it unlikely that Homer would describe these distant springs as "under the wall along the public way," where the "fair daughters of the Trojans used to wash their splendid garments."

The final test implications dealt with the topographic setting surrounding Troy: within view of the Aegean Sea (Implication VI), fronting onto a long plain where the battles took place (Implication VII), and located near the Scamander River (Implication VIII). The ruins of Burnarbashi were not built on a plain at all, but rather on a hill rising some 500 feet above the surrounding environs. Schliemann thought the battle could hardly have "surged between plain, and city walls"; the hill at Burnarbashi was simply too steep, rising almost to a peak near the top. Burnarbashi did not front onto a long, gently sloping plain, either, but rather was separated from the Aegean by a steep ridge of hills. How could Agamemnon look across from the sea to view the Trojan watch fires and hear the sound of flutes and pipes? And even discounting the hills, the ruins were over five miles from the Aegean coast. Schliemann considered it impossible for the two armies to return over such a long distance to home base each night after battle.

Thus Schliemann completed this first round of scientific investigation by rejecting the theory that the Burnarbashi ruins are those of ancient Troy. The physical ruins were wrong, the dating was wrong, the springs were wrong, the topography was wrong. End of cycle one.

What had Schliemann actually proved? Schliemann's preliminary work at

Burnarbashi proved exactly nothing. Cycle one had succeeded only in eliminating one competing hypothesis. It seemed unlikely that Burnarbashi could have been Troy.

Schliemann then turned his attention to Hissarlik. The eight test implications remain unchanged; only the physical locality varied.

Cycle Two: Schliemann's Campaign of 1870–1873

So it was with great planning and enthusiasm that Schliemann began his first large-scale excavations at Hissarlik in 1870. Fortified with olive oil to eradicate the bedbugs and quinine for the malaria, the Schliemanns established their field camp at the foot of Hissarlik. Digging in nineteenth-century Turkey was not an easy matter. First Schliemann was required to obtain a **firman**, an excavation permit issued rather reluctantly by the Turkish officials. This task alone took Schliemann years of cajoling, intimidating, and outright bribing of officials. Then he had been required to negotiate the hiring of his crew with the village headman of Renkoi. Skeptical at first, the headman finally arranged that his villagers would gradually appear at Hissarlik at first light. Finally, his initial trenching required him to split his massive crew, so Schliemann decided to train his wife, Sophie, to command her own crew of Renkoit workmen. Solving one complication after another, the Schliemanns finally penetrated the heart of Hissarlik, in search of ancient Troy.

It has been said that Schliemann's first seasons at Troy were "more a rape than a scientific examination" (McDonald 1967:17). While this may be true, we must recognize that the Trojan excavations were exemplary for their day, and certainly provided a model for further research. The excavations were not without gross blunders, as Schliemann readily admitted later, but it is hardly justified to accuse Schliemann of ignoring methods that evolved decades after the Trojan excavations.

What were these controversial excavation techniques? A glance at Figure 2–6 will indicate that excavating a site the size of Hissarlik is no minor task. Schliemann, assisted by his wife, Sophie, supervised a horde of inexperienced local workmen; the crew averaged 150 men per day. Because Schliemann was initially convinced that Homeric Troy lay in the very basal stratum of Hissarlik, he began a massive north-south trench to bisect the mound and expose Troy. In places, the excavations were 50 feet deep before reaching primary soil. This master trench was at the heart of Schliemann's strategy, and nothing was allowed to stand in its way. Using picks, shovels, wheelbarrows, even battering rams and giant iron levers, the workmen tore out all walls, structures, and foundations in order to penetrate to the earliest occupation. Schliemann detected four distinct strata, which he called "nations." The basal stratum was presumably Homeric Troy.

In 1872, however, Schliemann was forced to change his mind regarding the Hissarlik stratigraphy. His giant trench disclosed the bottom of the well-

Figure 2–6
Engraving from Schliemann's original description of Troy, showing the Trojan buildings on the north side and the "Great Trench" cut through the entire hill (*courtesy of The American Museum of Natural History***).**

preserved foundation of a great tower lying within the second stratum. Beside this tower had once stood a double gateway with a paved ramp leading from inside the fortress steeply toward the southwestern edge of the hill. This gateway quickly became to Schliemann the Scaean Gate, the fabled entryway to Troy. Now convinced that Homeric Troy lay in the second, rather than the first stratum, Schliemann quickly recognized an adjacent structure as the palace of Priam. Unfortunately, Schliemann's palace partially extended beneath the staff headquarters, so only part of the building could be exposed. But the terra cotta vases found inside the building were so well made, and the fact that a silver vase was found nearby, convinced Schliemann that he had indeed found King Priam's ancient dwelling.

Thus when Schliemann returned to Hissarlik in the spring of 1873, hopes were high. One day, while looking through the dust and rubble slightly west of the Scaean Gate, he spied a "large copper article of most remarkable form, which attracted my attention all the more as I thought I saw gold behind it" (1875:323). Sophie immediately dismissed the workmen, then joined her husband in excavating one of archaeology's greatest treasures:

> While the men were eating and resting, I cut out the Treasure with a large knife, which it was impossible to do without the greatest exertion and the most fearful risk of my life, for the great fortification-wall, beneath which I had to dig, threatened every moment to fall down upon me. But the sight of so many objects, every one of which is of inestimable value to archaeology, made me foolhardy, and I never thought of any danger. (Schliemann 1875:323–324)

Below the copper "shield" (which proved later to be a large basin) lay a copper cauldron, a silver jug, a globular gold bottle, and two gold cups. Further digging revealed more cups and vases of precious metals, lances, daggers, axes, knives, two gold diadems, and four gold earrings. Upon these lay 56 more gold earrings and 8,750 small gold rings, perforated prisms and dice, gold buttons, six gold bracelets, and more gold goblets (see Figure 2–7). Succumbing to one of his more eloquent flights of imagination, Schliemann reconstructed the contexts of his treasure this way:

> As I found all these articles together, forming a rectangular mass, or packed into one another, it seems to be certain that they were placed on the city wall in a wooden chest . . . such as those mentioned by Homer as being in the palace of King Priam. This appears to be the more certain, as close by the site of these articles I found a copper key [later identified as a chisel] . . . it is probable that

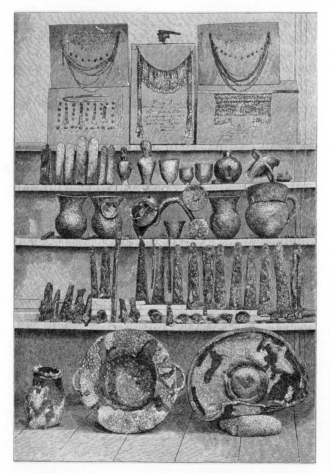

Figure 2–7
The "Treasure of Priam" as illustrated in Schliemann's original 1875 publication (courtesy of The American Museum of Natural History).

some member of the family of King Priam hurriedly packed the Treasure into the chest and carried it off without having time to pull out the key; that when he reached the wall, however, the hand of an enemy or the fire overtook him, and he was obliged to abandon the chest, which was immediately covered to a height of from 5 to 6 feet with the red ashes and the stones of the adjoining royal palace. (1875:332–333)

"Priam's Treasure" as it became known, further convinced Schliemann that Homeric Troy lay on the second, rather than the basal level of Hissarlik. Schliemann regretted this shift in context, because he "unfortunately, in 1871 and 1872, destroyed a large portion of the [second] city, for I at that time broke down all the house-walls in the higher strata which obstructed my way" (1875:347–348). Once again, archaeology emerges as the science that destroys its own data. Let me reemphasize the importance of analysis proceeding hand in glove with excavation strategy.

From this point on, the story of "Priam's Treasure" takes a sordid turn. After recovering the treasure, Schliemann immediately announced that the 1873 field season would terminate in two weeks. The thousands of gold pieces—all those necklaces, earrings, buttons, and beads—were hidden from Amin Effendi, the on-site Turkish guard whose duty it was to inspect all finds. Turkish law at the time required that half of the artifacts remain in the national museum at Constantinople. From its hiding place under the Schliemanns' bed, the golden treasure was carefully packed into three suitcases and Sophie's steamer trunk, designated as personal possessions, and shipped directly to Athens. In this way, Schliemann avoided the inspection mandated by his Turkish *firman.* Once in Athens, Schliemann hid the treasure in a secret storehouse. Only on selected days, such as Greek holidays, would he risk transporting any of the illicit artifacts. Little by little, the objects were cleaned, repaired and photographed for publication. Eight thousand gold beads were strung into two necklaces, one of eleven strands, the other of thirteen. Schliemann went so far as to photograph his wife, Sophie, wearing the best gold pieces of "Priam's Treasure"—the diadem, earrings, and one of the necklaces. It seems clear that Schliemann, contrary to modern protocol among professional archaeologists, regarded the priceless "Treasure of Priam" as his personal property. These underhanded dealings are one reason he is so often judged to have been only a treasure hunter and looter.[3]

In his report of the Hissarlik excavations, published in 1875, Schliemann boasted to the world that he had indisputably discovered the ruins of Homeric Troy:

I have excavated two-thirds of the entire city; and, as I have brought to light the Great Tower, the Scaean Gate, the city wall of Troy, the royal palace . . . I have also made an exceedingly copious collection of all the articles of the domestic life and the religion of the Trojans; and therefore, it is not to be expected that science would gain anything more by further excavations. (1875:349–352)

On what basis did Schliemann make such claims? To examine his reasoning, we must return to the initial eight test implications for Troy.

There seems to be little doubt that Implications I–III are verified. Truly had Schliemann discovered massive wealth (in the form of precious metals, just as he had predicted), ruined temples and public architecture, and a great fortification wall. With regard to Implication IV, that Achilles could have chased Hector thrice around the hill, Schliemann pointed out that his excavations disclosed that Homeric Troy would have been 37 feet lower than the present surface of Hissarlik. Furthermore, during the continuous occupation, the ridge would not only have gained in height, but also breadth. Even allowing for Homeric hyperbole, Schliemann thought the size of Hissarlik would not preclude the epic Homeric chase.

Furthermore, the topographic implications (VI–VIII) seemed to square with the modern topography of the Scamander Plain. In his initial campaign at Troy, however, Schliemann's work could not answer the ancient criticism of Demetrios, that the Aegean had formed a bay on the current alluvial plain. In addition, Schliemann found no spring near his "Scaean Gate."

Obviously, Schliemann's excavation argued strongly for Hissarlik, not Burnarbashi, as the site of ancient Troy. Not all the predictions were verified, but hypothesis B fared considerably better than hypothesis A, which was roundly rejected.

Unfortunately for Schliemann, the publication of his Trojan excavations received mixed reviews. Writing in 1891, C. Schuchhardt, director of the Kestner Museum of Hanover, raved that "the question is now decided forever. On the hill of Hissarlik Dr. Schliemann has uncovered the ancient palaces of Troy, has laid bare its colossal fortifications, and brought to light its treasures of gold and silver" (1891:18). But most scholars, trained in traditional values of archaeology, thought Schliemann's work fell badly short of the excavator's claims. While granting that an important early civilization had indeed been unearthed, most experts were critical of the methods and the conclusions he drew from them. Schliemann was even accused of salting his own site with objects of silver and gold (he was, after all, a wealthy man). Few scholars would allow any close connection between the artifacts of Hissarlik and the antiquities described in the *Iliad*. The architectural evidence was declared equivocal. In fact, Schliemann's bold correlations between the *Iliad* and archaeology became something of an open joke in the public press, as well as in scientific circles (McDonald 1967:26). All in all, the 1875 publication convinced few, and Burnarbashi remained the popular candidate for Homer's Troy (if indeed it existed at all).

The Third Cycle: Schliemann's Campaign of 1878–1879

Fortunately, science does not proceed by democracy; criticism leads only to further research and refined hypotheses. As one might expect, the deluge of adverse criticism of *Troy and Its Remains* spurred Schliemann to rise once again in defense of Hissarlik. After lengthy political and legal difficulties, Schliemann finally convinced the Turkish government to issue him a new excavation permit. Upon his return to the Scamander Plain in 1878, Schliemann had gained considerable experience in scientific excavation. Most notably, he had found and excavated the famous Shaft Graves at Mycenae. He approached the reexcavation of Hissarlik with a carefulness absent in his initial campaign.

In terms of scientific methodology, Schliemann's second Trojan excavations must be considered as the third loop in the scientific cycle. The first loop tested and rejected the Burnarbashi hypothesis. The second loop consisted of the initial excavations at Hissarlik. Although the evidence would not allow rejection of Hissarlik, the results were not compelling in either direction, as Schliemann's critics were quick to point out. In response to these critics, and in order to verify still untested implications, Schliemann commenced his campaign of 1878–1879.

The new excavations had two clear-cut goals. First of all, Schliemann intended to expose the ruins of the fortifications and of the large building in the second level, near where the treasure had been found. By this time, incidentally, Schliemann had ceased calling his finds the palace and treasure of Priam. The expedition successfully cleared the entire western half of the mound down to this second, or "Homeric" level. The stratigraphic column was reworked from the initial four "nations" into seven major occupation levels. Schliemann now correlated the Homeric Troy with the third stratigraphic level, superimposed on two prior burned cities. Several additional treasure hoards were found—ten in all—and his overall collection of ceramics and material culture was dramatically increased. The 1878–1879 excavations showed even stronger support for test implications I–III. There could be little doubt that Hissarlik was rich enough to have been Homeric Troy.

The second objective represented a rather major departure from his earlier approach. On his return to Hissarlik in 1878, Schliemann brought with him a battery of consulting scientists to conduct a broad-based ecological study of the Trojan plain—its topography, geology, flora, and fauna. One participating scientist, Professor **Rudolph Virchow**, was one of the nineteenth century's premier scholars. His sheer presence lent an air of credibility that had been lacking in the earlier Hissarlik excavation.

Virchow made a most important contribution during his stay at Hissarlik. As part of his naturalistic studies he examined the geology of the Plain of Scamander, excavating test holes to a depth of several meters. Nowhere did he discover buried marine deposits, and the implications were clear: Demetrios's ancient theory that the Scamander Plain had been submerged during Trojan times was false. Hence this proposition, obliquely dealt with in Implication VII, received independent verification.

A second benefit of the broad-based, naturalistic studies of the Trojan Plain was Schliemann's discovery of the much-disputed springs and washing troughs. Lying in an ancient rock channel at the foot of Hissarlik, the springs appeared to be precisely as described by Homer. The archaeological associations indicated that the springs had been continually used from early Mycenaean into Roman times. Schliemann was even able to relocate a "Scaean Gate" in this vicinity. Hence Implication V was also verified by the 1878–1879 fieldwork.

Schliemann summarized his second campaign in *Ilios: The City and Country of the Trojans* (1880), published in German, English, and French. This volume, while still failing to silence his most vociferous of critics, conclusively confirmed Schliemann's claim that he had indeed located and excavated Homeric Troy. Schliemann's gusto—tempered considerably by what Virchow termed "scientific poise and caution"—finally established the veracity of his extravagant claims.

Schliemann's excavations can be faulted on many, many grounds, but the fact remains that he did precisely what he had set out to do: to apply techniques of scientific excavation to pinpoint the location of ancient Troy. And he succeeded, for few modern scholars dispute the validity of the Hissarlik theory. But in so doing—as the old saw goes—Schliemann raised more questions than he answered. We will look briefly at the century of Trojan research that followed Schliemann's lead, not only because of the obvious historial implications, but also to see once again how hypotheses are progressively revised and refined as part of the continuing scientific cycle.

FURTHER EXCAVATIONS: WILL THE REAL TROY PLEASE STAND UP?

After Schliemann's second Trojan publication, the focus of research shifted. Debate centered not upon the existence and location of Troy—Hissarlik satisfied the Homeric implications all too well—but rather upon the precise level of Homeric Troy in the Hissarlik stratigraphy. Note carefully here how the initial research problem, although solved, gave rise to additional follow-up research.

While writing his second volume, Schliemann became progressively disenchanted with his identification of the "small town, the third in succession from the virgin soil" with Homeric Troy. Feeling compelled to recheck his findings once more, he returned to Hissarlik in 1882 for still further excavations. Working with two trained architects, Schliemann was forced to change his mind once more about the location of Homeric Troy. In *Troja*, published in 1884, Schliemann deleted all references to the third burnt city, reverting instead to his previous correlation of Homer's Troy with the second stratum. Thus Schliemann's thinking evolved from Level I, to Level II, to Level III, then back to Level II. In the final year of his life, Schliemann would even have changed the correlation to Level VI (and as we shall see, that correlation is also incorrect). But as McDonald (1967:39) has pointed out, such wavering is eloquent example of the self-correcting nature of hypothesis testing in archaeology: "Schliemann no doubt had an embarrassing habit of rushing into print: but no apology is needed in any scholarly field for a change of mind necessitated by new evidence. The unpardonable sin, indeed, is for a scholar to refuse to consider the possibility that a cherished theory may be mistaken."

Schliemann's work at Troy was continued by his young architect, Wilhelm Dorpfeld. Dorpfeld concentrated his 1894 excavations on Level VI, which both he and Schliemann now felt was Homeric Troy. Because of the presence of imported Mycenaean pottery, Dorpfeld concluded that Level VI dated roughly 1500–1000 B.C. Although vague, such was the best evidence available at the time. Also of interest were two "pre-Greek" settlements, labeled VII^1 and VII^2. Dorpfeld discussed the nature of these settlements in some detail, concluding that VII^1 probably resulted from a reoccupation of Level VI. In fact, many of the VII^1 houses were actually constructed against the ancient city wall. Dorpfeld felt that the newcomers were probably "ordinary people," whereas the Troy VI houses were sturdier, probably belonging to a "leader and dependents."

It was this transition from Troy VI to Troy VII^1 which spurred still further research at Hissarlik (now confidently called Troy by all). Carl Blegen of the University of Cincinnati led field expeditions to Troy for seven successive years, beginning in the spring of 1932. Applying evolved stratigraphic methods (discussed in Chapter 5), Blegen learned firsthand how complex the Hissarlik strata really were. Using a nine-part stratigraphic section, Blegen finally recognized forty-nine major and minor catastrophies and reconstructions throughout the site—a far cry from the initial four-part scheme first used by Schliemann.

Blegen also applied new techniques of ceramic analysis to demonstrate that Levels I through V represented essentially a continuous occupation over a thousand years. Schliemann had correctly interpreted the nature of these levels. The Cincinnati expedition also carefully mapped the location of all animal bone. Judging from the abundant sheep carcasses, the people of Hissarlik had already become major sheep raisers as early as Troy II times. Blegen even suggested that producing woolen textiles was a major activity at Troy.

A major break occurred in Troy VI, when a distinctive, wheel-made pottery was introduced. Blegen interpreted this as indicative of a full-blown invasion from the Greek mainland. Troy VI was apparently destroyed by a mighty earthquake about 1300 B.C. He found no support for Schliemann's final conclusion that the city had been destroyed by Agamemnon's troops. So when did the Greek siege take place?

Blegen's answer was Level VIIa (Dorpfeld's old Level VII^1). Blegen believed that the survivors of the Trojan earthquake returned to their ruined home "within a few days" to rebuild their homes on the ruins. The large number of storage jars and the maze of small rooms suggested to Blegen that Troy VIIa was badly crowded (perhaps in expectation of a siege?). The pottery found on the house floors of Troy VIIa suggest but a single generation of inhabitants. Using the evidence of Mycenaean trade wares, Blegen dated the level as the decade around 1270 or 1260 B.C.

What about the siege? How was Troy VIIa destroyed? Blegen argued that "the destruction was undoubtedly the work of human agency, and it was accompanied by violence and by fire." The 1930s excavations uncovered several complete and partial human skeletons, suggesting that the Troy VIIa people had been victims of a violent incursion.

Blegen concluded (1963:162, 164):

> Here, then, in the extreme northwestern corner of Asia Minor—exactly where Greek tradition, folk memory and the epic poems place the site of [Troy]—we have the physical remains of a fortified stronghold, obviously the capital of the region. As shown by pursuasive archaeological evidence, it was besieged and captured by enemies and destroyed by fire, no doubt after having been throughly pillaged, just as Hellenic poetry and folk-tale describe the destruction of King Priam's Troy. . . . It is Settlement VIIa, then, that must be recognized as the actual Troy, the ill-fated stronghold, the siege and capture of which caught the fancy and imagination of contemporary troubadours and bards who transmitted orally to their successors their songs about the heroes who fought in the past.

Did Blegen have the final word about Troy? Probably not. Current research is still attempting to unravel mysteries of the Mycenaean civilization. Areas of interest include the linguistic affiliation of the Trojans and their invaders, the presence of horse bones in Troy VI (were the middle Helladic folk horsemen?), the exact nature of Mycenaean economy and trade, and the continuation (or lack of it) from Mycenaean to Homeric times. The problems are never-ending; the more one knows, the more one needs to know.

On the whole, however, the research at Troy provides archaeology with a true success story. Not only has the Trojan war been explicated in marvelous detail, but the way in which the research was accomplished documents the growing sophistication of scientific methods of excavation and analysis. As Joseph Alsop has commented, "Homer has now been justified by the archaeologists, and every bit as fully as old Schliemann could have wished" (1964:81).

HEINRICH SCHLIEMANN: SCIENTIST IN ARCHAEOLOGY

The shortcomings of Schliemann's excavation technique need not detain us. Modern authors have stated—and overstated—these objections elsewhere (although it is interesting to note just how kind Schliemann's immediate successors, especially Dorpfeld and Blegen, have been). Of course Schliemann should not have ripped out walls indiscriminately; in fact, he unknowingly dug right through the most likely candidate for Homeric Troy (Level VIIa). And surely he was rash in his unfortunate use of terms like "Treasure of Priam" and the "Scaean Gate." Suffice it to say that Schliemann was a pioneer. Pioneers must be allowed occasional errors in practice and judgment.

But I will not over-apologize for Schliemann's archaeological technique. Old Heinrich made dozens of innovations in the art of archaeological excavation, innovations that are with us today. In fact, it is amusing to note how many of today's "revolutions in archaeology" have their roots in the Hissarlik campaigns of the late nineteenth century.

Consider for example the highly touted interdisciplinary approach to archaeology, which has received so much attention in recent years. Yet, after his first season at Troy, Schliemann recognized the necessity of taking along consultants to unravel mysteries that Schliemann knew he was untrained to solve: Virchow the naturalist, Emile Burnouf the French archaeologist and scholar, Dorpfeld and Hofler the architects, cartographers, photographers. Similarly, in analyzing his finds, Schliemann consulted professional help whenever necessary. In dealing with "Priam's Treasure" for instance, he consulted Carlo Giuliano, a well-known London goldsmith; Giuliano marveled at the purity of the gold, and puzzled as to how primitive goldsmiths could perform such fine work. As with today's prudent archaeologists, Schliemann knew when to call for help. Then, as now, no single scholar can hope single-handedly to deal with the entire range of complexity encountered in any one archaeological site.

Schliemann is also to be commended for his meticulous recording and publication of his archaeological finds. He wrote, "Archaeology shall on no account lose any one of my discoveries; every article which can have interest for the learned world shall be photographed, or copied by a skillful draughtsman, and published in the Appendix to this work; and by the side of every article I shall state the depth in which I have discovered it" (1875:219). These are notable statements of principle for the nineteenth century; in fact, I can think of more than a few modern archaeological site reports which do not even approach Schliemann's standards for adequate publication.

In sum, I think we must give Heinrich Schliemann rather high marks all the way around. His self-assertiveness irritated many, past and present, but as McDonald (1967:11) points out, without such characteristics he never could have forced himself to the attention of the learned world. I suggest that when modern archaeologists are tempted to label their works "new" or "revolutionary," they carefully check the writings and excavations of Schliemann. In many cases, Heinrich was there first.

SUMMARY

A scientist is one who uses scientific methods to abstract universals from a world of particulars, and it almost goes without saying that contemporary archaeology is a scientific endeavor. Archaeology's scientific laws are timeless and spaceless generalizations that tell how cultural processes work. These laws are found by use of the scientific cycle, which consists of three steps: hypothesis formation, bridging argumentation, and verification. Each round in the scientific cycle begins and ends with facts, each new set of facts suggesting new hypotheses which must themselves be tested. As a method, science implies a continuing upward spiral of knowledge. The principles and methods of science have been successfully applied for over two centuries in archaeology, and the scientific cycle provides the backbone for modern archaeological inquiry.

NOTES

1. Test implications can also be derived through induction, based on known prior probabilities of the various hypotheses (Salmon 1976:378); the present discussion has been kept purposely simple, and deals only with the deductive case.

2. All quotes from the *Iliad* are taken from Buckley (1873).

3. "Priam's Treasure" was ultimately presented by Schliemann to the Prussian government in 1881, and placed on display in the Berlin Museum. Tragically, the artifacts have disappeared. As the Russian army approached Berlin near the end of World War II, the curators of the Berlin Museum for Early History packed up the gold and hid (or buried) it. To this day, not a single gold bead from "Priam's Treasure" has surfaced. Rumors abound: it was bombed, or melted down, or confiscated, or stolen. Nobody knows.

3

What Is Anthropology?

I went to the University of Chicago for a while
after the Second World War. I was a student in
the Department of Anthropology. At that time,
they were teaching that there was absolutely no
difference between anybody. They may be
teaching that still. Another thing they taught was
that nobody was ridiculous or bad or disgusting.
Kurt Vonnegut Jr.

Everyone knows what anthropologists do. They study natives and fossils and
chimpanzees. Anthropologists write articles for *National Geographic* magazine
and they appear on the *Tonight* show on TV. Anthropologists are Margaret
Mead and Louis Leakey and Jane Goodall and Ashley Montagu.

What most people do not know is what these scientists share, what makes them all anthropologists. **Anthropology** is an unusual discipline; because anthropologists run in so many different directions at once, it is sometimes difficult to see the common thread. In fact, anthropologists sometimes get so involved with the minutiae of their own studies that they themselves forget what they are. What makes an anthropologist an anthropologist?

The answer is deceptively simple: what all anthropologists share is a perspective. This perspective holds that a true science of mankind can arise only from the holistic, all-emcompassing look. It is not enough to look at any single group—Americans, Chinese, Balinese, or **australopithecines**—to find the keys to human existence. Every human society, whether extant or extinct, is declared relevant to the study of mankind. On this all anthropologists agree.

This is not to say that all anthropologists study the same things: Margaret Mead has never excavated an archaeological site and Louis Leakey has never interviewed a native Athabascan speaker. Anthropologists, like most modern *Homo sapiens,* participate in a division of labor. The Renaissance anthropologist is dead because one scholar cannot hope to do all things well.

So anthropologists specialize. Before examining how modern archaeology articulates with the rest of anthropology, it is first necessary to see just what anthropology is, and how anthropologists have carved up the total pie of human existence.

KINDS OF ANTHROPOLOGY

The first basic division within anthropology deals with the very nature of human existence. **Physical anthropology** is concerned primarily with man as a biological organism; **cultural anthropology** views man as "the animal of culture" (Haviland 1974:8). While these are not wholly independent divisions, they do serve to bisect the range of humanity into manageable domains of study.

The origins of physical anthropology can be traced back into the eighteenth century, when Petrus Camper began measuring human skulls. **Anthropometry** arose as the practice of measuring human morphology, and, as anthropologists quickly discovered, human crania are terrific objects of study. There are so many things to be measured: length, breadth, height, cranial capacity, nasion-basion length, degree of cranial deformation. The list seemed endless. The study of human crania—craniometry—progressed so far, so rapidly, that some physical anthropologists (such as Boyd 1950) have argued that craniometry progressed too far, that preoccupation with skull measurements has retarded the overall development of physical anthropology as a science. Who knows? It is fair to say that craniometry (and anthropometry in general) kept the physical anthropologists off the streets and out of trouble until more relevant domains of study came along.

Contemporary physical anthropology has come a long way since the days of Petrus Camper and his cranial calipers. Modern physical anthropologists study a number of widespread aspects of the biological side of mankind. One major concern is the biological evolution of man. How did the modern species *Homo sapiens sapiens* come into being? An intricate family tree has been pieced together by physical anthropologists over the past century, working largely from fossil evidence and observations of living primates.

A second major focus of modern physical anthropology is the study of human variability. No two human beings are identical, even though we are members of a single species. The study of inherited—so-called racial—differences has become not only a critical domain of scientific investigation, but also a matter of practical concern for educators, politicians, and community leaders. To what extent, for example, are IQ scores the result of inherited (racial) differences? The answer has wide-reaching political and social significance.

Physical anthropologists provide a background against which to consider the workings of cultural anthropology. In the next section, we examine the concept of culture in some detail. For now, it is sufficient to recognize that culture consists of the rules by which societies operate; it is the way people think; and it can be studied in a number of ways. The **ethnologist** studies the culture of modern groups. By questioning and observing people throughout the world, ethnologists attempt to determine how diverse cultural elements intermesh and change in actual working societies. The **anthropological linguist** concentrates on one specialized segment of culture—language—and analyzes this phenomenon in detail: phonological structures, the relationship of language to thought, how linguistic systems change through time, the structural basis of language.

> **W**hat would I choose to do, if I had my life to live
> over again? I would be an anthropologist.
> *Margaret Mead*

This book is primarily concerned with the work of the third kind of cultural anthropology—**archaeology.** The archaeologist also studies culture, but techniques differ from those of the ethnologist and the linguist. The archaeologist usually studies extinct cultures, cultural systems that are no longer operative.[1] This places the archaeologist at something of a disadvantage: there is nobody to talk to. Because they lack living informants, archaeologists have developed a powerful array of techniques for analyzing the material remains of the past. We will examine these techniques in subsequent chapters. For now, it is important to see just how archaeology relates to the rest of cultural anthropology. There are characteristics in common, but there are differences, too.

"ARCHAEOLOGY IS ANTHROPOLOGY OR IT IS NOTHING"—WHY?

The past can be understood only through the present.

Albert Spaulding

For the past twenty years, students of archaeology have heard over and over again the phrase used in the title of this section: archaeology is anthropology or it is nothing. This dictum was first set down by archaeologists Gordon Willey and Philip Phillips in their influential book *Method and Theory in American Archaeology* (1958:2). In fact, the Willey-Phillips slogan has become something of a catch phrase in modern American archaeology. Just consider the titles of some recent publications: "Archeology as anthropology" (Binford 1962), "Archeology as anthropology: a case study" (Longacre 1964), "Archaeology as anthropology: a case study" (Longacre 1970), *Anthropological Archeology in the Americas* (Meggers 1968), "The future of archeology in anthropology" (Watson 1973), and most recently "Archaeology beyond anthropology" (Gumerman and Phillips 1978). It seems clear that American archaeologists want to be anthropologists, in one form or another.

What is less clear is why. Why should we believe that archaeology is nothing unless it is anthropology? Is it because most American archaeologists are trained in university anthropology departments? Is it because many archaeologists are employed by anthropology departments? Is it because many early American archaeologists were also practicing ethnographers?

Yes, archaeology is anthropology for all of these reasons—and one more. It is an unfortunate fact of life that the facts never speak for themselves. As discussed in the last chapter, facts are known and particular observations, and the general task of science is to transform these facts into universal statements called theories. The facts in archaeology are, in reality, contemporary observations made upon the material remains of the past. Archaeology requires a major anthropological input in order to *bridge the gap* between these contemporary observations and relevant statements about past behavior.

This is a critical point, perhaps best understood by analogy. Consider the problem faced by geologists. The geological record—like the archaeological record—consists only of objects and interrelationships between objects. A geological fact is really an observation made by a contemporary geologist on objects in the geological record. How do geologists move from their contemporary observations to meaningful statements about the remote geological past?

This difficulty was addressed by pioneering geologists long ago. The modern science of geology is said to have begun in the eighteenth century, largely through the efforts of James Hutton. A medical man and gentleman farmer, Hutton formulated a simple principle that provided the very cornerstone of modern geology. Hutton's principle, called the *doctrine of uniformitari-*

anism, states that the processes that now operate to modify the earth's surface are the same processes that operated in the geological past. It is that simple: the geological processes of the past and the present are identical.

Consider an example. We know from modern observation that as contemporary glaciers move, they deposit characteristic debris which range in size from microscopic to boulders weighing several tons. The rocks receive characteristic scratches (striations) as they move, and they are deposited in formations called moraines. The thorough study of modern glaciers has convinced geologists that moraines and striations are formed only through glacial action.

Now suppose a geologist finds moraines and striated rocks in Ohio, or California, or New Mexico, where no glaciers are present today. Armed with a knowledge of contemporary glacial processes, the geologist can frame and test hypotheses relating to ancient glacial action. *In other words, the observation of contemporary, ongoing processes provides the bridging arguments necessary to assign meaning to the objects of the past.*

Precisely the same logical stricture applies to archaeology. Archaeologists recover the material remains of past cultural processes. Like the geologist, the archaeologist can frame hypotheses that account for the formation and deposition of these physical remains. Input from contemporary anthropology supplies the bridging arguments necessary to translate general hypotheses into specific, observable outcomes which can be expected to appear in the archaeological record. Anthropology allows the archaeologists to bridge this important gap between contemporary observation and relevant statements about past behavior. This is why archaeology is anthropology or it is nothing.

Let us further illustrate this difficulty by borrowing an example from Lewis Binford (1978). As we will discuss in Chapter 8, archaeologists often study the abundance and distribution of animal bones to learn the composition of prehistoric diets, the nature of hunting practices, how animals were butchered, the season in which the hunt was conducted, and many other related questions.

Most of the faunal studies are based on the relative frequencies of various animal bones in archaeological sites. When analyzing the bones from Suberde, a seventh millennium B.C. Neolithic village in Turkey, Dexter Perkins and Patricia Daly noticed that the upper limb bones of wild oxen were usually missing. These facts (contemporary observations) were then interpreted as a result of the way in which the oxen were butchered: the animal must have been skinned, the meat stripped from the forequarters and hindquarters, with the bones thrown away. They suggested that the meat was piled on the skin, and the lower limb bones used to drag the hide bearing the meat back home (Perkins and Daly 1968:104). This interpretation seemed to explain why the upper limb bones were left at the kill site, while the lower limb bones were discarded at the habitation site.

R. E. Chaplin analyzed the bones recovered from a late ninth-century A.D. Saxon farm in the Whitehall area of London. The facts in this case also indicated a shortage of limb bones relative to the rest of the skeletal elements. Chaplin suggested that the limb bones (particularly those of sheep and cattle) disappeared because carcasses were being dressed and exported to market. Chaplin went on to discuss the nature of marketing and animal husbandry implied by such trade (Chaplin 1971:135–138).

Investigators also found that the upper limb bones of food animals were often missing from American Plains Indian sites. Theodore White analyzed these facts, suggesting that the bones had been destroyed during the manufacture of bone grease from the marrow (White 1954:256).

Note what has happened. Exactly the same archaeological fact—lower limb bones are more common than upper limb bones—have been interpreted in three very different ways:

1. The upper limbs were discarded at the kill site, and the lower limbs were transported with the meat back to the campsite (Perkins and Daly 1968).
2. The upper limb bones were selectively butchered and traded to market (Chaplin 1971).
3. The upper limbs were processed into bone grease, and hence destroyed at the campsite (White 1953).

All of the sites seem to have been well excavated and carefully analyzed. The relative frequencies of animal bones are the real data (the "facts") of archaeology. Yet these facts are merely contemporary observations made on the archaeological record. What do these facts indicate about past behavior? At least three very different behavioral interpretations have been suggested to account for the same facts.

Consider this difficulty in terms of the scientific cycle presented in the last chapter. The first step in the scientific method is *hypothesis formation,* during which one or more hypotheses are generated to account for the observable facts. Hypotheses are general statements, designed to cover not only the known facts, but also to predict facts as yet unobserved. The next step in the scientific method is to determine the *logical outcomes* of one's hypotheses. Because hypotheses are stated in general form, one must translate the generality into its specific outcomes. The translation from general to specific is accomplished through means of *bridging arguments,* logical statements which supply the necessary test implications. The scientific cycle is complete when the test implications have been tested (verified) by additional facts.

When the scientific cycle was presented in Chapter 2, I admitted that archaeologists have difficulty in supplying these bridging arguments, and the example of bone frequencies illustrates why this is so. The initial facts in this case are the bone frequencies at the various sites: lower limb bones are more common than upper limb bones. On these facts all archaeologists can agree (for these specific sites).

Three hypotheses were suggested to explain the facts. One suggestion was that the animals had been butchered some distance from the habitation area, and that some bones were discarded at the butchering area, while others were returned to camp with the meat. Let us call this first suggestion H_1. A second hypothesis, H_2, implies that, after butchering, some of the choice cuts were traded away, and this is why the upper limb bones did not appear in the archaeological record of the habitation site. A final hypothesis, H_3, suggests that a paste had been made from the larger bones; because only the larger bones would be used for bone grease, the smaller elements would appear more frequently in the archaeological record.

Literally dozens of additional hypotheses could be suggested to explain why upper limb bones seem to be less common than the lower limbs and feet. Perhaps certain bones were placed in a shrine away from the habitation area. Or perhaps the larger bones were made into awls and other bone tools. Or perhaps the largest bones were used as clubs. Remember that at this stage in the scientific cycle one is perfectly justified in using imagination (and genius, if possible) to generate worthwhile hypotheses. There are no rules governing how one gets a good idea.

But there are rules once the hypotheses have been suggested. Let us restrict our discussion to the three numbered hypotheses suggested above (H_1, H_2, and H_3). H_1, suggesting that bones were discarded at the site of butchering, is a generalized behavioral statement. A contemporary archaeologist can never hope to observe the butchering of a Neolithic wild ox. Neither can an archaeologist observe firsthand the making of bone grease by an American Plains Indian. The archaeologist can only hope to find the logical material consequences of oxen butchering or bison bone grease manufacture.

We are required at this stage to construct a series of *if . . . then* statements. *If* bone grease was manufactured *then* we should find artifacts X, Y, and Z, physical residues M, N, and O, bones distributed in patterns C, D, and E, and several bone elements (J, K, and L) should be missing altogether. Similarly, to test H_2, we must generate some *if . . . then* statements regarding the trading of meat and bones. What cuts are best to trade? How far can meat be traded before it spoils? Is meat marketed only in winter months? Are carcasses butchered in special ways so that cuts can be traded?

These *if . . . then* statements are the bridging arguments which translate general hypotheses into specific expectations which can be tested on the archaeological record.

But—I hope you are wondering—how do we know these things? How do we know that manufacturing bone grease involves artifacts X, Y, and Z? How do we know which bone elements are destroyed when bone grease is made? Any test of hypotheses can be only as strong as these bridging arguments. If we generate the wrong implication, then our hypothesis testing is worse than useless, it is misleading, because it brings us to the incorrect conclusions. The process of bridging the gap between hypothesis and implication is the subject of this chapter.

To date, anthropology has supplied the major bridging arguments to archaeology as *ethnographic analogy*. We will see in Chapter 8, for instance, how archaeologists have reconstructed a Paleo-Indian bison kill. The archaeological evidence consists only of stone and bone. But archaeologist Joe Ben Wheat used the nineteenth-century Plains Indians as an ethnographic analogy to interpret the behavioral meaning of the objects recovered in the archaeological excavation. In this case the ethnologist who recorded the nineteenth-century Plains Indian culture is analogous to the geologist who observes modern glaciers. In addition to supplying knowledge in the pure sense, both scientists also supply the bridging arguments necessary to interpret past events. In the case of the geologist, his observations on glacial processes will enable his colleagues to interpret glacial features found in the geological record. By the same token, the observations of the Plains ethnologist enable the archaeologist to read behavioral meaning into the archaeological record. Both geologist and anthropologist apply a version of the doctrine of uniformitarianism: the processes of the past and the present are identical. This, once again, is why archaeology is anthropology or it is nothing.

Having said this, I must admit also that simple ethnographic analogy has some limitations for archaeology. While it is true that ethnographers have stockpiled great quantities of data from primitive peoples, much of this research is irrelevant to archaeology. Many ethnographers focus only on the ideational aspects of culture: what people think, what people say, how people dance, what people call their grandmother. While these data are relevant to some brands of anthropology, ethnology has been guilty of ignoring many of the physical processes that also constitute human behavior. Time and time again, we find the ethnographer recording a thousand recipes for turtle soup, but never bothering to record what tools were involved, how the turtles were caught, what kind of fire was built, and what physical residues resulted from all of this activity. Yet it is only the tools and the physical debris that last in the archaeological record, long after the recipes have disappeared.

Thus, while accepting the dictum that *archaeology is anthropology or it is nothing,* we must also realize that some brands of anthropology are more relevant than others. Without an understanding of how modern anthropology works, it is quite literally impossible to see how archaeologists bridge the gap from inert objects to behavioral statements about the past.

> The truest kinds of thoughts—they are so
> profound that even their opposites are also true.
> *Niels Bohr*

THE NATURE OF CULTURE

> Where all think alike, no one thinks very much.
> *Walter Lippman*

Any number of academic disciplines purport to study **culture** (or at least cultural behavior): economics, sociology, political science, history, cultural geography, psychology, and so forth. A classical historian, for instance, might investigate Greek culture or Roman culture or Byzantine culture; his interest centers about the cultural phenomena that characterize these particular societies. But one does not expect to find the classical historian discoursing on the general nature of culture; if he did he would cease to be a classical historian. He would have become an anthropologist. In fact, the concept of culture is the central theme that weds together so many diversified (and sometimes conflicting) interests into a single, fairly unified anthropological approach.

And yet little general agreement exists among anthropologists about just what culture is (Goodenough 1970:101). In a classic study, A. L. Kroeber and Clyde Kluckhohn (1952) compiled over two hundred discrete definitions of culture, proposed by as many anthropologists and social scientists. Since that time, the number of definitions of culture must have tripled.

Fortunately, we as archaeologists need not be overly concerned with attempting to find the ultimate definition of culture. What is important to know is how culture works, and how archaeologists go about studying it. Let us begin the discussion with the classic definition offered by Sir Edward Burnett Tylor (the chap considered by many to be the founder of modern anthropology). Tylor's (1871) definition of culture appeared, interestingly enough, on the initial page of anthropology's first general textbook:

> Culture . . . taken in its wide ethnographic sense is that complex whole which includes knowledge, belief, art, morals, law, custom, and any other capabilities and habits acquired by man as a member of society.

Tylor's definition of culture provides a necessary baseline from which to begin scientific investigation of past cultural phenomena. Culture in this sense is *learned* and forms a body of tradition within society. But Tylor's definition is too general. We must make Tylor's definition operational by considering precisely how one goes about observing cultural behavior, both in the present and in the past.

This task is simplified by analogy. Following David Aberle (1960:14), we will examine first the workings of language, itself a subset of all cultural phenomena. The rather simple principles involved in language can tell us something about the more complex principles involved in general human culture (see also Goodenough 1970, 1971).

Linguistics is comprised of three components: the **idiolect**, the **language** (or dialect) per se, and the **system of communication**. Each speaker of a language employs a personal idiolect. No two speakers of a language pronounce every linguistic element in precisely the same manner—this is how we can identify specific voices on the radio or the telephone. But a major premise in linguistics is that an overall manner of speaking—what we call language— pervades the idiolects of all speakers within a speech community. The structure of a language (as analyzed by a linguist) consists of the shared speech patterns within a speech community. Each individual speaker pronounces his language in a distinctive manner. Language, in other words, consists of a generalized model which individuals approach to a greater or lesser extent.

The third aspect of linguistics, the system of communication, explains why languages exist in the first place. People speak because they have some message to communicate: please pass the acorn mush; go to your **wickiup;** do you have tickets for the football game? These are messages that are communicated by language. Furthermore, an entire repertory of hand gestures, facial expression, body *language,* even manner of dress and hair length, exists to enhance the system of communication. Most modern languages also rely upon a written component to facilitate communication.

But you must recognize a critical distinction between language itself and language as a vehicle of communication. "Language" is shared behavior, and speech communities are defined on the basis of these shared speech patterns. But people do not share a system of communication, they participate in it, because individual speakers occupy different positions within the chain of communications. People are involved in the system differently. Let us carefully distinguish the medium (language) from the function it serves (communication). Communication is why language evolved. The reverse is not true.

This linguistic analogy provides some interesting insights into culture in general (see Deetz 1967, Chapter 5). Just as linguistic phenomena have three components (idiolect, language, and a system of communication), so too can cultural phenomena be said to have three components (after Aberle 1960). The cultural idiolect is an individual's version of his or her culture. Like the linguist, the cultural anthropologist must sort through this diversified individual behavior in search of common threads.

We know that nineteenth-century Kwakiutl Indians practiced the potlatch; rural East Indians worship cows; the Tsembaga Maring (a New Guinea clan), nurture massive pig herds for ritual slaughter. In each case, these cultural activities and beliefs articulate with an enormous corpus of additional rules and prescriptions to form the cultural whole. Cultural events such as these have kept

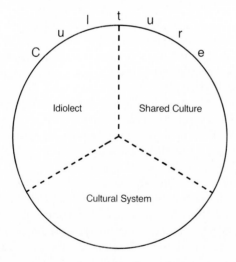

Figure 3–1
The major components of culture.

generations of anthropologists busy observing, participating, and describing. This is culture's shared, modal component.

But culture has a third component: the **cultural system.** Shared language exists to facilitate a system of communication and shared culture also exists to serve specific functions. Leslie White (a general anthropologist) pioneered the consideration of cultural systems, and more recently archaeologists have reworked White's thinking specifically to suit the study of extinct cultural systems. Lewis Binford (1964), following White's lead, defined the cultural system as a set of repetitive articulations among the social, technological, and ideological aspects of culture. These three aspects are not genetic. They are, in White's terminology, "extrasomatic," meaning *outside the body* (learned). Social, technological, and ideological aspects represent the nonbiological (cultural) mechanisms through which human populations handle their biological and derived needs. A cultural system embraces the structural elements basic to cultural adaptations, rather than emphasizing the mere aggregates of "cultural traits" that happen to be shared.

The point is this: *one does not share a cultural system—one participates in it* (Binford 1965). More precisely, one participates in a system of behavior that reflects, and is governed by, the underlying culture that itself constitutes a system. Participation is controlled by cultural roles, expressed often through intricate sets of statuses and roles.

This important point can be illustrated by the well-known case of rivalry **potlatch,** a custom best documented for the Southern Kwakiutl of Vancouver Island, and practiced by several late nineteenth-century tribes throughout the Northwest Pacific Coast of Canada and the United States. The post-contact potlatch consisted of competitive feasting, during which ambitious, status-hungry men battled one another for social approval by hosting massive, often opulent feasts. Kwakiutl custom dictated that the more food one gave away, the greater was the prestige accrued. Potlatch feasts were considered successful only when the guests had "eaten themselves under the table" and crawled groaning into the forest, only to vomit and return for more.

The potlatch is notable because the competitive feasting was extended far beyond simple gluttony. Late nineteenth-century potlatching culminated in the outright destruction of property—not only food, but also clothing, money, pieces of art, and even entire houses. The logic was this: the more goods destroyed, the greater the host's prestige. The guest chief, of course, belittled the host's efforts, and eventually held a return potlatch designed to show his own superior means, and hence superior status.

Potlatches proceeded by strict, culturally dictated rules. One person functioned in the role of host, inviting neighbors to his village for the feasting and festivities. The host parceled out gifts of varying degrees of worth: boxes of candlefish oil, baskets of berries, stacks of blankets, animal skins. As each gift was presented, the guests responded with a great degree of (culturally prescribed) dissatisfaction. They were being insulted by the host's generosity. Some guests served in the roles of "speaker" or "artist," and dancers assumed a variety of traditional poses, such as cannibal dancer, bear dancer, and food dancer.

The potlatch contains all three cultural components, if we are willing to look for them. The observer would initially be struck by the cultural idiolects. Each costume and mask is distinct; every dancer has his or her own style; each speaker strives to render the personal touch. This idiosyncratic behavior reflects culturally prescribed variance from group standards (Goodenough 1970:101–102).

The potlatch is also shared, modal behavior. All Kwakiutl believe in the institution of the potlatch. That is why they participate. By the same token, most Americans share a belief in the ballot box, a knowledge of American English, and the use of cash (Aberle 1960:14–15). The potlatch at this level consists of shared cultural beliefs.

But in a third sense the potlatch is not shared at all, it is participated in. And this participation is differential. A wide variety of culturally prescribed roles and statuses is evident. The host participates in a different fashion from that of the insulted guest; the hired dancer's role is quite different from that of the host's wife. This participation, of course, is not actually culture, but rather cultural behavior.

More importantly, the potlatch seemed to serve an adaptive function within the overall Kwakiutl cultural system as if it had been influenced by European culture. The shared behavior known as the potlatch served the cultural system. What could be adaptive about the destruction of personal property or the injurious personal insults hurled over potlatch fires? This question has puzzled generations of anthropologists who viewed the potlatch strictly as shared cultural behavior. The astonished observers of burnt blankets and flaming candle-fish oil saw only a destructive and wasteful cultural practice. It was "quaint." Ruth Benedict has called these people Dionysian, stressing the violent, frenzied nature of Kwakiutl culture: "The final thing they strove for was ecstasy" (Benedict 1934:175).

Another interpretation of the potlatch came after investigators looked beyond the obvious visual effects into the functions of the potlatch. What ecological, technological, and economic functions were served by such cultural beliefs? How did the potlatch serve Northwest Coast society? In a systemic perspective, the potlatch exhibits features that were not only adaptive but possibly essential to the survival of Northwest Coast Indians.

First of all, the rivalrous feasting between local groups may have increased overall regional productivity. People seem to work harder when personal prestige is at stake. Such regionalized feasts and ceremonies might also have functioned to distribute goods and services between villages, thereby overcoming the effects of localized failures in production (Suttles 1960; Piddocke 1965). If each Northwest coastal village was totally independent, then the failure of salmon to run up a particular stream could be locally disastrous. But through the potlatch system the less fortunate villages were invariably invited to several potlatches, hosted by more successful neighbors. Although the guest villagers had to endure insults, they left with full bellies. They had in effect traded some of their prestige for food, and, all else being equal within the ecological system, they will have had ample opportunity to redeem lost prestige when the neighboring villagers ran on hard times. But suppose that some villages suffered continued failure of subsistence items? There is even some suggestion that the potlatch served to shift population from the less productive to the more productive villages (Hazard 1960): economically successful villages could "boast" of (and demonstrate) their wealth at the potlatch ceremonies, thereby having induced guests to leave their impoverished situations and sign up with the more wealthy, more ecologically stable, village.

Cultural phenomena can thus be trisected into domains of study: the idiolect, the modal belief, and the underlying cultural system. The potlatch contained aspects of all three components. There is little disagreement among anthropologists that all three components of culture are real. But remarkably little agreement exists as how best to conceptualize these complex cultural components, and these philosophical issues color how the anthropologist views each component. Before narrowing the scope to archaeology, it is first necessary to look more closely at the mainstreams of current anthropological thinking.

> There are many roads to truth.
> *Paul S. Martin*

STRATEGIES IN CONTEMPORARY ANTHROPOLOGY

> The art of being wise is the art of knowing what to overlook.
> *William James*

The culture concept was presented in some detail because it provides the mainstay of all anthropological research. Culture is, in a sense, the baseline from which all of anthropology begins. But culture is not a monolithic concept. As you might expect, the kinds of anthropologists who study culture tend to emphasize one aspect over another.

The Ideational Approach

The basic theme of this approach is simple: "The realm of ideas, the force of symbols is centrally important in shaping human behavior" (Keesing 1976:137). Culture to the ideational theorist refers primarily to complex sets of ideas, of conceptual design, and of shared meanings which underlie the way people approach life.

Culture, in this sense, is mainly what humans learn, not what they do or make. This view of culture places primary emphasis on the realm of cognition:

ideas, thought, shared knowledge. Ideational culture does not consist of material things or events that can be counted or observed.

Clifford Geertz (1973:6–7) provides an illuminating example of culture in the shared ideational sense. Consider the difference between a wink and an involuntary eye twitch. These gestures are identical as physical behavior. We cannot measure the difference between them. Yet, culturally, the difference is manifest. A wink is a signal in a code of meanings that all Americans share, a code unintelligible to an Eskimo or an Australian aborigine. But an involuntary twitch is not a signal at all. It is a reflex. Even among winks, there can be subtle differences. Consider for example, a second winker, who derides the first for winking badly by producing a burlesque, intentionally inept wink. Such subtle behavior acquires meaning and conveys information only within a universe of shared cognitive meaning.

The ideational approach to culture holds that one cannot understand human behavior without postulating a *cognitive code* beneath it (Keesing 1976:142). One could measure forever and never capture the meanings of "wink," "burlesque wink," and "twitch." Much of what we perceive in the world, and endow with meaning, does not exist in the physical world at all. It exists only in our mind's eye. Robert Murphy (1976:52) has recently suggested that by ignoring the ideational perspective of culture, anthropologists will soon journey down rivers, watching the native women breaking rocks with their wet laundry. The ideational theorist insists upon "getting inside the informant's head."

Three fundamental mainstreams of thought can be recognized within the overall ideational strategy. *Cognitive anthropology* tends to focus on internalized folk classification as a key for discovering the rules for "appropriate" behavior. The second mainstream of the ideational strategy, *symbolic anthropology,* emphasizes the definition and use of symbols as a code for communication. To date, symbolic anthropologists have concentrated mainly on the study of religion and world view. The third major manifestation of the ideational strategy, *structural anthropology,* is the most influential. The objective of structural analysis is to discover the basic principles of human cognition; structuralists view culture as a set of shared symbolic structures, which together comprise the cumulative creations of the mind. Structuralists, led by Levi-Strauss, attempt to determine how the real world is culturally reduced into mental structure, primarily through the analysis of myth, art, kinship, and language.

The Adaptive Approach

We can contrast the ideational mainstreams of anthropology with a perspective that views culture primarily as an *adaptive* system. This approach explains cultural differences and similarities in terms of the technological, demographic, and ecological processes responsible for basic subsistence (Harris 1968a:240). Note the contrast:

> *Ideational strategy;* Ideas, symbols, and mental structures tend to shape human behavior.

Adaptive strategy: Technology, ecology, demography, and economics tend to shape human behavior.

Neither viewpoint says "always"; both seek only to isolate causes that "tend to" produce observed effects. Both the ideational and adaptive strategies allow for interplay and interaction between the mental and the material. The ideational approach simply argues that sociocultural phenomena are best understood by mentalistic factors; adaptivists feel that these sociocultural differences are better understood by identifying the precise nature of materialistic parameters.

Several points should be made about the adaptive view of culture. First of all, emphasis is squarely upon *culture as a system.* Both the cultural idiolect and the shared aspects of culture are momentarily set aside. It is the cultural system that functions to relate human communities directly to their ecological settings. Especially important in this adaptive sense are technology, modes of economic organization, settlement pattern, forms of social grouping, and political organization and religious practices.

Secondly, culture change is seen as primarily a process of adaptation, in a sense analogous to natural selection.

> Man is an animal and, like all other animals, must maintain an adaptive relationship with his surroundings in order to survive. Although he achieves this adaptation principally through the medium of culture, the process is guided by the same rules of natural selection that govern biological adaptation. (Meggers 1971:4)

In this manner, cultures function in dynamic equilibrium within their ecosystems. When changes occur in environment, demography, or technology, these shifts are ultimately ramified throughout the entire cultural system.

The prime movers of cultural systems are viewed as those elements of technology, subsistence economy, and social organization that are most closely tied to production. This view contrasts sharply with the ideational perspective discussed above. Although a certain amount of disagreement exists as to how cultures actually adapt (e.g. Harris 1968a; *contra* Service 1968), all cultural adaptationists agree that economics (in its broadest sense) and its social correlates are in most cases primary. Ideational systems are ultimately secondary (see Figure 3–3).

COGNITIVE ANTHROPOLOGY

For my thoughts are not your thoughts, neither are your ways my ways.
The Bible

Formalized only within the past two decades, this mainstream of cultural anthropology concentrates on the mentalistic, internalized folk classification as the focal point of inquiry. Terming the approach **cognitive anthropology**, Stephen Tyler has delimited a field of study that focuses on discovering how different peoples organize and use their cultures. This is not so much a search for some generalized unit of behavioral analysis as it is an attempt to understand the organizing principles of underlying behavior. Cognitive anthropology seeks to answer two questions (Tyler 1969:3): What material phenomena are significant for the people of some culture? How do they organize these phenomena? Cognitive anthropology thus tends to emphasize the *folk classification* as a key to how people organize their reality. Culture in this sense constitutes a system of knowledge. Ward Goodenough (1961:522) has succinctly summarized the cognitive approach: "Culture . . . consists of standards for deciding what is . . . for deciding what can be . . . for deciding what one feels about it . . . for deciding what to do about it, and . . . for deciding how to go about doing it." Cognitive anthropologists have adapted a number of techniques from descriptive linguistics for studying other cultural phenomena. Goodenough (1957) has argued that anthropologists should attempt to construct "cultural grammars" of behavior: What rules must a stranger know in order to operate in a manner acceptable to the members of society? Culture in this sense consists of the rules of "appropriate" behavior.

The most successful eliciting technique is the simple question-and-answer method, known as "frame analysis." A question, often taxonomic, is formulated in the informant's language. The informant is requested to answer the question. Further questions are formulated from the answers, the cycle repeating until the informant reaches the most specific term, which is not broken down into subspecies. Werner (1973:292) gives a simplified example of the technique:

A. "What kinds of animals are there?"
B. "There are . . . bears. . . ."
A. "What kinds of bears are there?"
B. "There are . . . brown bears. . . ."
A. "What kind of brown bears are there?"
B. "Can't think of any kind."

This hypothetical exchange between ethnographer and informant can then be translated into sentences:

The first pair: "Bears are animals."
The second pair: "Brown bears are bears."
The third pair: no sentence

These sentences could then be combined as a small fragment of a larger taxonomic classification of the animal kingdom.

Other cognitive anthropologists also follow a slightly different tack, using an investigatory technique known as **componential analysis** (see Buchler and Selby 1968, Chapter 8). Aimed directly at elucidating kinship terminology, the componential analysis attempts to elicit concrete, cognitively significant rules. By so doing, a bounded set of terms is defined according to semantic domains. The American kinship system, for instance, defines the term *father* as a male relative in the direct line belonging to the first ascending (higher) generation. The kin term *father* has thus been succinctly: male, direct, ascending (Brown 1965). All individuals in the American kinship system meeting these criteria will be *father;* no individuals not meeting the criteria will be *father.* Predictions made on the basis of this definition should be successfully verified on any informant participating in this kinship system.

Is cognitive anthropology relevant to contemporary archaeology? Not very. Cognitive anthropology involves intensive interaction with informants, often emphasizing the folk classification as a key to understanding culture. By devising a classification of "appropriate behavior," one learns how informants structure their own realities. Ethnographers construct their hierarchies and keys only through interaction with their informants. The methods of cognitive anthropology are designed to get inside the informant's head, to determine the structure of culturally acceptable responses.

When an archaeologist "gets into an informant's head," it is generally because he used his shovel incorrectly. Most of the information a cognitive anthropologist seeks disappeared with the death of the informant. While some evidence of cognitive patterning is surely manifested in surviving material culture, cognitive anthropologists themselves have paid little attention to it. In truth, there are too many informants to talk to for cognitive anthropologists to bother with the artifacts and garbage that are available to archaeologists.

Nevertheless, archaeologists have from time to time advocated a cognitive approach to archaeology, the best-known example being K. C. Chang's *Rethinking Archaeology* (1967).

Chang's argument went like this: since archaeologists spend 80 to 90 percent of their time classifying artifacts, these classifications should be designed to reflect the cognitive structures of the people who made and used the artifacts. Heavily influenced by **ethnoscience,** Chang proposed methods through which archaeologists could make their classifications "culturally meaningful." Chang reasoned that any archaeological *type* (a key concept considered in Chapter 7) that changes systematically through time "must have a structural base" (1967:87). Chang proposed that artifact classifications should be constructed like folk taxonomies, in order to unravel this hidden cognitive meaning.

The major difficulty is that Chang's "cognitively significant" classifications fall outside the scope of science. The scientific cycle, as we have seen, requires that hypotheses be validated by testing on independent data. How does one scientifically test a classification hierarchy?

Cognitive anthropologists can do this in good scientific fashion. They test their kinship analyses and folk taxonomies by asking informants tightly structured questions: Can "culturally meaningful" responses be generated from the anthropological model? If informants agree with the newly generated statements, then the model is good. If nonsense results, then the key does not adequately reflect the informant's mental categories. The ultimate test in cognitive anthropology is the informant's judgment of "appropriate behavior."

Chang wanted archaeologists to construct classifications to reflect the minds of the people who made the artifacts. The problem here is not building the typology—archaeologists can classify *anything.* The problem is how to test whether or not the categories mean anything to the people who manufactured the artifacts. Those mental classifications disappeared when the informants died. Cognitively significant classifications have not been constructed in archaeology because they cannot be tested. Cognitive anthropologists cannot construct their keys and folk taxonomies without native informants, and neither can archaeologists.

So cognitive anthropology has had little impact on mainstream archaeology. But having said this, I must inform you that a small group of contemporary archaeologists are indeed investigating the cognitive processes that operated in the past, and they are using archaeological materials as their data (e.g. Hall 1977; Marshack 1972a, 1972b, 1976; Kehoe and Kehoe 1973). The work of the **cognitive archaeologists,** as they call themselves, will be discussed in Chapters 11 and 13. This brand of cognition has relatively little to do with cognitive anthropology as such, except that both schools are attempting to cope with mental processes.

Other archaeologists, recognizing that cognitive anthropologists tend to ignore the relationship of material culture to ideas, have started doing their own fieldwork. This topic of **ethnoarchaeology** is considered in Chapter 12, and cognition is only one area currently being investigated.

To summarize: cognitive anthropology is a specialized methodology for determining what is going on in the heads of living informants. To date, this anthropological mainstream has had little impact on archaeology. Although the work of a small group of "cognitive archaeologists" may ultimately be fruitful, it is too early to tell.

SYMBOLIC ANTHROPOLOGY

> **M**an is what he believes.
> *Anton Chekhov*

A second ideational mainstream emphasizes the use of symbols in human culture. Although a number of anthropologists apply this approach (Dumont, Schneider, Geertz, Turner) it is necessary for us to focus this limited discussion on a very few **symbolic anthropologists.**

Geertz (1973) has criticized the views of Goodenough and the other cognitive anthropologists, arguing that the analysis of culture as primarily the cognitive, mentalistic systems of individual actors is a dangerous practice. To Geertz, culture is not merely a private common denominator between individuals, as Goodenough has suggested. Rather, culture is a public phenomenon transcending the cognitive realization of any single individual. Geertz emphasizes culture as a code for communication. Culture has a "collective magic" which cannot be understood from any single participant's perspective. In other words, Geertz sees culture as a stage play that has a public significance above and beyond the part of any individual actor. Because this shared consciousness transcends any single individual's experience, the collective understanding between two individuals of the same culture is far more than merely the sum total of their two individual parts. Geertz criticizes the cognitive anthropologists for describing culture as if it were individual and private. Culture is not private. Culture is shared and, in a real sense, public. Like language, culture is viewed as an abstraction, an idealized account, synthesized by the analyst and not wholly represented in the consciousness of any single native actor.

The premise that culture is both shared and public has led symbolic anthropologists to stress the distinction between the culture and the social system within which that culture operates. Geertz (1973) defines culture as "an ordered system of meaning and of symbols, in terms of which social interaction takes place"; the social system is "the pattern of social interaction itself."

Victor Turner (1968:135–138) uses a similar analogy to a concert orchestra. The culture of a group is analogous to the musical score of a symphony. The sheet music parcels out appropriate behavior to each musician in the orchestra. This score is the analogue of culture. But the interactions of the musicians with each other, and with the conductor, comprise the orchestral social system. Sometimes individual musicians are "out of synch" with the rest of the orchestra; they feud with one another and the conductor; they exchange grimaces and smiles.

When Turner studied initiation rituals among the Ndembu of Zambia, he was able to use the orchestra analogy to understand the interactions he was witnessing (see inset). The Ndembu are not "members" of a culture. They are a human population distinguished from surrounding populations in several important ways: they live in separate communities, they speak a common language, they share the same body of customs, and they interact more with one another than with outsiders. The Ndembu share and participate in a culture, an ordered system of meaning and of symbols; they are members of a society located in Zambia. The society is a kind of social system. Society has a social structure consisting of a set of roles and statuses that relate in recurrent patterns (Keesing 1976:143).

The overt emphasis on symbols and symbol systems leads Geertz, Turner, and the other symbolic anthropologists along a different path from that of the cognitive anthropologists. Instead of emphasizing folk taxonomies and kinship

Symbols in Ndembu Ritual

Symbolic anthropologists have concentrated on unraveling the particularly strong symbolism embodied in primitive ritual, as for example, Victor Turner's (1967) analysis of Ndembu ritual symbols. Turner sees Ndembu ritual symbolism as a set of major symbolic objects or qualities: specific colors, special trees, and other specified items deemed to be sacred in the Ndembu ecosystem. There is a sap-producing tree, *mudyi*, involved in a number of rituals. In Ndembu, the sap of this particular tree signifies a number of things: breast milk and nursing, mother-child interactions, matrilineal descent. The tree also signifies more general images of dependency and purity. The *mudyi* is but one of several symbolic objects that are integrated in Ndembu ritual. The total ritual involves a sequence of such objects, fitted together by Ndembu concepts of appropriate behavior. Here is where Turner uses the analogy of the musical score; the ritual objects are "orchestrated" in tightly defined ways. The ritual, in other words, has a syntax. A single rite might signify feelings about existing mothers and children, and also a general feeling of dependency upon one's ancestors. The differing levels of meaning also serve to relate the abstract with the mundane, emotional, day-to-day level. As Keesing points out (1976:404), such study marks the beginnings of a theory of symbolism that transcends the simplistic Freudian and purely social explanations: "The royal scepter is neither simply a phallic symbol nor a symbol of the unity of the state—it is both, and that is why it 'works'."

terms, the symbolists have made important strides in the study of religion, world views, and in unraveling the "musical score" that is seen as an unconscious substratum underlying human actions. Religion to Geertz (1966:4) consists of a system of symbols that defines the way the world is. Religion orders perspective so that one knows the appropriate actions to take toward the world—how to act and how to live.

Is symbolic anthropology relevant to contemporary archaeology? Only slightly. Symbolic anthropologists deal with how symbolism is reflected in actual behavior. Geertz, for instance, has attempted to discover specific ways in which religion, ritual, and symbol operate to structure contemporary world views. Symbolic culture tells people how to act and how to live. The task of symbolic anthropology has been to decode this ritual behavior in order to find its underlying significance.

But the same operational problem remains for archaeology: Lacking the testimony from participating informants, how does one test hypotheses about symbolism? How, for instance, does the prehistoric archaeologist test whether or not the sap from the *mudyi* tree actually represented breast milk and matrilineal descent? Such testing is difficult enough for ethnographers working with living informants.

Contemporary archaeologists are, to be sure, increasingly more involved with problems of how ritual, religion, and symbolism are manifest in material culture, as we will discuss in Chapter 11. But these studies are restricted to the in-the-ground evidence. Archaeologists have a great deal to contribute in terms of religion, but not the inside-the-head religion that symbolic anthropologists explore.

To summarize: archaeologists are working on the role of symbolism in extinct societies, but the results are likely to be very different from those of symbolic anthropologists working among extant cultures.

STRUCTURAL ANTHROPOLOGY

> Those theories of probable nature are seldom worth the proof.
>
> *George Gaylord Simpson*

The central figure in **structural anthropology** is **Claude Levi-Strauss**. Virtually all structural writings bristle with quotations from Levi-Strauss, whose publications have almost acquired the status of sacred texts. To the uninitiated, the multitudinous writings of Levi-Strauss seem so diverse and all-encompassing that they are like the Bible: any position on any issue can be supported by a carefully selected quotation. One critic has quipped that Levi-Strauss has interpreted structure; the task of structural anthropologists is to interpret Levi-Strauss.

Structuralists view culture as the shared symbolic structures which are *cumulative creations of the mind* (Keesing 1974:78). The objective of structural analysis is to discover the basic principles of the human mind as reflected in major cultural domains—myth, art, kinship, and language. To Levi-Strauss the real world can always be reduced to mental structure. This is an important premise because it implies that the material conditions of the real world— subsistence and economy—serve only to constrain human culture; adaptive considerations do not explain culture. When discussing the custom of primitive people to select totems, for instance, Levi-Strauss asserts that "natural species are not chosen because they are 'good to eat' but because they are 'good to think'" (1963b:89). Levi-Strauss concentrates his research on those areas that are least "constrained" by external, material considerations such as myth and religion.

Levi-Strauss set out to determine, then demonstrate, how the human mind operates on the "raw materials of experience" to produce endlessly elaborated conceptual schemes. To Levi-Strauss, the underlying logic of thought is always binary, comprised of two-way contrasts (+ or −, white or black, and so on). These symbolic polarities run throughout the fabric of a culture, and, in this way, the human mind is like a modern computer. In fact, the fundamental dualism is a constant, not a variable. Binary contrasts operate within all cultures.[2] In this sense, Levi-Strauss is more concerned with the workings of general worldwide culture rather than any particular culture.

Unlike the other ideational approaches already considered, structuralism has gone far beyond mere methodological discussion. Structuralism has produced a firm body of results (acceptable to the structuralists, at least). Prominent among the diversified interests of Levi-Strauss has been the study of myth, the cultural domain least constrained by the external conditions of subsistence, economy, and ecology. Levi-Strauss has set forth his theories in the monumental four-volume *Mythologiques*. The first volume, *The Raw and the Cooked* (1969b), deals with a complex of myths among South American tribes. Explanation relies heavily on cultural evidence. Subsequent volumes trace out mythological thought throughout the Americas, concluding with a "sweeping vision of culture, the mind and the human condition" (Keesing 1976:403).

At least as important to anthropological theory as the analysis of myths and mythic themes is Levi-Strauss's widely influential theory of marriage, exogamy, and exchange. **Alliance theory** attempts to explain why primitive groups consistently seek their mates from outside the local group. That is, why are most primitive residential groupings exogamous?

Levi-Strauss explictly rejects the adaptive explanation offered last century by E. B. Tylor and others, namely, that **exogamy** kept a growing tribe unified by exchanging mates between **clans**. In this way, "savage tribes must have had plainly before their minds the simple practical alternative between marrying-out and being killed out" (Tylor 1889:267). Levi-Strauss rejects the idea that exogamy functions to reduce intergroup competition.

Instead of focusing on descent and kinship, Levi-Strauss sees the exchange of women by groups of men as the key element in social structure. To Levi-Strauss, marriage and exogamy are neither the cause nor the underlying motive for exchange. The situation works the other way. Exchange is the central relationship in primitive societies. Exchange, in and of itself, has a positive value, and hence is basic to human culture:

> It is always a system of exchange that we find at the origin of rules of marriage. . . .
> But no matter what form it takes, whether direct or indirect, general or special,
> immediate or deferred, explicit or implicit, closed or open, concrete or symbolic, it
> is exchange, that emerges as the fundamental and common basis for all modalities
> of the institution of marriage. (1969a:478–479)

Marriage, exogamy, kinship, and descent have all evolved to facilitate this fundamental exchange. From this groundwork, Levi-Strauss goes on in *The Elementary Structures of Kinship* to analyze incest, dual organization, marriage of cousins, and to consider kinship systems throughout the world.

Critics and converts alike agree that the anthropology of Levi-Strauss is aesthetically elegant and logically coherent. But whether, in addition, his arguments are scientifically defensible has been the subject of considerable debate (Scholte 1973:680). Regardless of the outcome, Levi-Strauss undoubtedly emerges as one of the major driving forces in twentieth-century anthropology.

Many enemies, much honor.
Sigmund Freud

But is structuralism relevant to contemporary archaeology?

Levi-Strauss is no more germane to
contemporary archaeology than Charles de
Gaulle, Marcel Duchamp or Edith Piaf.
Personally, I prefer the latter two over Levi-
Strauss.

J. Jefferson Reid

Levi-Strauss and his followers attempt to unravel the structural intricacies of myth, kinship, and elementary mental organization. On the surface, it might seem that archaeologists, too, could become enmeshed in structuralism. After all, Levi-Strauss can see dual organization in the archaeological ruins of Tiahuanaco and Cuzco, can't he? In the inset, we see how Levi-Strauss explains the mysterious earthworks at Poverty Point, a site examined by both C. B. Moore and James Ford (Chapter 1).

As usual, Levi-Strauss puts forth intriguing possibilities. Some hypotheses, such as whether or not the Poverty Point people had eight clans or whether the cremations are "villages of the dead" or merely isolated burials, can perhaps be explored archaeologically.

But the crux of the Levi-Strauss approach is the binary mental organization which he says the Poverty Point earthworks represent. The issue of verification goes to the heart of Levi-Strauss's structuralism. In reviewing the empirical critique, Scholte (1973:688) has compiled an imposing roster of criticisms already launched at Levi-Strauss in this regard: the procedures on structuralism "are judged to be viciously circular, if not actually false. . . . it is subjective, selective, arbitrary, merely clever, even specious. It is abstract, rigid and dogmatic. It may even be meaningless and incomprehensible. It is certainly unverifiable and unempirical. In sum, structuralism is, at best, an aesthetic experience, at worst, a self-fulfilling prophecy."

Suffice it to say that the empirical status of structuralism is open to question. When these notions are applied to archaeological phenomena, the problem is compounded many times over.

The verification difficulty has pretty well removed structuralism from the arena of contemporary archaeology. We have been assuming that archaeology must proceed by scientific methods. How could one test Levi-Strauss's ideas about Poverty Point? Even if one could empirically establish that the Poverty Point people did have eight clans, it is a drastic jump to conclude that the earthworks symbolize a binary dualism as pervasive as male/female, sacred/profane, raw/cooked, bride-takers/bride-givers. Even with contemporary ethnographic evidence, these mental structures remain Levi-Strauss mysticisms. They may—or may not—have anything to do with the minds of the informants.

Archaeology may continue to provide fodder for the structures of Levi-Strauss, but so far, the outcomes of these inquiries have little to do with archaeology, or science, or maybe even reality.

What Levi-Strauss Sees at Poverty Point

As I [Levi-Strauss] write these lines, I have just learned of the archaeological discoveries at Poverty Point, Louisiana, in the Lower Mississippi Valley. Let me insert a parenthetical remark, for this Hopewellian town, dating from the first millennium before the beginning of the Christian era, offers an interesting resemblance to the Bororo village as it may have existed in the past. The plan is octagonal (recalling the eight Bororo clans), and the dwellings are arranged six deep, forming six concentric octagonal figures. Two perpendicular axes cross-cut the village, one running east-west, the other north-south. The ends of these axes were marked by bird-shaped mounds, two of which have been recovered (those at the northern and western ends). The other two were probably erased by a shift in the course of the Arkansas River. When we note that remains of cremation have been discovered in the vicinity of one of the mounds (the western one), we recall the two Bororo "villages of the dead," situated at the eastern and western ends of the moiety axis.

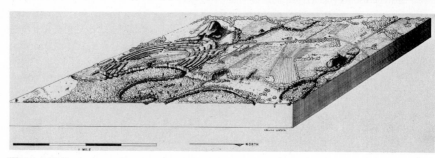

Figure 3–2
Reconstruction of the Poverty Point site, West Carroll Parish, Louisiana (*courtesy of The American Museum of Natural History*).

We are therefore dealing with a type of structure which in America extends far back into antiquity, and whose later analogues were to be found in pre-Conquest Peru and Bolivia and, more recently, in the social structure of the Sioux in North America and of the Ge and related tribes in South America. These are facts worthy of consideration. (1963a:138–139)

CULTURAL MATERIALISM

> Technology is the hero of our piece.
> *Leslie White*

The roots of **cultural materialism** as a strategy extend at least a century back in time. As before, we can identify this strategy largely with the writings of one or two highly influential scholars. Not that these writers represent the totality of thought in a particular area, but rather because these individuals tend to be the most vocal, the most zealous advocates for one posture or another.

Cultural materialism is largely associated with Marvin Harris, professor of anthropology at Columbia University. The cultural materialist philosophy suggests that anthropologists generally find the causes of sociocultural diversity in the mundane world: Techno-economic, techno-environmental conditions "exert selective pressures in favor of certain types of organizational structures and upon the survival and spread of definite types of ideological complexes" (Harris 1968a:241). This is the premise of cultural materialism.[3]

The modern origins of cultural materialistic thought are also closely intertwined with the writings of Leslie A. White. Basic to White's thinking is a division of the cultural system into three major portions: technological, sociological, and ideological (White 1949:364). The technological subsystem is broad-based, consisting of material, mechanical, physical, and chemical instruments, together with the techniques of their use. Technology articulates man with environment by means of the tools of production, means of subsistence, materials of shelter, and the instruments of offense and defense. The sociological subsystem is comprised of those interpersonal relationships which emerge as behavioral patterns: social organization, kinship, economics, ethics, and military and political organizations. The ideological system consists of the ideas, beliefs, and knowledge that are manifest in symbolic, cognitive form. To this point, White's subsystems are probably acceptable (to one degree or another) to both ideational and adaptive anthropologists.

Causality is where White parts company with the ideationalists. While related, the three sectors influence one another differentially (Figure 3–3), and, as a materialist, White assigns causal priority to the technological subsystem: "It could not be otherwise, the technical system is both primary and basic in importance; all human life and culture rest and depend upon it." Technology is the independent variable and the social system is the dependent variable. Social systems are considered secondary to technology; ideological systems are considered tertiary. Each mode of technology tends to involve rather distinctive

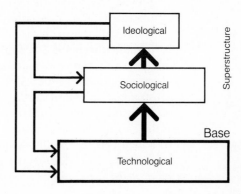

Figure 3–3
How the cultural materialist views ultimate causality.

ideological systems. Farmers think differently from hunter-gatherers, who view the world differently from industrialists. To White, technology is the key to understanding the growth and development of all culture.

The strategy of cultural materialism has been assailed for invoking simplistic, mechanical, monistic determinism (e. g., Service 1968; Friedman 1974): economy always determines social organization and ideology. Harris is quick to deny this accusation. Social phenomena are too complex to be explained by any single factor, materialistic or otherwise. A wide range of variables are considered to be causal, a position clearly traceable back to Frederick Engels:

> According to the materialist conception of history the determining element in history is *ultimately* the production and reproduction in real life. More than this neither Marx nor I have ever asserted. If, therefore, somebody twists this into the statement that the economic element is the only determining one, he transforms it into a meaningless, abstract and absurd phrase. The economic situation is the basis, but the various elements of the superstructure—political forms of the class struggle and its consequences, constitutions established by the victorious class after a successful battle, etc.—forms of law—and even the reflexes of all these actual struggles in the brains of the combatants: political, legal, philosophical theories, religious ideas and their further development into systems of dogma—all exercise their influence upon the course of the historic struggles and in many cases preponderate in determining their *form*. (cited in Harris 1968a:244–245)

Cultural materialists underscore the word *ultimately,* emphasizing that material conditions emerge as causal only given a sufficient number of cases and in the long run (Harris 1968a:245).

Is cultural materialism relevant to contemporary archaeology? Absolutely. I would guess roughly half of the practicing American archaeologists consider themselves to be cultural materialists, to one degree or another (see Leone 1972). There are two compelling reasons for this. The cultural materialistic strategy emphasizes technology, economy, environment, and demography, all aspects of the human existence that survive in the archaeological record. Almost by default, archaeologists have for decades concentrated on precisely the same factors that cultural materialism holds as primary.

Equally important, the cultural materialistic mainstream *needs* archaeology. In his influential book, *The Rise of Anthropological Theory* (1968a), Marvin Harris calls time after time for archaeological backup in his theories of human behavior. Elsewhere, Harris (1968b:359–360) has urged archaeologists to throw off the constraints imposed by current ethnographic theory: "[Archaeologists] are capable of defining entities whose reality, I assure you, is every bit as well grounded as the entities which are now being discussed at great length by ethnographers." Although Harris is hardly the first ethnographer to say this, *cultural materialism is important to archaeology in part because archaeology is important to cultural materialism.*

ECOLOGICAL ANTHROPOLOGY

> **M**an shapes himself through decisions that
> shape his environment.
> *René Dubos*

While neither new nor innovative, ecologically oriented research has become a main thrust of anthropological interest only within the past two decades. As with the other mainstreams, a certain amount of disagreement exists among practitioners as to what this field should properly be named: the new ecology, the newer ecology, new functionalism, neofunctionalism, human ecology, cultural ecology. I follow Vayda and McCay (1975) and Hardesty (1977) and simply use the term **ecological anthropology.**

The interests of ecologically oriented anthropologists are at once diverse and consistent (see Anderson 1973:193): problems involving population and demographic factors, human biobehavioral evolution, the relationship of ecology and cultural evolution, the ecological relationships within social organization, the study of latent functions (and dysfunctions), and the relevance of ecology to folk conceptualizations and decision making. In this brief treatment we can hope to scan only highlights of a wide range of interests.

Basic, of course, to delimiting a domain of study is the definition of key terms. "Anthropology" has already been considered, but **ecology** has not. Unfortunately, the great interest in things "ecological" has done the term a disservice. Ecology can mean anything from tending a victory garden, to protesting the Alaskan pipeline, to drinking one's beer only from recyclable glass bottles. Following Anderson (1973:182), let us define ecology as "the study of entire assemblages of living organisms and their physical milieus, which together constitute integrated systems." This definition embraces the entire range of organisms; bumblebees, birds, bunnies, and bushmen are all included in an ecological approach.

The definition of ecology also emphasizes the integrated system in which organisms interact. Generally termed an **ecosystem,**[4] this mechanism provides a key conceptual tool for ecologists, anthropological or otherwise. Like the concept of culture, a notion of ecosystem constitutes a framework into which relevant facts are interpreted. The ecosystem conceptually unites the physiology, behavior, structural organization, and actual functioning of all organisms (man, other animals, and plants) with inorganic components into a single structure (see inset). The concept of *ecosystem* allows anthropologists to articulate and coordinate their studies with those of other diverse sciences.

One goal of the ecological approach to anthropology is to explain how certain combinations of cultural traits behave within the human ecosystem. The concept of a *homeostatic system*, for example, has been shown to operate in some diverse social mechanisms—warfare, trade, rules of marriage, political organization, and even religion and ritual.

The Kula Exchange in Cultural Materialist Perspective

The **kula exchange** is practiced between the Trobriand Islanders, the Dobuans, and people on the southeast coast of New Guinea. One of the world's most fascinating tribal institutions, the kula exchange involved daring canoe voyages across long stretches of open sea. Men literally risked their lives to participate in this ritual exchange of long necklaces of red shell (called *soulva*) and *mwali,* bracelets of white trochus shell. The overall kula exchange (the kula ring) involved the systematic distribution of arm bands and necklaces; *soulava* went counterclockwise, the *mwali* traveled in clockwise fashion. The kula ring itself extended across several hundred miles of ocean, with no single trader involved in anything but a small portion of the total exchange.

Kula valuables were exchanged between lifelong partners, with a maximum of ceremony and precision, and there was a deep-seated sense of ceremonial honor and ethics in kula exchange, accompanied by a certain amount of jockeying for position. Although a voyager may have presented a particularly valuable kula gift, yet may return empty-handed, he knows that his kula partner will work even harder to make up for this gift at their next meeting.

Why all the fuss to exchange a few arm bands and necklaces? After all, the raw materials for such items lie all about. Why not simply manufacture a few more in one's spare time? That way, the dangerous voyage and possibility of shipwreck could be handily avoided.

Malinowski answered that kula valuables are not economic goods in the Western sense, and cannot be understood simply in subsistence terms. To Malinowski, the kula was "rooted in myth, backed by traditional law, and surrounded with magical rites." The kula objects themselves had no "practical" function. They were treasured heirlooms, valued for their age and history instead of intrinsic economic value.

Malinowski compared the arm bands and necklaces to the crown jewels, which, to him, were "ugly, useless, ungainly, even tawdry." But on reflection, Malinowski saw a magnificent parallel between the crown jewels and the kula valuables. Both were too valuable, too cumbersome to be worn, and both were heirlooms cherished because of the historical sentiment surrounding them. However, ugly, useless, and (perhaps) valueless an object might be, if it had figured in historic scenes it became an unfailing vehicle of important sentimental association. Every really good kula item had an individual name and a wealth of history and romantic tradition surrounding it. In other words, the kula objects, argued Malinowski, should be classed among the "ceremonial" objects of the world, laden with tradition and ritual. The kula ring thus joins the growing list of noneconomic, "irrational" acts by primitive peoples.

But must it? The reliance upon myth, tradition, ceremony, and magic are all ideational explanations, invoking the primacy of mentalistic considerations. The cultural materialist offers another explanation. Let us look toward the adaptive functions behind the symbols and myths and rituals.

A preoccupation with ritual could lead one to overlook one important fact: the "empty" canoes returning from faraway kula exchanges are not empty at all. The canoes are crammed to the gunwales with trade goods. These items might not be ritually important but they nevertheless play a vital role in daily Trobriand subsistence. As Harris

(1975:288) has suggested, "As long as everyone agrees that the expedition is not really concerned with such mundane necessities as coconuts, sago palm, flour, fish, yams, baskets, mats, wooden swords and clubs, green stone for tools, mussel shells for knives, creepers and lianas for lashings, these items can be haggled over with impunity." Viewed in this light, the kula provides the impetus for subsistence exchange. The islanders can actually be adversaries, competitors, even enemies: kula exchange functions as a regional peace pact, under which otherwise feuding neighbors can still engage in essential trade.

Such considerations were irrelevant to Malinowski, but, nevertheless, certain ecological details glimmer amidst his descriptions of kula myth and magic. *Lago,* for instance, is a concept that allows the ceremonial exchange of land for kula valuables. In this sense, sacred kula ornaments can be cashed in for subsistence items in the same manner that the Kwakiutl traded prestige for food in the potlatch ceremonies. Trobrianders also have extensive trade networks which serve to relate coastal fishermen to inland yam horticulturists, to redistribute yams for feasts (and hence build local prestige), for war, or for corvée labor. Once again, note the parallel to the materialistic views of the potlatch feasts. The kula network is fantastically intricate, and the cultural materialist emphasizes the details of mundane matters in order to understand the entangling economic networks.

To show how this ecological approach is applied, let us examine how ritual functioned in regulating the Western Shoshoni human ecosystem prior to white contact. The aboriginal Western Shoshoni were a simple hunter-gatherer people who lived in family bands throughout the Desert West (Steward 1938; Thomas 1973). In fact, the Shoshoni are often used as ethnographic analogies for the way archaeological groups must have been in Paleo-Indian times (see MacNeish 1964; Flannery 1966). The Shoshoni generally lived in small, family-based groups, rarely consisting of more than ten individuals (Steward 1938:240). But the Shoshoni and their Desert West neighbors did occasionally gather in much larger groups to celebrate temporary festivals or *fandangos.* Such celebrations were known to attract upwards of three hundred people (Harris 1940:53; Steward 1938:237) and provided an unusual opportunity for social interaction at the supraband level. Although *fandangos* varied from region to region, certain elements seemed practically universal: gambling, dancing, trading, philandering, courting, and praying for abundance of critical resources (particularly rain, berries, seeds, plants, fish, and land mammals). Steward described one rather typical *fandango* among the Reese River Shoshoni (1938:107):

> For five days the men drove rabbits daily and everyone danced at night. Dances were the round dance, the horn dance, which is a variation of the round dance, and the recently borrowed back and forth dance. Though danced primarily for pleasure, there was and still is, some belief that the round dance brings rain.

Some Shoshoni performed a "war dance"; exhibition dancers were occasionally imported and paid in both food and shell money (Steward 1938:90,122).

In general, the *fandango* coincided with the temporary availability of seasonal resources. Some groups, particularly those heavily dependent upon fishing, held their *fandangos* in the spring. But groups relying heavily on pine-nuts almost always held their celebrations in the fall, after the piñon harvest but prior to establishing the winter villages. This was about the only time when enough food could be stored to feed such a large gathering of people. Festivals were often planned and coordinated six to eight months in advance. In richer areas, pine-nut festivals were held at regular annual or biannual intervals.

The *fandango* has been interpreted in traditionally ideational fashion as a mechanism of social integration, an occasion during which kinship ties and group solidarity were strengthened. The function was seen as largely social: marriages were arranged, mourning ceremonies held for the past year's dead, and so on. Major Powell noted that "at the pine-nut festival, the Indians exchanged ornaments and clothing as an expression of their friendship. No person must wear away from the festival the articles in which he came" (cited in Fowler and Fowler 1971:248). Steward felt that the *fandangos* were of "essentially noneconomic motivation," involved only in dancing, feasting, and general visiting among long-lost friends.

Such an explanation, while surely correct to some degree, seems not to go far enough. Of course, *fandangos* promoted social integration, but the *fandango* also functioned in an ecological sense.

We know that it was food supply that limited the ultimate human density and distribution throughout the Great Basin (see Thomas 1972a). But it is also known that human societies almost never allow their population to reach this ultimate carrying capacity. Social sanctions generally keep the actual population well below the theoretical potential carrying capacity. Although food is the ultimate determinant of human demography, cultural factors generally intervene to determine the immediate and observed conditions of human abundance and distribution.

The Western Shoshoni, for instance, practiced birth control. The White Knife Shoshoni averaged only two or three offspring per couple; to have more children was an antisocial act. White Knife fathers encouraged their sons to practice withdrawal, and there was a ritual period of sexual abstinence among several groups. Abortion was induced by drugs, hitting the abdomen with a stone, or direct pressure.

Shoshoni also controlled their own death rate to some extent. Several groups routinely killed at least one twin upon birth. Although no stigma was attached to illegitimate children, they too were sometimes killed in times of famine, as were the aged and infirm. The Shoshoni realized the critical importance of controlling their population density, and they had limiting techniques at their disposal. But each limiting technique involved an individual decision. There were no inviolable rules in Shoshoni society: twins were not always killed, illegitimate children were often allowed to live, and the aged and sick were only occasionally abandoned. Each act required a separate, conscious decision. How were these decisions made?

Here is where we can apply the concept of the homeostatic system, which typically consists of three processes. First is the detection of changes in the state of the regulated variable. In a thermostat this operation is accomplished by a column of mercury or a bimetallic bar. Second, the value of the regulated variable is compared with a reference, or ideal, value. In the thermostat this value is fed in through a dial. Third, if there is a discrepancy between the reference and the detected value an error signal is transmitted to the effector, which initiates a corrective program. In the thermostat, the effector is a switch which turns the corrective program—heat from a furnace—on and off. The analogy of the homeostat can be used to examine the ecological function served by ritual behavior such as the Shoshoni *fandango*.

The *fandango* regulated human population density. The mere assemblage of three hundred people in the desert itself provided an indicator of the precise state of the regional population density. The productivity of the winter staple, piñon pine-nuts, was the least predictable of Shoshonean resources (Steward 1938). But future piñon productivity is in part predictable (Thomas 1972a), and the *fandango* served as a "clearing house" of such information (this idea stems from Rappaport 1971a, 1971b). People traveled for a hundred miles and from all directions to attend a *fandango*. Areas of potentially good (and bad) seed crops, regions of abundant and scanty rainfall, and locations of significant concentrations of herd animals were all prime topics of *fandango* conversation.

If these environmental indicators were bad, then some of the optional modes of population control could be more stringently applied, especially abstinence and abortion. In extremely lean years, more drastic means could be practiced, such as infanticide, senilicide, and abandoning the sick. Powell told of an old Shoshoni female who voluntarily went to her death in one such case (Fowler and Fowler 1971:162). But when these critical environmental indicators looked favorable, the optional regulator means could be ignored for the moment: the second twin would survive, the aging grandmother would be nursed along for another year, the illegitimate newborn would be spared.

The Shoshoni *fandango* can be interpreted in either ideological or adaptive fashion, depending upon one's research strategy. The cognitive anthropologist would concentrate on native categories of kinship and folk terminology, or perhaps determine the cognitive structure behind the Shoshonean world view of their own environment. The symbolic anthropologist would probably deal with the myths, songs, and dances evident at the *fandango* ceremonies. The structuralist would discuss deep-seated mental structures which conditioned the specific, external forms of the Shoshonean *fandango*. All such studies would be valuable in the attempt to understand how the Shoshoni themselves viewed the *fandango* and its relevance to their lifeway.

But the *fandango* is also an on-the-ground piece of observable behavior. It certainly had ritual significance to the Shoshoni, but it also had latent functions that are not apparent to its participants. One such latent function may have been the ritual regulation of human population. The *fandango* acted as a homeostat that kept Shoshonean population densities below the ultimate carrying capacities. The *fandango* functioned to detect changes in the state of the regulated variable (in this case, upcoming shortages of food). If the scuttlebutt about the *fandango* fires indicated a dire year ahead, then a series of "corrective programs" (infanticide, abstinence, and so on) could be undertaken. If indicators were positive, then these corrective programs did not need to be instituted.

The role of ritual and religion in ecological analysis will be considered in detail in Chapter 11. For now, two points need emphasis. Ideational and the ecological explanations are not mutually exclusive. Both are important for interpreting cultural institutions. The explanations are not right or wrong; they simply reflect differing strategies of inquiry.

> **E**cologists believe that a bird in the bush is worth
> two in the hand.
>
> *Stanley Pearson*

Is ecological anthropology relevant to contemporary archaeology? Yes. An ecological approach to the archaeological record is not new; archaeologists have been examining strategies of technology, subsistence, and economy for decades. As was the case with cultural materialism, the ecological approach opens dozens of avenues of potential research in archaeology. It is the same old problem: the archaeological record is full of ecological indicators, so archaeologists have tended to exploit them.

The ecological approach to archaeology will be considered in detail throughout this text. Ecological approaches themselves are evolving, particularly with regional perspectives in archaeology (see Chapter 9). We will also examine the role of ecology in religion (Chapter 11), the techniques of subsistence reconstruction (Chapter 8), and the underlying processes that seem to explain observable ecological adaptations (Chapters 12 and 13).

It is difficult to overemphasize the importance of ecology in contemporary archaeology.[5]

CULTURAL EVOLUTION

> **N**othing is permanent except change.
> *Heraclitus*

In Chapter 2 we briefly touched on the topic of **cultural evolution** when considering the nature of science. We distinguished, you will remember, between general and specific evolution, and discussed the law of evolutionary potential in order to see how lawlike statements operate within an anthropological framework. Now it is time to consider cultural evolution in more detail because in many ways it is the most important anthropological mainstream for practicing archaeologists.

The Ecosystem Concept in Action

Figure 3–4 depicts the state of Swat, in northern Pakistan. The anthropological problem is this: an area of less than a thousand square miles contains three radically different ethnic groups. *Pathans* are sedentary agriculturalists speaking the Pashto language; *Kohistanis* speak a Dardic language and they have large animal herds in addition to their agricultural fields; *Gujars* are nomadic herders who speak a lowland Indian dialect.

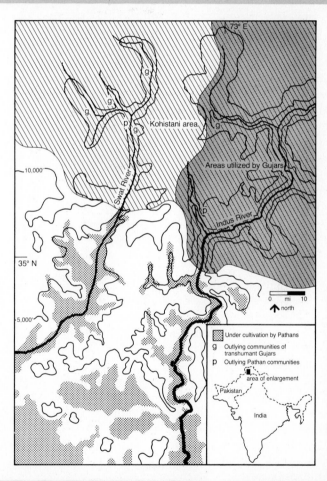

Figure 3–4
Map of ethnic distributions in Swat State, Pakistan. The cross-hatched area is used by the Kohistanis, the shaded area by the Gujars. The Gujar nomads spend the summer in the mountains depicted on the central and north portion of the map and the winter in the southernmost area of the map (*modified from Barth 1956:1084; courtesy of Fredrik Barth*).

How can this be? Three languages, three separate societies, and three distinct economies coexist within a 1,000-square-mile tract of land. And these groups are at peace with one another. If a primary objective of cultural anthropology is to explain cultural similarities and cultural differences, how are we going to explain these congeries of cultural traits?

The answer to this peculiar puzzle in human geography has been provided by Frederick Barth (1956) in a classic application of ecological principles of ethnography. The Pathans have a complex, stratified, multi-caste society. The lower-caste farmers use artificial irrigation systems to grow wheat, maize, and rice. Pathan farming settlements are clustered along the broad, fertile plains of the Swat and Indus rivers, and the nature of the intensive agricultural system constitutes an effective ecological check on further Pathan expansion. Pathan society is socially and economically powerful, always capable of expanding at the expense of their weaker neighbors. Yet Pathan territory is circumscribed to land where two crops can be raised annually.

The Kohistanis also practice plow agriculture, but because the more powerful Pathans control the fertile bottomlands, the Kohistanis live on the surrounding hillsides. Wheat and rice do not grow well in the hillside fields, so maize and millet are the Kohistani staples. Because of the higher elevations, the growing season is truncated and Kohistani fields produce a single crop each year.

Although Pathans and Kohistanis share the same agricultural technology, the net output is quite different. Pathan farmers produce surplus food to feed the nonagricultural segment of their society. The upland fields produce a single crop per year, so the Kohistanis must also herd sheep, goats, cattle, and water buffalo in order to survive. Kohistani people thus follow a *transhumant settlement pattern,* spending their winter months near their lower agricultural fields. During the warmer, summer season, they move to summer campsites at 14,000 feet. Neither mode, herding or agriculture, is sufficient to support the total Kohistani economy. But by careful integration of sedentary agriculture and nomadic herding, the Kohistani pattern supports over 30,000 people living in independent local villages and lacking the rigid caste structures of Pathan society.

The third ethnic group in Swat, the Gujars, are found in both Pathan and Kohistani territory. Gujars are a floating population of herders, with distinctive music, language, dance, and ceremonies. Like the Kohistanis, the Gujars herd sheep, goats, cattle, and water buffalo. But the Gujars are true nomads, not tethered to agricultural fields. The ecological adaptation is such that the Gujars can share the territory of both Pathans and Kohistanis.

When among the Pathans, the Gujars are more or less assimilated as a specialized occupational caste of herders. Gujars care for the animals either as servants of the landowner caste or as independent buffalo herders. They contribute milk products, meat, and manure for the fields; in exchange, the Gujars are permitted to rent the low-lying mountain slopes, useless to Pathans except for firewood. Thus the Pathans and Gujars coexist, but the interchanges are strictly economic and the societies remain socially distinct.

When Gujars move into Kohistani territory, a somewhat less satisfactory symbiosis exists betweeen guests and hosts. Kohistani societies are not caste-stratified, so the Gujars are not so readily assimilated as among the Pathans. In fact, the Gujars and Kohistanis are placed in direct conflict over grazing land. How is territory partitioned between these two partially competitive societies?

We must carefully distinguish between the concepts of *habitat* and ecological *niche.* All organisms, human or otherwise, live in a habitat. This is the place where one would go to find them. The ecological niche, on the other hand, does not refer to physical space occupied by an organism, but rather to the functional role of that organism within a community. The niche depends not only on where an organism lives, but also on what it does (what it eats, how it responds to modification in environment, how it is constrained by other species). In other words, the habitat can be said to be an organism's address, while the niche is the profession (Odum 1971:234).

The three ethnic groups share the same territory only in the habitat sense; the state of Swat is where we find them. But they fill quite different ecological niches within this habitat, and it is these niches that explain land use and even the sociopolitical configuration of the three ethnic groups.

The agricultural Pathans and nomadic Gujars avoid conflict because they participate in different niches. Similarly, the Pathans do not conflict with the Kohistanis. The Pathans are politically more powerful and hence have usurped the best agricultural lands. The Kohistanis live in fringe areas and supplement their agriculture with high-altitude herding. Their niches are such that the territories do not overlap.

But the Kohistanis would seem to be in conflict with the nomadic Gujars. Both societies herd animals, compete for pasturage, and hence occupy the same ecological niche. And yet warfare between Gujars and Kohistanis is rare. How did they strike a compromise?

The answer lies in the social, economic, and ecological details of Gujar and Kohistani society. The Kohistanis rely upon a mixed agricultural and herding economy; neither is sufficient in itself. The steep slopes on which Kohistani fields are located require complex terracing and irrigation, so they cannot practice shifting agriculture. The Kohistani habitat must necessarily provide careful balance between irrigated land suitable for agriculture and that available for pasturage. In effect, Kohistanis fill two complementary yet distinct niches.

Only part of Swat is suitable for this pattern of transhumance. In the Indus River drainage, the Kohistani fields can support a human and animal population of sufficient size through the winter. During summer months they move into the surrounding mountains with their herds. The Kohistani population hence utilizes both niches, and the habitat of Swat Valley does not allow for both niches. Deep snow tends to accumulate through the winter, remaining on the valley bottom until April or May. The Kohistani agricultural system of terraced and irrigated fields simply will not work in this habitat.

This is the crucial difference in habitat that allows for coexistence between the two herding groups. The Kohistanis must practice agriculture during the winter months, and they can do so only in the Indus drainage to the west. Kohistanis then move to upland valleys around the Indus Valley for the summer pastures. The Swat Valley lacks agricultural potential, cannot be utilized by the Kohistanis in winter, and hence summer pasturage in Swat cannot be used by Kohistanis either. This niche is thus left partly vacant and available. Nomadic Gujars are free to winter their herds on the low plains of Swat, an area suitable for pasturage but too cold for agriculture. As true nomads, the

Gujars simply move from one habitat to another, employing the identical niche. The two niches practiced by the Kohistanis have made western Swat essentially unlivable for them, eliminating the competition over the resources in this western area.

To summarize: the human mosaic in the Swat state of northern Pakistan is complex. The distribution of these three ethnic groups is not controlled by culture areas, superstition, world view, or symbolism. This peaceful solution to a complex habitat has evolved along solid ecological principles: "What appears as a single natural area to Kohistanis is subdivided as far as Pathans are concerned, and this division is cross-cut with respect to the specific requirements of Gujars" (Barth 1956:1088). The cultural geography in this case can be unraveled by recourse to an exceedingly simple concept: the ecological niche.

Many suppose that Charles Darwin introduced the term *evolution* into the scientific vocabulary of the nineteenth century, but this is not true. The truth is that the word *evolution* did not even appear in the first five editions of *On the Origin of Species;* only in the sixth edition, published in 1872, did Darwin actually use the term evolution, and even then it was used only six times, and left undefined at that.

Darwin avoided the term evolution because it already had a quite different meaning by the time *On the Origin of Species* was first published in 1859. Sociologist **Herbert Spencer** had preempted the term evolution in his *Social Statics,* published in 1851. At this early date, some eight years before Darwin's influential book, Spencer was already speaking of the evolution of societies, and, in the years to follow, Spencer refined and elaborated his thinking on the evolution of civilization. This is an important point, since many people suppose that cultural evolution is based on some kind of biological analogy; in fact, cultural evolutionary thought preceded Darwinian biological evolution (Carneiro 1973a).

What then is cultural evolution? Any number of definitions have been offered, but we will follow Carneiro's (1973b) slightly modified version of Herbert Spencer's original definition, which appeared in *First Principles* (1887:216): "Evolution is a change from a relatively indefinite incoherent homogeneity to a relatively definite, coherent heterogeneity, through successive differentiations and integrations" (Carneiro 1973b:90). Some points should be made about this concisely worded definition. Note first that evolution proceeds from homogeneity to more differentiated heterogeneity; that is, evolving societies become more complex. Similarly, although most ecological change is evolutionary, this is not necessarily so. Carneiro cites the example of the Amahuaca Indians of Peru (Carneiro 1973b:90) who, in order to survive raids from stronger tribes, split their settlements into smaller groupings and spread out through the jungle. That is, they simplified their social, political, and ceremonial organization in order to adjust to changing conditions. Although this settlement shift was adaptive, it was not evolutionary, because the change involved a fundamental simplification. This kind of change can be termed **devolution,** modification toward simplification rather than complexity.

The evolution of human society has been examined by a number of scholars over the past century, and any number of divergent schemes has been presented (and most of them have been criticized by opponents). It seems that cultural evolution is one of anthropology's most hotly contested theoretical positions. Cultural evolutionists often disagree among themselves; in order to simplify discussion, I follow Carneiro's (1973b) distinction of the four faces of evolution.

The first face, unilinear evolution, is in many ways the least complex. A unilinear evolutionist believes that throughout human history most societies have passed through similar (and unrelated) sequences of stages. That is, given similar environments and cultural backgrounds, independent societies will tend to evolve through similar stages. This is what is meant by unilinear.

The concept of a developmental stage is critical for the unilinear evolutionist, and literally dozens of evolutionary scales have been proposed. One notable effort was suggested by Lewis Henry Morgan, a Rochester lawyer who later turned to ethnography. Morgan has been called "the most important social scientist in nineteenth-century America" (Fenton 1962:viii). In *Ancient Society* (1877), Morgan divided the progress of human achievement into three major "ethnical periods"—savagery, barbarism, and civilization—which were scaled to seven categories according to status as follows:

1. *Lower status of savagery:* commenced with the infancy of the human race in restricted habitats, subsistence upon fruits and nuts. No such tribes remained into the historical period.
2. *Middle status of savagery:* commenced with acquisition of fish and use of fire. Mankind spread over greater portion of earth's surface. Exemplified by Australians and Polynesians.
3. *Upper status of savagery:* commenced with invention of the bow and arrow. Exemplified by Athapascan tribes of Hudson's Bay Territory.
4. *Lower status of barbarism:* commenced with invention or practice of pottery. Exemplified by the Indian tribes of the United States east of Missouri River.
5. *Middle status of barbarism:* commenced with domestication of animals in the Eastern Hemisphere, and in the Western with cultivation by irrigation and use of adobe brick and stone in architecture. Exemplified by villages of New Mexico and Mexico.
6. *Upper status of barbarism:* commenced with manufacture of iron. Exemplified by Grecian tribes of the Homeric Age and Germanic tribes of the time of Caesar.
7. *Status of civilization:* commenced with use of a phonetic alphabet and production of literary records; divided into ancient and modern.

Morgan's stages can, of course, be faulted on several scores, but such early classifications were important steps in sharpening the perception of cultural evolution.[6]

The tide of anthropological thinking turned, and about 1900, such unilinear schemes fell into disrepute, at least among American anthropologists. The basic research strategy for the first half of this century was largely formulated by Franz Boas, one of the most important figures in the history of social science. It has been said that Boas saw as his mission "to rid anthropology of its amateurs and armchair specialists by making ethnographic research in the field the central experience and minimum attribute of professional status" (Harris 1968a:250). Although Boas has been labeled by many as antievolutionary, the truth is that he was merely attacking the prevalent attitudes and standards of the late nineteenth century. Those prevalent ideas were, of course, dominated by unilinear evolutionists. Boas and his students did much to discredit the unilinear schemes of Morgan and others; many would argue that Boas made "evolution" a dirty word. Interestingly enough, it has really been archaeologists who have carried on the banner of unilinear evolution in the mid-twentieth century (Carneiro 1973b:91–97).

The second brand of evolutionism, termed **universal evolution,** has largely been promoted by the scholars Leslie A. White (see Chapter 1) and British archaeologist **V. Gordon Childe.** Both men were aware of the fallacies in the traditional schemes of unilinear evolution, and attempted to keep the concept of evolutionary stages alive by applying it not to particular societies, as did Morgan, but rather by considering the evolution of culture as a whole.

V. Gordon Childe attempted to distinguish a general evolutionary progression in human economic and social life. Heavily influenced by the writings of Morgan, Childe applied Morgan's scheme to humanity as a whole, especially as viewed through the archaeological record. Morgan's "ethnical period" of savagery coincided with Childe's Paleolithic and Mesolithic stages of prehistory. These were times characterized by intensive hunting and collecting of fruits, nuts, riverine resources, and wild seed crops. Childe proposed that a Neolithic revolution transformed hunter-gatherers to farmers (that is, society evolved, in Morgan's terms, from savagery to barbarism). We will consider Childe's theories on the origins of domestication in Chapter 13; for now, it is important to emphasize, as did Childe, the consequences of this domestication. Societies for the first time, controlled their own food supply; the population increased, a surplus of food accumulated, trade began on a large scale, a cooperative group spirit arose, and new religions emerged to ensure success of the crops. To Childe, the Neolithic revolution signaled a drastic reordering of technology and social organization of primitive society.

Childe also discussed a later urban revolution, the transformation from Morgan's period of barbarism to civilization. Humanity's second major revolution transformed society from organization based on equality and simple sex-age division of labor to a society dominated by social classes and organized political bodies. One key component is a formal army under the command of a central authority. Power is maintained by a formal legal system rather than kinship, and the economy is dominated by a market system.

Leslie White, the other major proponent of universal evolution, proposed a similar evolutionary scheme, but with a different emphasis. Both scholars had been deeply influenced by Marxian philosophy, White visiting the Soviet Union in 1929 and Childe doing so in 1934. While Childe emphasized the "revolutionary" and "class struggle" aspects, White (1959) approached the evolution of society in energy terms. We have already briefly discussed White's division of sociocultural systems into three parts: techno-economic, social, and ideological (see Figure 3–3). Culture, to White, was "primarily a mechanism for harnessing energy and of putting it to work in the service of man, and, secondarily, of channeling and regulating his behavior not directly concerned with subsistence and offense and defense" (White 1949:390–391).

Writing about universal evolution, Carneiro (1973b:100) points out that these broad generalizations, while based on a study of individual histories, are not meant to apply to any particular culture. That is, the generalizations might be exemplified by certain cultures, but not necessarily by all. The Childe and White sequences are designed to explain how and why human culture, as a whole, has developed the way it has.

The third kind of evolutionism, **multilinear evolution**, is most closely linked with the work of Julian Steward, who suggested that "multilinear evolution is essentially a methodology based on the assumption that significant regularities in cultural change occur" (1953:318). Steward, reacting in part to the universalism of White and Childe, searched for "parallels of limited occurrence" rather than of universals (Steward 1953). This view has been criticized by a number of evolutionists, suggesting that Steward limited himself too much: "Is this not like tying one hand behind one's back at the outset?" asked Carneiro (1973b:101; also see Harris 1968a:656).

Because of these self-imposed limitations, Steward is remembered more for his substantive contributions to the study of cultural change than for his thinking on evolutionary studies in general. Particularly important was his concept of *levels of sociocultural integration* (Steward 1951, 1955). The Inca Empire for instance, once existed at the state level of sociocultural integration, controlling the centralized political, military, economic, and religious institutions. When the Spanish conquered the Inca, Spanish institutions replaced those of the Inca Empire (that is, those at the state level). But the institutions at the community and family level were left relatively intact. Many native rulers were retained in local authority, and a large portion of village activities went on as in native times. All Peruvians became nominal Catholics, but many also maintained local shrines, ancestor worship, household gods, and shamanism.

The Cuna-Cueva Indians of the Isthmus of Panama experienced a quite different acculturative situation. Prior to the conquest, the Cuna-Cueva apparently also existed at a state level of sociocultural organization, and archaeological evidence shows an elaborate class-structured society. But the Spanish conquest struck with such force that all of the national or state-level institutions were wiped out (Steward 1955:61). Military incursions eliminated the upper classes and confiscated their wealth. As with the Inca, the native state-level traditions were eliminated; but in Panama, Spanish rule and the Catholic church were never effectively substituted. Left relatively unmolested and unable to regain their state-level organization, the Cuna simply resumed life on a community basis. This is a case of *devolution,* a change from relatively complex to relatively simple.

Steward also made the comparison to the Great Basin Shoshoni. The aboriginal Shoshoni were integrated only at the family level, lacking both community and state-level organization. For them, the family served all the primary social and ecological functions: "Virtually all cultural activities were carried out by the family in comparative isolation from other families" (Steward 1955:102). Because of this, the Shoshoni were spared the most disastrous aspects of acculturation. When white miners and ranchers entered the Great Basin a little over a century ago, individual families attached themselves to the white communities. Native hunting and gathering resources were destroyed (as discussed earlier in this chapter), and the Shoshoni began working for wages in the mines or on the ranches. But even with this major economic shift, the Shoshoni maintained their basic level of sociocultural integration, the nuclear family. "The difference between the Western Shoshoni and most other Indians is that the former did not have to experience the break-up of suprafamily-level institutions" (Steward 1955:58).

Steward's brand of evolution stressed limited comparisons such as these: given similar situations, societies integrated at similar levels of sociocultural integration will evolve in predictable ways.

The final evolutionary approach can be labeled **differential evolution** because of the emphasis on the differential rates of cultural change. Instead of simply comparing societies X and Z (as did Steward and Morgan), differential evolution examines how the various components within society change relative to one another: "If we can gauge how far society X as a whole has evolved, we can also gauge how far its economic organization, its legal system or its architecture has evolved" (Carneiro 1973b:105). Although an interest in differential evolution can be traced back over a century, anthropologists have only recently developed quantitative techniques sufficiently sophisticated to handle the amazing complexity of these data. Raoul Naroll (1956) devised the Index of Social Development, which provided the first objective, quantitative, precise, and practical means of assessing and expressing cultural complexity (Carneiro 1973b:105). This initial formulation has since been supported by similar objective measures of complexity (see Tatje and Naroll, 1970). In attempting to deal with the same problem, Carneiro (1962, 1968) has used *scale analysis* as a means of comparing cultural data on a large scale. In one example, Carneiro simultaneously compared one hundred societies, each scored on fifty discrete cultural traits. In effect, this scaling technique allows the investigator to arrange **synchronic** (single time period) data in order to infer the overall **diachronic** (evolutionary) processes involved. As Carneiro has pointed out, this mode of study is "still in its beginnings . . . [but] as work on cultural evolution continues and expands, we can expect more advances to be made" (1968:373–374).

Is cultural evolution relevant to contemporary archaeology? Yes, inextricably so. The aims and methods of cultural evolution are so closely intertwined that, at times, it is impossible to distinguish one from another. In fact, two of the evolutionists discussed above, Childe and Steward, were first-rate archaeologists in their own right. Investigating cultural evolution without using archaeology is like trying to climb a 20-foot ladder that is missing all but the top two rungs. It cannot be done.

Evolutionary thinking has been a major factor in archaeology for decades. In fact, we need go no further than the biographies in Chapter 1 to see the origins of evolutionary thought in American archaeology. Haag (1959:101) has discussed the "strong evolutionary slant" evident in nearly all of the writings of James Ford. Braidwood has briefly noted the evolutionism of A. V. Kidder and believes Nels Nelson "to have had the first leanings toward an evolutionary orientation in American archaeology" (1959:88). Both W. W. Taylor (1948:35) and Lewis Binford (1969) are self-proclaimed cultural evolutionists, as are most contemporary archaeologists (see Leone 1972). In fact, as we shall see in Chapter 13, it is virtually impossible to pursue archaeology's ultimate processual goals without a thorough grounding in cultural evolutionary theory (see also Willey and Sabloff 1974:178–182).

SUMMARY

Anthropologists believe that the true science of humankind can arise only from a holistic, all-encompassing perspective. The physical anthropologist views people primarily as biological organisms, while the cultural anthropologist analyzes people as the animals of their culture. Archaeology, as a branch of cultural anthropology, is deeply concerned with the concept of culture, the learned body of tradition that ties a society together. Cultural phenomena can be divided into three major domains of study. The cultural idiolect reflects an individual's version of his or her overall shared, modal culture. The cultural system is the underlying structural basis for a society's biocultural adaptation.

These three aspects of culture are reflected in different ways by various schools of anthropological thought. Contemporary anthropological thinking can be characterized by two major strategies of research. The ideational strategy deals with mentalistic, symbolic, cognitive culture. Cognitive anthropology focuses on the internalized folk classification as a key for discovering the rules which govern "appropriate" cultural behavior. Symbolic anthropology emphasizes the definition and use of symbols as codes of communication. Structural anthropology attempts to discover the fundamental underlying principles of human cognition, primarily through the analysis of myth, art, kinship, and language.

The contrasting adaptive strategy in anthropology emphasizes those aspects of culture which most closely articulate with environment, technology, and economics. Cultural materialism, cultural ecology, and cultural evolution are all mainstreams within this general adaptive strategy of research. To date, archaeologists have been most heavily influenced by these adaptive mainstreams, although many contemporary archaeologists are attempting to apply the ideational perspective as a mode of archaeological explanation. While some are more important than others, no single anthropological mainstream has dominant control in contemporary archaeology.

NOTES

1. Quite recently, archaeologists have been applying their techniques to the study of living, functioning societies. Discussion of these recent developments, particularly ethnoarchaeology and research on contemporary America, will be deferred until Chapter 12.

2. And perhaps, as Levi-Strauss suggests, this dramatic structure can be seen at major archaeological sites such as Tiahuanaco and Cuzco in South America (Levi-Strauss 1963a:131).

3. Although I have tried to be judicious in selecting labels for these mainstreams, the term "cultural materialism" causes special problems. In a real sense, all those described herein as employing an "adaptive" strategy are materialists, because they emphasize materialistic over mentalistic conditions. The appellation "cultural materialist" is reserved for those overtly adhering to the recent syntheses of Marvin Harris. It is true that many individuals grouped as "evolutionists" or "ecological anthropologists" are also cultural materialists, and the cultural materialistic strategy advocated by Marvin Harris surely "allows for" (in fact urges) evolutionary and ecological studies. Yet many evolutionists and ecological anthropologists object to being grouped with Harris, mainly because of specific disputes on matters of theory and emphasis. I have chosen to be a "splitter" rather than a "lumper," recognizing that the label "cultural materialist" can be said in a sense to overarch both evolutionary and ecological studies.

4. An *ecosystem* includes all the living organisms and their nonliving environment within a given area. The flow of energy through an ecosystem leads to a clearly defined structure, biotic diversity, and exchange cycles between the living and nonliving parts of the ecosystem (Odum 1971:8).

5. Some archaeologists such as Hall (1977), Kehoe and Kehoe (1973), and Trigger (1971), among others, have argued that archaeologists' preoccupation with ecology is so strong that they have been blinded to additional potentials in the archaeological record (see Chapters 11 and 13).

6. Lewis Henry Morgan's evolutionary classifications still provide the primary model for the reconstruction of prehistoric social life and customs by archaeologists in the People's Republic of China (Freeman 1977:93).

4

What Is Contemporary Archaeology?

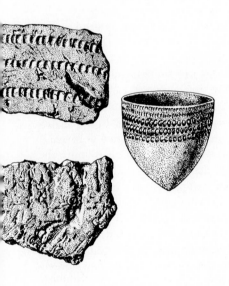

Chapter 3 presented in detail the objectives of anthropology relative to archaeology. The conclusion seems to be that archaeologists are a very special breed of anthropologists. Anthropology is comprised of six mainstreams of thought. Archaeologists, on the whole, have made few contributions to the cognitive, symbolic, and structural mainstreams of anthropology. This does not mean that archaeology can never deal with cognitive processes or symbolism or structures: in fact, some recent attempts will be discussed in subsequent chapters. Nevertheless, we must recognize that, to date, archaeological input has been concentrated toward cultural materialism, cultural ecology, and cultural evolution. These three mainstreams have been archaeology's bread and butter.

Despite the disparate views of culture and anthropological strategy, we find a remarkable agreement among contemporary archaeologists as to the ultimate aims of archaeology (e.g., Binford 1968c; Deetz 1970; Thomas 1974). Archaeology's initial objective is to construct **cultural chronologies** to order past material culture into meaningful cultural segments. The intermediate objective is to breathe life into these chronologies by reconstructing past **lifeways**. The ultimate objective of contemporary archaeology is to determine the **cultural processes** that underlie human behavior, past and present. These processes are expressed as lawlike statements and consist of timeless, spaceless universals.

Note that the objectives are rank-ordered, proceeding from chronology to lifeway to process. This ordering reflects the primacy given to each goal. Chronologies are important, but studying lifeways is more important. Elucidating cultural processes is ultimately the most important archaeological endeavor.

This ordering also reflects the growth of archaeology as a science. The initial research in most areas was chronological, designed to determine the nature and number of cultures that have lived there. Once a chronological ordering was available, archaeologists tended to branch out to examine how people in these cultures actually lived; this is research on past lifeways. Finally, after some information about lifeway is available, archaeologists can compare the information with relevant data to look for processes behind the adaptations.

But let me warn you not to oversimplify this relationship. In any actual piece of research, archaeologists often do a little of each objective at once. A single excavation, for instance, might well provide some data on refining the chronology and some new information about the lifeway, which can then by synthesized into a study of processual relationships. Modern archaeologists almost never encounter a wholly pristine situation in which absolutely nothing is known. Today, there is almost always some kind of chronology available. As research continues, this old chronology will probably be refined, sometimes because of new techniques, in other cases simply because of the availability of more data. So just because I have heuristically separated archaeology's objectives by a threefold division, do not take this to imply that the procedures will always follow such a simple, neat sequence. More often than not, archaeologists work on all three objectives simultaneously.

Another caution is in order regarding research priorities. I term chronology an initial goal, while process is our ultimate objective. This is true. But when one begins to research a problem, the archaeologist generally begins with a processual question (or series of them), then selects an area which is thought to contain the relevant data. Then fieldwork begins: chronological questions must be answered, and the details of lifeway supplied. Then ultimately these findings are incorporated into a series of processual statements. So in one sense, one actually begins and ends with process, working on matters of chronology and lifeway in the meantime.

Keeping these strictures in mind, let us examine the actual method and theory that enable contemporary archaeologists to pursue their three primary objectives.

Archaeologists wear many hats.
Richard I. Ford

INITIAL OBJECTIVE: CONSTRUCT CULTURAL CHRONOLOGY

> **C**hronology is at the root of the matter, being the
> nerve electrifying the dead body of history.
> *B. Laufer*

Chapter 3 emphasized that archaeology's major contribution to anthropological theory is time. Many ethnologists attempt to study cultural evolution and cultural change, but if they restrict themselves to ethnographic evidence, their studies are in danger of remaining shallow, short-term, and perfunctory. Only through an archaeological perspective can episodes of both short- and long-term cultural evolution be satisfactorily documented. The same holds true for human ecology. It is marvelous to study the ongoing adaptation of an existing human group, but this study takes on much broader significance only when one realizes how this adaptation came to be, which often requires archaeological examination.

Unfortunately, time depth is archaeology's double-edged sword. Before archaeologists can turn to the issues of cultural evolution, ecology, and process, the archaeological record must first be partitioned into appropriate temporal and spatial segments. Ethnographers have it easy because they work within a single time interval—the present. There is no need for an ethnographer to construct a temporal framework.

But consider the difficulties of organizing time at a major archaeological site, such as Gatecliff Shelter (introduced in the Prologue). Radiocarbon evidence tells us that people have lived intermittently at Gatecliff for at least eight thousand years. How many different cultures were there? Five? Ten? Eight thousand?

This is no mere exercise in typology and classification. Any discussion of a cultural system must assume that all systemic components existed at the same time. Suppose we are examining prehistoric trade networks. If we surmise a series of trading stations—*A* trades with *B*, *B* passes goods on to *C*, *C* returns something to *A*—it is obvious that *A, B,* and *C* must have been contemporaries. Or suppose that we are attempting to reconstruct a prehistoric seasonal round, such as that discussed earlier for the tribes of Pakistan (Chapter 3). We cannot define a group's spring, summer, and fall camps until we are sure that all these sites were occupied in the same year.

One cardinal principle of archaeology is that one must have a firm grasp on time before turning to the more advanced objectives. That is, archaeologists must know the *when* and the *where* before even considering the *how*, the *who*, the *what*, and especially the *why*. Temporal control generally involves two interrelated processes: dating the remains, then classifying the archaeological objects to reflect these temporal categories. These techniques are discussed in detail in Part Two.

A second point must be made about cultural chronology. This is a preliminary step; that is why I called it archaeology's "initial" objective. In 1948, W. W. Taylor strongly criticized his predecessors for concentrating strictly on chronology and cultural history. Kidder was, Taylor said, making chronology an end in itself. Archaeologists must avoid seeking the ultimate chronologies. Chronologies are hypotheses that are either satisfactory for the needs at hand, or not.

> **A**ll theoretical models are incomplete. By definition, they are abstractions and therefore leave things out.
>
> *Edwin T. Hall*

Chronology is merely a step toward an ultimate, anthropologically relevant goal; chronology must not be confused with that goal. In recognizing the preliminary nature of chronology, archaeologists are entitled to take certain shortcuts. Because chronology is only an initial objective, archaeologists are not required to take into account the entire range of cultural variability in their chronologies.

At the chronological step, archaeologists used a deliberately simplified definition of culture. Chapter 3 presented culture in three intersecting parts: idiolect, shared culture, and cultural system. Taken together, these three components comprise what most anthropologists refer to as culture. If archaeologists are serious about their role in social science—and if archaeologists are to provide a truly relevant input to social theory—then ultimately all aspects of culture must be considered.

Archaeologists discovered long ago that in order to establish this initial chronological ordering they must concentrate upon the shared aspects of culture that lend themselves more readily to chronological analysis than do the ideographic or systematic cultural components. That is, when archaeologists classify the remains of the past into chronological sequences they concentrate on the shared characteristics of material culture. One must therefore interpret a cultural chronology with due caution. Chronology building is grounded in a deliberately simplified, narrowly defined segment of the total cultural picture.

Chronology tells the archaeologist *when*. Chronologies do not tell us *what* or *why*. The *what* of culture consists of lifeway, the totality of an extinct society. This is archaeology's intermediate objective, and a change in our definition of culture is required to answer the *what* questions. Moreover, the *why* of culture—the processes behind human behavior—is an even more complex subject; it is archaeology's ultimate goal. Let us not make the mistake of using simplified chronological methods (archaeology's initial goal) to answer processual questions (archaeology's ultimate goal).

> **G**randma's Law: Eat your vegetables and then you can have your dessert.
>
> *Lawrence Peter*

INTERMEDIATE OBJECTIVE: RECONSTRUCT EXTINCT LIFEWAYS

Once a workable chronological framework has been established, the archaeologist is free to ascend to the second objective, that of reconstructing past lifeways. At this intermediate stage, archaeologists attempt to recall what Levi-Strauss once called "the ring of bygone harmonies" (1963a:114).

Chronology is a stepping stone, a necessary evil. By contrast, reconstructing man's past cultural adaptations is directly relevant to and comparable with modern ethnographic data. Ethnologists study adaptations for which firsthand descriptive observations are available; archaeologists, at this stage, study adaptations that existed in the past. Reconstructing past lifeways is what Heizer and Graham (1967) succinctly termed the "anthropology of the dead."

But what is a lifeway? It is the *what* and the *who* of culture. A lifeway encompasses all the recovered aspects of human existence: the settlement pattern, population density, technology, economy, organization of domestic life, kinship, maintenance of law and order, social stratification, ritual, art, and religion. While some aspects of lifeways are not preserved in the archaeological record, these lacunae are more than compensated for by the perspective of time, the long-term in situ evolution visible only in the archaeological record.

The archaeologist must adopt a different mind-set when approaching lifeways from that employed for constructing chronologies. When building chronology, one is free to pick and choose between cultural items, searching out those attributes that best reflect minute temporal and/or spatial change. But once the archaeologist graduates to paleoethnography, such cavalier treatment becomes inappropriate.

Consider once again the case of Gatecliff Shelter. So long as chronology was our major objective it was sufficient to excavate deep, vertical test pits—what Kent Flannery calls "telephone booths". These steep-sided excavation units exposed stratigraphic changes; we were looking for artifact forms that changed through time, and we found them. The actual cultural context within each stratum was largely irrelevant to the resulting chronology. All we cared about was that corner-notched spearpoints were manufactured before side-notched arrowheads. These time-markers could be used to date deposits at other sites and also to infer time ranges at isolated surface sites.

But archaeologists cannot let chronology alone rule their lives. Once the Gatecliff chronological sequence was pinned down with radiocarbon evidence, the excavation strategy changed markedly. We shifted to a "horizontal" perspective in the attempt to expose intact prehistoric campsites. The artifacts and features were carefully plotted, and we were able to construct the surface appearance of campsites occupied millennia ago.

To reiterate, once the *when* and the *where* questions were answered we could move on to the more relevant *what* questions:

What was the population density at Gatecliff Shelter?

What was the prehistoric social organization like?

What time of year did they live at Gatecliff?

What animals did they eat, and *what* hunting techniques were used to get them?

What were the trade networks, and *what* was traded?

What were the social relationships with neighboring societies?

The *what* questions proliferate indefinitely; once one is answered, five more spring forth to take its place.

It becomes clear that once we began to pursue lifeways at Gatecliff Shelter, the answer to the *what* questions would not necessarily lie inside the shelter at all. These were a nonsedentary people, moving several times each year. Gatecliff was only one small link in an intricate chain of settlements which probably extended fifty miles or so in all directions. In order to assess the total, year-round picture, it was necessary to learn much more about the region in which Gatecliff was situated. Archaeologists no longer rely on single isolated sites when attempting to reconstruct cultural adaptations of nonsedentary societies. That is like trying to reconstruct an entire digital computer by examining one single transistor. Isolated components provide some clues, but hardly the total picture.

In Part Three of this book we look at the techniques archaeologists use to reconstruct past lifeways. No longer is it sufficient to scrutinize only the shared, modal aspects of culture. When one examines a lifeway, it is necessary to view culture in its total systemic context. Building a chronology encourages one to look for the typical, the modal, the normal—what most people did. But those who study past lifeways do not stop with the average; variability is also an important aspect of lifeway. This variability can be due to technology, ecology, demography, social organization, and even ideology.

In other words, archaeologists seeking chronology can afford to make certain operational shortcuts, and traditional archaeology has long embodied these shortcuts. But once the archaeologist dons the mantle of paleoethnographer, chronological shortcuts become inappropriate. Lifeway transcends the shared aspects of culture to embrace the total systemic matrix in which that culture operated. This shift from the modal to the systemic requires different strategy and a rather different conceptual framework (discussed in Part Three). Although the same archaeological objects are often used for both chronology and lifeway, the data generated from these objects are different indeed.

> **B**efore the "why" of the past can be satisfactorily
> answered we must have available to us for
> analysis an essentially accurate "what" of the
> past.
> *H. B. Nicholson*

ULTIMATE OBJECTIVE: DEFINE CULTURAL PROCESSES

An archaeologist's ultimate goal should be to
stop doing archaeology.
David Hurst Thomas

The study of chronology and of past lifeways are both particularistic activities: particular artifacts from particular cultures that lived at particular times in particular places. Archaeologists have been kept busy for decades describing these particulars. Even the most articulate reconstruction of a society's ecological niche or its religion or social organization remains at the level of mere description. The phenomena being described are unique.

Archaeology's ultimate aim is to study the processes behind specific cultures. Culture, as we have seen, can be viewed as either a blend of shared traits or as a system that serves to articulate a society with its environment. The shared-culture approach is useful for deriving chronology, but for little else. To define past lifeways the archaeologist must view culture as a complex set of components.

And yet the components of a cultural system remain static until the processes that actually operate the system are defined. To do this, anthropologists consider the cultural system at a single point in time. Called *synchronic* analysis, this method studies how the various systems work with one another to meet society's needs. The synchronic approach is commonly used in ethnographic studies. We know, for instance, that the Nevada Shoshoni of the 1850s lived in small groups centered about the biological family. Describing the composition of particular Shoshoni families is a particularistic activity. But when he visited the Shoshoni, ethnographer Julian Steward became concerned with how the system worked, how social organization functioned to equip the Shoshoni for life in their harsh Great Basin environment. Steward demonstrated that the family band really links two complementary economic entities. The males spent most of their time hunting game animals, while the women gathered wild seeds, dug roots, and collected berries and nuts. Neither sex was ecologically self-sufficient, but when linked by marriage, the male-female dyad produced a remarkably stable ecological unit. In systemic terms, the social subsystem functioned to provide a critical survival function. Steward (1955) suggested that the family band form of social organization would be found throughout the world, and cited the Eskimo of North America and the Nambicuara, Guato, and Mura in South America as examples. The Nevada Shoshoni had given Steward the initial idea, but when he considered the underlying causes—those general rules that lie behind the specifics—he found that his family band was bound by neither time nor space.

Synchronic cultural processes can also be studied on archaeological data. Techniques of analysis differ vastly, but the objectives remain the same. Anthropologists—whether studying extant or extinct societies—attempt to define the dynamic cause-and-effect relationships that operate within functioning cultural systems.

Ethnographers can define cultural processes only for contemporary (or very recent) societies, but human societies from the past two million years are available to archaeologists: the complementary *diachronic* approach defines the cultural processes that allow cultural systems to evolve, to change through time. At best, ethnographic studies of culture change can measure time in terms of decades, but archaeologists approach cultural evolution with the perspective embracing the duration of mankind. Diachronic studies analyze how cultural subsystems evolve relative to one another, and how the overall system changes with respect to the external environment. One such change is the domestication of plants as food. How did societies evolve from simple collectors and hunters into farmers? Processual studies likewise examine stability: Why do some systems, such as that of the Nevada Shoshoni, remain almost unchanged for 10,000 years?

The study of cultural processes is hence the search for regularities that are both timeless and spaceless (Willey and Phillips 1958:2). These pan-human consistencies—the laws of archaeology—comprise archaeology's ultimate goal. Field archaeologists must first flesh out the specifics of chronology and lifeway. Once the data are explicated, they must be explained, and explanation consists of finding the processes behind the cultural system.

Part One of this book has examined in detail what science and anthropology really are. Chapter 2 emphasized that archaeologists use the steps within the scientific cycle as a method to truth: induction, bridging argumentation, verification. Chapter 3 presented what is happening in contemporary anthropology, synthesizing six mainstreams of anthropological thought.

Now is the time to bring these diverse topics together. While pursuing matters of chronology and lifeway the archaeologist is a highly skilled technician. The next several chapters detail the techniques that have evolved in order to solve the issues manifest in the physical archaeological record. How do archaeologists tell how old things are? How do we find out what extinct people ate? How are past environments reconstructed? How do archaeologists find their sites in the first place? Is there one proper way to dig an archaeological site? At this level, archaeological technique is combined with the steps of the scientific cycle to determine the specifics of the past.

But the specifics of radiocarbon dating and pollen analysis become irrelevant when archaeologists arrive at their ultimate goal. As I said at the outset of this section, the archaeologist's ultimate goal is to cease being an archaeologist at all. This judgment may sound heretical, but it is true. Defining a cultural process requires that the archaeologist rise above the details of the past. Processes are timeless, and once the archaeologist agrees to supersede the temporal and spatial he is obliged to look beyond the archaeological record into the world of contemporary events (and even into the future). As archaeologists turn to cultural process, they can no longer restrict their attention to those things preserved in the ground. The scholar who seeks process must utilize every source of information available—ethnography, history, sociology, economics—and once archaeologists do this, they are no longer archaeologists.

This is a thorny point, and I will explain it further by analogy. Robert Carneiro is a South American ethnologist, and when he takes to the field, say among the Kuikuru of Brazil, his days are filled with matters of ethnographic detail: photograph this activity, tape record this chant, weigh these food items, record how much forest is burned and when the crops are planted, map the settlement pattern and determine why camps are moved periodically. At this level, Carneiro is wholly absorbed by the specifics of Kuikuru ethnography. Events, thoughts, observations are recorded in detailed field notes, and when Carneiro returns from the field, he is faced with the staggering task of drawing his field notes into a comprehensive description of contemporary Kuikuru life. To this point, Carneiro has been generating ethnographic data.

But Carneiro, as an anthropologist, is concerned with more than just ethnographic description. He is also a leader of a major anthropological mainstream, cultural evolutionism, and some of his ideas were previously considered in Chapter 3. One of his articles (1970), presents his "circumscription" theory for the origin of the state (a topic considered in some detail in Chapter 13). Carneiro proposes that the state level of organization evolved initially in areas where major resources, such as prime argricultural land, were sharply restricted. When warfare occurs over these scarce resources, since the defeated peoples cannot escape into uninhabitable, or at least unproductive, hinterlands, they must submit to conquest and amalgamation by their victors. Although the theory is considerably more involved than just this, Carneiro argues that environmental and/or social circumscription eventually led to the evolution of the state level of political organization.

How does Carneiro support his argument? As a cultural evolutionist, Carneiro is required to look beyond the immediate ethnographic specifics. After all, processual theory is designed to explain the evolution of all state organizations, regardless of time or place. In fact, fewer than 30 percent of Carneiro's supportive data are drawn from ethnographic sources. Archaeological sources comprising more than 50 percent of Carneiro's supportive data are coupled with about 10 percent historical data. As a cultural evolutionist, Carneiro must consider all relevant information, be it ethnographic, historical, sociological, archaeological, or whatever.

Carneiro thus plays two roles. When he is sitting in a steamy Kuikuru village writing field notes, he is a field ethnographer. But when he is discussing theories of political evolution, he is a cultural evolutionist.

There is no contradiction here. Carneiro generated some ethnographic data relevant to state-level organization. In fact, he tells me that without his ethnographic experiences the idea of the circumscription theory might never have occurred to him. But once he gets out to test his theory, he is not—and cannot be—constrained by his own experience. It is perfectly logical for Carneiro to be a field ethnographer at one level and a cultural evolutionist at another.

Archaeologists also have split personalities. Many archaeologists spend years conducting field work. I personally worked at Gatecliff Shelter for thirteen months with a crew averaging about thirty-five people. The days of the field archaeologist are occupied with specifics: not only questions like "How old is geological unit 6-74" and "What is the provenience of this Pinto point?" but also mundane and even trivial matters such as "When will the cook get back from town?" and "What the hell do you mean you ripped the door off the pickup truck?" Archaeologists at this level are concerned with recovering and recording the archaeological objects in the best manner possible.

Archaeologists then retire to the laboratory, where the finds are analyzed and the final monograph prepared. The archaeologist at this level is analogous to the field ethnographer, although the specifics are as different as they can be. While Carneiro might be worried about truculent informants, convincing the Brazilian Air Force to fly him out of the jungle, and a rip in his mosquito netting, the field archaeologist will be troubled by sonic booms that threaten to cave in his sidewalls, by level bags that are improperly labeled, and by trying to correlate this year's excavations with last year's field notes. Ethnographers have specific techniques, problems, and needs, and so do archaeologists.

But these differences vanish at the processual level. Cultural evolutionist Robert Carneiro transcends the specifics of his ethnographic fieldwork to focus on the broader issues of cultural evolution. Analogously, archaeologists working at the processual level are freed from the nuances of reconstructing chronology or piecing together extinct lifeways.

The archaeologist analyzing the problems of plant domestication, for instance, is really functioning as a human ecologist. Or perhaps he is a cultural materialist. Or he might even be a cultural evolutionist. He will probably find more in common with a plant geneticist or an agronomist or a nutritionist than with his buddies in archaeological graduate school. But one thing is certain. The archaeologist, serious about isolating processes that transcend time and space, had better look far beyond the end of his archaeological nose. Human ecologists, cultural evolutionists, and cultural materialists can ill afford to restrict their input to any single source, archaeological or otherwise. This is why the ultimate goal of all archaeologists must be to cease doing archaeology.

CONSERVATION ARCHAEOLOGY: HOW CONTEMPORARY ARCHAEOLOGY IS DONE

> **T**he destruction of a prehistoric site is
> permanent. Like Humpty Dumpty, it cannot be
> reassembled.
>
> *Louis Brennan*

One final issue remains before we consider how archaeologists actually pursue the three major goals of chronology, lifeway, and process. American archaeology has traditionally been a strictly academic discipline, by which I mean that up until the 1970s most archaeologists have been employed as professors and teachers. But a revolution of sorts has recently overtaken the profession, and some archaeologists (such as Schiffer and House 1977) think the results will be as far-reaching as the conceptual revolution discussed in Chapter 1. The "conservation archaeology revolution" has already changed the operating structure of American archaeology, and we must examine the implications before proceeding further. For decades archaeologists have clamored about the importance of protecting archaeological sites, but it was not until the ecological awareness of the 1960s that some real progress was made. The mid-sixties saw demonstrations such as Earth Day, and heard thousands of people chanting non sequiturs like "Save the Ecology" or displaying bumper stickers like "I'm for Ecology." The voter-appeal of these popular movements was not lost on the legislators, whose ears picked up, and many of them became "conservationists" too. In fact, sufficient legislative power came down on the side of the ecologists that laws have been drafted to protect the nonrenewable resources of the nation.

But what are nonrenewable resources? Most people think either of beautiful things like redwoods and whooping cranes and baby seals, or else energy-related resources such as oil, coal, and uranium. But most legislators have a legal background, and in the course of arriving at a legal definition of nonrenewable resources, they realized they must also include properties of historic value. After all, how many Monticellos do we have? As illogical as it may sound, America's prehistoric sites are included as "historic" places under the law. As a result, archaeological sites were included in the ecological legislation of the late 1960s and the 1970s. Archaeological sites are now legally nonrenewable resources, just like the redwoods, the whooping cranes, and the shale-oil fields of Wyoming.

One of the important pieces of legislation is the Archaeological and Historic Preservation Act of 1974, more commonly known as the Moss-Bennett Act (see inset). Moss-Bennett requires that all federal agencies must consider the dangers posed by their activities on the archaeological sites on their land. And—here is the important part—these agencies are authorized to spend up to 1 percent *of their own money* for archaeological salvage. Congress thus provided a means for supporting large archaeological conservation without the necessity of going through the National Park Service or coming to Washington for special congressional authorization.

But even more pervasive than Moss-Bennett is the National Environmental Policy Act (NEPA) of 1969. Combined with two other measures—the National Historic Preservation Act and Executive Order 11593—federal agencies are now provided with quite rigid guidelines on how to assess the impact of proposed construction on archaeological sites (see inset). These acts actually define a new philosophy of governmental decision making, requiring that environmental and cultural variables be considered side by side with technological and economic benefits when planning future construction. These new

Qualifications for Recognition as a Professional Archeologist (as Stated by the Society of Professional Archeologists)

The minimal qualifications which an applicant must demonstrate for recognition as a professional archeologist are specified below. The applicant must agree to section I, must qualify under section II.1 or II.2, and must qualify for at least one emphasis under section III.

I. *Ethics:* By signing the application form, the applicant agrees to subscribe to the Code of Ethics, Standards of Research Performance, and Institutional Standards as adopted by the Society of Professional Archeologists.

II. *Education and Training:* The applicant must qualify under *either* II.1 or II.2.

II.1. The applicant must:

(A) have been awarded a postgraduate degree in archeology, anthropology, history, classics, or other germane discipline (or combination of disciplines) with a specialization in archeology, except where an equivalency to such a degree can be documented.

(B) have supervised experience in basic archeological field research, consisting of 12 weeks of field training (including both survey and excavation) plus 4 weeks of laboratory analysis and/or curating. The field experience must be in blocks of at least 2 weeks' duration.

(C) have designed and executed an archeological study, as evidenced by an MA or MS thesis or report equivalent in scope and quality. This report will ordinarily deal with archeological field research. Acceptable reports or substitutions for this requirement are detailed in sections III.3, III.5, III.6, and III.7.

II.2. The applicant must document that after 1 January 1962 and prior to 5 May 1976 s/he (a) engaged in the active practice of archeology for a total of 3 years and (b) must state that s/he did not violate the Standards of the Society of American Archaeology as adopted 5 May 1961. (This option will not be available to applicants after 5 May 1978.)

III. *Experience:* At least one year of experience in one or more of the following emphases (except Teaching, III.7) must be documented, or equivalent experience and training acquired prior to 5 May 1976. One year's experience must be gained in blocks of time of at least 4 weeks' duration.

III.1. *Field Research:* Field and laboratory experience under the supervision of a professional archeologist (to include 6 months of field and 3 months of laboratory experience), with a minimum of 6 months in a supervisory or other equally responsible role.

III.2. *Collections Research:* The analytic study of artifacts and/or other physical products and byproducts of human activities, in which the study focuses principally on the comparative treatment of the materials themselves rather than on their relationship to the general archeological context of a site or sites. Thus, the description and preliminary analysis of excavated collection(s) that is normally included in a site report is not "collections research" since it is a basic and necessary part of "field research." The report on collections research should have been published or otherwise be available to the scientific community, or be a thesis or dissertation on deposit in an institution's library. Examples of collections research: a study of rim sherds from late Woodland sites throughout the Northeast in an attempt to define social boundaries; microscopic analysis of edge-wear on utilized flakes; radiometric age determination. Applicants should indicate 6 months under a specialist, 6 months independent or supervisory work in collections research.

III.3. *Theoretical, Library, or Archival Research:* Archeological research on theoretical issues or on substantive problems using library or archival sources, resulting in a report equivalent in scope and quality to an MA or MS thesis. This report may also be used to satisfy the II.1(C) requirement.

III.4. *Archeological Administration:* The administration of an archeological research unit, a governmental agency office, a museum, or some other entity whose operations, while multifaceted, are archeological in orientation. "Administration" of a field project or acting as a Principal Investigator does not normally qualify as an example of archeological administration because it is a basic and routine part of directing "field research." The same holds true for direction of a field school. Service as the chairperson of an academic department does not ordinarily qualify as an example of archeological administration because it is not explicitly archeological. Examples of archeological administration are: service as chief of a university archeological research unit; service as head of a state or regional office charged with archeological research; service as the primary administrative officer in such an office.

III.5. *Cultural Resource Management:* Understanding and use of the laws, policies, and programs that contribute to the preservation and management of cultural resources. The conduct of archeological surveys for environmental impact statements or similar documents, and the conduct of salvage or mitigation projects, do not ordinarily qualify as examples of cultural resource management activities, since they are normally in no way different from field research. An exception to this generalization would be a case in which a survey was integrated by the archeologist into the development of a regional plan for preservation, or some other program that required cognizance of preservation law and policy. Examples of cultural resource management: preparation of a plan for the protection of cultural resources on a local, regional, or state level; preparation of archeological overviews or evaluations that are directly linked to management needs; major responsibility in an agency or firm to fulfill such management responsibility. A report qualifying under this section can also satisfy the II.1(C) requirement.

III.6. *Museology:* The application of professional museological methods and techniques to archeological material and data. Service as a museum administrator or curator qualifies as museology only if it requires that the applicant has gained an understanding and has applied museological methods and technics, otherwise such experience may qualify as archeological administration, collections research, or field research, depending upon the actual focus of the work accomplished. Examples of museology: preparation of displays; conservation of archeological specimens; organizations or implementation of modern classification and cataloguing systems. Since the title of "curator" is variously used in museums, applicants should describe their duties and responsibilities if they served in this capacity. Preparation of a major archeological exhibit area in a museum open to the public may also be used to satisfy the section II.1(C) requirement, provided the scope and quality of the research and execution are equivalent to those of an MA or MS thesis.

III.7. *Teaching:* One academic year of full-time teaching (teaching a total of 12 semester hours, at least 6 semester hours of which must be on archeologically oriented subjects). A person qualifying under this section may satisfy the section II.1(C) requirement by the production of a film on archeology, or publication of a report on archeology for use by students, colleagues, or the general public, provided the scope and quality of the film or publication are equivalent to those of an MA or MS thesis.

III.8. *Marine Survey Archeologist:* Background knowledge of coastal geomorphology and marine geology as this relates to cultural resources; training in the principles, proper set-up and operation of underwater remote sensing devices (including magnetometer, side-scanning sonar, sub-bottom profiler, and bathymetric sounder), and ability to interpret the output of these devices; training in navigation. The basic one-year experience requirement under supervision of a professional marine survey archeologist or equivalent, must include two weeks' offshore training or the equivalent, in the operation of the remote sensing devices; 6 months of the year should be in a supervisory or independent role.

requirements have created hundreds of archaeological contracts, which result in reports detailing the nature of the archaeological resources endangered, and how the impact of the projects should be mitigated, either by changing the proposed construction or by excavating the sites in question (see King, Hickman, and Berg 1977, Chapters 3–7).

The immediate result of the federal legislation has been to spotlight the need for accurate information regarding archaeological sites. Sometimes the federal agencies have qualified manpower to make such studies, but more commonly the agencies contract academic institutions, museums, and qualified private individuals to prepare the required reports. In fact, it has been estimated that in a couple of years 90 percent of all archaeological research in the United States will be contract related (Kelley 1977).

When in doubt, preserve!
Walter W. Taylor

The nature of conservation archaeology has also changed in recent years. Environmental impacts are no longer mitigated by merely finding a few sites that might be nice to dig. Federal agencies are now taking steps to locate *all* the archaeological sites of value that are within the agency's control or are potentially subject to damage (King 1977). This intensive survey requires more than a preliminary visit to the area in question. Modern legal regulations require intensive examination of all the federal lands involved. The archaeological sites discovered are then evaluated against a recent set of federal standards known as the *Criteria of Eligibility for the National Record of Historic Places* (see King, Hickman, and Berg 1977, Appendix A).

Federal procedures have thus created the unprecedented demand for trained archaeological personnel. Not only must contract archaeologists know the local pottery types and soil zones, but they must also be acutely aware of the provisions of NEPA and Executive Order 11593.

Contract work in archaeology has become big business. In recent years the Army Corps of Engineers and the Soil Conservation Service have spent considerably more annually for American archaeology than the National Science Foundation and other granting agencies combined (Schiffer and House 1977). Such huge sums of money are new to archaeology and inevitably raise the question, Who is a qualified professional archaeologist anyway?

One answer comes from the Society of Professional Archeologists (SOPA), incorporated in 1976. SOPA was created largely in response to the rapid growth of contract archaeology within the United States and Canada. As stated in the Articles of Incorporation, the purposes of SOPA are to:

1. Strengthen the identification of archaeology as a profession and of qualified archaeologists as professionals;
2. Encourage high standards in the training of archaeologists;
3. Require high standards of performance from practicing professional archaeologists;
4. Communicate to the public the importance of the proper practice of archaeology;

The Legality of Archaeology in the United States and Canada

The strength of the contract and conservation archaeological movement lies in the supportive network of legislation. The following paragraphs excerpt some of the relevant legal aspects of modern archaeology in the United States and Canada. For a discussion of the relevance of these and other acts, see McGimsey (1972), King (1977), and Schiffer and Gumerman (1977).

Canada. At present, the Dominion of Canada lacks a body of national legislation governing archaeological remains. Provincial laws vary somewhat; however, they generally provide strong protection for historic and prehistoric sites, once the sites have been identified. Canada sponsors a nationwide archaeological survey, and an agency called Heritage Canada.

United States. Legal archaeology in the United States is complicated somewhat by the structure itself. Protection for archaeological sites was first set out in the Antiquities Act of 1906, and the structure has since been strengthened by a number of pieces of legislation. Here is a brief summary of the most important individual acts:

Antiquities Act of 1906

AN ACT For the Preservation of American Antiquities, Approved June 8, 1906 (Public Law 59-209; 34 STAT.225; 16 U.S.C.431-433)
Be it enacted by the Senate and House of Representatives of the United States of America in Congress assembled, *That any person who shall appropriate, excavate, injure or destroy any historic or prehistoric ruin or monument, or any object of antiquity, situated on lands owned or controlled by the Government of the United States, without the permission of the Secretary of the Department of the Government having jurisdiction over the lands on which said antiquities are situated, shall upon conviction, be fined in a sum of not more than five hundred dollars or be imprisoned for a period of not more than ninety days, or shall suffer both fine and imprisonment, in the discretion of the court.*
SECTION 3. That permits for the examination of ruins, the excavation of archaeological sites, and the gathering of objects of antiquity upon the lands under their respective jurisdictions may be granted by the Secretaries of the Interior, Agriculture, and War to institutions which they may deem properly qualified to conduct such examinations, excavation, or gathering, subject to such rules and regulations as they may prescribe: Provided, *That the examinations, excavations, and gatherings are undertaken for the benefit of reputable museums, universities, colleges, or other recognized scientific or educational institutions, with a view to increasing the knowledge of such objects, and that the gatherings shall be made for permanent preservation in public museums.*

5. Assist governmental and other organizations which use archaeologists in the course of their activities to identify those properly qualified for the purpose.

A major function of SOPA has been to compile and maintain an up-to-date listing of professional archaeologists. That is, SOPA has initiated a certification

Historic Preservation Act of 1966

AN ACT To Establish a Program for the Preservation of Additional Historic Properties Throughout the Nation, and for Other Purposes, Approved October 15, 1966 (Public Law 89-665; 80 STAT.915; 16 U.S.C. 470)

TITLE I

Section 101

(a) The Secretary of the Interior is authorized—

(1) to expand and maintain a national register of districts, sites, buildings, structures, and objects significant in American history, architecture, archeology, and culture, hereinafter referred to as the National Register, and to grant funds to States for the purpose of preparing comprehensive statewide historic surveys and plans, in accordance with criteria established by the Secretary, for the preservation, acquisition, and development of such properties;

The National Environmental Policy Act of 1969

It is the continuing policy of the Federal Government, in cooperation with State and local governments and other concerned public and private organizations, to use all practicable means and measures, including financial and technical assistance, in a manner calculated to foster and promote the general welfare, to create and maintain conditions under which man and nature can exist in productive harmony, and fulfill the social, economic, and other requirements of present and future generations of Americans.

. . . all agencies of the Federal Government shall . . . include in every recommendation or report on proposals for legislation and other major Federal actions significantly affecting the quality of the human environment, a detailed statement by the responsible official on—(i) the environmental impact of the proposed action, (ii) any adverse environmental effects which cannot be avoided should the proposal be implemented, (iii) alternatives to the proposed action, (iv) the relationship between local short-term uses of man's environment and the maintenance and enhancement of long-term productivity, and (v) any irreversible and irretrievable commitment of resources which would be involved in the proposed action should it be implemented.

The President's Executive Order 11593

The heads of Federal agencies shall: . . . locate, inventory, and nominate to the Secretary of the Interior all sites, buildings, districts, and objects under their jurisdiction or control that appear to qualify for listing on the National Register of Historic Places.

program for professional archaeologists; individuals seeking to meet the qualifications for recognition as a professional archaeologist and certification must subscribe to SOPA's Code of Ethics, Institutional Standards, and Standards of Research Performance. The minimum qualifications for SOPA certification are reproduced in the inset.

In essence, SOPA, a self-policing agency, attempts to insure that individuals claiming professional competence are really qualified. The SOPA directory lists all archaeologists who have been accepted to date and is available to the public. Further information about the SOPA certification program can be obtained by writing:

> The Society of Professional Archeologists
> 919 18th Street NW, Suite 800
> Washington, D.C. 20006

Several departments of anthropology within the United States offer M.A. programs designed to prepare students as effective conservation archaeologists. For example, the Universities of Arizona and Arkansas, and the State University of New York at Binghamton offer programs that combine a solid foundation of archaeological method and theory with an up-to-date training in the specifics of contract archaeology. Recently the University of Arizona inaugurated the first curriculum in conservation archaeology at the Ph.D. level. Other programs are bound to follow.

The literature of conservation archaeology is difficult to discuss because of such rapid change. The interested reader is referred to *Public Archaeology* by Charles R. McGimsey (1972); McGimsey argues for the state-level program of conservation archaeology and provides state-by-state summaries of public support for archaeology, along with discussion of major pieces of relevant federal regulations that have influenced archaeology. Unfortunately, McGimsey's discussion is already dated by later legislation. Other useful books are *Rescue Archaeology* (Rahtz 1974), *Anthropology in Historic Preservation* (King, Hickman, and Berg 1977), and especially *Archaeology Conservation* (Schiffer and Gumerman 1977). The reader is also referred to Dixon (1971), Gumerman (1973), Lipe (1974), Lipe and Lindsay (1974), King (1971, 1976, 1977), Schiffer and House (1977), and Thompson (1975). A recent book by McHargue and Roberts (1977) provides an amateur's guide to the avocational practice of conservation archaeology in North America; also see Brennan (1973) and Feldman (1977).

> **O**ur ideals, laws and customs should be based
> on the proposition that each generation in turn
> becomes the custodian rather than the
> absolute owner of our resources—and each
> generation has the obligation to pass this
> inheritance on to the future.
>
> *Alden Whitman*

SUMMARY

Despite the wide variety of activities and interests evident among American archaeologists, three fundamental objectives emerge. Archaeology's initial goal is to construct cultural chronologies. It is a fact of archaeological life that chronology-building—the when and where of archaeology—must proceed prior to the more sophisticated modes of inquiry about the past. But chronology is merely a stepping-stone toward more anthropologically relevant objectives; it must not be viewed as an end in itself. Archaeology's intermediate objective is to reconstruct extinct lifeways, to study the anthropology of the dead. A lifeway encompasses all of the recoverable aspects of human existence: settlement pattern, population density, technology, economy, organization of domestic life, kinship, maintenance of law and order, social stratification, ritual, art, and religion. At the level of lifeway, the archaeologist's task is to reconstruct, in as complete a manner as possible, the totality of existence for a given culture at a point in time; this is paleoethnography. Archaeology's ultimate objective is to define the cultural processes that underly human behavior, past and present. Studying chronology and lifeway is a particularistic activity: particular artifacts from particular cultures that functioned at particular times in particular places. The ultimate objective of archaeology is to transend the specifics and particulars and expose the underlying processes, regularities which are both timeless and spaceless. Defining these processes requires that the archaeologist rise above the details of the past. Because these processes are independent of time and space, scholars seeking process must avail themselves of all conceivable scraps of relevant information—be it archaeology or sociology or economics. At the processual level, archaeologists can ill afford to restrict their attention to any single source of information, archaeological or otherwise. This is why the ultimate goal of all archaeologists must be to cease doing archaeology.

part **two**

Archaeology's Initial Objective: Construct Cultural Chronologies

Time is what keeps everything from happening at once.

Graffito, Bethel, Alaska

Because American archaeology is a subdiscipline of anthropology, archaeologists rely heavily on the concept of culture. Archaeologists in one sense deal with culture as would any other social scientist: culture has three components (cultural idiolect, shared culture, cultural system), and each functions as a necessary domain of study. But in another sense, the problem confronting archaeologists differs markedly from that facing anthropologists who specialize in ethnographic or linguistic studies. Archaeologists lack informants, making certain aspects of cultural belief and behavior inaccessible. But—almost as if to make up for this void—archaeologists have access to a wealth of material remains which add a time depth and overall perspective impossible in synchronic ethnography or linguistics.

This great diversity of data requires that archaeology derive special tactics for conducting the social science of the past. Each of the three cultural domains requires highly specialized treatment to bridge the gap between the lofty concept of culture and some practical guidelines that can be used in actual archaeological research. The section that follows considers in detail two of the three aspects of culture: shared culture and the cultural system. A consideration of past cultural idiolects will be postponed until Chapter 10.

The Modal Concept of Culture

Suppose you are an archaeologist facing a potentially rich yet archaeologically unknown region. You are faced with a bewildering variety of objects produced by societies ranging in complexity from relatively simple to exceedingly complex. Literally dozens of aspects of cultural behavior are represented within the archaeological objects: temporal variability, spatial variability, functional variability, technological variability, vandalism, and so on. We know that cultures, whether modern or prehistoric, are multivariate, complex phenomena, and each variation makes an input to the archaeological record at one time or another.

> Simplicity, simplicity, simplicity! I say, let your affairs be as two or three, and not a hundred or a thousand; instead of a million count half a dozen, and keep your accounts on your thumbnail.
>
> *Henry David Thoreau*

The archaeologist's initial task is to simplify. It is procedurally impractical (and generally impossible) to cope simultaneously with all of the variability inherent in any set of archaeological objects. Cultural items are just too complex. So the first assignment facing an archaeologist is to reduce the variability to manageable proportions. Control the variability within a couple of critical variables, then move on to consider more subtle inputs in the archaeological record.

How does this initial simplification take place? The answer is that we must provisionally adopt a simplified and purposefully limited concept of culture. We have already seen that culture consists of three related components: idiosyncratic cultural idiolect, shared aspects of culture, and the underlying cultural system. But archaeology has too great a data base, derived from too many objects, to be able to deal simultaneously with these three aspects of culture.

Thus at the outset, archaeologists are beset with twin difficulties: (1) archaeological data must first be controlled for time, and (2) all aspects of culture cannot be studied simultaneously. Some time ago, archaeologists stumbled upon an important postulate: *Temporal variability is best reflected by the shared, modal aspects of culture.* It is difficult to overemphasize how important this notion is to practicing archaeologists.

To repeat, when archaeologists set out to monitor chronological changes, most of the cultural complexity can (provisionally) be ignored. So long as one merely attempts to partition the archaeological record into manageable segments of temporal and spatial variability, both the cultural idiolect and the cultural system can be temporarily overlooked. Time-space divisions are most clearly reflected in shared, modal cultural behavior.

Why, one must ask, is time more readily available through the shared aspects of cultural remains? One answer is that we must start somewhere, and the shared aspects are the most obvious features of the archaeological record. But a more satisfying answer can be derived by considering the actual natures of time and space.

> There is no difference between time and any of
> the three dimensions of space except that our
> consciousness moves along it.
> *H. G. Wells*

Time is a linear variable. Time flows. Time can be represented as the vertical axis on Figure II–1. We can use the other dimension to represent the presence of

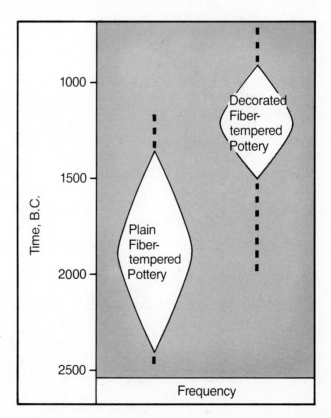

Figure II–1
Hypothetical changes in frequency of fiber-tempered pottery in archaeological sites along the Georgia Coast.

some shared cultural traits, such as the kind of pottery or perhaps the method of manufacturing stone tools. Note here that once we focus strictly on temporal variation, we are free to ignore the *why* and the *what* in favor of the *when* and the *where*. Never mind, for the moment, why a particular cultural item becomes more or less frequent or what its function was. It is enough that things change through time. Ignoring the *why* and the *what* allows archaeologists to choose any aspect of material culture, regardless of how it fits into the cultural system.

For precisely this reason, archaeologists often focus their efforts on seemingly trivial aspects of cultural behavior: what kind of temper people use in their pottery; how do people add notches to their spearpoints; do they sew their moccasins along the side or along the top? Archaeologists at the initial stage are seeking only a method for monitoring changes in time. Why these cultural items changed can be answered later.

Let us examine how the modal concept of culture actually works in archaeology. The oldest pottery known in North America is found in the southeastern United States, concentrated along the coasts of Florida, Georgia, and South Carolina, and extending inland along major waterways such as the Savannah River (Stoltman 1966). This pottery is quite distinctive (Figure II–2), consisting generally of bowl-shaped vessels with thick walls and flaring lips. Although some of the later varieties are decorated by impressions from sticks or fingernails, the vessels were never painted.

The most distinctive aspect of this earliest North American pottery is the **temper**, the foreign materials introduced into the clay to keep the pottery from cracking when fired. Prehistoric potters had a variety of potential temper materials from which to choose—sand, coarse grit, seashells, even ground up

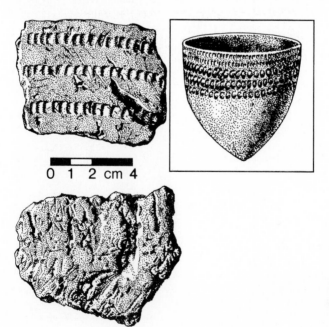

0 1 2 cm 4

Figure II–2
Plain and decorated varieties of fiber-tempered ceramics *(based on specimens from St. Catherines Island, Georgia).*

potsherds. The earliest North American potters chose to use plant fibers, probably grass or shredded palmetto fiber. Why these folks chose plant fibers over sand or seashells we will probably never know; it was a cultural decision that was followed almost without exception at the time.

On the basis of several radiocarbon dates, we now know that these earliest pots were first made about 2500 B.C. and seemed to die out about 1000 B.C. when potters began to temper their pots with coarse grit and sand. Put another way, when this distinctive fiber-tempered pottery is found in undisturbed archaeological contexts, the age of these deposits can be guess-dated between 2500 and 1000 B.C. based strictly on the ceramic association.

The earliest of the fiber-tempered wares are plain pots lacking decoration. But about 1500 B.C. potters began to decorate their vessels with simple designs applied before the pot was fired. Common motifs include small circles (probably made with a reed), cross-hatching, and interlocking frets. Once again, archaeologists will never know *why* the first design was added or exactly *what* the design meant to the potter. But we can be quite certain of *when* these pots were manufactured. Whenever a decorated fiber-tempered pot (or even a potsherd) is found in an undisturbed archaeological site, we hypothesize that the contexts date between 1500 and 1000 B.C. This hypothesis requires testing and retesting, by a variety of techniques.

Fiber-tempered pottery of the prehistoric American Southeast is thus a *time-marker,* and plotting the frequency of fiber-tempered sherds against time, we obtain a graph like Figure II-1. Plain, undecorated sherds are rare in 2500 B.C. As time goes by, the pottery becomes more popular and the sherds become more common in archaeological sites. About 1500 B.C., decorated sherds begin to appear in sites. Decorated pottery increases in frequency until about 1100 B.C., after which decorated, fiber-tempered pottery becomes rarer and rarer, finally disappearing from the archaeological record altogether.

It is precisely this kind of change that the archaeologist seeks to isolate initially: time has been partitioned using the details of material culture as a guide. As we will see, time-sensitive objects such as potsherds are grouped into divisions called **temporal types**. Time-markers enable one to place previously undated archaeological contexts into a time sequence. The next step is to synthesize several of these temporal types into divisions called cultural **phases**. These basic concepts will be discussed in some detail in Chapter 7. For now it is sufficient to recognize that before one can study the structure of extinct cultural systems, the cultures must be placed in time. It is senseless to compare components of a dynamic cultural system before we can be certain those subsystems were contemporary.

Moreover, the fiber-tempered pottery of the American Southeast demonstrates how archaeologists use the modal concept of culture. Even a single potsherd reflects various cultural inputs. The potter—probably female—molded the pottery along traditional, culturally determined lines. She probably learned how to make pottery from her mother or maternal relatives. Their notions influenced her own ideas, which were translated through the clay into a finished pot. Perhaps she added decoration to the vessel. If so, these designs reflect not only her own artistic inclinations and manual dexterity, but also the cultural standards of both contemporaries and ancestors. Vegetable fiber was added to keep the pot from cracking when fired. But sand works equally well, as does coarse grit or ground up potsherds or diatomaceous earth or clam shells. She chose vegetable fibers for her own culturally determined reasons. Literally dozens of decisions go into making that single pot, and evidence of these decisions is preserved in a single sherd.

Here is where the modal concept of culture becomes so critical. Setting aside the complexity for the moment, we can simplify. Looking at the pottery of the Georgia coast, one can ask simply, What changes? Eliminate the constants to search for variety. All pottery is made of clay, so that is a constant. All pots have been fired, so that is another worthless criterion. But by examining enough archaeological collections, one begins to see differences. The earlier pots are tempered with vegetable fiber; the later pots are tempered with sand, grit, or potsherds. Temper thus seems to be a useful variable. Because the earlier fiber-tempered pots are plain and the later fiber-tempered pots are decorated, surface decoration is another useful variable to partition time. And so on.

Why do pots made after 1500 B.C. tend to be decorated? Why is quartz grit not used for temper before 1000 B.C.? Why don't the fiber-tempered pots have outcurving rims? Do certain decorative motifs occur only in ceremonial contexts? These are all important questions, inquiries that may sometime tell us a great deal about the cultural milieu of the prehistoric Georgia coast. But these questions must be ignored for now because they speak to the more sophisticated goals of archaeology, not to the initial probing steps of analysis.

The really important point is that one must begin with a simplified scheme and gradually build in order to deal with multivariate cultural complexity. It is enough at the outset to isolate time-markers and to define some tentative cultural phases. Later one can build the structure of each phase. The initial phases are not inviolate; they are working hypotheses which will probably be modified. It is important to begin somewhere, and the modal concept facilitates that beginning.

The modal concept simplifies. People began making plain fiber-tempered pots about 2500 B.C. We do not know why; for now it is sufficient to know when. Then about 1500 B.C. the potters began decorating their pots. We do not know why they did that either, but the change provides a useful way to monitor the temporal context of our archaeological sites. Once the sites are suitably ordered, using simplified criteria such as these, we can begin to explain why these changes occurred. But we cannot explain before we explicate, and the modal concept of culture is critical for temporal explication.

> **T**ime is so thoroughly woven into the fabric of existence that we are hardly aware of the degree to which it determines and co-ordinates everything we do.
>
> *Edwin T. Hall*

To summarize, time varies in linear fashion, always progressing from before to after. By operationally focusing upon modal behavior—the shared aspects of culture—archaeologists are able to chart cultural changes along a temporal axis. Then these changes can be plotted on a map to determine spatial variability. This is how archaeology derives its basic analytical units.

But not all culture changes. Culture change is an extremely complicated business, and the modal concept of culture temporarily ignores the question of why. Initially, it is enough that change has occurred. Moreover, the change is generally apparent only in a very restricted range of archaeological objects. Suppose we have one hundred kinds of archaeological objects: potsherds, chipped-stone knives, grinding slabs, bone awls, and so on. Ninety-five of these items might remain constant through time. The modal concept of culture— culture as defined by what most people believe—allows one effectively to ignore the 95 percent of the cultural inventory that is stable in order to concentrate attention upon the important 5 percent that has changed. And keep in mind that the modal concept of culture is only a heuristic device, not an explanatory one.

Culture Chronology vs. Culture History

Archaeology's initial chronological aim makes two assumptions:

1. All variability not directly attributable to time is irrelevant; and
2. Temporal variability can best be isolated by monitoring only the shared aspects of cultural behavior.

That is, in chronological analysis, the archaeologist seeks to isolate segments of the archaeological record that differ only in time and/or space. Of course this assumption is simplistic; the archaeological record has abundant nontemporal variability. But it is precisely this complexity that leads us to simplify. For chronological purposes, any source of variability other than temporal or spatial is considered to be random noise, and temporarily irrelevant.

Let us consider the case of Shoshoni pottery to illustrate this point. Pottery appears suddenly in the archaeology of the Desert West about A.D. 1300, and the historic Shoshoni Indians are known to have ceased making pottery in most areas by about 1860. Shoshoni pottery is hence a time-marker implying certain limits: time—A.D. 1300–1860; space—the Desert West. Note that the early boundary (A.D. 1300) is only an estimate derived from radiocarbon dating, while the late boundary (1860) is based upon historical documentation. Hence the initial 1300 date is subject to considerably more error than the termination date. Such is often the case with time-markers, and this disproportionate error should cause no difficulties so long as we recognize it.

With the temporal parameters suitably established, Shoshoni pottery becomes a time-marker in the chronology of the Desert West. Sites exhibiting a significant number of these potsherds can be tentatively assigned to the A.D. 1300–1860 interval (subject of course to independent verification by suitable dating techniques).

But Shoshoni pottery, taken as a time-marker, leaves many more questions unanswered. Consider, for example, the origin of the ceramic complex in the Desert West. Is the post-1300 pottery introduced as the result of a migration of Shoshoni-speaking peoples? Or did the idea of pottery simply diffuse across the Desert West? Or did the peoples of the Desert West independently invent the idea of pottery?

These are deceptively simple questions, the answers to which require a thorough understanding of the cultural history of the Desert West. Can we document a population movement across the Desert West at A.D. 1300? If so, where did these newcomers come from? And what happened to the pre-1300 inhabitants of the Desert West? What conditions would allow replacement of one group of hunter-gatherers by another group? Are there signs of warfare at A.D. 1300? Is there evidence that the climate made the pre-1300 adaptation untenable, enabling the Shoshoni to invade the Desert West? Could it be that one ceramic-using population moved into the Desert West and intermarried with the previous inhabitants? Is there some change in ecological adaptation that makes use of ceramic vessels more efficient after A.D. 1300 than before? Are the vessels actually manufactured in situ in the Desert West, or are they traded in from neighboring ceramic-manufacturing areas? If so, what could the Desert West people be trading for the ceramics, and why did this trade begin only after A.D. 1300?

Questions of this nature could be elaborated ad nauseam. The point here—and this is a very important point indeed—is that the mechanics of cultural change cannot be understood strictly from an analysis of time-markers. By definition, time-markers are based on shared culture, and, as such, time-markers deliberately ignore the total cultural system. It should be clear that questions such as diffusion, migration, and independent invention are complex issues, reflecting changes in the underlying cultural systems. Time-markers, based only on shared aspects of the cultural experience, are woefully inadequate to unravel the mechanics of cultural systems. Thus, we must distinguish cultural chronology and cultural history: A **cultural chronology** documents the temporal and spatial changes of shared aspects of culture; a **cultural history** provides a fuller picture of what people actually did. Let me repeat. Cultural chronology does not equal cultural history. A cultural chronology strictly documents changes in cultural objects; the most convenient summary of chronology is the familiar **seriation** chart (Chapter 7). Cultural history, on the other hand, ultimately will attempt to explain how and why specific cultural systems have or have not changed.

The time-marker "Shoshoni pottery" tells us that distinctive potsherds occur in archaeological deposits dating A.D. 1300–1860 throughout the Desert West. Shoshoni pottery, as time-marker, cannot tell us why pottery was introduced in 1300. For some reason, a segment of the Desert West cultural system changed—people began using (if not manufacturing) pottery. This is a complex issue that can be studied after one has looked for related shifts in evidence from settlement pattern and demography, cultural ecology, social organization, and religion (such as rock art). Furthermore, if one posits that the pottery was introduced as part of a physical migration of people, then a second cultural system must be examined—the system operative in the area from which the newcomers migrated.

Issues of cultural history cannot be solved using time-markers, or using the modal definition of culture. A systematic definition is required. Time-markers document only changes in shared material culture; they do not tell us why such changes have occurred.

This warning is repeated several times throughout the text. It is a critical point which speaks to the very objectives of archaeology. One cannot study cultural systems prior to having a chronology based upon the modal concept of culture; one must then redefine one's units to consider the systemic content. These two complementary objectives must be kept quite separate, because to confuse the two is to commit an unpardonable archaeological sin.

> Many of the archaeological data we now possess
> are inadequate for the kinds of questions we
> now wish to ask about process in history.
> *Jeffrey Parsons*

5

Stratigraphy

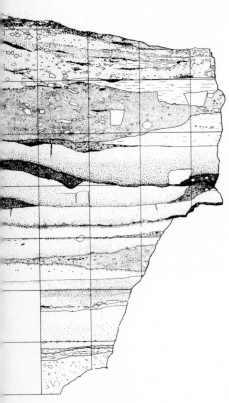

Adam was the only man who, when he said a
good thing, knew that nobody had said it before
him.

Mark Twain

Archaeology is a parasitic discipline because it relies so heavily on the findings of other sciences. It seems that archaeologists are forever borrowing methods, techniques, and theories from nonarchaeologists. In the chapter on dating, for instance, we will discuss physics, botany, and molecular biology.

Geology has been another useful mine for ideas. Geologists developed the major principles of the stratigraphic method, only to have archaeologists pirate these stratigraphic methods wholesale. In particular, two geological principles have been especially important for interpreting the archaeological record: the concepts of superposition and index fossils.

The **law of superposition** was initially formulated by Nicolaus Steno (1638–1687). Steno's law, simply stated, tells us that in any pile of sedimentary rocks that have not been disturbed by folding or overturning, the strata on the bottom were deposited first. The law of superposition, almost absurdly simple in principle, holds that—all else being equal—older deposits tend to be buried beneath younger ones. This principle facilitates the correlation of various geological exposures such as cliffs, stream valleys, and drill cores.

But geological correlation has its limits. It is impossible, for instance, to correlate the geological exposures at the Grand Canyon directly with those of the White Cliffs of Dover in England. Ever resourceful, the geologists developed a second principle—**the index fossil concept**—which assisted worldwide correlation.

In the early nineteenth century, a British surveyor named William Smith (1769–1839) began collecting data on the rock strata throughout England. Smith gradually became fascinated by the fossils he found while examining canals and various vertical exposures. As he became more familiar with the regional geology, he noticed that different exposures of the same stratum seemed to contain comparable fossils. Eventually, Smith became so knowledgeable that when somebody showed him a fossil he could guess the stratum from which it had come.

Smith's French contemporaries were making similar discoveries. While studying and mapping the fossil-rich strata surrounding Paris, Georges Cuvier (1769–1832) and Alexandre Brongniart (1770–1847) discovered that several of their fossils were restricted to specific geological formations. After first applying the law of superposition to arrange the strata in proper chronological order, they then arranged their fossil collection in stratigraphic order. The French fossil assemblages, it turned out, varied systematically according to the age of the parent strata. Cuvier and Brongniart then compared their fossils with modern species and discovered, rather expectedly, that the fossils characterizing later strata more closely resembled modern forms than did those of more ancient strata.

In other words, the fossils contained in a geological stratum are a clue to the relative age of the deposit. This is the *index fossil concept:* rocks containing similar fossil assemblages must be of similar age. Of course exceptions exist to both the index fossil concept and the more general law of superposition, but these two principles have enabled geologists around the world to correlate their stratigraphic sections into master chronologies. As we shall see, both principles are also critical in archaeology as guideposts to interpreting the record of the past. Let us examine both principles in detail.

ARCHAEOLOGY'S LAW OF SUPERPOSITION

Thomas Jefferson's examination of a Virginia burial mound was discussed in Chapter 1, and his excavation is generally acknowledged as the first use of stratigraphic principles in archaeology (e.g., Wheeler 1954:58). Jefferson's first-hand stratigraphic observations enabled him to reconstruct the various stages of construction of the site, and thereby allowed interpretation of the probable use of the burial feature. Stratigraphic techniques for analyzing burial mounds have changed very little since the time of Jefferson, as my own excavations on the Georgia coast illustrate.

McLeod Mound is located on St. Catherines Island, a barrier island about five miles off the Georgia coast (see Thomas and Larsen 1979). A rather small structure, the mound stands only one meter high and covers an area of approximately 300 square meters (Figure 5–1). When first examining the mound in 1974, we noted a small depression in the northeastern corner, probably the result of much earlier vandalism. Several oyster shells, presumably unearthed by the vandals, littered the surface of the mound.

Archaeology is a major focus of research on St. Catherines Island, and the strategy of excavation must be carefully designed to fit the situation. Archaeologists are generally forced to plan their excavations in order to protect their sites from vandals and pot hunters. I have worked on digs where we had to post a 24-hour guard (armed, appropriately enough, with bow and arrow) to protect the open excavation units from looters and treasure seekers. Most excavations must also be tediously backfilled once the scientific study is complete, in order to

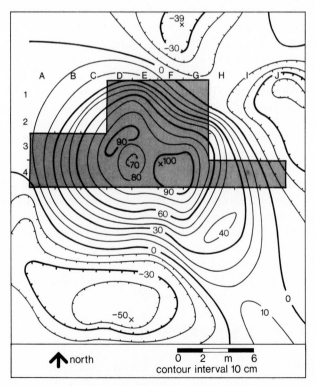

Figure 5–1
Topographic map of McLeod Mound, St. Catherines Island, Georgia; the shaded area was excavated in 1975 and 1976 *(after Thomas and Larsen 1979, figure 4; courtesy of The American Museum of Natural History).*

protect the archaeology from the curious public, and also the public from the dangers of open-pit archaeology.

But the only visitors to St. Catherines Island are scientists, who realize the research value of archaeological sites and leave the excavations untouched. It is thus possible to open a few test units on several sites, return to the laboratory to process the finds, then return to the more promising sites for more intensive excavation.

But the luxury of research freedom brings an added responsibility. Archaeology is a destructive science, ruining its sites in the very process of excavation. Sites can be excavated only once, so it is imperative to do things right. On St. Catherines Island, where the sites are not threatened in any way, we quickly decided that our strategy of excavation must be a conservative one: excavate only what is necessary to answer the specific question, and leave as much intact as possible for further investigators. They doubtless will have better questions to ask, and superior techniques with which to find answers. For this reason, we decided never to excavate more than half of any site, thereby preserving at least half of the deposits undisturbed for future generations of archaeologists. The topic of **conservation archaeology** has already been discussed in Chapter 4.

This stricture makes excavation somewhat tricky: obtain the maximum amount of information while minimizing the harm to the site itself. At McLeod Mound, we excavated only about 40 percent of the entire mound. A series of two-meter-square excavation units were opened in order to expose a large area of the pre-mound surface, but also to produce a continuous east-west profile of the mound stratigraphy. In this way, we could determine both the sequence of mound construction, and also the horizontal patterning of the ceremonial area beneath the mound.

Figure 5–1 shows how we implemented this strategy in the field. Once the excavation was completed, the twenty-meter profile was drawn and photographed in detail. Figure 5–2 illustrates the McLeod Mound stratigraphic profile, and Table 5–1 describes the major depositional units. Note that the thickness, texture, and general nature of each stratigraphic unit is described in detail. The number in parentheses, such as (10 YR 4/5: moist) is a description from the **Munsell Color Chart**, a device consisting of hundreds of color chips, graded along scales of value, hue, and chroma. When properly used, the Munsell Color Chart standardizes the descriptions of even the most subtle color gradations.

The stratigraphic profile and measured stratigraphic section thus provide our basic data from McLeod Mound. To this point, we would hope that any competent field archaeologist digging at McLeod would produce comparable data. Descriptions such as these are published in detail so that other archaeologists can compare the profile with sites excavated elsewhere.

Now comes the matter of interpretation. Although most archaeologists would probably produce the same data, the interpretation of these data is not at

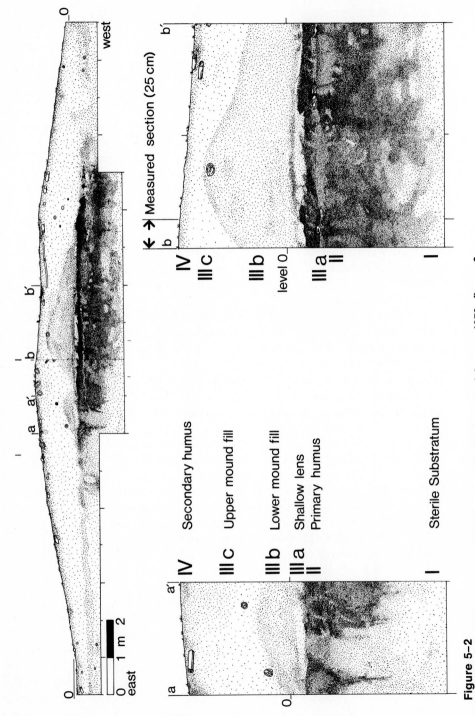

west

east

0 1 m 2

IV Secondary humus

IIIc Upper mound fill

IIIb Lower mound fill

IIIa Shallow lens

II Primary humus

I Sterile Substratum

Measured section (25 cm)

level 0

Figure 5–2
Stratigraphic section of McLeod Mound *(after Thomas and Larsen 1979, figure 9; courtesy of The American Museum of Natural History).*

Table 5–1

Measured Stratigraphic Section of McLeod Mound (for Location of Section, see Figure 5–2)

Unit	Thickness	Description
IV	10 cm.	*Secondary humus,* dark grayish brown sand, fairly dense root mat (10 YR 4/2: moist), formed as A horizon of Unit IIIc. Contact gradual over 4–5 cm.
IIIc	30–40 cm.	*Upper mound fill,* brownish yellow sand (10 YR 6/6: moist). Radiocarbon date: A.D. 130–110 ± 75 (UGA-1256). Contact distinct.
IIIb	50–65 cm.	*Lower mound fill,* dark brown sand (10 YR 3/3: moist), charcoal flecks throughout. Contact abrupt.
IIIa	4–5 cm.	*Shallow lens,* brownish yellow sand (10 YR 6/6: moist), occasional charcoal flecks present. Contact very abrupt.
II	90 cm.	*Primary humus,* very dark grayish brown sand (10 YR 3/2: moist), slightly mottled with abundant charcoal present, apparently disturbed with lens of shell embedded near center of mound, formed as A horizon of Unit I. Radiocarbon dates: 1600–1640 B.C. ± 70 (UCLA-1997E); 850–890 B.C. ± 65 (UGA-1557). Contact gradual.
I	30+ cm.	*Sterile substratum,* yellow sand (10 YR 7/8: moist), slightly mottled, uncompressed occasional charcoal flecks present year top. Bottom not exposed.

all mechanical. We must now translate observable stratigraphic phenomena into the behavioral patterns that produced the stratification. Here is where geology's law of superposition comes to the aid of archaeology.

Steno's law tells us that the older deposits will lie near the bottom of the stratigraphic profile, so we work from the bottom up. Unit I is a sterile yellow sand, and by coring in the vicinity of McLeod we found that the yellow sands of Unit I extend throughout the area. These sands were laid down during the Silver Bluff submergence of the **Pleistocene** period, some 40,000 to 25,000 years ago. At that time, the Pleistocene glaciers were at a maximum, capturing a massive volume of water and consequently lowering sea levels as much as 330 feet below current levels. The Georgia coastline at that time must have extended 70 to 80 miles eastward of the present beach. Georgia Sea Islands such as St. Catherines were formed as great onshore dune ridges, which then became isolated as islands when the glaciers melted some 18,000 years ago. Thus Unit I at McLeod is a dune formation at least 25,000 years old and has nothing to do with people.

Soil cores indicate that Unit I is always capped by a rich organic layer formed as a product of weathering. This thin soil horizon is rich in organic debris, and the black horizontal stain across the McLeod profile thus represents a *primary humus,* formed after the deposition of Unit I, but prior to any human activity at the site.

Charcoal and charred stumps in Unit II have been radiocarbon dated to about 1700 B.C. This fire was almost certainly set deliberately in order to clear the land. The fire must have been localized, because the charcoal concentration is restricted to the mound proper and does not appear in soil samples taken from the undisturbed forest surrounding McLeod. We interpret this burning as the initial human activity at the spot.

Unit III, subdivided into three subunits, poses a greater interpretive problem. A large central pit was dug throughout Units II and I sometime after the burning. Five females (see Chapter 10) were buried in this pit, then covered with burnt humus and a fine lens of oyster shell. These shells have been radiocarbon dated to about 500 B.C., indicating that the pit was dug quite a while after the area was burnt. By techniques discussed in Chapter 8 we even know that these shells were collected between November and May of the same year. The shallow yellow lens (Unit IIIa) in the profile represents backdirt from this central tomb. Unit IIIa is reworked sand from Unit I, piled up as the tomb was excavated.

Units IIIb and IIIc represent the actual building of the mound, after the tomb had been completed. Three large "barrow" areas are evidence on the topographic map in Figure 5-1; the mound builders evidently dug these pits in order to obtain sand from the mound fill. The color shift between IIIb and IIIc is due to the nature of these parent materials. While digging into burnt Unit II, the prehistoric excavator's backdirt was a dark gray. But once the barrow pits reached Unit I, the mound fill changed to the light yellow sand characteristic of the sterile substratum.

Finally a secondary humus zone formed over the top of the entire mound. This humus (Unit IV) is much lighter than the soil in Unit II because of the little amount of time available for formation (less than 2,500 years), and also because it was not burnt for clearing of vegetation.

This sequence of construction is inferred entirely from the stratigraphic column and profile on Figure 5-2. Almost identical sequences have been noted for eight additional mounds also excavated on St. Catherines Island (see Thomas and Larsen 1979). The law of superposition is the key to unlocking stratigraphic sequences of this nature, provided that the initial descriptions are accurate. Nothing in our interpretations departs radically from those made in 1784 by Thomas Jefferson, except that modern excavations are conducted more systematically and documented more completely. Jefferson would have interpreted the McLeod Mound stratigraphy the same way I did, had he been given Figure 5-2 and Table 5-1.

Mortuary sites such as McLeod are wholly constructed by human activities, and these activities can readily be reconstructed using the law of superposition. But habitation sites such as Gatecliff do not result from deliberate human activity. More commonly, the refuse simply accumulates haphazardly through time. Although this debris is patterned, the patterning is considerably more subtle than that seen at McLeod.

Figure 5–3 is the stratigraphic profile for Gatecliff Shelter. The entire column is forty feet deep, and spans about 9,000 years of human occupation. A simplified stratigraphic section is given in Table 5–2. Gatecliff Shelter has textbook stratigraphy, and that is why I discuss it here. The thin dark levels are habitation surfaces, or *living floors*. Each dark horizontal band, such as level 9, represents a single campsite. The thicker strata separating the dark bands are zones of naturally deposited, sterile debris. Layer 10, for example, is a flash flood deposit, devoid of artifacts. Another habitation surface lies on top of Unit 10, and this layer is in turn covered by another sterile unit.

In other words, Gatecliff Shelter contains forty feet of deposits which resulted from a complex interplay of natural and cultural factors. The living floors occurred as the result of human habitation, and these surfaces contain the firehearths, broken stone tools, grinding slabs, flakes, food remains, and occasional fragments of basketry and cordage. Chapter 10 discusses how the patterning of these artifacts on each floor allows reconstruction of the activities that occurred on each living surface.

But what makes Gatecliff so unusual is that the living surfaces were capped by sterile, noncultural layers of purely geological origin. Some units, such as 13, result from small ponds which occasionally formed at the rear of Gatecliff Shelter. The pond water acted as a sink for windblown dust particles, which settled out as finely laminated silts. Other units, such as 10, consist of coarser sediments grading from gravels at the bottom to fine sand silts at the top. Apparently, the ephemeral stream flowing in front of Gatecliff Shelter occasionally flooded and coursed through the shelter. The water of such flash floods would first deposit coarse sediments, such as pea-sized gravels. As the velocity of the waters diminished, the carrying capacity of the water decreased, and smaller particles were deposited. Finally, when the water slowed altogether, the tiniest silt particles would cap the stream deposits. Such floods occurred several times throughout the 9,000 years of the human occupation at Gatecliff, and each time the previous occupation surface was immediately buried. When the inhabitants returned to Gatecliff they lived on a new campsite, wholly separated from the previous one by as much as two feet of sterile alluvial sediments.

Gatecliff is thus like a giant layer cake. The sterile units are the layers of cake per se; the living surfaces are the icing capping each layer. At least one dozen discrete campsites were found at Gatecliff, each separated one from another by the geologically derived sands and silts. The silts formed impenetrable caps, insuring almost perfect separation between living surfaces, and virtually eliminating mixing between levels.

Archaeological sites with forty feet of stratified deposits are rare in

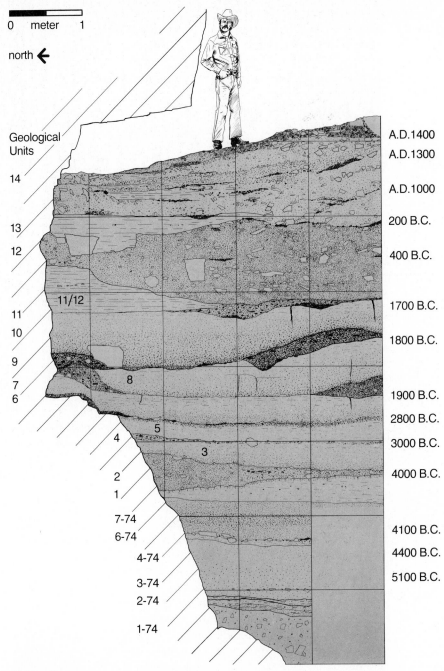

Figure 5–3
Master stratigraphic profile at Gatecliff Shelter. The cowboy stands exactly six feet tall
(courtesy of The American Museum of Natural History).

Table 5–2
Selected Living Floors at Gatecliff Shelter (Based on Preliminary Field Observations)

Phase	Geological Unit	Age	Contents
Underdown	Floor, Upper 14	A.D. 1300	Extensive bone bed, containing approx. 2 dozen individual mountain sheep carcasses; abundant butchering marks; 4 dozen discarded lithic tools.
Reveille	Floor, Lower 12	ca. 1000 B.C.	Surface approximately 5 cm. thick; apparently a base camp; heavy concentrations of grinding stones and choppers, California-type trade items; concentration of 90 incised limestone tablets in a 2-meter area. (an intentional circle?).
Early Reveille	Floor 11	1500 B.C.	Dense scatter of several hundred artifacts; few grinding stones, many bifaces (male hunting camp?), few trade goods, beads and awls.
Reveille/ Devils Gate transition	Floor 9	1600 B.C.	Dense scatter with abundant grinding stones, two large earth ovens, many female artifacts (winter village?).
Devils Gate	Floor 7	1650 B.C.	Brief occupation (suggesting perhaps base camps, but not for entire winter).
Devils Gate	Floor 6	2600 B.C.	Sparse occupation (temporary camp?).
Devils Gate (?)	Floor 4	2850 B.C.	Similar to 6.
Devils Gate (?)	Floor 2	4000 B.C.	Similar to 6.
Clipper Gap	Floor 6-74	4300 B.C.	Small hunting camp, with hearths and butchered animal bone.
Clipper Gap	Unit 4-74	4500 B.C.(?)	Too small a sample.
Clipper Gap	Floor 2-74	5000 B.C.	Too small a sample

archaeology, and these middens pose certain problems to the excavator. The profile in Figure 5–4 was not excavated in a single vertical cut because of the danger of collapse. In a similar situation, Don Fowler of the Desert Research Institute in Reno had cleared a fifteen-foot-high profile at a cave in eastern Nevada. It took two days to clean the section for final drawing and photography, and just as they began to make the final sketch an Air Force jet screamed overhead. The resulting sonic boom not only triggered the collapse of the stratigraphic profile, but also a fusilade of angry letters of protest from the

Figure 5–4
Basal stratigraphy at Gatecliff Shelter. The grid system divides the deposits into square meter units *(courtesy of The National Geographic Society).*

archaeologists. But like Humpty Dumpty, there is no piecing together of a collapsed stratigraphic profile.

The excavation units at Gatecliff Shelter were all stair-stepped, so that no walls stood higher than two meters (until the very last stage of the excavation). Should a collapse occur—as they did from time to time—there was no danger of excavators being totally buried. Figure 5-3 is a stratigraphic composite, drawn over a four-year period. The various aspects of the excavations will be discussed in later chapters, but the Gatecliff profile illustrates how the law of superposition—in this case, alternating cultural and natural deposits—facilitates archaeological interpretation.

THE INDEX FOSSIL CONCEPT

As we have seen, geologists surmised the law of superposition rather early in the game (1669), but fossils were not used for geological correlation until the work of Cuvier and Brongniart in the early nineteenth century. Similarly, archaeologists like Thomas Jefferson applied principles of superposition very early in the eighteenth century, but the use of artifacts as index fossils did not occur until the twentieth century. Nels Nelson, discussed in Chapter 1, is generally credited with the initial use of the index fossil concept in stratigraphic archaeology (see Spier 1931, Woodbury 1960). In 1912, Nelson toured European archaeological sites in order to become familiar with the most recent innovations. While at Castillo Cave in Spain, Nelson participated for several weeks in the excavation of tightly stratified Paleolithic remains. Castillo is a cave with layered stratigraphy not unlike that of Gatecliff Shelter. The Castillo grotto held deposits roughly forty-five feet thick, with thirteen layers of archaeological debris ranging from Paleolithic times through the Bronze Age. Nelson was impressed with the fine stratigraphic divisions of such sites, and he sought similar sites upon his return to the American Southwest the next year.

Nelson's initial stratigraphic excavations in the Galisteo Basin of New Mexico were disappointing. The trash heaps of the Southwest were badly disturbed, not like the crisp strata of European caves at all. Several sites were tested, but the middens were either too short in time span or else riddled by prehistoric grave digging.

Nelson finally found the stratigraphic profile he had been seeking at the Pueblo San Cristobal. Human burials had been exposed in an eroding creek bank, and Nelson explored the ruin for three years. When he returned to San Cristobal in 1914 he decided to try a new stratigraphic method.

Selecting an area with minimal disturbance, Nelson isolated a block of debris measuring three by six feet on the horizontal and nearly ten feet deep. Clearly the debris had accumulated over a long interval, and several distinct kinds of pottery were present. But the midden conspicuously lacked the sharp stratigraphy Nelson had observed in the Paleolithic caves of Europe.

Figure 5–5
General view of Nelson's early excavations at the San Cristobal ruins, New Mexico (*courtesy of The American Museum of Natural History*).

So Nelson did the next best thing: he created his own stratigraphy. He first divided his stratigraphic test block into one-foot vertical sections. Each twelve-inch level was excavated as one would dig a natural stratum, and the sherds were catalogued according to level. Nelson did not trust his workmen for this excavation and he later noted (1916:165), "I performed this work with my own hands, devoting fully three days to the task." The technique of arbitrary levels seems almost pedestrian today, but in 1914, Nelson's stratigraphic method was a brilliant innovation, immediately adopted by archaeologists as a fundamental tool of excavation.

At this point, Nelson could apply the principles of superposition to infer the character of the midden column (see Figure 5–6). Clearly the oldest deposits lay at the bottom, capped by more recent trash accumulations. But the dense midden lacked visible stratigraphy, and Nelson searched for time-markers in the form of diagnostic pottery types. The concept is precisely that of the index fossil used a century earlier by geologists Cuvier and Brongniart. Just as geologists could identify certain extinct life forms as characteristic of various rock strata, so too could archaeologists identify certain diagnostic artifact forms to characterize (and hence date) the strata of archaeological sites.

Thus Nelson applied the index fossil concept to the midden heaps of San Cristobal. Pottery was the most common of cultural remains, and the pottery styles apparently changed rather rapidly in the American Southwest. Nelson recovered over 2,000 sherds in his ten-foot section at San Cristobal. First grouping the sherds into obvious stylistic categories, he then plotted their distribution according to depth below the surface (see Table 5–3). Column 1 contains the frequency of corrugated pottery, the ware most commonly used for everyday cooking vessels. The frequency of the corrugated sherds was relatively constant throughout the occupation of San Cristobal, so Nelson rejected col-

Figure 5–6
Nelson's initial excavation by arbitrary levels in Refuse Heap B, San Cristobal Pueblo
(courtesy of The American Museum of Natural History).

Table 5–3
Potsherd Frequencies from Pueblo San Cristobal, New Mexico*

Depth Below Surface	Corrugated Ware (1)	Biscuit Ware (2)	Type I (black on white) (3)	Type II (2-color glaze) (4)	Type III (3-color glaze) (5)
1st foot	57	10	2	81	5
2nd foot	116	17	2	230	6
3rd foot	27	2	10	134	3
4th foot	28	4	6	93	0
5th foot	60	15	2	268	0
6th foot	75	21	8	297	1?
7th foot	53	10	40	126	0
8th foot	56	2	118	51	0
9th foot	93	1?	107	3	0
10th foot	84	1?	69	0	0
Total	649	83	364	1283	15

*After Nelson 1916:166.

umn 1 as a potential index fossil. Column 2 tabulated the frequencies of so-called biscuit ware, a dull white or yellow pottery which Nelson felt was probably traded into San Cristobal from other areas. The frequencies of biscuit ware did not change markedly in his stratigraphic column either, so it too was rejected as a stratigraphic marker.

Nelson concentrated on the three remaining columns—which he termed Types I, II, and III, and discovered, just as Cuvier and Brongniart had with their French fossils, that certain forms were associated with specific stratigraphic levels. Nelson's stratigraphy revealed that the most ancient levels at San Cristobal contained a predominance of black-on-white painted pottery (Nelson's Type I). Black-on-white sherds were most numerous *below* the eight-foot mark, and only rarely appeared above seven feet. Similarly, the Type II pottery—red, yellow, and gray sherds ornamented with a dark glaze—occurred most commonly *above* the seven-foot mark. Thus Type I sherds were diagnostic of the pre-eight-foot strata, while the Type II sherds characterized the upper deposits. Type III pottery (three-colored glazed ware), while rather rare at San Cristobal, was widespread throughout the Southwest and seemed to be still in use when the sixteenth-century Spaniards arrived in New Mexico. Accordingly, Type III pottery appeared only in the uppermost levels of Nelson's column.

Nelson's arbitrary levels revealed the presence of three time-markers, or index fossils. Not only could he document the specific ceramic changes at San

Cristobal, but the presence of these pottery types elsewhere provided clues to the age of undated archæological deposits. Chapter 7 discusses further how pottery types function as time-markers. For now it is sufficient to emphasize Nelson's innovative stratigraphic method. Creation of artificial stratigraphic units was a brilliant stroke and remains today a commonplace technique of excavation wherever visible stratigraphic units are absent.

Nelson thus charted the course, but it remained for A. V. Kidder to put Nelson's stratigraphic method to a major test. Kidder visited Nelson's excavations at San Cristobal and shortly thereafter adapted the technique for major excavations at Pecos Pueblo, less than twenty-five miles to the east. From his earlier excavations, Kidder surmised that Pecos (like San Cristobal) was characterized by early black-on-white pottery, followed by a series of later phases characterized by glazed pottery. The later of these, the Glaze 5 period, appeared some time before the Spanish conquest and lasted until nearly 1680 (Kidder 1924:104).

In 1915, Kidder located several rich deposits of the later phases, but the early black-on-white period was poorly represented. Kidder set out the next year to find the early Pecos occupation with a series of long exploratory trenches, cut at intervals of 100 feet or so. Because he found almost no refuse on the barren west slope of Pecos (probably because of the strong prevailing west winds that whistled through the Pecos Valley), Kidder concentrated his

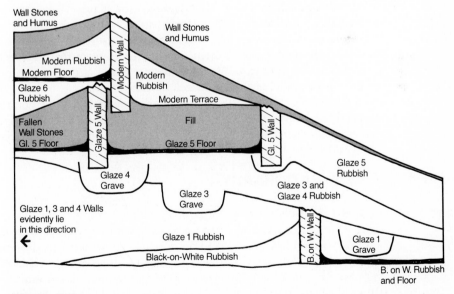

Figure 5–7
Cross-section of Pecos Pueblo, showing walls, burials and ceramics *(after Kidder 1924, figure 8; courtesy of Yale University Press).*

trenching along the leeward side of the ruin. Just inside the defensive perimeter wall Kidder located a series of chambers with ruined walls standing less than eighteen inches tall (see Figure 5–7). When only black-on-white rubbish was found stacked *against* these walls, Kidder concluded that he had found the earliest dwelling on the mesa at Pecos. Here lay the earliest settlement, the nucleus of the Pecos pueblo, and burials interred in the black-on-white rubbish comprised the first Pecos cemetery. As shown in Figure 5–7, the succeeding Glaze 1, 3, and 4 walls were located somewhat south of this early occupation, which in turn was buried by later Glaze 5 and 6 rubbish.

Kidder's Pecos investigations verified Nelson's techniques again and again. By carefully following the course of the various trash heaps—characterized by the time-marker sherds—Kidder reconstructed the several centuries of habitation at Pecos Pueblo. And when walls or burials were encountered, they could be dated by the associated midden.

Contemporary stratigraphic methods have come a long way since the days of Nelson and Kidder. At the Koster site in Illinois, an on-line computer terminal permits the information from about 60,000 excavation units to be retrieved in a nearby laboratory, enabling excavators to plan their next step in excavation (Struever and Carlson 1977). Several advanced chemical techniques are now available to help excavators distinguish minute soil changes in stratigraphic profiles (Cook and Heizer 1965; Cornwall 1969). Volcanism is even an aid in archaeological stratigraphy. Thousands of archaeological sites were blanketed in volcanic ash when Mt. Mazama (now Crater Lake National Park) erupted about 7,000 years ago, spewing ash and pumice throughout the northwestern United States. Archaeologists can now use the Mt. Mazama ash as a chronological marker bed in open sites and caves from that time period (e.g., Cressman 1977). Ash from Mt. Mazama was found at the bottom of Gatecliff Shelter (incidentally, in the final week of excavation).

These improvements and modifications notwithstanding, the principles of stratigraphic excavation were charted long ago by European geologists. Recent innovations remain only predictable links in a long-standing chain of progress.

HORIZONTAL STRATIGRAPHY

The overriding concern of geologists Steno, Smith, and Cuvier was verticality—how one sedimentary bed stacks upon another. But more recent geological investigation has also focused on the diversity within a single stratum. The paleogeography of single stratigraphic units is often well known; the oil-rich Permian Basin of West Texas, for instance, is known to have formed, in part, as stream deposits, elsewhere as back-reef, quiet-water lagoons. Stratigraphy quite obviously has a horizontal dimension.

Archaeologists, also aware of "flat stratigraphy," recognize that temporal variability is sometimes expressed horizontally. Archaeology's most dramatic

example of horizontal stratification occurs at Cape Krusenstern, a beach formation northeast of Nome, Alaska. The aerial photograph of Cape Krusenstern
(Figure 5–8) indicates that the cape is not one beach at all, but over a hundred
minor dune ridges. The beaches join to form a peninsula extending far into the
Chukchi Sea. The modern shoreline is a long, fairly flat surface comprised of
coarse sand and gravel; this contemporary beach is designated as Beach 1.
Behind this most recent beach is an older shoreline (Beach 2), which has
become stranded and landlocked. As one moves away from the Chukchi Sea,
one encounters a total of 114 such relic beach terraces. In most cases, the
ancient beaches are covered with a protective coating of grassy sod.

Archaeologist J. L. Giddings began investigating the archaeology of Cape
Krusenstern in 1958, and he spent four seasons excavating the archaeological
remains buried beneath the frozen sod. Giddings has excavated house pits,
burials, caches, tent sites, and even entire settlements of the peoples who have
lived on Cape Krusenstern (Giddings 1961, 1966).

The Cape Krusenstern ruins are as tightly stratified as the sediments of
Gatecliff Shelter or the trash heaps of Pueblo San Cristobal. But instead of
finding campsites stacked one on top of another, Giddings discovered that the
Cape Krusenstern sites are stratified *side by side.* A corollary of the general
principles of stratigraphy applies to beach terraces such as Krusenstern.

The principle of horizontal stratigraphy is that on any series of uneroded
beach surfaces, the youngest stratum will be seaward and the oldest stratum will
be inland. The modern Krustenstern beach contains house pits of very recent
Eskimo who camped there within the past century. Five beaches or so inland are
the multiple-roomed, deeply entrenched house remains of an ancestral pre-
Eskimo culture known as Western Thule. The late artifacts and distinctive
pottery found within these houses, pinpoint the Western Thule sites as similar
to those elsewhere in the Arctic known to date about A.D. 1000. Further inland,
about Beach 35, are the large square pit houses and clusters of shallow summer
lodges constructed by the Ipiutak peoples, a society known for their excellence
in carving ivory. Some fifteen beaches behind the Ipiutak sites, nearly a kilometer from the modern sea, are the hearths and tent sites of the Choris peoples,
characterized by large spearpoints strangely like those used on the Western
Plains to hunt extinct forms of bison.

Beach 35 contains a ruined settlement of deep, multiple-roomed winter
lodges, along with a few scattered summer settlements. Giddings terms this the
"Old Whaling" culture because of the abundant whale bones found in and about
the houses on this beach line. Further back, on Beach 78, are the hearths of the
culture known as the Denbigh Flint complex, and even more ancient tent sites
were found on Beach 104.

In all, the Cape Krusenstern archaeological sequence spans at least 5,000
years. Not only are the archaeological sites of interest in themselves, but they
provide valuable clues for interpreting the geological processes evident on Cape
Krusenstern. Studies of the ocean sediments indicate that the modern beach is

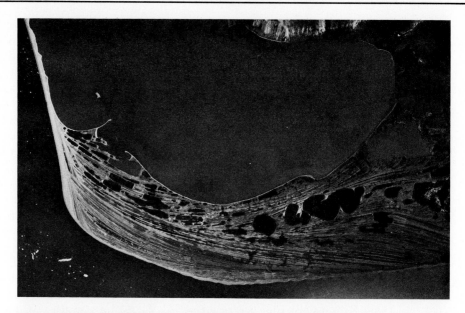

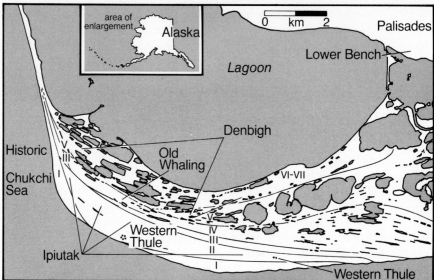

Figure 5–8
Aerial photograph and sketch map of beach ridges at Cape Krusenstern, Alaska. Most recent beaches are in the foreground, and oldest beaches are back toward the lagoon. Segment numbers I to VII correspond to Beaches 1 to 104 *(after Giddings 1966, figures 3 and 4; courtesy of the National Oceanic and Atmospheric Administration and the American Association of the Advancement of Science).*

built of gravels that slowly shift southward along the coast and move along by persistent long-shore currents. But the beachfront of Krusenstern has changed direction at least six times, changing some 20 to 32 degrees each time (Giddings 1966:131). Some geologists attribute this change to a shifting direction of prevailing wind, coupled with a slight rise in sea levels. Giddings, however, argues that because the early Denbigh Flint sites have never been washed over by water, sea levels could not have risen more than a meter or so over the past 5,000 years.

Here is one case in which the archaeological sites provide a fine-scale chronological control for the geological research. The horizontal stratigraphy evident on the beach ridges of Cape Krusenstern holds promise as an ideal laboratory for future geological studies of shifting sea levels and sea currents.

A similar application of the principle of horizontal stratigraphy has been undertaken by Chester DePratter of the University of Georgia. DePratter and Howard (1977) are studying the growth and erosion rates of the coastal Georgia shoreline using archaeological dating. The problem is basically geological: how did the Georgia Sea Islands come to be, and how are they being modified by ongoing erosion? The sea levels on the Georgia coast have evidently been fairly constant over the past 4,000 years or so, and the processes of deposition and erosion have formed a number of beach dunes along the margins of islands such as St. Catherines (the location of McLeod Mound, discussed earlier in this chapter). Geologists wish to study how the islands change, but lack a reliable method of dating the beach lines.

Once again, archaeology comes to the service of geology. The Indians of coastal Georgia have been living on the Sea Islands for the past 4,000 years, and their ecological adaptation depended heavily on the shallow marine environment. Shell heaps dot the beach lines of coastal Georgia, just as Eskimo and earlier sites accumulated on the shorelines of Cape Krusenstern in Alaska. The ceramic styles changed rapidly during this period, and the archaeological sites can be accurately dated by analyzing the potsherds found in the shell middens. Two factors—(1) the growing shoreline and (2) the rapidly changing pottery styles—result in a fine-grained chronology which permits geologists to measure the growth of the Georgia Sea Islands over the past 4,000 years. That is, the islands are progressively growing seaward. When the aboriginal occupation commenced some 4,000 years ago the shoreline must have been several hundred meters from the modern beaches. As on Cape Krusenstern, the archaeological sites will tend to cluster along the then-current shoreline. As younger beach ridges develop, the site localities move accordingly. Thus the more ancient archaeological sites are found on older beaches, and the more recent dunes contain the most recent archaeological sites.

Thus the distribution of prehistoric pottery can be used to date the age of sand dunes. In a pilot study on Tybee Island (near Savannah, Georgia), the following distribution of pottery types was discovered (see Figure 5–9). The

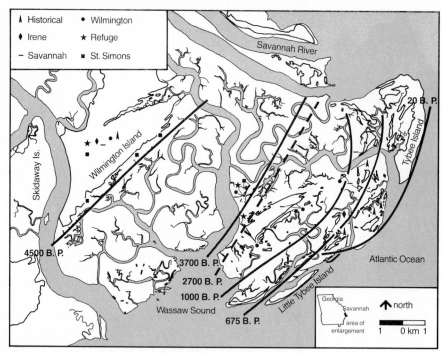

Figure 5–9
Distribution of archaeological sites and inferred prehistoric beach lines on Wilmington and Tybee Islands, Georgia *(after DePratter and Howard 1977, figure 2; courtesy of Chester B. DePratter).*

earliest pottery on the coast, fiber-tempered St. Simons ware (discussed in the Introduction to Part Two) is only found some three miles from the modern shoreline. Because St. Simons pottery is known to be older than 3,000 years, geologists can safely conclude that the shoreline must have been about three miles inland at 1000 B.C. St. Simons pottery will not be found closer to the shoreline because beaches had not yet formed. The next kind of pottery, known as Deptford, occurs up to two miles off the present beach line, but no closer. The conclusion is that the 500 B.C. shoreline must have been about two miles inland from the current beach. During the Wilmington—St. Catherines phases (some 850 years ago), the shoreline was about a mile inland, and the pottery of the protohistoric Irene phase is found much closer to the present beach. The geological processes still continue, of course, and one day future archaeologists might date the present beach front by the ubiquitous Coke bottles and beer poptops that litter today's beach line.

Several factors make DePratter's study an excellent example of horizontal stratigraphy. First of all, it was necessary to have a detailed cultural chronology, because without the radiocarbon-dated ceramic sequence the beaches could not be dated. In addition, the Georgia coastline was heavily populated over the past

4,000 years, thereby creating plenty of sites available for ceramic dating. On Tybee Island alone—an area of less than twenty-five square miles—almost a dozen archaeological sites were mapped and collected in less than two weeks. Furthermore, the Georgia coastline has been free of tectonic activity, which would disrupt the gradual development of beach dunes. Finally, because the Sea Islands are relatively undeveloped, most archaeological sites remain undisturbed and, in fact, undiscovered.

These last two studies point up a shifting relationship between the archaeological and geological sciences. Archaeology began as a parasitic science, borrowing concepts, techniques, and methods from the hard sciences such as physics, chemistry, and geology. But archaeological studies at Krusenstern, the Georgia Sea Islands, and elsewhere indicate that the borrowing is becoming reciprocal. Geophysics gave the technique of radiocarbon dating to archaeology. Archaeology is now using C-14 dating to establish ceramic chronologies, which in turn can date previously undated geological surfaces. Archaeology still has many scientific debts to repay, but pioneer studies such as those discussed here indicated that the balance may soon be redressed.

I start where the last man left off.
Thomas A. Edison

SUMMARY

Archaeologists are notorious for borrowing useful techniques and concepts from sister sciences. When dealing with stratigraphy, they have employed two important geological principles. The *law of superposition* holds that (all else being equal) older geological strata will tend to be buried beneath younger strata. A second principle, the *index fossil concept,* is that strata containing similar fossil assemblages must be of similar age. Although exceptions always exist, these principles have enabled geologists around the world to correlate individual stratigraphic sections into master chronologies.

Archaeologists commonly use the law of superposition to unravel complex sequences of stratification within archaeological sites. The stratigraphic record in sites such as burial mounds is the result of deliberate cultural activities; people have systematically deposited strata as cultural features. In many habitation sites, however, the stratigraphy results from accidental accumulation, often the result of complex interplay between agencies of natural and cultural deposition. The law of superposition provides an organizing principle through which such diverse archaeological sites can be interpreted and correlated.

Archaeologists have also modified the index fossil concept for use in archaeological contexts. Changing ceramic patterns, for example, can serve as clues for stratigraphic interpretation and correlation. The methods of establishing and monitoring such cultural change are discussed in Chapter 7.

A final means of correlation, horizontal stratigraphy, can be applied whenever successive cultural occupations are spaced along a systematically changing land surface. Beach lines are particularly good candidates for horizontal cultural stratigraphy. Whenever a shoreline is progressively growing, archaeological sites will tend to be arrayed along a temporal (and spatial) continuum: the older sites occur on inland beaches and the later sites cluster along the more recent (seaward) surfaces. Horizontal stratigraphy is useful not only for establishing the validity of cultural sequences but also as an independent means of establishing the absolute rate of beach deposit and erosion.

6

Establishing Chronological Controls

Time is but the stream I go a-fishing in.
Henry David Thoreau

The Fourth Egyptian Dynasty lasted from 2680 to 2565 B.C. The Roman Coliseum was constructed between A.D. 70 and 82. In the seventeenth century, Dr. John Lightfoot proclaimed that God created the entire Earth in 4004 B.C., at precisely 9 A.M. on October 23. Each date represents the most familiar manner of chronological control—the absolute date. Such dates are expressed in a specific unit of scientific measurement: days, years, centuries, or millennia. But regardless of how the measurements are derived—Lightfoot computed his estimate by projecting biblical lifespans back into time—all absolute determinations attempt to pinpoint a discrete interval in time.

Archaeologists also measure time in a second, more imprecise manner by establishing relative chronology. As the name implies, such temporal placement is not in terms of specific segments of scientific, absolute time but rather by a relative relationship: earlier, later, more recent, after Noah's flood, prehistoric, and so on. Often relative estimates are the only dates possible. Both forms of dating, absolute and relative, are means of controlling the dimension of time in the study of man's past.

In this brief survey only a few dating techniques can be considered, and we are forced to ignore such important techniques as counting annual varves in geological deposits, dating through decoding the Maya calendar, and many of the chemical methods such as the fluorine test, used in exposing the infamous **Piltdown hoax.**

> **T**ime has no divisions to mark its passing. There is never a thunderstorm to announce the beginning of a new month or year.
> *Thomas Mann*

DENDROCHRONOLOGY

Like many of archaeology's dating techniques, tree-ring dating (**dendrochronology**) was not developed by an archaeologist at all. The first systematic dendrochronologist was A. E. Douglass, an astronomer investigating how sunspots affect the earth's climate. Douglass knew that trees in temperate and arctic areas remain dormant during the winter and then burst into activity in the spring. In many species, especially conifers, this cycle results in the addition of well-defined concentric growth rings, evident in the stumps of most trees (Figure 6–1). Because each ring represents a single year, it is theoretically a simple matter to determine the age of a newly felled tree—just count the rings. Douglass reasoned further that since the rings varied in size, tree rings probably preserve information about past environments. The regular patterns of tree growth (that is, ring width) could be pieced together to establish a long-term chronological sequence.

Douglass began constructing a tree-ring chronology with living specimens, mostly yellow pines near Flagstaff and Prescott, Arizona. Douglass would examine a stump or a core from a living tree, count the rings, then overlap his sequence with a somewhat older set of rings from another tree and so forth (Figure 6–2). But dead trees and surface snags provided a chronology of only 500 years or so. Then dendrochronology turned to the prehistoric record. Douglass combed the known archaeological ruins of the American Southwest, sampling ancient beams and supports. Slowly, he constructed a prehistoric "floating chronology" which spanned several centuries but was not tied into the modern samples. With this sequence, Douglass could date various ruins relative to one another, but the hiatus between prehistoric and modern sequences defied

Figure 6–1
Cross-section of ponderosa pine, showing record of 108-year lifespan. Note particularly
the evidence of fire scarring: four scars can be seen around the growth center, another
is isolated by sound wood in the left center, and four others are evident at the far left
(courtesy of The American Museum of Natural History).

efforts at absolute dating. So Douglass was forced to work with two separate
sequences. The first could date with absolute precision ruins younger than about
the fourteenth century A.D., while the second relative sequence could date sites
only in relation to one another. The older sequence was expressed through
purely arbitrary numbers followed by the designation *R.D.* (Relative Date). But
there remained "the gap," an unknown span of time between the absolute and
the ancient sequence.

At this point the National Geographic Society, the American Museum of
Natural History in New York, and the Carnegie Institution of Washington
launched ambitious expeditions in an attempt to locate logs from the bother-
some middle period. The "gap hunters," as they were known, experienced little
initial success. The two sequences could occasionally be extended a year or two,
but the yawning gap remained. The problem was that Pueblo peoples had lived
in the large sites of Mesa Verde, Chaco Canyon, and elsewhere during the
relative sequence, but then they abandoned these sites for parts unknown. The
trail became clear again only in "post-gap" sites occupied during the Spanish rule
of the Southwest.

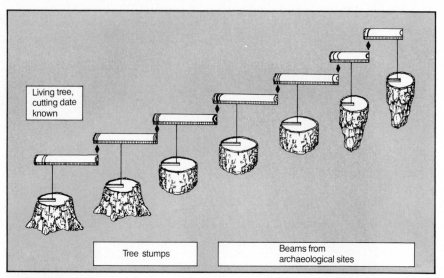

Living tree, cutting date known

Tree stumps

Beams from archaeological sites

Figure 6–2
Schematic representation of how a tree-ring chronology is built, starting from a sample of known age and overlapping successively older samples until the sequence extends back into prehistoric times.

One clue seemed to be modern towns of the Hopi, where people had perhaps lived during gap-times. After suitable arrangements were made between gap hunters and Hopi residents, borings were secured from the beams at Old Oraibi. The absolute sequence was extended back to A.D. 1260, but the gap remained.

Finally, in 1929, the archaeologists turned to the ruins underlying the modern villages in east-central Arizona. At the Showlow site, a rather unappetizing place to dig, the archaeologists excavated amidst the disarray of contemporary pigpens and corrals. But finally a small charred log was found, which was then preserved in paraffin and labeled HH39. Upon checking, Douglass discovered that HH39 neatly bridged the gap. The last year of the relative sequence was established at A.D. 1284. With the sequences united and the gap disposed of forever, the construction dates for the spectacular ruins of the Southwest could be dated with impunity: Mesa Verde had been built between A.D. 1073 and 1262, Pueblo Bonito in Chaco Canyon from A.D. 919 to 1130, the Aztec Ruin from A.D. 1110 to 1121.[1] Since that time, the dendrochronological sequence of the Southwest has been extended to 322 B.C., giving a total length of 2,300 years, and local sequences have been established for other areas, including Alaska, the American Arctic, the Great Plains, Germany, Great Britain, Ireland, Turkey, Japan, and Russia.

Not only has tree-ring dating spread worldwide, but its methods have become highly refined. In August of 1927, Douglass traveled to Betatakin, a large cliff dwelling in northeastern Arizona. The gap was still open at the time, and the Betatakin readings were subsequently joined to those of Pueblo Bonito and Aztec, setting the stage for the final union at Showlow. Douglass collected a couple of dozen samples and dated Betatakin within a decade of A.D. 1270. Dating with this sort of accuracy was astonishing for the time (and still is when compared with other techniques).

But contemporary archaeology is demanding even more from its dating techniques. Jeffrey Dean of the Laboratory of Tree-Ring Research at the University of Arizona spent two months collecting further samples at Betatakin in the summer of 1962. The total collection now represents 292 individual beams, and the growth of Betatakin can be documented literally room by room. Figure 6–3 shows Dean's architectural reconstruction (see also Figure 10–6).

Betatakin Cave was first occupied about 1250 by a small group of people who built a few structures which were later destroyed. The occupation was probably transient, with the cave serving as a seasonal camping spot for men who had traveled to plant fields at some distance from their home.

The actual village site was founded in 1267, when three room clusters were constructed. A fourth cluster was added in 1268. In 1269 this group of perhaps twenty to twenty-five people felled several trees, cut them to standardized length, and stockpiled them, presumably for use by future immigrants to the village. More stockpiling occurred in 1272, but the precut beams were not used until 1275, the beginning of a three-year period of immigration, which resulted in the construction of more than ten room clusters and probably one kiva. Growth at Betatakin slowed after 1272, reaching a peak of about 125

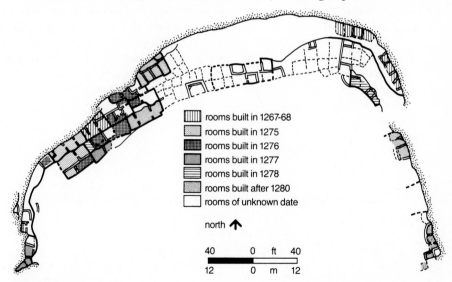

rooms built in 1267-68
rooms built in 1275
rooms built in 1276
rooms built in 1277
rooms built in 1278
rooms built after 1280
rooms of unknown date

north ↑

40   0   ft   40

12   0   m   12

Figure 6–3
Floor plan of Betatakin, Arizona, and the construction sequence as inferred from tree-ring evidence (after Dean 1970, figure 13; courtesy of Jeffrey S. Dean and the School of American Research).

people in the mid-1280s. The village was abandoned sometime between 1286 and 1300 for unknown reasons (after Dean 1970:158–159).

It can be seen that tree-ring dating provides absolute dates for archaeological sites, subject to the important limitation common to all such dating methods, for there must always be a clear association between the datable specimen and the cultural materials. One must assume that the wood was timbered at the time of occupation, because the use of dead trees or beams from abandoned structures can provide erroneously ancient dates.

Tree-ring dating can be applied to many but not all species of trees. The most commonly dated species is piñon pine, followed by ponderosa pine, Douglas fir, juniper, and white fir. Limber pine, bristlecone pine, and the giant sequoia have also been extensively studied. Even sagebrush is (sometimes) datable.

Matching unknown specimens to the regional master key has been a slow, laborious process requiring an expert with years of experience. Gradually, more automated means such as correlation graphs have been devised, and recently computer programs have been attempted (based upon the statistical theory of errors). To date, no truly successful computer program is available because the programs are unable to handle the problem of false and missing rings. Today's skilled dendrochronologist can still date samples much faster than can any computer.

In addition to providing calendar dates for sites, dendrochronology also has potential for providing climatic data. If tree-ring width is controlled by environmental factors such as temperature and soil moisture, then one should be able to reconstruct past environmental conditions by examining the band widths. But tree metabolism is a complex process, and progress in ecological reconstruction has not provided as many answers as could be desired. Perhaps the more sophisticated means of automated tree-ring analysis will provide more satisfying results. (I suggest Fritts 1976 as a reference for further reading on dendrochronology.)

OBSIDIAN HYDRATION

Obsidian (volcanic glass) has been used as a raw material for millennia. Anyone who has ever fractured an obsidian nodule is well aware of the razor-sharp edges, which can be fashioned into knives, scrapers, drills, and projectile points: obsidian has been used by flintknappers on every continent except Australia. Obsidian artifacts seem as ubiquitous as pottery in many archaeological sites and may one day be almost as useful for dating purposes (see Michels 1973, Chapter 13).

The potential of obsidian for prehistoric dating was initially explored in 1948 by two U.S. Geological Survey geologists, Irving Friedman and Robert Smith (see Friedman and Smith 1960). They discovered that obsidian hydrates (absorbs water), and they suggested that this *rate of hydration* is uniform.

Friedman and Smith knew that obsidian is a fairly "dry" rock, containing only about 0.2 percent water. But when a piece of obsidian is broken, and a new surface is exposed to the environment, water begins to be absorbed into the fresh surface. The absorption—or hydration—process continues until the obsidian contains approximately 3.5 percent water. This is its saturation point. These zones of hydration, called *rims,* are denser than the unhydrated inner portions, and the hydrated zone has different optical properties (see Figure 6–4). Every time an obsidian nodule is broken the hydration process begins from scratch on the fresh surface. Friedman and Smith reasoned the amount of hydration on an archaeological artifact should be a good measure of the amount of time elapsed since the surface was flaked by the flintknapper.

To measure the amount of hydration, it is necessary to prepare a thin section of the artifact edge. A wedge must be cut from the artifact with a diamond-impregnated saw. This wedge is ground thin on a lapidary machine, then mounted to a microscopic slide with Canada balsam. The wedge is ground once again, to a thickness of less than fifty microns. The slide is then placed under a microscope equipped with a polarizing light source. Figure 6–4 shows how the prepared specimen looks under the microscope.

The principle behind obsidian dating is simple: the longer the artifact surface has been exposed, the larger will be the hydration band. By assuming that obsidian artifact surfaces are exposed only by deliberate flintknapping, the hydration can be taken as a direct indicator of age.

Obsidian hydration dating has the distinct advantage of being simple,

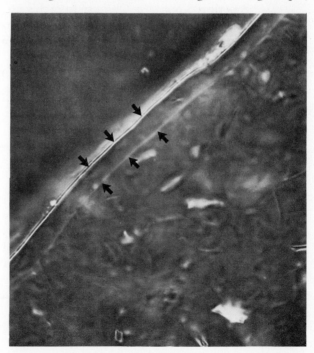

Figure 6–4
Photomicrograph of obsidian hydration band, taken at 490X. The specimen is a geological sample from Mono County, California. The band, denoted by arrows, is 4.2 microns thick *(courtesy of Frank J. Findlow).*

rapid, and cheap. At current commercial rates, twenty obsidian hydration dates can be obtained for the cost of a single radiocarbon determination. Students can be readily trained to prepare obsidian hydration samples, and several laboratories (such as those at Pennsylvania State University and UCLA) are currently in operation for such dating.

But obsidian dating is not without difficulty. After examining about 600 specimens, Friedman and Smith discovered that the rate of hydration is not uniform throughout the world. Of the several variables that seem to influence the hydration rate, atmospheric temperature seemed to be the most pervasive. Once sufficient samples were analyzed from around the world it was possible to construct a world map that described the correlation between climate and hydration rates.

Subsequent investigators then proceeded to derive rates of hydration for specific archaeological regions. Donovan Clark, then a graduate student at Stanford University, analyzed hundreds of obsidian artifacts from five prehistoric California sites and compared the hydration rims with known radiocarbon determination of the sites. Clark found that central California obsidian hydrates at slightly more than one micron per thousand years. Thus, by comparison with radiocarbon dating, Clark suggested a means of converting obsidian hydration from a relative to an absolute dating technique (Clark 1964; Ambrose 1976).

A recent study by Findlow and others (1975) shows how obsidian hydration can be used to date specific obsidian flows. The Government Mountain—Sitgreaves Peak area contains the most heavily used obsidian flow in the American Southwest. Obsidian from this area ranges from gray to shiny black in color, and the matrix is free of inclusions and **phenocrysts**. Its excellent fracturing qualities probably account for its wide distribution by trade throughout Arizona and southern Utah.

Obsidian from the Government Mountain–Sitgreaves source was found in a series of ten archaeological sites ranging in age from about 1500 B.C. to historic times. The samples were prepared for microscopic analysis and the hydration bands were read. The results were then synthesized into the following rate of hydration:

$$Y = 43.58 + 158.16 \, (x^2 - x)$$

where Y is the date (in years B.P.) and x is the hydration value in microns.

A couple of examples will illustrate how this hydration equation is used to date archaeological sites. Awatovi (Arizona) is a large Hopi city known to have been abandoned in A.D. 1630 (Brew 1941). Findlow and his associates dated ten artifacts made from the Government Mountain obsidian from the latest occupation at Awatovi. The hydration rims measured an average of 1.8 microns thick. The estimated age of this occupation is computed to be:

$$Y = 43.58 + 158.16 \, (1.8^2 - 1.8)$$
$$= 271 \text{ years B.P.}$$

This value converts to about A.D. 1680, a value that agrees fairly closely with the historically dated abandonment of Awatovi.

By the same procedure, stratum 3 at site CS 184 (Arizona) was also dated. The average thickness of the hydration rim was 5.2 microns, which converts to an absolute age of 3,498 years B.P. In this case the obsidian hydration value agrees rather closely with the date estimated by the radiocarbon method.

The present status of obsidian hydration dating remains somewhat clouded because of a number of lingering problems such as reuse of obsidian artifacts, short-term temperature fluctuations, and variable amounts of available moisture. Some archaeologists (such as Hole and Heizer 1973) remain apprehensive about the potential of obsidian hydration.

Michels and Bebrich (1971) have shown, for instance, that obsidians of different composition can also have different rates of hydration. In studying obsidians from the central Mexican highlands, Michels found that green rhyolitic obsidian hydrated almost three times as fast as the gray rhyolitic obsidian. That is, even under uniform temperature conditions, the green obsidian hydrates at a rate of 11.45 millimicrons^2 per millennium, while the gray obsidian hydrates at only a rate of 4.5 millimicrons^2 per 1,000 years. Fortunately, in this case, the different composition is obvious by superficial inspection, but the problem of differing rates is compounded when seemingly identical obsidians are of different composition.

It seems clear that *so long as the restrictions are kept in mind,* obsidian hydration does provide a useful technique for dating archaeological sites (e.g. Layton 1973; Johnson 1969; Erickson 1975). Michels (1973) has considered a number of such potential uses, including testing archaeological stratigraphy, testing for artifact reuse, and defining assemblages in the absence of reliable stratigraphy. There are certainly limitations on obsidian hydration dating, but even the best dating technique cannot be used without some restrictions and caution.

AMINO ACID DATING

Amino acids are protein compounds found in all living organisms. These compounds exist in two forms, which are mirror images of one another and can be distinguished only by their refractive properties. When placed under a polarized light one molecule bends light to the left; the mirror-image compounds bend the same light to the right. Left-handed compounds are called L-isomers ("lepto" is Greek for left). The right-handed amino acids are called D-isomers; "D" stands for the dextrorotation of the polarizing light.

Most of the proteins in living organisms are left-handed. When the organism dies, the protein molecules begin to flip over, more and more of them converting to the right-handed form. Geophysicists have converted this reaction into a dating technique. Because living forms contain primarily L-isomers and fossil materials have mostly D-amino acids, the D:L amino acid ratio is a measure of absolute age. The chemical reaction responsible for this change from L- to R-amino acid is called **racemization**. All amino acids (except glycine) undergo racemization, and the half-life of aspartic acid—about 15,000 years—is particularly useful for archaeological dating (Bada, Schroeder, Protsch, and Berger 1974).

Amino acid dating works like this: take a bone, stick it in an Automatic Amino Acid Analyzer and find the ratio of D-isomers to L-isomers. Racemization is a temperature-dependent reaction, occurring more quickly at higher temperatures, so it is necessary to "calibrate" the racemization ratio for the specific conditions. Sometimes a bone can be radiocarbon dated, then the D:L ratio can be converted to an absolute date. Samples are also calibrated according to the known temperature history of a locale. In any case, once a sample has been calibrated all the remaining bones in that site can be assigned absolute ages based strictly on the racemization ratio.

Amino acid dating has been developed by Jeffrey Bada and associates at the University of California, La Jolla Campus. Although the technique is still being perfected, amino acid dating would seem to offer several advantages over comparable dating methods. For one thing, amino acid dating requires very little bone. As we shall see, radiocarbon dating generally destroys hundreds of grams of bone for a single date. The racemization utilizes a single gram. Amino acid dating can also be accomplished more quickly than can radiocarbon assay. It is not uncommon for an archaeologist to wait six months (or even a year) for a radiocarbon laboratory to supply a suite of dates. Amino acid dating takes only a few days, assuming the sample is immediately processed by the laboratory (Bada, Schroeder, Protsch, and Berger 1974).

But the most significant aspect of amino acid dating is the potential time range. Radiocarbon methods cannot be used for materials older than about 70,000 years—there is simply not enough C-14 left to measure—and potassium-argon dating is useless for rocks younger than a million years. The disparity between these two common techniques leaves an undatable gap during which some very interesting archaeological events occurred. The effective range of amino acid dating seems to be about 5,000 to 100,000 years, thereby more than doubling the range of conventional radiocarbon dating (Bada, Schroeder, and Carter 1974).

To date, aspartic acid racemization has been applied to only a few dozen selected cases. A very small fragment of human femur was found at Abri Pataud, in the French Dordogne. The femur was the only human bone found at the site, and the fragment was much too small for radiocarbon dating. The D:L-amino acid ratio was quickly determined to be 0.123. Calibration was accomplished by comparison to radiocarbon-dated bone from Abri Pataud. The amino acid ratio was converted to an age of about 16,000 years, which proved to be in excellent agreement with cultural and geological associations. Amino acid dates have been compared to radiocarbon estimates for dozens of sites around the world, and the results seem to be quite close (Bada, Schroeder, Protsch, and Berger 1974).

But some difficulty has arisen with New World applications. For years, George F. Carter has argued from geomorphological evidence that man has been in the New World for at least 50,000 years; Carter's views sharply contradict the conventional wisdom, which holds that man had crossed the Bering Straits only about 20,000 years ago. Carter was particularly vocal about some human skeletal remains found near San Diego, California. Carter identified five bones that he thought were especially ancient, and Bada recently processed amino acid dates with the following results: 26,000 years; 6,000 years; 28,000 years; 44,000 years; and 48,000 years (Bada, Schroeder, and Carter 1974). These dates strongly support Carter's assertions of great antiquity for man in the New World; if accurate, Bada's amino acid determinations are the oldest direct dates available for New World hominids. These dates at least double the time conventionally assigned to man in the New World. But many archaeologists remain skeptical—not only about the extreme age, but about the accuracy of the new technique.

Whether the San Diego dates are upheld or not remains to be seen, and amino acid dating will never be a panacea. I recently submitted a series of bone scraps from Gatecliff Shelter to Professor Bada for aspartic acid racemization dating, but the results are not promising. Unfortunately, Gatecliff is a relatively cool site (mean annual temperature about 10° C). Because amino acid decay is a temperature-dependent process, too little racemization had taken place during the last few thousand years for satisfactory dating. Bones that have been heated also produce spurious results, so care must be taken to avoid bones that have been cooked or discarded into campfires. So far, aspartic acid dating does not approach the accuracy of radiocarbon dating, although the potential time range is over twice that of the C-14 technique. Investigations in the next decade should decide whether aspartic acid racemization lives up to its advance billing as a worthwhile method of dating archaeological bone.

RADIOCARBON DATING

Willard Libby, a physical chemist, announced to the world in 1949 that he had discovered a new physiochemical technique that would, when perfected, revolutionize absolute chronological controls in archaeology. Libby later won the Nobel Prize in chemistry for his discovery of the **radiocarbon method**. The early radiocarbon dates were limited to measurements of materials younger than about 30,000 years, but subsequent technical refinements have extended the effective range of the C-14 method to over 75,000 years (see Stuiver, Heusser, and Yang 1978).

The basic principle behind radiocarbon dating is deceptively simple. Cosmic radiation produces neutrons which enter the earth's atmosphere and react with nitrogen to produce the "heavy" carbon isotope carbon-14.

$$N^{14} + \text{neutron} = C^{14} + H$$

Carbon-14 is "heavy" because it contains fourteen neutrons in the nucleus, rather than the more common load of twelve. The extra neutrons render the nucleus unstable and subject to gradual radioactive decay. Libby calculated that it takes 5,568 years for half of the C-14 available in a sample to decay; this time span is termed the half-life of C-14. Whenever a neutron leaves a C-14 nucleus, a radioactive (beta) particle is emitted. The amount of radioactivity remaining can thus be measured by counting the number of beta emissions per gram of carbon.

$$C^{14} = B- + N^{14}+$$

With these fundamentals established, Libby could utilize radiocarbon decay as the basis for a chronometric tool. Plants and animals are known to ingest atmospheric carbon in the form of CO_2 (carbon dioxide) throughout their lives. When an organism dies, no further carbon is admitted into the body system, and that already present commences its radioactive decay. By measuring the beta emissions from the dead organism one can compute the approximate length of time since that organism's death.

Radiocarbon decay is a random process, because we never know which C-14 molecule will decay. It is an actuarial matter, like a life insurance table. It is possible to forecast next year's death rate quite accurately, although nobody can tell who will actually die; there is always a certain degree of error involved.

Over thirty-five radiocarbon determinations have been processed for Gatecliff Shelter. The procedure was fairly simple: collect the samples in the field, correlate samples with the known stratigraphy, then submit selected samples to a commercial radiocarbon laboratory. Radiocarbon dating is not cheap, current rates running about $125 and $150 per sample.

The radiocarbon lab reports a date like this:

UCLA 1926A   5,200 ± 120 radiocarbon years B.P.

This is an actual date from living floor 2 at Gatecliff. The first designation identifies the laboratory and sample: the University of California (Los Angeles) Radiocarbon Laboratory sample no. 1926A. The second part—5,200—estimates the age of the sample in *radiocarbon years* B.P., "B.P." being the abbreviation for "before present," which is arbitrarily taken to be 1950. Note also that the sample is measured in "radiocarbon years," not calendar years. As we will see, certain biases are inherent in radiocarbon dating, and the date must b corrected in order to reflect actual calendar years. The radiocarbon lab at UCLA is telling me that the age of my Gatecliff sample is about 5,200 radiocarbon years before 1950.

Note also that the date has "±120" attached to it. This is the "standard deviation" or "sigma," an estimate of the amount of error involved. Because of their statistical nature, radiocarbon dates are not precise. Some samples, like this one, have relatively small degrees of error (only ±120 years); but sometimes determinations have rather large errors—up to several hundred years—and the plus-minus factor warns the archaeologist about the degree of inaccuracy.

The standard deviation of a radiocarbon date determines the probable range in which the actual date falls. In UCLA 1926A, the figure of 5,200 radiocarbon years is an estimate of the actual age of the sample (which remains unknown). The standard deviation provides the range of estimation. Statistical theory tells us that there is a 2 in 3 (67 percent) chance that the true date falls within one "sigma." That is, by adding and subtracting 120 from the age estimate, we determine that the probability is 67 percent that the true age of UCLA 1926A falls between 5,080 and 5,320 radiocarbon years B.P. Because this is a matter of probability, we can never be absolutely certain that the true age falls into this interval, but chances are good that it does. If one wishes to be more positive, the standard deviation can be doubled; there is a 95 percent chance that the actual date falls within ±2 sigmas (why this is so is explained in Thomas 1976, Chapter 10). Thus there are 95 chances in 100 that the true age of UCLA 1926A falls within ±240 years, i.e., that is, between 4,960 and 5,440 radiocarbon years B.P.

The standard deviation estimates the consistency of the different "counting runs" performed at the laboratory. The standard deviation must never be omitted from the radiocarbon date, because without it one would have no idea how accurately the sample was actually measured. Statistical theory provides simple methods to test whether two radiocarbon determinations are the same or different (see inset). High standard deviations can be clues that something is amiss—either in the method of excavation or the laboratory analysis—and perhaps the date should be discarded.

Radiocarbon dating is based upon a number of key assumptions, perhaps the most important being that the radiocarbon level—that is, the ratio between carbon-12 and carbon-14—has remained constant in the earth's atmosphere. Libby assumed this constancy when developing the initial methods, but recent investigation has shown the assumption to be not quite true. We now know that the level of atmospheric carbon-14 has changed over the past few centuries. The first investigator to determine that the atmospheric assumption was incorrect was H. De Vries of Holland (De Vries 1958). De Vries cut several historic beams and determined the exact age of the wood by counting the tree rings. When he later radiocarbon dated the known-age specimens, De Vries found that the C-14 contrast was up to 2 percent higher than he calculated from the known age. At the time, however, scientists generally dismissed the work, since most of the errors De Vries discovered were only about 1 percent, and hence barely outside the limits of expected error. Finally, a joint investigation of the problem was conducted by laboratories in Copenhagen, Heidelberg, Cambridge, New Haven, Philadelphia, Tucson, and La Jolla. In one study, Hans

Table 6–1
Sample Size Desired for Common Archaeological Materials

Material	Weight Desired (gm)[a]	Minimum Weight
Charcoal	8–12	1
Wood	10–30	3
Shell (carbonate date)	30–100	5
Shell (conchiolin date)	500–2500	200
Bone (carbonate date)	100–500	50
Bone (collagen date, less than 5,000 years old)	200–500	100
Bone (collagen date, more than 5,000 years old)	400–1000	250
Iron (cast iron)	100–150	30
Iron (steel)		150
Iron (wrought iron)	1000–2500	500
Peat	10–25	3

[a]These refer to dry samples which possess average carbon contents.
From Michels 1973.

Suess of the University of California (La Jolla) analyzed dozens of wood specimens from the bristlecone pine tree.

Native to the western United States, some bristlecones live to be as old as 4,600 years, making them the oldest living organisms in the world. Using dead tree stumps, investigators have extended a tree-ring sequence back nearly 8,200 years by the technique discussed earlier in this chapter. By dating bristlecone wood of known age, Suess compared the true ages based upon tree-ring count with those computed by the radiocarbon method. The results indicate that significant fluctuations have occurred in atmosphere C-14 concentrations; the assumption of C-14 stability is false, and many previous radiocarbon determinations are in error. Dates younger than about 1500 B.C. seem to roughly correspond with the tree-ring data, but radiocarbon dates older than 1500 B.C. can be as much as 700 years too young. The fluctuations in carbon-14 appear to be worldwide because the earth's atmosphere is so well mixed. Once a gas is released into the atmosphere, it becomes evenly distributed throughout the entire global surface within a few years. Hence the discrepancy between tree-ring and radiocarbon ages, first noted by De Vries, must be independent of geographic origin.[2]

It is thus possible to "correct" for these errors by using a conversion table, such as that presented in Table 6–2. The Gatecliff date of 5,200 radiocarbon years converts, for example, to 4040 B.C. Note that the uncorrected date (3250

B.C.) is actually 790 years too young. Several corrected dates are available, and at this time, all "corrections" should be regarded as tentative.

Most regional sequences are unaffected by the correction factors. So long as all dating is by radiocarbon, the various subareas will remain in identical relationships, the only change being to alter the absolute dating. American cultural sequences, for example, remain intact, although all appear slightly older in absolute time. The Old World, however, is not so fortunate, because of a disparity in dating technique. In areas where writing was invented quite early, historic records provide the firm chronology, extending some 5,000 years in length. Radiocarbon dates for the Fertile Crescent and Egypt were corrected and supplemented by independent historical records. Western European chronologies, however, lacking historical evidence, were arranged strictly upon radiocarbon determinations. Over the years, Old World data have been almost universally interpreted as indicating that the early traits of civilization, such as metallurgy and monumental funerary architecture, were originally developed in the Near East, only later diffusing into the "culturally retarded" European area. The peoples of the Near East were considered the inventors and the barbaric Europeans the recipients.

The bristlecone correction changes much of that. Colin Renfrew (1971, 1973) speaks of a "second radiocarbon revolution," which has created a temporal "fault line." Most European chronologies are now placed several centuries earlier, but the classical Greek and Near Eastern chronologies remain unchanged. Stonehenge, for instance, was formerly considered to be the work of Greek craftsmen who traveled to the British Isles in 1500 B.C. Recalibration of the radiocarbon dates now indicates that Stonehenge (and the rich early bronze age of Britain) was well under way before the Mycenaean civilization of Greece had even begun. In fact, Renfrew (1973:16) now refers to Stonehenge as the world's oldest astronomical observatory. According to Renfrew, Europe can no longer be viewed as a passive recipient of cultural advances from the Mediterranean heartland. Monumental temples were built on Malta before the pyramids of Egypt. The elaborate British megalithic tombs now appear to date a full millennium prior to those in the eastern Mediterranean. It is no longer possible to believe that agriculture and metallurgy moved from Asia into Europe, and recent finds in Rumania may prove to be the earliest evidence for writing (Evans 1977). While diffusion of cultural traits remains an important process, the recalibration in some cases reverses the direction of the arrow; in other instances the whole concept of a "cradle of civilization" seems irrelevant. As Evans puts it, "If it is not yet time to write new textbooks on prehistory . . . it is time to discard the old ones" (1977:84).

The correction factors are but one example of possible sources of error in the radiocarbon method. Other potential problems include recent nuclear tests, which change atmospheric levels of radioactive materials, and the burning of fossil fuels, especially coal and petroleum products, affecting the level of atmospheric C-14.

Table 6–2
Calibration of Conventional Radiocarbon Dates (5568 Half-Life)

Radiocarbon Date		Calendar Date		Radiocarbon Date		Calendar Date	
bp	ad	AD	BP	bp	bc	BC	BP
50	1900	—	—	2050	100	95	2045
100	1850	1895, 1820	55, 130	2100	150	160	2110
150	1800	1685	265	2150*	200*	205*	2155*
200	1750	1650	300	2200*	250*	370*	2320*
250	1700	1625	325	2250	300	400	2350
300	1650	1580	370	2300	350	425	2375
350	1600	1495	455	2350	400	450	2400
400	1550	1470	480	2400*	450*	490*	2440*
450	1500	1440	510	2450*	500*	600*	2550*
500	1450	1420	530	2500*	550*	755*	2705*
550	1400	1400	550	2550	600	800	2750
600	1350	1375	575	2600	650	840	2790
650	1300	1350	600	2650	700	880	2830
700	1250	1315	635	2700	750	925	2875
750	1200	1255	695	2750	800	975	2925
800	1150	1220	730	2800	850	1030	2980
850	1100	1170	780	2850	900	1100	3050
900	1050	1070	880	2900	950	1175	3125
950	1000	1030	920	2950	1000	1250	3200
1000	950	990	960	3000	1050	1320	3270
1050	900	950	1000	3050	1100	1385	3335
1100	850	880	1070	3100	1150	1440	3390
1150	800	815	1135	3150	1200	1495	3445
1200	750	760	1190	3200	1250	1550	3500
1250	700	720	1230	3250	1300	1595	3545
1300	650	685	1265	3300	1350	1650	3600
1350	600	640	1310	3350	1400	1710	3660
1400	550	595	1355	3400	1450	1770	3720
1450	500	535	1415	3450	1500	1835	3785
1500	450	470	1480	3500	1550	1900	3850
1550	400	430	1520	3550	1600	1975	3925
1600	350	390	1560	3600	1650	2035	3985
1650	300	345	1605	3650	1700	2095	4045
1700	250	280	1670	3700	1750	2160	4110
1750	200	245	1705	3750	1800	2230	4180
1800	150	215	1735	3800	1850	2305	4255
1850	100	185	1765	3850	1900	2385	4335
1900	50ad	120AD	1830	3900	1950	2455	4405
1950	0ad	60AD	1890	3950	2000	2520	4470
2000	50bc	0AD	1950	4000	2050	2595	4545

Note: Calendar dates are rounded to the nearest 5 years.

*See supplementary table for calibration of dates in this region.

Table 6–2
Calibration of Conventional Radiocarbon Dates (5568 Half-Life) (*Continued*)

Radiocarbon Date		Calendar Date		Radiocarbon Date		Calendar Date	
bp	bc	BC	BP	bp	bc	BC	BP
4050	2100	2670	4620	5300	3350	4160	6110
4100	2150	2755	4705	5350	3400	4250	6200
4150	2200	2850	4800	5400	3450	4325	6275
4200	2250	2910	4860	5450	3500	4375	6325
4250	2300	2970	4920	5500	3550	4410	6360
4300	2350	3030	4980				
4350	2400	3095	5045	5550	3600	4450	6400
4400	2450	3175	5125	5600	3650	4485	6435
4450	2500	3245	5195	5650	3700	4520	6470
4500	2550	3310	5260	5700	3750	4555	6505
				5750	3800	4590	6540
4550	2600	3370	5320	5800	3850	4630	6580
4600	2650	3430	5380	5850	3900	4680	6630
4650	2700	3485	5435	5900	3950	4760	6710
4700	2750	3530	5480	5950	4000	4845	6795
4750	2800	3580	5530	6000	4050	4920	6870
4800	2850	3635	5585				
4850	2900	3685	5635	6050	4100	4975	6925
4900	2950	3730	5680	6100	4150	5030	6980
4950	3000	3785	5735	6150	4200	5085	7035
5000	3050	3835	5785	6200	4250	5130	7080
				6250	4300	5170	7120
5050	3100	3885	5835	6300	4350	5215	7165
5100	3150	3935	5885	6350	4400	5255	7205
5150	3200	3990	5940	6400	4450	5300	7250
5200	3250	4040	5990	6450	4500	5350	7300
5250	3300	4095	6045	6500	4550	5415	7365

Supplementary Table

Radiocarbon Date		Calendar Date(s)	Radiocarbon Date		Calendar Date(s)
bp	bc	BP	bp	bc	BP
2150	200	2155	2430	480	2510
2160	210	2165	2440	490	2530
2170	220	2175, 2270, 2285	2450	500	2550
2180	230	2190, 2250, 2305	2460	510	2565
2190	240	2230, 2315	2465	515	2575, 2620, 2655
2200	250	2320	2470	520	2585, 2605, 2665
2420	470	2480	2480	530	2680

How to Compare Two Radiocarbon Dates

This brief account demonstrates how two radiocarbon dates can be compared using the statistical theory of random errors. This description is "cookbook," in the sense that we ignore the mathematical nuances in favor of simple practicality; the reader is urged to examine the statistical theory behind these calculations in Thomas (1976, Chapter 10).

As an example, let us test the two raw radiocarbon dates cited earlier from Gatecliff Shelter:

UCLA 1926A	5200 ± 120 radiocarbon years
UCLA 1926E	5000 ± 80 radiocarbon years

The fieldnotes indicate that both samples were taken from charcoal scatters on a living floor approximately 430–440 cm. below datum. Stratigraphically, the two radiocarbon determinations should be synchronous. But the UCLA dates are 200 years apart. Is this an important difference or not?

We are really testing the hypothesis that the mean of date 1926A is equal to the mean of 1926E. Because we are dealing with samples, random variability could account for the difference. Alternatively, the samples really could be different. Statistical theory helps us decide between the two interpretations.

The student's **t-test** is appropriate in this case. We must first compute a value for t, then compare it with some fixed values, which are predetermined. The observed t is computed as follows:

$$t = \frac{\overline{X} - \overline{Y}}{S_{\overline{x}-\overline{y}}}$$

where:

$\overline{X}$ is the mean of the first sample

$\overline{Y}$ is the mean of the second sample

$S_{\overline{x}-\overline{y}}$ is the "standard error of the difference between sample means."
$S_{\overline{x}-\overline{y}}$ is computed like this:

$$S_{\overline{x}-\overline{y}} = \sqrt{S_{\overline{x}}^2 + S_{\overline{y}}^2}$$

where $S_{\overline{x}}^2$ and $S_{\overline{y}}^2$ are the "sigma" values attached to the radiocarbon date.
In the Gatecliff example:

$$S_{\overline{x}-\overline{y}} = \sqrt{120^2 + 80^2} = 144$$

So t in this case is found to be:

$$t = \frac{\overline{X} - \overline{Y}}{S_{\overline{x}-\overline{y}}} = \frac{5200 - 5000}{144} = 1.39$$

This $t = 1.39$ is the observed t value for the two radiocarbon dates. It must now be compared to theoretically predicted values of t.

$$
\begin{array}{|c|}
\hline
\text{Critical Values of } t \\
t_{.05} = \pm 1.96 \\
t_{.01} = \pm 2.58 \\
t_{.001} = \pm 3.29 \\
\hline
\end{array}
$$

These three values of t correspond to three different levels of probability: $t_{.05}$ means there is a 5 in 100 chance that your decision will be incorrect; $t_{.01}$ means there is only 1 in 100 chance you are wrong; and $t_{.001}$ indicates that only 1 in 1,000 decisions will be incorrect. There are no rules for which level one must choose; it depends on many factors, including the precision of the data, nature of the samples, and overall philosophy of the investigator. As a rule, archaeologists generally seem to stick to the 0.05 level (5 errors in 100), but there is nothing sacred about this level.

Returning to the Gatecliff example, suppose we decide to follow tradition and allow the chance of 5 errors in 100. This means that the theoretically expected value of t is $t_{.05} = \pm 1.96$. The observed t—which we computed above—must now be compared to the expected value. The rule is this:

If $t_{observed} > t_{expected}$, then the dates are probably different.

If $t_{observed} < t_{expected}$, then the dates are probably the same.

In the Gatecliff example, $t = 1.39$ is less than $t_{.05} = \pm 1.96$. Therefore we conclude that the dates are probably the same. Had t been computed to be greater than 1.96, we would have concluded that the dates are probably different.

This procedure can be used to compare any two radiocarbon dates, provided the same half-life has been used to compute them. Although I have left out the statistical details, it should be clear from examining the formula for t that the larger the standard errors—the "sigmas" attached to radiocarbon dates—the greater will be $S_{\bar{X}-\bar{Y}}$; because t is divided by $S_{\bar{X}-\bar{Y}}$, t becomes smaller as the sigmas become larger. It is common sense that the more error in the measurement, the greater chance the two dates will seem different.

This procedure rests on some rather sophisticated statistical theory (discussed in Thomas 1976, Chapter 10). But anyone can use these methods to test for differences in their radiocarbon dates. To summarize the procedure for testing:

1. Select a level of error, which then predetermines which theoretical value of t to use: $t_{.05}$ implies a willingness for one to be incorrect 5 times in every 100 tests.

2. Compute $S_{\bar{X}-\bar{Y}} = \sqrt{S_{\bar{X}}^{2} - S_{\bar{Y}}^{2}}$.

3. Compute $t = \dfrac{\overline{X} - \overline{Y}}{S_{\bar{X}-\bar{Y}}}$.

4. Compare the computed t with the expected value.

If the computed value is *larger,* then the dates are probably different.

If the computed value is *smaller,* the difference is probably due only to sampling errors, and no real difference exists between the dates themselves.

How to Compare a Radiocarbon Date to a Fixed Age

Sometimes occasions arise when a radiocarbon date must be compared to a fixed calendric age. Suppose, for example, that we had reason to suspect that Gatecliff living floor 2 (from which the previously cited dates came) actually dated to 4500 B.C. This evidence could come from other sources of dating or perhaps from dating on other sites. At any rate, how are radiocarbon dates compared to specific time periods?

First of all, we must be sure to use bristlecone-corrected dates, since the fixed ages are measured in calendric years. Let us compare the corrected date 1926A, 4020 B.C. ± 120 to the theoretical date of 4500 B.C.

The same theoretically expected values of t are used as when comparing two radiocarbon dates. Assuming a level of error at 5 in 100 (the 0.05 level), the expected value is $t_{.05} = \pm 1.96$.

Now we must compute an observed value of t comparing the radiocarbon age with the fixed age.

$$t = \frac{\text{radiocarbon age} - \text{fixed age}}{\text{sigma}}$$
$$= \frac{4020 \text{ B.C.} - 4500 \text{ B.C.}}{120}$$
$$= -4.00$$

Because $t = -4.00 > t_{.05} = \pm 1.96$, we conclude that the two ages are different: within an error of 5 in 100, living floor 2 could not be as old as 4500 B.C.

Suppose we wished to test date UCLA 1926A against the hypothesis that living floor 2 dates from 4000 B.C. The value of $t_{.05}$ remains the same, but the observed t must be recomputed:

$$t = \frac{4020 \text{ B.C.} - 4000 \text{ B.C.}}{120}$$
$$= -0.17$$

Because $t = -0.17 < t_{.05} = \pm 1.96$, we conclude that living floor 2 could easily date to 4000 B.C.

Despite the most cautious scientific controls and assumptions, the radiocarbon laboratory can date only the sample submitted to them. The onus remains upon the archaeologist to provide relevant and uncontaminated samples. Extreme care must be taken to date only undisturbed areas of sites. There is also the problem of humic acid, which, once formed in the soil, can contaminate all of the datable organics in that site. On the other hand, sometimes the humic acid itself can provide useful dates. The nature of the materials submitted for dating is likewise important: wood charcoal seems the best, followed by well-preserved wood, paper, parchment, and so forth. Particular care must also be taken to prevent contamination of samples after extraction from the site. Samples are generally placed immediately in aluminum foil or adequately labeled sterile jars. Many archaeologists (myself included) will not permit smoking on or near an excavation, lest a future C-14 sample become contaminated. These procedures help guarantee accurate laboratory assay, but the responsibility is always upon the excavator to submit only significant samples and to interpret the results in light of other clues of dating. For a more complete consideration of the methods, assumptions, and applications of radiocarbon dating see Michels (1973, Chapter 9), Ralph (1971), and Willis (1969).

POTASSIUM-ARGON DATING

Another absolute dating technique monitors the decay of potassium (K-40) into argon gas (A-40). Rather than estimating the rate of radioactive emissions (as in C-14 dating), the K-A method determines the ratio of potassium to argon particles in a rock. Since potassium decays through time, the more argon present, the older the rock. The initial datum in C-14 dating was the death of the absorbing organism, since C-14 acquisition ceases with death. The potassium-argon method is applied to rocks, so the age estimate refers to the latest significant lithological change, usually in the form of volcanism. Faul (1971), Gentner and Lippolt (1969), and Miller (1969) discuss the K-A method in more detail.

K-A dating involves assumptions not unlike those of radiocarbon analysis. There must have been no argon trapped at the time of formation, i.e., all argon must be the direct result of potassium decay and all argon must be retained in the rock structure without absorption by the atmosphere. It is known that some rocks, such as mica, tend to leak argon, so care must be taken in deciding which rock types to subject to potassium-argon dating.

The archaeological potential of potassium dating is more limited than that of radiocarbon, because the K-A time range is so great (as much as several billion years). Rarely are archaeological deposits so old. But some critically important early man sites in Africa have been successfully dated by the K-A method. At Olduvai Gorge, for example, the potassium-argon dates indicated to L. S. B. Leakey that his hominid fossils were roughly 1.75 million years old.

More recently, Glynn Isaac has discovered a mass of broken bones strewn across a twenty-foot area in the badlands of Kenya. Scattered among the bones (mostly hippopotamus) are remains of stone tools including flakes and a few pebble choppers. The site, termed KBS, is embedded in a volcanic tuff, and pumice cobbles within the tuff have been dated at 2.61 ± 0.26 million years by means of the potassium-argon techique (Isaac, Leakey, and Behrensmeyer 1971).

A BRIEF WARNING ABOUT ARGUMENTS OF RELEVANCE

We have considered several current methods of obtaining chronometric dates for archaeological sites, but one important issue has yet to be addressed. In the section on dendrochronology, for instance, I said, "It can be seen that tree-ring dating provides absolute dates for archaeological sites. . . ." This is true. But there lurks a major issue that was not discussed.

Archaeological sites can never be dated by simple equivalences. For example, a tree-ring cutting date provides the year, such as A.D. 1239, when a particular tree died. By itself, this date tells us exactly nothing about archaeology. The event actually being dated is the death of a tree, an inherently uninteresting event in itself. Trees die daily, and we are not in the business of conducting tree archaeology. The death of a tree assumes archaeological importance only when it can be argued that its death is relevant to a behavioral event of interest, such as the roofing of a pueblo room. The same argument applies to archaeology's other dating methods, which really only tell us when a clam died, or a piece of obsidian was broken, or a particular rock was heated.

In every case, the event dated must be demonstrated to be contemporaneous with a behavioral event of interest—roofing a pueblo, cooking a meal, or killing a deer (see Schiffer 1976:140–143). The demonstration of association is a key issue in archaeological dating, and the general topic of arguments of relevance will be considered in more detail in Chapter 12.

SUMMARY

Contemporary archaeologists are equipped with a powerful battery of techniques that can be used to date objects of the past. *Dendrochronology* (tree-ring dating) enables the archaeologist to establish the precise year of death for many species of trees commonly found in archaeological sites. These "cutting dates," when properly correlated with known cultural events, can often pinpoint the exact occupational history of a site. *Obsidian hydration* is a microscopic technique which measures the amount of water absorbed into the freshly broken surface of an obsidian artifact or piece of waste chippage: the older the artifact, the greater the degree of hydration. *Amino acid dating*—a relatively new and still controversial technique—measures the relative amount of decay of protein molecules within bone. *Radiocarbon dating* is a physiochemical technique which monitors the degree of radioactive emission from organic specimens. During life, all plants and animals ingest atmospheric carbon (including C-14); upon death, no more C-14 can be absorbed. Through the continuing process of radiocarbon decay, these C-14 molecules breakdown at a steadily decreasing rate. By determining the current rate of C-14 breakdown, one can estimate the length of elapsed time since the death of a plant or animal. Recently, physicists have discovered that the atmospheric level of radiocarbon has changed some-what over the last several millennia; many archaeologists now "correct" their radiocarbon dates using an absolute chronology based on radiocarbon dating of bristlecone pine samples of known age. *Potassium-argon dating,* like the radiocarbon method, monitors the rate of radioactive conversion, in this case, the conversion of potassium into argon gas trapped within geological strata. The maximum time-range of the radiocarbon method is roughly 75,000 years; potassium-argon dating can extend back several billion years.

It is important to recognize that these various dating techniques, by themselves, tell us nothing about cultural activities. Dendrochronology, for example, can only estimate when a certain tree died; obsidian hydration tells us only when a certain piece of obsidian rock was fractured. In each case, the event being dated must be demonstrated to be coeval with a behavioral (cultural) event of interest.

NOTES

1. An amusing and rather ironic sidelight to the Showlow story is that when HH39 was added to the picture, the former absolute and relative sequences were found to overlap forty-nine years. Apparently a long period of drought during the thirteenth century had formed rings so minute that they had been previously overlooked. That is, there had not been a gap at all! The data had been there since the earlier expedition to the Hopi town of Oraibi, but it took a specimen like HH39 to clarify the sequence. For a lyrical and charming personal account of the gap hunters, I highly recommend the book by Ann Axtell Morris (1933), wife of archaeologist Earl Morris and an early Southwest explorer in her own right.

2. The Egyptologists had warned Libby when C-14 was first introduced that his radiocarbon dates were in error. Libby thought that the disparity was due to experimental error. We now know that it was due to the differential production of atmospheric C-14.

7

Sorting Cultural Things in Time

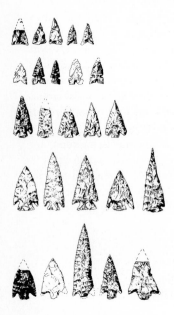

The new circumstances under which we are
placed call for new words, new phrases, and for
the transfer of old words to new objects.
Thomas Jefferson

All anthropologists recognize certain restrictions in their fieldwork. Ethnologists can work only at a single time level—now; the present ethnohistorians are restricted to written records, and linguists are restricted to studying either extant languages or the written versions of ancient languages. Archaeologists are limited to studying those cultural items that survive. Only rarely does the contemporary world get the chance to view the detail of a Pompeii. More commonly, archaeological remains are just patterned scatters of stone, bone, pottery, and dirt. Because relatively few obvious and tangible clues survive, pragmatic archaeologists have developed exacting techniques to extract the last morsel of information from their sites.

Archaeologists excavate two kinds of things: **artifacts** and **ecofacts**. Everyone knows what an artifact is—it is the obvious material remains from human activities, and, at one time, archaeology was almost totally artifact oriented. Archaeological sites were viewed as little more than mines from which to recover more (and better) artifacts. But within the last couple of decades archaeologists have come to realize that the person behind the artifact is more important than the artifact itself. Contemporary archaeology has shifted emphasis from simply obtaining things to fill museum cabinets to trying to find how people of the past actually lived. This reorientation required a shift in excavation strategy, from digging to find artifacts to a more sensitive field strategy designed to recover relevant ecological information as well. Bones, pollen grains, fish scales, seeds, and plant macrofossils are all of interest in today's ecologically aware archaeology. Lewis Binford (1964) coined the term *ecofact* to describe the nonartifactual remains contained in archaeological sites. Contemporary archaeology is largely involved with the recovery and subsequent analysis of artifacts, ecofacts, and their interrelationships.

> The path of civilization is paved with tin cans.
> *Elbert Hubbard*

TYPES OF TYPES

> Every animal leaves traces of what it was; man
> alone leaves traces of what he created.
> *Jacob Bronowski*

Archaeology's basic unit of classification is termed a **type**. Artifact types are abstract forms, ideal constructs created by the archaeologist to facilitate analysis. Instead of considering the thousands of individual specimens recovered from an excavation, the archaeologist generally abstracts his data into a few (dozen) typological categories.

Although the archaeologist excavates specimens, he analyzes types. There are many kinds of artifact types and the term *type* must never be applied without an appropriate modifier describing precisely which kind of type is being discussed. The word *type* is *naughty* when caught unmodified.

There are, of course, several ways of classifying the same set of objects. To illustrate this, consider a familiar set of modern artifacts: a workshop of woodworking tools. The carpenter classifies his tools as hammers, saws, planes, files, drills, and spokeshaves, since he is primarily concerned with tool function. But when this carpenter insures his workshop, the insurance agent would employ another set of classifications, the same tools being sorted into new categories such as "flammable" and "nonflammable." The insurance agent may also assign each tool to yet another set of classes based upon estimated value: "under $10," "between $10 and $25," and so on. Should our carpenter decide to relocate his workshop, the furniture mover will group these same tools into new divisions such as "heavy" or "light," or perhaps "fragile" and "nonfragile." The point here—and the main point of archaeological classification in general—is that each classification must be formulated with a specific purpose in mind; archaeology has no general, all-purpose classification. As Irving Rouse (1970) has cogently expressed this problem, the archaeologist must continually ask, "classification—for what?"

MORPHOLOGICAL TYPES

> Taxonomy in archaeology should be viewed as a system of working hypotheses which may be changed as the evidence warrants and opinion changes.
>
> *Walter W. Taylor*

To see how archaeologists create their types, let us return to Nels Nelson's study at the San Cristobal Pueblo in New Mexico. I stressed earlier that Nelson's method of stratigraphic excavation was an important step in the history of archaeology. But Nelson also made some important steps in classifying material culture. Nelson recovered over two thousand potsherds in his ten-foot section at San Cristobal. In Chapter 5, I just told you that he sorted these into five types, which he then plotted stratigraphically (Table 5–3). But I did not tell you how he arrived at these types (and I hope this bothered you). How did Nelson know there were five kinds of pottery at San Cristobal? Why not fifteen? Or fifty-five?

Put yourself in Nelson's boots. The date is 1914 and you are an archaeologist who has just spent several years excavating pueblo ruins throughout the American Southwest. You have no absolute dating technique at your disposal, and there is relatively little published literature for you to consult. It all really comes down to your own powers of observation.

As you approach the trash heap at San Cristobal (Figure 5–5), you are aware of certain basics about southwestern ceramics. You have seen some pottery with ornamental indentations, and you are aware that some wares are painted while others are glazed. You saw these while traveling in New Mexico and Arizona. But these are merely impressions, more perceived than explicit. You just spent three days excavating at San Cristobal, carefully peeling arbitrary one-foot sections and bagging the ceramics from each horizon. The level bags are hauled into a makeshift field laboratory, where they are washed and set out on the table. What would you do now?

What Nelson did was let his senses run free. He tried to discover what he called the "basic characteristics" (Nelson 1916:167). Nelson tried to overlook the minor variations in an effort to delimit major trends. Admitting that his procedures were "no doubt arbitrary," he sorted things out on his table. One by one, like sherds were grouped together until he had several stacks before him.

Then he assigned a name to each pile. The first stack was unpainted pottery with rough surface corrugations. A total of 649 corrugated sherds were recovered in the test excavation, and Nelson described the "leading characteristics" of the sherds as follows:

1. *Form, Size, etc.*—Normally a jar (olla), spherical body short neck, flaring rim; occasional shoe or bird-shaped pots with knobs suggesting wings and tails; bowls uncertain. Sizes range from miniature to medium, approaching large.

2. *Surface Finish*—Plain coil of primary and sometimes apparently secondary origin; indented coil (finger-nail or sharp implement being used) with occasional effort at ornamental effect. Coiling and indenting often obscured either by wear or by "wiping" during process of manufacture. Some specimens of later times show evidence of a micaceous wash.

3. *Paste Composition*—Gray colored clay, more or less tempered with coarse sand or crushed rock of crystalline nature. In early times some crushed pumice stone may have been added, while in later times micaceous substance was occasionally mixed in. Vessel walls are thin and brittle, the latter fact being due probably to constant use over the fire. (Nelson 1916:168).

> **I want observations, not agreement.**
> *Marshall McLuhan*

Moving down the line, his second stack of pottery consisted of 83 sherds of biscuit ware. This was a "peculiar kind of pottery, which can be detected even by the touch." One by one, Nelson worked his way through the stacks of pottery, until the "types" on Table 5–3 had been described and plotted.

Typology to Nelson was a matter of intuition, experience, and feel. Biscuit ware was "peculiar"; Type I pottery was "decidedly pleasing." In looking over the Type III sherds, he noted that "the new type of ceramics has gained in diversity of form and general adaptability, but it has lost not a little in decorative elegance."

Nelson's analytical procedures involved what we called the *modal concept of culture.* Establishing types at this level is merely an attempt to group like with like. Both the cultural idiolect and the cultural system are (temporarily) ignored. When Nelson stacked up his potsherds on the table, he simply focused on the most obvious aspects of the artifacts. He set aside the more complex questions of why pottery changes or how the pottery was made or what the different kinds of pottery were used for. These are important issues, but issues to be resolved at a later stage of analysis.

In more current terminology, Nelson was defining a series of *morphological* types (Steward 1954). Also called "descriptive," such types are designed to reflect the overall appearance of an artifact. Morphological types attempt to define broad generalities rather than focusing upon specific traits, simultaneously considering as many attributes as possible. Length, width, weight, material, color, shapes, and volume are just some of the attributes traditionally used to define morphological types.

> **A** weed is a plant whose virtues have not yet been discovered.
>
> *Ralph Waldo Emerson*

Because of this generality, morphological types are of limited value as end products; their primary function is descriptive, to convey the overall appearance of a set of artifacts or features. A modern observer examining the range of material remains left by extinct social groups will find many of the artifacts to be unfamiliar, often meaningless. The initial analytical step is a careful, accurate description of each artifact, grouped into morphological types. Consider, for example, one such description by Emil Haury, an eminent Southwestern archaeologist, in his site report on archaeological materials from Ventana Cave, Arizona (Haury 1950:329):

> *Discs*—Of the twenty-four stone discs, twenty-two are centrally perforated. They were all made of schist, from 36 to 74 mm. in diameter and averaging 8 mm. in thickness. The customary way of producing them was by breaking and then smoothing the rough corners by abrasion. . . . Only one was well made. . . . Drill holes are bi-conical and not always centrally placed. Two were painted red. Next to nothing is known about these discs. . . .

Even though the function and cultural context of stone discs remain uncertain, Haury illustrated and described the specimens in enough detail so that contemporary and future colleagues can visualize the artifacts without actually having to view them firsthand. The basis of initial archaeological analysis is accurate description.

Not only are morphological types basically descriptive, they are also abstract. Types are not artifacts. A type is the composite description of many artifacts, each of which is quite similar. Every morphological type encompasses a certain range of variability. Several colors may have been applied, the quality of manufacture may vary, size often fluctuates, and so forth. W. W. Taylor (1948:118) referred to this abstract quality as an *archetype,* emphasizing the rather elusive "ideal form" implicit in each morphological type.

To show how the modal concept of culture works in classification, let us return once again to Gatecliff Shelter. Remove yourself from Nelson's boots, and now pretend to be me. You have just spent six years excavating a Nevada rockshelter which turned out to be forty feet deep. How do you classify the tons of artifacts recovered? Where do you begin?

My best advice is to simplify: take one category at a time and work your way through. Archaeologists generally begin by creating morphological types as a first step, then incorporating these preliminary groups into special-purpose types. This initial sorting is often fairly informal, sometimes consisting of little more than grouping similar artifacts into piles on the laboratory table. This is precisely what Nelson did with his San Cristobal pottery in 1914, and exactly what now must be done with the Gatecliff artifacts. Do not worry about extraneous variables such as stratigraphy, time depth, cultural affiliation, or provenience. The main concern here is to reduce the complexity by creating homogeneous groupings.

Your first sort will be rather general, and it is usually conducted in the field. Potsherds can usually be separated from stone tools with little difficulty. Then the stone tools can be separated into piles: stone knives here, broken grinding slabs there, scraping tools over in the corner.

Figure 7–1 illustrates one of these preliminary piles. There are some projectile points from Gatecliff Shelter.[1] What do you do with the twenty-five projectile points? We need to form some morphological types, just as Nelson did for his San Cristobal sherds. But how many morphological types are there in Figure 7–1? Two? Six? Twenty-five?

If you are looking for a fixed rule of how many types to make, forget it. Sorting morphological types has progressed very little from the days of Nels Nelson. Morphological types, I must repeat, are merely descriptive groupings, which then must later be tested for changes in time or for specific function or for different technology. The point is this: get on with it, then be explicit about what you have done.

Look closely at Figure 7–1 and try to visualize how these twenty-five points differ from one another. If you are any kind of observer at all, you will notice that the points at the top of the page are smaller than those at the bottom. Another difference is how the points are notched for hafting to the spear or arrow shaft. Some points, such as numbers 7, 8, and 9 are notched from the side; numbers 14 and 15 are notched from the base; the points at the bottom of the page are notched from the corner; and those in the upper left-hand side are not notched at all.

You are observing what most archaeologists call **attributes**. No golden rule exists as to how many attributes to use. Use as many as seem useful. Nelson observed the kind of paint, the surface texture, and the color and pattern of the design on his San Cristobal sherds. That is, it is not which attributes you use, but how you use them. Morphological types can be created in dozens of ways—how you do it rests on your best judgment as an archaeologist. But once you have made your morphological types, you must be explicit about how you did it. In looking over the Gatecliff points in Figure 7–1, I mentioned two attributes: size and kind of notching. These two attributes, as we will see, are sufficient to create

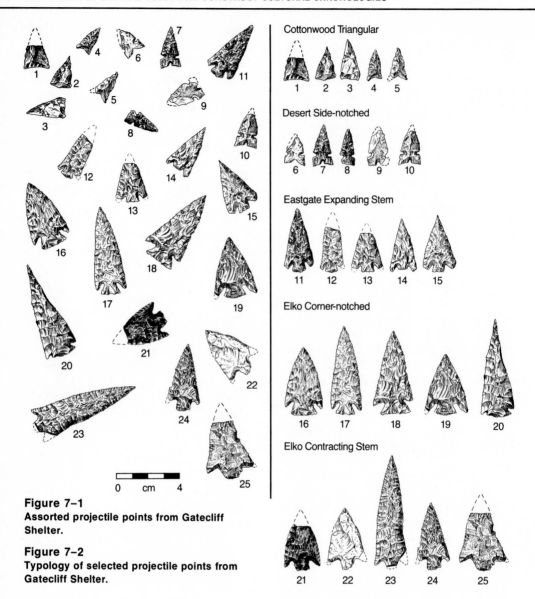

Figure 7–1
**Assorted projectile points from Gatecliff
Shelter.**

Figure 7–2
**Typology of selected projectile points from
Gatecliff Shelter.**

adequate morphological types. But it is not enough just to say "size" and "kind
of notching." I must explain precisely what I mean by the terms, so that you can
make identical observations.

Take size. We all know generally what size means, but it can be observed
in several ways. Measure the length of a projectile point and you are providing
information about its size. The width measurement also indicates size. You can
weigh the object to find its size or you could even drop it in a cup of water. The

amount of fluid displaced tells you its volume, which is still another way of measuring size. What size do you mean, anyway?

I have found weight to be a most useful measurement of projectile point size. The twenty-five Gatecliff points have been weighed, and the results appear in Table 7–1. When points are fragmentary, it is necessary to estimate what the original weight was before broken. The lightest point weighs only 0.4 grams and the heaviest (numbers 23 and 25) weigh 5.5 grams.

Table 7–1
Attributes for Gatecliff Projectile Points

Specimen Number	Weight in Grams		Proximal Shoulder Angle
	Actual	Estimated Total	
1	0.8	(0.9)	—
2	0.8	0.8	—
3	0.9	0.9	—
4	0.4	0.4	—
5	0.8	(0.9)	—
6	0.3	(0.4)	200
7	0.8	0.8	180
8	0.5	(0.6)	180
9	0.6	0.7	180
10	0.7	(0.8)	190
11	2.3	2.3	100
12	1.1	(1.5)	100
13	1.2	(1.4)	95
14	1.5	1.5	85
15	2.5	2.5	80
16	4.1	4.1	110
17	3.5	3.5	120
18	3.9	3.9	130
19	3.5	3.5	120
20	4.1	(4.2)	150
21	2.3	(2.8)	80
22	3.3	(3.4)	85
23	5.2	(5.5)	80
24	2.7	2.7	100
25	4.4	(5.5)	60

Weight is the initial attribute used in establishing the morphological types. The numbers in Table 7–1 are patterned, and, if you look closely, you will see certain natural breaks in the distributions. The following categories of projectile points seem apparent:

Small points: weight less than 1.0 gram

Medium points: weight between 1.0 and 2.5 grams

Large points: weight over 2.5 grams

Although these divisions are somewhat arbitrary, they adequately reflect categories implicit in Table 7–1. A certain amount of variability will naturally exist among projectile points, and the estimation of total weight in broken specimens introduces a certain amount of unavoidable subjective error.

But by and large, the categories are suitable. They are certainly replicable. If you visited my laboratory, you would come up with the same weights, within a small amount of measurement error. It is important that your "small points" are the same as mine.

The second attribute is notching. You will note that the only difference among the small points (those numbered 1 to 10) is that some are notched and others are not. Two categories are apparent here: small unnotched points and small side-notched points. The morphological types have been defined like this:

Cottonwood Triangular points (numbers 1–5)

Weight: less than 1.0 grams

Notching: absent

Desert Side-notched points (numbers 6–10)

Weight: less than 1.0 grams

Notching: present (from the side)

Archaeological convention dictates that the points receive first and last names. The first term generally refers to the site or region in which they were first recognized, and the second term describes some obvious morphological characteristic. "Desert Side-notched" points were named by M. A. Baumhoff and Byrne (1959). "Desert" refers to their general distribution throughout the arid West, and "side-notched" tells us what they look like. Similarly, "Cottonwood Triangular" points were first recognized at the Cottonwood Creek site in Owens Valley, California (Riddell 1951). The lack of notching makes them appear triangular. This is how we can type the smaller Gatecliff points.

Points numbered 11–15 are all medium-sized, weighing between 1.0 and 2.5 grams. The notching on these points creates a small base, or stem.

Eastgate Expanding Stem (numbers 11–15)

Weight: between 1.0 and 2.5 grams

Notching: present (generally from the base)

These points were first recognized by Heizer and Baumhoff (1961) at a small overhang near Eastgate, Nevada, about 80 miles west of Gatecliff Shelter. Once again, the first term tells us where the type was discovered, the second term is descriptive.

But we run into some trouble with the larger points. Numbers 16–25 all weigh in excess of 2.5 grams. If you look closely at Figure 7–1, you will notice that some have bases that expand, while others have bases that contract. But these are ambiguous terms, and I have found that archaeologists disagree about just what constitutes an expanding or a contracting stem. Look at point 24: I would call this stem *contracting,* but you could just as easily argue that it is *expanding.* Who is right?

Difficulties like this can be avoided with a little forethought. The stem is created by the notch, a slit added so that the point can be tied to a shaft. The edge of this notch actually forms an angle with the major axis of the point, and angles are interesting—they can be measured. Figure 7–3 shows what I mean. Draw an imaginary line along the notch of the point, then figure out the angle between that line and the cross-axis of the point. Angles such as this are easily measured using polar grid paper, within a measurement error of about ±5 degrees. I call this the **proximal shoulder angle** because it is the side of the notch nearest (most proximal) to the shaft of the tool.

The proximal shoulder angles for the ten large Gatecliff points appear in Table 7–1. Now the difference between expanding and contracting stems is apparent: points 16–20 have angles greater than about 110°, points 21–25 have angles less than 110°. The following types have been defined:

> *Elko Corner-notched points* (numbers 16–20)
>> Weight: greater than 2.5 grams
>> Proximal shoulder angle: greater than (or equal to) 110°
>
> *Elko Contracting Stem points* (numbers 21–25)
>> Weight: greater than 2.5 grams
>> Proximal shoulder angle: less than 110°

Elko points were initially recognized in Elko County, Nevada (Heizer and Baumhoff 1961). The types differ only in basal form, as described by the angle measurements.

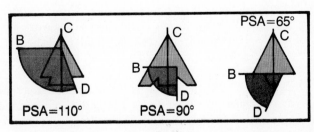

Figure 7–3
How to measure the
proximal shoulder angle
of a projectile point.

All of the twenty-five sample points have been grouped by type in Figure 7–2. I must, of course, emphasize that this example has been purposely simplified. A number of additional attributes are necessary to characterize the entire range, represented by the more than four-hundred points found at Gatecliff. But the fundamental procedures are the same, differing only in degree of complexity.

To many, these names and measurements may seem like mumbo jumbo. But this is the mumbo jumbo that archaeological facts are made of. It is a drag to memorize endless names (and archaeologists have the unfortunate tendency to overname things). Nevertheless, having five descriptive names is five times better than having to cope with twenty-five individual artifacts. And this is the function of morphological types.

> Science and taxonomy go hand in glove.
> *Edwin T. Hall*

TEMPORAL TYPES

Remember the caution under "Types of Types"? Archaeologists use the term *type* in a number of ways, and it is important to distinguish which type of type is meant. So far we have been talking strictly about morphological types, groups defined for descriptive purposes. It is now time to consider the second type of type, the temporal type. Temporal types, of course, have significance in time: they change.

To establish a set of time-markers, one first groups the individual artifacts into morphological types. The last section discussed how to do this. From this point forward, the archaeologist usually deals with abstract categories by studying the morphological types for significant temporal associations. If morphological type B is found only in strata dating between A.D. 500 and 1000, then morphological type B can be elevated to the status of a temporal type. When one finds several artifacts of temporal type B in future, undated contexts, the dates A.D. 500–1000 would be a plausible hypothesis for further investigation.

The formation of temporal types is a deductive process (see Chapter 2) because trial groupings are delimited strictly upon the basis of form (morphological types), and then these abstract groups are tested for temporal significance against independent, stratigraphic data. Temporal types can thus be formed in a manner wholly consistent with established scientific procedures.

Nels Nelson's work at San Cristobal shows how archaeologists go about defining their temporal types. Nelson, you will remember, began his typology by setting out his 2,300 sherds on a work table and sorting them into five piles. He named each category and published accurate descriptions so that other archaeologists could see how he performed his classification and use similar procedures on their own pottery.

Then Nelson examined the stratigraphic distribution of each of the five types (see Chapter 5). Two types—corrugated and biscuit ware—were found to be distributed throughout the ten-foot section. Nelson concluded that they were useless for chronological purposes and discarded them. But Types I, II, and III did change through time, and Nelson discussed their chronological significance in detail.

Procedures have changed little since 1914, but the terminology has. In the modern idiom, the five piles of potsherds were morphological types, created strictly on similarity in form. These are, in a sense, hypotheses to be tested against the stratigraphic record. Three morphological types (Types I, II, and III) passed the test. They did indeed have stratigraphic significance, and Nelson elevated them to the status of temporal types. When sherds of these three types were found in new, undated contexts, the San Cristobal stratigraphic associations suggest further hypotheses to be tested. And these hypotheses have been tested. Nelson's Type I, the early Black-on-White pottery, is now known as Santa Fe Black-on-White, and tree-ring dating suggests a temporal span from A.D. 1200 to 1350 (Breternitz 1966:95). Nelson's Types II and III (the two-color and three-color glazed pottery) are now placed in a ceramic series called Rio Grande Glaze. In general, the Rio Grande Glaze pottery begins about A.D. 1300 and the later types run into the historic period. In short, Nelson's temporal hypotheses have been wholly confirmed and refined, as one would hope after sixty years of archaeology.

The Gatecliff points work the same way. The morphological types derived in the last section are really hypotheses to be tested. Some of the types may have temporal significance, others may indicate different functions, and some may even differ between social groups. Once morphological types are formed, it is necessary to take these formal categories and test against other data available from the sites. For now, concentrate on the temporal differences.

The stratigraphy of Gatecliff Shelter was discussed earlier, in Chapter 5. At the time, I noted that the strata are stacked up in layer-cake fashion, and the law of superposition tells us that the oldest artifacts lie at the bottom, the later artifacts toward the top, with almost no mixing between the various stratigraphic units. Thus the Gatecliff deposits provide us with excellent temporal control.

Figure 7–4 plots the vertical distribution of the five morphological types defined earlier. These are the actual raw frequencies of projectile points recovered from each stratigraphic unit, and the points were classified according to the key presented above.

You will note that sharp stratigraphic differences exist at Gatecliff. Virtually all Desert Side-notched and Cottonwood Triangular points occurred in the uppermost geological unit. Similarly, every Eastgate Expanding Stem point occurred in geological unit Lower 14. From this figure alone, we can assign the following time ranges to each category.

Desert Side-notched:	post A.D. 1300
Cottonwood Triangular:	post A.D. 1300
Eastgate Expanding Stem:	A.D. 500–A.D. 1300
Elko Corner-notched:	A.D. 500–1500 B.C.
Elko Contracting Stem:	1500 B.C.–2500 B.C.

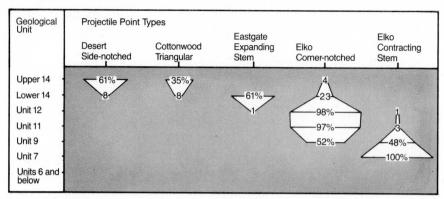

Figure 7–4
Relative proportions of selected projectile point types found at Gatecliff Shelter. Note how each stratum tends to be dominated by one or two extremely abundant time-sensitive types.

In other words, each of the five morphological categories has temporal significance. Our morphological types have become temporal types. Each time these points are found in undated contexts we now have a clue as to the time range of the deposit.

Note carefully what has happened here. The individual artifacts were initially grouped strictly on formal grounds. All that mattered for morphological types was what the artifacts look like. Then these morphological categories were tested against totally independent evidence, in this case, the Gatecliff stratigraphy and radiocarbon dates. When the categories were found to have differences in time, the morphological types were elevated to the status of temporal types. They sort in time.

But temporal types leave many important questions unanswered. In the beginning of Part Two, I stressed that archaeology can proceed with its initial objective—establishing cultural chronologies—only by making some very simplistic assumptions. Remember that the modal concept of culture focused attention on only the shared aspects of culture; the rest was temporarily ignored. Now you can see why that simplifying assumption was necessary.

Temporal types have been defined for Gatecliff Shelter according to this modal definition. Never mind (for now) what the artifacts mean—we care only if they change through time. Accordingly, some excellent temporal types have been discovered at Gatecliff.

But keep in mind that the modal concept is by itself incomplete. A great deal has been ignored in order to derive our temporal types. Although we now know that Desert Side-notched and Cottonwood Triangular points postdate A.D. 1300, much remains that we do not yet know. Why should two types exist simultaneously? Are two social groups living at Gatecliff in the post-1300 time period? Or are Desert Side-notched and Cottonwood Triangular points made by the same people and used in different ways? Perhaps the Desert Side-notched points are used for large game while Cottonwood points are for rabbits. Or could it be that the Cottonwood points are used for war arrows and left unnotched so that they cannot be pulled out once lodged? Or perhaps the difference is technological: could the Cottonwood Triangular points be unfinished, simply blanks intended to be notched later?

These guesses are really hypotheses that remain to be tested. But you should recognize that they deal with matters more complex than just time. In order to answer questions of this nature it is necessary to go beyond the restrictive modal concept of culture. Societal, technological, and functional differences are involved, and these issues require a more comprehensive, systemic approach to culture (discussed in detail in Part Three).

Temporal types are important stepping stones, and the modal concept of culture is a useful tool for deriving temporal types. But once the types have been found, it is necessary to go beyond the specifics of stratigraphy and dating techniques to view culture in its full systemic context.

SERIATION

Because there are so many duplicates of
everything, our culture can be said to be
fireproof.
Kurt Vonnegut Jr.

One upshot of the typological concept has been the technique of **seriation**. Seriation is a relative chronological method, allowing one to place stylistic periods as relatively earlier or relatively later than one another. Unlike the absolute dating techniques such as radiocarbon and dendrochronology, seriation works strictly with qualitative ordering.

The implicit assumption behind seriation is that all people are fickle in matters of style. New ideas are slow in catching on, with only a few pioneering individuals participating in the fad. But fads have a way of gaining popularity within a group and become superimposed upon earlier vogues. Since popularity is a fleeting thing, styles gradually fall into disuse (see Figure 7–5).

When one graphs the relative popularity of many fads, it becomes evident that they form a characteristic curve, and this property has been used for decades as a dating device in archaeology. One classic example of this kind of ordering was made by Sir Flinders Petrie (1899) who examined the contents of hundreds of Egyptian graves. After studying the ceramics in some detail, Petrie was able to seriate the pottery in time simply by looking at the characteristics of the handles.

To see how this works, let us return to Nelson's sherd counts from San Cristobal Pueblo (Table 5–3). When San Cristobal was initially occupied, black-on-white painting was the most common method of decorating ceramics.

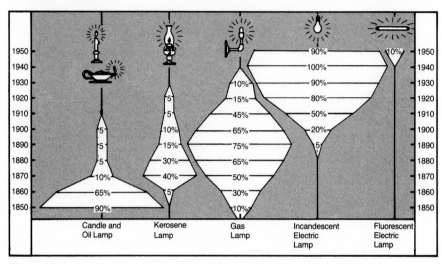

Figure 7–5
Seriation diagram showing how methods of artificial illumination change in Pennsylvania between 1850 and 1950 *(after Mayer-Oakes 1955, figure 15; courtesy of William J. Mayer-Oakes and The Carnegie Museum of Natural History).*

As one moves up in Nelson's stratigraphic column, it becomes clear that the two-color glaze rapidly takes over in popularity and black-on-white decoration fades out. Finally, near the top of the column, the three-color pottery comes into use. Even within the town trash heap the ceramic fads were preserved in the form of proportional changes.

Curves such as this have a characteristic form as styles are gradually introduced, flourish, and then slowly disappear. James Ford once characterized the popularity curve as "battleship-shaped," and its form has established the basis for the seriation technique. By arranging the proportions of temporal types into such lozenge-shaped curves, one can determine a relative chronological sequence.

Seriation has proved most useful in establishing chronological ordering in a series of discrete archaeological contexts (sites), representing several overlapping temporal periods. Such a situation is most frequently encountered with preliminary data from surface surveys, although excavated sites can be seriated as well. The seriation procedure goes like this:

1. Classify the artifacts into time-sensitive categories.
2. Compute the relative popularity of each category (percent frequency) within each assemblage.
3. Order the assemblage so that the percentages for each type tend to grade smoothly into each other, forming the types into battleship-shaped curves.

The inference is that this linear ordering is a chronological sequence. It only remains for the archaeologist to determine which end of the sequence is early and which is late, a final step based upon data external to the seriation.

> **A**bout five years ago I suddenly discovered a whole new world which wasn't even buried at all. It was all around me. It was called houses and cemeteries, and automobiles, and they're perfectly legal: you can do some pretty groovy things with hub caps and hood ornaments just as much as you can do with pre-Columbian ceramics.
> *James Deetz*

Let us now consider a hypothetical example that illustrates seriation procedures. A paleoethnographer interested in investigating cultural changes that occurred during the period of Anglo-Indian contact has discovered five historic Indian sites. If he can first order these sites in time, he can then determine the changes in group size, subsistence patterns, and material culture in general. A detailed surface survey was conducted on each site, and the surface artifacts adequately sampled. As is often the case in archaeology, only enough money is available for excavation of three of the five sites. In order to get an adequate picture of acculturative process, it is desirable to excavate sites from different time periods, so it is first necessary to order the five sites on a temporal continuum.

The most common debris in such historical sites is generally glass from broken bottles, and other household items. It is feasible, of course, to treat glass sherds in the same manner as broken pottery, namely, to create morphological types and then test for temporal significance. But by way of illustration, let us consider an alternative method of classification. In some cases—and glass is an excellent example—a single attribute is sufficient to sort the objects by time. This key attribute is called a **mode** (after Rouse 1960). Modes are particularly useful when dealing with small, badly broken artifacts such as glass. Depending on the mode, sometimes even the smallest sliver can be assigned a temporal span.

Three modes are particularly distinctive on historic glass artifacts: color, presence of pontil marks, and the method of adding the lip:

1. *Color.* Although antique bottle collectors have stripped all of the complete bottles from the sites, the surface is littered with glass sherds. These fragments seem to be of basically two colors. One kind is the crystal-clear glass common to most modern bottles, and the other kind of fragments have a distinctive purple cast. Although this glass was originally clear at the time of manufacture, exposure to sunlight has reacted with the manganese oxide in the glass to create the purple color. Since manganese was added to the molten glass

mixtures only prior to World War I, glass color can be considered a temporally significant mode.

2. *Pontil marks.* Many of the glass fragments are the bottoms of old bottles, and some have a distinctive scar known as a **pontil mark**. A pontil is a long iron rod which was formerly used to hold bottles during the finishing process. The bottle was empontilled after removal from the blowpipe so that the bottle maker could add the additional glass necessary to finish the neck. It was necessary to give the iron rod a sharp tap in order to detach the finished bottle from the iron pontil; as a result, all such bottles have a jagged scar on the outside of the bottom plate. Pontils were gradually replaced by devices called snap cases, which gripped unfinished bottles about the body rather than on the bottom. Thus, bottles made with a snap case have no pontil mark. Historic records show that snap cases were introduced in the United States during the late 1840s and had almost completely superseded the pontil by 1870 (Jones 1971). As a result, bottle bottoms lacking pontil marks found in archaeological sites can be considered post-1870, while the bottoms bearing pontil marks are generally older than about 1850–1870.

3. *Bottle seams.* During the nineteenth century, bottles were generally begun on a blowpipe and then formed in a two- or three-piece mold. At the joints, small ridges (mold marks) were left by the process of manufacture. It was then necessary to add the lip of the neck in a separate process. After about 1850, a lipping tool was used, which consisted of a plug placed into the unfinished neck and two forming arms which clamped about the outside of the neck. As the lipping tool rotated, it simultaneously smoothed the lip, removed the mold lines from the neck, and left the glass with a swirled appearance. Hence, in bottles made after about 1850, the mold marks were obliterated on the bottle neck. In 1903, a completely automated bottle machine was patented that produced bottles in a single mold. By this new process, the mold marks ran up the neck and onto the lip. The invention caught on quickly, and by 1920 the changeover was essentially complete, save for a few bottles produced by hand as novelties.

Table 7–2
Modes of Bottle Glass from Five Historic Archaeological Sites

		Modes							
	Total	Purple Glass		Pontil Mark		Seam on Lip		No Seam on Lip	
Sites	Fragments	#	%	#	%	#	%	#	%
Pete's Summit	903	452	50	181	20	90	10	271	30
Pony Canyon	462	139	30	46	10	139	30	92	20
Cold Springs	1096	658	60	548	50	—	0	438	40
Stony End	763	—	0	—	0	458	60	—	0
Cripple Creek	876	88	10	—	0	350	40	88	10

Bottle necks found with mold marks running onto the lip can thus be dated to the twentieth century (Lorrain 1968).

Through careful analysis of the glass refuse, the archaeologist can derive a chronology by seriating the collection, assuming that each historical site was adequately sampled. Had the archaeologist just poked around haphazardly, picking up only the large or brightly colored glass fragments, significant bias could easily have resulted. Table 7–2 presents the quantitative counts of glass fragments from the five sites.

The trickiest part of any seriation problem is to convert the table of percentages into the proper relative order. This means that the sites (rows) must be rearranged so that the percentages grade one into another. In effect, we are trying to create a battleship-shaped curve in each column. When only a few sites and types are involved this is a relatively easy matter. James Ford developed the

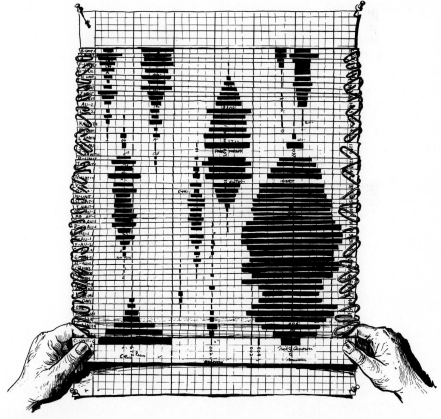

Figure 7–6
Constructing a seriation diagram literally by hand. Frequencies of types within each collection are drawn on individual slips, then moved along until the "battleship-shaped" curves become relatively smooth. Computer programs are currently available to do much of this tedious work *(after Ford 1957, figure 4; courtesy of Nicholas Amorosi).*

technique of placing individual sites on strips of paper, then moving the slips around until the best arrangement emerged (see Figure 7–6). Of course, when several sites and/or types are involved this method becomes too cumbersome, and a number of computer programs exist that can simultaneously arrange hundreds of sites and artifact types (e.g., Hole and Shaw 1967; Johnson 1968; LeBlanc 1975; Drennan 1976).

Figure 7–7 is the completed seriation diagram for the historic American Indian sites. The battleship-shaped monoliths are typical of successful seriation diagrams. One can readily see when each mode came into use, became more popular, and then trailed off in frequency as old styles were replaced by new. The relative order of sites is therefore Stony End, Cripple Creek, Pony Canyon, Pete's Summit, Cold Springs; but nothing in the seriation method tells us which end of the sequence is earlier, Stony End or Cold Springs. The archaeologist must resort to ancillary data to determine the directionality. In this case, we know that Cold Springs must be the most ancient site, in view of the high proportions of the older artifact types, especially purple glass (60 percent) and bottle necks lacking mold marks (40 percent). The graph grades from the earliest (bottom of the diagram) to the latest site, Stony End.

Using this relatively simple method of seriation, the archaeologist can obtain a serviceable sequence of these historic sites, and he can presumably make an intelligent decision regarding which sites to excavate. If he wishes to pick the earliest, the latest, and an intermediate site, he will decide upon Cold Springs, Stony End, and Pony Canyon.

It should be obvious that seriation, like the other typological tools discussed in this chapter, rests squarely on the modal definition of culture. All seriation diagrams make the implicit assumption that the observed variability is due to temporal change; that is, only the shared aspects of culture (styles) are reflected frequencies through time. Of course this assumption will be incorrect in many cases, since artifact frequencies often reflect functional, technological, and societal variability as well. When too much nontemporal variability is reflected, the collections simply do not seriate very well. But the fact that seriation diagrams do work so often indicates that the modal concept is once again useful, provided one realizes the limitations.

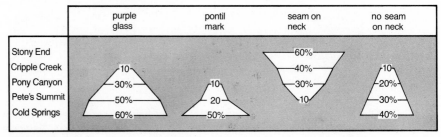

Figure 7–7
Seriation diagram for five hypothetical historical sites.

BASIC ARCHAEOLOGICAL UNITS

This chapter concludes the discussion of how archaeologists go about constructing cultural chronologies. But before moving on to the more advanced archaeological objectives we must still consider how the temporal types are synthesized into chronologies on a regional scale. In effect, temporal types are only the first building blocks which form the foundation for the regional chronology.

American archaeology has adopted a more or less standardized framework for integrating chronological information on a regional scale. This framework was set forth by Harvard archaeologists Gordon Willey and Phillip Phillips in an important book entitled *Method and Theory in American Archaeology,* published in 1958.

Although the terminology still varies somewhat from region to region, the Willey-Phillips nomenclature is the most generally accepted system in the Americas.

Returning to the temporal type, you will remember that individual artifacts are initially grouped into relative homogeneous categories, which we termed morphological types. These categories are then tested against a site's stratigraphy and internal dating. Those types that were found to change systematically were elevated to the status of temporal types.

The next analytical step is to see how the temporal types themselves cluster to reflect the overall cultural chronology of the site. The first critical unit in such supra-type synthesis is called a **component**—a culturally homogeneous stratigraphic unit within a single site. Of course "culturally homogeneous" is the catch phrase here, and the dividing line between homogeneous and heterogeneous rests on the excavator's best judgment. Many archaeological sites consist of a single component, meaning that the artifact assemblage is essentially similar throughout the entire site. Single-component sites are generally of quite short duration, so that no significant change has occurred; that is, the artifacts do not differ stratigraphically.

But most archaeological sites contain more than one discrete component. There can be no firm rules for defining archaeological components, since this definition rests on the intangible factor of "cultural homogeneity." In some sites, such as Gatecliff Shelter, the strata are obvious from the stratigraphic profile (see Figure 5–4). Distinct lenses of sterile (that is, noncultural) silt separate the deposits into distinct living floors. These living floors are then grouped together on the basis of shared time-markers, such as Desert Side-notched or Elko Eared points (as defined earlier in this chapter). Gatecliff contained five distinct cultural components, and each component was comprised of from one to six living surfaces. In other sites, such as San Cristobal, the trash heaps had been churned and mixed in the process of deposition. Components still exist, but they blend stratigraphically one into another without visible breaks. In such sites components must be isolated analytically without the obvious assistance of physical stratigraphy.

Components are thus site-specific. But the components from several sites must generally be synthesized in order to define an overall regional chronology. The next analytical step is called the **phase**, which consists of similar components as manifested at more than one site. Willey and Phillips have termed phases the "practicable and intelligible unit of archaeological study," and they define a phase as "an archaeological unit possessing traits sufficiently characteristic to distinguish it from all other units similarly conceived . . . spatially limited to the order of magnitude of a locality or region and chronologically limited to a relatively brief interval of time" (Willey and Phillips 1958:22). Like the component, the phase concept is encumbered by somewhat ambiguous terms such as "sufficiently characteristic," "similarly conceived," and "relatively brief interval." No matter how hard archaeologists try, there still remains a certain degree of subjectivity, and decisions must be based on simple familiarity with the archaeological data at hand.

> **D**espite all this progress, it is still better to be a
> smart "old" archaeologist than a dumb "new"
> archaeologist.
>
> *Kent Flannery*

Let us return to Gatecliff Shelter to see how the phase concept really works in archaeology. Table 7–3 summarizes the cultural chronology of this site. Gatecliff contained a total of five components, defined on the basis of shared time-sensitive artifact types. The uppermost component, for instance, was characterized by the presence of Desert Side-notched and Cottonwood Triangular projectile points, Shoshoni Brownware ceramics and distinctive snare trigger

Table 7–3

Provisional Cultural Chronology of Gatecliff Shelter (Based on Field Observations)

Phase Name	Time Range	Geological Units	Major Diagnostic Artifacts
Yankee Blade	A.D. 1300–historic period	Upper 14	Desert Side-notched and Cottonwood points, Promontory pegs, ceramics
Underdown	A.D. 500–A.D. 1300	Lower 14	Rose Spring and Eastgate points
Reveille			
Late	500 B.C.–A.D. 500	Upper 12	Elko Eared and Corner-notched points
Middle	1200 B.C.–500 B.C.	Lower 12	Elko Eared and Corner-notched points
Early	1500 B.C.–1200 B.C.	11	Elko Corner-notched points only
Reveille/Devils Gate transition	1600 B.C.–1500 B.C.	9	Elko Contracting Stem and Pinto points
Devils Gate	4000 B.C.–1600 B.C.	9- 7-74	Pinto points
Clipper Gap	ca. 6000 B.C.–4000 B.C.	6-74 and below	Black Rock Concave Base points

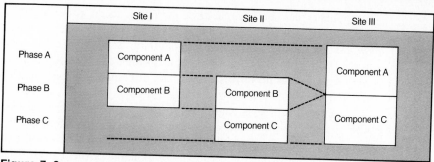

Figure 7–8
Relationships of the concepts *site, component,* and *phase.*

pins called **Promontory pegs.** This component began about A.D. 1300 and lasted until Anglo contact, about 1850. The other components are similarly defined, only using different artifact types and spanning other episodes of time.

So long as we are discussing only Gatecliff, the analytical unit remains the component. But we actually excavated nearly a dozen sites in the central Nevada area, and a number of these sites contained a late assemblage characterized by the same types found at Gatecliff. At the site level, these assemblages comprise a component; at a regional level, various similar components are synthesized into a phase, which we call Yankee Blade.

Figure 7–8 diagrams the relationship between the component and the phase. Three archaeological sites have been tested within a region, and, as is so often the case, no single site contains the entire cultural sequence. The first site has components A and B, the second site contains a new component called C. The third site in the series contains components A and C, but lacks component B. By analyzing the temporal types shared between the components it is possible to create a regional sequence of phases from these three sites.

So the component is site-specific while the phase applies to an entire region. The phase is thus archaeology's basic unit of areal synthesis, and in order to remain a viable concept the definition has been left purposely vague. Phases can be as short as a couple of generations, especially in areas where the chronology is based on painted ceramics. Phases can also span a long time period, such as the Reveille phase of central Nevada, which begins about 1500 B.C. and continues until A.D. 500. The length of the phase depends upon both the nature of the archaeological remains and our contemporary knowledge of these remains. The well-studied areas tend to have shorter phases.

In effect, the phase concept allows archaeologists to consider a continuous variable (time) as if it were a discrete set of points. The overall Gatecliff Shelter sequence lasted about 8,000 years. "Years" are a perfectly viable means of handling time, but years create difficulties in archaeological sites. It is better to consider Gatecliff as a set of five components, one stacked upon another. Each component has an array of dates and a set of characteristic artifacts. These components can be compared to components at other nearby sites and a regional chronology can be constructed. By using the phase as our smallest unit we can establish regional contemporaneity. Strictly speaking, two events are never contemporary, even if we measure time down to the nearest millimicrosecond. Time has no intrinsic units, and our smallest subdivision can always be subdivided.

But archaeology's phase concept imposes a set of minimal units on time. The phase is that minimal unit. When we discuss the Yankee Blade phase, we are considering the time span from A.D. 1300 to A.D. 1850 as if it were an instant. We are stipulating that two components of the Yankee Blade phase are simultaneous, provided that "simultaneous" is understood to last 550 years. As our knowledge of the Yankee Blade phase increases, we may be able to distinguish divisions within the phase. We might be able, for instance, to distinguish an early Yankee Blade component from a late Yankee Blade component. When this happens, our initial phases can be subdivided into subphases. This increasing subdivision is a function of the amount of research accomplished on each phase, and it underscores the real point that our knowledge of the archaeological record is a contemporary phenomenon.

SUMMARY

Archaeologists recover two kinds of things in their excavations: artifacts and ecofacts. Artifacts are the material cultural remains of human activity. At one time, archaeology was almost exclusively artifact-oriented, but within the past couple of decades, archaeology has employed more sensitive field techniques designed to recover relevant ecological information as well. The term ecofact describes the nonartifactual remains found in archaeological sites: bones, pollen grains, fish scales, seeds and plant macrofossils (analysis of ecofacts is considered in detail in Chapter 8).

The basic unit of artifact analysis is the type, an ideal construct that allows archaeologists to transcend the individual artifact and consider more generalized categories. The morphological type reflects the overall appearance of a set of artifacts, emphasizing broad similarities rather than focusing upon specific traits. Morphological types are above all descriptive, enabling the archaeologist to summarize large sets of individual artifacts into a few ideal categories.

The temporal type serves a more specific function, namely, to describe how artifact categories change through time. Temporal types are best defined through stratigraphic analysis, employing the index fossil concept (introduced in Chapter 5).

Seriation is a relative chronological method which enables the archaeologist to monitor systematic artifact change through time. Seriation operates on the implicit assumption that stylistic change tends to begin gradually, then picks up speed as the style catches on. After this peak of popularity, the frequency of the style tapers off gradually, until it ultimately disappears from the archaeological record entirely. Thus relative popularity takes on a characteristic "battleship-shaped" curve. Seriation has traditionally been accomplished by graphic means, and now several computer-assisted methods are available.

A number of basic archaeological units apply to the supra-artifact level of analysis. The archaeological component is a culturally homogeneous stratigraphic unit within a single site: components are thus site-specific. Similar components are at different sites and can be synthesized into phases which are archaeological units of internal homogeneity, limited in both time and space. In general, phases comprise the basic archaeological building-blocks for regional synthesis.

NOTE

1. I am discussing, of course, only 25 of the 400 projectile points recovered at Gatecliff.

three

Archaeology's Intermediate Objective: Reconstruct Extinct Lifeways

rchaeology is often defined as the study of
antiquities. A better definition would be that
it is the study of how men lived the past. . . .

Grahame Clark

Some of the methods, assumptions, and procedures by which archaeologists manufacture culture chronologies were presented in Part Two, considered as "Archaeology's Initial Objective." Constructing chronology is indeed one of archaeology's goals, but only the initial one. In fact, in Chapter 5, I suggested that chronology is best viewed as a stepping stone, almost as a necessary evil. Of course it is true that many archaeologists have spent their entire careers working out the nuances of one regional sequence or another. But chronology must not be allowed to become an end in itself; rather, chronology is an absolutely necessary first step in setting up more sophisticated inquiries.

What are these "more sophisticated inquiries," you might ask. Archaeologists tend to subsume the various intermediate-level reconstructions under the general rubric of **lifeway**. To an archaeologist, the term lifeway describes the multifarious aspects of human existence: population, density, settlement pattern, cultural ecology, technology, economy, social organization, kinship, legal systems, social stratification, ritual, sanctity, art. Year by year, archaeologists are expanding the horizons of what is known as lifeway.

The study of extinct lifeways—called **paleoethnography**—proceeds quite differently from the construction of cultural chronologies. One shift is in field technique. When constructing chronology, one seeks the largest, deepest, most clearly stratified site. It does not really matter where the artifacts come from within a level, so long as the mixture between the levels is minimized. In the past, many archaeological sites have been mined for time-sensitive artifacts; in these cases, horizontal provenience was simply not relevant to the temporal objectives. But in so doing, data potentially important to future problems are lost forever.

This field strategy must change when one begins to reconstruct a lifeway. Archaeologists must pay close attention to where artifacts come from within the stratigraphic units, that is, to the contexts of the artifacts. A pottery vessel containing the bones of an infant tells us something quite different from a vessel containing piñon meal.

The focus must also shift from a site orientation to a regional orientation when reconstructing past lifeways. Single sites may be sufficient to define the relevant time-markers in a region, but no isolated site can be expected to exhibit the entire range of variability operative within a region. One site might be a major ceremonial or administrative center, while others might serve as outliers, or satellite sites, subservient within the structure of the region.

Paleoethnography also requires the archaeologist to pay more attention to the nonartifactual contents of a site. The archaeologist concerned only with cultural chronology will view a fire hearth as a means of obtaining radiocarbon dates. But the fire hearth is a wealth of additional information to the paleoethnographer. Hearths often contain the remains of tiny seeds and hulls, which provide clues as to which wild or domestic crops were harvested. Burnt bones within a hearth can indicate not only which animals were eaten, but also which season the campsite was occupied. Even the structure of the charcoal itself can be important, telling the observant archaeologist where the people gathered their firewood and also something about past environments of the surrounding area.

Underlying these procedural shifts is the most critical difference between constructing chronology and reconstructing the lifeways of those now dead. At the root of the issue is one's definition of culture. When isolating temporal types one could simply follow a modal definition: culture is what people share. Styles of making projectile points and decorating ceramics change because peoples' shared conception of what is proper has changed through time. Culture, at this level, encompasses the beliefs that a society holds in common.

Contemporary archaeology transcends the shared, modal concept of culture when analyzing extinct lifeways. Cultural systems have evolved through time so that societies are equipped to adapt to their social and natural environments. It is this adaptation that comprises a society's lifeway. As we proceed through the subsequent chapters be certain to note specific instances in which the systemic conception of culture leads archaeologists to study individuals' participation in culture, rather than merely their sharing of it.

The chapters that follow in Part Three present the methods and techniques that contemporary archaeologists use to reconstruct past lifeways. As before, we will proceed largely by example, so that you can see how these techniques work in actual cases of archaeological inference. But my examples are chosen not only to illustrate techniques; they also serve to introduce the broad nature of lifeways with which archaeologists work. Although each individual case is unique, it is possible to categorize the various lifeways in terms of their relative sociopolitical complexity. Figure III–1 presents one such classification. Many of the societies listed in this figure will be taken as examples of archaeological technique and method.

In addition, the following chapters employ some key terms that define the various levels of social and political organization. These terms will be introduced here, so that the subsequent examples can be viewed in their proper evolutionary sequence (after Flannery 1972:401–404):

Bands are the simplest of human societies. Bands are **egalitarian**, integrated largely on the basis of kinship and marriage; leadership is informal and temporary; the division of labor is allotted generally by sex and age. The Great Basin Shoshoni are an excellent example of band structure, and we will have occasion to discuss the Shoshoni frequently (see Chapters 3, 8, 9, and 10).

Tribes are also egalitarian societies, but they are organized into much larger political units. Kinship is more complex and formalized than in band society, and the economy is often based on agriculture rather than foraging. The Pueblo Indians are one well-known example of tribal structure, and these groups are discussed in Chapters 8 and 10.

Chiefdoms involve a basically unequal or ranked sociopolitical organization; people are born into their cultural stations. The chief is a person of noble birth and is often held to be divine. Chiefdoms occur in the prehistoric and ethnographic American Southeast, as discussed in Chapter 10.

States are characterized by a strong and centralized government with a professional bureaucratic ruling class. The society lacks the kinship bonds evident in the less evolved political forms, and the structure is highly stratified by class. States maintain their authority through true law, and have the power to wage war, levy taxes, and draft soldiers. States generally have populations numbering (at least) in the hundreds of thousands, and the urban centers generally exhibit a high level of artistic and architectural achievement. A state religion is generally practiced, even in areas of linguistic and ethnic diversity. The Classic Maya and the Aztecs are examples of state-level organization (see Chapters 9 and 11), and the evolution of the state is considered in some detail in Chapter 13.

These four categories provide a broad evolutionary framework within which individual societies can be categorized. As the subsequent chapters unfold, you

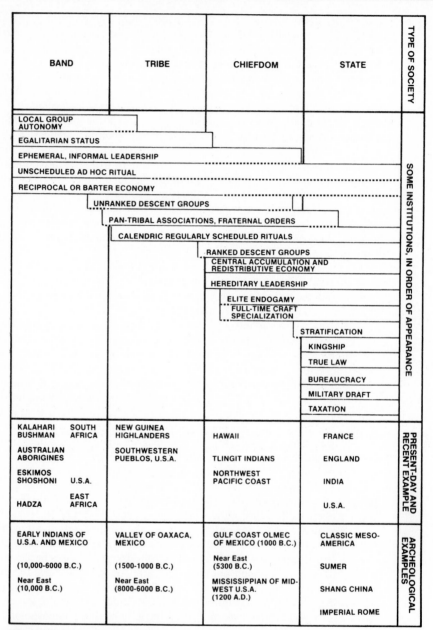

Figure III–1

Levels of sociopolitical complexity (*modified from Flannery 1972, figure 1; courtesy of Kent V. Flannery and Annual Reviews, Inc.*).

should be sure to understand into which level of sociopolitical complexity each society falls. Part Three considers how archaeologists go about reconstructing various aspects of each lifeway: subsistence, settlement pattern, social organization, religion, and ideology. Then Part Four will examine the process of evolution from simpler to more complex lifeways.

8

How People Get Their Groceries: Reconstructing Subsistence Practices

Undoubtedly the desire for food has been, and still is, one of the main causes of great political events.

Bertrand Russell

Down in the valley the little stream flowed gently southward. Pleasant groves of trees were heavy with their new burden of early summer leaves. . . . To the north, a small herd of 200 to 300 long-horned bison—cows, bulls, yearlings, and young calves—were grazing in the small valley. A gentle breeze was blowing from the south.

As the bison grazed, a party of hunters approached from the north. Quietly, under cover of the low divide to the west and the steep slope to east, the hunters began to surround the grazing herd. Moving slowly and cautiously, keeping the breeze in their faces so as not to disturb the keen-nosed animals, they closed in on the herd from the east, north and west. Escape to the south was blocked by the arroyo. Now the trap was set.

Suddenly the pastoral scene was shattered. At a signal, the hunters rose from their concealment, shouting and yelling, and waving robes to frighten the herd. Spears began to fall among the animals, and at once the bison began a wild stampede toward the south. Too late, the old cows leading the herd saw the arroyo and tried to turn back, but it was impossible. Animal after animal pressed from behind, spurred on by the shower of spears and the shouts of the Indians now in full pursuit. The bison, impeded by the calves, tried to jump the gully, but many fell short and landed in the bottom of it. Others fell kicking, twisting and turning on top of them, pressing them below even tighter into the confines of the arroyo. In a matter of seconds, the arroyo was filled to overflowing with a writhing, bellowing mass of bison, forming a living bridge over which a few animals escaped. Now the hunters moved in and began to give the coup de grace to those animals on top, while underneath, the first trapped animals kept up the bellows and groans and their struggle to free themselves, until finally the heavy burden of slain bison above crushed out their lives. In minutes the struggle was over.

One hundred ninety bison lay dead in and around the arroyo. Tons of meat awaited the knives of the hunters—meat enough for feasting, and plenty to dry for the months ahead—more meat, in fact, than they could use. Immediately, the hunters began to butcher their kill. . . . As it was cut off, some of the flesh was eaten raw, but most of the meat was laid on the skin to keep it clean. . . . Some carcasses were wedged well down in the arroyo, and these were too heavy for the hunters to move. The beautifully flaked spear points which had killed these animals went unretrieved. Wherever a leg jutted up, it was cut off, and other accessible parts were butchered; but much remained which could not be cut up.

For many days, the butchering, feasting, preparation of hides, and meat-drying went on. In time, however, the meat remaining on the carcasses became too "high" for use, and the hunters had dried as much meat as they could carry; so finally they moved on, leaving the gully filled with bones and rotting flesh . . . .

Several thousand years passed before this last remnant of the arroyo was filled. . . . By 1880, there were no bison left, and the last Indians began to be replaced by White cattlemen. In 1947, the sod was broken for planting; shortly thereafter, the combination of drought and fierce winds that marked the early 1950s began to erode away the upper deposits that had covered the gully. . . . By 1957, the bones that filled the one-time arroyo were once again exposed on the surface. (Wheat 1972:1–2).

This account was written by Joe Ben Wheat, the archaeologist who excavated the Olsen-Chubbuck site in eastern Colorado. During his excavations, Wheat studied the jumble of bones upon bones, the scanty stone tools, and the bone-dry sands and silts that formed the ancient arroyo (Figure 8–1). But Wheat was fortunate to possess the vision to look beyond the bones and rocks: to him, Olsen-Chubbuck was "a picture so complete within itself, whose action was so brief and self-contained, that, except for minor details, one could almost visualize the dust and tumult of the hunt, the joy of feasting, the satisfaction born of a

Figure 8–1
The "river of bones" found at the Olsen-Chubbuck site, Colorado (*from Wheat 1972, figure 1; courtesy of Joe Ben Wheat and the University of Colorado Museum*).

surplus of food, and finally, almost smell the stench of rotting corpses of the slain bison as the Indians left the kill scene" (Wheat 1972:2). We will be examining the Olsen-Chubbuck excavation in some detail. Not only does this site contain the remains of a remarkably well-preserved Paleo-Indian bison kill, but the efforts of Joe Ben Wheat show us a great deal about how archaeologists reconstruct extinct subsistence patterns.

Decades of anthropologists have studied the subsistence practices of both primitive and industrial peoples. The ethnologist generally focuses on mechanisms of gift and ceremonial exchange, trade and barter, forms of money and wealth, standards of living, land tenure and territoriality, population size and economic surplus. For the archaeologist, however, the study of subsistence has a more restricted meaning, generally focusing on the business of how people went about feeding themselves. To most archaeologists the study of subsistence practices quite literally means examining how people get their groceries.

Figure 8–2 shows how Richard MacNeish (1967) reconstructed the various subsistence activities in the Tehuacan Valley of Mexico, based on archaeo-

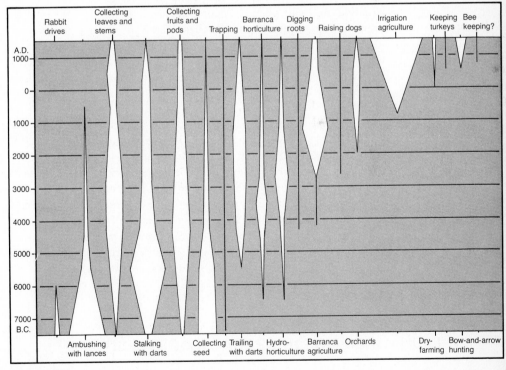

Figure 8–2
Relative importance of various subsistence activities in the Tehuacan Valley, Mexico (*after MacNeish 1967, figure 188; courtesy of Richard S. MacNeish and the University of Texas Press*).

logical excavation and analysis (see also Chapters 2 and 10). About 9,000 years ago the earliest inhabitants of the Tehuacan Valley secured their food through a variety of hunting and trapping techniques, combined with the collection of wild plant leaves, stems, fruits, pods, and seeds. Individual hunting patterns continued to change until about 4000 B.C., when hunting became a less important subsistence activity.

Figure 8–2 also indicates how plant cultivation gradually grew in importance in the Tehuacan subsistence system. People began growing hardy squash plants in the *barrancas* (steep-sided gulleys) near their cave sites as early as 6500 B.C. About this time, people also planted avocado trees and chili plants near springs, or along the flanks of the Rio Salado, where the plants received a steady year-round supply of water. These minor subsistence activities accounted for only about 2.5 percent of the total diet in 6500 B.C. But later in time this rudimentary horticulture was supplemented by full-blown *barranca* agriculture, the planting of grains such as corn and amaranth in fields, in the gulley bottoms, or on terraces where they would receive moisture from runoff during the rainy season. As agriculture became more important, the overall contribution of hunting and wild plant collecting declined. At about 800 B.C., the advent of irrigation agriculture drastically changed the subsistence pattern in the Tehuacan Valley, corresponding to increasing social and religious complexity.

How could MacNeish reconstruct these various subsistence practices from the archaeological record of the Tehuacan Valley? How did Joe Ben Wheat reconstruct the exact mode of bison hunting and butchering at the Olsen-Chubbuck site?

Archaeologists have a well-stocked arsenal of methods and techniques available for reconstructing the subsistence activities of the past. In this chapter we will discuss three of the major techniques in some detail. The Olsen-Chubbuck site provides an excellent example of **faunal analysis**, illustrating how the archaeologist studies past hunting and dietary practices. The analysis of **plant macrofossils** is rapidly becoming another important tool by which archaeologists determine what wild and domesticated plant foods were utilized in the past. Finally, we discuss **pollen analysis**, a technique by which the fossil pollen grains from archaeological sites are extracted. Not only does pollen analysis enable the archaeologist to reconstruct past vegetation, but several studies show how analysis of fossil pollen can directly contribute to the study of past dietary practices.

FAUNAL REMAINS IN ARCHAEOLOGICAL SITES

In 1957, Jerry Chubbuck, an amateur archaeologist, was driving through a ranch near Cheyenne Wells, Colorado. Chubbuck noticed an eroded area with a discontinuous outcropping of large bones protruding from the surface. Upon investigation, Chubbuck found a Paleo-Indian projectile point and an endscraper. Chubbuck wrote to Joe Ben Wheat describing his find, but Wheat was momentarily occupied on another dig and was unable to inspect the site. Meanwhile, Chubbuck also told Sigurd Olsen about the site; by an odd coincidence, Olsen had, in 1937, found the tip of another ancient spear point near the same spot. At the suggestion of curators at the Denver Museum of Natural History, Olsen and Chubbuck began to dig test pits into the site. On the basis of their test findings, Olsen and Chubbuck were convinced of the importance of their site; once again they contacted Wheat, who first visited the site in April 1958. Olsen and Chubbuck refrained from further excavation so that Wheat could field a crew from the University of Colorado Museum. The summers of 1958 and 1960 were spent excavating at the site. The site was named, incidentally, after a toss of a coin established the sequence of names.

When Wheat first visited the Olsen-Chubbuck site, a deep furrow had been plowed lengthwise through the outcropping of bones. This furrow, coupled with the pits excavated by Olsen and Chubbuck, revealed a "river of bones" lying within a filled-in gulley, or arroyo (Figure 8–1). Wheat established a baseline to the south side of the bones, then divided the baseline into two-meter sections, providing the basic units of excavation. Wheat's crew began digging the odd-numbered sections, starting from the western end of the site. In this manner they determined the margins of the site and also created profiles of the arroyo and bone bed every two meters. Once the profiles had been drawn and photographed, the even-numbered sections could be excavated, exposing the entire bone bed.

Trowels, various small knives, dental tools, and brushes were used to excavate the bones and artifacts. Shovels were used only to move backdirt and to trim the sides of the trenches. Each bone and carcass was wholly exposed in place and recorded. Wheat devised a method of **photomapping** whereby a large frame was strung with cord at regular intervals, then placed over the bones. Half of each section could be photographed at each exposure. A twelve-foot ladder-tripod was erected over the grid, and the camera was leveled before the exposure was made. The photomap from Olsen-Chubbuck is reproduced in Figure 8–3.

The major problem at Olsen-Chubbuck was, of course, how to analyze the roughly 190 bison that had been killed there. Wheat devised a series of terms to assist in the task. Completely articulated individuals (those so deep in the arroyo as to preclude butchering) were catalogued as animal units. Partially butchered skeletons were treated similarly: pelvic-girdle units, rear-leg units, front-leg units, etc. All animal units were drawn and photographed, and the associated artifacts (if any) were also photographed in situ. In addition to the animal units, over 4,000 unarticulated, disassociated bones were present at Olsen-Chubbuck.

The animals ambushed at Olsen-Chubbuck are an extinct form of bison. Modern bison is characterized by short, curving horns and is known as *Bison bison*. The animals at Olsen-Chubbuck have been identified as *Bison antiquus* (Joe Ben Wheat, personal communication). Not only does *Bison antiquus* have

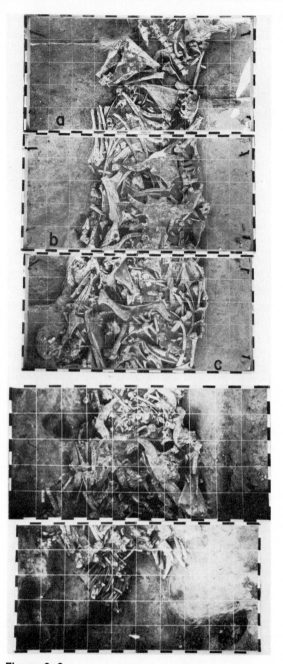

Figure 8–3
Vertical photo-map of the Olsen-Chubbuck site (*from Wheat 1972, figure 33; courtesy of Joe Ben Wheat and the University of Colorado Museum*).

nearly straight horns, but the Olsen-Chubbuck individuals average at least 25 percent larger than *B. bison.* This means that the adult males at Olsen-Chubbuck weighed about 2,250 pounds, as compared with 1,800 pounds for the modern bison bull. The females probably weighed up to 1,000 pounds.

Because the bones were meticulously plotted and catalogued, Wheat could make certain inferences regarding the herd composition at Olsen-Chubbuck. Both sexes and all ages were represented in the single bison kill. About 6 percent of the bison were juveniles; most of the young bison appeared to be a month or two old, although a couple of animals could not have been more than a few days old. Reasoning from figures for modern American bison, Wheat estimated that the kill could have occurred as early as April or as late as August, but the evidence points to a time fairly late in the calving season, probably late May or early June. Although he could not count the ones that got away, Wheat estimated that nearly all of the herd was ambushed, since 200 is near the optimal modern herd size.

Careful analysis revealed even more details about that late spring day some 10,000 years ago. Wheat's description of the bottommost animals bellowing and ultimately suffocating is supported by the physical data. The lower half of the arroyo contained skeletons of forty whole or nearly whole animals who were virtually inaccessible. Of these, fifteen had been violently twisted on or around the axis of the vertebral column. Many bison had backs broken just behind the rib cage, and the forepart of the animal rotated up to forty-five degrees. Three animals had been completely doubled up into a *U* shape, wedged against the sides of the arroyo. The herd had obviously been stampeded from north to south, based on orientations of the unbutchered carcasses.

A very limited array of cultural items was found associated with the Olsen-Chubbuck bones. As you might expect, these were artifacts directly involved in the killing and subsequent butchering of the bison: projectile points, scrapers, knives. Most striking were the two dozen beautifully flaked spearpoints found that were directly associated with the bison carcasses. Wheat used this evidence to infer that the hunters had been stationed along the path to the arroyo. Noting that projectile points were found lodged in the bodies of the lowermost animals in the arroyo, Wheat concluded that the very first animals to the arroyo had been ambushed. These animals were inaccessible to later butchers and could only have been shot as they were charged by the awaiting hunters. Spears were probably heaved at the flanks of the moving herd, striking the lead animals and coercing the herd toward the awaiting arroyo. These animals would have tumbled into the arroyo first, precisely where Wheat found them.

The Olsen-Chubbuck site is an excellent illustration of the principles behind the reconstruction of extinct lifeways and stands as a vivid counterpoint to the chronologically oriented excavations considered in Part Two.[1] We know that Joe Ben Wheat excavated Olsen-Chubbuck in order to reconstruct the lifeways of those ancient bison hunters. But suppose he had been interested only in chronology. How would his strategy have changed?

Although no contemporary archaeologist would do so, the Olsen-Chubbuck site could have been excavated for strictly chronological purposes. The scenario would go something like this. Chronological analysis is grounded in shared, modal behavior. Thus, any part of the site is as useful as any other. A trench would probably have quickly been sunk through the bones, in order to determine the stratigraphy. Then lateral trenches could be extended through the densest concentration of bone. Two aspects are important for chronology: obtain a decent sample of cultural items, and then satisfactorily date these artifacts. In effect, the site could have been mined for the projectile points, of which several were obtained. Then the bones themselves could be dated by the radiocarbon method. The results would be the statement: "Firstview projectile points date roughly 8200 ± 500 B.C." In addition, the archaeologist concerned with chronology would surely note the presence of the extinct *Bison antiquus,* the bones of which are themselves time-markers.

When one is concerned strictly with chronology, it makes little difference where the artifacts come from within a site. Nelson established the relative chronology and stratigraphy at San Cristobal by digging in arbitrary one-foot units; it mattered not at all where the individual potsherds occurred within each of the ten levels. Similarly, had Olsen-Chubbuck been excavated merely for chronology, one could have rapidly trenched the site, collecting bones for radiocarbon dating, and begun building a decent sample of cultural items.

Of course there is not a qualified contemporary archaeologist around who would approach Olsen-Chubbuck in this manner. Reconstructing aspects of extinct lifeways is *de rigueur* in today's archaeology—everyone is a paleoethnographer. I merely wish to emphasize the point that the techniques of chronology building permit certain shortcuts, in both excavation and analysis. These shortcuts—especially applying the modal concept of culture and ignoring horizontal stratigraphy—are justified only in the extremely rare case when a regional chronology is wholly unknown. In truth, a paleoethnographic strategy can (and does) encompass all of the objectives of chronology building, and yet preserves the contextual information necessary for reconstructing the details of lifeways long since past.

Recovery of Faunal Remains

Faunal materials are found in two contexts within archaeological sites. Sometimes archaeologists discover bones and shells resting precisely where they were butchered or eaten. Called **primary refuse** (Schiffer 1972), these deposits offer archaeologists an opportunity to reconstruct the sequence of events that transpired prior to the abandonment of the site. A **kill site**, such as Olsen-Chubbuck, is an excellent example of bones occurring in their primary contexts. In many cases, the butchered carcasses can be carefully exposed and mapped in situ. Analysis is facilitated in such cases because the animal units are often intact, and the archaeologists can readily infer the activities that occurred.

But primary refuse is not restricted to kill sites. Campsites, such as Gatecliff Shelter, often have trash piles or middens containing faunal materials. At Gatecliff over 60,000 animal bones (mostly bighorn sheep and rodents) were recovered; many of the bones were found precisely where the food had been prepared and the scraps discarded.

Bones also occur as **secondary refuse**, discarded away from their immediate area of use (Schiffer 1972). Although Nelson saved only the ceramics from the San Cristobal trash heap, literally hundreds of bone scraps were also present. Today's more ecologically aware archaeologist would attempt to recover and analyze these faunal materials, in addition to the ubiquitous potsherds.

The contexts of the faunal materials condition, in large measure, the recovery techniques used in excavating archaeological sites. Primary refuse is commonly mapped in place, then removed to the laboratory for further study. The isolation of **living floors** enables analysts to determine rather accurately the nature and composition of archaeological faunal assemblages.

Secondary refuse creates more difficulties. Because these consist of reworked trash heaps, the primary contexts have been destroyed. Archaeologists generally excavate secondary refuse middens by screening the debris. The matrix is often passed through a standard mesh screen, and all bones retained in the screen are bagged, labeled as to provenience, and returned to the laboratory. Of course the nature of the faunal remains dictates the appropriate mode of recovery. Thomas (1969) has shown that the mesh size of the sifter screen can markedly skew the kind of bones recovered. The standard one-quarter-inch mesh is entirely adequate when the midden contains only bones of large animals such as bighorn or bison, but significant numbers of medium-sized animals, such as rabbits and rodents, are lost through the one-quarter-inch gauge. A one-eighth-inch mesh screen is recommended whenever the faunal assemblage includes these smaller mammals. In fact, even significant amounts of small mammal bones are lost through one-eighth-inch screen. When one is concerned with recovering animals the size of, say, pack rats or small birds, a flotation method of recovery is strongly recommended (Struever 1968a; also see discussion later in this chapter). Casteel (1970, 1976a) has shown that standard methods of excavation often overlook fish bones altogether. He recommends that archaeologists dealing with fish remains should not screen their sites at all, but rather take column or core samples, which are then sorted by hand in the laboratory. It is clear that the nature of the archaeological debris must be seriously considered before selecting a method of excavation.

Analysis of Faunal Remains

Once the faunal materials have been removed from the site, the archaeologist is faced with the task of identification and analysis. Many graduate programs in archaeology offer courses in the identification of faunal remains, and a number of field archaeologists are also highly qualified in the identification of mammal, bird, mollusk, and even fish bones. In addition, there are a number of specialists who are experts in the analysis of archaeological faunas.

The identification of archaeological faunas is a complex procedure. The analyst must first assign the specimen to a particular bone of the skeleton. Is it a rib or a pelvis or a skull fragment? This requires a working knowledge of comparative anatomy. Then the specimens are identified as to taxon, the identification being as accurate as the condition of the specimen (and the expertise of the analyst) permits. In many cases, the elements are so fragmentary that they can be identified only to family or even class. Where possible, the bones are then identified by sex and age of the animal. Many departments of anthropology have assembled their own comparative faunal collections, so that archaeological specimens can be readily and routinely identified. Often, archaeologists must do a "first sort" before consulting a faunal expert to deal with the more truculent and fragmentary specimens. A number of manuals exist to assist archaeologists in the identification of bones from their sites (e.g., Cornwall 1956; Chaplin 1971; Casteel 1977; Ryder 1969; Olsen 1960, 1964, 1968).

Analysis to this point is fairly routine and really concerned only with the zoological nuances of the material recovered. But analysis beyond the mere identification stage requires a serious archaeological input. Were these bones found in primary or secondary context? Have the specimens been butchered? Or worked into tools? Has the deposit been disturbed by erosion, or predators, or by later scavenging? Questions such as these can be answered only by a careful, step-by-step consideration of the archaeological contexts.

Jumping from bones to lifeway requires a large step. How do we proceed beyond mere identification of archaeological bones? In kill sites, the procedure is straightforward. Individual animals (Wheat's "animal units") can often be recognized during excavation and are readily assigned to taxon; and they can often be sexed and aged. At sites such as Olsen-Chubbuck, one can readily determine the number of animals involved (about 190), the sex distribution (about 57 percent were female) and even the season of the kill (late May or early June).

But in habitation sites, where both primary and secondary refuse may be involved, faunal analysis is considerably more difficult. Articulated bones in such contexts are rare, and the analyst is faced with the problem of making inferences from hundreds, or more commonly, thousands, of isolated bone fragments.

The most tempting mode of analysis is simply to take the raw bone counts as an indicator of relative frequency: if one has excavated a hundred bighorn bones and only five antelope bones, then bighorn must have been twenty times more important than antelope. Unfortunately, using the number of identified specimens poses a variety of problems. First of all, one is never certain whether the various bone fragments are all independent of one another (Grayson 1973). It could well be that the one hundred bighorn bones came from a single animal, while each antelope bone came from a different individual (in that case, antelope would be five times more abundant than the bighorn). The animals may also have been butchered differently, so that some bones have been highly frag-mented (and hence have disappeared from the archaeological record) or else identifiable elements, such as teeth, become dispersed and inflate the overall count. Other investigators have used the raw weight of the identifiable bones with varying degrees of success (see Ziegler 1973; Reed 1963; and Chaplin 1971:63–70).

Because of the difficulties in using raw frequency or raw weight, archaeol-ogists have turned to another technique of comparing animal frequencies, called the *minimum number of individuals* method. Long used in paleontology, this method determines "that number of individuals which are necessary to account for all of the skeletal elements of a particular species found in the site" (Shotwell 1955:272). That is, if one has one hundred fragments of bighorn bone, what is the minimum number of individual bighorn required to account for the one hundred bones? To find out, one simply tabulates the bones by element (left femur, right tibia, hyoid . . .) to find the most common skeletal element. If four right femurs are involved in the one hundred bones, then it is clear that at least four bighorn must be represented. In this way, one can reduce large collections of bone fragments into the minimum number of individuals required to account for the bones. Refinements on the minimum individuals approach can be found in Flannery (1967:157), Ziegler (1973), and Grayson (1973).

A number of problems also arise from the use of the minimum individuals approach. When the bones are highly fragmented, it is entirely possible that the four right femurs are only represented by fragments of one whole bone. Then it is necessary to see whether or not two fragments could have come from a single animal; if so, then only a minimum of three individuals are represented. Moreover, the results depend on what one takes for a universe. In unstratified sites, some investigators have computed minumum individuals over the entire occupation. This approach has the unfortunate consequence of reducing hundreds of bone fragments to a single individual or two; this is clearly an untenable solution for sites occupied over millennia (see Heizer and Baumhoff 1961:135). Investigators often choose to calculate their minimum numbers based on stratigraphic breaks observed during excavation. But once again, the minimum number per species depend on how fine one wishes to draw the stratigraphic boundaries. As Grayson (1973) has pointed out, the minimum number of individuals is directly dependent on the size of the stratigraphic units involved. Because of this difficulty, results may not be comparable, since the minimum number has been computed in different ways. In general, the mini-mum number approach functions best when fine stratigraphic divisions are involved, containing bones that are not overly fragmented.

Objectives of Faunal Analysis

With these procedures in mind, we can turn to a brief look at the objectives and potential of faunal materials from archaeological sites. This discussion covers only the highlights, and ongoing studies will doubtless point up new directions for the analysis of faunal remains.

The Olsen-Chubbuck site was discussed in some detail at the beginning of this chapter. A major objective of the analysis was to determine the quantity of meat consumed by the Paleo-Indian hunting party. Wheat estimated that 190 bison were killed at Olsen-Chubbuck (1972:114); of these animals, about 10 percent were not butchered in any way. Over 6,000 pounds of usable meat were wasted. Taking into account the sex and age distribution of the herd, the degree of butchering, and the amount of usable meat per individual, Wheat estimated that the hunters at Olsen-Chubbuck obtained almost thirty tons of usable meat from this single kill (Wheat 1972:114). Moreover, roughly 4,400 pounds of tallow and nearly 1,000 pounds of marrow grease would have been available.

How long did this butchering take? Once again, Wheat could use well-preserved data from Olsen-Chubbuck to make a working estimate. Relying on relevant ethnographic sources, Wheat estimated that approximately 210 man-hours were required for the heavy butchering, and another fifteen hours or so for the partly butchered animals. In other words, one hundred men could have completed the butchering in about two and a half hours; or a party of ten could have butchered the entire herd in less than three days.

Some additional clues emerge from the Olsen-Chubbuck bone bed. The distribution of the hyoid bones (from near the throat) suggests that many tongues were removed—and presumably eaten—before or during the early stages of the butchering. Similarly, the distribution of the bison shoulder blades suggests that some of the animals were butchered early to get at the internal organs, the hump, and the ribs. Judging from the distribution of the ribs, these choice pieces were probably cooked immediately and consumed while the remainder of the herd was being butchered. Feasting was a common occurrence among historic Plains Indians, and the evidence suggests that a victory feast was indeed held at Olsen-Chubbuck. Wheat goes on to note that even the heftiest bull was wholly butchered. Because the neck meat from these massive animals was generally so tough as to defy chewing even when dried, he suggests that the Olsen-Chubbuck Indians must have been making pemmican, which was the only really effective way of using neck meat from bulls.

Olsen-Chubbuck is something of an ideal case, as few archaeological sites provide such clues regarding past behavior. More commonly, the archaeologist is forced to infer dietary intake from the thousands of disarticulated food bones that lie strewn about living sites. In one such study, I analyzed the food bones recovered from Smoky Creek Cave, a small site located in the high desert of northern Nevada (Thomas 1969). Here the bones represented several species, and no two bones articulated with each other. After the sample of bones had been identified to species, I tried to construct the overall food intake represented at Smoky Creek Cave. It is clear that a mouse bone represents somewhat less available meat than does an antelope bone. In order to correct for the size bias, the total raw counts of fragments were multiplied by the meat potentially

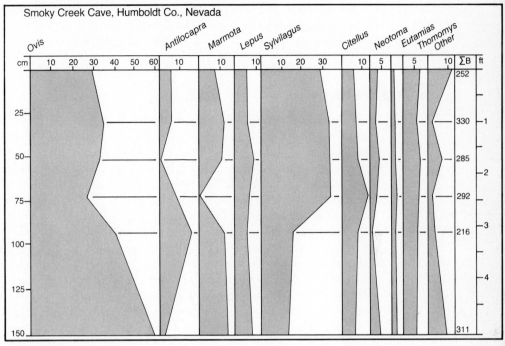

Figure 8–4
Estimates of the relative protein intake at Smoky Creek Cave, Nevada (*after Thomas 1969, figure 1*).

available from each species. Deer, for instance, are known to provide an average of 100 pounds of usable flesh per animal, while a jackrabbit contributes only about three pounds per individual. This means, of course, that one must kill over thirty rabbits in order to obtain as much meat as that available from a single deer carcass. These figures have been combined into a chart which provides a rough idea of the relative importance of food animals hunted in the Smoky Creek Cave vicinity. Figure 8–4 indicates that bighorn sheep *(Ovis)* declined in overall dietary importance during the occupation of Smoky Creek Cave, while the cottontail rabbit *(Sylvilagus)* increased markedly in significance. The bottom of the site, about 150 cm., dates about 1000 B.C. and the site was abandoned about A.D. 600, so the decrease in importance of mountain sheep seems to have occurred about A.D. 1 in this site. Whether this change is due primarily to environmental shifts or different hunting patterns remains to be determined.

You should note that Figure 8–4 differs from Wheat's (1972) estimates in an important way. At Olsen-Chubbuck, Wheat was able to deal with actual individuals (the 190 *Bison antiquus*), while the Smoky Creek Cave data are relative. When dealing with isolated bones, one has no way to tell how many individuals were involved; a single bone could represent an entire animal or only one small part, which was perhaps scavenged and brought into the cave. The

Olsen-Chubbuck estimates provide us with data about the probable number of calories consumed, while the Smoky Creek Cave estimates are only relative to one another and cannot be translated into an absolute figure.

Hunting Practices

Bones also provide clues about the hunting practices of prehistoric peoples. We already noted how much detail could be inferred from the Olsen-Chubbuck bison kill: we know that the herd numbered between 200 and 300 individuals; the prevailing breeze was probably from the south; the hunters shot at the lead animals as they led the stampede into the arroyo. Once again, Olsen-Chubbuck is an ideal case, demonstrating what archaeologists can do when the factors of preservation and luck are right.

Hunting practices can, of course, also be inferred from lesser sites. But to do so requires an added dose of ingenuity and common sense to interpret the archaeological evidence. Consider the case of the postglacial "readaptation" in the Americas. The conventional wisdom has been that the New World was initially occupied by people who survived by hunting large, now-extinct herbivores such as mammoths, mastodons, and the *Bison antiquus* found at Olsen-Chubbuck. This interpretation argues that once the climate changed and these animals became extinct (about 8000 B.C.), the human populations turned from their specialized big-game hunting economy to a broad-based hunting and gathering economy, in which the game was smaller than before. The species involved include deer, moose, caribou, even rodents, fish, and shellfish.

But many archaeologists do not accept this reconstruction. At Levi Rock Shelter in Texas, for example, most of the archaeological bones were those of small animals—coyotes, skunk, cottontail, packrat, etc.—even though mammoths and mastodon were known to have roamed nearby during the occupation of the site (Alexander 1963). Archaeologist Richard MacNeish has suggested that his colleagues may have overreacted to the dramatic image of the big-game hunter. MacNeish (1964:14) has quipped that the Paleo-Indians "probably found a mammoth once in their lifetime and never stopped talking about it—like some archaeologists."

To examine the nature of the postglacial readaptations in Middle America, Kent Flannery (1966, 1968) has identified the animal bones from Coxcatlan Rock Shelter, near Tehuacan, Mexico (see also Chapters 2 and 10). Although few extinct animals were found in the deposits, several species did occur that are no longer present in the immediate area. Flannery suggests that a shift in hunting patterns did take place in that area between 9000 and 7000 B.C., but that shift was not from big to small animals, but rather from large to small bands of hunters.

In analyzing these bones, Flannery noted some interesting correlations between animal behavior and hunting practices. Flannery observed that the remains of antelope and jackrabbit will tend to co-occur in archaeological sites because they are hunted in a similar manner. Both antelope and jackrabbit are communal animals, in the sense that they are best hunted by large groups of hunters, who drive the animals (whether jackrabbits or antelope) into specially prepared corrals or ambushes. By contrast, both deer and cottontail rabbits are more solitary animals, best hunted by stalking or ambushing by a very few individuals. The principle here is simple. When frightened, jackrabbits take flight, for they have evolved for speed. But when you frighten a cottontail rabbit, he will hole up in one of several previously prepared dens. Thus jackrabbits will herd while cottontails will not. The same principle applies to deer and antelope; one antelope is profitably hunted by large communal drives.

Flannery suggests that the terminal Pleistocene hunters of Tehuacan hunted mostly antelope and jackrabbits. To do so required large communal hunts. Between 9000 and 7000 B.C., the open, treeless steppe environment was gradually replaced by thorn-cactus-scrub forest; correspondingly, the antelope and jackrabbit gave way to the modern populations of deer and cottontails. These noncommunal animals could only be profitably hunted by small groups of men, who ambushed individual animals.

Note that Flannery makes his case *on faunal remains alone* (plus, of course, a knowledge of the behavior of modern species): this readaptation is reflected neither in the artifacts nor in the settlement pattern. Satellite activities such as communal drives leave few archaeologically visible remains, and of course ambushing a single deer would generally leave no archaeological traces. Flannery's argument—that bands were reduced in size in postglacial times—is observable only through the faunal remains.

Following Flannery's line of argument, we can make some attempts at interpreting the bone frequencies from Smoky Creek Cave (Figure 8–4). Deer are not present at this site, but bighorn sheep can be considered to be the functional analogue of deer (Thomas 1969). That is, neither animal can be profitably hunted by a communal drive, and they are best taken by a few lone hunters (see Steward 1938:37; Heizer and Baumhoff 1962:216). If this is so, we see at Smoky Creek Cave an argument for the absence of communal hunting near this site. The Smoky Creek Cave faunal assemblage is dominated by animals, namely bighorn and cottontail rabbit, that are best taken by a very small band of hunters. Those animals that are best hunted communally—antelope and jackrabbit—are conspicuously rare. This suggests that few people were necessary for efficient operation of the Smoky Creek Cave technology. The cave itself is quite small and could have supported only one or two nuclear families. It appears that the inhabitants did not engage in communal hunts of antelope or jackrabbit while living at Smoky Creek Cave, although they may have joined others for this purpose elsewhere. In this case, the faunal evidence points toward a pattern not unlike the Western Shoshoni and Paiute, for whom "it was physically impossible for families either to remain in one place for any considerable time or for more than a few families to remain in permanent association" (Steward 1938:257). Of course such inferences must be supported by evidence from elsewhere in the archaeological record, but the procedure illustrates how

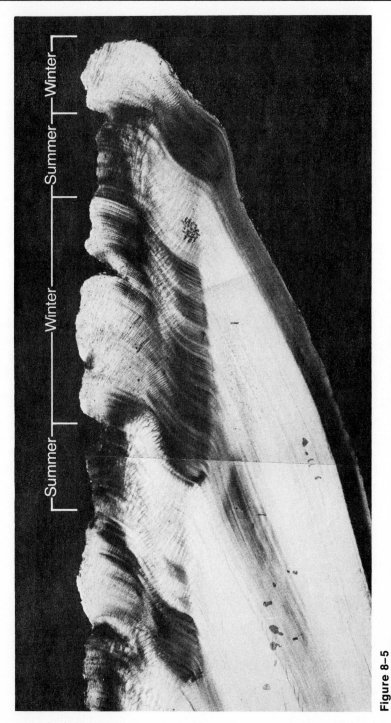

Figure 8–5
Photomicrograph of clam shell found in the Central Tomb of McLeod Mound, St. Catherines Island. Light-colored bands result from rapid winter growth and the nearly dormant summer period appears as the darker colored band. Note that growth ceased sometime during the period of winter activity, probably December or January. Other clams from this same feature have been radiocarbon dated to approximately 450 B.C. (courtesy of George R. Clark II and The American Museum of Natural History).

faunal remains can be helpful in interpreting hunting patterns and overall cultural-ecological adaptation.

Seasonality

Animal bones can also tell archaeologists when in the year the sites were occupied. Remember that Joe Ben Wheat determined that the Olsen-Chubbuck bison kill must have occurred fairly late in the calving season, probably in late May or early June. In another classic example of faunal analysis, Hildegarde Howard (1929) demonstrated the potential of such noncultural remains for reconstructing lifeways by identifying the avifauna (birds) from the Emeryville Shellmound on the San Francisco Bay. Howard identified several of the bones as cormorants, birds that nest on offshore islands in the early summer. After about a month, these nestlings move onshore, where they were killed by prehistoric hunters. Since the bones found in the mound were relatively immature birds, Howard reasoned that the prehistoric hunts must have taken place between the middle of June and the end of July. Cormorants were found throughout the midden, leading Howard to infer that the site was occupied at least during the summer months. This early example of paleoecological reconstruction has been emulated by many archaeologists in the decades since Howard's pioneering work.

Margaret Weide (1969) used a somewhat different technique to attain similar results at the Edwards Street shell midden in southern California. The most common shellfish was the Pismo clam *(Tivela stultorium).* While excavating the site, Weide noticed that the shells were remarkably uniform in size and shape; after further investigation, she discovered that such uniformity is because the clams had been harvested at the same time each year. Clams, like trees, add growth rings each year, so a careful examination of such shells can disclose when growth ceased, i.e., when the harvest took place. Weide determined that the bulk of shell collecting at the Edwards Street site must have occurred during January, although the total gathering season probably extended from late winter through early spring. It seems ironic that archaeologists are sometimes able to determine seasonality within a margin of a few weeks, and yet often cannot determine the absolute age of the site within several hundred years. It is as though we could look at a clock and see that it is exactly thirty-five minutes after the hour, but we are unable to tell whether this hour is two, three, or four o'clock.

The seasonal dating of mollusks has progressed considerably since Weide's study (see Coutts 1970, 1975; Coutts and Higham 1971; and Koike 1975). McLeod Mound on St. Catherines Island, Georgia, was discussed earlier in Chapter 5; remember that the central tomb at McLeod was covered with a thick lens of mixed oyster and clam shells. These shells were radiocarbon dated to about 450 B.C. It is also possible to determine the season of the year during which these clams were harvested. This research has been conducted by George R. Clark II, who has analyzed samples of both modern and prehistoric clams

(Mercenaria mercenaria) from St. Catherines Island. It seems that the maximum growth in this species occurs during the winter and spring months, the clams lying nearly dormant during the summer and fall (Clark 1979). But unlike the Pismo clams studied by Weide, the growth patterns of *Mercenaria* are not visible on the surface of the shell. For *Mercenaria,* it is necessary to use a diamond-bladed saw to thin-section each shell, then mount this section on a microscope slide. When so mounted, it is possible to observe the internal patterning, which appears much like a dendrochronological cross section (see Figure 8–5). Using this method, Clark determined that the shells placed in the central tomb at McLeod had been killed during the winter months, probably in December or January. In addition, the McLeod clams exhibited an unusually poor winter

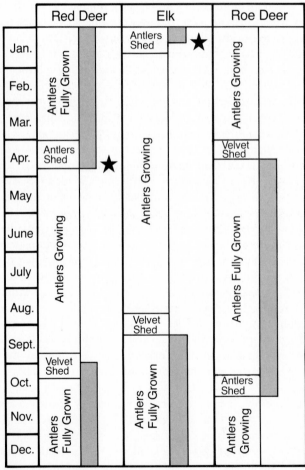

★ Indicates times at which site must have been occupied

▨ Indicates period during which animals could have been obtained

Figure 8–6
Indications of seasonality at Star Carr (*after Clark 1954, figure 5; courtesy of Cambridge University Press*).

growth during the second winter before they were harvested. The fact that all the shells exhibited the same episode of poor growth indicates that the shells were harvested in a single season, and probably on the same day.

A number of additional faunal techniques are available for seasonal dating of archaeological sites. Antlers, for instance, provided the major source of seasonal information at Star Carr, a **Mesolithic** site in northern England, occupied about 7500 B.C. (Clark 1954, 1972). The major food animals at Star Carr were roe deer, red deer, and a few elk. Red deer remains were the most abundant, and virtually every red deer stag had been killed while he still carried his antlers. Based on modern populations of red deer, we know that modern red deer carry their antlers from mid-October until late April (see Figure 8–6). Assuming that red deer of 9,500 years ago behaved similarly, it is possible to infer that Star Carr must have been occupied at least during the winter months. Additionally, a great number of shed red deer antlers were found at Star Carr; these must have been retrieved almost immediately after they had been shed, else the deer themselves would have devoured them. This piece of information means that Star Carr must have been occupied until at least early April, when red deer normally discard their antlers. The high frequency of unshed roe deer antlers also suggest an April occupation (see Figure 8–6). When the occupation began at Star Carr is a more difficult question. Nearly half of the elk stags had antlers, indicating that they were killed sometime prior to December, and perhaps as early as October.

Other studies have shown that mammal teeth also contain records of seasonal growth, and seasonality can be estimated from thin-sections of these teeth (Bourque, Morris, and Spiess 1978). Fish remains are also highly sensitive seasonal indicators, especially the vertebrae, otoliths (ear bones), and scales (Casteel 1972a, 1976b).

A note of caution is required here. Each of these techniques can tell an archaeologist only when one or more animals died. Weide's Pismo clams seem to have died in January, the *Mercenaria* in McLeod Mound also died in December or January, and some cormorants died at Emeryville in June or July. Once again, the archaeologist must be aware of the *arguments of relevance* (see the caution in Chapter 6). By itself, the death date of a clam or a deer is uninteresting to the archaeologist. In each case, the archaeologist must demonstrate that these items are somehow contemporaneous with a specific behavioral event of interest. Without the demonstration of such relevance, the seasonal dates might tell us something about clam or cormorant archaeology, but nothing about people.

PLANT MACROFOSSILS: DOWN TO SEEDS AND STEMS

One method of studying the history of vegetational fluctuations and human diet is to find actual plant parts (**macrofossils**) that have been preserved.

One common, and rather surprising, source of macrofossils in the Desert West is in the ancient nests of wood rats *(Neotama)*. Like some humans, the wood rats lived in shallow caves and rockshelters. Their nests were constructed of locally available plant materials, and because of the very small home range of the wood rat, one can infer that plants present in the midden must have come from the immediate vicinity of the nest itself. Wells and Berger (1967) have excavated and radiocarbon dated a number of fossil wood rat nests from the Nevada Test Site (scene of the recent nuclear explosions). Their study showed conclusively that the junipers, common throughout southern Nevada, grew as much as 3,000 feet below their present range within the last 12,000 years (Wells and Berger 1967, Figure 1; also see Mehringer 1977:133–134).

Archaeological sites in arid climates also provide readily available macrofossils for climatic analysis. The fill of Danger Cave (Jennings 1957; Harper and Alder 1972) and Hogup Cave, Utah (Harper and Adler 1970), was comprised almost entirely of plant seeds, hulls, and chaff. Virtually no dirt was present inside these caves, despite the fact that the deposits were deeper than ten feet. From column samples of the fill, Harper and Alder (1970, 1972) were able to reconstruct the vegetational history and climatic change in the vicinity of both Danger and Hogup caves. Particularly important over the last 10,000 years was the ubiquitous pickleweed *(Allenrolfea)*. Oddly enough, remains of piñon pine, a staple during ethnographic times, were absent from the early sediments of Danger and Hogup caves. The study indicates that present plant distributions can be potentially misleading when analyzing the cultural ecology of even the fairly recent past (see Mehringer 1977).

Unfortunately for the archaeologist, such readily available plant macrofossils are hard to come by; the Great Basin samples are preserved only because of the general aridity of the environment. In more humid climates, plant remains generally preserve only when they have been burned, and hence carbonized. The most common method of recovering such plant remains is **flotation**, a technique that has become almost standard procedure within the last decade or so.

There are several procedures for floating archaeological samples (see Watson 1976). In an early application, Struever (1968a) floated soil samples from 200 features attributable to the Middle Woodland component at the Apple Creek site, Illinois. The samples were hauled to nearby Apple Creek, where they were placed in mesh-bottomed buckets, then water-separated by students who worked midstream. Over 40,000 charred nutshell fragments, 2,000 carbonized seeds, and some 15,000 identifiable fish bones were collected in this manner. Standard dry-land excavation techniques would have missed them all.

While excavating at Salts Cave in Kentucky, Patty Jo Watson and her associates were not blessed with a nearby flowing stream, so they were required to improvise (Watson 1974). The sediments to be floated were placed in double plastic bags, then carried outside the cave. The samples (weighing a total of 1,500 pounds) were then spread in the shade to dry. Two fifty-gallon drums were filled with water, and then the dry samples were individually placed in metal buckets with their bottoms replaced by window screens. The buckets were submerged in the fifty-gallon oil drums, which had been filled with water. After a few seconds, the investigator skimmed off the charcoal and carbonized plant remains using a small scoop made from a brass carburetor screen. Both light and heavy fractions were then placed on labeled newspaper to dry once again. Sediments at Salts Cave yielded carbonized remains of hickory nuts and acorns, seeds from berries, grains, sumpweed, chenopods, maygrass, and amaranth (Yarnell 1974).

Despite the popularity of flotation, many archaeologists still seem to think that flotation is (1) too expensive or (2) too impractical for universal application. In part to counter these arguments, Kent Flannery (1976a:104–105) has described what might be the simplest flotation method yet devised:

> Gray ash and black ash are good bets for flotation samples; so is ashy brown earth with visible charcoal flecks. White ash is usually not so good, because the burning is too complete and the oxidation too strong to promote carbonization. Take as big a sample as you can. A 2-kilo sherd bag is good, but a 5-gallon wicker basket lined with newspaper is better. Let the sample dry for a week, very slowly, in the shade; if it dries in the sun, the seed coat shrinks faster than the inner seed, and it cracks.
>
> Now fill a plastic washtub with water, and add a couple of teaspoons of sodium silicate ("water glass") to each liter of water. The silicate acts as a deflocculant, to disperse the clay and bring the charcoal to the surface clean. Pour in some cupfuls of dirt from the sample, stir, and when you think all the carbon is floating, pour it off into a screen before it starts to waterlog. Be generous with the water, and pour only carbon, not mud, into your screen. When the screen is full, let it dry for a day in the shade, slowly. And *there* are your carbonized seeds.
>
> Remember, a 5-mm mesh will only stop avocado pits and corncob fragments. A 1.5-mm mesh will stop chile pepper seeds. But if you want the chenopods, amaranths, and smaller field weeds, you have to turn to carburetor mesh.

It is important to emphasize that flotation need not be an expensive or even a particularly time-consuming process. Flannery's flotation operation required only a couple of buckets and a few minutes. Flotation techniques can (and should) be fitted to the local requirements. Alternatively, Jarman, Legge, and Charles (1972) have described an elaborate power-drive machine in use at Cambridge University which separates specimens by "froth-flotation." But technology is not the issue. What is important is that for decades archaeologists meticulously saved, catalogued, and identified all scraps of bone but flatly ignored the plant remains. The resulting skewness led archaeologists to overemphasize the hunting aspects of economy and ignore the gathering component altogether. Now that flotation techniques have come into their own, archaeologists are coming to place proper emphasis on the gathering of wild and domesticated plant foods.[2]

PLANT MICROFOSSILS: POLLEN ANALYSIS

The analysis of ancient plant pollen and spores—known as **palynology**—has recently become one of archaeology's best methods for examining prehistoric ecological adaptations. Most plants shed their pollen into the atmosphere, where it is rapidly dispersed by wind action. Pollen grains are thus present in most of the earth's atmosphere, including, of course, archaeological sites. Small wonder, since a single pine branch produces as many as 350 million individual pollen grains.

While the interpretation of pollen concentrations is quite difficult, the initial steps in extracting and identifying pollen are rather simple. Pollen samples are generally taken from the sidewall of test pits or trenches, special care being taken to prevent contamination of the sample with foreign pollen. A suitable sample generally consists of a fist-sized dirt clod called a **ped**. Samples are usually taken at five- or ten-centimeter intervals to provide a continuous record of the pollen rain throughout the period of deposition at the site. Careful stratigraphic drawings are made to facilitate correlation between the pollen record and the archaeological remains. The pollen grains are isolated in the laboratory through use of acid baths and centrifuging. Microscope slides containing the fossil pollen grains are then scanned and analyzed. The standard procedure is to identify and enumerate the first 200 pollen grains encountered on each slide. These figures are converted to percentages and integrated into a pollen spectrum, indicating the proportional shift between stratigraphic levels within the site. The pollen profiles are then correlated with the known absolute and relative dates for each stratum.

The pollen diagram can be interpreted for various purposes, one of which is the reconstruction of past environments. The archaeological samples are statistically compared with the pollen rain from known extant plant communities. The ratio of tree (**arboreal**) to non-tree pollen, for example, generally indicates the degree of forestation. Pollen percentages that fluctuate through time indicate shifts in prehistoric habitats. The postglacial climatic sequence in Europe, well known from hundreds of pollen samples, contains notable fluctuations in the forest cover, as indicated by the frequencies of hazel, oak, birch, and grass pollen.

Figure 8–7 presents the major pollen diagram from Star Carr, the important Mesolithic site introduced earlier. The diagram reflects pollen frequencies which were determined from small uncontaminated samples of peats or lake muds. These samples were arranged in stratigraphic order, with the oldest at the bottom. Pollen was then extracted from each sample, and the various pollen grains identified and counted. The stratigraphic profile is divided into seven zones, with Star Carr spanning the transition from Zone IV to Zone V. Figure 8–7 expresses the pollen frequencies as percentages of the total tree pollen; note that the tree pollen frequencies are black, while the herbaceous vegetation is represented by white polygons.

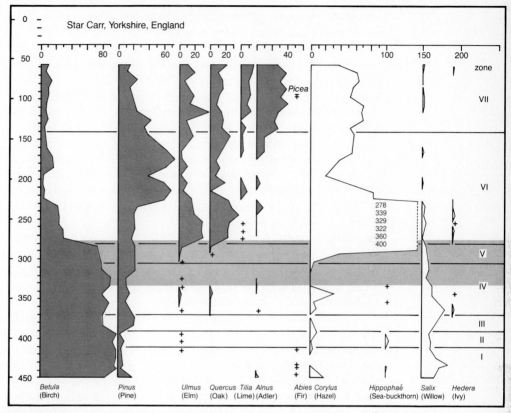

Figure 8–7
Pollen diagram from alluvial deposits near Star Carr. The occupation of the Star Carr site is denoted by the shaded horizontal band (*after Clark 1954, figure 2; courtesy of Cambridge University Press*).

Figure 8–7 is only one of several pollen profiles available from the Star Carr vicinity. These profiles, coupled with the identification of preserved plant macrofossils, enabled Clark's collaborators, D. Walker and H. Godwin, to reconstruct the ecological development of the Star Carr area (see Clark 1954:38–69). Zones I, II, and III represent the late glacial period. The vegetation was apparently a park tundra dominated by herbaceous communities, with dense stands of birch or pine trees. This vegetation lasted until the occupation of Star Carr, roughly 7500 B.C. About this time the vegetation shifted to birch and pine forest, the park tundra disappearing altogether. Note in Figure 8–7 how the increasing abundance of hazel pollen suggests a shift to woodland conditions. Pollen diagrams from nearby localities also reflect the presence of species that attest to warming climates during this time. In Zone VI, after the abandonment of Star Carr, hazel achieved dominance in the forest, and elm and oak also became more abundant. This shift reflects the transition from birch woodland to mixed oak forest. Later pollen profiles from this area document the extension of herbaceous plant communities, which were produced by human deforestation.

The pollen evidence provides a clear picture of what the Star Carr landscape must have looked like during Mesolithic times. It is particularly interesting to note that the pollen diagrams show absolutely no indication of any large-scale deforestation during the occupation of Star Carr. The abundant faunal remains indicate that while the Mesolithic people took advantage of the rich forest fauna, they left the forest itself virtually untouched.

Figure 8–8 presents another pollen diagram, this time from the Lehner site in southern Arizona (Mehringer and Haynes 1965). Excavations at Lehner in 1955 and 1956 yielded several Clovis fluted points, butchering tools, and charcoal in association with mammoth, horse, bison, and tapir remains (Haury et al. 1959). Four radiocarbon dates are available from the Lehner site, averaging about 11,200 radiocarbon years ago.

Beginning in 1962, palynologist Peter Mehringer set out to determine the nature of the environment of the early big-game hunters and their prey. Pollen analysis at Lehner is complicated by the repeated cutting and filling in prehistoric times, and it is difficult to find a single locality at Lehner that contains a continuous and unbroken pollen record.

Figure 8–8 shows the results of three different pollen profiles, each of which partially overlaps the others. Note that the form of the Lehner pollen diagram differs somewhat from that at Star Carr. The Lehner profile is obviously dominated by high frequencies of pollen from **composites** (herbs such as ragweed and sagebrush) and **cheno-am** (plants of the goosefoot family and amaranth). This dominance is common in postglacial pollen profiles of this area and creates a problem because it masks the presence of the less common (yet more ecologically sensitive) indicators. In order to counter the high frequency of composite and cheno-am pollen, Mehringer applied the technique known as the *double fixed sum* (Mehringer and Haynes 1965:19). The black profiles in Figure 8–8 are based on a standard 200-grain summary for all pollen types. That is, exactly 200 grains from each sample were counted, and then percentages computed. A total of 25 individual 200-grain samples are represented in Figure 8–8. While the dominant cheno-am and composite pollen undoubtedly represent locally occurring species, they are insufficient by themselves for interpreting regional vegetation or climate. For this reason, a second, 100-grain, count was instituted, which is represented by the hatched area in Figure 8–8. The percentages for the second count were computed by ignoring the high abundance of cheno-am and composite pollen, counting only the other, rarer pollen types. By comparing the results of both counts, one can study both gross frequencies of the dominants and also the presence of the rarer species, which are in fact most sensitive ecological indicators.

The pollen from stratigraphic units *i, j,* and *k* reflects the climatic conditions that prevailed during the mammoth-killing episode. The frequencies during this period are quite similar to modern samples collected nearby. The

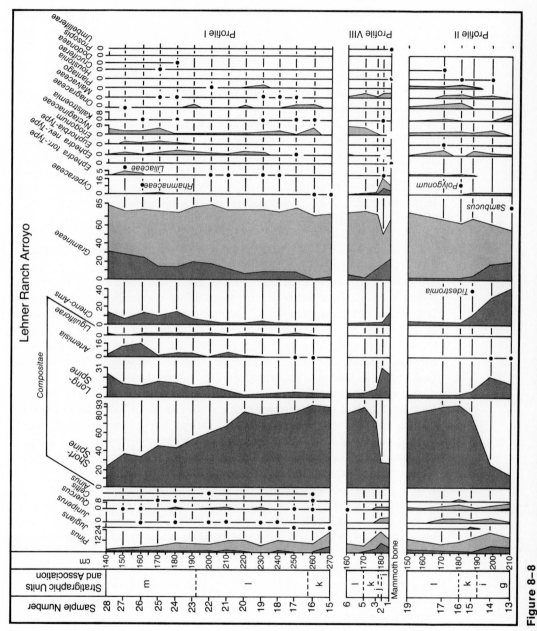

Figure 8-8
Pollen diagram from the Lehner Ranch site, Arizona (after Mehringer and Haynes 1965, figure 8; courtesy of Peter J. Mehringer).

267

slightly greater abundance of pine, oak, and juniper pollen may indicate some-what more moist or cool conditions prior to and during the deposition of the lower part of unit *k*. Somewhat later, in unit *l*, one sees a gradual shift within the composite categories. In all, the vegetation represented by the pollen spectra shown in Figure 8–8 is most probably a desert grassland, which today occupies more favored sites near the Lehner site. Mehringer and Haynes (1965:23) "do not believe that the climate at the Lehner site 11,000 years ago could have differed from the present by more than a 3- to 4-in. increase in mean annual rainfall . . . and a 3 to 4°F. decrease in mean annual temperature."

Once several pollen diagrams from an area have been analyzed and integrated, a regional sequence can be constructed. At this point, pollen analysis can even function as a relative dating technique. That is, an undated site can be placed in proper temporal sequence simply by matching the unknown pollen frequencies with the dated regional frequencies, just as in dendrochronology. In eastern Arizona, pollen analysis has even assisted in the reconstruction of the sequence of pueblo room construction (Hill and Hevly 1968). The regional pollen profile indicates that during the occupation of the Broken K pueblo, from A.D. 1100 to 1300, the relative frequency of tree pollen was decreasing. Through careful excavation, the floors of about fifty rooms were located and pollen samples taken. Samples from room floors are assumed to represent the pollen rain during site occupation. Each room was placed in temporal sequence by measuring the relative frequency of tree pollen (since earlier rooms have higher arboreal pollen counts than the later rooms). The sequence of room construction compiled in this fashion corresponded precisely with the sequence based upon architectural superposition and soil stratigraphy.

Broken K pueblo provides another application of palynology (see also Chapter 10). Hill and Hevly were able to isolate room functions through the analysis of the fossil pollen spectrum. During the excavation of the site it became clear that several different sorts of rooms were represented. Many of the rooms contained fire hearths and stone slabs for grinding corn; these were interpreted as habitation rooms, where daily activities generally occurred. A second type of room, considered to be storage facilities, was not only smaller than the habitation rooms but also lacking in the artifacts and features involved in food processing. A third type of room, markedly different from the others, was round in plan view and completely sunken below the ground surface. Both context and artifact yield convinced the excavators that these rare rooms must have been ceremonial, analogous to the modern pueblo kivas. Thus, on the basis of conventional archaeological reasoning, Hill and Hevly were able to discern three sorts of rooms: habitation, storage, and ceremonial. What did the pollen from these rooms indicate?

Pollen counts from Broken K pueblo were divided into "natural" and "economic" categories, the latter dominated by domestic maize (corn), squash, prickly pear cactus, and other edibles. The economic varieties were assumed to be largely introduced into the deposits by man, while the natural pollen was probably windblown. As expected, the economic pollen was most common in the storage rooms, since stored crops probably dropped their pollen as they were stacked in the room. Habitation and ceremonial rooms had some economic pollen grains, but in lower frequencies than the storage rooms. Two kinds of pollen, Mormon tea *(Ephedra)* and buckwheat, were particularly abundant in the ceremonial rooms. It seems likely that since both species are considered sacred by modern Hopi and Zuni Indians these species served a similar function in prehistoric ceremonies. Although this example is somewhat trivial in the sense that we already knew the room functions on the basis of other evidence, the Broken K pollen analysis provides a useful, scientifically valid method for reconstructing the nature of subsistence (and even ceremonial) activities within archaeological sites.

SUMMARY

For the archaeologist, the study of subsistence generally focuses on the way in which people go about feeding themselves. A wide variety of techniques is now available to assist the archaeologist in such subsistence reconstructions. Faunal analysis—the study of animal remains in archaeological sites—can be directed toward a number of relevant objectives. In some cases, the faunal remains provide direct evidence of which species were hunted (or collected) for food, how these animals were captured, and the butchering methods employed. Some sites can provide clues as to exactly how many animals were killed at a time, and how much meat was subsequently consumed (or wasted). Sometimes the reconstruction of hunting practices implies the presence of correlated patterns of social organization, as for example the coordinated bison hunts that occurred on the American Plains. Bones and shells can also provide data regarding seasonality, the time of year during which sites were inhabited.

Plant remains are also important sources of data regarding past subsistence practices. Macrofossils (intact plant parts) have been important not only in paleoclimatic reconstruction but also as direct evidence of which plant species were exploited, the season during which these plants were collected, and exactly how the various plant parts were cooked. Flotation is the most commonly used method for recovering plant macrofossils from archaeological sites. Plant microfossils—pollen grains and spores—are also of interest to archaeologists. Fossil pollen grains can be systematically recovered from archaeological deposits, and then used to construct a pollen diagram, which plots the changing frequency of pollen throughout the occupational history of the site. Coupled with relevant data on modern plant biogeography, the pollen diagram can enable the archaeologist to reconstruct the distribution of prehistoric plant communities and to document how these floral associations have changed through time. A regional pollen analysis can also be used as a relative dating technique. The frequencies of economic pollen types can also serve as clues to economic functions of specific intrasite areas, such as storage rooms and ceremonial areas.

NOTES

1. Of course this reconstruction relies heavily on a knowledge of the behavior of present-day bison, as well as the knowledge of how Plains Indians went about hunting bison in historic times. This is yet another instance of mid-range theory, a topic mentioned in Chapter 3 and developed in detail in Chapter 12.

2. This is particularly interesting in light of the relatively new ethnographic knowledge that plants seem to account for most of the food eaten by hunters and gatherers (see Lee and DeVore 1968, for instance). That is, many "hunters" really hunt very little.

9

Why People Live Where They Live: Reconstructing Settlement Patterns

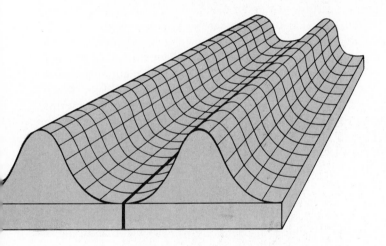

Santa Barranza! Something as common as pig tracks! Under our very noses all the time! So obvious we never stepped back to see it for what it was!

Tom Wolfe

After the doldrums of World War II, archaeological research underwent a resurgence of sorts. Many archaeologists were seeking a new direction. One group of South American archaeologists working at Columbia University observed, quite rightly, that there had never been a big dig along the Pacific coast of Peru. Although a great deal of earth had been moved in this region, most of the archaeology had been restricted to test pit excavation, designed only to provide a workable temporal-spatial framework.

Among this group was Gordon Willey, who assembled a team of archaeologists to undertake a major excavation in coastal Peru. Willey and his team finally decided that they should attempt the large-scale regional survey of one of the several valley systems that line the Peruvian coast. The Virú Valley was ultimately selected for a number of reasons: some of the Columbia faculty had previously worked there, the valley itself was relatively small and could be reasonably surveyed by a small crew, and a regional chronology already existed which could be used to date sites on the basis of surface pottery. In 1946, Willey and his team traveled to the Virú Valley to begin their big dig along the Peruvian coast.

Willey's Virú Valley Project received inspiration and guidance from a number of sources, but nobody was more important than Julian Steward, then of the Columbia University faculty. Although technically a social anthropologist, Steward had conducted a number of his own archaeological excavations in the Great Basin during the 1930s, and he maintained a keen interest in the evolution of civilizations throughout the world. As Willey firmed up his plans for the Virú Valley, Steward urged him to look beyond traditional spatial-temporal aims toward problems of more general anthropological significance. Specifically, Steward argued that Willey should be concerned with the forms, the settings, and the spatial relationships of the sites themselves, and what these relationships might imply about the societies that constructed them. As Willey put it nearly thirty years later: "Steward began to convince me that archaeology should be something more than potsherd chronicle, and his settlement pattern suggestion showed me a way in which it might be done" (Willey 1974:157). Steward's own research among the Pueblo societies of the American Southwest (Steward 1937a) had demonstrated how environmental-cultural-social relationships could be revealed in settlement distributions over the wider landscape, as well as how societal patterning could be revealed by settlement arrangements within individual communities.

The objectives of the Virú Valley Project were clearly modeled after Steward's concern with context and function: How did the different communities of the prehistoric Virú Valley interrelate and function during the various periods of human occupation? To implement this strategy, Willey defined a **settlement pattern** as

> the way in which man disposed himself over the landscape on which he lived. It refers to dwellings, to their arrangement, and to the nature and disposition of other buildings pertaining to community life. These settlements reflect the natural environment, the level of technology on which the builders operated, and the various institutions of social interaction and control which the culture maintained. Because settlement patterns are, to a large extent, directly shaped by widely held cultural needs, they offer a strategic starting point for the functional interpretation of archaeological cultures. (Willey 1953:1)

In the course of the Virú Valley survey the research team visited and collected pottery from over 300 site locations. The sites were characterized according to their inferred function into categories such as dwelling sites, pyramid mounds, cemeteries, fortifications, and so forth. The ceramic typology for the area allowed Willey to determine the time of occupation for most sites, and then the dated site types were synthesized into a series of overall community patterns. To do this, he prepared a series of valley site maps, with different symbols for the different functional classes of sites. Operating on the basis of site proximities, Willey attempted to define sustaining areas in order to determine which villages were aligned with which ceremonial center. At the conclusion of the Virú Valley monograph, Willey offered some cautious speculations regarding the meaning of settlement pattern in terms of population size and sociopolitical organization.

The Virú Valley Project stimulated a great deal of settlement pattern research during the 1950s. Willey himself edited a seminal volume entitled *Prehistoric Settlement Patterns in the New World* (Willey 1956). The overall importance of the regional approach was highlighted by the Society for American Archaeology's 1955 seminar entitled "Functional and Evolutionary Implications of Community Patterning" (Meggers 1956). This seminar marked a turning point in the history of American archaeology because it signaled archaeology's attempt to reach far beyond matters of mere chronology and typology. The focus was clearly comparative as the participants attempted to define the various kinds of community patterning by combining ethnographic and archaeological data from throughout the world. A series of community patterns were defined—such as "free wandering," "central-based wandering," and "advanced nuclear centered"—and the presentation concluded with an explicit discussion of the functional and evolutionary implications of the overall scheme (Meggers 1956:150–153).

Settlement pattern archaeology has flourished since the days of the Virú Valley Project, and major research efforts have taken place throughout the Old and New Worlds (see Chang 1968). In Mesoamerica alone, a number of significant surveys have been conducted. MacNeish directed the monumental Tehuacan Valley Project, which located 370 sites and excavated over two dozen of them (MacNeish 1964, 1978; MacNeish et al. 1972). The ambitious Teotihuacán Mapping Project has been under way since 1960, and the published results are beginning to appear (Millon 1973; Cowgill 1968). Major settlement pattern surveys have also been conducted in the Valley of Mexico (Parsons 1971; Sanders 1965), the Oaxaca Valley (Flannery 1976a; Blanton 1978), and at some major Maya ceremonial centers such as Tikal (Haviland 1965, 1970). In North America, settlement pattern surveys have now been conducted in nearly every culture area including the Northwest Coast (Dancey 1976), the Great Basin (Thomas 1973; Bettinger 1977; O'Connell 1975), the Great Plains (Zimmerman 1977; Loendorf 1973), the Midwest (Struever 1964, 1968b), and the Southeast (DePratter and Howard 1977), to name only a few.

One particularly significant development in regional archaeology has been the establishment of the Southwestern Archaeological Research Group, or

SARG (Gumerman 1971; Euler and Gumerman 1978). Recognizing the need for broad-scale planning and coordination, several top archaeologists have pooled their talents to create a "master research design" for the American Southwest. Although the actual surveys are still conducted independently, archaeologists affiliated with SARG have agreed to adopt standardized archaeological field techniques and strategies, so that their data can focus on the solution of major questions regarding regional settlement pattern and demography.

Probably the greatest change in settlement pattern archaeology has been the reliance on established sampling theory in the design of such regional surveys. The early projects such as that by Willey in the Virú Valley were conducted on a largely hit-and-miss basis: "Survey was pursued to some extent by convenience and to some extent with an eye to covering all portions of the valley, all types of terrain, and all of the functional categories which began to emerge in the course of the work" (Willey 1974:161). Modern archaeologists have since come to regard archaeological site sampling as simply a special case of the general survey sampling theory. A number of theoretical and statistical considerations are now generally applied to the issue of regional site sampling in archaeology (and some of these considerations are discussed briefly in this chapter).

In this chapter we will examine how the contemporary archaeologist conducts research on a regional scale. It is first necessary to consider the fallacy of the so-called typical site, and why archaeologists have come to rely on the regional approach. Then we will examine the Reese River Valley as an extended example to show how settlement pattern archaeology really works. The relative completeness of the archaeological record and the ample ethnographic data available for the Great Basin make Reese River an appropriate way to introduce some important sampling considerations that are involved in most regional surveys.

While emphasizing how much research has been conducted on settlement pattern archaeology, I do not wish to create the false impression that there is one single settlement pattern approach. There is not. The final portions of this chapter discuss four rather different perspectives that are currently being applied to settlement pattern problems: the *ecological determinants* approach (illustrated, once again, by the Reese River case), a *locational analysis* approach (using Classic Maya settlements as examples), a *site catchment* approach (as applied to Formative villages in Mexico), and a *biocultural* approach (illustrated by Woodland burial practices in Illinois). These four cases not only provide actual settlement pattern data from cultures of different levels of sociocultural complexity, but they also underscore the desirability of applying different theoretical perspectives to the issues of modern archaeology.

When new questions arise, methods must be
altered to allow for their solution.
                                                Lewis R. Binford

THE FALLACY OF THE "TYPICAL" SITE

Part Two discussed the explicit assumption that culture can be considered as a collection of shared beliefs: culture is what most people accept as appropriate. This definition was acceptable to archaeology only when the objectives were purely chronological. When dealing with temporal change, it was perfectly permissible—in fact, quite advantageous—to accept a purposely restricted view of cultural phenomena.

But Part Three has developed the point that the modal definition of culture is unacceptable for studying past lifeways. The "typical" can no longer be the focus of study. Instead, culture is viewed as an adaptive system, and no single representative—be it artifact, component, or site—can be taken as "typical" or "normal." Culture in this sense is not shared at all, but rather participated in (Binford 1965:205). And because this participation is differential, archaeologists pursuing the lifeways of the past must design their fieldwork to consider the full range of variability in cultural systems, rather than looking for the typical, normal, or modal.

Nowhere is contemporary archaeology's concern with cultural variability more apparent than in regional prehistory. The dangers of applying a modal perspective at this level are manifest. Take a look at Figure 9–1, which is a graphic rendering of the seasonal round of the Western Shoshoni. Ethnographer Julian Steward attempted to reconstruct, where possible, the seasonal movement of aboriginal groups, based on informant testimony collected between 1925 and 1936. A nonagricultural people, the Western Shoshoni based their subsistence on seasonally ripening plant foods, supplemented to some degree by hunting.

Look closely at the pattern for the Reese River Valley, in the northwestern portion of Figure 9–1. The numbered village sites in the Toiyabe and Shoshoni ranges are winter villages, sites established seasonally to exploit the ripening piñon nuts. Sites are also present along the Reese River, and these localities were established in the summer to exploit seeds and roots, and also to collect rabbits and occasionally hunt antelope. Other satellite sites were also established for ceremonial purposes—such as the *fandango* held each fall (see Chapter 3)—and in the upland areas to exploit berries and hunt bighorn sheep.

Figure 9–1 was constructed from informant testimony, and these informants were often recalling events that had not occurred within the past fifty years. Yet despite the large amount of information that was irretrievably lost, a staggering amount of complexity remained. Figure 9–1 demonstrates how intricate and complex a seasonal round the Western Shoshoni actually practiced.

Figure 9–1 also illustrates the *fallacy of the typical site.* Suppose an archaeologist had the opportunity to locate and excavate just one of Steward's Western Shoshoni sites. Which one would he or she choose? Winter village sites are of interest because they represent the lengthiest occupation and probably contain remains of a great variety of activities. But winter village sites are almost always

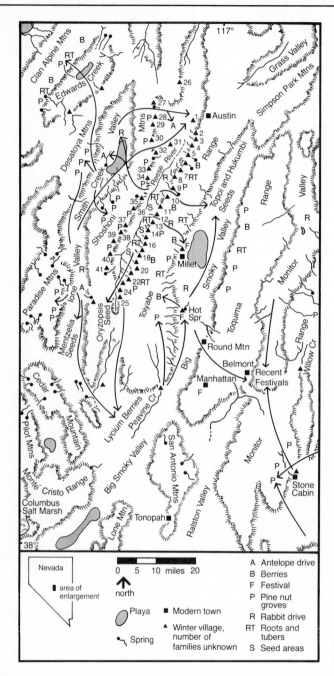

Figure 9–1
Seasonal round of the Western Shoshoni and Northern Paiute in the central Great Basin (*after Steward 1938, figure 8; courtesy of the Smithsonian Institution Press*).

located on windswept ridges, and all that is preserved are stone tools and ceramics. Perhaps one should seek out one of the small upland shelters where hunters briefly camped while pursuing bighorn sheep. The preservation in these shelters is often good, and chances are excellent of finding remains of sandals, snares, and perhaps even pieces of bows, arrows, and fire-making apparatus. But these small shelters represent only a very small portion of the overall Shoshoni pattern. Women were not present on such small hunting parties, and the men were concerned only with a limited range of activities. Or perhaps one would choose to excavate the site of a *fandango,* or a seed-gathering camp, or an antelope drive, or a women's camp established to gather lycium berries.

The difficulty is clear: no matter which site is selected, a great deal will be missed. No single Shoshoni site is sufficient to manifest the total range of cultural variability. One cannot just sample here or there, because there is no typical site.

Let us take this difficulty one step further. Suppose that archaeologist *alpha* excavated a piñon-gathering station in the Toiyabe Range. *Alpha*'s reconstruction of the lifeway might (correctly) suggest that the economy of that site was involved with harvesting piñon nuts, that the camp contained between one and two dozen people, that the men were engaged in manufacturing stone tools and repairing their weapons, and that the women spent a great deal of time preparing piñon meal and sewing skin clothes. This is all correct, so far as it goes. But now suppose that archaeologist *beta* elected to excavate the scene of a *fandango. Beta*'s reconstruction would suggest a grouping of 200 to 300 people who subsisted on communal hunting of jackrabbit and antelope and who spent a great deal of time dancing, gambling, and "living off the fat of the land."

In other words, archaeologist *alpha* would reconstruct a hardworking society comprised of small social groupings (extended families), while *beta* would see a more festive society which lived in large aggregations and was particularly concerned with rite, ritual, and feasting. Yet in truth, both sites are involved in the seasonal round of the Western Shoshoni, and neither site can be taken as typical.

This is not just a hypothetical difficulty: instances of precisely this misinterpretation have occurred in archaeological literature. Consider the case of the prehistoric Fremont and Promontory cultures of Utah.

The **Fremont culture** was initially recognized by Morss (1931) as a fairly sedentary society which subsisted mainly on maize-beans-squash horticulture. The Fremont culture flourished from about A.D. 500 to 1400 (Aikens 1966) and occurred throughout much of the state of Utah. Fremont people lived in pithouse villages and aboveground pueblos, manufactured a distinctive black-on-gray and corrugated pottery, occasionally hunted bighorn sheep and deer, and painted characteristic pictographs on cave walls. To most archaeologists, the Fremont seemed to be a northern extension of the well-established Puebloan cultures which occurred throughout the American Southwest.

The **Promontory culture** was defined by Julian Steward (1937)—yes, this is the same Steward who conducted the ethnographic fieldwork mentioned above—on the basis of excavations in the Promontory Caves, located north of Salt Lake City. Steward "guess-dated" the Promontory manifestations at about A.D. 1000. Unlike the horticultural Fremont, the Promontory people seemed to be more Plains-like, subsisting mainly by bison hunting. No signs of agriculture were found in Promontory sites, and the "pure" Promontory sites never contained architectural remains, such as pit-houses or pueblos. Promontory pottery consisted of a poorly made black plainware, and Promontory sites contained distinctive moccasins made of bison hide and several other well-made leather items such as bags, pouches, and mittens.

The distinction seemed clear. About A.D. 500, Utah was occupied by a group of Fremont horticulturalists, who exhibited obvious ties to the Puebloan peoples of the American Southwest. Then, about A.D. 1000, these agricultural peoples were displaced by the bison-hunting, cave-dwelling Promontory peoples, who had probably moved out from the Great Plains. Not only were the economies quite different, but so was the pottery, the architecture, the settlement pattern, and indeed most of the artifact inventory.

A great deal of archaeological evidence has been assembled since the 1930s regarding the Fremont and Promontory cultures, and this evidence renders the traditional model untenable. Of primary importance is Fremont-Promontory chronology. Excavations by Aikens (1966) have shown Fremont and Promontory pottery, once thought to be distinct, to be in "complete association" in a number of sites. Moreover, radiocarbon dates seem to show that Fremont and Promontory materials existed together for a considerable span of time in northern Utah (Aikens 1966:74). In addition, hundreds of Fremont sites have been found throughout the eastern Great Basin, but Promontory manifestations are now known to be limited to the Salt Lake region of northern Utah. The once distinctive Promontory moccasin and pottery now seem to be little more than northern variants of the overall Fremont pattern.

In short, the two-culture model does not work. The newer interpretation is explained by Aikens (1966:74): "Promontory does not in fact represent a cultural grouping distinct from the Fremont, and . . . the 'Promontory culture' is an artifact of archaeological misinterpretation of a few variant items of material culture from seasonal Fremont hunting camps." It is not surprising that little overlap exists between sites of the so-called Promontory culture and Fremont. The classic "Fremont" sites were more or less permanent habitation sites, areas where horticulture was conducted and substantial dwellings were built. The "Promontory" occupations were simply seasonal bison-hunting stations, inhabited only sporadically and used for special, limited purposes. Small wonder there is little overlap between the material culture of the two manifestations: one site represented a year-round, full-scale village, and the other was only a short-range seasonal stopover.

The Fremont-Promontory problem is but one example of how archaeologists are becoming aware of the intracultural variability inherent in archaeological sites. The Fremont-Promontory confusion occurred because Steward applied the modal concept of culture to problems of reconstructing lifeways, and so long as artifacts and sites were taken as "typical" of their cultures, the confusion lasted. But once archaeologists, such as Aikens, began viewing cultural remains in systemic contexts, the misinterpretation became clear. The remainder of this chapter will discuss the modern methods by which contemporary archaeologists deal with the variability involved in regional archaeological systems.

THE REESE RIVER VALLEY, NEVADA: A CASE STUDY IN REGIONAL ARCHAEOLOGY

> The probability of making surface finds decreases in inverse ratio to the square of the distance between the ground and the end of the searcher's nose.
>
> *Louis Brennan*

Traditionally, archaeologists anxious to examine past adaptations have attempted to find deep, stratified sites with a high degree of preservation. Caves and grottos such as Gatecliff Shelter are particularly fruitful in this regard. Plant and animal remains can be carefully excavated and analyzed using methods discussed in the last chapter. Recently, however, archaeologists have come to recognize the finite nature of their data. Many rivers have been dammed, flooding in the process many of the heavily occupied river bottoms; subdivisions are rapidly encroaching upon wilderness areas where sites formerly remained untouched; some misguided amateur collectors, eager to obtain artifacts and unmindful of scientific purposes, have wantonly destroyed some of the richest sites. Archaeologists are running out of sites. It has been estimated that in California alone over 1,000 sites are destroyed annually. While this situation is distressing, the worst is yet to come. It is only a matter of time until archaeologists can no longer rely upon stratified deposits for keys to the past, for most such sites will be gone.

Contemporary archaeologists are mindful of this problem and are looking for new avenues of prehistoric research. One relevant resource is the **surface site**, an area in which archaeological remains have simply lain on stable ground surfaces rather than becoming buried by sand, silt, and gravel. In regions that have been spared the plow, archaeologists have the unparalleled opportunity of collecting artifacts literally where they were dropped, often thousands of years ago.

Not only do those surfaces offer a laboratory for studying prehistoric remains, but they also represent adaptations different from the more traditionally excavated midden sites. Until recently, surface sites had been largely ignored, since they lack the contextual relations (stratigraphy) necessary for establishing cultural chronologies. But current archaeology is examining more than merely time-space sequences, and surface sites provide unique data regarding past man-land relationships. This section considers one such area, the Reese River Valley of central Nevada. This project is presented as an illustration of some of the modern techniques used to reconstruct past lifeways.

The Great Basin Shoshoneans

The Great Basin is, as the name implies, a massive geographic unit of interior drainage. The few river and stream drainages flow into large sinks or playas, so water escapes the Basin only through evaporation. The physiographic boundaries are formed by the Sierra Nevada mountain range to the west with the Wasatch Mountains flanking the eastern Great Basin. The volcanic Columbian plateau forms the northern margin, which gradually tapers into the arid Mojave and Colorado deserts to the south. As cyclonic storms move eastward from the Pacific Ocean, the Sierras act as a significant topographic barrier, causing the moisture-laden clouds to lose most of their precipitation on the Sierra's western face. The eastern scarp of the Sierras and the Great Basin is therefore relatively arid. This *rainshadow effect* is repeated on a reduced scale throughout the western Great Basin itself, so that the comparatively moist west-facing slopes tend to support more verdant stands of trees and shrubs than do the eastern slopes.

The semiarid steppe environment of the Great Basin hosts a varied array of vegetation communities. Often called *lifezones,* these biotic associations provide dramatic contrasts within a relatively small area. In recent times, at least, sagebrush has been the ubiquitous ground cover, often interspersed with rabbit-brush and wild rose in the more moist areas. A riparian association of cotton-wood, aspen, and willow is often so dense near the waterways that it obscures the water itself from view. A thin belt of piñon and juniper trees grows on the numerous mountain ranges. Piñon are replaced at higher elevations by scrubby mountain mahogany, which eventually yield to sagebrush again at the summits. The overall visual effect is of a low, monotonous carpet of sagebrush punctuated by fringes of riparian or montane shrub communities (see Figure 9–2).

This unique environment fostered an equally distinctive cultural adaptation. Historically, the Great Basin was inhabited by groups of Northern Paiute, Western Shoshoni, and Southern Paiute (or Ute), divisions based largely upon linguistic boundaries. The Indians of the Great Basin can be collectively termed the Shoshoni-speakers or Shoshoneans, for short. Their ecological adaptation depended upon a meticulous and exacting exploitation of Great Basin **microen-vironments**. Since the Shoshoneans practiced no true agriculture, they had to travel from one habitat to another to harvest the local wild crops as they became available. This seasonal round, considered briefly in the previous section, required the aboriginal groups to schedule their itinerary in such a way as to

Figure 9-2
Vegetational zonation in the Reese River Valley, showing the riparian association in the foreground and the piñon-juniper zone on the Shoshone Range in the background.

fully exploit local productivity. Nuts of the piñon tree, a staple Shoshonean resource, ripened in the late fall and usually provided enough food for the winter. Buffalo berries and currants also became available in the low foothills about this time. Indian ricegrass seeds were usually ripe during the summer months so camp was moved from the piñon forest to the flat valley floor in late spring (see Figure 9-3). Many other local foods were utilized in the same cyclical fashion. Because of their intimate relationship with the natural environment, the Shoshoneans were able to weld isolated native foodstuffs into a solid economic subsistence cycle.

The vicissitudes of successful adaptation to the Great Basin habitat also were reflected in the social aspects of their lifeway. By its nature, the Shoshonean ecological adaptation required a sparse, mobile population. The native seed crops could only support between twenty and thirty people in every 100 square miles, and even these small groups moved frequently to new seed areas throughout the year. Large permanent social groupings were impractical and generally impossible to maintain. Only the extended family (i.e., the parents, their unmarried children, and perhaps a grandparent or two) remained in permanent year-round association. Small enough for mobility yet large enough for efficient seed harvesting, these foraging groups (called *family bands*) were the ideal basic unit in the Great Basin ecosystem.

A spirit of pragmatism pervaded the entire Shoshonean social sphere. Marriage was ad hoc and primarily an economic affair. Females gathered the seed crops, thereby providing the bulk of the diet. Husbands spent much of

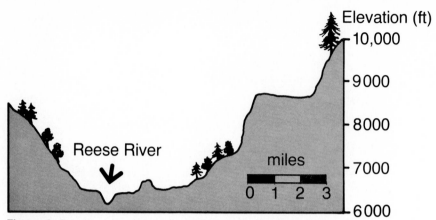

Figure 9–3
Cross-section of the Reese River Valley, showing the distribution of major biotic communities (*after Thomas 1973, figure 2*).

their time hunting game, mostly antelope and mountain sheep, to supplement the vegetal diet. The marriage alliance was a brittle one, easily dissolved and reshuffled. Pubescent children married early, with economic provisions overshadowing most other considerations, including romantic inclinations. There was little margin for "useless," i.e., nonfunctional, cultural norms ("You really should marry your mother's brother's eldest daughter"). What mattered was the creation of an economically viable dyad, suited to surviving the rigors of Great Basin life. No elaborate mortuary practices were observed, for death was accepted as the logical and necessary conclusion to life.

The Shoshoneans, along with the Bushmen, the Eskimo, and the Australians are often taken as representing the minimum possible cultural adaptation (e.g., Lomax and Arensberg 1977, Fig. 3). For more basic, simpler social groupings, one must presumably look to the nonhuman primates. Small wonder that in addition to serving as the cultural baseline, the Shoshoneans have also been important in anthropology as analogies in reconstructing the even more remote adaptation of prehistoric groups, such as the early Pleistocene hunters of Africa.

It was not until the 1930s that anthropologist Julian Steward attempted major ethnographic fieldwork in the central Great Basin. Most Shoshonean informants had been born about 1870, after the initial silver boom. Could these informants, born and enculturated in the midst of such disruptive conditions, be expected to recall the precontact "pristine" lifeway of the Shoshoneans? Some anthropologists, such as Elman Service (1962), think not. Furthermore, some archaeologists feel that Great Basin prehistory does not correlate with Steward's overall interpretation of the historic period (e.g., Cowan 1967; Napton 1969). The primary questions concern the prehistoric Great Basin lifeways. Were the informants questioned in 1930 accurate in their descriptions of precontact conditions, or had acculturation to the Anglo-American invasion significantly hampered their ability to relate an accurate description of past lifeways?

There are several methods of attacking this important question. New ethnographic fieldwork is one such approach, but modern informants can shed only limited light on socioeconomic practices that vanished over a century before. An ethnohistoric study of written sources would perhaps be helpful, but the biased accounts of miners, ranchers, and farmers seem almost invariably to distort and deride Indian culture. Furthermore, such sources document only the acculturated period, not the critical prehistoric era. The most workable approach to determine precontact economy and demography is to examine the remains of the prehistoric material culture. That is, the question of prehistoric ecological adjustment can be solved only through carefully planned and executed paleoanthropological research; the Reese River Project was initiated with these purposes in mind.

Prerequisites for Archaeological Research

To be anthropologically relevant, prehistoric data of this sort must satisfy three basic criteria. First, the critical facets of the seasonal round must be represented; it is not enough to generalize from a single site. These people moved about from place to place every year, so information from any single site (like Gatecliff Shelter) can tell only part of the story.

The data must also be unbiased, since capricious sampling techniques can lead the archaeologist astray in assessing the relative importance of the various hunting-gathering sites. The best scientific way to insure unbiased results in this situation is through judicious use of *probability sampling theory.* To conduct such a probability sample, one must first choose the **sampling elements** that are the objects of study. In many cases, these elements are archaeological sites, in the traditional sense. All of these elements taken together form a set of all possible elements, the **sampling universe**. Each element is assigned a consecutive number from 1 to N, and numbers are randomly selected so that each has an equal probability of selection, $1/N$. In this manner, a subset, called the **sample**, of the N elements is chosen, so that each member of the universe has an equal chance of inclusion.

In addition to providing relatively unbiased samples, random procedures have the added benefit of providing data amenable to further statistical manipulation. Also, since statistical analysis generally requires a random sample, the archaeologist who accepts a biased sampling design immediately and unnecessarily ties his own hands.

Finally, the research design must provide useful *negative evidence.* In addition to telling the archaeologist what activities did take place, the data must likewise indicate those activities that did not occur in a particular area or lifezone. It is a relatively simple matter, for example, to determine the presence of piñon harvesting sites within the piñon-juniper zone, but the archaeologist should also determine that such sites do not also occur (1) near a river, (2) on the sagebrush-covered flatlands, or (3) on the high mountain peaks. The requirement for negative evidence, only recently recognized as relevant to archaeological research, imposes severe yet necessary qualifications upon fieldwork. Only by paying strict attention to the quality of data can archaeologists hope to derive anthropologically viable conclusions.

RESEARCH DESIGN

The research design that best satisfies the above requirements is an *inclusive regional random sample*. The study area (the universe) is selected to include an entire seasonal round (see Figure 9–4). In the central Great Basin, this universe is a single valley system, situated between the north-south trending mountain ranges. The universe is then gridded into a series of large squares

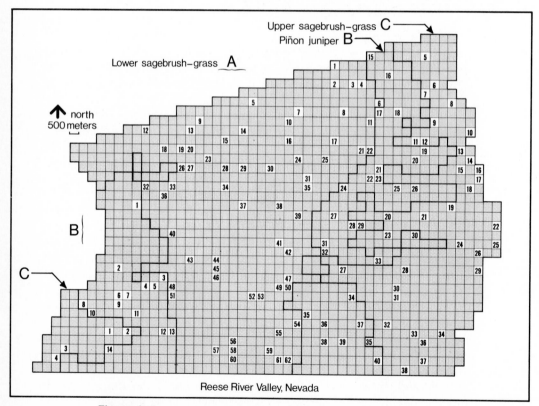

Figure 9–4
Grid sampling scheme used at Reese River. Each square is 500 meters on a side, and a 10 percent sample was randomly selected for survey. Note the three major "strata," which correspond to the environmental zones evident on Figures 9–2 and 9–3 (*after Thomas 1973, figure 6*).

(**tracts**), which are each considered as a sample element. Every tract will be completely searched for all visible remains of prehistoric subsistence activities. In this case, archaeological sites per se cannot serve as elements, since prior to survey one does not know how many of what kinds of sites are involved in this particular valley. Finally the tracts are numbered from 1 to N, and a random sample of size n is selected. Economic vicissitudes—time and money available, scope of the project, estimated unit variability, and so forth—determine how many tracts can be selected. The sampling fraction is expressed as n/N.

With this generalized strategy in mind, it remains to determine the specific tactics necessary for application in the Great Basin. Such a design assumes that archaeological material will be present on the land surfaces, rather than buried underground. While this assumption is invalid for many geographic areas, the Reese River area is notable for its relatively stable land surfaces and for its paucity of buried sites. The tract survey procedure also requires complete cooperation from local landowners, since all possible tracts must be totally accessible to the field teams. Additionally, amateur artifact collecting (**pothunting**) must be minimal so the archaeologist is able to recover reliable samples. Aerial photographs and serviceable access roads are also desirable. A final consideration in selecting an area for research is that the archaeologist who lives where he is working is often able to make observations and gain valuable insights into some of the significant local ecological exigencies. For this reason, most archaeologists prefer to camp near the excavation site or survey area.

THE REESE RIVER VALLEY

The upper Reese River Valley of central Nevada was chosen as the area best satisfying the prerequisites outlined above. The Reese River is a lazy little stream less than fifteen feet wide, which originates about forty miles south of Austin, Nevada. Flowing northward between the Shoshone and Toiyabe mountain ranges, the Reese finally empties into the Humboldt River. The valley itself is about fifteen miles wide and over a hundred miles long. For survey purposes, a cross section was selected to provide a suitable universe, which, you will remember, should enclose roughly the area of an annual seasonal round of the historic Shoshoneans. The overall study area comprised a tract of land about fifteen miles wide by about twenty miles long.

The valley floor in this area lies about 6,500 feet above sea level and is presently dominated by sagebrush shrubs. The piñon-juniper belt, so critical for winter forage, reaches between about 7,000 and 8,500 feet, covering the low flanks of the mountains. Thick stands of buffalo berries, currants, wild rice, and a host of other native foods also grace the montane forest belt. Above 8,500 feet, trees yield again to low sagebrush. The mountain peaks, some of which tower over 11,000 feet, are tundra-like, practically devoid of vegetation. A riparian zone consisting of willow, aspen, and cottonwood flanks all montane streams, which gradually wind their way toward the Reese River.

Psychic Archaeology???

> It is well to open one's mind but only as a preliminary to closing it . . . for the supreme act of judgment and selection.
>
> *Irving Babbitt*

> If you keep your mind sufficiently open, people will throw a lot of rubbish into it.
>
> *William Orton*

The most frequent question I get from nonarchaeologists is how I know where to dig. How are sites found, anyway? In the Prologue, I discussed how we found Gatecliff Shelter, based on a hint from a local miner. In Chapter 2 we saw how Schliemann found Troy through painstaking analysis of clues provided in Homer's *Iliad.* In this chapter, I mention how the theory of probability is used for systematic site survey.

Probably the most colorful method of finding sites has recently surfaced as **psychic archaeology**, the use of ESP and other parapsychological powers to explore past events and objects. The operating premise of such studies is that deep within the human mind is a faculty which, when properly unlocked, can be used to explore ancient mysteries; Goodman (1977:xv) calls this faculty the "psychic porthole to the past." In some cases, psychics claim the ability to psychometrize artifacts, that is, to hold an object, concentrate upon it, and then recall details about the ancient people who made and used the artifact. Another version of psychic archaeology calls on the psychic to predict locations of archaeological sites by contemplating maps or aerial photographs. Such map dowsing has been practiced for years in search of water and oil, and some police departments are using psychics to find bodies and solve crimes. Now some believers are advocating the use of psychic powers in search of archaeological sites.

The most publicized effort is probably Jeffrey Goodman's search for very ancient man near Flagstaff, Arizona. In his book *Psychic Archaeology: Time Machine to the Past,* Goodman describes his "research" with a mystic. The endeavor started when Goodman dreamt of finding artifacts and human bones in a creek bed somewhere in the American Southwest. Then a student studying archaeology at the University of Arizona, Goodman contacted a psychic to help him explain the whereabouts of his "dream site." Through a series of tapes, the psychic gradually pinpointed an area near Flagstaff, Arizona, telling Goodman that he should find both stone tools and human skeletons if he would dig in that exact spot. Goodman excavated a deep shaft, as directed, and he did find a small collection of rocks. Goodman claims that his Flagstaff site has clear-cut human occupations at 25,000, 30,000, 45,000, and 100,000 years ago. If true, this changes the accepted chronology by a factor of four! Although some qualified archaeologists seem to agree with Goodman's interpretations, most archaeologists who have examined the finds deny their validity (see Goodman 1977, Chapters 4 and 5). As you can imagine, the Flagstaff site has sparked heated feelings on both sites of the debate.

J. Norman Emerson, of the University of Toronto, has also used mystics in what he calls "infinite archaeology." Not overly concerned about the psychic or metaphysical arguments, Emerson argues simply that psychics have helped him find and interpret archaeological sites, and he refuses to ignore this evidence. Specifically, Emerson has used mystics to locate the remains of buried house sites near Ontario and to psychometrize artifacts from British Columbia (Emerson 1973, 1974). Psychics also have been used by archaeologists in Ecuador, Great Britain, and the Soviet Union (see Goodman 1977, Chapters 7 and 8; Asher 1974).

It is clear that the entire topic of parapsychology is only now receiving serious attention in the scientific community. In fact, the Parapsychological Association has been recognized as a component science of the American Association for the Advancement of Science, largely at the urging of anthropologist Margaret Mead. Serious investigation is still in its infancy, and it is certainly too early in the game to render a decision about the validity (or invalidity) of parapsychological phenomena.

The same is true for so-called psychic archaeology. In truth, the evidence presented to date for the effective use of psychics in archaeological research is unconvincing. The point, however, is this: whether or not the psychic time machine ultimately proves out, use of the psychics in archaeology is in no way "unscientific." In Chapter 2, I emphasized that when using proper scientific procedure, it matters not at all where one gets hypotheses; psychics can be as good a source in archaeology as Ph.D.s. The true test of hypotheses is always in their ability to predict unknown phenomena. If psychics can ultimately help archaeologists find buried sites and explain events of the past, then so much the better. I personally remain unconvinced, but I am inclined to agree with Goodman when he challenges his archaeological skeptics to "put your shovel where your mouth is!" (Goodman 1977:195). The truest test of psychic archaeology is in the ground, not in the mind.

> **W**hat determines the soundness of a hypothesis is not the way it is arrived at (it may have been suggested by a dream or a hallucination), but the way it stands up when confronted with relevant observational data.
>
> *Carl Hempel*

These lifezones of the Reese River Valley were clearly defined and easily discerned in the field (see Figure 9–2). Four lifezones were isolated for study: lower sagebrush-grass, piñon-juniper, upper sagebrush-grass, and the riparian zone, including both upland stream margins and the immediate vicinity of the Reese River. This universe was circumscribed on aerial photographs and divided into about 1,400 tracts, each of them 500 meters (about one-third of a mile) on a side. Each tract was numbered, and a 10 percent random sample was selected. Each tract was considered as a *sampling element* in this study (see Figure 9–4).

The actual fieldwork consisted of locating each of the 140 tracts of the sample on the ground and then surveying the entire 500-meter square for signs of prehistoric occupation. All artifacts and waste chippage, whether an isolated find or part of a dense concentration, were mapped, catalogued, and collected. The most efficient survey unit was a team of six archaeologists, primarily instructors and students from the Universities of California (Davis) and Nevada. Each crew could survey one or two such tracts daily, depending upon accessibility and local terrain. This sampling design attempted to minimize bias by forcing archaeologists to look in *every* topographic locale, even those unlikely to have habitation residue. It is not enough to say that people could not possibly have lived in a particular situation, for such statements are highly colored by the archaeologist's preconceived ideas and are unacceptable in scientific research. The random survey established (within statistical sampling error) precisely which types of localities were or were not occupied, with little bias or ethnocentrism involved. Artifacts recovered were then analyzed to determine prehistoric man-land relations.

Analysis

The Reese River fieldwork took about four months to complete, with a field crew varying in size from twenty-three to forty-five people. Approximately 3,500 artifacts were recovered from the surface of the 140 tracts. About a dozen attributes were measured on each artifact and then an IBM card was prepared for each specimen. Artifacts were then analyzed and classified using a computer, in this case a Burroughs 5500. The initial computer output was in terms of *temporal types,* which ranged from roughly 5000 B.C. to historic times. After the temporal range of the samples had been determined, the temporal categories were collapsed in favor of more useful *functional types,* divisions based upon distinctive attribute modes such as cutting-edge angle, degree of blade curvature, and others (for details of the computer work, see Thomas 1971, 1972b, 1973).

The primary aim of analysis was to evaluate the presence of consistent artifact tool kits that corresponded with the prehistoric exploitation of the lifezones. Areas of extensive hunting, for example, were expected to exhibit a distinctive and male-oriented artifact assemblage: spent projectile points, butchering tools, and flaking debris resulting from resharpening rather than from primary artifact manufacture. Habitation areas, on the other hand, ought to reflect both male and female tasks such as tool manufacture, clothing preparation and repair, remains of cooking activities, house foundations, campfires, ritual paraphernalia, and so on. The computer was used in predicting artifact distributions (see Thomas 1971, 1972b). Given the proper ethnographic input, such as the activity sequences and the tool kits involved, we predicted the relative frequency of each artifact within each lifezone. These predictions were actually the artifact distributions which could be expected from Julian Steward's model of Great Basin subsistence patterns. The primary objective of the fieldwork at Reese River was to confirm or reject those theoretical predictions, and, by implication, the overall Steward model. In a sense, the project was testing anthropological theory through the use of archaeological data.

Results at Reese River

The fieldwork and laboratory analysis resulted in an overall synthesis of the archaeology of the Reese River Valley. The pattern of local cultural ecology can be described as a "subsistence-settlement system." That is, the results depict an ecological adaptation that lasted from about 5000 B.C. to the historic era in the Great Basin. In a strict sense, the Reese River ecological pattern holds only for the Reese River locality, but further research will probably indicate that similar patterns exist throughout much of the central Great Basin.

The Reese River subsistence-settlement system can be characterized by two types of settlements. The *shoreline settlement* consists of a series of large sites located on permanent water sources within the lower sagebrush-grass zones. The artifact assemblage indicates that economic focus was upon the wild grass and root crops that ripen in the late spring and early summer. The shoreline settlements consist of massive linear scatters of artifacts—often a couple of miles long—which lay parallel to the source of the flowing water. In this context, the "site" was anywhere along the river or stream, for no specific village areas were consistently reoccupied. These campsites were probably situated near scattered caches of harvested summer seeds, and the only structures were mere brush windbreaks and sunshades. The waste chippage indicates that much of the stone tool manufacture took place in the summer camps. The seed diet was doubtless supplemented by rodents and rabbits, both of which could be easily hunted on the nearby flats.

The other primary focus of habitation, the *piñon ecotone settlement,* was located in the dense stands of piñon and juniper trees, generally on long, low ridges which finger onto the valley floor. This "edge effect," as it is called, is a rather common form of ecological adaptation that allows exploitation of dual lifezones: in this case, both the piñon belt and the nearby valley floor. These sites are also linear scatters of artifacts and chippage, but unlike the shoreline settlements, the piñon ecotone sites consisted of more densely concentrated artifact clusters. There are only a limited number of suitable flat-topped ridges in the area, so the potential areas of habitation were more limited than those along the river. The piñon sites were occupied just after the fall pine cone harvest, so the villages could be established only when the nut crop of the immediate area was successful. In other years, the winter village had to be relocated in some more distant portion of the forest where the piñon nuts were available. The artifact inventory of these sites indicates that most of the hide preparation and clothing manufacture took place during the winter encampments. Deer and mountain sheep probably supplemented the diet of piñon nuts. Houses consisted of domed **wickiups**, sometimes surrounded by stone circles and covered with piñon tree bark or juniper boughs. These houses were often placed in shallow pits up to 18 inches deep. Although only about five families could live on each ridge-top, there might be several such villages within a one-mile radius.

In addition to the habitation sites, the remains of several special-purpose sites were located and mapped. On the flat valley floor several butchering assemblages were recovered (knives, scrapers, and resharpening flakes), presumably resulting from communal hunting of both jackrabbits and antelopes. Scattered about in the same area were additional artifacts (seed knives and grinding stones) which resulted from women's seed-gathering forays. Evidence was also recovered that suggests that deer and mountain sheep were hunted in the piñon belt and also in the high, more barren mountains that flank the Reese River. All of these *task-group assemblages* represent short-term, ancillary subsistence activities undertaken by small groups of relatives, working out of the more permanent habitation sites.

The Reese River subsistence-settlement system can be characterized as a central-based wandering pattern, defined by Beardsley (1956:138) as a "community that spends part of each year wandering and the rest at the settlement or 'central base,' to which it may or may not consistently return in subsequent years . . . a half-sedentary community [which] represents an adjustment to . . . a storable or preservable wild food harvest such as acorn or mesquite beans. . . ." The Reese River system can be more properly considered a *dual central-based wandering pattern,* since two storable foods are involved: piñon nuts and wild seeds. Each crop dictated a distinct area of habitation which was an "on the fence" compromise between wandering and sedentary life. This lifeway provided the flexibility required to succeed in the harsh, unstable Great Basin environment.

Implications

This extended example has been presented as a case study indicating precisely how archaeology attempts to reconstruct an extinct lifeway. The initial step was to establish a local cultural chronology and then to impose the chronological controls necessary for further investigation. Some specific research objectives were then outlined and an archaeological strategy framed to gather the relevant data. In the Reese River case, the more conventional approach of excavating a few large stratified sites such as Gatecliff Shelter would not answer the questions under consideration. A new research design based upon the systematic random sampling of an entire valley was therefore devised to suit the problem at hand. As archaeological research progresses in its anthropological endeavors, the archaeologist will have to adapt more and more nontraditional techniques.

Let us tally the overall anthropological significance of the Reese River Ecological Project. First of all, the survey determined the temporal parameters of the area. The Reese River Valley was not significantly occupied prior to about 5000 B.C. Secondly, the project attempted to reconstruct the aboriginal seasonal round of the prehistoric Indians of Reese River. Their seasonal round, based as it was upon piñon pine-nuts and Indian ricegrass, permitted a flexible and enduring man-land relationship. The overall adaptation hedged against short-term environmental fluctuations because the seasonal round depended upon several crops, not upon a single food resource. There appear to be no significant subsistence changes in 7,000 years.

This demographic pattern can now be compared to similar data from any other group—historic or prehistoric. If anthropology seeks to understand the mechanisms of human ecology then the focus must not be restricted to those social groups that survived into the ethnographic present. Extinct, unsuccessful cultural adaptations must be as carefully studied and documented.

SOME SAMPLING CONSIDERATIONS

The archaeological fieldwork at Reese River depended heavily on the theory of random error, and it is now necessary to look at this theory in more detail. Archaeologists are becoming increasingly aware of how important it is to think through their sampling procedures. Archaeologists have always dealt with samples, of course, but the recent trend has been toward drawing samples in accordance with the accepted principles of probability. Several sources discuss archaeological sampling procedures, and the present discussion is only intended to highlight some of the more important aspects (see Mueller 1974, 1975; Thomas 1976, 1978; Ragir 1967; Plog 1976).

The first key sampling concept is that of **population**. In general usage, "population" refers to a group of living organisms of a single species which are found in a circumscribed area at a given time; this is a breeding population. Cultural anthropologists also commonly use the term "population" to denote a specific society, and archaeologists are often heard speaking of "prehistoric Pueblo III populations" or the "Shoshoni-speaking population." Proper sampling, however, requires us to adopt a more restricted statistical usage for the term population.

Statisticians use the term population to refer not to physical objects (people, lemurs, or microbes), but rather to observations made upon these subjects. The difference is both subtle and important.

Shoshoni Indians could comprise a biological or sociocultural population, but they could never be a statistical population. Only a set of related variates— such as stature, body weight, daily caloric intake, or presence of the Rh blood factor among Shoshoni Indians—could comprise a statistical population. A **statistical population** is a set of variates (counts, measurements, or characteristics) about which relevant inquiries are to be made (Thomas 1976:35). Statistical populations thus differ from "populations" in the common usage; statistical populations are arbitrary and must be carefully defined.

Some populations may consist of finite number of variates, such as the stature of all living Shoshoni Indians. But "population" can also be defined to include not only the living Shoshoni but also all Shoshoni who lived in the past, and even those who will live in the future. So populations can also be infinite. It would be troublesome indeed for an anthropologist to attempt to interrogate, measure, observe, or photograph the entire physical population of living Sho-shoni. And, if the statistical population had been defined to include Shoshoni of all times and all places, complete observation would be impossible. Because of this, most statistical populations are incompletely observable: physical anthro-pologists can never hope to measure the cranial capacity of *Australopitbecus robustus,* and archaeologists can never measure the length of every Clovis point.

This is why archaeologists nearly always deal with samples. A **sample** is defined as any subset of a statistical population, whether randomly, haphazardly, or capriciously selected. The objective behind probability sampling is to obtain samples that were selected from the statistical population *with a known probability.*

There is no single best way to select a sample; too many practical and logistical matters enter into the decision. In the Reese River example, the physical population included 1,400 tracts of land, and each was 500 meters on a side. Each tract contained archaeological objects, and each of the archaeological objects could be observed in a number (an infinite number) of ways. Thus in the single physical population we could define an infinite number of statistical populations; this is why it is important to specify the research objective prior to taking the sample.

One objective at Reese River was to find the density of archaeological objects, say, projectile points such as were discussed in Chapter 7. Because it was impractical to find the density of points in each of the 1,400 squares, we elected to measure that density in only 140 of them, and then extrapolate to the entire statistical population. The only way such an estimate could be unbiased is from a sample in which every element had an equal probability of selection; in this case, the probability of selecting any individual tract was exactly 1/1,400.

SQUARES, RECTANGLES, OR CIRCLES: WHICH IS THE BEST RESEARCH DESIGN?

Literally dozens of strategies exist to enable archaeologists to select their samples. When we gridded the Reese River area into 500-meter squares (see Figure 9–4), we were employing a **quadrat** technique. This method, derived from quantitative sampling in plant ecology, has been used in several archaeo-logical applications, including Cedar Mesa, Utah (Lipe and Matson 1971), Kingman, Arizona (Matson 1971), and Owens Valley, California (Bettinger 1977).

Another popular method of archaeological sampling is called the **transect** technique. Instead of employing square sampling units the transect sample defines long linear units. Teams of archaeologists can thus survey in long, straight lines. Transect sampling is often easier than quadrat sampling because access time is minimized; the team simply walks from point A to point B without having to travel throughout the region in a checkerboard fashion. There is some evidence that transect samples tend to be statistically more efficient than quadrat samples (see Plog 1976:151 and Judge, Ebert, and Hitchcock 1975).

Figure 9–5 shows how transect sampling works. In this case, we wanted to find out how archaeological sites distribute along the margins of Pleistocene Lake Tonopah, about 100 miles south of Reese River, Nevada. Some 12,000 years ago the lake was full and the shoreline stood at about 4,800 feet above sea level. Presumably, the early Paleo-Indians in this valley would have lived near the beach line. Then, as the climate became hotter and drier, Pleistocene Lake Tonopah began to shrink. One thing we wanted to learn at Lake Tonopah was how later Paleo-Indian groups changed their settlement pattern in response to receding beach levels.

Lake Tonopah is now completely dry, and the area could have been gridded and sampled in a manner like Reese River. But because we were primarily concerned with the relationship of cultural materials to fossil beach terraces it made more sense to run a series of transects across the dry lake, laid out so as to intersect the known beach terraces (see Figure 9–5). East-west transects were selected so that they intersected the beach lines in a perpendicular manner.

The Lake Tonopah example differs in another important way from the Reese River sampling design. You will remember that at Reese River the 1,400 sampling tracts were divided into homogeneous strata (based on modern life-zones) and then a 10 percent sample was selected within each stratum. Technically speaking, the Reese River design was a *stratified random quadrat sample.* At Lake Tonopah the climate had changed so drastically that environmental strata were less important, so they were not included in the sampling strategy.

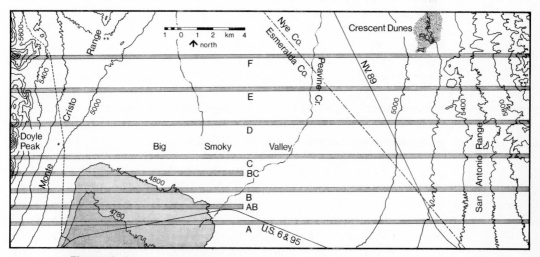

Figure 9–5
Transect sampling method used at Pleistocene Lake Tonopah, Nevada. Each transect is 150 meters wide, and the shaded portions indicate approximate lake levels during the late Pleistocene.

Moreover, because we wanted to obtain an overall picture we elected to use a systematic (rather than random) method of selection.

Look at Figure 9–5. The universe of transects is really a large series of 150-meter-wide strips running across dry Lake Tonopah. For reasons of time and budget we decided to select a systematic sample. A *random* method of selection would have us number every strip and then select random numbers to define which strips would become transects in the sample. In a *systematic* sample, only the first sampling unit is selected at random, and the remaining transects are chosen at intervals to complete the 7.5 percent sample. There are statistical advantages and disadvantages to both sampling schemes (see Kish 1965, Chapter 4; Cochran 1963, Chapter 8); at Lake Tonopah we selected a systematic transect sample because we thought it would provide us with the best overall coverage of the zones in question.

Several other options exist for sampling designs in archaeology. In fact, it is easy to be led astray by the theoretical and statistical advantages of one sample design over another (see Thomas 1978). At least as important as the abstract statistical characteristics of each design are the practical archaeological considerations, and archaeologists should never feel tied to any single sampling strategy. Random quadrats were used at Reese River because I wanted to know distributions of artifacts and sites within discrete lifezones. Systematic transect sampling was employed at Lake Tonopah in order to provide clear-cut data on the relationships between archaeological sites and the extinct Pleistocene beach terraces.

One final example should underscore the point that archaeologists must be flexible in designing their samples. While digging Gatecliff Shelter we needed to conduct a regional sampling operation in order to examine additional components of the seasonal round; Gatecliff represents only a fraction of the overall transhumance pattern. So we devised a method of sampling the surrounding Monitor Valley. One key question was to find how the sites related to water.

Water can occur on the landscape in a number of ways. At Reese River, water was a *linear* resource, concentrated in streams that flowed year-round out of the mountains; these streams were then collected in the Reese River, which ran north-south up the valley. At Pleistocene Lake Tonopah, water was a *circular* resource contained in a massive lake basin; thus, the transect samples were designed to cross-cut the Lake Tonopah beaches.

Monitor Valley presented yet a third option for distribution of water. With a couple of exceptions, Monitor Valley lacked the permanent streams of the Reese River area, and the dry lake in Monitor Valley was never an important Pleistocene lake. Water in Monitor Valley occurred primarily in springs that bubbled forth, flowed a short distance, then disappeared. That is, water at Monitor Valley was neither circular nor linear—it was a *point* resource.

In order to compare how water-determined settlement patterns vary between valleys, we needed to sample the archaeological sites of Monitor Valley. Our survey area (Figure 9–6), contained a total of thirty permanent springs, each of which seemed to hold potential for prehistoric exploitation.

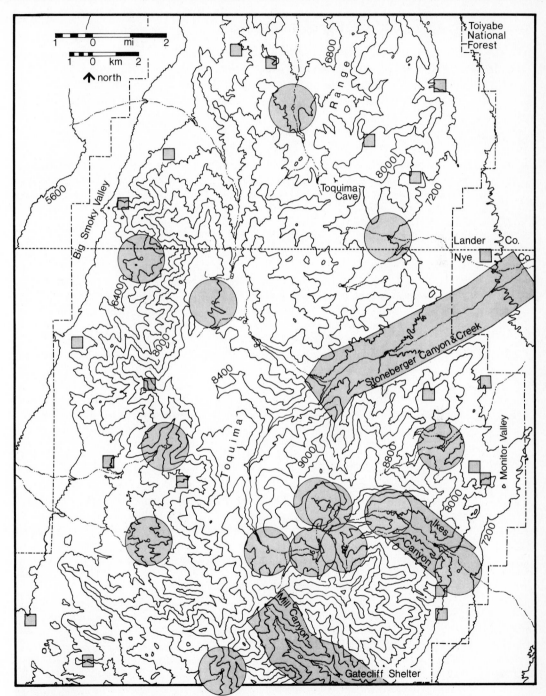

Figure 9–6
Sampling strategy used in the Toquima Mountains near Gatecliff Shelter. Note that both circular and square sampling grids were involved.

The Pros and Cons of Random Sampling

The general topic of random sampling is still hotly debated by archaeologists: some swear by it, others only swear at it. In the dialogue that follows, Kent Flannery creates the traditional Real Mesoamerican Archaeologist (R.M.A.) and the methodologically oriented Skeptical Graduate Student as foils to illustrate both sides of the sampling question (Flannery 1976b:132–135).

The Real Mesoamerican Archeologist doesn't like probability sampling. He regards it as (1) a waste of energy, (2) too time-consuming, (3) not as reliable as his intuition, and (4) not applicable to complex societies. He even has reservations about applying it to such "simple" political units as Formative villages. He and I have had acrimonious debates on the subject, neither of us backed up by very much data or mathematical expertise, and each of us continually harassed by the Skeptical Graduate Student, who claims to have both.

The argument began in the Quinta Las Rosas, a now-defunct "nocturnal center" on the outskirts of Veracruz.

While the waiter filled our order, R.M.A. drew on a paper napkin the outline of the Río San Jacinto drainage and the pattern of sites he had found so far. Reaching the end of the paper, he concluded, " and to the south, it looks as if there were no more Formative sites—just Early Classic, and some small Post-Classic sites."

Near his elbow, the Skeptical Graduate Student quickly added, "but we can't be sure of that, because our sample of sites is inadequate and our survey so far has been very haphazard and unsystematic."

Now, short of calling attention to a whole projectile point on his backdirt pile, there is probably no easier way to make a Real Mesoamerican Archaeologist angry than by telling him that his survey techniques are inadequate. In fact, R.M.A. is still overheated from having read Binford's 1964 article "A consideration of archaeological research design." Fortunately, he believes that he saw Binford subjected to the ultimate put-down. He tells the story often. In fact, he tells it every time his Skeptical Graduate Student brings up the subject of sampling.

"It was at the 1964 meetings of the American Anthropological Association, held in Detroit," he says. "Everybody was talking about Binford's article. Well, Bill Mayer-Oakes and Ronald Nash had tried out some of his techniques on Bill Sanders' Teotihuacán survey area, and they presented a critique . . ." (Mayer-Oakes and Nash 1964, 1965).

At this point, the Skeptical Graduate Student always rolls his eyes straight up at the ceiling and shakes his head is disbelief. The action was not lost on R.M.A., but he was interrupted by the waiter, who had just brought three rum-and-cokes. Three young ladies followed the waiter, circling our table with little attempt at subterfuge. One was clearly trying to see if R.M.A.'s lap would support her full body weight; I doubted it, but I've been wrong before.

"What Mayer-Oakes and Nash did was to take Bill Sanders' survey map of the Teotihuacán Valley, showing the location of all 500-odd sites he had found," R.M.A. went on. "To this, they applied the 'stratified random sampling program' that Binford had recommended. First, the 750-sq-km valley was divided into seven 'strata' or environmental zones: the Río San Juan delta, the Patlachique Range, Cerro Gordo, the lower valley, middle valley, upper valley, and northern valley. They then gridded the whole map with squares .6 km on a side, and selected a 20% sample of those squares at random. The sample was allocated so that various 'strata' received squares in proportion to their area—more squares in the biggest areas, and so on. Finally, they placed their grid with its

sample areas over the map of Sanders' sites, to see how many they would have found." He smiled triumphantly. "And you know what they found? Do you know?"

"I can't imagine."

"They missed Teotihuacán. For God's sake, the largest Pre-Columbian city in the New World, 20 sq km, an estimated 125,000 population, and they missed it. Now why, for God's sake, should I use a technique that won't even find Teotihuacán? I could find it with my eyes shut and my hands tied behind my back."

"Yeah, it is hard to miss," I admitted.

"Well, they did it. And what's more, as Mayer-Oakes and Nash pointed out, the 20% stratified random sample recovered none *of Sanders' 'Proto-Classic urban sites',* none *of his 'Cuanalán phase large villages', and only* one *of his 'Zacatenco phase hamlets'."*

"Not too good, I guess."

R.M.A. adjusted his position slightly to accommodate the ample young lady who now occupied his left knee. "And do you know what Mayer-Oakes and Nash concluded?"

"Lay it on me."

"They said, and here I am going to quote them exactly to the best of my memory, 'given the same amount of time, we believe that an archeologist working by instinct (parenthesis) i.e., expertise (close parenthesis) could certainly locate a greater number of sites' (Mayer-Oakes and Nash 1965:16). Now, isn't that what I do every day? Hell, I found 33 sites last week without a table of random numbers."

The Real Mesoamerican Archeologist sat back in satisfaction while we finished our rum-and-cokes and ordered a round for our newly arrived companions. We hadn't heard from the Skeptical Graduate Student yet, which was unusual, but I figured he was too smothered under the weight of the young lady in his lap to reply. I was wrong, of course; he's never that out of breath.

"I have never," said S.G.S., "heard such a gross distortion of what went on at that session of the meeting."

"How would you know? You weren't even born yet."

"I was there," said S.G.S. "That was back when I was a Skeptical Undergraduate *Student. As I remember, Mayer-Oakes and Nash were rather temperate in their criticism, and even said, "it seems clear that Binford's theoretical framework and specific sampling techniques offer much of interest and value to archaeologists working anywhere' (Mayer-Oakes and Nash 1965:21).*

"It seems to me," S.G.S. went on, "that you and several others who heard that talk have a complete misconception of what a 20% random sample is supposed to do. Somehow you seem to think that its purpose is to find a lot of sites—more than Sanders could find in his total survey, or more than I could find in a comparable period by racing around the Teotihuacán Valley with a bag over my head, picking up sherds.

"That isn't what it's supposed to do at all.

"And you, and many others, missed Binford's most important comment, since it came at the end of the conference session during a three-way conversation between Mayer-Oakes, Deetz, and Ascher."

"I don't remember a thing," said R.M.A.

"Mayer-Oakes had, in the interests of impartial scholarship, provided Binford with a copy of his results before the talk. It showed the following recovery of sites by the 20% sample (Mayer-Oakes and Nash 1965:13):

Aztec sites
    (i) Urban—4
    (ii) Rural—61

Toltec sites
   (i) Urban—2
   (ii) Rural—30
Classic Teotihuacán sites
   (i) Urban—1
   (ii) Rural—23
   (iii) Traces of occupation—11
Proto-Classic Hamlets—5
Cuanalán hamlets—1
Zacatenco hamlets—1
Pre-Classic hamlets—1
Preceramic sites—1

"These Binford communicated to the assembled crowd."

"What a memory," I marveled.

"Then Binford compared these with the totals for each type of site found by Sanders. And do you know what?"

"I can already guess."

"Virtually every type of site recovered by the 20% stratified random sample—'rural Toltec sites', 'rural Aztec sites', and so on—was recovered in approximately the proportion it contributed to the whole site universe. If one type of site made up, say, 40% of the total 500-odd sites, it also made up about 40% of the sites recovered by the sample. As Binford put it: 'the results are an excellent confirmation of the value of stratified random sampling'."

"Fantastic."

"You see," S.G.S. went on, "what the critics misunderstood was that probability sampling is not a discovery technique. *It isn't a better way to find lots of sites. As Mayer-Oakes and Nash themselves said, 'we are not saying that Sanders has done a better survey, because . . . he has sampled more than 20% of the area, and it is not as if we can pit one approach against the other . . . this is*

From other work at Reese River we had a theory that the prehistoric inhabitants tended to camp about 450 meters from their water source. At Reese River this could be tested by walking linear strips along stream courses. But the Monitor Valley water was concentrated at single points, small springs scattered throughout the Toquima Mountains.

So we designed a sampling design to look at the relation of sites to these springs. Monitor Valley contained a total of thirty springs, and neither quadrats nor transects seemed appropriate for sampling these springs. We elected to use a circular sampling unit in Monitor Valley: each spring was considered a point, and we surveyed the surrounding area using a radius of 1,000 meters. That is, we looked for all sites within 1,000 meters of water.

But we did not have time enough to survey all thirty springs, so we numbered them one through thirty and selected a 50 percent random sample (see Figure 9–6). These 1,000-meter circles were then completely surveyed in order to locate, map, and collect all of the associated sites.

The Monitor Valley survey was also concerned with sites located away from water (that is, more than 1,000 meters from a spring). We thought there would be few such sites, but, as a control, we overlaid a 500-meter grid system *about what we would find with 20% areal coverage" (Mayer-Oakes and Nash 1965:14). Surveying the entire area is always preferable to surveying only 20% of it. But what you and most other people do is survey about 20% in a haphazard fashion. We can never know if you have recovered each site type in the same frequency with which it occurs in the total universe of sites. On the other hand, if you took a 20% sample according to probability sampling techniques, you could multiply each type of site by 5 and have some confidence—*in fact, a mathematically definable confidence—*that the results would approximate the real site universe."*

R.M.A. sighed impatiently.

"A 20% random sample isn't designed to find Teotihuacán," S.G.S. continued, "or any other type of site that is unique or represented by only a few examples. If, in a universe of 500 sites, there are only five 'Zacatenco phase hamlets', then such sites make up only 1% of the universe; the chances are that, in a 20% sample, you would recover only one of them. In the case of 'Cuanalán phase large villages', there are only two in the whole universe; small wonder the sample didn't recover any at all. Probability sampling isn't the best way to find sites—it's just the best way to get a representative *sample of sites, if you can't go for the whole universe as Sanders did."*

"It's too complicated and it takes too long," R.M.A. replied. "And as Mayer-Oakes and Nash pointed out, 'increasing the areal coverage to find the rarer types of sites is a waste of time and resources'" (Mayer-Oakes and Nash 1965:14).

"Why would it take any longer than your techniques?" asked S.G.S. "We spend most of our time pushing the Jeep out of the mud anyway."

Sitting in the slowly moving shadow of the ceiling fan, listening to Sonia prattle in one ear and S.G.S. in the other, I realized that opinions would always differ on what had happened in Detroit. Some people had gone away feeling vindicated, pleased to hear that traditional survey techniques would recover more sites, that probability sampling wouldn't find unique features like Cuanalán phase large villages or the Pyramid of the Sun. Others had gone away convinced that only probability sampling would produce reliable, statistically valid samples whose confidence levels could be defined in mathematical terms. There was no hope of rapprochement.

(like that used at Reese River) and then drew another random sample for survey. In this way we were forced to look even where we thought there would be no sites.

These three examples point out the importance of fitting the samples scheme to the topography and to the nature of the questions being asked. The basic sampling unit at Reese River was the 500-meter-square quadrat; the unit at Pleistocene Lake Tonopah was a 150-meter-wide transect; the sampling unit in Monitor Valley was a 1,000-meter circle. The Reese River and Monitor Valley samples were selected randomly, while the Lake Tonopah sample was determined systematically. The sampling fractions also differed: Reese River, a 10 percent sample; Monitor Valley, a 50 percent sample; and Lake Tonopah, a 7.5 percent sample. Do not be misled into thinking there is a single best sampling scheme. There is not.

STRATEGIES IN REGIONAL ARCHAEOLOGY

This book has a number of common threads, archaeological trends that I want to emphasize. One important point is the notion of strategy. There is no single strategy in modern archaeology; there are several. This is why we spent so much time discussing the major anthropological mainstreams in Chapter 3, in order to see how differing approaches and assumptions can be applied to the same cultural phenomena.

The four sections that follow are also provided to illustrate the multiple-strategy concept. We will consider four individual cases of regional archaeology and discuss the underlying rationale and motivation for each. Although the ultimate objective is similar, the means for obtaining that goal vary considerably. There is no conflict here. In fact, it seems to be a healthy sign that contemporary archaeology is capable of mustering so many diverse approaches to tackle the fundamental issues.

An Ecological Determinants Approach: Reese River Piñon Ecotone Settlements

The first of four settlement models to be discussed explains the patterning of human settlements by examining relevant ecological parameters. Not to be confused with environmental determinism, the **ecological determinants approach** recognizes simply that human settlements are often located in response to a specific set of environmentally determined factors. As a model, the ecological determinants approach assumes that, all else being equal, a particular constellation of environmental parameters strongly conditions the placement of habitation sites. The approach will be illustrated by further research in the Reese River Valley of central Nevada; other applications can be found in Baumhoff (1963), Judge (1973), Schalk (1977), and Gumerman (1971).

The last section discussed the initial archaeological survey of the Reese River Valley in some detail. The upshot of the computer modeling and subsequent fieldwork was to test one theory—Julian Steward's theory about the ethnographic Shoshoni Indians—and then to propose another—the prehistoric Reese River settlement pattern. The scientific cycle had taken a single turn, and it became time once again to test the new theory. Basically, the synthesis of the Reese River fieldwork suggested that a bimodal settlement pattern operated prehistorically in this region: winters were spent in piñon camps located in the low foothills, and summer camps were established on the banks of the Reese River. The preliminary survey results indicated that these summer, riverine settlements were simply long, linear scatters of artifacts which paralleled the Reese River. The test of this pattern would involve little more than walking the banks of the Reese River. This would be an interesting project because the sites seem to be distributed nonrandomly along the river, but that fieldwork has not yet been done.

More complex was the structuring of the winter camp locations, those small and nucleated settlements that can be found scattered throughout the foothills of the ranges in central Nevada. Particularly intriguing was the high degree of predictability involved with the placement of these sites. After two years of working in the area, my crew and I came to the point at which we could predict the presence (and absence) of sites in places we had never been. This was fun, and to see why these predictions worked so well we listed all the environmental criteria we could think of relating to these sites. That is, we knew we could find the sites intuitively, so we tried to pin down our hunches in the form of objective criteria. Then we invested another year of fieldwork to test our set of site determinants.

We called each of these predicted site localities a **locus**, to distinguish it from the location of actual, known sites. We found that seven criteria were sufficient to predict the presence of known piñon ecotone settlements at Reese River (after Williams, Thomas, and Bettinger 1973: 226–227):

1. The locus should be on a ridge or saddle.
2. The ground should be relatively flat (less than 5 percent slope).
3. The locus should be in the low foothills (less than 250 meters above the valley floor).
4. The locus should be within the extant piñon-juniper lifezone.
5. The locus should be near the piñon-juniper ecotone (within 1,000 meters).
6. The locus should be near a semipermanent water source (within 1,000 meters).
7. The locus should be some minimal distance from this source (greater than 100 meters).

We settled on these seven criteria based on our previous fieldwork in the area. After seeing many piñon ecotone sites, we were fairly sure that these seven criteria were the best predictors of site location.

But no single criterion was sufficient in itself to predict sites. That is, all sites were not on ridges or saddles, but most were. Similarly, although the ground was usually flat (less than 5 percent slope), we did find sites from time to time that had more than 5 percent slope. No single criterion was perfect, so we decided that a combination of criteria might be the best predictor. We framed a **polythetic definition** of site location: if at least five of the seven environmental criteria are met, then we can expect to find a piñon site. (The polythetic concept is discussed by Clarke 1968:668 and Williams, Thomas, and Bettinger 1973:227–228.)

Note that the predictors are based strictly on noncultural, environmental parameters. We decided to test our predictions on a twelve-mile strip of mountains to the east of the Reese River. We obtained aerial photographs of the area and studied them closely, trying to find spots that satisfied at least five of the seven critical determinants. These archaeological sites are invisible from the air, so the site predictions were based strictly on environmental criteria.

A total of seventy-four potential site locations were found on the aerial photographs. Then we took to the field to see if sites actually occurred in the seventy-four locations. And we also wanted to see if we could find any sites that were not on the predicted spots.

The survey took about a month, with a crew of twenty archaeologists and

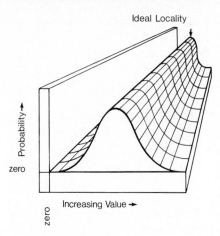

Figure 9–7
Three-dimensional probability model which describes how archeological sites in Reese River could be predicted from (1) percentage slope, (2) distance to the piñon ecotone, and (3) elevation above the valley floor (*after Thomas and Bettinger 1976, figure 64; courtesy of The American Museum of Natural History*).

students. We found archaeological sites on sixty-three of the seventy-four predicted locations, so our polythetic predictions were about 85 percent accurate. We also found only two sites that were not located on the potential loci (97 percent accuracy).

This fieldwork not only verified the fact that one can predict archaeological site locations on strictly environmental grounds, but also proved that the initial random survey of the Reese River provided a satisfactory picture of where the piñon ecotone settlements were located.

Of the polythetic criteria, it was found that four factors (distance to water, distance to ecotone, elevation above valley floor, and percent slope) were sufficient to account for most of the observed variability in site location. Parameters were determined for each variable, and it was found—to our surprise—that the Reese River sites fell into almost perfect normal-curve distributions. In no case was the observed distribution statistically different from the expected normal frequencies.

These determinants can be summarized even further in terms of two simple probabilistic models. The first such model is the familiar bell-shaped curve, projected into three dimensions (Figure 9–7). This model applies to three of the four settlement pattern determinants: percent slope, distance to piñon ecotone, and elevation above the valley floor (transformed to square roots). All three variables truncate at zero and increase in a single direction ("steeper," "further from the ecotone," and "higher"). The ridge along the top of the curve represents the maximum probability and corresponds to the parametric mean of the three-dimensional distribution.

A second model is presented in Figure 9–8, which applies to distance from the campsites to water. Previously (Figure 9–7), the two distance variables (from ecotone and above valley floor) logically progressed in a single direction: up. This was specified in the polythetic definitions of site location. But the distance to water is different because direction is unspecified. By considering a stream flowing out of the Toiyabes as a perfectly straight line, the bell-shaped probabil-

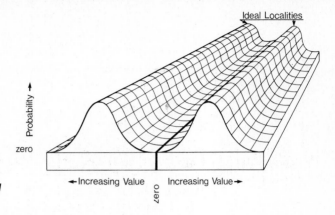

Figure 9–8
Three-dimensional probability
model which shows how the
distance to water can be used to
predict the presence of
archaeological sites in the Reese
River Valley (*after Thomas and*
Bettinger 1976, figure 65; courtesy
of The American Museum of Natural
***History*).**

ity curves must extend on both sides of that stream (Figure 9–8). Let us stand at a water source (zero distance) and then walk away in a perpendicular direction. As this distance increases, so does the probability of finding an archaeological site. The most probable spot is located at the parametric mean (in this case estimated by $\bar{X} = 450$ meters). Once past this point, the probability of finding a campsite diminishes and ultimately approaches zero. Had we chosen to walk the other direction from the stream (180 degrees away), exactly the same probability distribution would have been involved. In other words, because the water sources at Reese River tend to flow linearly (as ephemeral streams), the sites are predicted by two bands of probability, each running parallel to the water source.

We find these two probabilistic models to be useful descriptions of our Reese River data. The piñon ecotone camps can be viewed as a sample of $n =$ sixty-five sites, drawn at random from a hypothetical universe of all possible samples that exist under similar conditions (Thomas 1976 discusses the hypothetical universe concept in detail). The probabilistic models in Figures 9–7 and 9–8 are thus theories, to be tested in other localities. Pragmatically speaking, the true role of science in archaeology is to take such primitive theories and see just how well they perform in predicting phenomena elsewhere. By so doing, we can ultimately define the hypothetical population from which the Reese River sample was drawn.

A Locational Analysis Approach: Classic Maya Settlements

The preceding example from Reese River followed in the basic tradition of cultural ecology: relevant environmental factors were isolated, and these in turn were used to predict prehistoric patterns of human settlement. The assumption was that people tend to live in places that best satisfy primary technological and ecological requirements. As it turned out, these environmental factors did predict the Reese River settlement pattern to a remarkable degree.

But Chapter 3 went to great lengths to demonstrate that modern anthropology is really comprised of several alternative mainstreams, each of which suggests a particular method and perspective for approaching the same cultural phenomena. Cultural ecology is merely one of the anthropological mainstreams. While pervasive, cultural ecology by no means has an exclusive hold on current archaeological thinking. In the example that follows we will demonstrate how a more humanistic approach can be brought to bear on the issue of settlement patterns.[1]

One of America's most intensively studied societies is that of the Classic Maya, who lived in the lowland forests of the Yucatán Peninsula from about A.D. 250 to 900.

The bare facts of Maya settlement are well known. The Maya constructed impressive centers of population and government throughout the lowlands, sites typified by monumental architecture, elaborate hieroglyphic monuments, and, in some cases, lavish tombs. Several minor religious and governmental centers were also known to exist, and spread around these lesser sites were the scattered hamlets of the Maya peasantry.

Interpreting these facts, however, requires an explicit theoretical structure, and this is where archaeologists differ in their interpretation of the Maya civilization. Some archaeologists, operating within the overall framework of traditional cultural ecology, have pointed to environmental parameters which conditioned the Maya settlement pattern. William R. Bullard (1960) attacked the problem by conducting a broad-scale site survey throughout northeastern Petén, Guatemala. Bullard's survey consisted primarily of conducting compass traverses, which were carried out on muleback. The heavily forested tropical terrain hampered the survey efforts, making sites almost invisible even from fifteen meters distant.

Habitation sites seemed to cluster in some areas and be wholly absent in others. Bullard (1960:364) suggested that this distribution was linked with the accessibility of well-drained level ground adjacent to dependable sources of water; houses occurred all around Lake Yaxha, and they also seemed to occur almost continuously around the edges of the large *bajos*. Sites were clustered near the natural and artificial *aguadas*, large circular basins dug into the clay soil of swampy places, and house ruins seemed always present near large arroyos and stream beds. To Bullard, the Classic Maya settlement pattern seemed best explained by water use.

Another archaeologist, William Rathje (1971), has considered different features of the Maya landscape. Because the lowland environment is "redundant" in access to resources, transportation of goods is difficult, and irrigation agriculture impractical. Rathje believes that the environment of the Maya provides an unlikely setting for the development of such a high-level civilization (Rathje 1971:275). In particular, the Maya territory is uniformly deficient in resources essential at the individual household level: mineral salt, obsidian for tools, and hard stone for grinding slabs. Rathje suggests that the Maya lowlands were divided into an outer buffer zone which bordered the highlands (and hence where resources were in short supply) and an inner core or central area "landlocked" and secluded from resources by the buffer zone. Perhaps the very exigencies of everyday trade made the isolated inner core a suitable spot for the development of complex societies. That is, the Maya settlement pattern can be explained as a complex sociopolitical response to the need for procurement and allocation of critical resources or services (Rathje 1971:278).

These interpretations of the Maya settlement pattern fall under the broad umbrella of "ecological determinants approaches," which I illustrated earlier for the Reese River Valley. Such studies resort to the distribution of resources within the physical environment to explain the patterning of human settlements.

Recently, an alternative mode of reasoning has been brought to bear on the problems of the Maya settlement pattern. Joyce Marcus (1973, 1976) has combined recent discoveries in Maya epigraphy with techniques of **locational analysis** to propose what might be called a "cognitive" solution to explain the settlement hierarchy of the Maya.

Marcus began with an examination of the Maya world view. By citing relevant ethnographic information, Marcus proposed that for the Maya heaven was a quadripartite and multilevel region, supported by four divine brothers known as *bacabs* (Marcus 1973:912). The Maya also conceived of Earth as comprised of four parts (see Figure 9–9), and each of the four directions was associated with a color, a system known to be widespread among North American Indians.

Marcus then argued that modern cosmology provides clues to ancient organizational principles, suggesting that the Classic Maya landscape was commanded by four capital cities. Although power shifted from one center to another through the years, there were always four regional capitals at any given time, and, regardless of their actual location, they were viewed as occupying the

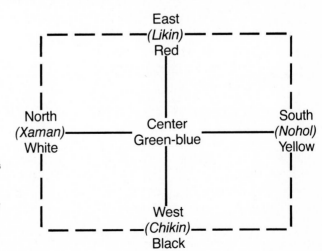

Figure 9–9
The Maya conception of the earth's quadripartite organization, with world-directions and associated colors (*after Marcus 1973, figure 2; courtesy of Joyce Marcus and The American Association for the Advancement of Sciences*).

four quadrants of the Maya universe (heaven and earth). The freestanding carved stone monuments, **stelae**, tend to support this contention. One such stela at Copan, Honduras, dates to A.D. 730 and speaks of four contemporaneous capitals (Copan, Tikal, Calakmul, and Palenque). They are associated with the world-directions. Each capital had a distinctive "emblem glyph," a hieroglyph that stood for that specific site. Even more interesting is the fact that while the monuments at the four major sites were permitted to mention each other by name, no secondary center ever mentions a primary center except the one to which it was subsidiary. Marcus argues that it is possible to document exactly which secondary centers are attached to which major regional center.

Marcus then expanded this cosmological framework by calling on the basic tenets of **Central Place Theory**. A variant of locational analysis, Central Place Theory was initially proposed as a series of models, designed to explain how settlement hierarchies function and to determine demography within a modern market economy; Flannery (1972), Crumley (1976), and Johnson (1972, 1975) have discussed the relevance and application of Central Place Theory to archaeology. Briefly stated, the location theory suggests that a hexagon is the most economical geometric form for the equal division of an area between a number of points. Employing the hexagon as the fundamental building block, the locational theory goes on to explain the spacing of towns and cities that act as centers for distribution of goods and services to smaller towns and the rural hinterland (see Flannery 1972:418). Several assumptions are made: (1) uniform distribution of population and purchasing powers; (2) uniform terrain and resource distribution; (3) equal transport facility in all directions; and (4) all central places perform the same functions and serve areas of the same size. In theory, the most economic arrangement of service centers results in a hexagonal network or lattice.

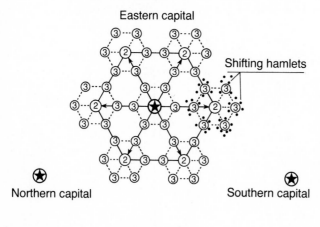

Figure 9–10
Joyce Marcus's hypothesis of how the Lowland Classic Maya organized their territory from regional capitals to outlying hamlets. Circled stars indicate the four regional capitals; circled 2's represent the secondary centers; and circled 3's represent the tertiary centers. The small dots represent shifting hamlets around the tertiary centers (*after Marcus 1976, figure 1.12; courtesy of Joyce Marcus and Dumbarton Oaks Research Library*).

Figure 9–10 shows the idealized lattice for the Classic Maya. The smallest unit of settlement is the village hamlet, probably little more than a cluster of thatched huts occupied by groups of related families (marked by the "3" in Figure 9–10). These tertiary centers were spaced about the secondary ceremonial-civic centers, which contained pyramids, carved monuments, and palacelike residences for the local priesthood. The secondary centers were in turn spaced in hexagon fashion around major Maya capitals. These centers, such as Copan and Tikal, contained acropolises, multiple ceremonial plazas, and a great number of monuments. Linking the centers of the various hexagons were marriage alliances between members of royal dynasties.

Marcus suggests that out of the several large primary centers existing, the Maya selected four as regional capitals. In accordance with their cosmology, these capitals were associated with the four quadrants of heaven, regardless of their physical location. According to Marcus (1973:915), "So strong was the cognized model that, despite the rise and fall of individual centers, there seem always to have been four capitals, each associated with direction and, presumably, with a color."

All of this, of course, is only enlightened speculation. The crux of the issue is how well the actual Maya settlement pattern corresponds with the Marcus model. The answer is that the sites fit the hexagonal distribution remarkably well. Consider the case of Calakmul, in the Petén of Guatemala (see Figure 9–11). Marcus identified Calakmul as one of the four major Mayan regional centers. Surrounding Calakmul are five to eight virtually equidistant secondary centers. The Marcus model suggests that between A.D. 600 and 900 Calakmul was the "central place" of a hexagon consisting of Naachtun, Altamira, La Muñeca, Oxpemul, Sisilha, and Uxul. The stelae at these secondary centers share the single emblem glyph of the major center, Calakmul. Other "central

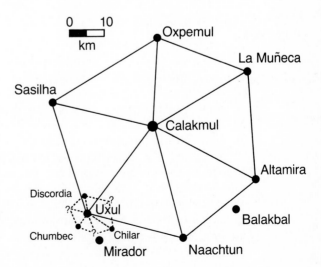

Figure 9–11
Calakmul, one of the four regional capitals in Figure 9–10. Note how the six secondary centers are almost exactly the same distance from Calakmul (*after Marcus 1976, figure 1–15; courtesy of Joyce Marcus and Dumbarton Oaks Research Library*).

places" such as Tikal and Naranjo display similar hexagonal arrangements of secondary centers.

Moreover, the secondary centers themselves seem to be at the center of smaller hexagonal lattices of tertiary sites. Uxul, for example, is encircled by Discordia, Chilar, and Chumbac (Figure 9–11). Analysis at the tertiary level is hampered by incomplete archaeological surveys of the lowlands, but the available data seem fairly consistent with the hexagonal model.

Aside from presenting the specifics of Maya ceremonialism and settlement, this example points up an important scientific principle. Archaeologists are obviously participating in more than one anthropological mainstream. Archaeologists such as Rathje and Bullard have presented largely ecological explanations for the patterning of Maya sites. Marcus has synthesized data from cosmology, epigraphy, and Central Place Theory to propose an alternative theory for Maya settlement pattern. Other models could presumably be generated, grounded in other a priori assumptions.

What sets archaeology apart from theology is that each model—regardless of how it was derived—must then be tested against the independent archaeological data. As described in Chapter 2, some theories may survive the initial testing, others will fail outright. Then it is time to revise the surviving theory and test once again. It seems to be too early in the scientific cycle to see which of the competing Maya theories will prove victorious. Particularly important in the future will be systematic archaeological surveys designed to locate the small village hamlets, so often overlooked in previous archaeological surveys of the lowland rain forest. At this point, the Marcus model is tenuous and, in all likelihood, no single theory will emerge triumphant. But the alternative processes of induction and deduction progressively bring scientists closer to the truth.

A Site Catchment Approach: Formative Villages in Oaxaca

The site catchment approach was introduced to archaeology by C. Vita-Finzi and Eric Higgs (1970:5). They defined the objective as "the study of the relationships between technology and those natural resources lying within the economic range of individual sites." The **catchment principle** is quite simple: all else being equal, the further away from the site, the less attractive is a resource. That is, the longer one must travel to exploit a particular resource, the less rewarding that exploitation becomes. Ultimately, there is a certain distance beyond which resources are probably not exploited at all—it is simply easier to move and establish a new site adjacent to the resource in question. The Kalahari Bushmen women, for instance, almost never forage further than ten kilometers from their base camp. Small groups of men may occasionally travel further while hunting, but they generally make a separate overnight camp to avoid excessive travel (Lee 1969).

Vita-Finzi and Higgs applied their catchment concept to late Paleolithic and early **Neolithic** sites in the eastern Mediterranean. They drew circles of five-kilometer radius around the sites in question, reasoning that most resources used at these sites would come from within the circle. That is, the 7,900-hectare area surrounding a site forms a *catchment*. Vita-Finzi and Higgs then analyzed the land within the catchments in terms of potential for agriculture. Sites with low percentages of arable land (less than 20 percent) were thought to have been unlikely spots for agriculture.

The pioneering effort of Vita-Finzi and Higgs has been followed by other archaeologists anxious to explore the potential of catchment analysis; the original method is not without its defects, however, and several modifications have been made in the analysis of site catchments (e.g., O'Connell 1975; Flannery 1976a; Rossman 1976; Zarky 1976; and Peebles 1978). To see how catchment analysis really works, let us examine an application by Flannery (1976a).

The site of San José Mogote is an Early Formative village located in the Etla region of the Valley of Oaxaca, Mexico. The site was occupied from approximately 1150 to 850 B.C. and consists of several household clusters which, taken together, form a nuclear riverside community. The site itself was excavated during four field seasons by crews from the University of Michigan under the direction of Kent V. Flannery. Preservation of archaeological remains at San José Mogote was exceptional, and samples of carbonized seeds, wood charcoal, pollen, and animal bones were recovered. On the basis of these excavated samples Flannery attempted to reconstruct the site catchment of San José Mogote. His method differs from the original Vita-Finzi and Higgs catchment analysis in that Flannery began with the actual resources exploited and then tried to reconstruct the necessary catchment, rather than taking the catchment radii as given.

Figure 9–12 summarizes the catchment areas operative at San José Mogote. The catchment areas really consist of a series of ever-widening concentric circles (Flannery 1976a:109). Flannery concludes that San José Mogote needed a circle of less than a two-and-a-half kilometer radius to satisfy all of the basic agricultural requirements. Within a few hundred meters of the village were domestic dogs and turkeys (both eaten) and several wild plants such as prickly pear and hackberry. The Atoyac River flowed less than one kilometer from the site, and villagers could obtain mud turtles, opossum, and raccoon, in addition to necessary building materials such as reeds and sand for making adobe. Most important, of course, is that within a two and one half kilometer radius, the San José Mogote villagers had available to them more than 1,400 *ha* of arable alluvium, and Flannery (1976a:107) estimates that this land had an agricultural potential of over 400 metric tons of maize. Flotation samples from house floors at San José Mogote indicate that teosinte also grew in the nearby cornfields. In essence, the two and one half kilometer catchment easily provided the basic agricultural potential for supporting the estimated 80 to 120 households at San José Mogote.

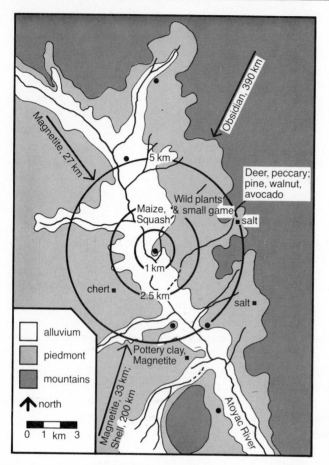

Figure 9–12
Site catchments for the village of San José Mogote, Oaxaca (*after Flannery 1976a, figure 4–6; courtesy of Kent V. Flannery and Academic Press*).

But a catchment of five kilometers' radius was required to satisfy the mineral resource requirements, and also to provide some important wild sea-sonal plants, such as agave, prickly pear stem, rabbits (both jackrabbit and cottontail), and birds like quail, dove, and pigeon. An excellent source of chert for making stone tools was available only three kilometers to the southwest, and a salt source was also available within the five-kilometer radius. The five-kilometer radius is probably the threshold beyond which agricultural activity would yield decreasing returns.

Moving even further out, a circle with a fifteen-kilometer radius probably supplied the necessary deer meat, house construction materials, and pine, the preferable wood for cooking fires. Several other long-distance inputs can be noted in Figure 9–12, such as magnetite (used to make small iron-ore mirrors) and obsidian (used for utilitarian and ritual purposes).

Flannery then juxtaposed the San José Mogote catchment with those of similar Early Formative villages scattered along the Atoyac River (Figure 9–13).

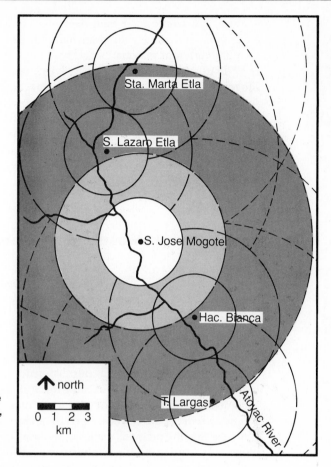

Figure 9–13
Catchments for Early Formative
villages along the Atoyac River,
Oaxaca (*after Flannery 1976a,*
figure 4–7; courtesy of Kent V.
***Flannery and Academic Press*).**

It is interesting to note that circles of radius of two and one half kilometers do not overlap; each village was able to approximately satisfy its basic agricultural requirements without competition from neighbors. The five-kilometer circle for San José Mogote overlaps with neighbors on both sides, and the seven and one half kilometer radius intersects with the catchments of the four nearest neighbors. The fifty-kilometer radius overlaps with all villages, and exclusivity to resources disappears, producing a single large catchment for the entire Valley of Oaxaca.

Flannery interpreted the San José Mogote catchment areas in human terms. The innermost catchment circle consists of a small area of river bottomland, and upland where the village site is located. Most of the agriculture occurs here, and this is the place of burial. This inner circle was probably aggressively defended. The five-kilometer area contains the area where people forage for wild plants and animals, and they expect to encounter neighbors from nearby villages. Still further out is the area of overlapping utility, where women do not venture, but where men hunt deer and attend to mountain-top shrines. This outer zone is shared with even more distant strangers, probably even those speaking different dialects.

Thus a catchment analysis of the resources actually used at San José Mogote gives clues to how these early agricultural peoples related to the surrounding territories and to neighboring groups. The realities of site catchment areas, combined with relevant social factors, ultimately determined the actual location of villages, and the spacing between neighboring communities. As Flannery stated (1976a:117), "It is this interplay between social distance, subsistence needs, and the geometry of location that makes the complex settlement systems of the Formative such an interesting challenge."

A Biocultural Approach: Woodland Mortuary Practices

> *De mortuis nil nisi bonum*
> **(say nothing but good of the dead)**
> *Kurt Vonnegut Jr.*

The distinction was made in Chapter 3 between physical and cultural anthropology, stressing that archaeology deals with cultural phenomena. Like most black-and-white criteria, this distinction is not really as clear-cut as I have led you to believe. But in books like this it is necessary to begin somewhere, so I excluded physical anthropology from our immediate domain of interest. Now it is time to redress the balance. In truth, archaeologists have been guilty of rather badly mistreating their colleagues in physical anthropology. All too often archaeologists excavating mortuary sites have called in a physical anthropologist (or osteologist) primarily as a technician whose job is to produce some tables and figures about the bones. Before 1970 or so it was rare for the archaeologists to even invite the osteologists to the site, much less solicit advice about the best way to go about testing the site and removing the human burials.

But recently one branch of physical anthropology has indeed worked closely with field archaeologists with the express purpose of studying the prehistoric biological system. Called **biocultural anthropology**, this new subdiscipline recognizes the need for cooperation between archaeologist and biologist in working toward a common goal. Of particular interest in the past decade or so has been the study of prehistoric health and demography.

Archaeologists have traditionally focused on problems of prehistoric settlement patterns and cultural ecology by studying the density and distribution of cultural debris. Biocultural specialists study similar questions but they examine instead the biological remains. That is, while archaeologists gravitate toward potsherds and arrowheads, biocultural anthropologists look among the bones for their answers.

The biocultural approach has recently been expanded to a regional scale by Jane Buikstra and her colleagues. Working in the lower Illinois Valley, Buikstra (1976, 1977) has applied the regional perspective to issues of human biological variability. Buikstra has limited her study to the period between about 150 B.C. and A.D. 1000. The initial part of this sequence is known as the **Middle Woodland period**, which lasted until about A.D. 400. The well-known **Hopewell** burial mounds are a product of the Middle Woodland period in this area. Following the Middle Woodland is a period conventionally defined by the absence of elaborate Hopewellian artifacts and structures. The period from A.D. 400 to A.D. 1000 is known as **Late Woodland**.

The transition from Middle to Late Woodland has been the topic of discussion for decades. Basing their arguments largely on changing elements of artifact style and burial disposition, investigators have often depicted the Late Woodland period as the "dark ages" or a period of "cultural decline" (Buikstra 1977:73). The transition period has been variously ascribed to migration, climatic change, disease, stress, and "cultural fatigue." Buikstra has recently mounted an integrated program of biocultural research to look beyond the specifics of artifact style and mortuary pattern to examine the complex interdependence between biological and cultural systems during Woodland times.

Buikstra's research combines the traditional human osteological studies with the more recent advances in archaeological field technique. The study of biological and cultural variability during Middle and Late Woodland times requires a large, unbiased mortuary sample from both periods called a *paleoseries.* Significant error can be introduced by generalizing from a few, unrepresentative skeletons. At the Koster site, for instance, several individuals were buried in the central midden of Horizon VI. But these were only the old and abnormally diseased individuals; obviously the remainder of the population had been buried elsewhere. For the purposes of examining the influence of disease and diet, this kind of sample is clearly inadequate.

The problems faced by Buikstra are similar to those faced by other archaeologists looking at settlement patterns. Realizing this, Buikstra initiated her program of *regional sampling* for mortuary sites in the lower Illinois Valley. She quickly realized that burial sites in this area are far more numerous than the published archaeological literature would suggest. Previous work sites had centered on a few spectacular sites and had overlooked dozens of less flashy or less accessible sites. Another advantage of the mortuary site survey is that the archaeological resources can be effectively conserved, minimizing both expense and damage to archaeological sites. Buikstra's survey provided a mass of high-quality observational data. She systematically collected data, for instance, that indicated the soil attributes of each site, which further defined which areas would preserve human bones and which areas had soil conditions that probably destroyed the osseous material. Combined with data on site location and appearance, the decision of where to dig could be made intelligently, rather than in a haphazard fashion.

Buikstra, as a biocultural anthropologist, combines the relevant attributes of both osteologist and archaeologist. Not content to act merely as a technician, she designed a regional archaeological site survey to locate the mortuary sites she needs. Then, once the sites have been delimited, certain special areas are selected for detailed excavation, which she directs. In so doing, she has been able to obtain data heretofore escaping the attention of the prehistorian.

Specifically, Buikstra and her colleagues have developed contrasting biocultural models for Middle and Late Woodland periods. The Middle Woodland model can be summarized as follows (after Buikstra 1977:73–74):

1. Mounds comprise the major mortuary facility during Middle Woodland times.
2. Middle Woodland communities lived in evenly spaced villages along watercourses.
3. A system of social ranking can be identified within Middle Woodland communities.
4. Individuals of paramount rank within Middle Woodland communities controlled the redistribution of key economic resources.

By contrast, the Late Woodland period utilized mortuary areas other than burial mounds, so the skeletal series is sometimes skewed. As a result of Buikstra's site survey and excavation techniques, Late Woodland cemeteries adjacent to burial mounds have been identified and studied for the first time, suggesting that previous samples from Late Woodland mounds were seriously biased. Buikstra and her colleagues systematically carried out reconnaissance, rather than relying on simple, intuitive methods.

A number of general points regarding the Middle-Late Woodland transition emerged. Although Late Woodland burials lack the exotic and spectacular burial goods noted for Middle Woodland Hopewell sites, the social organization reflected by these burials does not appear to become less complex through time. That is, despite discontinuities at the artifact level, the underlying system of ranking appears to be relatively stable. In fact, more social change seems apparent within the Late Woodland period than between Middle and Late Woodland (Buikstra 1977:75).

The patterning of genetic traits also supports the Middle-Late Woodland continuity. Buikstra analyzed the minute cranial and postcranial characteristics on eight Woodland paleoseries and found that the hypothesis of a population movement between Middle and Late times is extremely unlikely. But she did find evidence of another interesting discontinuity. During Middle Woodland times, the gene pool extended in an almost linear fashion up and down the major rivers of the area. This finding is completely consistent with the suggestion (based on cultural and environmental evidence) that Middle Woodland populations spaced themselves along the rivers and oriented to them as their primary means of interaction. But during Late Woodland times the genetic interaction appears to be more circular than linear, suggesting an orientation that included the surrounding upland regions. It would seem that a marked population increase occurred during Late Woodland times, leading to a circumscription of plant-collecting territories, and a relative localization of gene pools. Of course these suggestions are based on preliminary assessment of the skeletal evidence, and must be tested against other relevant biological and cultural data.

Going even further, Buikstra and her colleagues used the site survey data to estimate overall population densities during Late and Middle Woodland times. As expected, the population density did increase between 150 B.C. and A.D. 1000. But, rather surprisingly, there was no striking increase associated with any particular segment of the Late Woodland period. Instead, the population gradually increased, perhaps associated with some shift in subsistence practices in areas that had minimal access to arable land.

Coupled with this population increase was a suggestion that life within Late Woodland times was "more biologically stressful" than during the Middle Woodland period (Buikstra 1977:78). The life expectancy at age fifteen was a full five years less in Late Woodland times than in Middle Woodland. The suggestion of increased dependence on agriculture is strengthened by patterns of dentition. From combined studies on the amount of stable strontium in the bone, the number of cavities, and the attrition rates, the pattern emerges that carbohydrate intake increased markedly in the later Late Woodland sites.

Although the complete summary of the findings of Buikstra and her research team remains to be published, it is clear that the findings integrate a holistic concern with prehistoric ecology, stressing relationships between variables relevant to prehistoric social organization, subsistence strategy, and biological (that is, genetic) factors. Not only do the biocultural data provide a new avenue of research per se, but they also open significantly new possibilities for further archaeological testing.

SUMMARY

The regional approach has become a major theme in American archaeology in the last three decades or so. Focussing on overall man–land relationships, settlement pattern archaeology transcends the single site in order to determine the overarching relationships between the various contemporary site-types employed by societies. The regional approach thus precludes the taking of single sites as somehow "typical" or "normal" for a culture. Instead, emphasis is upon variability between sites within the settlement pattern. Nonstratified—or "surface"—sites are often critical to the regional approach, and a number of probability-based sampling designs are currently being employed to minimize bias in recovering settlement pattern data.

Four major strategies are apparent in the regional approach to archaeology. The ecological determinants approach stresses the key underlying environmental and technological factors that condition the placement of archaeological sites; in some cases, strictly environmental criteria can be used to predict the locations of undiscovered archaeological sites. The locational analysis approach examines the relationship of key regional centers to outlying secondary sites. These organizational principles are sometimes manifest as a hexagonal lattice arrangement, in which the settlement pattern minimizes transport of goods and services between major population centers and the outlying rural hinterland. The site catchment approach also focuses on the mode of procurement of subsistence items, but emphasizes the strategic placement of major habitation areas. Such analyses assume that people tend to minimize travel between their places of residence and the location of key resources. Catchment areas thus involve a series of concentric circles that radiate from the major habitation sites. When a critical resource distance is exceeded, new habitation sites will be established in a more centrally located spot. The biocultural approach represents an important synthesis between strictly archaeological and physical anthropological research; this relatively new subdiscipline focuses on mortuary patterns and attempts to explore ways in which biological factors (such as rates of mortality, disease, and genetic distance) are related to sociocultural phenomena such as site placement, systems of social ranking, and redistribution of key economic resources. All four of these approaches are currently being applied to problems of regional patterning of archaeological sites.

NOTE

1. This example presages an approach termed "cognitive archaeology," discussed in more detail in Chapter 11.

10

How People Relate to One Another: Reconstructing Social Organization

The shift in prehistoric archaeology, as I see it, is from talk of artifacts to talk of societies.
Colin Renfrew

Not long ago, the conventional wisdom in archaeology held that the archaeologist could learn very little about the social organization of extinct societies. As an undergraduate, I was once counseled that "nobody ever excavated a kinship system" and that archaeologists who insisted on speculating about social organization would really do better to spend their time gluing potsherds back together. That is where the real culture is!

In the past few years, however, archaeologists have made some strides toward inferring social organization from the archaeological record. Throughout this book I have emphasized the point that so long as chronology remained the major objective, it was possible to apply a simplified modal definition of culture; the objective in such cases was to find the typical in a particular region, locality, or archaeological site. A few test pits or trenches were generally satisfactory for obtaining the diagnostic artifacts necessary for constructing cultural chronologies. Culture in this sense is shared and homogeneous; relatively little attention was paid to variability within sites or within regions.

But this shared, modal view of culture cannot be applied to the problems of lifeway, and particularly to reconstructing aspects of extinct social organization (Binford 1965, 1968c; Hill 1970a). The systemic view of culture was discussed in some detail in Chapter 3, the major point being an emphasis on the variability inherent in the archaeological record. From the systemic point of view, archaeological sites are not homogeneous, and the strategy of excavation must be carefully tailored in order to reveal intrasite and intraregional variability (see Hill 1970a:17–19). Cultural systems are internally heterogeneous, made up of a number of internal distributions which directly reflect the social system that produced them. Pueblo San Cristobal, for example, contained not only potsherds that could serve as time-markers (Chapters 5 and 7), but also the physical remains left by households, activity groups, and political organizations. There is even evidence of the status of the various individuals who produced the debris.

Pueblo San Cristobal contained the right objects, but the sociocultural *data*—relevant observations made on these objects—were not recovered. The data do not exist because Nelson simply was not asking questions of this nature when he dug the site. The same site can produce either chronological or sociocultural data (or both), depending on the questions asked by the investigating archaeologist. When dealing with sociocultural reconstruction the context of an artifact is critical. As Hill (1970a:18) has pointed out, a pot may serve for years as a water storage vessel. Then, upon the death of its owner, the same pot may function as a symbol of status in a burial. A single artifact can even function in several different sociocultural contexts simultaneously; a ceramic vessel might be manufactured primarily as a cooking vessel but may also possess certain design elements that serve to identify it as belonging to a specific lineage.

The discussion that follows provides several concrete examples of how archaeologists go about reconstructing past sociocultural behavior. Although the study of social organization is not new in archaeology, such research has only recently been pushed into the mainstream. The tools remain relatively crude and the accomplishments modest, but archaeologists are taking their social organization seriously, and progress is bound to come in the years to follow.

A policy of wait-until-all-the-evidence-is-in can
stunt the growth of archaeology.
Walter W. Taylor

WHAT IS SOCIAL ORGANIZATION?

We can define the general scope of **social organization** by following Walter Goldschmidt's (1960:266) advice on the subject: "The structure of a society involves two things: first, there is a division into smaller social units, which we call groups; and second, there are recognized social positions (**statuses**) and appropriate behavior patterns to such positions (roles)." In this chapter, we will follow this primary distinction: the *group* is a social subdivision, distinct from the network of *statuses* which define and influence the conduct of interpersonal relations.

The **social group** can be either residential or nonresidential in character. **Residential groups** consist of domestic families or households, territorial bands, or community-level villages. Consisting of relatively permanent aggregations of people, the residential group is spatial, local, and territorial (Service 1971:12). By contrast the **nonresidential group** (or **sodality**) consists of associations formed to regulate some specific aspect of society. Residential and nonresidential groups have quite different origins and courses of development. Residential groups are physical agglomerations of people; residential groups are truly residential. But the nonresidential group is a group only in the abstract sense, and, as such, nonresidential groups do not necessarily ever convene. The spirit of the nonresidential group is most commonly maintained through the use of symbols such as names, ceremonies, mythologies, or insignias of membership. In a sense, the residential group functions to regulate discrete spatial matters, while the nonresidential group operates to bind these territorial units together.

Societies are also integrated along status lines. Sometimes these statuses correspond closely to residential or nonresidential groups, but more commonly the status divisions crosscut conventional social groups. The statuses *male* and *female* might, for instance, comprise two separate residential groups, but more commonly they do not (Service 1971:15). Similarly, membership in a specific nonresidential group might confer some degree of high status, or it might not.

Probably the most commonly studied status organization is that of the **kinship** network. The kinship "group" is an organized bunch of people who are related somehow to one another. Kinship statuses are really just special cases of the overall status framework of a society. That is, kinship terms are really just familistic and egocentric status terms (Service 1971:16).

Joining the social group with social status requires a series of guidelines that prescribe "appropriate behavior" within a given cultural matrix. In general, such rules govern where a couple will live upon marriage, how one behaves toward particular categories of people.

Social organization thus embraces the structure and functions of the groups within a society, including how individual statuses articulate one with another. Kinship, marital residence, and descent reckoning are all part of a society's internal organization.

With this as general background, let us see how archaeologists go about reconstructing social organizations that functioned in the past. We begin with the topic of *residential groups* and how they are recognized archaeologically at a variety of levels. Then we will extend the discussion of social organization to consider how the archaeologist analyzes *social status,* and particularly how ranked statuses are recognized in the archaeological record. Finally, we will turn to a consideration of the *role of the individual* in prehistoric social organization, a topic that has only recently come into focus for archaeology.

> The archaeologist has to rely upon circumstantial evidence and much of his time is taken up with details which may appear to be trivial, although as clues to human action they can be of absorbing interest.
>
> *Graham Clark*

RECONSTRUCTING RESIDENTIAL GROUPS

> Here is a problem to face, not one to dodge by bemoaning the inadequacy of the archaeological record.
>
> *Walter W. Taylor*

Reconstructing previous social organization requires one to make certain statements about past behavior; but the behavior itself has long since vanished and is therefore beyond direct archaeological recovery. The task of the archaeologist is to examine the products of this previous social behavior—the artifacts, the sites, the structures—because material culture is presumed to reflect past behaviors in some systematic fashion. Following James Deetz (1968) we will consider four different levels of social behavior; and fortunately for the archaeologist, each behavioral level corresponds to a distinctive kind of archaeological patterning.

Individual behavior patterning is reflected at the *attribute* level of the archaeological record. The attribute (you will remember from Chapter 7), is a distinctive feature of an artifact, a characteristic that cannot be divided into smaller constituent units. Of course, a great deal of cultural behavior is shared by a large number of individuals, but it is the individual alone who actually combines the culturally prescribed attributes into concrete material culture. It is the individual who decided to put side notches (an attribute) on the small (another attribute) projectile points illustrated in Figure 7–1. Similarly, it is the individual who decided to combine a cord-impressed surface with a flared rim on a pot. Deetz (1968:42) suggests that this patterning of attributes at the individual level is "archaeology's only case of perfect association." No amount of rodent activity, sloppy excavation, or miscataloguing in the laboratory can destroy the primary association between a cord-marked surface impression and a flared rim on a potsherd. Absolutely perfect patterning does not occur at any of the higher levels of archaeological patterning.

Material culture is patterned at a second level as the direct result of action by members of various minimal groups of interacting individuals: for example, families, hunting groups, and war parties. This group behavior is reflected in the archaeological record as the patterned combinations of artifacts that are called **tool kits.** Unlike groupings of attributes, tool kits are identified only by their contexts. Hence the tool kit is extremely vulnerable to pre-excavation disturbance, as well as actual blunders in excavation technique. In some cases, archaeologists can fail to recognize the presence of a tool kit during excavation, and the items are analyzed as isolated artifacts. In this case, the second level of patterning could be missed altogether.

The third kind of patterning occurs at the community level, and the archaeological correlate is the household. Households, in turn, are commonly arranged into larger order units, several of which constitute a community.

Finally, behavior at the society level is reflected in the overall settlement pattern, as in the case of the Reese River camps or the Classic Maya hierarchical network. This settlement pattern level of behavior was considered earlier in Chapter 9, and those examples have relevance for the reconstruction of social organization as well as for the analysis of settlement pattern. For the purposes of this chapter, we will restrict our examination to how residential groups are reconstructed at the three lower behavioral levels, as reflected by *attribute patterning, tool kit patterning,* and *household patterning.*

Patterning at the Attribute Level

As always in any discipline which, like archaeology, progresses by the method of "successive approximation," the need is for more data and for more intensive, yet broader, study upon them.

Walter W. Taylor

Artifact attributes can be analyzed for a number of purposes (including chronology), but we will limit the present discussion to the reconstruction of residential groups. Specifically, we will examine how attribute analysis has been used for the study of prehistoric patterns of postmarital residence.

One nearly universal requirement in human societies throughout the world is that married couples should live together. Because incest taboos prohibit marriage between people of the same family, one inevitable consequence of marriage is that a new household must be established; both the bride and groom simply cannot remain living with their parents. One or the other—or both—must move. The possible alternatives for this shift in residence are few, and all societies express one or more culturally preferred modes of residence.

Five major patterns of postmarital residence are possible (after Murdock 1949:16):

Matrilocal residence: a man may live with his wife and her mother.

Patrilocal residence: a woman may live with her husband and his father.

Avunculocal residence: a woman may live with her husband and his maternal uncle.

Bilocal residence: the couple may be permitted to live with either set of parents, depending on economic and personal factors.

Neolocal residence: the newly wedded couple may establish a home independent of both sets of parents.

Although other rules of residence are theoretically possible, these five alternatives are sufficient to describe nearly every known ethnographic situation.

Why do societies practice such different kinds of residence patterns? Murdock (1949) has suggested that the explanation is largely economic. Matrilocal residence occurs in societies in which cooperation among women is crucial for subsistence, particularly among horticultural societies. Patrilocal residence is particularly common in societies heavily dependent upon pastoralism; male cooperation is assured in this case by having men bring their wives home to keep the male herding group intact. Neolocal residence often occurs in societies emphasizing the integrity of the nuclear family. The bilocal residence pattern occurs among relatively unstable bands such as the Shoshoni, where economic and ecological necessity favors a flexible pattern of postmarital residence. Avunculocal residence is somewhat rare, generally developing as an evolved (and replacement) form of matrilocal residence.

Many archaeologists in the early 1960s turned to the study of prehistoric social organization, and a major effort was directed at the detailed analysis of design elements on ceramics (e.g., Cronin 1962; Freeman 1962; Whallon 1968). This era produced three studies that seem to have assumed the status of classics in the literature of American archaeology. William Longacre, then a graduate student studying under Lewis Binford at the University of Chicago, began fieldwork at the Carter Ranch pueblo in eastern Arizona during the summer of 1959. The excavations lasted for three summers, and in 1963 Longacre completed his doctoral dissertation (Longacre 1968, 1970). Longacre was specifically concerned with reconstructing the postmarital residence patterns at Carter Ranch, and his study involved analysis of 175 design elements which were observed on more than 6,000 sherds (also see Freeman and Brown 1964).

A second, related project was carried out by James Hill (1968, 1970b), also a graduate student at Chicago, who excavated the Broken K pueblo during the summers of 1962 and 1963. Among other things, Hill was concerned with extending Longacre's earlier work on matrilocal residence patterns. Since Broken K was almost three times as large as the Carter Ranch site, Hill thought that

Broken K should probably have contained a larger number of residential units, perhaps of an equivalent nature (Hill 1970b:58). By using a combination of computer-related statistical techniques and detailed stylistic analysis, Hill (1970b:72) was "reasonably certain" that matrilocal residence groups existed at Broken K about A.D. 1300.

The Longacre and Hill studies are mentioned here largely for historical reasons, as they both are classic cases that indicated the new directions in which archaeologists of the 1960s were pushing. The Hill and Longacre projects have been both praised and criticized in detail elsewhere (e.g., Watson, LeBlanc, and Redman 1971:34–45; Clarke 1968:255–258; Binford 1977:3–4; Stanislawski 1972; S. Plog 1976; Friedrich 1970; Dumond 1977).

The third such classic residential pattern study was conducted by James Deetz (1965), who examined the change in social organization experienced by the eighteenth-century Arikara Indians in South Dakota. Deetz began with a detailed analysis of Arikara culture history. The Arikara were settled village horticulturalists who lived along the Missouri River. A number of critical social and environmental factors influenced the Arikara between A.D. 1600 and 1800, ultimately producing a profound change in Arikara economy and social organization. The lack of wood for construction, for example, required that the Arikara move frequently, reestablishing villages at short intervals. Trading for European goods changed aboriginal patterns of wealth in favor of the male Arikara population. Disease, largely smallpox, drastically reduced Arikara populations from about 4,000 able-bodied men to about 500.

This combination of factors caused the lives of the eighteenth-century Arikara to change radically. Their strongly matrilineal, matrilocal social system broke down, becoming more flexible as the system adapted to new physical and social environments. The residence pattern was influenced particularly by the rapid decline in population, as well as by the increasing male status due to trading and the resulting accumulation of wealth. The overall effect was the destruction of the aboriginal matricentered social organization, replaced by a more mobile and amorphous system.

It was against this ethnohistorical background that Deetz approached the analysis of ceramics from a three-component Arikara site called Medicine Crow, located on the Missouri River in South Dakota. The three archaeological components at Medicine Crow occurred in two spatially distinct areas of the site. The datings, based on house forms, pottery typology, and limited stratigraphic control, are as follows (Deetz 1965:39):

Component A	1750–1780
Component B	1720–1750
Component C	1690–1720

Medicine Crow was but one of the stops in the northward movement of the Arikara. More importantly, Medicine Crow was inhabited at precisely the time during which the social organization of the Arikara was apparently undergoing the rapid acculturation and change.

Deetz analyzed 2,500 rim sherds from the Medicine Crow site in order to document the social change using archaeological evidence. The analysis began with the explicit statement that he intended to inquire regarding the relationship between the material and nonmaterial aspects of culture (1965:1). His efforts, like those of Hill and Longacre mentioned above, are based on an extremely important postulate which relates the ceramic complex to the society that produced it:

> Under a matrilocal rule of residence, reinforced by matrilineal descent, one might well expect a large degree of consistent patterning of pottery design attributes, since the behavior patterns which produce these configurations would be passed from mothers to daughters, and preserved by continuous manufacture in the same household. Furthermore, these attribute configurations would have a degree of mutual exclusion in a community, since each group of women would be responsible for a certain set of patterns differing more or less from those held by similar groups. (Deetz 1965:2)

Note that Deetz assumed that (1) the pottery was manufactured by women; (2) since ceramic designs are handed down from mother to daughter, a matrilocal form of postmarital residence should result in a more consistent set of ceramic designs than would follow from a patrilocal pattern; and (3) each matrilocal group would tend to have its own distinctive kinds of ceramic decoration.

Deetz selected twenty-four primary ceramic characteristics for study, including observations of the surface finish, the overall profile, the lip profile, and decoration. Using a computer, he tabulated how often each of the attributes co-occurred with the others. How often, for example, does a square lip have a single dotted design? How often does a square lip have a curvilinear design? And do the proportions of these associations change during the ninety-year occupation of the Medicine Crow site?

Overall, the Medicine Crow ceramics show a marked tendency toward reduced attribute association between Components C and A. That is, through time, the Arikara ceramic complex became more randomized. The ceramics of Component C—the earliest occupation at Medicine Crow—was fairly uniform, producing a consistent series of attribute associations. The stylistic designs of Component B pottery were less consistent, and the ceramics of the late Component A were extremely variable. In other words, in less than a century Arikara pottery underwent a radical stylistic change from relative consistency toward relative randomness.

Deetz had demonstrated two things up to this point. Based on ethnohistorical sources, he had established that the eighteenth-century Arikara underwent a change in social organization characterized primarily by abandonment of their matrilocal pattern of residence. This change was precipitated by a major ecological and economic readjustment, reinforced by stresses from hostile neighbors and encroaching Europeans. The ceramics produced by the Arikara women also changed in stylistic patterning, characterized by a reduction in the degree of regular association between traditional design attributes. Deetz (1965:86) then asked, "To what extent, if any, are these two phenomena of change and transformation related?"

Three possibilities were considered:

1. There is no relationship between change in social organization and change in ceramic patterning;
2. Some outside factor (perhaps now unrecognized) might be responsible for the coincidental change in eighteenth-century Arikara social organization and Arikara ceramics;
3. The changes in ceramic attribute patterning and social organization are indeed directly (and causally) related.

Deetz rejected the first two possibilities and cautiously concluded that "the possibility of a functional and real connection between kinship change and pottery design is very high" (Deetz 1965:98). Deetz also entered the standard caution that his conclusions were tentative—"a mere beginning"—and that future research should be directed toward the relationship of material culture to social organization.

Deetz's Arikara study is now an archaeological classic, a pioneering effort in the study of social change. As such, literally dozens of critics have analyzed Deetz's methods, his assumptions, and his conclusions. The percentage method of comparing ceramic attribute frequencies has been criticized (e.g., Whallon 1968; Clarke 1968:595–601). In addition, Deetz has been accused of oversimplifying the patterns of descent and residence (Allen and Richardson 1971:44) and also of not considering the influence of ongoing acculturation on the manufacture of pottery styles (Dumond 1977:335).

But the heaviest criticism has been directed at the sociocultural model employed by Deetz, in which he relates matricentered social organization to the specifics of ceramic design. These same criticisms have also been leveled at Longacre's analysis of the Carter Ranch pueblo and Hill's Broken K study. Stanislawski (1972), for instance, conducted ethnographic research among modern Hopi potters and reached conclusions markedly different from those of Deetz, Longacre, and Hill. Stanislawski noted that there are at least four ceramic teaching models in current use, which crosscut villages, settlement areas, and even tribal and linguistic groups. Modern potters make up to twenty different pottery types during their lifetime, and individual women make pottery quite different from their mothers. In addition, women learn throughout their careers and feel quite free to apply any designs and styles they wish. On this basis, Stanislawski rejected Deetz's hypothesis that ceramic training is channeled along kinship and residence lines: "There are simply too many variations from such an ideal, or norm" (Stanislawski 1972:121).

A Biological Approach to the Problem of Postmarital Residence

This chapter has approached the issue of postmarital residence practices strictly through analysis of attribute-level artifact patterning. While it is true that most of what we know about past residence patterns has come to us from attribute analysis, other approaches are possible for solving the same problem.

Lane and Sublett (1972), for instance, have suggested that residence can be analyzed in terms of its genetic implications. They suggest that within the maximal residence kin group, it should be possible to detect clusters of skeletal traits that reflect the following residence patterns:

1. male-male genetic relationship
2. female-female genetic relationship
3. neither of the above.

Note that these relationships do not equate strictly with patrilocality, matrilocality, and neolocality. The male-male relationship, for example, might reflect a father-son genetic link (patrilocal residence), but it could just as well reflect the mother's brother–sister's son link (the avunculocal pattern). These are genetically identical situations.

Lane and Sublett examined the burial context and settlement pattern based on a number of burials which were exhumed and relocated during the building of the Kinzua Dam near Warren, Pennsylvania. The graves were those of Seneca Indians who had died between the 1850s and the early 1930s.

Ethnohistorical literature and interviews with older informants indicated that during the reservation period the Seneca practiced almost exclusively patrilocal residence. This being the case, one would expect to find a male-male genetic relationship, which would be manifest as follows:

1. Males and females within a single cemetery should be genetically heterogeneous;
2. Males and males between cemeteries should be genetically heterogeneous; and
3. Females and females between cemeteries should be genetically homogeneous.

The results from the Seneca cemeteries were striking because they so closely matched the patrilocal model. The male skeletons within each cemetery were genetically quite similar, but there were great differences between the male populations in each of the cemeteries. On the other hand, female burials were roughly similar, regardless of the cemetery. In other words, the males had been buried near close blood relatives, while the females apparently had not. These preliminary findings are entirely consistent with the known ethnographic practice of patrilocal residence and indicate that similar genetic analyses may be able to supplement the more conventional design analysis studies for the examination of past practices of postmarital residence.

Similarly, Friedrich (1970:332) has argued that the Deetz, Hill, and Longacre studies "have often rested on a naive view of culture as consisting of sets of objective elements correlated with one another in a limited and mechanical fashion." Based on a study of contemporary potters in a Tarascan village, Friedrich noted that design elements are not nearly as relevant as design structure. Stanislawski and Friedrich also criticized Deetz and company for assuming that spatial patterning of artifactual debris will reflect prehistoric social organization in such a straightforward manner. For additional critical comment, see L. Johnson (1972), S. Plog (1976), and Watson (1977).

The Longacre, Hill, and Deetz design studies have been presented not so much for their conclusions—which will probably be modified—but rather to show how they operated at the attribute level. Taken together, these projects comprise a forceful statement of archaeology's contemporary willingness to tackle problems of social organization and cultural change. For more recent research on design and attribute analysis see Washburn (1976), Pyne (1976), and LeBlanc and Watson (1973); also see the excellent review article on this subject by Watson (1977).

> The next thing to having a question solved is to have it well raised.
>
> *John Stuart Mill*

Patterning at the Tool Kit Level

The next level of archaeological pattern is the **tool kit**—a related scattering of artifacts, waste products, and/or raw materials found in a spatially discrete assemblage (see Whallon 1973:226). Tool kits are by no means ubiquitous in the archaeological record. In fact, for a tool kit to come down to the archaeologist "in one piece," as it were, requires that the tools were discarded nearly simultaneously and that the association has not been destroyed by postdepositional factors.

Archaeologists have been aided in their study of prehistoric tool kits by the common practice of burying an individual in the presence of his or her favorite possessions. These grave associations can provide rare and valuable clues as to the composition of diverse prehistoric tool kits.

One important discovery was made in the Valley of Mexico by George Valliant. While excavating at Ticoman, Valliant discovered two human burials, both of which were accompanied by tool kits used for working hides into finished leather. Burial 17 at Ticoman was an elderly male, buried with the tools of his trade. Amidst these tools

> were found two spongy horn grainers or chisels, much worn and with both ends shaved down to edges. These might have been used to detach the flesh from the hide. Their function was supplemented by three small obsidian scrapers. For

perforating holes in the leather there were three large bone awls made from deer radii, the distal portions of which were smoothed to a point. Two bodkins were used presumably to push the thread or sinew through the holes perforated by the awls. A small shovel-tipped tool of bone has no explicable use unless for fine work in the preparation of the hide or as an implement for weaving mats and baskets. (Valliant 1931:313)

Also included were sixteen pocket gopher mandibles, each containing a sharp, chisel-ended incisor (see Figure 10–1). Nearby, burial 34 was uncovered with a kit of fifteen stone and eleven bone tools, which Valliant suggested were for "finer work, like perhaps the tailoring of a hide." Beyond the specifics of leather-working technology, these two burials—both elderly men—suggest a high degree of craft specialization at this site. Moreover, one suspects that leather working was probably a male-dominated activity.

Unmistakable tool kits also occur in archaeological contexts as **caches**; dozens of "cache pits," for instance, have been excavated throughout the Desert West and wherever arid climatic conditions favor the preservation of perishables. At Lovelock Cave, Nevada, a prehistoric basket-manufacturing kit was recently found (Ambro 1970). The small bundle consisted of two main elements, an outer cover made of Canada goose skin, and an inner folded pouch of red fox pelt. Inside the pouch were two completed bone awls and a bone awl blank, a coil of willow splints, and a small chert flake. One bone awl was made of antelope (?) bone, and the other two were manufactured from a pelican leg bone. The chert flake was unremarkable except for its simplicity; one end had a steep scraping edge, while the other edge was quite sharp and had obviously been used in a slicing motion. The wad of willows had been carefully cut and shaped. Ambro (1970:76) suggests that the cache must be older than about 500 years, based on its stratigraphic association.

This simple bundle of hide, stone, bone, and wood would seem pedestrian to most, but it provides some salient clues to the observant archaeologist. The antelope bone awl is much larger than those of pelican bones, suggesting that different tools were used for various stages of basket manufacture. When examined under the microscope, the bone awls exhibit minute yet unmistakable striations along the tip. And the willow splints have been obviously prepared for use in a coiled basket. Hence, the wear patterns on the bone tools almost certainly result from coiled basket manufacture, and the patterns can be used in the future to determine the function on bone awls not found in such tight association with coiled baskets. Moreover, ethnographic accounts suggest that willow splints were probably gathered in the winter, when the leaves were absent from the bushes (Wheat 1967:92). Even the raw materials are informative since Canada goose, red fox, antelope, and pelican are all locally extinct.

Although the association is less firm, analogy to modern and historic Shoshoni indicates that basket making was exclusively the activity of females (Wheat 1967:91). The cache even indicates something about the nature of the seasonal round; Lovelock Cave must have been only one stopover during the

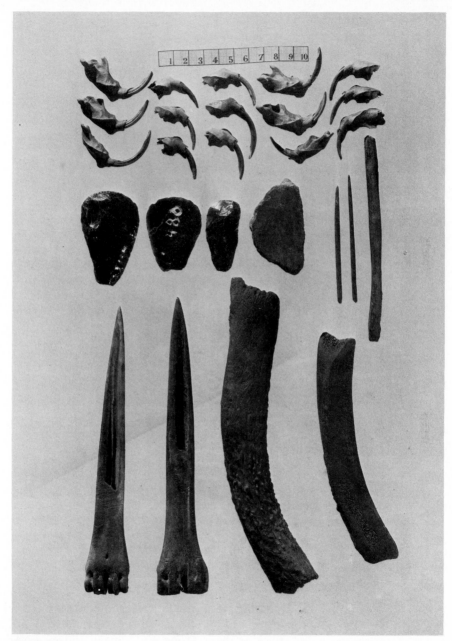

Figure 10–1
"Leather-worker's kit" associated with Skeleton 17 at Tikoman, Valley of Mexico. Top three rows: 15 gopher mandibles; fourth row (left to right) 3 obsidian scrapers, 1 fragment pottery disc, 2 small bone bodkins, bone chisel. Bottom row (left to right) 2 awls of deer metapodial, 2 hide grainers of deer antler (*after Valliant 1931, Plate XCI; courtesy of The American Museum of Natural History*).

year, but the fact that this bundle (as well as several dozen other caches) was left here denotes the intention to return to Lovelock Cave within the near future. This suggests a rather stable pattern of seasonal movement, necessitated, no doubt, by various wild crops available throughout the band's territory.

Grave associations and cache pits are unfortunately all too rare in the archaeological record, and most archaeologists must rely on other analytical techniques to infer the composition of prehistoric tool kits. One of the best examples of working with the tool kit concept is found in the research in the Tehuacan Valley of Puebla, Mexico.

Coxcatlan Rock Shelter is a deeply stratified site initially tested by Richard MacNeish during reconnaissance of the Tehuacan Valley in 1960. Extensive excavations began in 1961, and lasted through 1963. The physical stratigraphy of Coxcatlan was quite clear, and separation of zones of occupation was easily accomplished. The site was initially occupied at approximately 10,000 B.C., and debris continued to accumulate until about A.D. 1300 or so.

Coxcatlan Shelter contained twenty-eight living surfaces and a total of forty-two actual "occupations." During excavation, concentrations of the artifacts, ecofacts, and features from each occupation were carefully mapped. These field data were then computer coded and a series of "living-floor maps" plotted by a Cal. Comp. line plotter. Thus the data were not only available for immediate analysis, but this procedure also allowed the zones and floors to be published in sufficient detail to allow future investigators to analyze the patterns at Coxcatlan.

Figure 10–2 shows one of the living-floor maps produced by the Tehuacan Valley study. Figure 10–2 represents Zone XXIII of Coxcatlan Shelter, with a key to the ecofacts and artifacts. Zone XXIII has been radiocarbon dated between approximately 7200 and 6700 B.C., and occupation occurred during the Ajuereado Phase. This floor contained dark gray occupational debris, and, although no fire pits were located, the dark color of the soil strongly suggests that fires had been built on this surface. The thickness of the floor was about fifteen centimeters, and it covered almost forty square meters. Fowler and MacNeish (1972:242) note that no breaks occurred in the deposition of the debris.

Analysis of the artifacts, bones, and plant remains in Zone XXIII discloses three separate activity areas (Figure 10–2). Activity Area A contained a variety of scraper-planes, projectile points, side- and end-scrapers and several deer bones, a deer antler, and one cottontail rabbit limb bone. The presence of the fully developed deer antler indicates an occupation during the winter months (see Flannery 1967:158), and the abundance of bones, along with the associated projectile points, suggests that hunting was a major activity in Area A. The cottontail rabbit humerus also indicates that some trapping occurred, since cottontail rabbits are more readily trapped than driven (see Flannery 1968, and discussion in Chapter 8). The excavators suggest that butchering, skin preparation, and flintknapping may also have taken place during the brief winter visit.

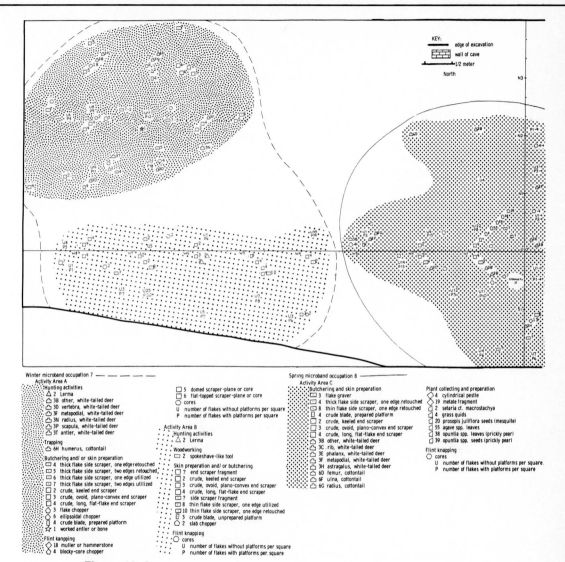

Figure 10–2
Activity areas present in Zone XXIII at Coxcatlan Shelter, Tehuacan Valley, Mexico (*after Fowler and MacNeish 1972, figure 104; courtesy of Richard S. MacNeish and the University of Texas Press*).

Activity Area C occurred to the east of A. The artifacts include side- and end-scrapers, a metate, other grinding stones, and a variety of deer and cottontail bones. Perhaps most important, however, is the storage pit (labeled Feature No. 35). Found within this basin-shaped depression were the leaves and seeds of *Setaria,* mesquite, and *Opuntia* (cactus). These plant remains indicate not only the food preferences of the Ajuereado occupants, but also the seasonal nature of Activity Area C, since this particular selection of seeds would only be available during the spring. The associated artifacts suggest that Area C was a relatively short occupation by a few individuals who came to Coxcatlan Shelter to perform specific tasks. The seeds and grinding stones—along with the thin scattering of animal bones and the absence of projectile points—are indications that seed collecting was the major activity, rather than hunting or trapping. The scraping and graving tools suggest hide preparation, and the core and flakes may denote some flintknapping during the spring occupation of Area C.

Spatially intermediate between A and C is Activity Area B. No animal or plant remains were found and seed-grinding tools were also absent. Area C is tentatively interpreted as similar to A, involving hunting, skin preparation and/ or butchering, woodworking, and flintknapping.

Zone XXIII of Coxcatlan Shelter is only a small part of the living floor analysis conducted for the Tehuacan Valley. MacNeish and his colleagues isolated over seventy-five occupations from about a dozen sites. Taken together, these data allow reconstruction of the subsistence pattern, ecology, and social organization of this area over the past 12,000 years. For the Ajuereado Phase, for instance, eighteen occupational surfaces were excavated, and Zone XXIII at Coxcatlan Shelter is one of the five components that can be regarded as a single occupation (MacNeish, Peterson, and Neely 1972:361).

MacNeish (1972:497) reconstructs the Ajuereado social pattern, from about 10,000 B.C. to 6800 B.C., as consisting of two or three nuclear families or linked individuals. During the late Ajuereado Phase—that is, during the occupation of Zone XXIII—the climate was much like that of today, and the seasonal round was probably designed to exploit seasonally available plants and animals. There is no evidence that sites were occupied longer than either one wet or one dry season, strongly suggesting a nomadic settlement pattern. The cycle was "scheduled," in that the Ajuereado people had a "hierarchy of priorities in the temporal ordering of selected options." The group probably lacked defined territories and used the entire Tehuacan Valley as home base. MacNeish terms this pattern a "nomadic microband community pattern." The Ajuereado technology was not complex; they practiced minimal ceremonialism, and their subsistence pattern was predominantly one of hunting and trapping, with seed and plant collection occurring only during the short seasons when these items were available. MacNeish feels that no modern ethnographic analogies fit the pattern; this way of life has vanished from the earth. That is, living primitive peoples "do not represent this pristine evolutionary type at all, but rather evince a few minimal similarities because they have regressed from a more developed stage, due to decimation and social disintegration under European contact" (MacNeish 1972:497). If we accept the MacNeish reconstruction, the settlement pattern and social organization of the Ajuereado people are available to modern scholars only through archaeological research. Once again, we need only reiterate the point—made more forcefully in Chapter 4—that the true anthropologist cannot proceed without considering the available archaeological evidence. To ignore prehistory is to assume that nothing has become extinct, and we know that this assumption is false.

In truth, archaeologists have only been actively concerned with the reconstruction of activity areas and tool kits for the past couple of decades. The examples discussed above are really somewhat ideal cases, instances when the tool kit associations seem to jump out at the archaeologist. More commonly, the field archaeologist will come upon a living surface that can be identified stratigraphically but not directly partitioned spatially. That is, while the vertical separation might be excellent, the horizontal, contextual nature of the floor is often obscure. A number of investigators have suggested statistical means for analyzing activity areas in such cases (see Whallon 1973, 1974b; Speth and Johnson 1976; Fletcher 1977).

Before we leave the topic of tool kits, I must mention some recent difficulties with the tool kit concept. Specifically as a result of ethnoarchaeological observations, investigators have pointed out that the "living floor" is an assumption that simply does not hold for many modern societies. Based on his recent work among the !Kung Bushmen, for example, Yellen (1977:97) cautions archaeologists against assuming that tools found on living surfaces must be related to a single task or must form part of a single tool kit. At !Kung campsites, for instance, stone hammers and anvils are used to crack mongongo nuts, and these tools are often found in nuclear camp areas, which are also commonly littered with high concentrations of bone. But the stones have no relationship to the faunal remains. Both are physical remains of very different activities, and they occur together only fortuitously (see also Chapter 12). It should be apparent how violating the assumption of the single tool kit could drastically influence the interpretation of Coxcatlan Zone XXIII.

Binford (1973:242–243) has cautioned archaeologists of similar dangers regarding living floor analysis. Binford's work among the Nunamiut Eskimo suggested to him that the Nunamiut have an almost exclusively **curated technology**. That is, the Nunamiut hunters carry their artifacts about to such a degree that the tool inventories of their sites have precious little to do with the original activities that took place there. The problem for archaeologists—at least those dealing with Nunamiut sites—is that there may be little relationship between activities performed and where artifacts are discarded.

These and other problems will be discussed in more depth in Chapter 12; for now, I only mention the potential difficulties in dealing with living surfaces and tool kits.

Patterning at the Household Level

Family and community social patterning is reflected in the archaeological record largely at the household level. Probably the simplest form of a household is a simple brush structure. The Shoshoni, for example, were known to have

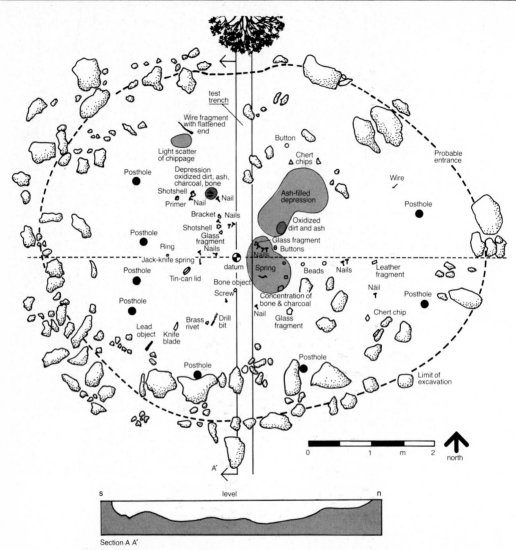

Figure 10–3
Distribution of historic artifacts in House A at the Flat Iron Ridge site, Reese River Valley, Nevada (*after Thomas and Bettinger 1976, figure 36; courtesy of The American Museum of Natural History*).

constructed brush structures, or **wickiups** (see Figure 10–3). Sometimes these temporary structures were surrounded by a ring of stones which presumably held the uprights in place. The stone "house rings" are a common archaeological feature throughout sites in the Desert West. Robert Bettinger and I excavated one such structure on a ridge overlooking the Reese River, in Nevada. While making a surface collection of the area, we discovered dozens of small glass trade beads and a flat clothes iron cached beneath a grinding slab; apparently they used the flat iron in lieu of a hand stone (or **mano**). We named the site Flat Iron Ridge and, thinking that the site was a historic Shoshoni house, we decided to excavate the well-preserved rock ring. The house floor surface was found to be littered with historic artifacts (Figure 10–3), and from the square nails recovered, we estimated the duration of occupation to be from about 1870 to 1890 (Thomas and Bettinger 1976:323–324).

Close examination of Figure 10–3 indicates some interesting relationships between the artifacts within the structure. From the placement of the hearth, and the scatter of burnt bones, it seems clear that food preparation occurred in the eastern half of the house. The doorway was nearby, to admit light and permit the smoke to escape. The larger number of nails found in this area suggests that boards were probably salvaged from other settlements nearby and used for firewood.

A concentration of tools such as knife and cartridge parts was found on the western section of the house, suggesting that the area was used for storing bundles of work items. It also seems likely that this is where the inhabitants slept.

Such patterning is precisely what one would suspect for a Shoshoni house of the early historic period. As discussed earlier in Chapter 9, Shoshoni social organization centered around the nuclear family. According to Steward (1938:239), "Among Western Shoshoni the household was very nearly a self-sufficient economic unit and as such an independent social and political unit." The house on Flat Iron Ridge was probably built to shelter just such an independent household. In aboriginal times this area was used extensively for piñon harvesting in the late fall, and perhaps this is also why the historic house was built. But there is ample evidence of lumbering in the vicinity, and it could well be that the Flat Iron Ridge household was engaged in cutting timber for the nearby ranches and mines. Too little archaeology has been done on the historic Shoshoni for us to offer more than tentative suggestions.

More complex patterning of house remains has been found in the Valley of Oaxaca, Mexico. Flannery and Winter summarize (1976:44) evidence from a sample of twenty-two carefully excavated houses at several Oaxacan sites (see Figure 10–4). In every house they found evidence of grinding stones (for preparing corn), storage pits (generally filled with corn kernels and prickly pear seeds), large storage jars, bones of cottontail rabbits, fragments of pottery, and charcoal braziers (Flannery and Winter 1976:36). They conclude that food procurement, preparation, and storage were carried on by each individual household between 1500 and 500 B.C. This pattern may suggest that houses were virtually autonomous in terms of their food supply, regardless of any additional specialization.

Evidence of tool preparation was also found in each household. Chert cores and core fragments were universal, as were broken stone tools and waste debris. Each household seems to have had access to local stone, and every household produced its own cutting and scraping implements.

Some evidence for household specialization did exist. One house, for

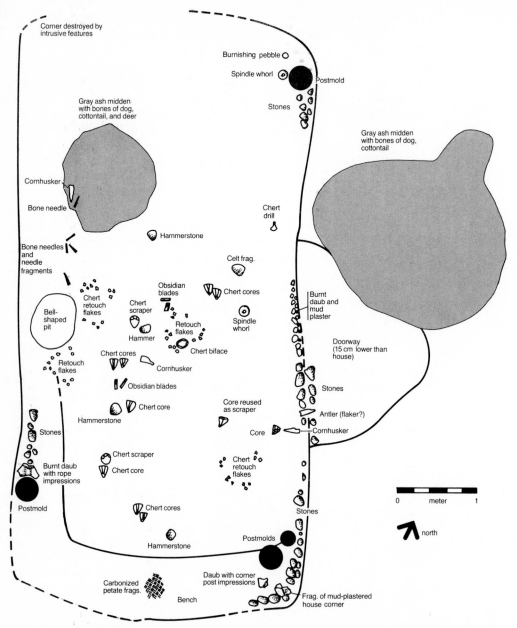

Figure 10–4
Distribution of selected artifacts in House 1, Area A at the Tierras Largas site, Oaxaca (*after Flannery and Winter 1976, figure 2–17; courtesy of Kent V. Flannery and Academic Press*).

instance, contained a bell-shaped pit, which contained a cache of chert waste flakes. The excavators interpreted this as the workshop of a part-time toolmaker who probably made the more refined stone implements for the village. Another house contained a storage pit with a cache of deer bones, some of which were unmodified, while others had been cut to produce socket-type handles and bone rings. Once again, although all households used bone tools this single individual seems to have done a great deal of the tool manufacture for his neighbors. These tool kits seem wholly analogous to the leather-working and basket-making kits discussed earlier; the inference about specialization depends largely on the placement and context of the tool kits within the community.

Another common analytical tool in studying residential patterns is to characterize artifacts as either male or female. The leather-working kits are found, for example, only with males, and we used ethnographic analogy to suggest that the basket-making pouch belonged to a female. Using a similar ethnographic analogy from the highland Chiapas, Flannery and Winter (1976:42–45) have made some tentative suggestions about intrahousehold patterning in Oaxaca. They suggest that women's tools included grinding stones, pottery charcoal braziers, pots showing a crust where maize had been soaked in lime, some hammerstones for preparing food, special deer-bone tools for husking corn, spindle whorls for weaving, and needles for sewing. Most of the flintworking would have been conducted by males using antler flakers; projectile points, chert knives, and scrapers also seem to be men's tools. Men also probably used bone hide-working tools (like those found in the leather-working kits), celts for clearing land, and tools for making other tools, such as shaft smoothers and burins.

The Oaxaca houses seem to be divided along the midline, with the women's area on one side and the men's on the other. Figure 10–4, for instance, seems to have all the male artifacts—chert cores, scrapers, retouched flakes, and a biface—lying to the left of the door as one enters. To the right are the bone needles, deer-bone cornhuskers, and pierced pottery disks that probably function as spindle whorls. Moreover, the gray ash indicates that the cooking also occurred on the right or women's half of the house.

The Oaxaca houses do not, of course, stand in total isolation. Associated with each house is a cluster of related activity areas, including outside storage pits, trash midden, burial area, and oven (see Figure 10–5). These household clusters are then grouped into the total community. The village of San José Mogote is estimated to have contained several of these discrete yet related household clusters.

A rather different case of inferring social organization from the residential structures is found at Betatakin, the Tsegi Phase cliff ruin in northeastern Arizona. Chapter 6 already discussed how Jeffrey Dean (1970) used tree-ring data from nearly 300 trees to determine the construction sequence of rooms with almost year-to-year accuracy, from initial occupation in 1250 to abandonment shortly after 1286. But Dean's objectives went far beyond mere architec-

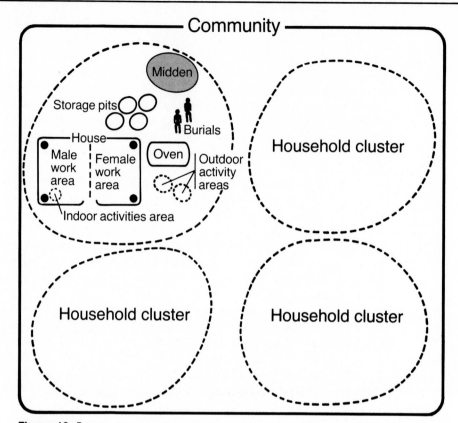

Figure 10–5
Diagram showing the relationship between the concepts of *activity area, feature, male and female work area, house, household cluster,* and *community (after Flannery and Winter, figure 2–18; courtesy of Kent V. Flannery and Academic Press).*

tural dating. He was able to use the tight dendrochronological sequence to infer a great deal about Tsegi Phase social organization at the Betatakin ruin.

Dean (1970:153–157) recognized several functionally different room types at Betatakin:

Living rooms: Features that typify living rooms are one or more jacal walls, low-silled doorways, leveled and plastered floor, fire pits, mealing bins, interior wall plaster, and interior smoke blackening.

Courtyards: These are unroofed, irregularly shaped areas, which generally have plastered floors, fire pits, mealing bins, and storage pits; generally surrounded by living and storage rooms.

Granaries: These rooms are designed to keep insects, rodents, and weather out; they have high-silled doorways, stone slab doors, finely finished and chinked masonry.

Figure 10–6
Betatakin, a cliff dwelling in the Tsegi Canyon, northeastern Arizona (*courtesy of Jeffrey*
***S. Dean and the Laboratory of Tree-Ring Research, University of Arizona*).**

Storerooms: These small rooms lack distinctive features of dwellings and granaries; probably used to store nonperishable items such as tools, ceremonial paraphernalia, and pottery.

Grinding rooms: These rooms have a battery of two to four stone slab bins, which held a series of graded metates.

Ceremonial chambers: The kivas are quite variable, ranging from completely subterranean to completely above ground, from circular to rectangular in shape.

These various types of rooms are grouped into what Dean calls room clusters: at least one living room, one to six storage chambers (granaries and storerooms), occasionally a grinding room, and, in all but a few cases, a courtyard. The rooms within a cluster open directly into the courtyard, or are connected with other rooms that do. The room cluster seems to be the basic architectural unit of Tsegi

Phase villages such as Betatakin. That is, the sites are not merely agglomerations of individual rooms, but are rather an agglomeration of room clusters.

Dean's detailed analysis of Betatakin architecture makes it clear that not only was the room cluster the basic unit of residence, it also provided a more or less exclusive territory for the resident social unit. Each room cluster was undoubtedly occupied by a household, the basic localized unit of modern Pueblo society. Room clusters with a single living room were probably occupied by nuclear families, while clusters with more than one living room must have been the home of multifamily households. Analogy with the Hopi would suggest matrilocal residence, but this proposition was not considered archaeologically (Dean 1970:163).

Interestingly enough, although in modern western Pueblo groups the extended families always occur within the larger lineage, there is no architectural unit that could correspond to a lineage at Betatakin. Therefore, if lineages once existed at Betatakin, they were nonlocalized and hence not visible in the archaeological record.

Beyond the room cluster complex, the only architectural unit that can be isolated during the Tsegi Phase is the village itself. Communities such as Betatakin possessed all necessary mechanisms for mobilizing and directing cooperation of the villagers in community projects. There is no firm correspondence between **kivas** and subvillage residence units, suggesting that kivas must have functioned in conjunction with nonlocalized social units comprised of members of several households. These social units could have been the nonlocalized clans or, alternatively, ceremonial sodalities whose membership cut across clan lines (or both). It is also interesting to note that dual organization (such as **moieties** at Mesa Verde or Chaco Canyon) is lacking at Betatakin.

Dean thinks Betatakin provides evidence of how the Tsegi Phase villagers coordinated labor for community projects. Dendrochronology shows that tree cutting at Betatakin was a communal rather than an individual or household activity: a group of perhaps twenty people felled a number of trees, cut them to standardized primary and secondary beam length, and stockpiled them for future use, perhaps by later immigrants to the village. This occurred in 1269 and again in 1272, but the beams were not used until 1275 when a three-year period of immigration resulted in the construction of more than ten room clusters and one or more kivas.

Dean interprets these data to mean that Betatakin was settled by a group of people who already constituted the functioning community. That is, "Betatakin, *as a social unit,* existed somewhere else prior to the founding of the village known by that name" (Dean 1970:159). The cave was carefully planned for habitation—probably by community decision—and the society had sufficient sanctions to carry out the task. A preplanned move such as this would require a strong leadership structure. The first settlement of Betatakin took the form of three or four spatially isolated room clusters, and subsequently the village grew by accretion of individual room clusters, presumably as additional families arrived.

To summarize, the exceptionally well-dated ruin of Betatakin was probably occupied by (matrilocal?) extended family households, each of which occupied a room cluster. Households were probably grouped into sodalities, and the village itself had a tight sociopolitical structure able to amass a labor force necessary for community works programs. It seems likely that there was also a formalized intervillage social structure.

RECONSTRUCTING SOCIAL STATUS

Success is counted sweetest/By those who ne'er succeed.

Emily Dickinson

Status consists of the rights, duties, privileges, powers, liabilities, and immunities that accrue to a recognized and named social position (after Goldschmidt 1960:266 and Goodenough 1965:2). In other words, a single social status consists of a collection of rights and duties. Consider the typical father-son relationship in our own society. The status "father" is determined by a series of duties owed to his son, and the responsibilities he can legitimately demand of his son. Similarly, the son owes certain obligations to his father and can expect certain privileges in return.

Social status is apportioned through a number of culturally determined criteria. Nearly all societies categorize their members in terms of their age and their consequent position in the cycle of life. Bohannan (1965:149) notes that for African societies the list of male age categories generally runs like this: newly born infant, child on the lap, uninitiated boy, initiated bachelor, married man, elder, and retired elder. The specifics vary from culture to culture, of course, but the underlying principle of age almost always influences one's social standing within the society at large.

Another ubiquitous status category is sex. It is true, of course, that people are inescapably male or female, and that fact is obvious to all. As Robert Lowie noted dryly in *Social Organization,* "Sex . . . is an effective social sorter" (1948:6). But it's interesting that rarely do societies assign status strictly along sexual lines. That is, sex rarely splits a society into two antithetical halves. Sexual links are more commonly merged with other principles of alignment in the definition of status.

Another related conditioner of status is **kinship**. As with sex and age, kinship in a sociocultural sense depends on a biological counterpart but is rarely identical with it (Lowie 1948:7). Kinship terms provide cultural labels for the social positions that determine how interpersonal relations are conducted.

An obvious yet important point to be made here is that each individual simultaneously possesses several different social statuses, or what Goodenough (1965) terms *social identities*. For a given adult male, "father" is only one of several statuses that are operative. That individual may also be a colonel in the

Air Force, a captain of the bowling team, and a Harvard graduate. Each social position has its own collection of rights and duties. Which identity is currently operating depends upon with whom the individual is interacting. The composite of the several identities maintained by a single individual is termed his (or her) *social persona* (Goodenough 1965:7; also see Binford 1971:17). As we will see, it is this encompassing social persona that is reflected in the archaeological record, along with individual status categories such as sex and age.

Linton (1936:115) has observed that "most of the business of living can be conducted on the basis of habit, with little need for intelligence and none for special gifts." Societies have developed two rather different ways of assigning statuses, through ascription and through achievement. An **ascribed status** is assigned to individuals without regard to innate differences or abilities. Ascribed statuses are determined at the moment of birth, and the training for that status begins immediately. Alternatively, a society can provide for statuses to be **achieved**, requiring special qualities of the individuals (Linton 1936:115). Achieved statuses are not assigned at birth, but rather are left open and are ultimately filled through competition and individual effort.

The concept of status allows us to leap from the level of the individual to the level of the entire society. A society is termed **egalitarian** when the number of valued statuses is roughly equivalent to the number of persons with the ability to fill them (Fried 1967:33). That is, egalitarian societies lack the means to fix or limit the number of persons capable of exerting power. Therefore, egalitarian societies are characterized by generally equal access to important resources. One example of an egalitarian society is the Great Basin Shoshoni. Shoshoni leadership is simply assumed by those best capable of leading others, and authority among the Shoshoni was restricted to a particular situation. A particularly good hunter might, for instance, assume a position of leadership when a group of men joined to hunt bighorn. Or a particularly good dancer might take charge of *fandango* arrangements. A particularly good talker might keep the villagers informed about the ripening of plant foods in different areas, and urge the people to cooperate for the group good (Steward 1938:247). The key to leadership in an egalitarian society is experience and overall social standing.

A **ranked society**, on the other hand, is one in which "positions of valued status are somehow limited so that not all those of sufficient talent to occupy such statuses actually achieve them" (Fried 1967:109). The social structure of a ranked society embodies an intrinsic hierarchy in which relatively permanent social stations are maintained and people have unequal access to the basic life-sustaining resources. Although distribution of labor is conditioned by sex and age in both egalitarian and ranked societies, ranked societies tend to have economies that redistribute goods and services throughout the community. The tribes of the American Northwest Coast (see Chapter 3) are an excellent example of a ranked society. The localized kin groups—not the individuals—control the resources, and the major economic goods flow in and out of a finite center (Fried 1967:117).

The categories *egalitarian* and *ranked* define the ends of a social spectrum that can be traced archaeologically. Social status, as we have seen, is one aspect of the overall social organization. And at times the ranking of social statuses can be reflected in the archaeological record.

One common method an archaeologist uses to examine the workings of extinct social systems is analysis of the mortuary practices. An important assumption comes into play here: that persons who are treated differentially in life will be treated differentially in death (Peebles 1971:68). Death, in a sense, is a period of separation and reintegration for both the deceased and also those left behind. The dead are separated from the living and must be properly integrated into the world of the dead. Social ties existed between the living and the once-living, and the ceremonial connections at death reflect in large measure these social relations. Peebles (1971:69) has emphasized the importance of studying human burials as the fossilized terminal statuses of the individual. While these terminal statuses are often different from the statuses most commonly studied by ethnographers, those models defined archaeologically are every bit as real as those observable among ethnographic cultures (Harris 1968b:359–360).

Let us begin with a very simple case, that of McLeod Mound on St. Catherines Island, Georgia (Thomas and Larsen 1979). Chapter 5 has already discussed the stratigraphy of the McLeod Mound. Now let us see what we can tell about the people who were buried in the site.

The vegetation on the McLeod site was apparently burned off, and radiocarbon dates suggest this initial burning occurred about 1600 B.C. Sometime later a large pit was excavated in the center of the clearing, and the remains of five women were laid out. The physical evidence indicates that, although buried together, these people died at different times (see Figure 10–7). The bones of two of the women (burials 13 and 17) were bunched together into a bundle, and this would have been possible only after all the flesh had decayed (or had been removed). Under natural conditions, this decay would have taken at least six months or so. Although we lack the specifics, it seems that the bones of these two people must have been stored someplace else before their final burial in the central tomb at McLeod.

Burial 14, another adult female, died somewhat later. Her body had largely deteriorated, but one hand and some vertebra were still articulated at the time of burial. Although she had died some time before she was buried, no more than six months or so elapsed because the hand and back ligaments were still somewhat intact. Comparison with forensic cases studied in the Washington, D.C., area suggest that decomposition is complete after six months or so, and would also suggest that individual 14 was buried within a few months after death.

The two remaining burials (15 and 16) were both between twenty and thirty at the time of death, making them somewhat younger than the other adults. Their bones were in perfect anatomical order, indicating that interment occurred almost immediately after death. Then the tomb was covered with clam

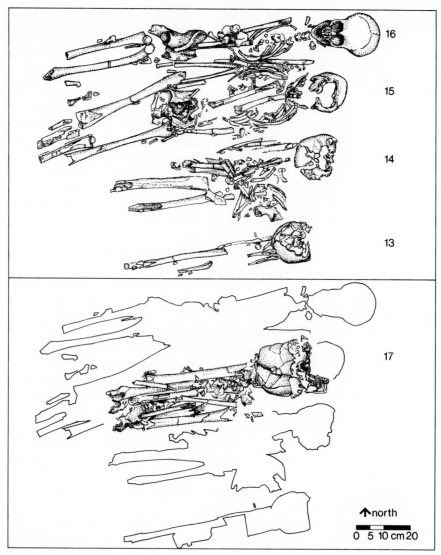

Figure 10–7
Female burials found in the Central Tomb of McLeod Mound, St. Catherines Island, Georgia (*after Thomas and Larsen 1976, figure 13; courtesy of The American Museum of Natural History*).

and oyster shells, perhaps collected from a nearby trash heap; microscopic studies indicate that the shells were collected between December and January (see Chapter 8). The shells themselves have been radiocarbon dated to about 450 B.C. A conical mound about four feet high was then built to cover the tomb.

McLeod Mound was visited several times thereafter, and more burials were placed in the upper part of the mound fill. Although the total site has not been excavated, we can estimate that somewhere between thirty-five and forty people were placed in these later, intrusive graves. Of the fifteen intrusive burials excavated, five were determined to be female, three were male, and seven were too fragmentary for sexual determination. No grave goods accompanied any of the burials.

The evidence here is skimpy, and the skeletons are badly decayed, but we can still find out something about the social organization of the people who built and used McLeod Mound. The social system corresponds to that expected for an egalitarian society, a setting in which there were sufficient statuses for those who achieved them. Note, for instance, that no infants were found in McLeod Mound. In fact, roughly seventy-five burials have been excavated from this time period on St. Catherines Island, and not a single individual younger than about twenty years of age was found. It would seem that the higher status individuals were buried in a mound, while those of lower status were disposed of somewhere else. We know that at McLeod the bones of some adult females were saved for at least six months prior to burial.

The absence of children and infants suggests that achievement of high status came only through experience and demonstrated ability (as among the Shoshoni). Although advanced age does not insure prestige, youth certainly precludes it. Moreover, the lack of grave goods at McLeod would suggest that the individuals buried there were roughly of the same status, both male and female. There is not evidence for elaborate ranking above the level of "mound burial" and "non-mound burial." The entire situation comfortably fits within the model of an egalitarian society.

By contrast, let us examine the ranking of social status evident at Moundville, the second largest ceremonial center in the United States (Peebles 1971, 1974). Located on a bluff overlooking the Black Warrior River in Alabama, Moundville covers about 300 acres and consists of twenty major ceremonial mounds surrounding a large plaza. Unlike simple burial mounds such as McLeod, Moundville consists largely of **temple mounds**, large flat-topped earthen structures designed to function as artificial mountains to elevate the temples above the landscape. Moundville was a major site in the Mississippian tradition, which reached its peak about 200 to 300 years prior to European colonization.

Initial archaeological investigations at Moundville were conducted by the ubiquitous C. B. Moore in 1905–1906 (see Chapter 1). Moore excavated both platform mounds and village areas, and published his findings in two volumes (Moore 1905, 1907). As might be expected, Moore's work is not up to contemporary standards, but his data are still quite usable. The Alabama Museum of Natural History then excavated at Moundville from 1929 through 1941; over half a million square feet of the village areas at Moundville were excavated during this twelve-year period, in part by workers under the Civilian Conservation Corps (Peebles and Kus 1977:435).

More than 3,000 burials have been excavated at Moundville, and they have provided an excellent data base for studying Mississippian social structure. The task is complicated by the different methods of excavation employed, but Peebles's success clearly indicates that a kind of "salvage archaeology"—salvaging museum collections excavated decades ago—can be fruitful indeed.

Peebles began his analysis by studying the various grave goods, which were abundant. Moundville is a major site in the so-called **Southern Cult** or Southeastern Ceremonial Complex (Waring and Holder 1945; Brown 1976). The Southern Cult objects are characterized by a series of distinctive motifs such as the cross, the sun circle, the bi-lobed arrow, and the forked eye (see Figure 10–8). Peebles terms these Southern Cult artifacts *supra-local* because of their widespread distribution throughout the South. In fact, Southern Cult artifacts are known from as far north as northern Georgia and as far west as Spiro, Oklahoma. Whatever the Southern Cult really was—and archaeologists are still debating the point (see Brown 1976)—it seems clear that the complex crosscut the boundaries of many distinctive local cultures.

Peebles recognizes a second kind of distinctive grave goods, which he calls *local symbols*. These artifacts are specially constructed animal effigy vessels, or parts of animals such as canine teeth, claws, and shells. Although the localized symbols are widely distributed in form, they have a very distinctive and structured context within the Moundville area (Peebles 1971:69). The local symbols seem to have functioned as status items within a single site (that is, presumably within a single community), but the supra-local symbols designated the rank of individuals within the overall region.

Each of the mounds at Moundville appears to contain a limited number of high status adults. Grave goods include copper axes, cooper gorgets, stone discs, various paints, and assorted exotic minerals such as galena and mica. Each mound also contains some less well accompanied (presumably lower status) individuals, accompanied only by a few ceramic vessels. Since the Moundville mounds appear to have once supported ceremonial structures (temples), Peebles infers that the high status burials from these mounds were associated with these temples. The lower status burials—particularly the infant and skull burials—were probably ritual accompaniments to the high status individuals.

Peebles has taken the Moundville status hierarchy even further. The very highest status individuals in the mounds were accompanied by several supra-local symbols, including ceremonial axes and sheet copper plumes that depict the "eagle being" and the "dancing priest." Presumably these individuals had status and reputation which spread throughout the entire Moundville culture.

By correlating the presence of higher and lower status symbols, Peebles could then make limited inferences about the mechanisms of ranking at Moundville. The very high prestige items tended to be buried with individuals of all ages and both sexes. This means that status at Moundville was probably assigned at birth. That is, one's social position was inherited and automatically assigned to all family members. This inference is reinforced by the fact that even infants and

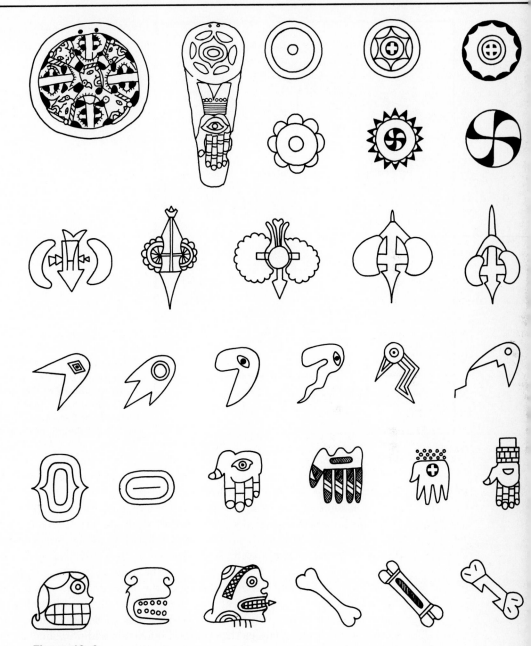

Figure 10–8
Various Southern Cult motifs that occur on shell ornaments, ceramics, and pipes.

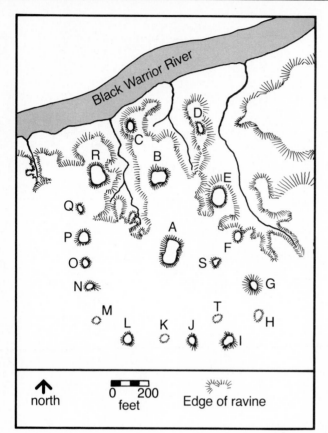

Figure 10–9
Topography of the Moundville site, Alabama (*after Peebles and Kus 1977, figure 1; courtesy of Christopher Peebles and The Society for American Archaeology*).

children—clearly too young to have accomplished anything very noteworthy in life—were buried with lavish grave goods. These individuals were important because of who they were, not what they did.

On the basis of comparison with ethnographic cases, Peebles and Kus (1977:431) predicted that the Moundville burials should be divided into two major classes: the superordinate and subordinate dimensions. Subordinate ranking is a social ordering based on symbols and energy expenditure, a ranking determined exclusively by age and sex. The rule here is the same as that suggested for McLeod Mound: the older the individual, the greater was his opportunity for accomplishment, and therefore the higher will be his rank. In the main, adult burials will be more complex than those of children, and child burials will be more complex than those of infants. In addition, men and women will not share all grave goods because some will be sex linked. The subordinate divisions consist of the "commoners" within a ranked society.

The superordinate division is a partial ordering based on criteria other than age and sex. In this case, class membership is determined by one's geneology. Within the superordinate (that is, the ruling) dimension, some

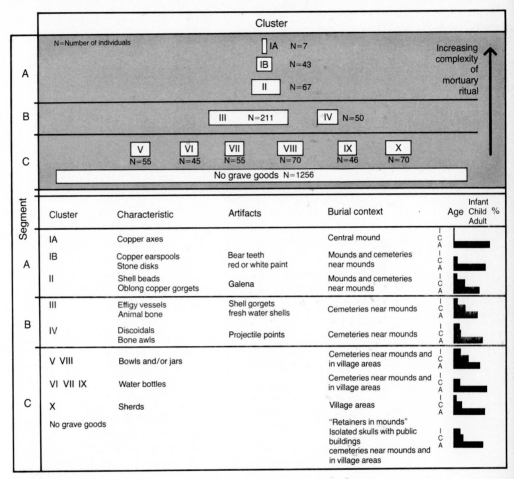

Figure 10–10
Diagramatic representation of the hierarchical social clusters represented in burials at Moundville (*after Peebles and Kus 1977, figure 3; courtesy of Christopher Peebles and the Society for American Archaeology*).

individuals will be infants, some children, and the rest adults. All groups will occur in every ranked category, except the paramount division. This supreme class will contain only adults, and generally only adult males.

In sum, Peebles and Kus predicted that the statuses should divide into a pyramid-shaped distribution. At the base of the pyramid are the commoners, whose statuses are determined strictly by sex and age. The next step up the social ladder consists of those few "special" individuals with ascribed (that is, inherited) status. Finally, at the top will be the paramount individuals, individuals upon whom are lavished all the emblems of status and rank available within the society.

This model was then tested by performing in-depth statistical analysis on 2,053 of the best-documented burials from Moundville (see Figure 10–10). The supreme division (Cluster IA) is presumably the chief. The seven individuals in Cluster IA clearly represent the highest of statuses and the ultimate political authority. These individuals, probably all males, were buried in large truncated mounds and were accompanied by a lavish array of material culture, plus infants and human skulls presumably sacrificed for the occasion. The large copper axes found in the graves seem to be the material representations of the offices held by these individuals. Cluster IB individuals were also buried in or near the truncated mounds and have other Southern Cult artifacts along with several mineral-based paints as part of their grave goods. These peoples were probably the second-order ritual or political officers whose duties included the ceremonial application of body paint or tattoos to others. This cluster contains both children and adult males. The final clustering of this superordinate dimension included adults and children who were buried in cemeteries near the mounds, and in charnel houses near the main plaza; grave goods include chest beads, copper gorgets, and galena cubes.

The important difference between the individuals of the superior Cluster A and those of subordinate Clusters B and C is that the latter are ascribed status strictly on the basis of sex and age. Within Cluster III, for instance, stone ceremonial celts are found only with adult males, while infants and children have "toy" vessels, clay "playthings," and unworked freshwater shells. Unworked deer, bird claws, and turtle bones were found only with adults. The individuals in the lowest segment, C, were generally found away from the mounds and major ceremonial areas at Moundville.

This second set of data clarify the nature of ranking within the Moundville society. The upper class of social elite were buried in a sacred area and accompanied by symbols of their exalted status. The Moundville elite apparently lived in larger, more complex dwellings than did the commoners. Elite membership was conditioned by geneology, and because social position is inherited within the elite, even children occupy such social positions.

Further down the ladder, the villagers' graves also reflected their social positions in life, but that position was conditioned largely by sex and age distinctions rather than inheritance. The less glamorous grave goods were distributed in a quite different manner. The graves contained pottery vessels, bone awls, flint projectile points, and stone pipes, which were distributed quite unevenly (mostly to older adults). Peebles infers that these individuals were required to achieve—rather than inherit—their social status. The prize artifacts in this social setting went to the "self-made individuals," who had achieved status on their own (Pfeiffer 1977:97). Over half of the Moundville graves examined by Peebles were of commoners who were buried without any grave goods at all.

Peebles has placed his studies of ranked status at Moundville into a regional framework. All the twenty-plus sites of the Moundville phase are part of a single polity. This cultural system was glued together by a common social organization and a common ritual. Part of the production of this society as a whole was used to support a number of specialized politico-religious offices (see also Steponaitis 1978). Most of these offices were physically associated with the major Moundville site itself, but others were part of the minor ceremonial centers and villages in the hinterlands. The recruitment to these high offices was probably limited to members at the apex of the social organization. Nevertheless, the bonds of clanship and reckoned geneological relationship probably pervaded the whole of the society.

Peebles goes on to suggest that Moundville conformed to a *chiefdom* model (Fried 1967) characterized by a status framework containing fewer valued positions than there are individuals capable of handling them. The economy was probably redistributive, Moundville serving as a center of regional distribution of key goods. Since Peebles's work at Moundville, a ranked form of social organization has been recognized at other Mississippian sites in Tennessee, Georgia, Oklahoma, and the lower Illinois Valley (see Peebles 1977). In all cases, burial populations served as the mode of inference.

RECONSTRUCTING INDIVIDUAL BEHAVIOR

> Society in its full sense . . . is never an entity separable from the individuals who compose it. No individual can arrive even at the threshold of his potentialities without a culture in which he participates. Conversely, no civilization has in it any element which in the last analysis is not the contribution of an individual.
>
> *Ruth Benedict*

Chapter 1 discussed briefly the role of the individual in anthropological explanation. We were concerned, you will remember, with the role of several luminaries—Thomas Jefferson, A. V. Kidder, Lewis Binford, and others—in the development of archaeology as a discipline. I quoted Leslie White at length on the relevance of individuals to anthropology. The gist of White's quote was that the history of Egypt would have been largely unchanged had Ikhnaton been a bag of sand. This principle was then applied to the development of archaeology: contemporary archaeology would be little changed had Jefferson, Kidder, Binford, and the others all died in early childhood. Major ideas are products of their time, and if one individual does not develop the idea, then somebody else will.

Ignoring the individual is fine when looking for broad trends in cultural evolution, but archaeologists have recently been poking about to see if anything important is obscured by ignoring the role of the individual in the past. In the discussion of the nature of culture (Chapter 3), we developed the point that culture actually consists of three interrelated components: idiolect, shared perspective, and the underlying cultural system. The shared aspects of culture were discussed in detail in Part Two of this book, particularly as they related to the formation of temporal artifact classification. The cultural system as a concept has been elaborated throughout this section, dealing with the reconstruction of past lifeways.

But what about the idiolect—those aspects of culture that do not transcend the individual? Is contemporary archaeology justified in wholly overlooking the role of individuals in the past?

Until very recently, the answer to that question was yes. To hell with the individual! Archaeologists deal with long-range trends over time, and individuals are merely the instruments of that change, never the primary cause. But other academic disciplines have made detailed studies of individual behavior (as discussed in Muller 1977). Art historians, for instance, have been isolating the work of individual artists for decades. Art critic Bernard Berenson dealt specifically with the question of identifying schools of art, and even specific individuals (Berenson 1962). In his studies of Italian Renaissance painting, he has isolated certain specific attributes, such as specific types of faces and certain compositions and groupings to characterize specific schools of painting. Moreover, Berenson (1962: 129) has isolated specific details which are of use in separating individual painters. These aspects are, in a sense, peripheral to the overall intent of the work, characteristics which are not vehicles of expression and which are not designed to attract attention. Painters of the Italian Renaissance, for instance, can often be distinguished by the way they paint ears. They employ almost an artistic shorthand, and individuals are readily recognized by their idiosyncratic usage of this shorthand. Similar "keys" are utilized by art dealers when attempting to detect forgeries (Jeppson 1970).

Psychologists, educators, and physicians have also focused attention on individual variation. Crime detection units have studied individual characteristics such as handwriting to distinguish the work of specific suspects (see Hill 1977).

Within the past few years, some archaeologists have begun to look into this neglected third aspect of culture. A number of studies have appeared recently which suggest that individual variation can indeed be approached in the archaeological record. A symposium was held on the topic at the 39th Annual Meeting of the Society for American Archaeology in 1974, and the results of the session were recently published as *The Individual in Prehistory* (Hill and Gunn 1977). Let us examine a couple of recent investigations of individual behavior.

One elementary example is the recognition of ancient Peruvian potters' marks (Donnan 1971). As part of a systematic survey of the Santa Valley in northern Peru, Christopher Donnan noticed a number of previously unrecognized marks on fragments of plain Moche style pottery (the Moche style dates between A.D. 100 and 800). These marks occurred on about 10 percent of the vessels, and they ranged from simple punctations, to parallel scratches, to combinations of lines and dots (see Figure 10–11). There was no question that

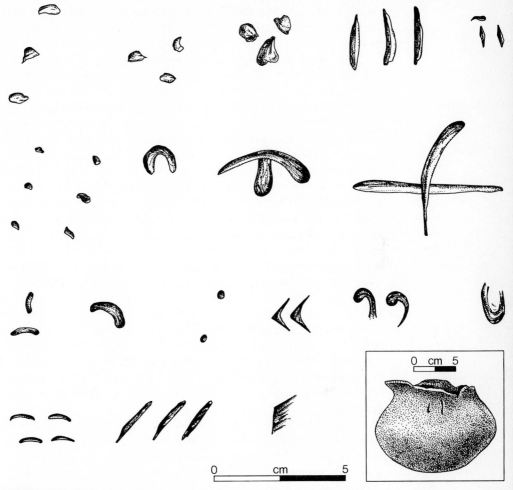

Figure 10–11
Ancient Peruvian potters' marks on Moche vessels from the Santa and Trujillo Valleys
(*after Donnan 1971, figures 2 and 3; courtesy of Christopher B. Donnan and The Society for American Archaeology*).

the marks were deliberate, all being made while the clay was still quite moist. The marks always occurred on the necks of the vessels and they were clearly not decorative features.

To interpret these curious marks, Donnan turned to the modern potters of the central sierra of Peru. People living in these communities obtain their pottery from two sources, either at established markets where potters bring their finished wares for sale, or from traveling potters who bring the unfired clay to the communities and make pots on request in the individual villages. Donnan found that modern Peruvian potters often place an individual mark or *signál* on their pots before firing them. The modern *signál* is simply a way of distinguishing the work of one potter from another, as the pots are often fired together in order to save fuel.

The modern analogy has enabled Donnan to interpret the curious markings on the Moche pottery as ancient makers' marks. In both modern and ancient times, the marks seem to be restricted to plain, everyday cooking ware. Also in both cases, the marks appear on only about 10 percent of the vessels, those pots that for one reason or another are fired with the pots of two or more potters. In addition, some of the individual Moche marks are almost indistinguishable from those used today, and the modern potters invariably identified the Moche marks as *signáles*. Of course, ethnographic analogies such as this only open avenues of possible explanation and do not themselves contribute proof (see Chapter 2). But the suggestion that the curious scratches on the Moche potsherds are indeed makers' marks is a concrete proposal which can be examined and tested in the future.

A variety of additional studies have been recently conducted, not only on ceramics (see Gifford 1960; Hill 1977; Hardin 1977), but also on basketry (Adovasio and Gunn 1977) and stone tools (White and Thomas 1972; Gunn 1975).

In truth, these initial studies of the role of the individual in prehistoric society are not very convincing. The topic is a difficult one, and investigators have only begun to look in this direction.

But the surface has been scratched, and the studies above are pioneering in the sense that they point up new directions of research and also indicate concepts and ground rules that seem necessary to really get at past individual behavior.

As one intermediate step, Redman (1977) has proposed the concept of the analytical individual. While generally sympathetic with the attempt to isolate and study behavior of individuals, Redman questions the effectiveness of those studies. It is certainly possible to suggest that objects were made by the same person, but it is extremely difficult to prove it. Redman has suggested that a preoccupation with identifying individuals will lead to such detailed debate as to displace our primary concern, for the processes to be explicated from these data. That is, too much concern with individual behavior of individuals is an inefficient use of the prehistorian's research effort (Redman 1977:42).

Redman has suggested that prehistorians can sometimes sidestep the reconstruction of past events and lifeways altogether, thereby not relying on the difficult-to-demonstrate interpretation of individual behavior. Instead, the concept of the analytical individual asserts only that some objects are more closely similar than other objects, and this similarity can be the basis of measuring interaction between members of a group. Ceramics, for instance, are classified strictly according to empirical criteria; the pots that are the most different are assigned to the largest interaction group (with little contact), whereas objects with great similarities are assigned to the smallest interaction group (intense contact). This smallest interaction group might represent an individual craftsman, or it might not. It is an "individual" only in the analytical sense. Redman and his colleagues are presently using this concept to study the hierarchy of stylistic variation in the El Morro Valley of western New Mexico.

Other preliminary studies have examined underlying principles of individual behavior. We might call these principles the constants of idiosyncratic behavior. Hill (1977), for instance, has conducted a series of experiments on individual craftsmanship using design elements on 3×5 cards, a specially constructed set of pots from Tiajuana, Mexico, potsherds from a thirteenth-century pueblo in eastern Arizona, and handwriting from four nineteenth- and twentieth-century British novelists. This is admittedly quite a range in materials, but Hill thinks that certain principles of organization are beginning to emerge.

Certain variables, for instance, seem more conducive to isolating the works of individuals than others. In ceramic styles, variables that deal with angles, relative heights, shapes, and areas seem to function quite well. That is, people tend to use design in an idiosyncratic manner. The least sensitive variables are absolute lengths of design elements. Hill argues that these variables should hold for all materials, not just ceramics (Hill 1977:100). These variables are seen as reflecting individual specific behavior that is not susceptible to change over time, changes in scale of the materials, errors in execution, or even periods of fatigue, illness, or stress. Interestingly enough, Hill also argues that the context of learning is also relatively unimportant, that is, that brothers and sisters or those taught by the same teacher will not necessarily produce similar artifacts (Hill 1977:57). Hardin (1977:135) disputes this finding, asserting that social relationships such as family ties do indeed influence design strategies.

A final point deserves mention. Do not get the impression from the preceding section that individual behavior is being studied for its own sake. The research discussed above is ultimately directed at the study of human population behavior, not simply individual behavior. Studying the individual in prehistory is important because it is necessary for the archaeologist to distinguish individual variation from other kinds of variation that influence the form of artifacts. Ultimately, it is hoped, archaeologists can learn to control for individual variation with a knowledge about the attributes of use, technology, conscious stylistic variations, and so on. In other words, the major goal of the individual variation studies is to contribute toward the development of a general theory of form. In this way, individual variation might ultimately be used as a measure of various critical aspects of prehistoric social organization.

> **W**hatever you may be sure of, be sure of this—
> that you are dreadfully like other people.
> *James Russell Lowell*

SUMMARY

Contemporary archaeologists have been making important strides toward inferring the nature of prehistoric social organization from the archaeological record. Social organization encompasses two elements: the division of a society into smaller groups (or social units), and the allocation of a recognized set of social positions (statuses) which are accompanied by appropriate behavior patterns (roles). Archaeologists are presently examining both social groups and social statuses.

Reconstructing extinct residential groups is accomplished by analyzing the problem at four primary levels. Individual behavior is most commonly reflected in material culture at the attribute level of patterning. This is the initial level of analysis. Behavior of various minimal social groups—for example, families, hunting associations, and war parties—is most commonly reflected in the archaeological record at the tool-kit level. Community social patterning is generally evident in terms of individual households, which themselves are commonly arranged into larger-order subsistence units. Finally, behavior at the overall societal level is reflected in the regional settlement pattern, as discussed in some detail in the last chapter.

Archaeologists also attempt to reconstruct extinct patterns of social status and ranking. Status can be apportioned in one of two ways: an ascribed status is assigned to individuals at birth, without regard to innate differences or abilities; status can also be achieved in those societies which prefer to allocate status as a reward for competition and group effort. Egalitarian societies are those in which the number of such valued social positions is roughly equivalent to the number of persons available to fill them. In ranked societies, the number of valued status positions is somehow limited, creating an intrinsic social hierarchy and unequal access to the basis of subsistence. Archaeologists are now capable of dealing with the mechanisms of status allocation, largely through the study of mortuary patterns. The critical assumption in such research is that persons who were treated differentially in life were also treated differentially upon death. In other words, human burials represent the fossil terminal status of the individual, a basis on which the archaeologist can reconstruct patterns of ranking throughout societies.

The final archaeological approach to social organization is through the study of individual behavior. Such research is ultimately directed at the reconstruction of human population behavior. But isolating the role of the individual in prehistory is important so that archaeologists can learn to differentiate individual stylistic variation from more complex social patterning. The major goal of individual variation studies is to contribute to the development of a general "theory of form"; in this way, individual behavior patterns can be used as a measure of critical aspects of extinct social organization.

How People Relate
to Their Cosmos:
Religion and Ideology

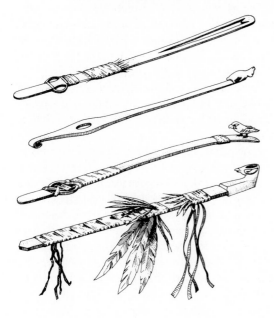

An honest God is the noblest work of man.
Robert Ingersoll

The religions and ideologies of the past have been of compelling interest to archaeologists since the very beginning of the discipline. We saw in Chapter 1 how Nabonidus, the sixth-century B.C. Babylonian king, searched among the ruins of his empire to pursue his worship of the ancient gods. The same was true of Petrarch, the early Renaissance scholar who turned to the religions of classical antiquity for moral guidance.

In this chapter we discuss the major features of religious behavior and what clues remain for the archaeologist. But what is religion? Are there certain characteristics that are common to all religions?

A basic premise of every religion is a belief in the existence of souls, supernatural things, and supernatural forces. Religion, in effect, is a society's mechanism for relating these supernatural phenomena to the everyday world. Religion is a set of rituals, rationalized by myth, which mobilizes supernatural powers for the purpose of achieving or preventing transformations of state in man and nature (after Wallace 1966:107). Wallace's succinct definition contains three operative elements: (1) transformation of state, (2) myth, and (3) ritual. Let us briefly examine each.

1. *Transformation of State.* Religion is universal because of the ubiquitous cultural desire to influence change in people and nature. Sometimes the objective is to effect the quickest possible transformation; sometimes the goal is to prevent an undesired change from occurring. The target of the transformation can be either a group or an individual, and the change itself can be minor or radical. Regardless, the prime objective of religious behavior is to influence the course of this change by appeal to a supernatural power—a power quite separate from those of the muscles, the brain, or the elements of nature (Wallace 1966:107). It follows that if humankind were wholly satisfied with (or resigned to) the status quo there would be no need for religion, and, indeed, religious behavior itself would atrophy.

2. *Myth.* A major component of society's overall cosmology, myths identify and explain the nature of the relevant supernatural entities. That is, myths define how human beings articulate with the supernatural and rationalize the various actions that are directed toward these supernatural structures. In the more primitive societies myths generally take the form of a narrative, describing events in the careers of the supernatural beings; more technologically advanced societies (with professional priesthoods) tend to codify their myths into an official mythology such as the Bible, the Koran, and other sacred texts.

3. *Ritual.* Religious beliefs are manifest in everyday life in terms of a "program of ritual," a succession of discrete events such as prayer, music, feasting, sacrifice, and taboos. These stereotyped sequences are the cultural mechanisms by which individuals attempt to intercede with the activities of the supernatural.

It is thus fair to say that ritual comprises the fundamental aspect of religion. Myth becomes the secondary element, the cultural theory that rationalizes the ritual. Myth functions in explaining the nature of the powers involved, in setting forth the proper sequence of actions, in accounting for the observed successes and failures (Wallace 1966:106–107). *Overall, religion consists of ritual, supported by myth, directed at a desired transformation of state.*

In this chapter we examine how past religions can be explored in the archaeological record. Wallace's anthropological definition of religion is particularly relevant to archaeology because of the explicit emphasis on ritual and the de-emphasis of myth. Most rituals, after all, are closely related to material culture and, as such, are often represented in the archaeological record. Myth has few real-world correlates and is rarely preserved. The analysis of ritual behavior is thus archaeology's major contribution to the study of past religions.

Religion: A daughter of Hope and Fear,
explaining to Ignorance the nature of the
Unknowable.

Ambrose Bierce

RECONSTRUCTING RITUAL BEHAVIOR

We have argued that the primary feature of religious behavior is ritual, the stereotyped, often obsessively repetitive behavioral sequences (Kluckhohn 1942:78). Ritual sequences themselves consist of a number of individual acts, what Wallace has termed "the smallest religious things" (1966:67). Prayer, for example, is one part of many rituals, comprising a standardized, stylized manner of conveying one's feelings to the supernatural. Music—including dancing, singing, and playing instruments—is another component of ritual that is present in nearly every religion. Some rituals employ various artificial manipulations designed to produce the proper spiritual state, with drugs and/or sensory or physical deprivation. Rituals are generally reinforced with a sacred oral or written literature, a set of sacred objects which often possess supernatural power (mana), a sequence of taboos, a variety of feasts and/or sacrifices, and, of course, a wealth of symbolism.

Although myth and ritual are universally associated, ritual can be shown to have priority, and often myths have been invented to rationalize the performance of certain rituals. According to Wallace (1966:102), "The primacy of ritual is instrumental: just as the blade of the knife has instrumental priority over the handle, and the barrel of a gun over the stock, so does ritual have instrumental priority over myth. It is ritual which accomplishes what religion sets out to do."

Wallace goes on to distinguish kinds of ritual, analyzing rituals as technology, as therapy, as social control, as salvation, and as revitalization (Wallace 1966, Chapter 3). Of particular importance to archaeologists are technological rituals, as these are the aspects of religion most often reflected in the archaeological record. Some technological rituals attempt to extract ecological information directly from nature (divination), while other such rituals attempt to control hunting success (through availability and fertility of game) or agricultural productivity or safety of flocks and herds. These so-called rites of intensification are directly aimed at protecting the techno-economic base of the society.

In the remainder of this chapter, we will make the distinction between calendrical and critical rituals (Titiev 1960). Because of their nature, rituals based on calendrical events can be scheduled and announced long in advance of their actual occurrence. The calendrical ritual has the advantage of providing its participants ample time to develop a sense of shared anticipation, and a chance to prepare for the big event. The gigantic Shalako figure appears in Zuni every December, just as the western world celebrates Christmas annually on December 25. Both of these are examples of calendrical rituals.

But because the timing of calendrical rituals is so tightly circumscribed, these rites cannot possibly function to satisfy the immediate desires for supernatural assistance or divine comfort; this is the function of the critical ritual. Unlike the calendrical ritual (which is invariably communal), the critical ritual can be designed to benefit either the entire society, a relatively small group, or even a single individual (Titiev 1960:294). Sometimes critical rites are held to counteract a public emergency, but more often they are held when some important object has been stolen, somebody has become ill, and at such inevitable, yet noncalendric events as birth and death.

The analysis of past religion begins with a discussion of such critical rituals, as we examine first the evidence for Neanderthal burial customs and then turn to a recent study on the evolution of public ritual areas in prehistoric Oaxaca, Mexico. Then we examine how archaeologists are studying calendrical rituals, including methods of recognizing the various ways in which primitive and nonliterate peoples keep track of the progress of the year. While not new, astroarchaeology has recently provided a major focus of attention from both astronomers and archaeologists. The findings remain tentative, but we are now seeing marked progress in the study of past calendrical reckoning and the rituals that accompanied such primitive calendars.

CRITICAL (NONCALENDRICAL) RITUALS IN ARCHAEOLOGY

Archaeologists are most familiar with critical ritual behavior through evidence of human mortuary practices. In fact, anthropologists such as Wallace (1966, Chapter 5) rely heavily on burial practices in reconstructing the origins of religion. The general mode of thought holds that, as early Paleolithic populations increased in size, people grew more accustomed to social living and their universe became more culturally oriented and distinct from the natural environment. Families became more closely united, and archaeologists generally believe that an elaborate body of cosmological belief existed as early as Middle Paleolithic times, say, 75,000 years ago. Human burials are especially indicative of this ideological reification. The logic goes like this: "The mere fact of intentional burial implies that the living felt sufficient concern for the recently deceased that disposal of their body was a matter of group planning and execution. Intentional burial further implies that there existed beliefs concerned with an after life. Thus we have the beginnings of what may be termed religion" (Hester 1976:146).

One of the most ancient human burials was discovered at Shanidar Cave,

Figure 11–1
Skull of Neanderthal burial at Shanidar Cave; this person was probably killed by a roof fall inside the cave *(courtesy of Ralph Solecki).*

Iraq, by Ralph Solecki of Columbia University. Shanidar Cave had been occupied sporadically over about 100,000 years, with cultural remains spanning from the Middle Paleolithic to fairly recent times. During his fourth season at Shanidar, Solecki and his crew discovered a Neanderthal skeleton which appeared to have been intentionally buried, roughly 60,000 years ago (see Figure 11–1). The skeleton, called Shanidar IV, was a poorly preserved adult, lying on its left side facing west (Solecki 1971:232). The skeleton was hemmed in by stones on three sides and so fragile that the entire block was removed in a plaster jacket, earth and all. The box containing Shanidar IV was transported to the Iraq Museum where it remained unopened for two years. It was later discovered that the Shanidar IV grave actually contained four individuals—three adults and an infant.

Following his routine field procedures, Solecki took soil samples from around and within the area of Shanidar IV. Although he had no specific purpose for collecting the samples, Solecki had learned in previous work on American Indian burial mounds in Ohio that soil samples can provide unexpected dividends (Solecki 1971:245). Some eight years later, these soil samples would provide "significant, if not startling results."

Mme. Arlette Leroi-Gourhan, the project paleobotanist, tested the Shanidar IV samples for pollen and—to everyone's surprise—pollen was preserved in great quantities in the Neanderthal grave site. Microscopic examination of the pollen spores indicated that Shanidar IV had been accompanied by a bouquet of at least eight species of brightly colored wildflowers including grape hyacinth, bachelor's button, and hollyhock. Leroi-Gourhan (1975) suggests that the flowers were woven into the branches of a pinelike shrub, which apparently grew nearby on the Ice Age hillside. Moreover, the individuals found in the Shanidar IV grave were laid to rest sometime between late May and early July.

Archaeologists conventionally interpret such intentional burial practices as indicative of religious beliefs. On the basis of Shanidar IV, Solecki concluded:

> With the finding of flowers in association with Neanderthals we are brought suddenly to the realization that the universality of mankind and the love of beauty go beyond the boundary of our own species. No longer can we deny the early men the full range of human feelings and experience. (Solecki 1971:250)

Evidence of critical rituals is also available to the archaeologist in the form of architectural remains. A recent study by Flannery and Marcus (1976) has attempted to reconstruct the evolution of public spaces in prehistoric Oaxaca, Mexico. The period from 2000 B.C. to A.D. 1 is particularly important because this is when established village life evolved, bringing with it the origins of social ranking and ultimately the rise of the Mesoamerican state. Flannery and Marcus demonstrated that in addition to the well-known ecological consequences of settled village life, certain structural changes in social and religious structure also occurred. The physical development of "public spaces" is interesting because it indirectly mirrors the ritual behavior during these changing times.

During the preceramic era, architecture—public or otherwise—was virtually unknown. Dwellings were probably similar to the temporary structures noted earlier in the discussion of the Reese River Shoshoni. One site in Oaxaca, Gheo-Shih, provides some clues. The site was occupied between about 5000 and 4000 B.C., probably by a macroband during the rainy season of July and August.

The most interesting feature at Gheo-Shih consisted of two parallel lines of boulders, running for about twenty meters. The seven-meter space between them was swept clean, containing virtually no artifacts. Flannery and Marcus (1976:207) suggest that this feature is analogous to the cleared "dance grounds" of the Great Basin Shoshoni. Writing specifically about the Reese River Shoshoni, Steward noted (1938:107):

> When visitors arrived [at the fall pine-nut festival] Tutuwa assigned each family a place in the camp circle which surrounded the dance ground . . . it had an opening on the eastern side, directly opposite which Tutuwa camped, and a pine-nut tree or post in the center. People merely erected temporary windbreaks for shelter.

Using the Shoshoni analogue, Flannery and Marcus infer that the early Oaxacan hunter-gatherers placed their public structure near the heart of camp, and whatever activity occurred there could have been observed by the entire camp; it could not have been used for "secret rites" (such as take place in the underground kivas of the American Southwest). Moreover, such temporary features were likely used for ad hoc critical ritual, requiring neither maintenance nor particular architectural skill. Similar temporary open areas persisted at San José Mogote until about 1600 B.C. in the form of small open areas, set apart from residential areas by a double line of staggered posts.

The first real public buildings at San José Mogote appear about 1500–1300 B.C. In the western portion of the hamlet, a special area seems to have been set aside for construction of a public building, and domestic houses were not found in this area. These structures were rectangular, one-room buildings; all structures contained an altar built against the southern wall. Directly north of this altar was a storage pit. The entire floor and pit were plastered with white stucco.

Developments continued with the erection of an impressive acropolis atop Mound I at San José Mogote. Faced with roughly cut limestone blocks (often weighing over a ton), the acropolis contained the remains of an adult sacrificial victim, buried beneath one retaining wall. The acropolis is the earliest example of a complex public building "removed from the heart of the village and raised to a new position some fifteen meters above" (Flannery and Marcus 1976:215). While the acropolis would have been visible for a great distance, the buildings themselves had a more limited access by members of the community.

This trend culminated about 500 B.C. in the founding of Monte Albán, located on a mountaintop some 400 meters above the valley. The plaza itself is about 300 meters by 150 meters and is located on one of the least accessible spots in the Valley of Oaxaca.

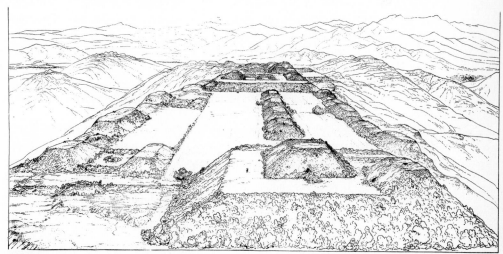

Figure 11–2
Panoramic view of the mountaintop ruins at Monte Alban *(courtesy of The American Museum of Natural History).*

Somewhat later (about A.D. 1), an entirely new kind of public building appeared—the palace, or royal residence. The ceremonial ball court also appeared about this time.

Setting architectural details aside, the evolution of public buildings tells archaeologists a great deal about the evolution of ritual behavior as well. Even during the initial hunting-gathering period, a portion of the village was set aside for "public" purposes; the space was accessible to all, and the rituals were observable by everyone. Somewhat later, precincts were set aside from ordinary habitation areas, but the citizens still had full access to the area. Flannery and Marcus refer to these structures as "generalized public buildings" (1976:220).

Two new trends occurred during the Middle Formative period. Ceremonial buildings were grouped by threes or fours facing inward to a common patio, rather than toward the domestic structures. These structures were also placed on low hills, elevated over the community. The ultimate step in Oaxaca was the founding of Monte Albán, located atop a 400-meter mountaintop and looking out over the entire valley.

The Flannery-Marcus architectural study spans the transition from the time of seminomadic hunting-gathering bands to that of sedentary village farmers. We also presume that ritual life underwent some profound changes. The early foragers seem to have engaged primarily in unscheduled critical rituals, such as initiation ceremonies, gambling, dancing, and athletic competition. These ad hoc rituals gradually transformed into the more scheduled calendrical rituals which are more characteristic of sedentary agricultural villages; often, such time-structured ceremonies were closely related to the predictable harvest and planting cycles. In later times carved monuments were erected, involving the typical Mesoamerican 260-day calendar. Finally, by A.D. 1, a lavish set of public institutions was headquartered at Monte Albán atop the mountain dominating the Oaxacan landscape. By this time the agricultural village had evolved into a full-scale state organization (see Chapter 13).

But we should not create the false impression that calendrical rituals occur only among advanced societies. The section that follows discusses in detail the recent developments in astroarchaeology: we will see not only how calendrical rituals function, but also examine some evidence of how they evolved.

RECONSTRUCTING CALENDRICAL RITUALS THROUGH ASTROARCHAEOLOGY

The fault, dear Brutus, is not in our stars but in ourselves.

William Shakespeare

The endless shifting of the sun, the moon, and the stars is one constant that must have influenced—in one way or another—every society on earth. Michael

Coe has suggested, for instance, that "if any one trait can be said to be distinctive of native cultures of prehispanic Mesoamerica, it is a deep concern with the heavenly bodies and the passage of time as marked by the apparent movements of these objects" (Coe 1975:3). And yet, until quite recently, professional archaeologists have almost totally ignored the field of *archaeoastronomy* (or **astroarchaeology,** if you prefer). Because of this reluctance, the study of past astronomical practices has been the subject of almost violent speculation, often by the "crackpot fringe" that seems to haunt the archaeological profession: if it wasn't the visiting aliens, it must have been the survivors from Atlantis.

The situation has changed recently as legitimate archaeological and ethnographic inquiries are being made into the relationship of religion and cosmology to astronomical phenomena. Before turning to these archaeological interpretations let me first demonstrate how astronomical phenomena can function in ritual by introducing briefly the idea of a horizon calendar. The Hopi Indians of Arizona begin their agricultural season in February with a clearing of the fields, and the cycle ends in the final days of September when the last maize (corn) and beans are gathered. Although the precise time of each agricultural operation is determined by general weather conditions, the entire cycle can be anticipated by a "horizon calendar." That is, both the ritual and the actual agricultural practices are regulated by the daily shift in the position of the sunrise on the horizon (Forde 1963; Fewkes 1893, 1898; Parsons 1925). Even the smallest irregularity on the skyline is known to the Hopi, and reference points were established to pinpoint each change in the sun's position (see Figure 11–3). Many of these points were in turn associated with rituals or agricultural operations, due to commence when the sun rose behind the designated spot. "For a well-educated Hopi such terms as *neverktcomo* and *lohalin* have as precise a significance as have for us May 3rd and June 21st with which they correspond" (Forde 1963:227).

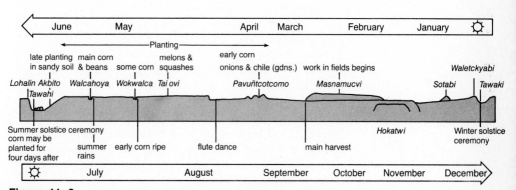

Figure 11–3
Horizon calendar **used by the Hopi at the First Mesa Pueblo of Sihmopovi. This calendar, which serves to indicate appropriate dates for agricultural operations and ceremonies, is provided by the daily shift in the position of sunrise on the horizon** *(after Forde 1963, figure 75; courtesy of Methuen & Co., Ltd).*

The daily observation of these solar positions is the responsibility of the "sun watcher," a religious official whose duty it was to forewarn the people of upcoming important dates; he also kept a tally on a notched stick.[1] The Hopi solar observations are perfect examples of what Titiev (1960) referred to as calendrical rituals.

But it is one thing to discuss the significance of solar ritual in a documented ethnographic case such as the Hopi, and quite another matter to establish such behavior prehistorically. The emerging field of archaeoastronomy is still, quite frankly, met with a great deal of skepticism by many archaeologists. In the following examples we will see how scholars are attempting to study cosmology and ideology through study of astronomic indicators. Many cases involve the introduction of methods and techniques quite alien to many conventional archaeologists. These innovations only add to the controversial nature of the findings.

One of the most controversial and influential investigators of such phenomena is Alexander Marshack, who for the last fifteen years has been studying the nature of Upper Paleolithic engraving from throughout the Old World. In *The Roots of Civilization* (1972a), Marshack discusses how his research began as a relatively straightforward search for the origins of scientific thought; to his surprise, Marshack found that he was able to trace scientific thinking back only to the Greeks; then the trail disappeared. Largely because he felt "something missing," Marshack has personally studied almost the entire body of the engraved, symbolic materials from the Upper Paleolithic. We can only discuss a small part of his work in this chapter.

Marshack's technique can be demonstrated by his analysis of an incised bone artifact from the Upper Paleolithic site of La Marche in central France (Marshack 1972b). Several hundred stone and bone artifacts were excavated at La Marche in 1937 and 1938, the majority of them coming from Magdalenian levels, approximately 12,000–13,000 B.C. One of the visually less exciting pieces is a discolored, deteriorated bone fragment, which has been engraved with a faint series of marks and lines (see Figure 11–4). Marshack first encountered the bone on display, without caption, at the Musée de l'Homme in Paris; the excavator had noted that the fragment contained engraved horses and punctations, but made no further comment.

Marshack analyzed the La Marche bone over a three-year period, and his results reveal an unsuspected complexity. The bone had apparently been a shaft straightener that had broken and been reshaped to serve as a pressure flaker in the manufacture of stone tools. But of more interest are the intricate engravings which microscopic analysis indicates were placed upon the bone before it was used as a flaker and then presumably during the period of its use as a flaker.

Figure 11–5 presents a schematic rendition of the La Marche bone. Note particularly the two horses carved near the bottom. The unbroken horse was added second, and seems to represent a pregnant mare with a rounded belly. Careful line-by-line analysis indicates that this mare in fact possesses three eyes, three ears, a second mane, and two backs. Marshack's microscopic technique is

Figure 11–4
Three views of the La Marche bone; note the faint and indistinct engravings *(after Marshack 1972, figure 1; courtesy of Alexander Marshack and the American Association for the Advancement of Science).*

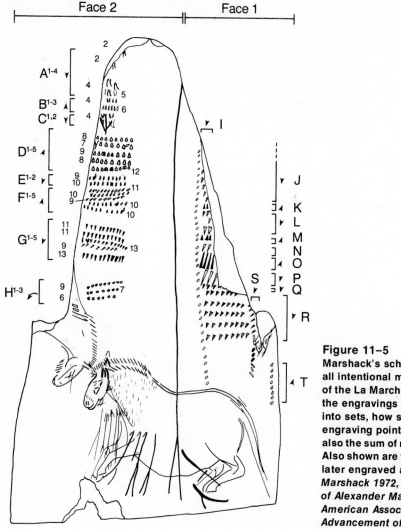

Figure 11–5
Marshack's schematic analysis of all intentional marks on both faces of the La Marche bone. Note how the engravings are broken down into sets, how several different engraving points were used, and also the sum of marks in each set. Also shown are the two horses, with later engraved additions (*after Marshack 1972, figure 10; courtesy of Alexander Marshack and The American Association for the Advancement of Science*).

very similar to a ballistic analysis used in law enforcement. Each minute scratch is examined to determine the nature of the tool that performed the carving. Some stone tools are relatively flat and blunt, creating a deeper, more V-shaped groove. Such analysis revealed that each of the mare's three ears was carved by a different stone point, presumably at different times.

In addition, note that the horse has been ritually "killed" a number of times by the addition of at least nine darts, many of which have realistic points and feathers. Once again, microscopic analysis indicates that at least four different tool tips were used to engrave the darts.

Comparable renewals and ritual killings are known to occur in a number of the famous European painted caves, and Marshack suggests that the La Marche bone provides strong evidence that these complex cave compositions were accumulated within a relatively short cultural period (Marshack 1972b:823). In addition, Marshack stresses the nature of the animals often represented in the cave paintings and on the La Marche bone. Particularly during the Magdalenian period, we do not see generalized game or species, but rather *specific* animals in *specific* seasons and of *specific* sex. The La Marche horse is a pregnant mare, and other scenes are known to depict stags in velvet and bison in the molting stage. To Marshack, the killings "seem more applicable to periodic ritual or sacrifices at specialized times than to random acts of magic intended for success in the hunt for food" (1972b:823).

Marshack then turns to analysis of the tiny marks that cover the rest of the La Marche bone. These marks seems to comprise a complex sequence of engraving that is neither random nor decorative. Marshack claims these incisions are a complex form of notation from which sequence and structure can be determined through careful microscopic analysis. Note first of all that the marks occur in blocks (or sets). While generally similar, each block is quite distinct when closely examined. Row H, for instance, has been inscribed by a cutting edge that flares near the top, creating an irregular angle in cross section. The marks are created by a turning or twisting stroke, set at an angle of about 15° to the baseline of the bone. By contrast, the engravings above row H are perpendicular to the axis of the bone and involve only a single downward stroke.

Marshack's microscopic analysis indicates that at least six different tool tips were used to engrave the various sets of dots and lines. The internal complexity of the marking sequence suggests that the marks were accumulated through time. The two surfaces were probably carved at different times (perhaps by the same hand) and almost certainly within the same cultural contexts.

But what do these tiny marks mean? A number of hypotheses have been considered to explain engravings such as those on the La Marche bone. Some investigators, such as Absolon (1957), suggest that the marks are hunting tallies, with the implication that some sort of decimal system was involved. Frolov (1970, 1971), influenced by Marshack's early work, suggests the recurrent reuse of the number seven, suggesting that that number had special ritual significance.

Marshack proposes that the La Marche bone and similar artifacts be consistently tested against the lunar model. That is, could these intentionally accumulated sets be expressing observed phases of the moon? Figure 11–6 shows Marshack's "lunar test" of the La Marche engravings. Beginning with block A in the upper right corner, the counts are arranged sequentially, as indicated by microscopic analysis. Then an overlay of modern astronomic observations is placed atop the counts. The darkened circles represent invisibility, the white circles represent the full moon.

The fit with the lunar model is surprisingly close. Of twenty-three subsets of marks observable on the single face of the La Marche bone, only four (E^2, F^2,

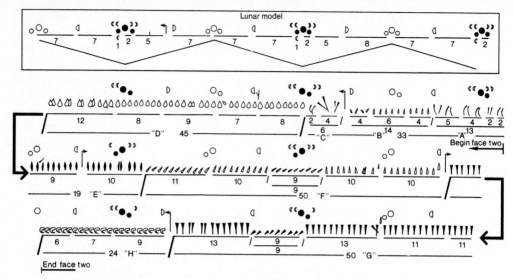

Figure 11–6
Marshack's "test" of the La Marche engravings against a standard lunar model. This chart begins at the upper right and proceeds sequentially in alternate directions along each line, ending at the bottom left. One space in each two months (the right-angle arrow) represents zero, providing the proper total of 59 marks for two months in a model scaled to 60. The lettered sets, subsets, and cue marks are indicated, along with the astronomically correct observation point. The differences in the engraving points are schematically rendered *(after Marshack 1972, figure 16; courtesy of Alexander Marshack and The American Association for the Advancement of Science).*

$G^{1,2}$) fail to begin or end at normal phases of the moon. Of these, three subsets correspond to the difficult period of the crescents and new moon, when precise observation is difficult. According to this interpretation, the marks cover a span of seven and a half months.

But why would a Magdalenian hunter-gatherer concern himself some 14,000 years ago with recording the phases of the moon?

Marshack is concerned with understanding the cognitive strategies implied by the use of such a complex notational system. Marshack notes that despite the wide range of Native American cultures (from hunter-gatherers to pure farmers) almost all maintained lunar counts in one form or another. In general, the months were named according to their seasonal and regional significance, triggering appropriate ritual or economic responses. Such counts were often kept by specialized shamans, and Marshack believes that the Upper Paleolithic notations, such as the La Marche bone, were also maintained by ritual specialists. If, for instance, the La Marche count began with the late March thaw, then the notation would have ended in mid-November, approximately the time of first snow. Such a sequence depends only on sequential marking, and can be maintained even without named or recognized months or a complex arithmetic. Marshack suggests that both the counting ritual and the reuse of animals on the La Marche bone strongly argues for a "scheduled," "time-factored" cultural year, even in Upper Paleolithic times.

To Marshack, the cognitive strategies utilized in the La Marche (and many other) notations differ from those employed by later record keepers living in settled farming villages. He thinks that the Upper Paleolithic engravings were made and used by the engraver alone. As later cultural and ecological pressures changed, notational systems of necessity became more stable and interpersonal, leading ultimately to the development of true writing.

Marshack's research can only be described as pioneering, and reactions to it are characteristically mixed. Many archaeologists are frankly skeptical, suggesting that Marshack has "gone beyond the data" (Lynch 1972), ignored "all likely alternative explanations" (Rosenfeld 1972), and failed to present the data necessary to support his hypotheses (Brose 1972). But other archaeologists have lauded Marshack's analytical approach, using terms such as "significant breakthrough" (Kurtén 1972 and Sieveking 1972) and "breaking new ground" (Kessler 1972). A number of investigators find his evidence "impressively persuasive" (Hosley 1972) and "a valuable contribution to the study of prehistoric art" (Anati 1972). In fact, the author of one introductory world prehistory text goes so far as to rave that Marshack "has come as close as any archaeologist ever to reading the mind of ancient man" (Hester 1976:181).

My personal feeling is that final judgment (either pro or con) is grossly premature. Marshack has introduced a new method for examining the symbolic artifacts of the past, and his microscopic techniques will doubtless influence coming generations of archaeologists. Marshack is virtually alone in his use of these techniques at present, and his research must be replicated by independent investigators before it can be firmly accepted or rejected. Marshack is also the only scholar who has examined all of the symbolic objects, but this makes him neither correct nor incorrect. We should also point out that the lunar correlations discussed here constitute only a fragment of his research on symbolic artifacts; the more general implications of Marshack's work are discussed in Chapter 13.

At this point, Marshack's research on Upper Paleolithic astronomical phenomena stands by itself, but a number of investigators have conducted research on later archaeological materials. The most famous of such sites is Stonehenge, where a variety of scholars have attempted to unravel the possible astronomical significance (see inset).

Another influential Old World astroarchaeologist is Alexander Thom, Emeritus Professor of Engineering Science at Oxford. Shunning most of the publicity that invariably accompanies this spectacular brand of prehistoric research, Thom has plugged away for nearly three decades, surveying and interpreting a staggering number of prehistoric British and French sites.

Stonehenge Decoded?

Stonehenge—what Colin Renfrew (1973:214) calls that "huge and problematical monument"—has already been briefly discussed in Chapter 6. Situated on the broad Salisbury Plain in southern Britain, Stonehenge consists of a series of massive upright stones supporting great horizontal lintel slabs. Stonehenge was built over several centuries; the major portions (Stonehenge III) were probably erected between 2100 and 1900 B.C. (Renfrew 1973:226). The monumental scale of the structure, standing some fifteen feet overhead, dwarfs the onlooker and lends an increased measure of power and intensity to this strange archaeological site.

Stonehenge (which means "the hanging stones") quite naturally became a focus of speculation for all intrigued by British antiquity. One twelfth-century writer suggested that the great Merlin, court wizard to King Arthur, magically situated the enormous stones in place. Stonehenge appeared in the seventeenth-century diaries of John Evelyn and Samuel Pepys, and in the poetry of Wordsworth. Stonehenge was variously ascribed to visiting Romans, to the Danes, and to the legendary Druidic Celts. Theories of the function of Stonehenge ranged from a temple to the sun to a temple of the serpent, from a shrine of Buddha to a prehistoric planetarium or astronomical model of the planets, and from a Roman racecourse for chariots (!) to a gigantic gallows on which British leaders were hanged in honor of the Saxon god Woden (see Brown 1976:59).

So it came as little surprise when in 1963 another Stonehenge theory appeared: not only was Stonehenge a moon and sun observatory, it was also an extremely sophisticated counting device (a "Neolithic computer") that had been used for predicting the earlier theories. This time, (1) the theoretician was Dr. Gerald Hawkins, a respected professor of astonomy affiliated with Boston University, and (2) the theory was published in the pages of *Nature,* one of the most influential scientific journals in the world (Hawkins

Figure 11–7
The ruins at Stonehenge, England *(courtesy of The American Museum of Natural History).*

1963, 1964). Hawkins later detailed his theory in a book entitled *Stonehenge Decoded* (1965).

Hawkins's analysis is highly mathematical and difficult for most archaeologists to follow. In its simplest form, Hawkins suggests that the fifty-six holes (the "Aubrey holes") which surrounded the perimeter of the upright stones could have functioned as an eclipse predictor. The Aubrey was, according to Hawkins, a giant marker that was operated by knowledgeable priests: if a stone was moved around the circle, one hole each year, then the extreme positions of the moon and the eclipses of both sun and moon might be predicted. Hawkins suggests that if six tally pebbles were spaced at intervals of 9, 9, 10, 9, 9, and 10, and then moved counterclockwise each year, the Aubrey circle would accurately predict "every important moon event for hundreds of years" (Hawkins 1964).

Eclipses, to be sure, held great fascination for primitive peoples throughout the world. Eclipses are important in the ritual folklore of the Orient and the Maya, for instance, and are discussed in Sumarian texts going back to 3000 B.C. The intrepid Christopher Columbus once even saved his starving crew in Jamaica using an eclipse. Forewarned from his almanac that a lunar eclipse was due on March 1, 1504, Columbus threatened the natives that he would take away the light of the moon until they brought him food. Columbus confidently retired to his cabin, and once the predicted eclipse began, his terrified Jamaican hosts provided him all the provisions he desired (Morison 1974:261).

The eclipse theory for Stonehenge has been refined by Hoyle (1966a, 1966b). Although agreeing with Hawkins that the Aubrey holes had indeed functioned as eclipse predictors, Hoyle disagreed totally with how they had been used. The problem was that the foreteller could predict only a small fraction of all actual eclipses. Hoyle presented an extremely complicated scheme for moving the marker stones about the Aubrey holes so that "almost every eclipse" could be predicted (although only about half would in fact be visible from Stonehenge).

The Hawkins-Hoyle interpretation of Stonehenge calls for extreme mathematical and astronomical sophistication on the part of the Neolithic priesthood. Most archaeologists who have worked with sites of this period refuse to grant such sophistication. In two scathing reviews entitled "Decoder Misled" and "Moonshine on Stonehenge," Atkinson denounced Hawkins's research as "tendentious, arrogant, slipshod and unconvincing" (1966a, 1966b). Atkinson accused Hawkins of using an outdated map of Stonehenge, of arbitarily accepting a ± 2° rate of error, and of overlooking the archaeological facts in search of astronomical elegance. Somewhat later, Jacquetta Hawkes (1967) took up the battle with Hawkins, accusing him of playing to an enthusiastic, if uninformed, public: "Evidently they were getting the Stonehenge they desired" (1967:175). After considering the various archaeological evidence, Hawkes asked: "Is it possible that Neolithic or even Bronze Age Britain was a nest of calculating geniuses? . . . Perhaps it is just possible, but very, very unlikely" (1967:179, 180).

Friction between astronomer and archaeologist has become commonplace as astronomical studies of archaeological sites proceed. The astronomer is most commonly accused of ignoring the archaeological evidence, and the archaeologist is almost always woefully unequipped to deal with the mathematical and astronomical data.

> True genius resides in the capacity for evaluation of uncertain, hazardous, and conflicting information.
>
> *Winston Churchill*

Thom has concentrated on Megalithic sites consisting largely of tombs and sacred monuments constructed during the middle Neolithic period, roughly the second millennium B.C. Thom has personally mapped 450 **Megalithic** sites, meticulously recording the positions of the remaining stones and features (see Thom 1967, 1971). He has also paid special attention to horizon features (similar to the Hopi horizon calendar) which could have been used as engineering "foresights" and "backsights" during the construction phase.

In the process of mapping the monuments, Thom was deeply impressed with the unusually high degree of skill with which the ritual alignments were constructed. Thom suggests that the builders of these monuments used standard units of measurement, which he calls the Megalithic yard (2.72 feet) and the Megalithic fathom (5.44 feet). Thom notes that his Megalithic yard is almost identical to the Old Spanish *vara,* which was introduced throughout the New World by the conquistadores. Although Thom has interpreted the spread of the Megalithic yard in terms of large-scale prehistoric migrations, it seems more plausible that the Megalithic yard closely approximated the human pace, and the Megalithic fathom is close to a double pace (which can be traced back to Roman times).

After establishing the Megalithic yard (at least to his satisfaction), Thom moved on to consider the problem of exactly how the hundreds of Megalithic ritual circles were planned and built. While many investigators had noted that the Megalithic circles are slightly out of round and lopsided, most simply wrote off the distortion to crude or sloppy construction methods. But Thom looked more deeply into the problem. Although the geometry is too complicated to consider here, Thom finally decided that the circles were distorted because Megalithic man simply refused to accept the actual value of *pi* as 3.1416. Instead, the Megalithic builders appear to have rounded off pi to the nearest whole number and then proceeded on that basis. Thom notes over and over again that many of the smaller circles tended to have a diameter of about twenty-two feet; these circles are exactly eight Megalithic yards in diameter, built on a pi value of roughly three. Thom ultimately classified Megalithic ritual stone rings into categories (egg-shaped, ellipses, compound and concentric circles). On the basis of sophisticated mathematical reasoning, Thom postulated that not only did the circle dimensions conform to integral numbers, but that the builders must also have discovered the principle of Pythagorean triangles.

Thom was also deeply impressed with the accuracy of Megalithic construction. The sprawling site of Avebury, in Wiltshire, England, for instance, was constructed with an accuracy approaching 1 in 1,000 (accuracy that can be achieved today only by experienced surveyors with excellent optical equipment). Thom proposed that an elaborate construction technique was used at Avebury based on complex geometrics and the Megalithic yard. He also cites a list of over 250 alleged alignments with the stars, the sun, and the moon (Thom 1967:97–101). Thom argues that the stars were harnessed as timekeepers, noting how Capella, for instance, has extreme importance in agricultural and husbandry rituals of northern Europe. Thom even postulates some ideas about how the Megalithic calendar operated: at least 16 equal divisions ("months"), each made up of 22-23-day periods. Thom concluded: "One can only surmise that, having no pen and paper, [Megalithic man] was building in stone a record of his achievements in geometry and perhaps also in arithmetic" (Thom 1966:126).

The work of Alexander Thom directly places much traditional archaeological interpretation in question. Should Thom be correct, then the Megalithic builders and priests possessed sophisticated astronomical and arithmetic capabilities, far greater accomplishments than we have given them credit for. Although archaeological opinion changes slowly, Thom's meticulous and sophisticated research has already convinced many that he is correct (e.g., Atkinson 1966b and Renfrew 1973: 337–339). The recent statement by Atkinson (1975:51) is enlightening in this regard:

> It is hardly surprising that many prehistorians either ignore the implications of Thom's work, because they do not understand them, or resist them because it is more comfortable to do so. I have myself gone through the latter process: but I have come to the conclusion that to reject Thom's thesis because it does not conform to the model of prehistory on which I was brought up involves also the acceptance of improbabilities of an even higher order. I am prepared, in other words, to believe that my model of European prehistory is wrong, rather than that the results presented by Thom are due to nothing but chance.

Research on astroarchaeological ritual is under way worldwide, and results are rapidly becoming available for study and synthesis. I recommend Baity (1973) as a first-rate source on the general status of astroarchaeological studies throughout the world; P. Brown (1976) provides an excellent nontechnical summary of the European Megalithic research (see also Renfrew 1973). Aveni (1975, 1977) provides a great deal of material regarding New World astroarchaeology; and for specific studies see Aveni (1972), Aveni and Gibbs (1976), Eddy (1974), Dow (1967), Fuson (1969), Nuttall (1906), Thompson (1974), and Wedel (1967).

ANALYZING THE FUNCTIONS OF RITUAL

When people perform rituals their intentions are explicit: they want to control nature, or make people well, or make people sick, or save souls, or revitalize their society.

But a second, related question invariably arises: How successful is religious ritual in achieving these goals? The problem, of course, is how to deal with such adaptive functions. To most anthropologists the "function" of a cultural element is the contribution it makes to the survival of the society (see Wallace 1966:169). Archaeologists have relatively little difficulty in determining the "function" of a particular hunting strategy, or the "function" of a Clovis point, or even the "function" of a burial mound. All of these activities are closely linked to the technological, ecological, and demographic adaptation of the society, and the linkages are not difficult to make even in the archaeological record.

But to determine the "function" of expressly religious behavior is more difficult, precisely because the obvious technological and ecological linkages are lacking. Vogt (1952), for instance, conducted a classic study of water witches (or dowsers); even today, thousands of rural American farmers and ranchers employ water witches to help them find the best location to drill for water. Despite the lack of empirical support, these farmers steadfastly hold onto the custom of dowsing for water. Why?

Or consider the case of voodoo death. Throughout South America, Africa, Australia, and New Zealand, deaths due to voodoo curses have been repeatedly reported by competent observers (e.g., Cannon 1942). Both American water witching and voodoo are examples of contemporary ritual behavior. But what is the function of these rituals? Does water witching really find water? If not, why is the custom still practiced so widely today? Does voodoo really kill people? If not, why is the ritual practiced in so many contemporary cultures?

In one sense, these functional interpretations depend on the empirical evidence alone. How well do dowsers really perform in predicting the location of underground water? Not very well, according to Vogt (1952). Or what about voodoo? Can black magic really cause death (yes, by literally frightening the victim to death, according to Cannon 1942)?

But the facts rarely speak for themselves. As explained in Chapter 3, anthropological interpretation really depends on one's theoretical perspective. Some mainstreams of anthropological thought assign strategic priority to matters of technology and ecology; other approaches emphasize symbolic, structural, or cognitive components.

Archaeological thinking follows similar lines. In the remainder of this chapter we will examine how one's theoretical perspective colors one's interpretations of the actual data. Although we are specifically concerned with the function of past ritual, we will also examine how some current schools of thought operate within contemporary archaeology.

An Adaptive Approach to Past Ritual and Religion

Several examples were presented in Chapter 3 to suggest adaptive functions for ethnographic religious practices. The elaborate potlatch complex of the American Northwest Coast was one case in point; adaptively oriented ethnologists suggested that the potlatch feasts were one way in which social status could be converted to material subsistence items (especially food) in times of ecological stress. The kula exchange of the Trobriand Islanders was also viewed as a ceremonial apparatus which fostered functional trade networks among potential enemies.

Archaeologists have also relied on the adaptive perspective to explain prehistoric religious practices. To cite one example, consider this problem: Why was the pig domesticated as early as 6000 B.C. in parts of the Near East (like the Zagros Mountains) but apparently never domesticated in prehistoric times throughout other areas such as the Khuzistan steppe (Flannery 1965)?

The ideational perspective might argue that some religious taboo or dietary law must have been involved, probably the same religious tradition that today bans pork from the tables of Jews and Moslems. The Bible (both in the book of Genesis and again in Leviticus) denounces pigs as unclean beasts, forbidding tasting or even touching them. Somewhat later, Allah told Mohammed that followers of Islam should forever be forbidden to eat pigs. This perspective would suggest to archaeologists that the absence of pig bones in many Near Eastern sites is due to religious prohibitions, which persist even today among millions of Jews and hundreds of millions of Moslems (see Harris 1974:35–37).

But an ecological alternative has been suggested by Flannery (1965) and elaborated by Harris (1974). The environment of the Khuzistan steppe is one of extremes, marked by erratic and unpredictable storms in the winter, followed by arid, scorching winds during the summer. The most successful human adaptation seems to have been transhumant herding, that is, moving flocks from plains to mountains. A mixed economy evolved about 7000 B.C.; the villagers grew crops of wheat and barley and tended flocks of domestic goats and a few sheep (Hole, Flannery, and Neely 1969: 342–345). This mixed economy survived until late prehistoric times.

The ideal pastoral animal is one that is biologically adapted to arid environments in the first place—the sheep and the goat. These beasts have digestive tracts that evolved to allow them to subsist on high cellulose diets, and the villagers of Khuzistan ran herds of goats as early as 7500 B.C. (Hole, Flannery, and Neely 1969: 243–244).

Pigs, it turns out, are poorly suited to such a lifeway. Pigs are lowland creatures who evolved in forests and riverbank environments. Not equipped with a ruminant stomach, pigs are inefficient converters of the high cellulose foods of the steppes. Wild pigs occur today on the Khuzistan steppe, but since they do best when fed foods such as nuts and fruits, pigs are found only near the lower reaches of river bottoms. Most importantly, pigs like grain and even invade modern grain fields in the spring. This places the pig in direct competition with man.

Harris (1974:42) also points out the pig is "thermodynamically ill-adapted" to areas with hot, dry upland climates. Pigs cannot sweat to maintain their body temperature, and experiments show that pigs will die when exposed to even moderate amounts of direct sunlight. Wild pigs survive only in environments that permit them to keep their skin dampened, thereby requiring external moisture to maintain body temperature.

Pigs pose other ecological problems. For one thing, pigs simply will not flock the way sheep and goats do. Any transhumant society would quickly find any attempt to herd their pigs just simply not worth the effort. Not only that, but pigs have an extremely limited lung capacity. They are winded easily and cannot travel as tirelessly as sheep and goats.

This combination of factors conspires to make the pig a poor herd animal indeed (Flannery 1965:1254). At 6000 B.C. there is a striking difference between archaeological sites in the oak-pistachio belt and those of the steppe. The relatively low site of Jarmo had permanent mud-walled houses, with courtyards and ovens, and the Jarmo villagers kept goats, sheep, and domestic pigs, along with two strains of wheat and one of barley. But the contemporary sites on the upland steppes show only goats and sheep and probably reflect a seasonal pattern of herding.

Thus an adaptive interpretation looks beyond religious factors for ecological factors to explain the absence of domestic pigs in parts of the prehistoric Near East. The prehistoric Hebrews of 2000 B.C. were a society that subsisted on a mixed economy of herding and seasonal agriculture. Their herds of sheep, goats, and cattle provided the economic mainstay, and hence, from an adaptive standpoint, Jahweh (and later Allah) rendered some sound ecological advice in prohibiting pork from the diet.[2]

Another recent example of an ecological approach to ritual can be found in Harner's highly controversial interpretation (1977a, 1977b) of Aztec sacrifice and cannibalism. Cannibalism is a topic that anthropologists encounter more commonly on TV talk shows than in their everyday research. Anthropologists Garn and Block (1970) have analyzed the nutritive value of cannibalism, concluding that "while human flesh may serve as an emergency source of both protein and calories, it is doubtful that regular people-eating ever had much nutritional meaning." One recent episode occurred in which a plane carrying an amateur rugby-team from Uruguay crashed in the remote Andes on approach to Santiago, Chile. Stranded in the wreckage for eighteen days, the surviving Uruguayans resorted to full-scale cannibalism of their dead teammates and friends. This case is probably unique in our own culture: the sixteen survivors were later assured by the archbishop of Montevideo that the Catholic Church sanctioned cannibalism when undertaken for survival purposes (Read 1974).

Cannibalism is most commonly interpreted as no more than a bizarre custom or as a short-run survival method for a few desperate people.

This conventional wisdom is manifest in almost all treatment of Aztec sacrifice and cannibalism. Estimates of the magnitude of Aztec sacrifice vary widely; the most commonly cited figure is 20,000 victims per year (see Harner 1977a:119). The account of the conquest by Bernal Díaz del Castillo (1956) describes human sacrifices in nearly every Aztec village encountered between 1519 and 1521. Here is one fairly typical episode:

> I remember that in the square where some of their *cues* stood were many piles of human skulls, so neatly arranged that we could count them, and I reckoned them at more than a hundred thousand. I repeat that there were more than a hundred thousand. And in another part of the square there were more piles made up of innumerable thigh-bones . . . in this town of Tlascala we found wooden cages made of lattice-work in which men and women were imprisoned and fed until they were fat enough to be sacrificed and eaten . . . these prison cages existed throughout the country (Díaz 1956:138,183).

Structural anthropologist Levi-Strauss (discussed in Chapter 3) suggests that the Aztecs possessed a "maniacal obsession with blood and torture," a trait that is evident in all human cultures, but reaching its fullest expression only among the Aztecs (Levi-Strauss 1970:388). Eric Wolf suggests another explanation, namely that the Aztec constituted an extreme psychological type, "driven by imaginary and real indignities, cruel against himself and others . . . even engaged in fulfilling his prophecies of destruction by acting upon the assumption of imminent catastrophe" (1962:145). Kroeber (1955:199) concurs in the assessment of the Aztec as an extreme form of cultural behavior.

These conventional interpretations of Aztec sacrifice and cannibalism by Levi-Strauss, Kroeber, and others fall squarely in the ideational mainstream of anthropological thought. Michael Harner's recent works (1977a, 1977b) provide an interesting, if controversial, counterpoint because he operates within a wholly adaptive framework.

Rather than concerning himself with the regularities of sociocultural evolution, Harner turns to the extremes: How does population pressure influence peculiar or unusual cultural developments (Harner 1977a:117)? Of concern here is not so much the number of people sacrificed—and recent evidence suggests as many as one-quarter million victims per year—as what happened to their bodies after the sacrifices. Harner documents case after case of ethnohistorical evidence to show that the Aztec victims not only provided a ritual outlet, but their flesh also provided a major source of protein and calories. According to Harner (1977a), the flesh of victims was boiled, roasted, stewed with salt, peppers, and tomatoes, but rarely wasted. In fact, at a feast hosted by Montezuma, Díaz (1956:225–226) worried that he could not tell whether dinner was human or something else, since they served fowls, turkeys, duck, venison, pigeons, and rabbits along with their human dishes.

Harner views sacrifice as a ritual response to increased population pressure. Meat was at a shortage in the Mexican Highlands during Aztec times, and ethnohistoric sources note that while the nobility had a rich diet, the commoners would eat most anything; famine was not uncommon. Harner argues that as the population pressure of the Central Highlands increased, so did the incidence of cannibalism. During its peak, the cannibalism rate may have reached as high as five victims per each one hundred people.

While not suggesting that cannibalism constituted a major portion of the total Aztec diet, Harner does attempt to explain the extremity of the Aztec sacrificial complex. According to this explanation, the Aztecs sacrificed people not to satisfy "some maniacal obsession," as Levi-Strauss argues, but rather to fulfill subsistence requirements. Moreover, the Harner hypothesis may explain other puzzling aspects of Aztec society. For example, through supernatural sanctions, the priesthood motivated the bulk of the population to participate in major military operations; the Aztecs marshaled an effective and aggressive war machine. The power of the Aztec priesthood was also reinforced by cannibalism, which Harner calls a fail-safe system: "If the priests failed in the supplications to bring food in the form of local crop harvests, then with the aid of the nobility and the forces under their command, they almost automatically caused food to be brought from other regions in the form of sacrificial captives" (Harner 1977a:130–131).

The mode of Aztec warfare always puzzled their Spanish captors. Why did the Aztecs wage such aggressive warfare, then fail to consolidate the conquered territory? The Aztecs simply conquered, then withdrew. Harner suggests that the Aztecs did not eat their own polity—this would have been socially and politically disruptive. Instead, the Aztecs waged war to obtain captives; Harner calls the Aztec state a "cannibal empire."[3]

Harner's hypothesis of Aztec cannibalism and Harris's ideas on the sacred pig have been discussed here for two reasons. First of all, they demonstrate how ecological, technological, and economic perspectives are being applied to religious strictures and ritual behavior. More importantly, however, is the role of archaeology in such an explanation. Cultural anthropologists such as Harner and Harris cannot pursue their adaptive strategies in explaining cultural behavior without recourse to archaeology and archaeological data. We have seen that ideational or adaptive cases can be made to explain Aztec sacrifice. But such cases are hypothetical and circumstantial. Where is the evidence?

The evidence comes from archaeology. Few Aztec sites have been excavated, partly because the Spaniards destroyed so much, and partly because of the wealth of ethnohistoric documentation available. But as Aztec studies proceed archaeology will play a major role, especially because most of the Aztecs' own documents were destroyed, and those of the Spaniards were drastically biased.

In his articles (1977a, 1977b), Harner attempts to bolster his arguments by citing the relevant archaeological data. Mexican archaeologists working in the Plaza de las Tres Culturas at Tlateloco in Mexico City have found various deposits which contain more than one hundred human skulls. The evidence indicates that the eyes, brains, and other flesh parts were removed prior to their ritual display. At the same site, Eduardo Contreras found headless human rib cages, from which the limbs had been removed. Associated with these bones were obsidian blades, which could have been used for the butchering (see Harner 1977a:126).

These archaeological data are scanty and equivocal, but what is not debatable is that hypotheses such as Harner's and Harris's remain only bold speculations until they are tested. And the only means of conducting such tests is through future archaeological excavation and analysis.

A Cognitive Approach to Past Religion and Ideology

> **H**umanists must cease thinking that ecology "dehumanizes" history, and ecologists must cease to regard art, religion, and ideology as mere "epiphenomena" without causal significance. In an ecosystem approach to the analysis of human societies, everything which transmits information is within the province of ecology.
>
> *Kent Flannery*

It is no secret that most archaeological research is adaptive, in the sense that archaeologists first examine how societies function within their physical ecological framework. This emphasis is understandable, given the ecological, technological, demographic, and economic biases inherent in the archaeological record itself.

But since 1970, alternative explanations have appeared in the archaeological literature. A small but growing cadre of archaeologists have turned to an ideational emphasis in their research, examining the active role ideology can play in shaping the ultimate social, and even technological, structure of societies. Chapter 9 introduced one example of this approach when discussing Joyce Marcus's controversial explanation of Classic Maya settlements. Rejecting a strictly ecological—that is, adaptive—model of Maya settlement patterns, Marcus emphasized the importance of cosmology and world view in determining the location of Classic Maya sites. Marcus is only one of several archaeologists who have recently expressed a dissatisfaction with a strictly ecological mode of archaeological explanation.

This point of view has probably been best expressed by Kent Flannery (1972), who has argued that modern cultural ecological approaches are simply too narrow. Human ecosystems are characterized by exchanges of matter, energy, and information within an ecosystem. Flannery accuses traditional paleoecologists of focusing strictly on the matter-energy exchange and ignoring altogether the informational aspect (art, religion, ritual, writing systems, etc.).

Flannery has further argued that cultural ecologists and cultural materialists have focused too heavily on what Harris (1968a) calls techno-environmental factors. "To read what the 'ecologists' write, one would often think that civilized people only ate, excreted and reproduced" (Flannery 1972:400).

Flannery proposes an encompassing "ecosystem approach" which would include all information-processing mechanisms as part of the ecological whole. The problem here, of course, is that ritual, religion, cosmology, and iconography have traditionally been considered almost the exclusive province of the ethnographer, and archaeology lacks established analytical procedures for dealing with such "intangible phenomena" (Flannery and Marcus 1976).

Flannery and Marcus are not alone in their increased emphasis on the ideological aspects of extinct ecosystems. Robert L. Hall (1977), for instance, has recently accused modern archaeology of *econothink,* of placing undue emphasis on changing tactics of technological adaptation and ignoring "what it may have been that prehistoric peoples found worthwhile to live for." Hall has urged archaeologists to put as much effort into the study of the "cognitive core" of societies as they have in assessing the techno-environmental, techno-ecological core. To illustrate his point, Hall uses the calumet—or peace pipe—as an example of how his cognitive archaeology can broaden the horizons of archaeological investigations.

Hall goes back to the Hopewell period of eastern United States prehistory. Probably the most famous Hopewell artifact is the platform pipe (see Figure 11–8), often found as grave goods in the burial mounds of the Hopewell. Hall contends that contemporary archaeology has concentrated strictly on the economic aspect of the Hopewellian exchange network and has ignored the symbolic and "affective" possibilities implied by ceremonial Hopewellian artifacts. Hall cites Michael Coe's indictment of most adaptively oriented eastern archaeologists:

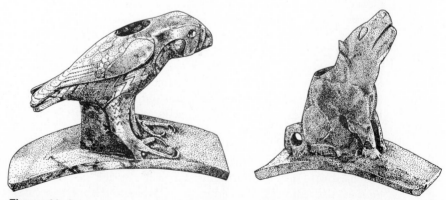

Figure 11–8
Sculptured bird and animal effigy Hopewell pipes, from the Tremper Mound, Scioto County, Ohio.

> Those pipes, for instance, which have come to us from Hopewell and Mississippian cultures of the southeastern and eastern United States, are usually explained away in the following terms: well, these Indians had access to some rare stones, and they grew some tobacco, and they stuffed it in these pipes, and this was part of their leisure time, especially if they were high up in a well-stratified society, and they must have been so since they had such and such an economy. (Coe 1975:195)

Coe and Hall argue that eastern archaeologists have spent so much time emphasizing economy and ecology that they have entirely overlooked the symbolic importance of the very artifacts they dig up. Hall asks, for instance, why the long stem of a ceremonial pipe should symbolize anything more important than the pipe bowl, or why the peace pipe used historically to establish friendly contact is almost always in the form of a weapon. Or why the famous Hopewellian pipes take the form they do.

Hall (1977:502–503) begins with a model familiar to all. Everyone engages in certain culturally dictated customs, the exact meaning and origin of which may be lost. The rite of "toasting" originally involved the sloshing and spilling together of two persons' drinks to reduce the possibility that one planned to poison the other. But how many of us who have toasted friends realized the origin of the custom? Or saluting: Did you know that it originally represented the act of raising visors on armored helmets in order to expose the faces of the two persons encountering one another? Hall suggests that while the original function of the gestures lost practical significance, the acts survive as elements of etiquette or protocol.

Hall applies similar reasoning to the Hopewell platform pipes. Throughout historic times in the eastern United States, Indian tribes observed the custom of smoking a sacred tribal pipe: when the pipe was present violence was absolutely ruled out. Moreover, the calumet (or peace pipe) was generally manufactured in the form of a weapon. Among the Pawnee, for instance, the pipe was fashioned in the form of an arrow, and the Osage word for calumet means "arrowshaft" (Hall 1977:503) Hall argues that the weaponlike appearance is the result of a specific ceremonial custom: the peace pipe was a *ritual weapon*.

This notion is then extended to the prehistoric Hopewell, who manufactured these pipes between 1,600 and 2,100 years ago. These pipes were also ritual weapons, but they were made before the introduction of the bow and arrow. The common Hopewell weapon was the **atlatl**, or spear thrower (see Figure 11–9). Hall suggests that the common Hopewell platform pipe symbolically represented a flat atlatl with an effigy spur. The animal on the bowl is almost invariably carved precisely where an atlatl spur would be needed on a spear thrower, and the curvature of the platform corresponds with the curvature on an atlatl. Hall concludes: "I see the Hopewell platform pipe as the archaeologically visible part of a transformed ritual atlatl, a symbolic weapon which in Middle Woodland times probably had some of the same functions as the calumet of historic times, itself a ritual arrow" (1977:504–505).

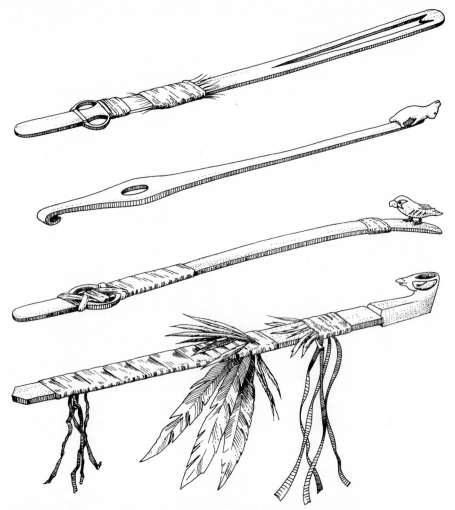

Figure 11–9
Some representations of atlatls in aboriginal North American art *(after Hall 1977, figure 2; courtesy of Robert Hall and the Society for American Archaeology)*.

The importance of the Hopewell pipe goes beyond mere symbolism. Hall suggests that the platform pipe was not merely one of many items exchanged between groups, "It may have been part of the very mechanism of exchange." And here is the potential contribution of Hall's work.

Adaptively oriented research on eastern United States prehistory has defined the Hopewellian Interaction Sphere primarily in economic and environmental terms. Hall suggests that the cognitive archaeology approach can add a larger understanding of the Hopewell lifeway. Arguing from historic American Indian analogies, he suggests that peace pipe ceremonialism served to mediate interaction over a vast central portion of the United States and Canada. While one cannot ignore the economic and political ramifications of such interaction, Hall urges archaeologists also to consider the symbolic details of Hopewellian exchange and mortuary practice. He argues that through "peace pipe diplomacy," the Hopewellian Interaction Sphere tended to reduce regional differences and promote friendly contact and communication between discrete groups.[4]

Of course, archaeologists have speculated about ritual and religion for decades, but the blending of the ecological with the ideological is a relatively new development. The work of Flannery, Marcus, Hall, Lathrop (1973), Marshack, and others can be grouped under the rubric of cognitive archaeology. As noted in Chapter 3, the direction of cognitive archeology has relatively little to do with the work of cognitive anthropologists. While both schools are ideational in the sense that they look for nonmaterial explanations, the day-to-day procedures and assumptions of the two schools have virtually nothing in common. It is difficult to assess the overall significance of cognitive archaeology because so few concrete studies have appeared to date. But it is clear that this approach will supplement the strictly "ecological" studies of the 1960s and the 1970s.

ECOLOGY, IDEOLOGY, AND SCIENTIFIC METHODS

Why shouldn't truth be stranger than fiction?
Fiction, after all, has to make sense.
Mark Twain

Some of the statements in this chapter might seem to be outright contradictions, particularly when archaeologists attempt to determine the function of past ritual behavior. Is Robert Hall (1976:363) right when he states that "the challenge for archaeologists is to think in Indian categories"? Or is Betty Meggers (1955:129) correct when she notes that "there is considerable advantage in being forced to deal with culture artificially separated from human beings"?

This chapter presents both sides of the fence. We examined an adaptive explanation for why the pig had been domesticated in some areas of the Near East for nearly 8,000 years, yet apparently was never domesticated in neighboring areas. The adaptive strategy pointed up a number of ecological disadvantages for the domestication of pigs in parts of the prehistoric Near East. Alternatively, the more traditional (ideational) explanation pointed toward a long-standing religious prohibition against pork.

This example shows how competing strategies operate in archaeology. In truth, most American archaeologists have felt more comfortable working within the adaptive framework of research, and for good reason. Not only does the adaptive explanation seem to explain the distribution of animal bones in Near

Eastern sites, but the model also proposes how different lifeways operated in this area.

What about the ideational strategies? Anthropologists working with contemporary cultures, or societies with historic documentation, are free to examine ideational alternatives, namely that religious dictations prohibited the eating of pork. Harris (1974:35–45) discussed this proposition in detail, citing evidence from biblical and Koranic texts, exploring the pig taboos during Renaissance times and discussing the modern Jewish and Moslem explanations for continuing the taboo today.

But problems can arise with the introduction of archaeological evidence. How does one take an ideational explanation—that pigs were not domesticated due to religious sanctions—and test it? Archaeological sites of the relevant periods contain no written records. There are no informants to interrogate and the actual legal sanctions seem unretrievable. This is why ideational strategies have not fared well so far in archaeology.

But some ideational studies do indeed show promise for testability. Marcus's work on Maya settlement patterns is eminently testable. Either her scheme explains the distribution of Maya hierarchical centers better than the strictly environmental explanation or it does not. The data are readily available in the form of regional settlement pattern surveys. The same is true of Hall's ideas on Hopewell exchange. Either the peace pipe analogy tells something about Middle Woodland interaction or it does not. But of course it remains for Hall and others to translate their ideas into explicitly testable propositions, as Marcus has done.

This is the crux of the issue. Chapter 2 emphasized that within the framework of established scientific methods it is irrelevant where one's hypotheses come from. Hypotheses can come from daydreams, computers, textbooks, or geniuses. Explanations are never judged on their points of origin. Explanations are only judged on their ability to explain phenomena. Thus, strategies of research are neither right nor wrong. Research strategies either open up useful avenues for research or they do not.

Adaptive explanations have prospered in archaeology because they are relatively easy to test; that is, traditional ecological explanations do indeed open useful avenues of research. Ideational explanations in archaeology are more difficult to translate into concrete, testable propositions. Whether the ideational strategy will be fruitful or not remains to be seen. But one thing is manifestly clear: archaeologists can ill afford to ignore any potential source of understanding, whether it is ecological, technological, societal, religious, or cosmological. No anthropological mainstream has an exclusive pipeline to the truth.

> **F**alse views . . . do very little harm, for everyone takes a salutary pleasure in proving their falseness; and when this is done, one path towards error is closed and the road to truth is often at the same time opened.
>
> *Charles Darwin*

SUMMARY

Religion consists of three interrelated aspects: a set of rituals, rationalized by myth, designed to mobilize supernatural powers for the purpose of achieving (or presenting) transformations of state in man and nature. Of these three elements—ritual, myth, and transformations of state—ritual emerges as the primary factor. This is an important fact for archaeology, since ritual is most closely related to material culture, and as such, is the most conspiciously represented element in the archaeological record.

Rituals are either calendrical or critical in nature. Calendrical rituals are always scheduled in advance and publicly announced long before their actual occurrence. Archaeologists are presently attempting to recognize such calendrical practices in the archaeological record and relating this time-factored behavior to the evolution of ritual activity. But because the calendrical ritual is by nature planned beforehand, these rites cannot meet all of the religious requirements of a society. That is, the calendrical ritual is insufficient to cope with emergency requests to the supernatural: this is the function of the critical (noncalendrical) ritual. Certain life crises (such as birth, death, and marriage) are simply not calendrically determined, so societies also have a mechanism for involking supernatural aid at infrequent intervals.

It is assumed that ritual behavior—and in a larger sense, religious behavior in general—functions for the good of society. That is, religion probably has some sort of long-term survival value. But functional explanations invariably arise from implicit research strategies. Archaeologists are presently studying the function of prehistoric religious behavior from both adaptive and ideational perspectives; some investigators emphazise ecological and demographic functions, while others emphasize more ideational factors to explain religious phenonema. As discussed in detail in Chapter 3, such strategies of research are neither "right" nor "wrong"; research strategies either open up useful avenues of explanation or they do not. Archaeologists are presently exploring several possibilities.

NOTES

1. Ellis (1975) has discussed the Pueblo observatories in some detail, emphasizing their recognition from archaeological remains. Recently, investigators have searched Chaco Canyon, New Mexico, for evidence of such horizon-observing stations once used by the prehistoric Anasazi Indians (see Williamson, Fisher, and O'Flynn 1977).

2. Diener and Robkin (1978) take strong exception to Harris's interpretation of pig taboos. They argue that Harris has distorted both fact and theory. The Diener-Robkin paper and the discussion that follows it are highly recommended for those interested in the way in which theory influences one's view of factual evidence.

3. Ortiz (1978) has vigorously challenged Harner's ecological interpretation of Aztec sacrifice. While admitting that the Aztecs obviously practiced human sacrifice and cannibalism, Ortiz interprets the practice as a thanksgiving ritual, which operated on a strict calendrical base. Ortiz questions Harner's assertion that human flesh could have contributed a significant protein source and argues that the Aztec diet was entirely satisfactory without introduction of human protein. Ritual sacrifice was, according to Ortiz, an institutionalized means for Aztec warriors to achieve social status.

4. An important point must be made regarding the nature of explanation employed in the examples presented in this section. Each of the cases discussed in this section relies on a *functional argument* to explain the operation of ritual phenomena. We examined, for instance, an argument that attempts to explain how pork prohibition functioned in parts of the ancient Near East. We also considered evidence that Aztec sacrifice might have served an ecological function. We also considered Hall's suggestion that ritual involving the Hopewell platform pipe might have served specific economic and trade functions.

The common premise in these examples is that the cultural traits and ecological variables are already present. That is, the investigator attempted to explain only how an ongoing system operates—how it functions. Nowhere did the investigator attempt to explain where the traits came from. No matter how well Harner's hypothesis, for instance, may or may not account for the operation of Aztec cannibalism, the hypothesis cannot explain why cannibalism arose in the first place. The functional argument is designed only to demonstrate how a particular custom might be adaptively advantageous; this form of logic is insufficient to account for the origins or presence of cultural traits (see Collins 1965; Hempel 1959). The problems of origins—or more properly, of cultural evolution and change—are considered in Chapter 13.

part four

Processual Studies in Archaeology

S cience is facts; just as houses are made of
stone, so is science made of facts; but a pile of
stones is not a house and a collection of facts is
not necessarily science.

Henri Poincaré

The last four chapters considered how archaeologists go about reconstructing past lifeways.
The focus of these studies—regardless of whether the subject is ecology, social organization,
or ideology—was on specifics. A lifeway is firmly bound in both time and space: the Maya
subsistence-settlement pattern, the bison kill at Olsen-Chubbock, and the alleged periodicity
of the La Marche bone.

As discussed in Chapter 4, the ultimate objective of archaeology is to define the processes that underlie human behavior. A lifeway must be distinguished from a process. The term **lifeway** is used to refer to a single cultural system at a fixed point in time and space; by contrast, a **process** exists at a much more basic level, quietly directing the overall evolution and operation of the cultural system.

The interest in cultural processes is an indirect call for more attention to archaeological theory. *Theory* is a term we have not used so far, but it is important nevertheless. Social scientists use the word theory in a number of different ways. In one usage, theory is an untested explanation, which would probably be false if ever properly tested. We might speak of Von Daniken's "Chariots of the Gods theory," which argues that the major cultural advances on earth result from visitation by extraterrestrial beings (Von Daniken 1969). Many archaeologists would call this a "theory," an improbable and untested generalization. In this sense, theory is almost a dirty word.

Theory is also used to refer to a general set of untested principles or propositions. In this sense, one deals with theory as opposed to practice. Thus a new invention to harness solar energy might work in theory (that is, on paper), but would require extensive field testing before one could decide whether or not it was a successful design. If the solar device functioned as expected, the theory would be valid; if the device failed, the theory would be held invalid ("back to the drawing board").

While both usages are not uncommon, they are of little interest in a discussion of general archaeological theory. A more useful application of the term theory is as a description of the overall framework within which a researcher operates (Brown 1963:166). A social scientist might speak of his "basic orientation" or his "general theory." Such theories generally involve a set of procedural rules and a classification system which can be shared with colleagues who hold the "same basic theory." Although I did not use the term, the six anthropological mainstreams introduced in Chapter 3 are theories of this kind. Each mainstream sets forth a series of assumptions and terms that define a strategy of research. The structuralists, you will remember, concentrate their efforts on myth and religion because these aspects are less constrained by external, material considerations (Levi-Strauss 1963a). The cultural materialists, on the other hand, concentrate on precisely those material conditions, because cultural materialistic theory holds that the variables of economy, ecology, technology, and demography will ultimately prove to be causal (Harris 1968a:245). In other words, the basic theoretical orientation leads Levi-Strauss (and the structuralists) to concentrate on the ideational sphere, while Marvin Harris (and the cultural materialists) focuses on the external conditions of the mundane world. The ultimate test of all such theoretical frameworks is in their ability to explain and predict cultural phenomena.

There is one final usage of the term theory to be considered. One frequently hears that the social sciences lack any formal theory. The critic in this case is lamenting the fact that the social sciences have, to date, been unable to come up with the elegant theoretical structures common in the physical sciences. A formal theory in this sense begins with a set of axioms which are assumed to be true. A series of theorems are then deduced from the axioms, and it is these axioms that make testable predictions about the real world. Anyone who has ever taken a college course in physics, chemistry, or mathematics is well aware of how such formal theories operate.

Formal theory in the social sciences is another matter entirely. First of all, one should not expect to find such a creature as *formal archaeological theory*. Remember the point made in Chapter 4, that the ultimate goal of archaeologists must be to quit doing archaeology. This is because the archaeologist is ultimately after timeless and spaceless generalizations, and such generalizations cannot be made without recourse to data from ethnography, history, and the study of contemporary, functioning societies. Thus, at this level, archaeology cannot have a unique body of theory; that theory must be shared with the rest of social science.

> **It is a mistake to believe that a science consists of nothing but conclusively proven propositions, and it is unjust to demand that it should. It is a demand only made by those who feel a craving for authority in some form and a need to replace the religious catechism by something else, even if it be a scientific one.**
>
> *Sigmund Freud*

The truth is that, with the exception of economics, social science has made very little progress at establishing a formal theory (see Brown 1963, Chapter 11). Part of this difficulty has to do with the nebulous kinds of data with which social scientists must work. Social scientists lack the "intuitively evident quantities" with which Newton began: length as measured by sticks, time as measured by clocks, force as felt in the muscles (Rapaport 1959:351). Social scientists must spend a great deal of time and effort on defining even the most elementary units of observation (as discussed in Chapter 7).

Beyond the methodological problems, there are others who contend that, as a matter of basic principle, it will be impossible for the social sciences to become truly "scientific." We are told that inanimate objects do not obey strict laws, that free will makes human behavior unpredictable. But these arguments have been adequately dealt with elsewhere by philosophers of science (e.g., Kemeny 1959; Hempel 1965, Chapter 7; Rudner 1966).

The fact that social science has so little formal theory rests more in pragmatics than in principle. The laws of social science are more difficult to isolate because of the ambiguous measures employed by social scientists and because of the emotive involvement between subject and scientist. Predictions are difficult to make because of the difficult mathematics implied by many social science problems (see Kemeny 1959:252). And even when predictions are made, social scientists have difficulty carrying out precise experiments to determine whether or not the propositions have been verified. Moreover, the nature of social science is such that progress must be made in much smaller steps than occurs in the physical sciences. For all of these reasons it is not surprising that the social sciences have lagged far behind.

Given the primitive nature of general theory in the social sciences, we will concentrate in this final section more on *how* archaeologists go about studying theory, and we will de-emphasize the actual theories and processes involved. In this context it is most important to understand how a processual study works in archaeology; the actual theories and processes involved are really incidental to our purposes.

Chapter 12 discusses the processes involved in forming the archaeological record. More and more, archaeologists have come to realize how little is actually known about site formation processes. Also called *mid-range theory,* these processual studies provide archaeologists with the bridging arguments necessary for adequate interpretation. In particular, we will consider ethnoarchaeology, experimental archaeology, and the heralded "Garbage Project" as examples of how archaeologists study the processes of site formation.

In Chapter 13 we will consider the study of more general evolutionary processes. The focus of discussion will be purposely limited, considering particularly the origins of agriculture, the origin of the state, and some recent investigations into the ideational processes that are reflected in the archaeological record.

> **P**rocessual archaeology has its dreamers, its missionaries and its prophets. For the most effective pursuit of laws of culture process that directed past human behavior, everyone must get into the act.
>
> *Stanley South*

12

Processes That Create the Archaeological Record

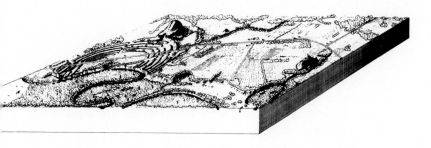

Perhaps *how it comes to be* is really more
distinctive . . . than what it *is*.
Alfred Kroeber

In Chapter 3, I stressed the importance of mid-range theory in archaeology. Because the facts are incapable of speaking for themselves, it is necessary for archaeologists to provide firm bridging arguments to breathe behavioral life into the objects of the past. In an analogy between archaeology and geology, I cited the doctrine of uniformitarianism: the processes that now operate to modify the Earth's surface are the same processes that operated within the geological past. It is necessary to understand the ongoing geological processes in order to provide the bridging arguments necessary to assign meaning to the objects of the geological past. One must have, for instance, a knowledge of contemporary glaciers in order to interpret the glacial features of the remote past. Precisely the same issues face contemporary archaeologists when they attempt to interpret the material remains of past cultural processes; the archaeologist must also frame hypotheses to account for the formation and deposition of these physical remains. Bridging arguments are then required to translate the general hypotheses into specific outcomes, which can actually be observed in the archaeological record.

Once the need for mid-range theory is recognized, it becomes clear that one of archaeology's most pressing goals is the systematic development and synthesis of bridging arguments. Although archaeologists (and, to a lesser extent, ethnographers) have collected relevant data on these topics for decades, it is only within the last few years that this large body of detailed, particularistic facts has been pulled together into a single coherent framework. Michael Schiffer, now of the University of Arizona, has recently synthesized the various types of cultural formation processes into a single terminological framework (see esp. Schiffer 1972; 1976, Chapter 3; 1977).

Schiffer begins with the important concepts of **archaeological** and **systemic context**. The artifacts, features, and residues with which archaeologists work were once involved in an ongoing behavioral system. Arrowheads were manufactured, used for specific tasks, often repaired, and then lost or discarded. Potsherds were once part of whole pots, which were manufactured and decorated according to prescribed cultural criteria, used for utilitarian or ceremonial functions, and then either broken or deliberately discarded, perhaps as part of a rite or ritual. Food bones are the organic residues resulting from a succession of activities—hunting, butchering, cooking, and consumption. While these materials are being manufactured and used they exist in their *systemic context.* These items are part of the actual behavioral system.

By the time the cultural materials reach the hands of the archaeologist they have ceased to participate in this behavioral system; the artifacts, features, and residues that the archaeologist deals with were found in their archaeological contexts. The function of mid-range theory (or bridging arguments) is to bridge the gap between the known, observable archaeological contexts and the unknown, unobservable systemic context. This is why mid-range theory is necessary to provide relevance and meaning to archaeological objects.

Based on this important contextual distinction, Schiffer (1976) has defined four kinds of processes that directly influence the formation of archaeological sites. It is necessary to review briefly these processes before we examine some concrete examples. Schiffer uses the term cultural deposition (S-A process) to characterize the transformation of materials from systemic to archaeological context. S-A processes are those operations that are directly responsible for the accumulation of archaeological sites. Cultural deposition processes are relatively easy to study, and they constitute the dominant factor in forming the archaeological record. When a pottery vessel is broken and discarded into the trash heap it has ceased to function in the behavioral system and becomes incorporated in its new archaeological context: this is cultural deposition. Similarly, when an individual dies and is buried, his physical being has been transformed from systemic to archaeological contexts. S-A processes need not involve deliberate discard or ritual; one major S-A process is the simple loss of functioning artifacts. In this case, the transformation from systemic to archaeological context is accidental, generally involving artifacts that are still capable of performing tasks within the behavioral system. Archaeologists are generally quite familiar with cultural deposition processes because they are directly relevant to conventional archaeological interpretation.

Although the processes of cultural deposition are complex, there seem to be certain general principles that govern S-A processes. Size, for example, seems to have an influence on how items are deposited into the archaeological record. One study (cited by Schiffer 1977:21) of discard behavior was conducted on the campus of the University of Arizona. Small items (those less than four inches in overall dimensions) were discarded almost independently of the location of trash cans, but larger items almost always found their way into trash cans, when they were available. Schiffer terms this principle a cultural-transform (or c-transform), and a number of similar c-transforms have been suggested relating to the deposition of faunal materials, artifacts, and ecofacts (see Schiffer 1976, Chapter 4).

Somewhat more elusive is reclamation (or the A-S process). As the name indicates, reclamation involves a transition of cultural materials from the archaeological back into the systemic context. It is not uncommon to find evidence that archaeological artifacts are scavenged for reuse by both primitive and industrial peoples. Whenever a discarded projectile point is resharpened, a potsherd picked up and used to scrape hides, or an old brick reused in a new fireplace, reclamation has occurred. The act of archaeological excavation is itself an A-S process: artifacts are being removed from their archaeological contexts and integrated into the functioning behavioral system of the archaeological profession. A common and recurring problem when dealing with surface sites (such as those discussed in Chapter 9) is to recognize and account for previous collecting on the same site. Heizer and Clewlow (1968), for instance, have shown that as an archaeological site is repeatedly collected, the larger, more complete artifacts are the first to disappear; as collection continues, the remaining complete artifacts are removed, along with the smaller, harder-to-find artifacts; after sufficient collecting pressure, all that is left is a scatter of barely recognizable bits and pieces. The archaeologist oblivious to the ongoing reclamation processes will be tempted to produce a differing (systemic) interpretation for the same site, depending on the stage of previous collecting. Unlike cultural deposition, reclamation has received relatively little attention from archaeologists.

These first two cultural formation processes deal with transformation of materials between archaeological and systemic contexts. But the archaeological record is also heavily conditioned by transformations that occur within the archaeological and systemic context. Disturbance (the A-A process) changes the contexts of materials within the archaeological site itself; examples include such diverse mechanisms as dam building, farming, and heavy construction, as well as noncultural activities such as freeze-thaw cycles, landslides, and simple erosion. Although the A-A process has few direct implications for systemic contexts, modification (and, indeed, preservation) of archaeological sites is a major and pressing problem facing modern archaeology.

The final relevant mechanism is called reuse (the S-S process), involving the transformation of materials through successive states within the behavioral system. The reuse process moves a single object through a series of different behavioral settings. Potsherds, for example, are sometimes ground up to use as temper in manufacturing new vessels, and broken arrowheads are occasionally rechipped into scrapers.

These four processes are involved in nearly all archaeological sites, and their explicit recognition is necessary in order to project contemporary meaning into our observations of the past. As Schiffer (1976:42) has put it, "The structure of archaeological remains is a distorted reflection of the structure of material objects in a past cultural system." These distortions occur as the result of both cultural and noncultural processes, and the regularities in such processes are a major concern of the contemporary archaeologist. Although it is too early to expect much in the way of concrete results, in this chapter we will examine some of the methods by which archaeologists are attempting to define the processes that control the formation of the archaeological record.

ETHNOARCHAEOLOGY

> The certainties of one age are the problems of
> the next.
>
> R. H. Tawney

It should be clear that archaeologists concerned with mid-range processual studies cannot restrict their attention to the dead. In order to define relevant bridging arguments, archaeologists must observe firsthand the workings of culture within its systemic contexts. This is why archaeologists are turning to living peoples for clues to the interpretation of prehistoric remains. Although people are never considered to be data, the insights gained by participation in a functioning society often open the eyes of the modern archaeologist.

Archaeologists studying the material remains of contemporary peoples are known as **ethnoarchaeologists**. Richard Gould, trained as an archaeologist at the University of California, spent months living with the aborigines of Australia and the Tolowa of northwestern California. Gould was conducting basic ethnography in order to define the processes involved in forming the archaeological record. Why, he would quiz his informants, are arrowheads made in a particular manner? How does one go about surviving in a harsh environment without benefit of agriculture or industry? Exactly who lives with whom, and what would these houses look like a hundred (or a thousand) years from now?

On one field trip Gould asked his Tolowa informants to inspect his archaeological excavations in order to solicit their ideas regarding puzzling aspects of his site.

Gould had begun his excavations under the standard assumption that habitation areas are best located by looking for surface concentrations of broken artifacts and midden deposit. He was somewhat chagrined when, after repeated digging, he was unable to locate any prehistoric house remains on a site that seemed to hold promise for such finds. When asked about the problem, his Tolowa informants were quite amused, telling him that "them old-timers never put their houses in the garbage dump . . . they don't like to live in their garbage any more than you would" (Gould 1966:43). They pointed to a steep slope on the edge of the "site." Although this hillside had seemed to Gould an unlikely spot on which to construct a house, he followed their suggestions. After only twenty minutes of digging, he came upon a well-preserved redwood plank house buried only eighteen inches below the surface. Gould's Tolowa informants only grinned knowingly.

Archaeologists rarely worked with informants until the mid-1960s; since then, ethnoarchaeology has become a fairly common practice. Archaeologists have come to realize the importance of establishing a relevant mid-range theory, and the study of living peoples is perhaps the best single way to do so.

As archaeologists supersede their initial, chronological goals, analysis rests on a number of critical assumptions, many of which can be tested for accuracy and relevance through ethnoarchaeological research. Consider the tool-kit concept, discussed earlier in Chapter 10.

> The aim of such analysis is generally to define "tool kits," or clusters of artifacts and other items which occur together on occupation floors as a consequence of having been used together in certain activities. It is hoped that inferences concerning patterns of prehistoric human activity can be made by interpreting these "tool kits" in terms of their contexts and their position on the occupation floors. (Whallon 1973:266)

Note the implicit bridging argument here which allows inference from the archaeological remains: tools found in spatial association on an occupation surface (archaeological context) reflect a single task (systemic context). This underlying assumption has conditioned a great deal of recent archaeological research into spatial patterning and, ultimately, past social organization (see Chapter 10).

It certainly sounds logical enough to infer that tools found together on a living surface must have been discarded from a single or a few related tasks. But how do we know this is necessarily so? Just because the bridging argument

Figure 12–1
A Bushman village near Gomodino Pan *(courtesy of The American Museum of Natural History).*

sounds plausible is insufficient reason. Similar reasoning in geology would lead to the interpretation of morainal features as glacial deposits just because the explanation "sounds logical" or "seems plausible." Geologists certainly do not do this. They go out and personally investigate active, ongoing glaciers to see whether or not they in fact produce moraines. If so, exactly what do these moraines look like? In other words, geologists have for centuries realized the importance of relating the "facts" of the geological record to systemic, processual contexts. Archaeologists have only recently come to this realization.

Fortunately, archaeologists have begun critically to examine their concepts and assumptions. Consider, for instance, the work of John Yellen (1977). Although trained at Harvard as an archaeologist, Yellen spent over two years in Botswana (southern Africa), studying the behavior and material culture of the !Kung Bushmen. Although never fluent in the language, he did learn sufficient !Kung so that he could dispense with an interpreter and conduct his own direct interviews. Yellen's goal was to draw plans of !Kung campsites in order to provide fundamental data to be used in mid-range theory formation. Yellen was particularly concerned with recording how long each camp was occupied, exactly what activities occurred there, and how these activities were reflected in the archaeological record.

Yellen mapped sixteen such !Kung camps, and was able to make some generalizations. The !Kung camp is circular in shape, with huts located along the circumference of the circle and entrances facing toward the center. The hut serves primarily as a place in which to store belongings, and very few activities actually take place inside it. Only during rainstorms do people sleep in huts at night. A hearth is located in front of each hut, providing warmth in winter, a place to cook food, and also serving as a focus for domestic activities. In all camps a characteristic amount of debris accumulates around each hearth, including vegetable remains (such as nut shells and fruit and melon skins), bone fragments, and waste products of manufacturing activities (such as bits of ostrich egg shell, bone, wood shavings, and fiber used for making string). A few fist-sized nut-cracking stones are the only items of value left at a campsite when abandoned. The staples of the !Kung tool kit—iron knives, axes, and adzes—are never left behind, and Yellen only found one such lost tool in over two years of research.

!Kung camps are thus divided into public and private areas. The public portion includes both the center of the camp circle, as well as the space outside of it. The primary, or family, area consists of the hearth, the hut, and the immediately surrounding space. The individual's space within a !Kung campsite is thus divided into three parts: the area belonging to one's own family, similar spaces belonging to other families, and the communal area shared by all.

These sixteen campsites formed a data base for Yellen to examine the concept of the tool kit. He was impressed with the number of disruptive factors that conspired to mix and jumble the archaeological context of these sites. The exact area being utilized depends on a number of transient factors, such as the continually shifting pattern of sun and shadow. The huts themselves provide some shade, and, in some camps, the charcoal and nut scatters tend to lie to the east and north of the huts. In other camps it is more convenient to use shade provided by individual trees and shrubs. Thus, the same general areas used for skin drying and the roasting of animal heads are also occupied to take advantage of shade. Children also run and play continually, scattering and discarding debris. There are also some adults who maintain their own huts and hearths, but they are dependent largely on others for food. At these huts, living debris is either scanty or absent.

Nevertheless, a certain pattern of occupation does emerge for all !Kung camps (Figure 12–2). Activities do not occur at random, and the by-products of such cultural activities do indeed tend to cluster across the camp spaces. Yellen defines four basic activity areas. The *communal activity area* is characterized by negative evidence only: nothing ever appears in this central area. The *nuclear activity area* includes the hut, the hearth, and associated debris; this is the site of most domestic activities. Outside the hut circle one finds a *shade area* and a *special-use area* used for drying of skins and so on.

What does this evidence tell us about tool kits? Yellen finds little support for the common assumption that artifacts found in similar archaeological contexts must have been involved in similar systemic contexts (1977:96–97). The debris from subsistence activities (cooking and preparing vegetable foods) is

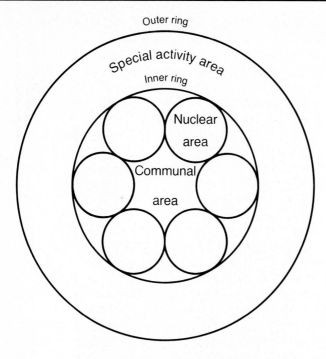

Figure 12–2
Schematic interpretation of activity
patterning at a !Kung camp *(after*
Yellen 1977, figure 12; courtesy of
John Yellen and Academic Press).

found scattered about with debris resulting from manufacturing activities, such as making ostrich egg shell beads or poison arrows. There is no spatial separation in the archaeological record because there is no spatial separation in the systemic context. Similarly, the debris from a single activity, such as cracking nuts, can be found in several different places within the !Kung camp. Nuts are usually cracked within the nuclear family context, but people also crack nuts in the shady area outside the hut circle.

Research such as Yellen's work among the !Kung points up many fallacies in archaeological interpretation; Yellen (1977:11) refers to this as a "spoiler" function, noting that "it takes only one pin to prick the balloon." More important, however, is the body of mid-range theory that will grow up from such ethnoarchaeological studies. Yellen's research provides a starting point, and his notions of camp patterning among the !Kung can be refined by parallel studies among other similar groups elsewhere in the world. The function of mid-range theory is to provide the arguments necessary to bridge the gap between observable archaeological contexts and nonobservable systemic contexts. These propositions, by their nature, will apply to systemic contexts both present and past. Ethnoarchaeology is based on the premise that if they cannot adequately cover the contemporary contexts, they cannot be viewed as adequate generalizations.

The tool kit concept has also been examined by Lewis R. Binford, who conducted ethnoarchaeological research among the Nunamiut Eskimo. After analyzing the patterns of faunal distributions in Middle Paleolithic sites in southwestern France, Binford became concerned with the S-A processes involved with hunting behavior, and studied caribou hunting among the Nunamuit. But Binford emphasizes that "the focus on fauna and my study of the Nunamuit were not research choices made because of an abiding interest in either fauna or Eskimos. My primary interest was in evaluating the utility of certain concepts commonly employed by the archaeologist" (Binford 1978).

Binford accompanied Nunamuit hunters on practically all of the various kinds of hunting practiced today. Like Yellen, Binford was concerned with recording what the hunters did at each locality, and what debris would be left for the archaeologist. Also like Yellen, Binford (1973:242) was struck by the general lack of correlation between the systemic activities and the artifacts that remained. Binford has characterized the Nunamiut technology as "almost exclusively **curated**," meaning that artifacts are reused and transported so much that they are rarely deposited (lost) in contexts that reflect their actual manufacture and use. The problem for archaeologists is that localities that are demonstrably different in behavioral (systemic) terms produce archaeological sites that are almost identical. Differentiation between activities is only possible through artifacts, which are very rare and nearly always broken and heavily modified through use. The more that artifacts are curated, preserved, and transported, the less correspondence there will be between the systemic and archaeological contexts of given sites.

Both Yellen and Binford studied the way in which relatively primitive people patterned their archaeological sites. Effective mid-range theory also requires that archaeologists understand the processes involved at the artifact level. In some ways this is more difficult: the artifact level is more difficult to study because western technology has intruded on most contemporary societies, regardless of how remote. The Nunamuit hunters that Binford studied, for instance, conducted most of their hunting with the aid of snowmobiles and high-powered rifles. While these technological advances do not necessarily change the process of site formation, many processes involved in bow-arrow-spear technology remain unknown.

The problem is that many prehistoric techniques have perished with their practitioners. Consider the manufacture and use of stone tools. Fortunately for the archaeologist, flintknapping is a messy business; archaeological sites are commonly littered with broken stone artifacts and waste from stone tool manufacture. As discussed in Chapter 7, the superficial outline of a stone artifact is often sufficient to define a series of temporal types: side-notched projectile points might, for instance, occur later in one region than corner-notched points.

But stone tools can provide more than just chronological information, if we can understand how they were manufactured and used. To be sure, native aboriginal stoneworkers are rare in this modern world, but such groups do exist, and archaeologists have recently recognized their potential contribution to relevant mid-range theory. Not only can these peoples provide information about the physical technology involved in making stone tools, but questions can also be asked regarding the sociological and idiosyncratic implications of stone artifacts and the debris from their manufacture. Do distinctive social groupings, such as villages or bands, manufacture their tools in characteristic ways? How do group norms condition the finished artifact? Do primitive artisans tend to think—like archaeologists—in terms of artifact types? Are individual preferences expressed in stone tool assemblages? Questions such as these can be answered only through research involving informants who have learned the techniques of stoneworking within their native cultural matrix. The following example discusses one such project designed to learn about the sociology of stone tool manufacture.

It was in 1964 as a graduate student at the Australian National University that J. Peter White first visited the highlands of New Guinea. Although he was trained primarily as a field archaeologist—his doctoral dissertation was the first ever written on the prehistory of New Guinea—White was delighted to find a few local residents who still manufactured tools of stone. Realizing the scientific potential of this situation, White framed a research strategy and returned to New Guinea in 1967 to study this vanishing craft, its social implications, and its correlates (for more details on this project, see White and Thomas 1972 and Thomas 1978).

The informants in his study are the Duna-speakers of the western New Guinea highlands who subsist primarily upon sweet potatoes and domestic pigs. The Duna live in social groups called **phratries**—loosely structured communities numbering between one hundred and one thousand; they experienced initial contact with European technology less than three decades ago. Although adult males now prefer to use steel axes and knives, each was raised by his parents with a complete knowledge of stone tool manufacture and repair. Until just a few years ago, one either made tools from stone or did without.

To make a tool, the Duna first collect the proper raw materials, in this case, chert nodules from a nearby stream. Sharp stone chips are then fractured from the raw nodule, which is called a **core**. Fracturing is accomplished in basically two ways. The most direct means is by holding the nodule in one hand and then striking it with another rock; this is one direct percussion technique. Alternatively, one may exert more control by placing the core upon a large platform stone, called an **anvil**. The core is then smashed with a stone hammer into dozens of sharp flakes (see Figure 12–3). The large amount of lithic debris apparent in Figure 12–3 is precisely the same sort of garbage that accumulates in most archaeological sites; sometimes the remains range over thousands of years. Cores are occasionally wrapped in bark so that the resulting flakes tend to be longer and narrower, i.e., they are more bladelike. The bark wrapping also keeps the stone chips and waste flakes from scattering about upon impact.

After observing this process for some time, White questioned the Duna about the kinds of artifacts they were making. In Duna, no linguistic distinction is made between the initial core and the flakes driven from it: both are called

Figure 12–3
Aluni clansman fracturing flakes from a chert core *(courtesy of J. Peter White).*

aré. These sharp little tools are used in wood carving, stripping fibers, and drilling shells. Figure 12–4 shows one such *aré* carving barbs upon a Duna hunting spear. Although steel knives hold a better edge, completely adequate work can be accomplished with the lithic counterpart. Some flakes are selected for a more specialized function. These flake tools, called *aré kou* by the Duna, are tied with orchid fibers into the handle of cane or wood and then used for drilling holes or shredding fibers. The point for archaeologists is that the Duna distinguish two types, distinct in morphology, function, and cognitive significance. The point to a Duna is that the archaeologist has made a lot of fuss about nothing; these are simply old-fashioned tools which nobody bothers to make anymore. But archaeologists are accustomed to being scoffed at for their unusual interests in the garbage of others.

In planning his research among the Duna, White elected to examine some previously unexplored social correlates of artifact manufacture. Specifically, given an assemblage of similar stone tools, what can one tell regarding the cultural matrix in which they were manufactured? This amounts to identifying and interpreting the social variables of flintknapping. Technological aspects of stone tool making—method of flaking, selection of flakes for hafting, and so

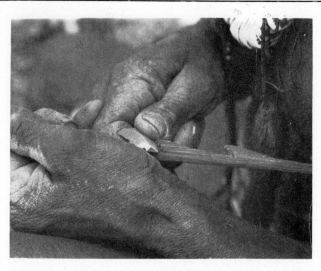

Figure 12–4
Aré **being used to carve barbs into a wooden arrowhead** *(courtesy of J. Peter White).*

forth—are somehow related to functional variables and to differences in raw material. These in turn ought to be observable in the local tool traditions in the villages. Individual variation also affects the final appearance of the tools. In order to study these aspects in an objective manner, a research design was formed which held all variables constant save the one under immediate study.

The first such variable concerned fluctuation of tool morphology in artifacts manufactured by the same worker. Making crude stone tools like this involves an element of randomness, reflecting both the haphazard nature of stone fracture and the range of tolerance for acceptable tools. Perhaps these tolerances vary from day to day, even when made by the same worker. Once this variation per individual can be properly isolated, these figures can serve as a baseline against which to compare further, independent variables. Another source of patterned variation is that between workers, since some men are likely to be more consistent in their artifact manufacture, or perhaps more skilled in the mechanics of flaking stone. There could also be differences between the local villages—the phratries—since daily face-to-face contact could be expected to condition group norms for tool manufacture. What could be considered a decent tool to one group might seem odd or sloppy to their neighbors.

Three independent variables were isolated in the stone tool complex of the Duna: functional differences, idiosyncratic variations, and group norm patterns. White's project attempted to determine which, if any, of these dimensions of variability could be detected in the stone tools. If patterns could be isolated in the ethnographic sample and collected under strict control, then similar forms of variability could be postulated for prehistoric assemblages where such external controls are lacking. This study could also provide some anthropological data about the contemporary culture of the Duna, especially the relationship of the psychological importance of material culture to systems of norms. Once again, the operational boundary between archaeology and ethnography becomes a fuzzy one.

Two phratries were selected for study. Hareke, a dispersed grouping of 375 people, is situated about fifteen miles—a five-hour walk—from Aluni, a smaller community with a population of only 160. White initiated his project by observing the overall range of techniques used by the Duna in artifact manufacture. After he understood the basics of Duna technology he asked several knappers in each phratry to prepare batches of tools for him. Eighteen men were selected as informants, ten from Hareke and eight from Aluni. Every day, these men produced between twenty and seventy-five individual tools, both *aré* and *aré kou*. Each individual's daily output was catalogued as a unit, so the basic element of analysis was a single worker's daily output for each tool type. This analytic unit was termed a *TMD*, a type-man-day. In this manner, tools could be analytically separated in the laboratory; stoneworker output could be sorted by maker to study individual bias, by daily output to examine the worker's variations from day to day, and also by village to study the relationship of tool traditions in each phratry. Through such a priori deductive reasoning, White constructed a research design in which the three variables under analysis—variation between types, variation between individuals, and variation between villages—could be held constant relative to other sources.

After a couple of months, over nine thousand artifacts had been procured in this experiment, and the problem became how to analyze effectively such a bulk of data. The first step was to measure individual attributes that seemed to best reflect variation in each assemblage (TMD). On these rather amorphous flakes one is limited in quantitative analysis, since only a few measurable variables exist on such crude tools (see Figure 12–4). White selected six attributes that the Duna themselves felt were important: length, width, thickness, edge angle, weight, and length/width ratio. The informants, of course, do not think of their tools in terms of measurable attributes, but they do have rather strong feelings about what makes a serviceable tool ("It should be so long, about this wide, very sharp . . .").

These measurements resulted in a tremendous mass of data, too much for an individual to handle by pencil-and-paper means, so White enlisted the aid of a computer in handling the tedious analytical operations. Measurements were transferred to IBM cards and processed on a Burroughs 5500 computer at the University of California, Davis. After the machine routinely accomplished the thousands of calculations, it drew graphs to indicate the distributions of each of the attributes. The machine was then directed to analyze further the data by a rather advanced statistical technique known as **principle component analysis**. Although these computations were performed in a manner of minutes by the computer, it would have taken several trained men their entire lifetimes to perform similar mathematical operations.

The initial conclusion, indicated by statistical testing, is that without doubt the men of Hareke differ from their Aluni neighbors in their standards of tool

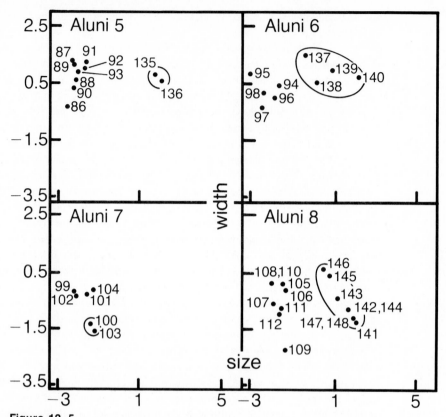

Figure 12-5
Statistical analysis of New Guinea stone tools, plotting the supervariables size against width. The circled area represents *aré* and the uncircled area depicts *aré kou (modified from White and Thomas 1972; courtesy of J. Peter White and Methuen Co.).*

manufacture. Although both communities consist of an apparently homogeneous group of individuals (that is, they are of the same culture), *aré* and *aré kou*
from Hareke are generally longer, wider, thicker, and heavier than those of
Aluni. This is significant because workers of both phratries adamantly maintain
that there is no difference between the tools of the two groups. In this simple
study, the archaeologist with his measurements and his computer is able to
distinguish meaningful size differences that the actual tool makers are unaware
of. These mathematical results can be interpreted in terms of more concrete
human behavior.

Figure 12–5 represents a small portion of the computer output, comparing
four of the Aluni men. The vertical dimension is the length-width ratio of
individual artifacts, while the horizontal axis represents total size. Each numbered point represents a single TMD, a type-man-day. The shaded areas represent *aré,* while the striped zones depict *aré kou.* Initially, we can easily distin-

guish between tool types, since *aré kou* are always smaller than *aré*. This is particularly interesting since the informants were unaware of any significant difference between the two types.

Looking at the statistical analysis from within each village, a second significant pattern emerges: technicians have a clear conception of type. That is, each man has a mental template which directs how each artifact should be. Individual number five from Aluni—his name is Daka—consistently manufactures more bladelike *aré kou* than either individual seven, Agele, and artisan number eight, Tage. Aluni worker number six is less careful in the manufacture of his tools, since he tolerates a wider range of total size, especially in his *aré*. The overall effect is analogous to a marksmanship contest. Everyone has individual targets, but some men are better sharpshooters than others. The more skilled participants shoot with tight patterns, closely grouping their consecutive shots. Other less skilled individuals seem to hit all over the target. Although it may be that nobody ever hits the dead center of his target, most workers consistently shoot near the bull's eye. This same clustering pattern is apparent in Figure 12–5. Mental templates are merely a set of slightly differing targets; statistical manipulation of the data is necessary to separate the shot pattern from the actual target at which each contestant aims.

Figure 12–5 thus provides information about the remaining sources of variation, variation within and between workers. In general, people exhibit parallelisms in their artifact classifications. One fellow makes his tools consistently larger, wider, and sharper than a colleague who is content to put up with more variability in his tools. Instead of aiming at a different target (mental template), the workers are just exhibiting different degrees of marksmanship. It is also interesting to note, once again, that the workers themselves are totally unaware of these differences. Yet the analyses leave no doubt that such differences exist. The observed variations are unquestionably the result of mental templates carried about in the head of each artisan; the informants, however, are ignorant of the existence of such templates.

In looking at the overall implications of this study, one is first struck by the fact that sociocultural parameters can be accurately defined using metric limits of artifact classes. The size, length-width ratio, and edge angle components can, almost without exception, separate the nine thousand tools by artifact type and by phratry of manufacture. This indicates that two distinctions are implicit in the Duna mental template. Each phratry has established implicit size limits for its two types of tools: *aré* must always be longer than *aré kou*. The larger *aré* are held in the hand while the *aré kou* are more delicate in order to fit into their cane handles. The abrupt boundary in sharpness suggests an equally rigid demarcation in the Duna mental template.

The tools from Hareke are always, in a statistical sense, larger than those from Aluni. Each village made the same tool types, for the same functions, but— setting aside differences in raw materials—apparently the Hareke mental template dictates that their tools should be larger than those manufactured at Aluni, although the Duna are consciously unaware of such distinctions. This study validates the sometimes disputed premise that socio-technological behavior is often coded, as it were, in the stone artifacts, and that metric attributes are the proper means to decode such clues.

Peter White's work also tells us something about the concept of archaeological type. In past discussions, some archaeologists have suggested that archaeological classifications should always attempt to mirror mental patterns in the mind of the maker (see Chapter 3). That is, regardless of whether one is dealing with temporal or functional types, this argument states that these types are also cognitive types, corresponding to a prehistoric mental template. The Duna artifacts were formed into discrete types based upon metric attributes, and these preliminary categories did in fact correspond quite well with the natively defined categories, *aré* and *aré kou*. But upon close questioning, the Duna uniformly stated that this size difference was not significant to them. They were also unaware of the differences in stone tools between individual flintknappers. White's New Guinea experiment suggests that salient differences between important artifact assemblages may go unrecognized by the stoneworkers themselves, and that people are not necessarily aware of the mental templates they carry about in their own heads.

This study also has implications in the study of idiosyncratic variation, discussed previously in Chapters 3 and 10. Stoneworkers, like many other artisans and craftsmen, have characteristic methods of performing their craft. It is conceivable that much of the so-called typological variation that archaeologists note in prehistoric assemblages is no more than variation between contemporary craftsmen.

EXPERIMENTAL ARCHAEOLOGY

The last section discussed how ethnoarchaeologists are working to generate archaeological mid-range theory. These studies attempt to examine systemic processes which operate in functioning societies. Processes can also be studied through experiment by re-creating the necessary conditions, then looking for the linkage between systemic and archaeological context. This research, known as **experimental archaeology**, has the same function as ethnoarchaeology. The major difference is that ethnoarchaeologists work within a functioning behavioral system, while experimental archaeologists attempt to define processes through experimental replication.

One of the earliest studies in experimental archaeology can be traced back to Saxton Pope, in a touching episode of early anthropology.

In 1911, a beaten and defeated Indian, later to be named "Ishi," was found crouching in a slaughterhouse corral near Oroville, California. His family had either been murdered or had starved, and Ishi himself had given up the will to live. Obligingly, the local sheriff locked him in the jail, since "wild" Indians were not allowed to roam about freely in those days. Through good fortune, Alfred

Kroeber, a young anthropologist at the University of California, learned of Ishi's plight and arranged for his release. Kroeber brought Ishi to San Francisco, where he secured quarters in the university museum. From that time until Ishi's death in 1916, Kroeber and his staff taught Ishi the ways of civilization, while the Indian exchanged his secrets for survival in backland California; clearly Ishi had more to offer. Before long, Ishi developed a hacking tubercular cough—which would later cost him his life—and he was treated daily by Dr. Pope, a surgeon from the nearby University of California Medical Center. Over their short association, Pope and Ishi found common ground in their interest in archery. What an odd combination they must have been: Pope, the urbane physician and scholar paired with the Yahi Indian, hair singed in tribal custom, together shooting arrows through the parks of downtown San Francisco. Pope was a good student, learning what Ishi had to teach. After Ishi's death, Pope continued his research into the almost lost art of archery, studying the bows and arrows preserved in museum collections, and often test-shooting the ancient specimens. Pope ultimately wrote a book describing his experiments in archery, emphasizing techniques and strategy. This book, *Hunting with the Bow and Arrow* (1923), not only provided important information for ancient finds, but also quickly became the bible of the bow-hunting fraternity. Apparently, as many urbanites as archaeologists were intrigued by the nuances of the nearly extinct art. Now, of course, archery is big business. This is but a single example of how the techniques of a nearly lost survival art were salvaged by timely observation and experimentation.

Unfortunately, many prehistoric techniques have perished with their practitioners, and archaeology has been forced to rediscover the lost technology. Most aboriginal flintknappers, for instance, are now dead, and with them perished the trade secrets that could enable archaeologists to learn more from the stone tools so commonly found in sites. Fortunately, a few dedicated scientists have spent years experimenting with stone tools. Don Crabtree, affiliated with the Idaho State University Museum in Pocatello, undertook a series of carefully documented studies to uncover the true nature of prehistoric stoneworking. One of Crabtree's projects was to discover what techniques were necessary to replicate the **Folsom projectile points** discovered at the Lindenmeier site in Colorado. Folsom points, surely some of the world's most exquisite stone artifacts, were originally made between 12,000 and 11,000 years ago. Mounted on spear shafts, these artifacts were used for hunting extinct forms of American bison. Although the spearpoints are only about two inches long, Crabtree counted over 150 minute sharpening flakes removed from their surface (see Figure 12–6). The distinctive property of Folsom artifacts is the **flute**, or channel flake, removed from each side. The purpose of the groove is unclear; some archaeologists suggest that flakes were removed to facilitate hafting on the spear shaft, while other scholars maintain the groove allowed for more rapid release of blood, like "blood grooves" on modern daggers. At any rate, Crabtree insisted on finding exactly how such flutes could be duplicated.

Crabtree, who had been interested in flintknapping for most of his life,

Figure 12-6
Replicas of Folsom spear points,
manufactured by Don Crabtree.
Note the two "fluting" flakes which
were removed from the bottom two
specimens (courtesy of Don
Crabtree).

began his work on the Folsom problem shortly after the Folsom complex was initially documented in 1926. The technical quality and intrinsic beauty of the Folsom point intrigued Crabtree; while most arrowheads can be fashioned in a matter of minutes, the Folsoms required hours, assuming that one understood the elusive technique in the first place. In the experimental period, which lasted over forty years, Crabtree tried every conceivable method of making the Folsom points. In his final report on his experiments, Crabtree (1966) described eleven different methods of trying to remove such flakes. Most methods proved unsuccessful: either the technique was impossible with primitive tools or the flute removed was too dissimilar to those on the Folsoms. One method in fact only succeeded in driving a copper punch through Crabtree's left hand.

Crabtree concluded that there were only two realistic methods of removing such a flake from an artifact. The first way was to place an antler shaft on the bottom of the unfinished artifact and then strike this punch with a sharp hammer blow. Because of the critical placement of the antler punch, this technique requires two workers. Further investigation led Crabtree to a historic source which described aboriginal American Indian flint-working techniques. Particularly interesting were the observations of a Spanish Franciscan Friar, Juan de Torquemada, who traveled through the central American jungles in 1615:

> They take a stick with both hands, and set well home against the edge of the front of the stone, which also is cut smooth in the front of the stone, which also is cut smooth in that part; and they press it against their brest [sic], and with the force of the pressure there flies off a knife. . . . Then they sharpen it [the tip of the crutch] on a stone using a hone to give it a very fine edge; and in a very short time these workmen will make more than twenty knives in the aforesaid manner (quoted in Crabtree 1968:449).

Although Torquemada was describing removal of flakes from a polyhedral core, Crabtree thought the method might possibly produce similar results to those evident on the Folsom artifacts. Crabtree manufactured a chest crutch following Torquemada's descriptions, padding one end to avoid painful chest injuries and equipping the other end with a sharp antler flaker. An unfinished Folsom point was tied tightly in a vise of wood and thong and then gripped between the feet of the flintknapper. Using this crutch braced against the chest, fluting flakes were driven off between the feet. The resulting artifacts were almost identical to the Lindenmeier Folsom points. Figure 12–6 illustrates several of the Folsom specimens re-created by Don Crabtree in this manner.

Although the archaeologist can never be certain that this was the precise method employed over 10,000 years ago, Crabtree's experiments plus the 250-year-old description by a Spanish friar give the archaeologist a much firmer foundation upon which to base further hypotheses. Scientists such as Crabtree have contributed greatly to our knowledge of how stone tools are manufactured (see also Flennikan 1978).

Another recent direction of study has been to determine the function of prehistoric stone tools. As the stone tools were used in their behavioral contexts, the edges often became damaged and dulled. Tools found in the archaeological record often contain such distinctive edge damage. Sometimes stone knives are found to have minute **striations** or scratches, which often reveal the direction of force and the nature of tool use. Sickles used to harvest grain seem to acquire a characteristic sheen from abrasion by silica contained in the plant stalks. Tools used for piercing or drilling often seem to have small nicks or polishing on the surfaces that protrude. And so on.

The patterns of edge damage (often called **microwear**) on a stone tool is archaeological evidence regarding some previous behavior. But, given only the stone tool, how do we know that the edge damage resulted from a specific action? How, for instance, do we know that the sickle sheen came from harvesting plants rather than from scraping hides? How do we know that the striations on a stone knife came from gritty inclusions contained in meat rather than from cleaning it off or from putting it in a sheath?

Once again, this is an issue requiring a bridging argument. Archaeologists who use microwear patterns to infer tool function must in each case demonstrate the relationship between the wear pattern observed (archaeological context) and the previous behavior act that produced that wear (systemic context).

A number of experiments have been conducted to provide precisely this sort of one-to-one relationship between edge damage and tool use. Although microwear studies can be traced well back into the nineteenth century (see Tringham et al. 1974), the trend was established by Sergei Semenov, whose major work, entitled *Prehistoric Technology,* was first published in the Soviet Union in 1957. Semenov documented the results of over two decades of experimentation with primitive tools, some of the studies dating back to the 1930s. Semenov experimented with a variety of techniques to replicate prehistoric tools, manufacturing artifacts of both stone and bone. His major contribution was the definition of three kinds of microwear: polishing, coarse abrasion (such as grinding and striations), and rasping of the edge. Semenov argued that the direction of the microscopic striations seems to be the most important key in the discovery of unknown functions of ancient implements.

The translation of *Prehistoric Technology* into English in 1964 spurred a flurry of microwear research throughout the world. One such follow-up study was conducted by Ruth E. Tringham, who studied with Semenov for a year in Leningrad, then moved her experiments to the University College of London and ultimately to Harvard University (see Tringham et al. 1974). Tringham and her associates conducted a wide range of experiments in the tradition of Semenov, with some important differences. While Semenov's work was largely intuitive and unsystematic, Tringham followed rigorous methods to determine the exact extent and nature of tool wear in a number of different media. She attempted to reproduce working edges, then bring each into contact with a specific material working in a given direction. Experiments consisted of making a tool from British flint, then systematically applying tools to a variety of media such as antler, bone, wood, skin, flesh, and plant fiber. Then the tool was used, carefully maintaining constant direction of force and counting the number of strokes involved. Some of the tools were hand held, while others were placed in a haft.

Then the experimental tools were examined under a low-power stereoscopic microscope. Photographs were taken to document each stage of wear. Among other things, Tringham found that Semenov's striations were not as universal as he had thought. Striations appear slowly, and sometimes not at all. Instead, Tringham concentrated on **microflaking**, the minute edge chipping that occurs as stone tools are used. This approach allowed Tringham to characterize the kind of wear resulting from a variety of functional movements. Cutting, for instance, produced a series of tiny uneven flake scars along both sides of the working edge. Planing, however, produced flake scars only on the surface opposite from that in direct contact with the worked material. Boring produced distinct trapezoidal flake scars, especially on the sides of the tool. In addition, the edge damage varied with the nature of the materials being worked.

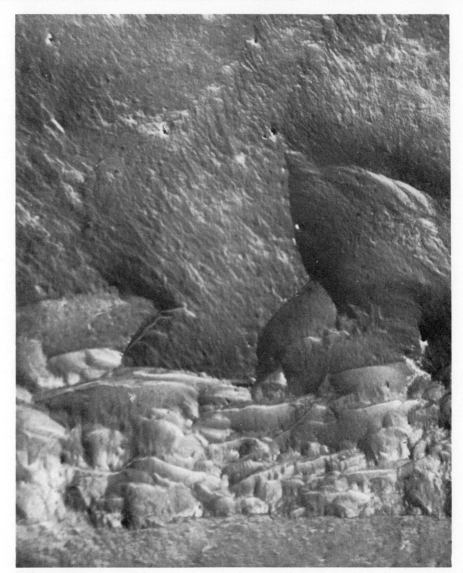

Figure 12–7
Photomicrograph of a scraper, dating 400 B.C. from Gatecliff Shelter. The photograph was prepared by a Scanning Electron Microscope, at approximately 50X magnification. The broad, smooth flaking at the top of the picture is retouch, part of the manufacture of the artifact. The small step scars at the bottom are the result of edge damage during use. This evidence indicates that this tool was used to scrape a relatively hard surface, perhaps antler or bone (*courtesy of Robert Rowan and The American Museum of Natural History*).

Soft worked materials such as skin and flesh produced only scalar-shaped scars, while hard materials such as antler and bone produced crushing and eventually dulled the edge so that it would no longer cut at all.

Tringham's experiments, while hardly definitive, do point the direction for functional analysis of stone tools and also provide some of the theory necessary to bridge from archaeological to systemic contexts. At this stage of investigation, microwear studies cannot distinguish between species of plant or animals being worked or determine whether flesh or skin was being worked, but the studies do enable one to tell whether the edges were used on soft as opposed to medium or hard surfaces (but see Keeley 1974). This is an important beginning.

The last two sections have focused primarily on experimental and ethnoarchaeological research conducted on stone tools. This focus is important in archaeology because in so many cases stone tools are all that survive. But the experimental approach is hardly limited to lithics. Literally hundreds of experiments have been conducted within the last couple of decades in order to test prevalent theories regarding the relationship of culture to the physical world in which it exists. Experiments range from the daring transatlantic and transpacific voyages of Thor Heyerdahl (1950, 1971) to the lesser-known experiments in clearing agricultural fields using stone tools (e.g., Iversen 1956; Saraydar and Shimada 1971). Entire fortifications have been constructed, only to be experimentally burnt to the ground and then excavated (see Coles 1973, Chapter 2). In addition, a large number of experiments have been conducted to determine the methods of lost crafts such as ancient pottery manufacture (Shepard 1956; Mayes 1962) and primitive metallurgy (Coghlan 1940; Wynne and Tylecote 1958). *Archaeology by Experiment* (Coles 1973) provides a useful summary of these and many other experiments designed to provide insights as to how the archaeological record has been formed (also see Coles 1967).

THE GARBAGE PROJECT: ARCHAEOLOGY OF YESTERDAY'S LUNCH

We are tomorrow's past.
Mary Webb

The final example of archaeological mid-range theory is the Garbage Project. Emil Haury has been an archaeologist at the University of Arizona for decades (we have already mentioned his excavations at Ventana Cave briefly in Chapter 7). A specialist in southwestern prehistory, Haury continually taught his students that "if you want to know what is really going on in a community, look at its garbage." Apparently Haury's advice was not lost on his students and colleagues because in 1971 the University of Arizona launched a long-term, in-depth study of just that—garbage. But it must have surprised Haury when he found out which community the Garbage Project decided to study; they were after the garbage of contemporary Tucson.

Figure 12–8
Archaeologist William Rathje, director of the Garbage Project, with an array of choice "artifacts" *(courtesy of William Rathje).*

The Garbage Project is directed by William Rathje, a Harvard-trained archaeologist who had previously specialized in the Classic Maya (we mentioned his Maya research in Chapter 9). By initiating the Garbage Project, Rathje was attempting to apply archaeological methods to the analysis and description of modern societies. Rathje objects to the traditional restriction in archaeology that the lifeways being reconstructed must be extinct. Rathje contends that we still have a great deal to learn about contemporary lifeways, and a century of archaeological experience with material culture should be brought to bear on relevent issues of modern society.

> **A**ll archaeologists study garbage; the Garbage Project's raw data are just a little fresher than most.
>
> *William L. Rathje*

Conducting the archaeology of contemporary society is an unusual concept, and one rarely considered. Basic to Rathje's thinking was a dissatisfaction with the available research techniques for dealing with contemporary society. Specifically, a group of concerned sociologists and psychologists began to question their own methods, particularly the dependence on interviews and questionnaires. They recognized that the very act of conducting an interview and administering a questionnaire intrudes, as a foreign element, into the social setting that is being studied. That is, the respondents are continually aware of their status as subjects, and the test measure itself can act as an agent of change and bias (Rathje and Hughes 1975:152).

Once the sociologists and psychologists began searching for alternative methods, they discovered that their disciplines had become largely the science of administering questionnaires and interviewing informants. Nothing in the training of a sociologist or a psychologist equipped them to deal with actual physical evidence.

Archaeologists, of course, have been learning how to deal with mute material evidence for over a century. But why restrict ourselves to behaviors that have become extinct? Beginning in 1971, Rathje began looking for methods to apply established archaeological methods and theory to the analysis of contemporary behavior.

The key term here is nonreactive. Whereas conventional questionnaires condition the nature of the response, material culture is static and relatively easy to quantify. The Garbage Project has been the first large-scale attempt to apply archaeological techniques to ongoing lifeways.

Rathje's Garbage Project focused on Tucson, an urban community with a population slightly over 360,000. A strict sampling design was initiated to assure proper correlation with relevant socioeconomic variables. Garbage was picked up from randomly selected households with selected sampling tracts. In 1973, 236 households were sampled, and 388 more in 1974 (Rathje and Hughes 1975). By 1975, the Garbage Project had examined and coded more than 70,000 individual items and it still continues (Rathje 1975).

Over three hundred volunteers from the University of Arizona sorted the garbage on special sorting tables provided by the Sanitation Department maintenance yard in Tucson. As with all archaeological fieldwork, the student workers were provided with appropriate field equipment, in this case, laboratory coats, surgical masks, and gloves. They were also required to take the appropriate inoculations. Students sorted garbage items into two hundred categories of food, drugs, sanitation products, amusement and educational items, communication, and pet-related products. The data were recorded on forms for computer processing (see Figure 12–9). Here is where the standard principles of archaeological classification provided objective, repeatable categories of data retrieval.

Of course the University of Arizona archaeologists are hardly the first people to snoop in somebody else's garbage can. Probably the most publicized garbage snooping occurred in 1971, when A. J. Weberman—a self-proclaimed garbage guerrilla—investigated the private lives of celebrities, as reflected by their garbage. In one sense, Weberman was following up the same discrepancy that bothered the sociologists—people say one thing, yet often do another. Pop singer Bob Dylan, for instance, proclaimed a benign disinterest in popular fan magazines; he boasted that he never bothered to read what they wrote about him. But when Weberman surreptitiously ransacked Dylan's New York garbage pail, "The many rock magazines wasted Bob's claim that he didn't follow the rock scene" (Weberman 1971:114). Dylan, of course, was outraged, and report-

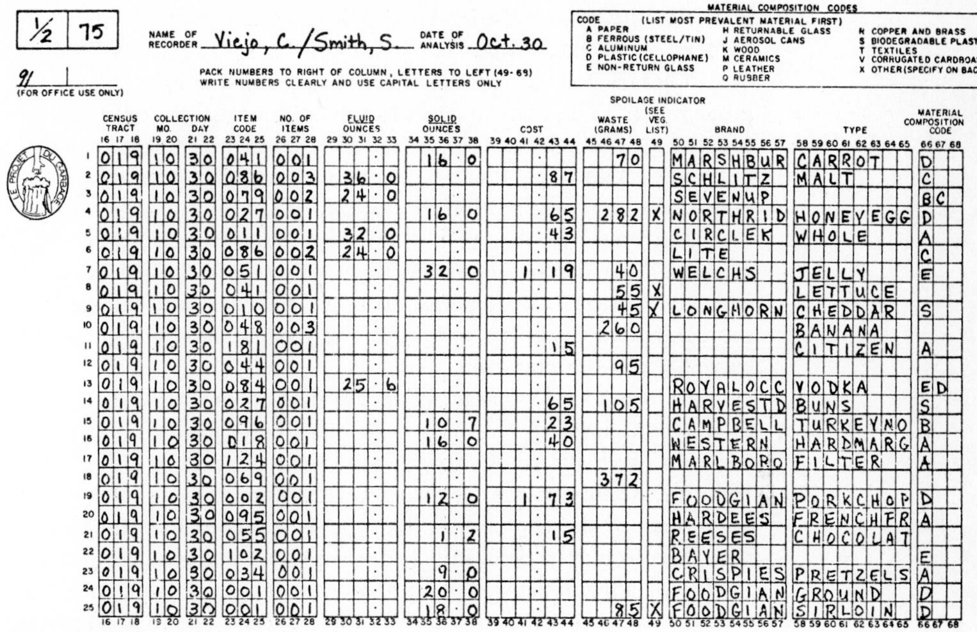

½ | 75

91 | (FOR OFFICE USE ONLY)

NAME OF RECORDER Viejo, C./Smith, S. DATE OF ANALYSIS Oct. 30

PACK NUMBERS TO RIGHT OF COLUMN, LETTERS TO LEFT (49-69)
WRITE NUMBERS CLEARLY AND USE CAPITAL LETTERS ONLY

MATERIAL COMPOSITION CODES
CODE (LIST MOST PREVALENT MATERIAL FIRST)
A PAPER
B FERROUS (STEEL/TIN)
C ALUMINUM
D PLASTIC (CELLOPHANE)
E NON-RETURN GLASS
H RETURNABLE GLASS
J AEROSOL CANS
K WOOD
M CERAMICS
P LEATHER
Q RUBBER
R COPPER AND BRASS
S BIODEGRADABLE PLASTIC
T TEXTILES
V CORRUGATED CARDBOARD
X OTHER (SPECIFY ON BACK)

	CENSUS TRACT (16 17 18)	COLLECTION MO. (19 20)	COLLECTION DAY (21 22)	ITEM CODE (23 24 25)	NO. OF ITEMS (26 27 28)	FLUID OUNCES (29 30 31 32 33)	SOLID OUNCES (34 35 36 37 38)	COST (39 40 41 42 43 44)	WASTE (GRAMS) (45 46 47 48)	SPOILAGE INDICATOR (SEE VEG. LIST) (49)	BRAND (50–57)	TYPE (58–65)	MATERIAL COMPOSITION CODE (66 67 68)
1	019	10	30	041	001		16.0		70		MARSHBUR	CARROT	D
2	019	10	30	086	003	36.0		.87			SCHLITZ	MALT	C
3	019	10	30	079	002	24.0					SEVENUP		BC
4	019	10	30	027	001		16.0	.65	282	X	NORTHRID	HONEYEGG	D
5	019	10	30	011	001	32.0		.43			CIRCLEK	WHOLE	A
6	019	10	30	086	002	24.0					LITE		C
7	019	10	30	051	001		32.0	1.19	40		WELCHS	JELLY	E
8	019	10	30	041	001				55	X		LETTUCE	
9	019	10	30	010	001				45	X	LONGHORN	CHEDDAR	S
10	019	10	30	048	003				260			BANANA	
11	019	10	30	181	001			.15				CITIZEN	A
12	019	10	30	044	001				95				
13	019	10	30	084	001	25.6					ROYALOCC	VODKA	ED
14	019	10	30	027	001			.65	105		HARVESTD	BUNS	S
15	019	10	30	096	001		10.7	.23			CAMPBELL	TURKEYNO	B
16	019	10	30	018	001		16.0	.40			WESTERN	HARDMARG	A
17	019	10	30	124	001						MARLBORO	FILTER	A
18	019	10	30	069	001				372				
19	019	10	30	002	001		12.0	1.73			FOODGIAN	PORKCHOP	D
20	019	10	30	095	001						HARDEES	FRENCHFR	A
21	019	10	30	055	001		1.2	.15			REESES	CHOCOLAT	
22	019	10	30	102	001						BAYER		E
23	019	10	30	034	001		9.0				CRISPIES	PRETZELS	A
24	019	10	30	001	001		20.0				FOODGIAN	GROUND	D
25	019	10	30	001	001		18.0		85	X	FOODGIAN	SIRLOIN	D

Figure 12–9
Garbage Project data recording form *(courtesy of William Rathje)*.

edly directed his housekeeper henceforth to deliver his trash directly to the sanitation man. Weberman conducted similar garbage exposés on other celebrities such as Muhammed Ali, playwright Neil Simon, and yippie Abbie Hoffman.

Rathje terms such tactics an invasion of privacy, a "rip-off . . . a threat to the conduct of garbage research as a means of quantifying the resource management strategies of population segments" (Rathje and Hughes 1975:154). To combat the adverse publicity that resulted from the Bob Dylan and Muhammed Ali cases, the Garbage Project instituted elaborate safeguards in their collection procedure to insure the complete anonymity of particular individuals and households. The sample garbage is collected strictly by the Sanitation Department foremen, but these foremen are not present when the bags are opened, and they are forbidden access to Garbage Project data. Personal data such as names, addresses, photographs, or financial statements are never recorded; such variables are not analyzed. The Garbage Project field director and/or one senior Garbage Project field supervisor are always present during analysis to insure that no personal items were examined or saved. Participating students were required to sign pledges against even looking at such personal items. No garbage of any kind was saved; all aluminum was recycled, and the rest of the garbage was used as sanitary landfill.

The Garbage Project has used its accumulated data to study a number of contemporary social issues, one of them being the rate of alcohol consumption.

In 1973, the Pima County Health Department conducted interviews with 1 percent of the households in the city of Tucson. Questions were phrased like this: "On the average, how many cans or bottles of beer does ——— have in a usual week?" The sample was carefully chosen using conventional sociological procedures and informant anonymity was assured. The Health Department then published its findings, which were taken by many as an accurate indication of the rate of alcohol consumption in Tucson.

But how well do the questionnaire results stack up against the material evidence? The garbage volunteers carefully record the presence of beer bottles and cans as part of their routine sorting. They also note the kind and volume of the containers discarded and have even attempted to control the amount of recycling of aluminum cans.

Rathje is fond of pointing out the discrepancy between front door answers provided to interviewers and back door behavior as reflected by the actual contents of the trash. Garbage cans don't lie, and the differences from the Health Department questionnaire were striking. In one tract, for instance, only 15 percent of the respondent households admitted to consuming beer, and no household reported drinking more than eight cans in a week. But the Garbage Project data from that same area showed that over 80 percent of the households actually had beer containers in their garbage cans, and fully 54 percent discarded more than eight cans each week. In fact, those households averaged about two and one half six-packs each week (Rathje and Hughes 1975:157).

Although the specifics varied between sampling tracts, the patterning was always the same: significantly heavier beer consumption—in the form of more drinkers and higher rates of drinking—than was reported to the interviewers.

The conclusion that interview data are distorted should astound nobody. People simply drink more beer than they own up to. But the degree of distortion is noteworthy, and the analysis of the material remains even provides future interviewers with a means for correcting this inevitable bias. The skewing, it turns out, is also correlated with socioeconomic factors. The low-income Mexican-American households typically distorted their interviews by reporting no consumption at all (Rathje and McCarthy 1977:268). By contrast, while the middle-income Anglo respondents typically admitted to limited beer consumption, they significantly underreported the amount of beer actually consumed. These preliminary findings point up future directions not only for garbage research, but also in the administration of health questionnaires.

The Garbage Project data also disclosed some surprises about the effectiveness of recent recycling campaigns. The advertising media have given great coverage to campaigns by beverage companies and aluminum factories to recycle aluminum cans; Boy Scouts sponsor newspaper drives to raise money and to save trees, and more Christmas cards are printed on recycled paper each year. As Rathje (1975) puts it, "We think of ourselves today as ardent recyclers."

But the facts are otherwise. In 1975, the households of Tucson recycled only 19 percent of all wood fiber; this figure stands in marked contrast to the 35 percent national average that was recycled during World War II. Similarly, studies in a mid-1800 trash deposit in Magdelena, Mexico, show that only broken bottles were discarded, and these had apparently been reused extensively before breakage. In the 1970s, the average Tucson household discarded about 500 whole bottles each year; of these, over 10 percent were made of returnable glass and could have—ideally—been used up to forty times if they had been returned.

Perhaps the most interesting finding to emerge from the Garbage Project is data on how people cope with economic adversity. Most economists simply assume that as the economic squeeze gets tighter, people will economize, particularly by using cheaper products more efficiently. But such is not the case.

Consider the 1973 beef shortage. Prices increased dramatically, and beef became considerably less available in retail stores. Garbage Project data confirmed that purchase behavior changed immediately as shoppers experimented with new cuts of beef. Purchasing occurred in new quantities, and while some people stocked up, anticipating even higher prices, other shoppers cut down on beef purchases (Rathje 1975).

But at the same time, something unexpected happened with the amount of beef waste (Rathje 1975; Rathje and Hughes 1975). Common sense tells us that when prices go up, and a commodity is scarce, people will waste less of the scarce, expensive item. This did not happen with the beef shortage. In the spring of 1973, a time when beef prices were astronomical and there was considerable economic pressure to conserve beef, the amount of beef waste hit an all-time high—9 percent of the volume purchased (excluding weight of bone and fat). That is, for every one hundred pounds of beef purchased, which went in the front door, nine pounds of edible and expensive beef was discarded out the back door. A year later, when beef had become relatively inexpensive, and plenty of beef was available on the market, beef waste dropped to 3 percent of the total volume. Common sense—and economic theory—misled us again. The Garbage Project determined empirically that when beef was expensive, it was wasted; when prices went down, beef was conserved. Why?

Rathje has derived a "food discard equation," based on his findings. This equation suggests that as prices change, so will shopping behavior; but experimentation can lead to behavior that is far from efficient. Only as prices stabilize, and people adjust to the new conditions, will the amount of waste decrease. While this hypothesis remains untested, Rathje successfully predicted food discard frequencies resulting from the sugar shortage in 1975.

The Garbage Project findings remain tentative and, at this stage, serve primarily to point up directions for future study. But the notion of using archaeological methods to discern modern, ongoing trends is so radical that comparable data are almost nonexistent. Only future research will determine whether Rathje's findings are fluke or fact. But it seems clear that the Garbage

Project has projected archaeological method and theory firmly into the contemporary social scene.

If efforts such as ethnoarchaeology, experimental archaeology, and the Garbage Project live up to advanced billing, then the basic character of archaeology will be changed. Archaeology can no longer be considered the study of extinct behaviors, but must truly be considered the science of material culture—regardless of the material or the culture. If this is true, then the distinction between ethnography and archaeology will be permanently blurred, a trend already under way in ethnoarchaeological research, considered earlier. Once archaeologists are free to study material culture from all time periods—including the contemporary—then archaeology's inferiority complex will forever be eradicated.

SUMMARY

The "facts" of archaeology are incapable of speaking for themselves; it is therefore necessary for archaeologists to employ bridging arguments to breathe behavioral life into the objects of the past, which have actually existed in two discrete contexts. The artifacts, features, and residues without which archaeologists could not work were once related to an ongoing behavioral system; while these artifacts were being manufactured and used, they existed in their systemic contexts. But by the time they reach the hands of the archaeologist, the objects have ceased to participate in their behavior system and have passed into archaeological contexts.

The formation of archaeological sites involves four basic processes: cultural deposition, reclamation, disturbance, and reuse. Each process has certain regularities, but archaeologists are only beginning to understand the complex mechanisms involved. One way to supply these bridging arguments between archaeological and systemic contexts is to study first hand the workings of ongoing societies. As contradictory as it may seem, a number of archaeologists—the ethnoarchaeologists—spend their time studying living societies, observing artifacts, features, and residues while they still exist in their systemic contexts. To date, ethnoarchaeological studies have examined, among other things, the processes determining settlement pattern and intrasite patterning, the reality of the tool-kit concept, the mechanisms of artifact curation and reuse, and the social correlates of stone-tool manufacture and use. Ethnoarchaeologists are also examining the relationship of material culture to modern industrial society, as is illustrated by the well-known Garbage Project at the University of Arizona.

Archaeological formation processes are also currently being defined by experimental archaeologists. Although sharing a primary interest in midrange theory, ethnoarchaeologists work within a functioning behavior system, while experimental archaeologists attempt to derive relevant processes through experimental replication. Much of this initial experimental work has concentrated on the manufacture and use of stone tools, although archaeologists are currently experimenting on a wide range of problems including tool efficiency, processes of site destruction and preservation, and methods of ceramic manufacture. Thor Heyerdahl's epic trans-Atlantic and trans-Pacific voyages can even be considered to be a variety of experimental archaeology.

13

General Theory
in Archaeology

If you, like Jack London, are seeking to gaze on the face of Truth, I am afraid you will not find it in this chapter. Although my intention is to discuss general theory in archaeology, I must confess at the outset that archaeologists are still groping. Truth, I fear, has yet to be located. But let me tell you something about the search.

In this chapter, I present some examples of how archaeologists are working to define the **processes** that underlie (and explain) cultural behavior. You will remember that back in Chapter 3 we examined how Leslie White divided cultural phenomena into three interrelated spheres: technology, sociology, and ideology. We will be considering an example from each of these spheres of human behavior in order to see how social scientists deal with matters of process.

But be certain not to confuse the upcoming discussion with Truth. The processual explanations that follow are bound to change, and I have deliberately chosen several examples for their overall historical significance. It is more important right now to concentrate on *how the questions are framed*. More satisfying answers will come later.

TECHNOECOLOGICAL CHANGE

Throughout this book I have stressed that contemporary archaeology embraces a number of sometimes complementary, often conflicting anthropological mainstreams. Although a number of archaeologists are currently turning to the ideational perspective for answers, the fact remains that the archaeology of the 1960s and 1970s has been dominated by cultural materialistic, cultural evolutionary, and cultural ecological thought (see Part One of this book). As stated over and over again in Chapter 3, these mainstreams are really strategies which direct research. The materialistic perspective suggests merely that the variables of demography, technology, ecology, and environment will *ultimately* prove to be most successful in predicting cultural variability and change. These variables are obviously more readily inferred from the archaeological record.

Let us examine how contemporary archaeologists go about studying these technological, ecological, demographic, and environmental processes in contemporary archaeology. It is impossible, in a book of this scope, to consider the entire range and substance of theory available. Rather, I wish to focus on two major areas of study—hunter-gatherer dynamics and the origins of agriculture—to demonstrate how archaeologists go about studying processes, and to discuss briefly the nature of the processes themselves. Once again, let me caution you that my emphasis is more on the search and less on the actual explanation offered.

We know that the first humans on earth were hunter-gatherers, and we also know that this lifeway persisted for over 99 percent of the human past (Lee and DeVore 1968:3). Anthropologists—many of them archaeologists—have conducted in-depth projects aimed at defining the processes that underlie this hunting-gathering existence, and we have already had occasion to mention John Yellen's ethnoarchaeological work among the !Kung (discussed in Chapter 12). Yellen was concerned largely with defining the demographic and ecological processes that structure the contemporary !Kung campsite. Why are the dwellings placed in a circle? What is the relationship between this camp patterning and !Kung social organization? Why, and when, do the !Kung abandon one campsite in favor of another?

In a related study, Richard Lee (1969) found water to be the single most important resource in determining !Kung demography and settlement pattern. Since flowing water is practically unknown on the Kalahari Desert, Bushmen must anchor their camps to a few well-known springs. Throughout the entire 2,500 square miles of the Dobe and Nye Nye regions, only five waterholes are considered to be permanent, and of these, three have been known to fail. According to Lee, the seasonal movements of the !Kung "must be continually revised in light of the unfolding rainfall situation throughout the growing season and beyond." In years of relatively abundant rainfall, camps are established according to the availability of food and the known locations of neighboring groups. In moderately dry winters, the !Kung must establish themselves near the five relatively reliable water sources. But in drought years, Lee found as many as seven normally autonomous groups coexisting at a single waterhole. This is how the availability of water structured the !Kung settlement pattern.

The Lee and Yellen studies are excellent examples of how ethnographers and ethnoarchaeologists go about studying an ongoing lifeway. Their data relate to a single group of people (the !Kung) who exist in a specific place (the Kalahari Desert) at a specific time (the mid-twentieth century). In Chapter 9, we discussed some of the environmental factors that condition population movements of the Great Basin Shoshoni. This was another hunting-gathering lifeway specific in time and place. The challenge for anthropology is to define the processes that underlie the specifics and condition all hunter-gatherer existence, regardless of time and place.

One such effort is a classic study by Joseph Birdsell (1953), who also examined the relationship between settlement pattern and distribution of water, this time over the entire Australian continent. By plotting the territorial size of 409 independent aboriginal tribes against the mean annual rainfall figures, Birdsell found a surprisingly high correlation: rainfall indeed predicted Australian aborigines' settlement pattern with a remarkable degree of accuracy. Elsewhere, I examined this same relationship between population and precipitation in the aboriginal Great Basin and found a much weaker relationship (Thomas 1972a). In these cases, a single variable—water—has been examined to see whether it bears any processual relationship to hunter-gatherer dynamics.

In another effort to define the processes conditioning hunter-gatherer existence, Wilmsen (1973) proposed a generalized model of hunter-gatherer spatial organization. Beginning with the perspective of locational geography, Wilmsen began by borrowing a theory initially defined for blackbirds: this biogeographic model suggested that blackbirds tend to space themselves throughout their territories according to a precise mathematical formula. Wilmsen then examined how well the model seemed to account for known hunter-gatherer patterns, and suggested how the revised model could be tested against archaeological evidence. In another study, William Divale (1972) argued that because of the prevalence of prehistoric warfare, ancient hunter-gatherers must have been forced to practice extensive female infanticide in order to keep the sexual ratios in relative balance. Similarly, Casteel (1972b) has provided mathe-matical methods for computing maximum possible population figures for prehis-toric groups (also see Wobst 1974; Zubrow 1971). To date, relatively little has come of these various theories, but they do illustrate how archaeologists and ethnographers are attempting to explicate the processes that condition the hunting-gathering lifeway.

Studies of this sort are critical not only because of the processual informa-tion they provide about hunting-gathering dynamics, but also because they provide a baseline from which to explore the evolution of more advanced technology, such as the origins of agriculture and pastoralism. Countless theo-ries have been suggested to account for the initial efforts at domesticating plants and animals. Anthropologists of the eighteenth and nineteenth centuries were concerned largely with constructing worldwide evolutionary schemes, yet lacked the relevant archaeological data. The cultural evolutionists relied instead on analogies with contemporary primitive societies and linguistic evidence. In *Ancient Society* (1877), for instance, Lewis Henry Morgan suggested that animal domestication (pastoralism) must have preceded agricultural villages throughout the Eastern Hemisphere. His evidence? Read this:

> That the discovery and cultivation of cereals by the Aryan family was subsequent to the domestication of animals is shown by the fact that there are common terms for these animals in the several dialects of the Aryan language, and no common terms for the cereals or cultivated plants (Morgan 1877:23).

Morgan viewed plant domestication mostly as an expedient means for providing food for the already domesticated herds.

Through the years, a number of other theories appeared, and these have been nicely summarized by Wright (1971). The evolution of the various theories is instructive, indicating major avenues of thought. One of the more pervasive explanations—termed the "oasis theory"—was offered in the 1940s by British archaeologist V. Gordon Childe. Briefly stated, Childe's theory held that as the Pleistocene (Ice Age) glaciers melted, the world's climate became warmer and generally more arid. In the desert areas, especially those of the Near East, the acquisition of water became a major problem for survival. As both men and animals flocked to the oases and exotic desert streams in the difficult search for nourishment, the forced association between man and beast eventually pro-duced a symbiotic relationship. In time, this situation grew from mutual benefit to mutual dependence. The mechanisms (processes) for the beginnings of animal domestication were explained in rather simple terms by Childe (1951b:68–69):

> The huntsman and his prey thus find themselves united in an effort to circumvent the dreadful power of drought. But if the hunter is also a cultivator, he will have something to offer the famished beasts: the stubble of his freshly reaped fields will

afford the best grazing in the oasis. Once the grains are garnered, the cultivator can tolerate half-starved mouflons or wild oxen trespassing upon his garden plots. Such will be too weak to run away, too thin to be worth killing for food. Instead, man can study their habits, drive off the lions and wolves that would prey upon them, and perhaps offer them some surplus grains from his stores. The beasts, for their part, will grow tame and accustomed to man's proximity.

The domestication of animals was possible in Childe's scheme only after man has become a successful cultivator of plants. In order to find the roots of floral domestication one needed to look no further than the nearby Nile Valley. The "nobler grasses"—ancient ancestors of modern wheat and barley—apparently grew in abundance on the banks of the Nile, where they were subjected to annual flooding and enrichment by the rich alluvial soil. Childe felt that plants of the Nile Valley were controlled by nature's perfect irrigation cycle, and that it remained only for "some genius" to produce similar artificial irrigation conditions elsewhere.

While Childe and others felt that the Egyptian area held the key to early domestication, a second, competing hypothesis—called by Wright (1971:455) the "Natural Habitat Zone Model"—had been proposed by Harold Peake and H. J. Fleure (1927). The Peake-Fleure model highlighted a number of preconditions which they felt were critical in the origin of domestication:

1. The natural area must have hosted a regular and reliable harvest each year.
2. The geography must have been rather restricting, so man was required to stay put and change rather than simply moving elsewhere with his old adaptation.
3. The area could not have been forested or swampy, since early technology did not allow for clearing of forests or filling of swamps.
4. The area could not have been isolated, for contact with other cultures was necessary to facilitate the breakdown of custom and taboo which could have inhibited change.

Peake and Fleure examined a number of candidates, eventually concluding that only Southwestern Asia met their requirements. Especially critical in their theory was the natural distribution of wild plants suitable for domestication (particularly wild wheat, emmer, and einkorn), wild cattle and goats would also have been available. The Peake-Fleure argument held that climatic change ultimately precipitated domestication of plants and animals, but only in areas of their natural occurrence.

Shortly after World War II, Robert Braidwood of the University of Chicago traveled to the foothills of Iraq to spearhead a series of strategic excavations designed to test the competing hypotheses regarding the origins of domestication. Braidwood's excavations employed a bevy of natural scientists, and the results questioned the very existence of significant post-Pleistocene climatic shifts in the Near East. Instead, Braidwood and his team found that the climate had been essentially stable during the period of animal and plant domestication; in light of these data, Childe's oasis theory was rejected. Braidwood suggested a new explanation, which came to be known as the "hilly flanks theory." Rather than calling upon environmental processes to explain the origins of agriculture, Braidwood and his colleagues suggested that, because climate had been essentially constant, a post-Pleistocene readaptation (the **Mesolithic**) would have been unnecessary in the Near East.

Braidwood suggested instead that agriculture had arisen in the Near East as a "logical outcome" of culture elaboration and specialization. The hunters and gatherers simply "settled in" during the post-Pleistocene, becoming intimately familiar with their plant and animal neighbors. As culture evolved further, so did more efficient means of exploitation and agriculture, which formed another quite natural link in the long evolutionary chain. The hilly flanks theory is thus an elaboration of the earlier Peake-Fleure model, yet without the climatic elements and environmental deterioration.

Although the Childe, Peake-Fleure, and Braidwood theories employ different data and reach conflicting conclusions, they do agree on the fundamental processes that triggered initial domestication of Old World plants and animals. All three theories make the implicit assumption that humanity continually seeks to improve its technology and subsistence. Whenever the proper conditions come along, it is "logical" that plants and animals will be domesticated, because domestication provides a more technologically advanced economic base.

This assumption is fundamental. Childe, Braidwood, and the others are basically Malthusians, in that they share the basic economic premises set forth almost two hundred years ago by T. R. Malthus. In order to understand the implications of Malthusian theory, we must first understand who Malthus was and why he said what he said.

Thomas Robert Malthus (1766–1834) was born into a wealthy eighteenth-century English family (see Figure 13–1). Robert's father, Daniel, was the embodiment of the Age of Reason, well-connected in intellectual and philosophical circles. To this entire generation, the world was on the threshold of paradise: the Laws of Reason would eventually eradicate all poverty, misery, and suffering.

Yet despite this rosy outlook from the British gentility, there were problems only a few miles away. These were the years that Charles Dickens called "the best of times, the worst of times" and revolution was sweeping France. Being gentlemen of leisure, the Malthus family debated the significance of the French Revolution. Father Daniel held undampened enthusiasm; he still argued that "reason" would be sufficient to lift humanity from darkness, superstition, and cruelty.

But young Robert Malthus disagreed, and he brooded about the future of civilized humanity. How can society be perfected when population growth will so obviously outstrip the available resources? Father and son Malthus went

Figure 13–1
Robert Thomas Malthus, as he appeared shortly before his death in 1834 *(courtesy of The American Museum of Natural History).*

round and around, arguing their positions at their British country estate. Finally young Malthus prepared a treatise so that he could more effectively marshal his arguments against his father. Daniel Malthus was so impressed with the document that he encouraged his son to publish it, which he did (anonymously) as *An Essay on the Principle of Population as it Affects the Future Improvement of Society* (1798). Five years later, Malthus published a second essay, documenting his speculations and answering his numerous critics.

The Malthusian essays explore the relationship between human population and the resource base available to support this population. The Malthusian argument holds that because human fertility is essentially constant, human population will be governed only by a changing mortality rate. Population size will grow unchecked until something dramatic happens. Population size can be reduced only by what Malthus termed "vice and misery," by catastrophies such as war, epidemic, or disaster.

The basic Malthusian position remains an important force in contemporary economics, although the neo-Malthusians (such as Kenneth Boulding) reject Malthus's assumption that man's capabilities for production and redistribution cannot exceed population. The neo-Malthusian premise is that population growth is a dependent variable, ultimately determined by preceding changes in subsistence potential.

This is why the Childe and Braidwood theories are fundamentally Malthusian in nature. Why were plants and animals domesticated? The Malthusian argument suggests that domestication occurred simply as a natural consequence of man's continual struggle to improve technology. Because growing crops and keeping flocks are more advanced means of subsistence, people quite naturally stopped foraging to become full-time farmers and herdsmen. Once agriculture was adopted the human population was free to increase dramatically. The wholesale shift to domestication came to be known as the **Neolithic Revolution.**

Recently, anthropologists have begun to turn away from Malthusian explanations. Particularly difficult for many to accept is the economic and ecological determinism implied by the neo-Malthusian position (see Zubrow 1976). Childe argued that when the climate changed, people readily turned to domestication. Braidwood rejected Childe's notion, arguing instead that domestication arose as an evolutionary elaboration of the "settling in" process.

An important alternative has been recently expressed by the Danish economist Ester Boserup in her influential book *The Conditions of Agricultural Growth: The Economics of Agrarian Change under Population Pressure* (1965). Boserup reverses the classic Malthusian equation. Instead of regarding population growth as a response to changing economic and ecological potential (as did Malthus), Boserup argues that population growth is itself the autonomous or independent variable. Population growth as such is held to be a major factor in determining agricultural development and productivity (Boserup 1965:11).

Concerned primarily with contemporary agrarian societies, Boserup asks, What happens when population increases? In low-density, primitive agricultural areas, excess land is available, and such societies practice *slash-and-burn* agriculture. People move from one plot to another, eventually coming back to the original plot. All of this occurs within home territory. In such a system, the land is given sufficient time to replenish its resources through lengthy fallow periods. Slash-and-burn methods were common in Europe prior to World War I, and today support some 200 million people in Africa, Latin America, and Asia.

But as population increases, the land must be used more intensively and the fallow periods become increasingly shorter. People must work harder as land becomes scarce, and technology increases in the form of agricultural machinery, fertilizers, and pesticides. Boserup sees the frequency of cropping as a key variable and argues that economic systems can be viewed along a continuum. At one end is the society with excess uncultivated land; at the other extreme is the society with multicropped land, in which a second crop is sown as the first is reaped. Boserup argues that all forms of primitive land use can be viewed along this continuum, that population growth is the prime mover causing societies to evolve from one stage to another.

Note that the Malthusian argument is essentially pessimistic, with starvation and misery increasing as human population increases toward the carrying capacity. The Boserup model is a more optimistic one, suggesting that technological responses will become available "when they are needed."[1] The perspectives differ in their view of population growth: Is it a cause or an effect?

Many contemporary theories of plant and animal domestication tend to focus on population growth as a key factor (see Dumond 1965; Spooner 1972;

Carneiro 1968, 1972). While some investigators retain the more traditional Malthusian perspective (such as Polgar 1972; Hassan 1974, 1975; Cowgill 1975a, 1975b), others have actively applied the ideas of Boserup to the prehistoric evidence (particularly Flannery 1969, 1973; D. Harris 1972). As Lewis Binford (1968a:327) points out, the Malthusian perspective implies that man will continually attempt to increase his food supply, and this is why the Childe, Peake-Fleure, and Braidwood explanations of domestication discussed above are fundamentally Malthusian. Yet despite these arguments the archaeological record clearly shows long periods of technological and economic stability. How can such stability be explained in the face of Malthusian progress?

Binford employs the *niche* and *habitat* concepts, discussed earlier in Chapter 3. Habitat, you will remember, refers to the environmental setting in which an organism lives, while the way in which they exploit that habitat is called a niche. An animal's habitat is his "address" while his niche is his "profession." Binford views plant domestication as merely another one of man's possible ecological niches. We know of many ethnographic and archaeological cases in which well-developed hunting-gathering societies (such as the California Indians and groups on the Northwest Pacific Coast) never grew crops at all, yet they lived in rather large, settled villages. Why, they might ask, adopt the risks of some new method when the old one seems to work well enough?

Why, indeed? Binford prefers the theoretical position advanced by Boserup in which people adapt to new energy sources (such as domesticated plants) only when forced to do so. Binford thus rejects Braidwood's notion that agriculture developed because "culture was ready for it." On this point, Binford agrees with Childe's earlier argument that domestication constitutes a new niche, one imposed by changing conditions. But while Childe called upon climatic and environmental changes as the initiating factors, Binford proposes that the true stress on these groups was pressure from other human populations.

Specifically, population pressure was exerted by groups of people with an extremely successful Mesolithic adaptation who were occupying the same habitat within the Fertile Crescent. The post-Pleistocene emphasis upon riverine and lacustrine food sources (fish, shellfish, sea mammals) permitted a more sedentary and comparatively lavish existence in contrast to more traditional hunter-gatherer modes of subsistence. The competitive pressure upon the nonsedentary, non-Mesolithic peoples must have been severe, and it is in these marginal areas, Binford suggests, that people first turned to domestication for survival.

Binford's hypothesis attempts not only to explain most of the known facts, but also to provide directly testable implications for further archaeological fieldwork. Specifically, Binford's theory predicts (after Wright 1971:461):

1. There must have been a population increase due to a new and efficient Mesolithic lifeway in the optimal zones prior to the first domestication.
2. The earliest evidence of domestication should come not from these optimal zones where the Mesolithic lifeway functioned, but rather in the marginal, less favored areas (as the law of evolutionary potential would suggest).

3. The material culture of the earliest Neolithic populations should be essentially similar to their Mesolithic neighbors.
4. There should be no circumscribed center of domestication; the process should have occurred simultaneously in several areas under population pressure.

Kent Flannery (1969, 1973) has applied Binford's "density equilibrium" model to the archaeology of the Near East. Following Binford's arguments to their logical conclusion, Flannery suggests that the "optimum" habitats should have been the centers for population growth, with the marginal areas receiving the emigrant overflow. Flannery discusses a "broad spectrum" revolution that began about 20,000 B.C. and amounted to a major broadening of the subsistence base from mostly hunting to include larger amounts of fish, crabs, water turtles, molluscs, and migratory water fowl (Flannery 1969:77). To Flannery, this change in subsistence was due less to post-Pleistocene climatic change than to a simple overuse of prime land. Demand for the previously ignored invertebrates, fish, water fowl, and plant resources would have increased in precisely those "marginal" areas in which Binford suggests the initial domestication of plants occurred. Flannery, like Binford, argues that population increase (à la Boserup) could have functioned as a major factor, encouraging hunting-gathering groups to begin cultivation of plant crops. In both cases, population pressure becomes the major independent variable.

Even now, the processes that triggered plant and animal domestication are still poorly understood. The Flannery-Binford model has been roundly criticized by Meyers (1971) and Cohen (1977:7–8), who claim that the archaeological record simply lacks evidence of inland migration near the early agricultural centers. Cohen also suggests that the "broad-spectrum" adaptation was not restricted to seacoasts, and that agriculture actually arose earlier and in areas other than those recognized by Flannery and Binford.

Flannery (1973:284) has criticized even his own theory, noting candidly that "although [the theory] has won an almost frightening acceptance among some of my colleagues, it is still unproven and highly speculative . . . our archaeological data (such as they are) do not show strong population increases in 'optimum' areas like the Lebanese woodland, but the very opposite . . . the model comes too close to making population growth and climatic change into prime movers." Clearly the final word remains to be written regarding the origin of plant and animal domestication.

We have discussed the topic in some detail here not to define the exact moment somebody first planted a seed or monkeyed around with the genetics of penned animals, but rather to illustrate how the search for processes proceeds.

Progress in archaeology (or any science) does not occur in a theoretical vacuum. Note that Braidwood made certain (Malthusian) assumptions about the nature of human evolution: culture evolves on its own. Several recent investigators followed Boserup by assuming that cultures change only when forced to do so, as population increases. As Chapter 12 emphazised over and over again, the facts in archaeology will never speak for themselves. We arrive at the truth only by framing theories which are then used to predict future finds in the archaeological record. Some processes predict the past successfully, others do not.

SOCIOPOLITICAL CHANGE

In Chapter 3 we discussed in some detail how contemporary social scientists study the societal and political dynamics of cultural institutions. There were, you will remember, two basic research approaches. The *synchronic* procedure emphasizes the in situ analysis of functioning cultural systems. This is the basic concern of ethnographers, sociologists, economists, psychologists, and (as we saw in the last chapter) ethnoarchaeologists. Synchronic studies provide a picture of the dynamics of a system which operates at a single point in time: now. Part Three discussed the ways in which archaeologists too can conduct synchronic studies of another time period: then. In effect, the general objective of reconstructing past lifeways is an attempt to unravel the specifics and dynamics of single societies.

Anthropology's second fundamental approach is called *diachronic,* emphasizing the development of societies over a span of time. While the ethnographer can justly point to the richness of the detail available in contemporary society, such studies invariably fall short in an evolutionary sense because the time factor is lacking. Of course archaeological data lack the great ethnographic detail, but archaeology can provide a chronicle of in situ cultural developments without which diachronic studies cannot proceed.

The last section considered some theories of plant and animal domestication, one of the most critical technoecological developments in the history of human evolution. We now turn to the evolution of sociopolitical institutions as another example of how archaeologists are working to develop general theories to account for stability and change.

Some specifics of sociopolitical change were introduced briefly in Chapter 3, and various ethnographic and archaeological bands, tribes, chiefdoms, and states have been considered throughout the text. In Chapter 10, for instance, we examined how archaeologists go about distinguishing a ranked, chiefdom-level society from an egalitarian band (such as the Shoshoni), based strictly on the archaeological record. We also considered some mechanics of settlement patterning within a state-level society, the Classic Maya. But it remains for us to examine how these various sociopolitical structures—the band, the tribe, the chiefdom, and the state—came to be. That is, we have considered some aspects of synchronic dynamics, but have so far ignored the issue of diachronic evolution. We will rectify this situation immediately by focusing on the most complex political structure, the state. First we will examine some general theories that explain the origin of the state, and then we will look at a specific instance, the evolution of the Mesoamerican state.

The **state** has been defined in a number of ways over the years, and to simplify this discussion, we will follow Flannery's (1972:403–404) definition:

> The state is a type of very strong, usually highly centralized government, with a professional ruling class, largely divorced from the bonds of kinship which characterize simpler societies. It is highly stratified and extremely diversified internally, with residential patterns often based on occupational specialization rather than blood or affinal relationships. The state attempts to maintain a monopoly of force, and is characterized by true law.

States generally have powerful economic structures and often involve a true market system. The state economy is controlled by an elite, which maintains authority by a combination of law and differential access to key goods and services. States generally have populations numbering at least in the hundreds of thousands, and this population is often centered in large cities. Much of the population consists of economic specialists, dependent on the labor of others for subsistence. States are also known for a high level of artistic achievement, monumental architecture, and an overall state religion.

The state is thus a complex form of sociopolitical organization, and any number of contemporary examples could be cited (such as modern France or England or the United States). Ethnographers and other social scientists have studied the modern state for decades, and its dynamics are relatively well understood.

But it is clear that these contemporary states are the products of a long chain of sociopolitical evolution, and how they came to be remains an unanswered question. Archaeological states are evident throughout the world in such diverse places as Classic (or maybe Formative) Mesoamerica, the Near East, Shang China, Egypt, India, and imperial Rome. While contemporary ethnographic studies can satisfactorily unravel the synchronic dynamics of functioning state-level organization, no amount of study on modern states will explain their evolution. The state as we know it today is a worldwide phenomenon, with a long history preserved in the archaeological record. Only through a consideration of the archaeological evidence can an accurate diachronic study be made of societies as they develop to the state level.

Theories of the origin of the state go back to the nineteenth-century cultural evolutionists, discussed briefly in Chapter 3. A number of causal factors have been suggested to account for the development of the state: irrigation, warfare, population growth, circumscription, trade, cooperation and competition, and the integrative power of great religions (see Flannery 1972:405–407 and Wright 1977).

In order to see how archaeologists, as social scientists, attempt to unravel the evolution of the state, we will concentrate first on two general theories: Wittfogel's "irrigation" hypothesis and Carneiro's "warfare and circumscription" hypothesis. These are both general theories in that they attempt to explain the origin of the state regardless of when or where. Then we will drop down one level of abstraction and examine how such general theories are brought to bear on state-level evolution in a single area, that of Classic Mesoamerica. Once again, I am more concerned with the nature of the search than with providing the ultimate truth.

One well-known theory for the origin of the state was expressed by Karl A. Wittfogel in his influential book *Oriental Despotism* (1957). Wittfogel asserted that the mechanisms of large-scale irrigation are directly responsible for creating the state. He argued that the great Oriental societies (China, India, Mesopotamia) followed a radically different evolutionary course than did the societies of Western Europe and elsewhere. The state evolved because of special conditions required by large-scale irrigation: the imposition of inordinately strong political controls to maintain the hydraulic works, the tendency for the ruling class to merge with the ruling bureaucracy, the close identification of the dominant religion with governmental offices, and the diminution of private property and economic initiative. Wittfogel argued that, after a creative period in which the bureaucracy was begun, stagnation set in, producing a corruption of power and ultimately creating a despotic and feudal system. Wittfogel saw the hydraulic society as an initial step to totalitarianism, and his theory of the state was clearly framed with twentieth-century perspectives in mind; in fact, "It was my belief in these values that put me behind the barbed wire of Hitler's concentration camps" (Wittfogel 1957:v).

Wittfogel's theory has been translated into a simple flow chart in Figure 13–2. The state, according to this interpretation, evolved in direct response to the demands of large-scale irrigation. The need for coordinated labor, massive

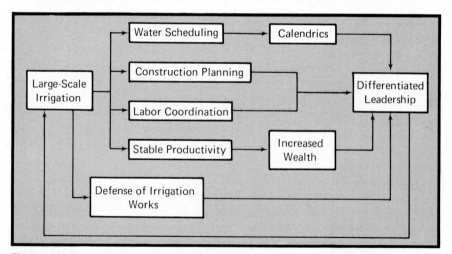

Figure 13–2
Schematic diagram of Wittfogel's irrigation hypothesis for the origin of the state *(after Wright 1977, figure 7.1; courtesy of Henry Wright and the School for American Research).*

construction, and so forth, led to increased wealth, military strength, and ultimately to the powerful ruling bureaucracy that characterized state development (see Wright 1977).

A second explanation for the origin of the state, offered by Robert Carneiro, rests on a very different initial premise: he assumes that autonomous political units will never willingly surrender their sovereignty (Carneiro 1970, 1972). Carneiro terms Wittfogel's irrigation hypothesis a "voluntaristic" theory, one requiring that "at some point in their history, certain peoples spontaneously, rationally, and voluntarily gave up their individual sovereignties and united with other communities to form a larger political unit deserving to be called a state" (Carneiro 1970:733). This is why he objects to the irrigation hypothesis of Wittfogel and others. Carneiro argues that egalitarian settlements will be transformed into chiefdoms, and chiefdoms into kingdoms, only when coercive force is involved, and warfare is especially critical in this transformation. Of course some tribes might agree to cooperate in times of stress, but such federations are temporary and voluntarily dissolve once the crisis situation has passed. Carneiro's initial premise stipulated that political change of lasting significance will ultimately come about only because of coercive pressure. Warfare is the only mechanism powerful enough to forcibly impose bureaucratic authority on a large scale. Thus warfare—the world's major coercive device—plays a major role in the origin of the state.

But it is clear from the archaeological record that warfare is considerably older and more widespread than the state. Because warfare does not invariably lead to state formation, Carneiro is quick to add that, while necessary, warfare is insufficient in itself to account for the state.

According to Carneiro, it is in areas where agricultural land is at a premium—areas that are environmentally "circumscribed"—that warfare predictably leads to state formation. Competition over land arose first where arable land was restricted by natural barriers such as mountains, deserts, or seas. The vanquished peoples had no place to flee and were required to submit to the expanding political units of the victors. Carneiro points out that the early states near the Nile, the Tigris-Euphrates, the Indus Valley, and the valleys of Mexico and Peru all evolved in areas of circumscribed agricultural land. Conversely, in areas where agricultural land was plentiful—such as northern Europe, central Africa, and the eastern woodlands of North America—states were quite late in developing, if they developed at all.

Figure 13–3 expresses Carneiro's circumscription theory as a flow diagram. The combination of population growth and circumscribed agricultural resources leads to increased warfare, which in turn ultimately leads to the centralized political organization characteristic of state-level complexity.

Both the **irrigation** and **circumscription** hypotheses are examples of general theory in anthropology. Each proponent would claim that, all else being equal, his or her theory will explain the origin of the state throughout the world, at any time. Let us bring the discussion more down to earth and consider one

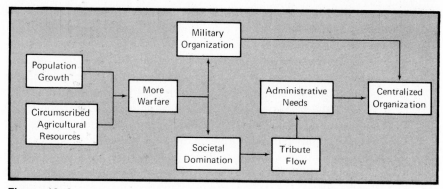

Figure 13–3
Schematic diagram of Carneiro's circumscription and warfare hypothesis for the origin of the state *(after Wright 1977, figure 7.3; courtesy of Henry Wright and The School of American Research)*.

specific instance of how general theory operates to explain specific cases. We will focus on the case of Mesoamerican states and examine how general theory tends to guide specific interpretation.

Regional syntheses appear from time to time in archaeology. While some of these studies attempt only to provide a convenient summary of the available facts, others attempt to explicate the underlying cultural processes that have conditioned the development within that region. Not only do such syntheses provide a convenient summary of the available data, they also can function as a "rallying point," a focus for further discussion.

One such regional synthesis is *Mesoamerica: The Evolution of a Civilization* (1968), by William Sanders and Barbara Price. Although now largely out of date, the Sanders and Price formulation provides a useful point of departure for this discussion of the evolution of the Mesoamerican state. As we shall see, not only have Sanders (1972, 1973, 1977; see also Logan and Sanders 1976) and Price (1977) refined their own ideas, but their effort has spurred a new wave of data and interpretation. This is how science progresses, through a continuing dialectic between synthesis and critical revision.

Sanders and Price operate within the general framework of cultural materialism, adopting an ecosystem approach to civilization in Mesoamerica. They posed a number of salient questions in their consideration of sociopolitical evolution: "Why were the early civilizations restricted to certain areas?" "Why were the rates of evolution different in these areas?" "Can civilization be considered 'inevitable' under given circumstances?" Such heady questions probed the very heart of modern cultural evolution, and more germane to this book, they can be answered only through detailed scrutiny of the archaeological record.

Sanders and Price summarily stated that "civilized society is above all else stratified society" (1968:227). The implication is that at least two subgroups must exist within every civilized society: the rich and the poor. Although archaeologists can never excavate an intact stratified social system, such lifeways leave unmistakable markers. The construction of monumental architecture, for example, usually implies a viable system of technological controls such as taxation, a corps of specialized craftsmen, and a relatively efficient bureaucracy to administer the entire operation. Stratification also is evident in the differential wealth from burials (see Chapter 10). Thus, although the clues come from material culture, the inferences aim specially at processes.

Sanders and Price isolated what they felt to be the three primary evolution processes operative in New World civilization: population growth, competition, and cooperation. Of these, *population growth* is considered fundamental, since absolute population size can be interpreted as a measure of society's productive potential. In its most simplified form, this thesis is that "organizational stresses occur as a society increases in size; size is broadly limited by population density, and such stresses stimulate the development of more effective systems of social controls (*i.e., civilizations*)" (1968:84).

The issue of population pressure was discussed in the last section, and Boserup's arguments are relevant to the Sanders–Price model. It is clear that Sanders and Price are in general agreement with Boserup: given a choice, cultivators will select extensive systems of cultivation over intensive ones (Sanders 1972:147). But Sanders feels that the Boserup model underestimates the amount of environmental variability that influences agricultural technology (Sanders 1973:333–334). It is these variations in environmental potential that, according to Sanders (1972:148), often explain why populations grow gradually in one area and rapidly in another.

With ecological theory close at hand, Sanders and Price then attacked the problems of the evolution of civilization in Middle America. Archaeologists working in the rich pre-Columbian ruins of Mexico and Guatemala have traditionally divided the Mesoamerican culture area into two rather distinct segments. The Mexican highlands consists of the arid montane basins of central Mexico. The past civilizations of the Teotihuacános, the **Toltecs**, and the Aztecs were all born, flourished, and died within the ecological milieu of the highlands. The second major region lies within the humid jungle habitats of the Yucatán peninsula and the Gulf Coast plain where Classic Maya civilization evolved by the second century A.D. and then collapsed some 600 years later.

In its boldest form the Sanders–Price theory attempted to explain how these ecological differences influenced the trajectories of the Mesoamerican civilizations. While the highland-lowland dichotomy should not be overdrawn, there seem to be major cultural as well as ecological distinctions between the two regions. Probably the most salient difference was urbanism. It has been estimated that in its heyday, the highland city of **Teotihuacán** covered an area over 19 kilometers square and perhaps hosted a total population of some 85,000 people (see Figure 13–4). A city in the true sense, Teotihuacán contained a downtown section complete with marketplaces and a planned urban core that

Figure 13–4
Aerial view of the city of Teotihuacán, Mexico. The Pyramid of the Sun is in the foreground and the Pyramid of the Moon is in the upper right *(courtesy of The American Museum of Natural History)*.

was probably devoted to bureaucratic and sacred functions. A peripheral zone consisted of the ruins of several housing complexes which gradually gave way to the outskirts of the city, where the bulk of the Teotihuacános must have dwelt. Tula, the capital of the later Toltec empire and the Aztec city of Tenochtitlán (which today lies beneath modern Mexico City) were also true cities, tightly nucleated and socially stratified.

Sanders and Price argued that the Classic Maya probably lacked such urban centers. They suggested that the largest Maya sites are better characterized as ceremonial centers, serving both secular and sacred functions but lacking the large stratified populations characteristic of the highland cities. Critical to this argument is Tikal, a massive Maya site lying some 300 kilometers north of modern Guatemala City (see Figure 13–5). Sanders and Price (1968) estimated that only 10,000 people probably lived at Tikal, which was 16 kilometers square during Classic times.

Sanders and Price also argued that the highlands and lowlands differed in technology. Although the farmers in both areas grew primarily corn, beans, and squash, their horticultural technologies were rather different in detail. The Maya practiced *milpa*, a system of shifting cultivation in which the fields were partially cleared and burnt prior to planting and much of the natural vegetation was reduced to ashes. Not only were the fields cleared by burning but the standing biomass was converted to ashes and the natural nutrients were returned to the soil, thereby enriching the productive potential. The swidden method generally required that the land be left fallow between several years of planting in order to allow the successful growth of the natural vegetation, thus enriching the depleted soil. Depending upon local soil conditions, this fallow interval lasted from a single growing season to decades. According to information from modern *milpa* farmers, 80 to 90 percent of the available land in most areas was not out of production in any given year.

In the Mexican highlands (especially the basins of Mexico, Puebla, and upper Balsas) the soil was relatively richer and unencumbered with the dense jungle vegetation typifying the lowlands. In certain areas of the highlands the natural processes, such as alluviation of montane valleys, permitted nearly continuous usage of bottomlands without any form of artificial fertilization. Elsewhere in the highlands the soil was developed through the addition of animal (and sometimes human) waste products and the organic garbage from nearby farming settlements. But the most significant highland agricultural advance was the discovery of floodwater irrigation, a technique through which suspended particles of soil, organic nutrients, and minerals could be artificially returned to depleted fields. Recent archaeological evidence suggests that irrigation was perhaps practiced in the Teotihuacán Valley by Early Classic times, some 2,300 years ago. Sanders and Price felt that the valley slopes may have been terraced and inundated by floodwater in a manner not unlike the Aztec system Cortez observed in 1519 (1968:149).

The distribution of these two agricultural systems was thus closely correlated with the two primary ecological provinces of Mesoamerica; according to Sanders and Price, the lowland Maya practiced a mixed economy based largely upon *milpa* agriculture, while irrigation was restricted to the central valleys of the highlands. In terms of modern ecological principles, each distinctive habitat apparently required its own equally distinctive niche. But even more important in the study of cultural evolution is that each ecological niche closely conditioned the sociocultural institutions of each group, for the highlanders lived in cities, and yet the Maya probably did not. According to Sanders and Price this differentiation is intelligible in terms of three critical underlying ecological processes: population increase, competition, and cooperation.

At one time all the Middle American peoples were hunters and gatherers of wild plants who were ignorant of plant domestication. In areas such as the Tehuacan Valley studied by MacNeish, plants were apparently domesticated quite early, and as these discoveries passed between groups, the specific agricultural techniques evolved to suit differing habitats. Assuming that early modes of agriculture involved slash-and-burn technology, Sanders and Price (1968:133) suggested that the tropical lowlands would have been the most favorable environment in Mesoamerica. The more humid areas of the highlands were intermediate in potential, and the arid uplands were probably least favorable due to drought, erosion, and the short growing season. Thus it was the humid jungles that experienced the earliest population growth due to the added productivity of New World agriculture. Yet the available evidence indicates that the earliest experiments in labor-intensive techniques of agriculture took place in the ecologically disadvantaged regions of the arid uplands. With the development of more highly productive techniques of floodwater hydroagriculture, the population density of the highlanders rapidly overtook the lowland *milpa* farmers. The cumulative effect of the irrigation process was to nucleate the population; as the absolute number of people increased, so did the population density within the proto-cities.

It is here that Sanders and Price (1968) rely heavily on the irrigation hypothesis, presented earlier in this section. The Wittfogel theory argues that, like the spread of agriculture itself, irrigation fundamentally alters the power balances within major areas. In this case, the balance of power shifted from the lowlands to the nuclear highlands. Wittfogel argued that the labor and managerial needs of the hydraulic agricultural systems are so strong as to stimulate the development of a highly centralized, bureaucratically structured despotic state. Price (1977:214) emphasizes different points than Wittfogel, but the basic theory is the same: the state evolves as a result of the mechanics of hydraulic agriculture. The "intensification" that occurs in a hydraulic system is precisely what Boserup's model would predict to maintain the higher population densities.

Sanders and Price admitted, of course, that the rise of urbanism involved factors other than merely the technology of irrigating one's crops. The groups in areas favorably suited for irrigation quickly gained power and dominated the peoples in areas less well adapted to the new super-agriculture. Not only did the irrigationists have a more viable subsistence, but they had the political organization necessary to marshal effective military expeditions, for administration of the canals, dikes, and levies. It was necessary to distribute food from the fields to the non-farming specialists who could be supported in the non-affluent society. The explosive population growth in time led to extensive trade networks, and markets flourished within the inner city. At this point, societies involved in irrigation were firmly stratified into identifiable social classes, based largely upon differential access to critical economic resources.

The growth of urban centers thus tended to accompany hydraulic agriculture, for highland cities arose only in those areas of Mexico where hydroagriculture was feasible. But the ecology of the Yucatán lowlands created a rather different situation. Sanders and Price argued that the mixed economy based upon *milpa* agriculture supported only a relatively low population density, so settlements grew in a rather dispersed fashion. According to Sanders and Price, there simply was not the ecological potential for the progressive cycle of population growth–competition–cooperation witnessed in the highlands. The largest centers among the Maya were interpreted as "ceremonial," with only a small resident population comprised primarily of clergy. The absence of cities greatly reduced the potential for the social inequity characteristic of more complex societies. Sanders and Price concluded that left to itself, the Maya lowland region would not have attained civilization. They argued that the lowland "civilizations without cities" arose as a response to stimuli different from those associated with the hydraulic agriculture of the highlands. At the heart of the Sanders–Price thesis lies the relationship between a strong, aggressive society and its lesser neighbors. Sanders stressed the importance of the mechanism of group-to-group diffusion: "What is essential here is that the really significant development in the evolution of any civilization is the increase of societal size and internal heterogeneity, that is, the emergence of class and occupational divisions; and this is a process, not an invention to be diffused from place to place" (Sanders 1972:152).

The presence of a powerful society on a small community's borders stimulates the smaller group to readapt itself for survival. In the case of the Maya, this reorganization (evolution, if you will) involved the adoption of the sociopolitical organization of the highlands. Mayan civilization still required the critical prerequisites for the state (especially a minimal population level and a stable economic base), but the urban sites simply never developed in the lowlands. The earliest nucleated states of the Mexican highlands, according to the Sanders–Price synthesis, evolved primarily through inner responses to ecological stimuli. The non-urban civilizations also responded to ecological factors, but the form of the response came from outside the existing fabric of local society.

A great deal of field research has taken place in the Maya area since the Sanders–Price model was first proposed in 1968. In fact, *Mesoamerica: The Evolution of a Civilization* is of interest today primarily for historical reasons. The Sanders–Price formulation has been quite heavily criticized over the past decade, and the nature of this criticism is instructive. The scientific method often proceeds through the critical process: this is how theories are examined and reexamined before they are accepted. The last thing we want in archaeology—or any science, for that matter—is to accept blindly the theoretical in statements of others based strictly upon alleged expertise or reputation. The only useful theories are those capable of surviving critical scrutiny. Let us examine the Maya case in some more detail.

One major point of disagreement is the issue of urbanism. Sanders and Price, you will remember, argued that, unlike the Mexican highlanders, the Maya lacked true urban centers. William Haviland (1969, 1970, 1978) has vigorously challenged this position, asserting that Tikal met all the criteria of urbanism. Haviland (1978) argues that the boundaries of Tikal are much greater than those suggested by Sanders and Price; overall population figures for Tikal

Figure 13–5
Temple 1 at Tikal, Guatemala *(courtesy of The American Museum of Natural History).*

could be about 45,000 (Haviland 1970:193). Sanders (1973:356) and Price (1977:217) reject the high population density figures for Tikal, objecting to Haviland's assumption of absolute contemporaneity of occupation of all structures and his average family size of 5.6 people. Sanders, while revising his estimate upward to 20,000 to 25,000 people for Tikal (1973:357), still maintains that the Maya lacked true cities and the nucleation at Tikal may be due merely to favorable local soil conditions (1973:338).

The exact figures aside, there remains the larger question of why so many people gathered at Tikal in the first place. Sanders (1973:358–359) argues that "the stimuli for this nucleation at Tikal lies in the socioeconomic sphere with major stimuli being the needs for political integration and for defense against attack. A secondary factor would be the increasing degree of economic specialization among the Tikal Maya peasantry." Price (1977:217) also questions urbanism at Tikal, suggesting that there is "a strangely fugitive quality about much of this evidence."

To Haviland, (1970, 1978) not only does Tikal meet two of the stated criteria for urbanism (large population and nucleation), but it also had considerable socioeconomic diversity, which is also important in the true city. Haviland points out that the residents of central Tikal could not have supported themselves, because land was too scarce in the middle of the urban center; they must have been supported by a large peasantry. Part of this support implies trade, which is evidenced by the number of granite, jade, slate, and obsidian artifacts that were excavated at Tikal; all of these items required long-distance transport. Haviland cites archaeological evidence for a number of economic specialists including flintworkers, architects, astronomers, and administrative bureaucrats, and he speculates that a number of other occupational specializations (butchers, brewers, weavers, etc.) occurred but did not leave archaeologically visible remains. Recent evidence is also available (Coggins 1975) to suggest that the Maya had hereditary state organization prior to influence from the Mexican highlands (see Haviland 1978:180).

In short, Haviland questions the Sanders-Price theory because it fails to account for the specifics at Tikal. His criticisms are important because they require that theoreticians pay close attention to their data; but archaeologists also face the danger of seeing the entire world through the narrow perspective of "their site." Fowler (1977) has referred to this later approach as the "view from . . . syndrome." Archaeologists interested in general theory must tread a fine line between empirical myopia and boundless overgeneralization.

> **A**rchaeology is now in possession of a vast body
> of information before which the student quails
> and indeed before which the professional
> boggles. The problem is how to organize and
> interpret this material meaningfully, a problem
> from which so many . . . archaeologists turn
> with a sigh of relief to their own cabbage-patch.
> *Glyn Daniel*

The Sanders and Price theory has been criticized on rather different grounds by Robert Carneiro (1977). At the beginning of this section we discussed Carneiro's circumscription hypothesis for the origin of the state. At the outset, therefore, it would seem likely that Carneiro would disagree with the Sanders–Price model because of their heavy reliance on the competing hydraulic hypothesis of Wittfogel. And such is precisely the case. Carneiro (1977:222) objects to Price's recent formulation of the Sander–Price theory on a number of grounds (see also Webster 1977). For one thing, Sanders and Price have proposed a voluntaristic theory for the origin of the state: "It holds that the state arose when, out of enlightened self-interest, autonomous villages voluntarily surrendered their individual sovereignties and joined peacefully to form larger political units" (Carneiro 1977:222). Such an argument, Carneiro asserts, "flies squarely in the face of the historical facts." In addition, reliance on the hydraulic hypothesis proposes a causal relationship between hydraulic technology and the state-level bureaucracy. Carneiro points out that such an argument requires the explicit demonstration that irrigation did in fact precede state-level organization, and Price did not demonstrate this. Carneiro also cites the cases of the Elgeyo of Kenya, the Sonjo of Tanzania, and the Kalinga of Luzon, all of whom practice intensive irrigation but lack a state organization.

Carneiro restates his position on the origin of the state: "Whatever the *circumstances* of state formation, the *mechanism* was warfare. Without the agency of war the problem of state origins remains obscure. With it, it readily yields to a solution" (Carneiro 1977:223).

Price calls Carneiro's criticisms "quaint." While agreeing that warfare will always be a universal component in the evolutionary process, she asserts that the Sanders–Price theory encompasses Carneiro's argument, "reducing his to a special case without in any sense invalidating it."

New data have also come to light regarding the nature of Maya agriculture. The Sanders–Price model emphasizes that the ancient Maya, like their modern descendants, lived principally on maize grown by *milpa* (slash-and-burn) agriculture. Because this mode of farming can support a relatively low population density, Sanders and Price argued that the state must be the result of cultural contact (diffusion) with the Mexican highlands: by itself, *milpa* agriculture was held to be insufficient to support such a sociopolitical superstructure.

Recent evidence now shows that the Maya population was not in fact relatively light and uniform, but rather that some areas were very densely settled (Harrison and Turner 1978). The most solid proof of more intensive agricultural techniques among the Maya is the remains of drained or ridged fields, which seem to predate the Classic Maya period (Hammond 1976:11; Netting 1977:319). Although less dramatic than the extensive irrigation and **chinampas** evidence in the Mexican highlands, these improvements doubtless increased the carrying capacity of the land. Moreover, the amount of labor involved in their construction implies a more permanent policy of land use than the simple shifting slash-and-burn technique suggested by Sanders and Price. Extensive terracing of fields has also been reported (Wilkin 1971); once again, the work of protecting the fields from erosion is inconsistent with the common notion of lengthy fallow periods for fields.

In addition, there is evidence that the Maya supplemented their maize cultivation in a number of ways. Apparently they spared breadnut and zapote trees while clearing their fields, and each household maintained an easy access to these highly nutritious foods (Haviland 1970:194). Wilkin (1971) has studied modern Maya practices and suggests that the ancients may well have upgraded their agricultural productivity by using the agricultural techniques of terracing and chinampas (like the so-called "floating gardens" of modern Xochimilco). Cultivation of ramon orchards also occurred in some Maya areas (Sanders 1973:340–341). It is also quite likely that the Maya collected lakeshore foods and edible plants, exploited marine resources, and often hunted locally available wild animals, especially deer.

The effect of this agricultural technology and population pressure has a major significance for the origins of the Maya state. Webster (1977) cites evidence that indicates that during the first two millennia of pre-Classic agricultural colonization of the lowlands, the Maya population was expanding at a rapid and startling rate. Webster asserts that the carrying capacity of the lowlands had already been exceeded as early as 500 B.C., a full 500 years prior to the Classic Maya period. If true, this calculation implies that even during pre-Classic times, emigration may no longer have been a viable choice to alleviate population pressure. Especially in the core Maya areas, social circumscription (in the sense of Carneiro) would already have been a compelling factor leading, of course, to conflict and open warfare. This evidence would indicate that warfare (its apparent sociopolitical consequences) played a much more major role in the rise of Maya civilization than attributed in the original Sanders–Price formulation, as Sanders (1977:287) now admits.

At present, there exists no overall consensus regarding the precise processes involved in the origin of the Maya state (see Adams and Culbert 1977:17). A recent symposium on the topic (Adams 1977) discussed the issue in some depth, and Willey (1977) has summarized the thinking in terms of a single "overarching" model. The core of Willey's synthesis remains ecological and demographic, relying heavily on the earlier Sanders–Price model. Once again reflecting the perspective of Boserup, Willey (1977) stresses the overall heterogeneity of the lowland Maya environment (see also Sanders 1977 and Webster 1977). Because some areas were vastly more productive than others, Maya population growth proceeded unevenly. The environmental potential of areas such as Tikal, for instance, directly led to a differential buildup of population and ultimately to shortages of agricultural land in these areas. In time, intergroup competition increased and ultimately social ranking and stratification developed. A secondary cause—also a subsistence-demographic factor—was the concomitant rise of warfare in areas of greatest population pressure. Although never a viable solution to the crises of population pressure, warfare did apparently play a significant role in spurring the rise of sociopolitical complexity among the Maya.

Competition for prime agricultural land also involved increased trade, as the larger, more complexly structured social units enjoyed a competitive advantage over the smaller, less complex groups. The production and exchange of trade goods had an important feedback effect on Maya sociopolitical development, once certain societies had reached a critical size and density of population.

Thus, while the Sanders–Price emphasis on ecological and demographic factors has survived, the emphasis has changed. No longer can the Maya be viewed as responding only to the rapidly growing civilization in the Mexican highlands. Rather, the ecological processes involved in the Maya lowland as such seem to be sufficient to account for the initial rise of the state in that area. The combined evidence suggests that the Maya state evolved in a "pristine" condition, rather than as an outgrowth of developments among the irrigation-based states of the Mexican highlands.

A final point needs to be made. The discussion of the Sanders–Price model and its subsequent modification illustrates the search for cultural processes operative in the archaeological record. We cannot help but note how frequent synthesis and reflection—even if incorrect—serve to stimulate additional fieldwork, and these new data generally serve as the basis for reinterpretation and modification. But we must also recognize the pervasive influence of overall theoretical perspectives in the search for processes. Time and time again, I have stressed how one's general anthropological orientation colors archaeological interpretation, the reason we spent so much time in Chapter 3 examining the dominant mainstreams in contemporary anthropological thought. The initial Sanders–Price model and subsequent reformations of it, generally operate from an *adaptive* perspective, relying on theoretical arguments borrowed from cultural ecology and cultural evolution.

As you might expect, this adaptive strategy is vulnerable to criticism from less materialistic, more ideationally oriented archaeologists, and such is precisely the case. René Millon has directed a long-range project to map the expansive ruins at Teotihuacán, Mexico. You will remember that Teotihuacán is important in the Sanders–Price model, and Millon uses this critical site as a point of departure. He is generally critical of the overall ecological approach Sanders and Price used, and he specifically questions the pivotal role given the irrigational complex at Teotihuacán. Millon (1973:47–49) notes that there is still no direct archaeological evidence for irrigation during Teotihuacán times, but he thinks that irrigation works probably did contribute significantly to the growth of the city once it had reached a critical size. Millon calls it "little short of absurd" to argue, as do Sanders and Price, that the mechanism of irrigation could account for the "phenomenal growth of the city, in its social, economic, or political organization." He prefers to look at other factors—such as the obsidian, maguey, and nopal cactus resources available—to account for the rise of Teotihuacán. He also points up the strategic importance of its location in manufacturing, commercial, and political terms.

But beyond the specifics, Millon is also highly critical of the overall framework: "The ecological approach as used by Sanders and Price is made to carry too heavy a burden." Millon feels that a "single-minded concentration on ecology" has caused Sanders and Price (and others) to overlook the importance of Teotihuacán as a religious center, which came to dominate much of central Mexico during its heyday. Millon points to the "cultural magnetism" of the Teotihuacán metropolis and argues for a "more balanced" approach to understand urbanism at Teotihuacán.

Millon's comments carry implications that extend far beyond the Mesoamerica state. In Chapter 3, I spent a great deal of time discussing various mainstreams within contemporary anthropological thought. I concluded that although one can isolate six different mainstreams, only three have had a significant impact on modern archaeological theory. Whether or not one agrees with the perspectives, one cannot argue with the generalization that cultural materialism, ecology, and evolution have dominated archaeological theory for the past few decades. Millon reacts to this domination by pointing out that the ecological approach cannot be allowed to carry such a heavy burden. Although the alternatives are still poorly defined, a number of contemporary archaeologists tend to agree with Millon that modern archaeology must broaden its perspectives beyond the materialistic and the ecological, to embrace the other modes of anthropological explanation. This dissatisfaction has been recently expressed by a number of archaeologists, including Kent Flannery (see Chapter 11), Hall (1977), Trigger (1971), and Willey (1976). If this book has a single point, it is that alternative strategies exist to explain archaeological phenomena, and the success of archaeological explanation in the future rests in large measure on the ability of archaeologists to draw upon these various perspectives.

IDEATIONAL CHANGE

In the last analysis magic, religion, and science
are nothing but theories of thought.
Sir James Frazer

Part Four of this book deals with cultural processes and how archaeologists go about finding (and understanding) them. I made the point in Chapters 2 and 4 that these processual statements are really timeless and spaceless generalizations. While a statement about lifeway must be firmly bound by the when and the where, processual statements presumably hold independently of time and space.

Having said this, I must point out that this assertion can be challenged. Human beings are governed, as it were, by the second law of thermodynamics and the laws of gravity. Humanity is ultimately a pawn at the mercy of the immutable laws of the universe. Unfortunately, recognition of this fact does not lead to the explanation of cultural uniformity and diversity: humans are not like electrons.

Unlike electrons, humans have the ability to perceive, to know, and to humanize themselves. It is said that although animals know, only humans know they know. While the electron is oblivious to our measurement of it, the human mind is not. Because the human subject knows the object of his inquiry, he can reflect on his behavior as both subject and object, and he can change some aspects of himself and nature.

This human awareness may make the prediction of future states of humanity impossible. That is, if one follows this line of argument the laws governing the form and pattern of human behavior may not be so immutable after all. While the social sciences can to some degree explain the present and predict the past, one can be less sure about predicting the distant future because of the human interaction. Once a prediction is made, human cognition may interact with that very prediction and alter the evolutionary course.

This may seem to be a picky philosophical point, but let me take the argument one step further. I argued earlier, in Chapter 4, that cultural laws are independent of time and space. Arguing that the laws of culture are timeless and spaceless implies an assumption that human cognition has remained a constant. How else could such laws be independent of time?

But cognition is not a constant. It is intuitively apparent that the cultural laws that governed human life some two million years ago will not explain the range of variability in human behavior today. Aside from the obvious taxonomic difficulties of classifying early hominid fossil remains, we are also faced with the problem of dealing with the emergence of human cognition. Did *Australopithecus africanus* have modern cognitive powers? Undoubtedly not. Did *Homo erectus* "think" in the same way we do? I doubt it. What about Neanderthal (*Homo sapiens neandertalensis*)? Did they think, talk, and communicate as we do? And what about the artists who painted the bulls on the walls of Lascaux some 15,000 years ago? What were they thinking about? All of these questions are germane to the original point: How far back in time are we entitled to generalize the laws of cultural behavior?

Archaeologists have been traditionally reticent to pursue such questions. This is partly due to the domination of archaeology by the cultural materialistic and cultural ecological mainstreams, and also because of the difficulty of treating past systems of ideology and symbolism. As Lewis Binford (1967:234) has stated the problem, "We would be paleopsychologists, and our training equips us poorly for this role." And yet, as archaeology pushes toward its processual objectives, it becomes clear that archaeologists must indeed become concerned with matters of cognition, symbolism, and ideation.

So little work has been conducted in this direction that it is difficult even to discuss the relationship of cognitive processes, past and present. In truth, we are dealing with an area that archaeologists have not really investigated. In fact, many contemporary archaeologists are afraid of even asking pertinent questions.

A major theme of this book has been that archaeologists have three basic goals: chronology, lifeway, and ultimate process. Before we can successfully analyze the processes we must thoroughly understand both the chronology and the specific lifeways involved. Chapter 11 discussed a number of investigations that are attempting to deal with cognition and ideation at the level of lifeway. Unfortunately, lifeway studies remain so tenuous that generalized conclusions at the processual level are presently premature. But let us examine what is being done in this important direction.

For example, Alexander Marshack's technique for analyzing Upper Paleolithic engravings was discussed in some detail in Chapter 11. Marshack contends that the La Marche bone could have been used as a notational device for keeping track of the phases of the moon. This "lunar hypothesis" has received a great deal of critical attention by archaeologists; in one sense, this is unfortunate, since it represents but a single aspect of Marshack's highly innovative research.

At a different level of abstraction, Marshack is also concerned with finding the cognitive processes and strategies implied by the Upper Paleolithic engravings and cave art. The lunar notations—if, in fact, that is what they are—comprise a single symbolic system, a prewriting, prearithmetic mode of symboling. But these notations were undoubtedly only one of many symbol systems that operated during the Upper Paleolithic. The same cultures created an elaborate complex of cave paintings; yet these paintings involved a very different symbolic system. Doubtless there were many other such systems of symbol use which simply have not preserved in the archaeological record.

Thus, at the level of lifeway, Marshack is examining the symbolic artifacts to determine their function within the specific cultural setting. But simultaneously, Marshack raises profound questions concerning the evolution of human cognitive and intellectual capacity. Surely an evolving notational system that spans some 25,000 years implies something about the developing cognitive powers of the people whose symbols they were. In another study, Marshack (1976) has examined artifacts made by Neanderthals, to determine whether the level of symbolic complexity represented on the artifacts necessarily implies that the Neanderthals had language.

These are extremely complicated questions, and few answers are available at this time. And yet archaeologists are becoming increasingly aware of the need to deal with matters of ideology. Like Marshack's work, Alexander Thom's research raises issues that cannot be ignored. Should Thom be correct—and the current evidence seems to be on his side—then British archaeologists will be forced to grant an extremely high degree of cognitive ability to the Neolithic peoples responsible for Stonehenge and the megalithic tombs (Renfrew 1973:239). The same is true of Hall's research on Hopewell symbolic systems (Chapter 11); if correct, then archaeologists should be able to understand matters of prehistoric ritual, religion, and even trade in much greater depth.

But significant research on the evolution of cognition has only begun. Binford was correct when he noted that archaeologists are poorly trained as paleopsychologists. Perhaps this is why some of the major advances seem to be made by scholars such as Marshack and Thom who began their research without the conventional archaeological training. One thing is for certain: no matter what happens to the processual theories of Marshack, Thom, Hall, and the others, the questions they raise are important, and we will undoubtedly see a fluorescence of research on such ideational matters in the next few years.

A FINAL WORD ABOUT PROCESSUAL STUDIES IN ARCHAEOLOGY

Throughout these pages I have emphasized the sequence of archaeological research: chronology, lifeway, and process. The entire text has been organized precisely to reflect this progression. Now that processual studies have been examined in some detail, let me return for one last word about how archaeologists go about actually conducting their research.

The study of cultural processes is contemporary archaeology's ultimate goal. In order to learn about processes, however, one must first control the specifics of chronology and lifeway. Consider how Richard MacNeish conducted his search for the origins of Mesoamerican agriculture (Chapter 3). MacNeish actually began with a clear statement of the process he was interested in—in this case, the process of plant domestication. Little by little, he narrowed his scope until he had focused on the area of greatest potential—the Tehuacan Valley of Mexico. Although he was ultimately concerned with process, MacNeish first was required to develop a workable chronology and then reconstruct the lifeways of the Tehuacanos over 10,000 years. Only after years of research on chronology and lifeway could MacNeish finally return to his ultimate objective—cultural processes.

Contemporary archaeologists really begin and end their research with process. Archaeologists start with processual questions and fill in the chronological and lifeway information as necessary in order to answer the initial processual question. This is a matter of priorities—beginning and ending with processual statements—and the importance of this sequence cannot be exaggerated.

SUMMARY

The establishment of general theory in archaeology requires that archaeologists transcend the specifics of chronology and lifeway to examine the relevant processes that condition human behavior in general. Archaeological theory still remains to be defined, partly because data are lacking on so many key issues and also because archaeologists are only now beginning to search in earnest for explanations and processes.

The bulk of archaeological theory deals with matters of technoecological and sociopolitical change, and this emphasis reflects the recent domination of archaeology by cultural materialistic and cultural ecological thought. At one time, archaeologists phrased their theoretical arguments largely in Malthusian terms, viewing population growth largely as a dependent variable, generally preceeded by technological innovation. In Malthusian perspective, culture was seen as constantly struggling to improvise new and more efficient modes of production. The past decade has seen a fundamental shift in perspective, and many archaeologists have explicitly rejected the neo-Malthusian premise. In its stead are substituted the views of Ester Boserup, who argues that population growth is not merely a response to evolving technology, but rather population growth is itself the key *independent* variable. According to Boserup, technological innovation occurs largely as the result of an already increasing population density, not the Malthusian reverse. The conflicting theoretical viewpoints of both Malthus and Boserup are manifest in many current attempts at the explanation of technological and sociopolitical evolution.

Contemporary archaeologists are much less well-equipped to deal with the evolution of ideology and human cognition. In fact, this issue has been seriously raised only within the past decade or so. Progress along this line has been very slow, partly because of the intrinsic difficulties in studying cognition through archaeological remains and partly because archaeologists have traditionally been reluctant to stray far from the relatively safe ground of technology, environment, ecology and demography. The trend in contemporary archaeology seems to be away from a single monolithic school of thought, and several archaeologists seem perfectly willing to transcend the mainstreams of cultural ecological and cultural materialsistic thought in order to examine the ideational perspectives available in general anthropology. Whether this diversification will actually lead to progress in the study of cognitive evolution remains to be seen.

NOTES

1. The fact remains, of course, that populations increase exponentially, while resources do not; food production probably cannot be intensified infinitely. There are implied limits even under the Boserup model.

2. I am indebted to Christopher Peebles and Susan Kus for their thoughts on this issue.

Glossary

Acculturation   The adoption of a trait or traits by one culture from another; the influence one culture has on another.

Achieved status (see **Status**)

Aguada   A large circular basin dug into the clay soil of a swampy area.

Alliance theory   A structural explanation for marriage, exchange, and exogamy.

Alluvium   Deposits of gravel, sand, and soil that are caused by flowing water.

Analogy   A means of reasoning based on the assumption that if two things are similar in some respects, then they must be similar in other respects.

Anthropology   The study of humankind, extant and extinct, from an all-encompassing holistic approach.

Anthropometry   A subdiscipline of physical anthropology that specifically examines the measurements of human morphology.

Antiquarian   A term used in the eighteenth and nineteenth centuries referring to one who collected antiquities.

Anvil stone   A rough stone artifact upon which other lithics or food (such as nuts) are placed and smashed with a stone hammer.

Arboreal   Pertaining to trees.

Archaeological contexts (see **Contexts**)

Archaeology   The study of the human past. Archaeology's initial objective is the construction of cultural chronology; its intermediate objective is the reconstruction of past lifeways; and its ultimate objective is the discovery of the processes which underlie and condition human behavior.

Aré   A term, according to the Duna of the New Guinea Highlands, used for both the initial core and flakes broken off the core.

Aré Kou   Tools used by the Duna of the New Guinea Highlands; the term refers to flakes tied with orchid fibers into a cane or wooden handle that are used for shredding fibers or drilling holes.

Artifact   Any object used or manufactured by humans.

Artifact, sociotechnic   A tool that functions primarily in the social subsystem.

Artifact, technomic   A tool that functions primarily to cope with the physical environment; variability is explicable largely in ecological terms.

Ascribed status (see **Status**)

Astroarchaeology   The study of the relationship between astronomical events and past cultural behavior; also known as archaeoastronomy.

Atlatl   An Aztec term for "spear-thrower," a wooden shaft used to propel a spear or dart. The *atlatl* functions like an extension of the arm, providing more thrusting leverage.

Attributes   Individual characteristics that distinguish one artifact from another, that is, size, surface texture, design pattern.

Australopithecus   The most ancient and most primitive grade of man, dating back roughly five million years in South Africa.

Avunculocal residence   The case in which the residence of a married couple is with the mother's brother.

Awl   A bone or stone tool tapered to a point and used to pierce holes or make decorations.

Aztec   The last major pre-Columbian civilization in Mesoamerica; the capital, Tenochtitlán, lies under the modern Mexico City.

Band   The simplest form of human society. It is egalitarian and based largely on kinship and marriage; the division of labor is generally determined by age and sex.

Bandelier, Adolph (1840–1914)   An early traveler throughout the American Southwest, his journals are still a rich source of information regarding the northern Pueblo Indians.

Bat Cave   A site in southwestern New Mexico that yielded some of the most primitive corncobs in the world, roughly between 4,000 and 5,000 years old.

Biface   A stone tool that has been flaked on both sides.

Bilocal residence   The case in which a married couple can reside with either spouse's relatives, depending upon personal and economic factors.

Binford, Lewis R. (1930–   )   An influential contemporary archaeologist, considered by many to be the father of the New Archaeology.

Biocultural anthropology   A research strategy that combines physical anthropology and archaeology in the investigation of prehistoric biological systems.

Biological population (see **Population**)

Boucher De Perthes, Jacques (1788–1868)   A controller of customs at Abbeville, England, who, in the early part of the nineteenth century, found bones of now extinct mammals associated with stone tools in the ancient gravels of the Somme.

Bridging arguments   Established mathematical or physical properties that are used in deductive reasoning to arrive at specific outcomes from generalities.

Burial Mound Builders   The nineteenth century term used to describe the prehistoric American Indians who constructed the burial and temple mounds that are widespread east of the Mississippi.

Burin   A flaked stone artifact with a narrow chiseled edge, used for engraving stone and bone.

Burnarbashi   Ruins near Balli Dagh, Turkey, once thought to have been the site of ancient Troy.

Cache   A collection of artifacts and/or ecofacts which has been deliberately stored for future use.

Cairn   A memorial or landmark, often indicating where something valuable was stored.

Catchment   The resource area around an archaeological site which is within convenient walking distance.

Central Place Theory   A series of theoretical models designed to explain how settlement hierarchies function and determine demography within modern market economies.

Cheno-am   Plants of amaranth and the goosefoot family.

Chiefdom   A ranked sociopolitical organization where people are born into their place in the society.

Childe, V. Gordon (1892–1957)   A British archaeologist who promoted a universal view of cultural evolution.

Chinampas   Artificial islands used to provide for more agriculturable land; also known as "floating gardens."

Circumscription theory   A hypothesis, largely associated with Robert Carneiro, suggesting that warfare, due to increasing population density and environmental (and social) circumscription. ultimately led to the development of the state.

Ciriaco (1391–ca. 1449)   An Italian Renaissance scholar who helped establish the modern discipline of archaeology.

Clan   A unilineal kin group, usually exogamous, that provides security and social control.

Classical archaeology   The study of Old World Greek and Roman civilizations.

Clovis point   A spear point manufactured by American Paleo-Indians, roughly 12,000 years ago. Characterized by one or more "fluting" flakes, Clovis points are found throughout the United States and, to a lesser degree, Canada.

Cognitive anthropology   A subdiscipline of anthropology that attempts to understand the organizing principles underlying behavior, especially mentalistic, internalized folk classifications.

Cognitive archaeology   The study of past mental processes, as viewed through the archaeological record.

Component   A culturally homogeneous stratigraphic unit within an archaeological site.

Componential analysis   An investigatory technique in cognitive anthropology aimed at elucidating kinship terminology.

Composites   Herbs such as ragweed and sagebrush.

Conjunctive approach   As defined by W. W. Taylor, the explicit connection of archaeological objects within their cultural contexts.

Conservation archaeology   A movement within contemporary archaeology which involves the explicit recognition of archaeological sites as nonrenewable resources.

Contexts, archaeological   Artifacts, features, and residues as found in the archaeological record.

Contexts, systemic   Artifacts, features, and residues as they functioned within the behavioral system that produced or used them.

Coprolites   Dessicated remains of human or animal feces which can reveal both dietary and climatic information.

Core   A piece of stone from which other pieces of stone are flaked off to make artifacts.

Crescent   A crescent-shaped stone tool generally restricted to the Paleo-Indian period and almost always found in association with extinct Pleistocene lakes. Sometimes known as Great Basin Transverse points, these artifacts may have been used for hunting large shorebirds.

Cultural anthropology   A subdiscipline of anthropology, emphasizing nonbiological aspects—the learned social, linguistic, technological, and familial behaviors of man.

Cultural chronology   The ordering of past material culture into meaningful temporal segments; the "when" of culture and the initial goal of archaeology.

Cultural ecology   The study of the relationship between human populations, other organisms, and their physical milieus, which together constitute integrated systems.

Cultural evolution   A subdiscipline of anthropology that emphasizes the systematic change of cultural systems through time.

Cultural materialism   A research strategy which emphasizes technoecological, technoeconomic and demographic factors as ultimately causal in cultural evolution.

Cultural population (see **Population**)

Cultural process   The cause-and-effect relationships not bound by time and space; the "why" of culture and the ultimate aim of archaeology.

Cultural system   The nonbiological mechanism which relates the human organism to its physical and social environments; whereas one shares cultural traits, one participates in the overall cultural system.

Culture   The nonbiological mechanism of human adaptation.

Curated technology   When artifacts are reused and transported so often that they are rarely deposited in contexts which reflect their actual manufacture and use.

Data   Relevant observations made on objects, serving as the basis for study and discussion.

Deduction   A means of reasoning from the general to the specific; in deductive arguments, the conclusions must be true, given that the premises are true.

Dendrochronology   Tree-ring dating.

Denticulate   An artifact with small tool-like projections on the working edge.

Devolution   Cultural evolution from relatively more complex toward relatively simpler.

Diachronic   Referring to two or more reference points in time.

Differential evolution (see **Evolution**)

Ecofacts   The nonartifactual remains found in archaeological sites such as seeds, bones, and plant pollen.

Ecological anthropology   A subdiscipline of anthropology that emphasizes cultural behavior as being embedded in the overall ecosystem.

Ecological determinants approach   A research strategy in settlement archaeology which emphasizes the location of human settlements in response to specific ecological factors.

Ecology   The study of entire assemblages of living organisms and their physical milieus, which together constitute an integrated system.

Ecosystem   The living organisms and their nonliving environment within a given area; the flow of energy through an ecosystem leads to a clearly defined structure, biotic diversity, and system of exchange cycles between the living and nonliving parts of the ecosystem.

Egalitarian society   One in which the number of valued statuses is roughly equivalent to the number of persons with the ability to fill them.

Empirical   Based on practical experience and physical evidence.

Endscraper   A stone tool with an acute edge used for flensing or softening hides.

Eolith   An extremely crude stone object, once thought to be the work of man, but now known to have been created through natural processes.

Ethnoarchaeology   The study of contemporary peoples in the attempt to determine processual relationships which will aid in unraveling the archaeological record.

Ethnocentrism   The belief that one's own ethnic group is superior to all others.

Ethnography   A primarily descriptive study of contemporary or modern cultures.

Ethnoscience   An anthropological approach that seeks to determine how people perceive and operate in their cultural world through the systematic analysis of cultural labels.

Evolution   A gradual on-going process that reflects adaptive change; cultural evolution involves change from relative homogeneous to relatively heterogeneous; biological evolution involves significant changes in the gene frequencies of a species' gene pool.

Evolution, differential   An approach to cultural evolution that emphasizes various components within societies and how these components evolve relative to one another.

Evolution, general   The overall direction advance or progression stage-by-stage, as measured in absolute terms; the evolution from heterogeneity toward homogeneity.

Evolution—Law of evolutionary potential   The group with the more generalized adaptation has the greater evolutionary potential (potential for change) than the group with the more highly specific adaptation.

Evolution, multilinear   An approach to cultural change advocated by Julian Steward, suggesting that given similar initial conditions, societies integrated at similar levels will evolve in predictable ways.

Evolution, specific   The increasing adaptive specializations which improve the chances for survival of species, cultures, or individuals.

Evolution, universal   A general approach to cultural change which emphasizes evolution of culture as a whole rather than change within specific societies.

Exogamy   A requirement for marriage outside a particular social group or range of kinship.

Experimental archaeology   A means of studying archaeological process through experimental reconstructions of necessary conditions.

Fandango   A seasonal festival, practiced by the Shoshoni, that promoted social integration and served to regulate human population density.

Faunal analysis   The study of animal remains from archaeological sites to illustrate past hunting and dietary practices.

Fetish An inanimate object that has been associated with a spiritual being or magical powers.

Firman A permit issued by a government to allow archaeological excavations.

Flakes Lithic fragments (usually debris) resulting from the manufacturing of stone tools. Sometimes the flakes are merely waste from a core; in other cases, flakes themselves can function as tools.

Flintknapping The art of manufacturing stone tools.

Flotation The use of fluid suspension to recover tiny plant and bone fragments from archaeological sites.

Fluted points Points that have characteristic "fluting" or thinning flakes running longitudinally from the base up toward the point.

Folsom point A spear point characterized by a single, well-made flute and fine pressure flaking. Folsom points were made from about 12,000 B.C. to 11,000 B.C. and are generally found only on the Great Plains and in the American Southwest.

Ford, James A. (1911–1968) Working mainly in the American Southeast, Ford's major theoretical contribution to archaeology was the development of the seriation technique of chronological ordering.

Fremont culture An agricultural, Puebloan people who lived throughout most of Utah from about A.D. 500–1400.

Gastrolith Stones or pebbles found in the stomachs of fish, reptiles and birds; used for grinding food.

General evolution (see **Evolution**)

Graver A stone tool with a protruding edge or point used for cutting, scraping, and slicing.

Habitat The physical environment in which an organism lives.

Haliotis The genus of abalone.

Hematite A reddish mineral commonly used in body paint and for pictographs.

Hissarlik The massive ruins above the Scamander Plains, Turkey, that Schliemann established to be the ruins of ancient Troy.

Homer A ninth century B.C. Greek poet, known for writing the *Iliad* and *Odyssey,* as well as numerous other epics and hymns.

Homo erectus The ancestor of modern man who emerged from *Australopithecus,* contained a brain about two-thirds the size of contemporary man, and established a number of flake tool traditions.

Hopewell Associated with the Middle Woodland period in the American Midwest from about 50 B.C. to A.D. 400, the Hopewell culture is characterized by dome-shaped burial mounds, large earthen wall enclosures, and finely decorated pottery and clay pipes.

Hypothesis A statement that goes beyond bare description; a suggestion that must be tested upon independent evidence.

Hypothetico-deduction A means of testing hypotheses by using deductive reasoning to find and verify the logical consequences.

Ideotechnic Something that reflects most clearly the mental, cognitive component of culture.

Idiolect The reflection of individual variation; the way in which an individual speaker pronounces his language or practices his culture.

Index fossil concept Strata containing similar fossil assemblages will tend to be of similar age; in archaeology, this concept indicates that diagnostic artifact forms enable archaeologists to characterize and date strata within archaeological sites.

Induction A means of reasoning from the particular to the general such that the conclusions contain more information than the premises.

In situ A term referring to the position in which an artifact or ecofact was initially located.

Irrigation hypothesis A theory, largely associated with Karl Wittfogel, suggesting that the mechanisms of large-scale irrigation are directly responsible for the origins of the state.

Jefferson, Thomas (1743–1826) The third president of the United States and considered by many to be the father of American archaeology because of his meticulous excavation of a Virginia burial mound.

Kidder, Alfred V. (1885–1963) A prominent Southwestern and Middle American archaeologist, known especially for his early stratigraphic excavations at Pecos Pueblo and for his multidisciplinary approach to archaeology.

Kill site The deposit of bones in the location where the animals had been butchered, in their primary context.

Kinship Socially recognized relationships based on real or imagined descent and marriage patterns.

Kiva An underground circular chamber associated with historic and prehistoric Pueblo Indians of Arizona, Colorado, and New Mexico; used primarily by men and for ceremonial purposes.

Kula exchange An intricate ceremonial and economic rite practiced by Trobriand Islanders, the Dobuans, and several peoples of southeastern New Guinea; participating members traveled hundreds of miles to exchange symbolic necklaces and bracelets.

Language The overall manner of speaking that reflects general shared speech patterns.

Late Woodland The time period from about A.D. 400–A.D. 1,000 in the American Midwest; it follows the Middle Woodland era but lacks the elaborate Hopewellian artifacts and structures.

Law of evolutionary potential (see **Evolution**)

Law of superposition In any pile of sedimentary rocks which have not been disturbed by folding or overturning, the strata on the bottom were deposited first.

Laws Universals in nature that are statements of what has been, what is, and what shall be.

Levi-Strauss, Claude (1908–) The founder of the structuralist approach in anthropology.

Libby, W. F. (1908–) An American physicist who received the Nobel prize for his discovery of the radiocarbon dating technique.

Lifeway The "what" and "who" of culture: settlement pattern, population density, technology, economy, organization of domestic life, kinship, social stratification, ritual, art, and religion.

Lightfoot, Dr. John (1602–1675) The Master of St. Catharine's and Vice-Chancellor of the University of Cambridge, who in 1642 declared that man, heaven, and the earth were all created by the Trinity on October 23, 4004 B.C. at nine o'clock in the morning.

Linguistics A subdiscipline of anthropology that emphasizes the relationship of cultural and linguistic behavior.

Living floors The exposure of in situ refuse within an archaeological site.

Locational analysis approach A research strategy in settlement archaeology which emphasizes the location of human settlements relative to the tenets of Central Place Theory.

Locus A predicted archaeological site locality.

MacNeish, Richard "Scotty" (1918–) A New World archaeologist who has pioneered research on the evolution of agriculture; also an important figure in the development of regional archaeology.

Malthus, Thomas Robert (1766–1834) The proponent of the theory that population growth will overrun available resources unless it is controlled by catastrophes such as war, epidemic, or natural disaster.

Mano A smooth stone tool held in the hand and used to crush grain or seeds on a metate.

Matrilocal residence The case in which the residence of a married couple is with the wife's kin; also known as *uxorilocal.*

Megalithic Of or pertaining to the Middle Neolithic period; characterized by the presence of large stone monuments.

Mesoamerica The area in Central America in which various Classic and Postclassic civilizations developed, including the Olmec, Teotihuacán, Aztec, and Maya.

Mesolithic The Middle Stone Age; a period of transition from hunting and gathering into agriculture, featuring settlements based on broad-spectrum wild resource exploitation.

Metate A stone upon which grain or seeds are crushed with a mano.

Microblade A long, narrow flake ranging in length from about 15 mm to 45 mm and in width from about 5 mm to 11 mm.

Microenvironment A characteristic biotic assemblage, often exploited by a distinctive ecological niche.

Microflaking The minute edge flaking that occurs as stone tools are used.

Microwear Patterns of edge damage and use on lithic material.

Midden Refuse deposits resulting from human activities, generally consisting of soil, food remains such as animal bone and shell, and discarded artifacts.

Middle Woodland   The time period during which the Hopewell culture flourished throughout the American Midwest, roughly 50 B.C. to A.D. 400.

Milpa   The Mayan term for slash-and-burn agriculture.

Mode   The single or multiple attribute clusters which vary through time and space.

Moiety   A division of a society into two distinct social categories or groups, often on the basis of descent.

Moore, Clarence Bloomfield (1852–1936)   Considered to be one of the forefathers of American archaeology, he traveled along the Southeastern coast in the "Gopher" excavating major sites along the way. Moore's major contributions to archaeology were his excavations at Moundville, Alabama, and Poverty Point, Louisiana.

Morphological type   A descriptive and abstract grouping of individual artifacts; the focus is on overall similarity rather than specific form or function.

Mortar   A stone bowl in which grain and seeds are ground with a pestle.

Mound Builder People   A mythical, non-American Indian people, postulated in the nineteenth century as responsible for the construction of the thousands of burial mounds in the eastern United States.

Multilinear evolution (see **Evolution**)

Munsell color chart   A chart that consists of hundreds of color chips, graded along scales of value, hue, and color; a standard means of describing all color gradations.

Nabonidus (555–538 B.C.)   The last king of the Neo-Babylonian Empire; often considered to be the first archaeologist because he searched among the ruined temples of ancient Babylon to answer questions about the remote past.

Neanderthal *(Homo sapiens neandertalensis)*   An extinct species of the human species dating about 100,000–50,000 years ago and predominantly associated with the Mousterian culture in the Stone Age.

Nelson, Nels (1875–1964)   Though Danish born, Nelson moved to the United States at an early age and had a profound effect on twentieth-century North American archaeology. Working primarily in the Southwest, though he traveled and excavated sites throughout the world, Nelson is best known for his contributions to the stratigraphic method of excavation.

Neolocal residence   The case in which the residence of a married couple is established independently of the residence of either spouse's parent's residence.

Neolithic   The New Stone Age, during which self-sufficient agriculture developed; characterized archaeologically by the use of polishing and grinding stones and the origin of ceramics.

New archaeology   A term commonly associated with Lewis R. Binford and his students.

New World   The Western Hemisphere, North and South America and, the neighboring islands.

Niche   The functional role of an organism within a community; not only where that organism lives, but what it does and eats, and how it responds to the environment.

Nock   The groove into which the bowstring is inserted on an arrow.

Nomothetic   The search for general laws and theories.

Object d'art   An object of artistic value.

Obsidian hydration   The technique of dating obsidian artifacts by measuring the microscopic amount of water absorbed on fresh surfaces.

Ocher (or ochre)   An iron ore compound generally mixed with earth, clay, or grease to be used as paint.

Olla   A Spanish term for a ceramic vessel generally used to store and cool water.

Paleoethnography   A fundamental focus in contemporary archaeology; the study of extinct lifeways.

Palynology   The study of plant pollen and spores.

Patrilocal residence   The case in which residence of a married couple is with the husband's kin; also known as *virilocal.*

Pecos Conference   A convention of Southwestern archaeologists orginally established in 1927 by A. V. Kidder to determine a uniform cultural chronology and a relatively consistent terminology; the conference is still held today.

Ped   A fist-sized clod of dirt created in the soil formation process.

Pedology   The study of soils and their structure.

Petrarch (1304–1374)   Often considered to be the first humanist and perhaps the most influential individual of the early Renaissance. He provided a strong impetus for archaeological research by looking to antiquity for moral philosophy. His humanism led to a rediscovery of the past.

Petrie, Sir Flinders (1853–1942)   A British Egyptologist who developed the technique of sequence ordering known as "seriation."

Phase   An archaeological construct possessing traits sufficiently characteristic to distinguish it from other units similarly conceived; spatially limited to roughly a locality or region and chronologically limited to a relatively brief interval of time.

Phenocryst   Crystals embedded in igneous rock.

Photomapping   A technique of recording archaeological living floors by use of precisely scaled photographs.

Phratry   A group of clans related by traditions of common descent or historical alliance based on kinship.

Physical anthropology   A subdiscipline of anthropology which views man as a biological organism.

Phytolith   The tiny silica particles contained within plants; sometimes these fragments can be recovered from archaeological sites, even after the plants themselves have decayed.

Pictograph   A rendering, often painted on the walls of caves or cliffs, that represents a form of nonverbal communication and often employed by nonliterate people.

Piltdown hoax   Bones were found at Piltdown, England, which supposedly provided the "missing link" between fossil and modern man; flourine tests subsequently indicated that the Piltdown fossil was a clever and deliberate combination of a modern skull with the jaw of an orangutang.

Plant macrofossils   The preserved or carbonized plant parts recovered from archaeological sites.

Pleistocene   The geological period characterized by the appearance and recession of glaciers and the development of early man.

Pollen analysis   The analysis of fossil pollen in order to reconstruct past vegetation and climate.

Polythetic definition   A class is polythetic if a large number of the members share most of the individual characteristics; there is no necessary or sufficient criterion of membership.

Pontil mark   A mark on the bottom of a glass bottle caused by the removal of the long iron rod that was used to hold the bottle during the finishing process.

Population, biological   A group of organisms of a single species, at a given time, that are capable of interbreeding.

Population, cultural   A specific society, such as the Shoshoni or Arikara.

Population, statistical   A set of variates (counts, measurements, or characteristics) about which relevant inquiries are to be made.

Pothunting   Amateur (illegal) artifact collecting.

Potlatch   A custom of nineteenth-century Northwest Coast Indians which involved competitive feasting for prestige.

Prehistoric   The time period before the appearance of written records.

Primary refuse   The occurrence of archaeological debris in contexts where they were used and discarded.

Principle component analysis   A multivariate statistical technique designed to reduce redundancy in a body of data and to clarify underlying structural relations.

Projectile point   A chipped stone artifact used to tip an arrow or atlatl dart.

Promontory culture   Once thought to be a bison-hunting, cave-dwelling people in northern Utah; now recognized as a seasonal variation of the Fremont culture.

Promontory peg   A carved wooden artifact, probably used as the trigger for a snare; first recognized at the Promontory Caves, north of Salt Lake City, Utah.

Proximal shoulder angle   The angle on a projectile point formed by the hafting notch and the axis of the shaft.

Psychic archaeology   The use of ESP and other parapsychological powers to explore past events and locate sites.

Quadrat sampling (see **Sample**)

Quid   The fibrous remains of rhyzomes which were chewed by many hunting-gathering peoples.

Racemization   The action of changing from an optically active compound into a racemic (or optically inactive) compound.

Radiocarbon dating   A physiochemical method of estimating the length of time since the death of an organism.

Random sample selection (see **Sample**)

Ranked society   A society in which there is unequal access to the higher status categories; many people who are qualified for high status positions are unable to achieve them.

Residential group   Physical agglomerations of people at the domestic, territorial, or community level.

Rock art   Inclusive term referring to both pictographs (designs painted on stone surfaces) and petroglyphs (designs pecked or incised into stone surfaces).

Roughout   An early stage in the manufacture of bifacially chipped stone tools; roughouts are often manufactured in quarry areas, then later reworked into finished artifacts.

Sample   Any subset of a population.

Sample, quadrat sampling   A means of archaeological research design in which the sampling element is a square or rectangular grid.

Sample—random sample selection   A method of selecting a sample in which every element has a known and equal probability of selection.

Sample—systematic sample selection   A method of selecting a sample in which the first element is drawn randomly and the others are selected at predetermined intervals.

Sample—transect sampling   A means of archaeological sampling in which the sampling element is a fairly long linear unit.

Sampling elements   The objects of study in a probability sample.

Sampling universe   The set of all possible elements to be considered in a probability sample.

Scapula saw   An artifact manufactured from the shoulder blade of a big-horn sheep or antelope.

Science   The search for universals in nature by use of the established scientific method of inquiry.

Schliemann, Heinrich (1822–1890)   A one time German businessman who retired to study Greek archaeology. Often considered the progenitor of contemporary archaeological method, he established scientific excavating procedures in an effort to prove the historic validity of Homer's city of Troy.

Secondary refuse   Deposits of artifacts, bone, shell, and other habitation debris discarded away from the immediate area of use.

Seriation   A temporal ordering of artifacts based on the assumption that cultural styles (fads) change such that the popularity of a particular style or decoration can be associated with a certain time period.

Settlement pattern   The distribution of human populations throughout their habitat.

Shaft straightener   An artifact manufactured from a coarse (often volcanic) stone, with a groove used as a rasp to finish spears and arrowshafts.

Shoshoni   The American Indian group which inhabited much of the Great Basin during both historic and prehistoric times.

Side-scraper   A stone tool with one sharpened edge and a blunt back side.

Signál   Individual marks which distinguish one potter's work from another.

Slopeface   The merging of a slope and an attitude, that being the orientation of a spacecraft relative to its direction of motion.

Social organization   The structural organization of a society involves two things. First, there is a division into smaller social units, which are called *groups*. Second, there are recognized social positions (*statuses*) and appropriate behavior patterns for these positions (*roles*).

Sociotechnic artifact (see **Artifact**)

Sodality   A nonresidential social group based on common interest or voluntary participation.

Sondage   An exploratory excavation or test pit, designed to expose stratigraphy and determine whether a thorough excavation should be conducted.

Southern cult   A ceremonial complex widely distributed throughout the American Southeast in Mississippian times, characterized by distinctive motifs such as the cross, the sun circle, the swastika, and the forked eye; also known as the Southeastern Ceremonial Complex.

Specific evolution (see **Evolution**)

Spencer, Herbert (1820–1903)   A British philosopher and social scientist who pioneered the study of the evolution of societies and civilization.

Spokeshave   A stone tool with a semicircular concavity used for smoothing spears or arrowshafts.

State   A strong centralized government with a professional ruling class; leadership is not based on kinship affiliation, though it does occur, and the structure is highly stratified by class.

Statistical population (see **Population**)

Status   The rights and duties associated with a particular social position.

Status, achieved   The social rights and duties attributed to individuals according to achievement, rather than by inherited social position.

Status, ascribed   The social rights and duties attributed to an individual at birth, regardless of ability or achievement.

Stelae   Free standing carved stone monuments.

Strata   The various layers of human or geological origin which comprise archaeological sites.

Stratigraphy   An analytical interpretation of the structure produced by deposition of geological and/or cultural sediments into layers (or *strata*).

Striations   The microscopic scratches on stone tools which often reveal the direction of force and the nature of tool use.

Structuralism   A theory of culture that emphasizes the underlying structure of the mind.

Surface site   An area in which archaeological remains occur on stable ground surfaces.

Symbolic anthropology   The study of shared systems of symbols that underlie human behavior.

Synchronic   Referring to a single period in time.

System of communication   The underlying motive for language, to communicate information between individuals.

Systematic sample selection (see **Sample**)

Systemic contexts (see **Contexts**)

t-test   A univariate statistical test designed to test for differences between relatively small samples of variates.

Talisman   A charm or fetish thought to produce unusual, extraordinary happenings.

Taylor, Walter W. (1913–   )   Considered a revolutionary figure in twentieth-century American archaeology, Taylor proposed the "conjunctive" approach to archaeology, emphasizing the connection of objects to their cultural contexts.

Technomic artifact (see **Artifact**)

Temper   The foreign material introduced into clay to keep pottery from cracking when fired; also known as "grog."

Temple mound   A large flat-topped earthen structure designed to function as artifical mountains and that set the temple above the landscape.

Temple Mound Period   Time period from about A.D. 700 to European colonization when Indians of the Mississippian tradition built large flat-topped earthen structures designed to function as artificial mountains, elevating the temples above the landscape.

Temporal type   Morphological types which have been shown to have temporal significance; also known as "time-markers."

Teotihuacán   A major urban center which flourished during the Classic period of Mexican prehistory, roughly 300 B.C. to A.D. 900; located about 25 miles north of modern Mexico City.

Toltecs   The prehistoric culture from central and southern Mexico dating about A.D. 1000; founded the city-state of Tula.

Tool kit   A spatially or functionally patterned combination of artifacts.

Tract   The sampling element in a quadrat research design.

Transect sampling (see **Sample**)

Tribe   An egalitarian society generally consisting of a group of bands;

kinship is more complex than that of the band and economy is often agricultural rather than foraging.

Trojan War A ten-year struggle, during which, according to Homer's *Iliad,* the Greeks invaded Troy to recover Helen, wife of Spartan King Menelaus.

Ungulate A term referring to the hoofed animals, including ruminants, swine, horses, tapirs, rhinoceros, and elephants.

Uniface A stone tool that has been flaked only on one side.

Universal evolution (see **Evolution**)

Varve A stratified deposit of silt often caused by annual melting of glaciers.

Virchow, Rudolph Ludwig (1821–1902) A German scientist and naturalist who conducted a broad-based ecological study of the Trojan Plain in conjunction with Schliemann's excavations at Hissarlik.

Warp In weaving, the foundation threads that run lengthwise over and through which the weft crosses at right angles.

Weft In weaving, the horizontal threads that interlace through the warp.

Whetstone A hone stone used to sharpen other tools.

Wickerwork Woven basketry that is composed of a flexible thin weft and a thick warp.

Wickiup A domed hut used by the Shoshoni Indians, sometimes surrounded by circles of stone and covered with piñon tree bark or juniper boughs.

Xerophyte A plant that grows in arid conditions.

Zoomorph An animal form symbolized in art.

Bibliography

A Aberle, David F., 1960, The influence of linguistics on early culture and personality theory. In *Essays in the science of culture,* Gertrude E. Dole and Robert L. Carneiro, eds., New York: Thomas Y. Crowell, pp. 1–29.

Absolon, Karel, 1957, Dokumente and beweise der fähigkeiten des fossilen menschen zu zählen in mahrischen Paläolithikum. *Artibus Asaie* 20: 123–150.

Adams, Richard E. W., ed., 1977, *The origins of Maya civilization.* Albuquerque: University of New Mexico Press.

Adams, Richard E. W., and T. Patrick Culbert, 1977, The origins of civilization in the Maya lowlands. In *The origins of Maya civilization,* Richard E. W. Adams, ed., Albuquerque: University of New Mexico Press, pp. 3–24.

Adovasio, J. M., and Joel Gunn, 1977, Style, basketry and basketmakers. In *The individual in prehistory,* James N. Hill and Joel Gunn, eds., New York: Academic Press, pp. 137–154.

Aikens, C. Melvin, 1966, Fremont-Promontory-Plains relationships in northern Utah. Salt Lake City: *University of Utah Anthropological Papers,* No. 82.

Alexander, Herbert L., Jr., 1963, The Levi site: A Paleo-Indian campsite in central Texas. *American Antiquity* 28: 510–528.

Allen, William L., and James B. Richardson III, 1971, The reconstruction of kinship from archaeological data: the concept, the methods, and the feasibility. *American Antiquity* 36: 41–53.

Alsop, Joseph, 1964, *From the silent earth: a report on the Greek Bronze Age.* New York: Harper & Row.

Ambro, Richard D., 1970, A basket maker's work kit from Lovelock Cave, Nevada. Berkeley: *Contributions of the University of California Archaeological Research Facility* No. 7: 73–79.

Ambrose, W. R., 1976, Intrinsic hydration rate dating of obsidian. In *Advances in obsidian glass studies,* R. E. Taylor, ed., Park Ridge, N.J.: Noyes Press.

Anati, Emmanuel, 1972, Comment on *Upper Paleolithic engraving* by Alexander Marshack. *Current Anthropology* 13: 461.

Anderson, James N., 1973, Ecological anthropology and anthropological ecology. In *Handbook of social and cultural anthropology,* John J. Honigmann, ed., Chicago: Rand McNally, pp. 179–240.

Asher, Maxine, 1974, Theories of intuitive perception applied to ancient anthropological inquiry. Ph.D. diss., Walden University, Naples, Florida.

Atkinson, R. J. C., 1966a, Decoder misled, Review of *Stonehenge decoded* by Gerald S. Hawkins. *Nature* 210: 1302.

———, 1966b, Moonshine on Stonehenge. *Antiquity* 40: 212–216.

———, 1975, Megalithic astronomy—a prehistorian's comments. *Journal for the History of Astronomy* VI: 42–52.

Aveni, Anthony F., 1972, Astronomical tables intended for use in astroarchaeological studies. *American Antiquity* 37:531–540.

———, ed., 1975, *Archaeoastronomy in Pre-Columbian America.* Austin: University of Texas Press.

———, ed., 1977, *Native American astronomy.* Austin: University of Texas Press.

Aveni, Anthony F., and S. L. Gibbs, 1976, On the orientation of Pre-Columbian buildings in central Mexico. *American Antiquity* 41: 510–517.

B Bada, Jeffrey L., Roy A. Schroeder, and George F. Carter, 1974, New evidence for the antiquity of man in North America deduced from aspartic acid racemization. *Science* 184: 791–793.

Bada, Jeffrey L., Roy A. Schroeder, Reiner Protsch, and Rainer Berger, 1974, Concordance of collagen-based radiocarbon and aspartic-acid racemization ages. *Proceedings of the National Academy of Science* 71: 914–917.

Baity, Elizabeth Chesley, 1973, Archaeoastronomy and ethnoastronomy so far. *Current Anthropology* 14: 389–449.

Barth, Fredrik, 1956, Ecologic relations of ethnic groups in Swat, North Pakistan. *American Anthropologist* 58: 1079–1089.

Baumhoff, Martin A., 1963, Ecological determinants of aboriginal California populations. Berkeley: *University of California Publications in American Archaeology and Ethnology* 49: 155–236.

Baumhoff, Martin A., and J. S. Byrne, 1959, Desert Side-notched points as a time marker in California. Berkeley: *University of California Archaeological Survey Report* No. 48: 32–65.

Beardsley, Richard K., 1956, Functional and evolutionary implications of community patterning. *American Antiquity* 22: 129–157.

Benedict, Ruth, 1934, *Patterns of culture.* Boston: Houghton Mifflin.

Berenson, Bernhard, 1962, *Rudiments of connoisseurship: study and criticism of Italian art.* New York: Schocken Books.

Bettinger, Robert L., 1977, Aboriginal human ecology in Owens Valley: prehistoric change in the Great Basin. *American Antiquity* 42: 3–17.

Binford, Lewis R., 1962, Archeology as anthropology. *American Antiquity* 28: 217–225.

———, 1964, A consideration of archaeological research design. *American Antiquity* 29: 425–441.

———, 1965, Archaeological systematics and the study of cultural process. *American Antiquity.* 31: 203–210.

———, 1967, Smudge pits and hide smoking: the use of analogy in archaeological reasoning. *American Antiquity* 32: 1–12.

———, 1968a, Post-Pleistocene adaptations. In *New perspectives in archeology,* Sally R. Binford and Lewis R. Binford, eds., Chicago: Aldine, pp. 313–341.

———, 1968b, Some comments on historical versus processual archaeology. *Southwestern Journal of Anthropology* 24: 267–275.

———, 1968c, Archeological perspectives. In *New perspectives in archeology.* Sally R. Binford and Lewis R. Binford, eds., Chicago: Aldine, pp. 5–32.

———, 1969, Conceptual problems in dealing with units and rates of cultural evolution. *Anthropology UCLA* 1: 27–35.

———, 1971, Mortuary practices: their study and their potential. In Approaches to the social dimensions of mortuary practices, James Brown, ed., *Society for American Archaeology Memoir* No. 25, pp. 6–29.

———, 1972, *An archaeological perspective.* New York: Seminar Press.

———, 1973, Interassemblage variability—the Mousterian and the "functional" argument. In *The explanation of culture change: models in prehistory,* Colin Renfrew, ed., London: Duckworth, pp. 227–254.

——— ed., 1977, *For theory building in archaeology.* New York: Academic Press.

———, 1978, *Nunamuit ethnoarchaeology: a case study in archaeological formation processes.* New York: Academic Press.

Binford, Lewis R., and Jack B. Bertram, 1977, Bone frequencies—and attritional processes. In *For theory building in archaeology,* Lewis R. Binford, ed., New York: Academic Press, pp. 77–156.

Binford, Lewis R., and W. J. Chasko, Jr., 1976, Nunamuit demographic history:

a provocative case. In *Demographic anthropology: quantitative approaches,* Ezra B. W. Zubrow, ed., Albuquerque: University of New Mexico Press, pp. 63–144.

Birdsell, J. B., 1953, Some environmental and cultural factors influencing the structure of Australian aboriginal populations. *American Naturalist* 87: 171–207.

———, 1972, *Human evolution: an introduction to the new physical anthropology.* Chicago: Rand McNally.

Blanton, Richard E., 1978, *Monte Albán: settlement patterns at the ancient Zapotec capital.* New York: Academic Press.

Blegen, Carl, 1963, *Troy and the Trojans.* London: Frederick A. Praeger.

Bohannan, Paul, 1965, *Social anthropology.* New York: Holt, Rinehart and Winston.

Boserup, Ester, 1965, *Conditions of agricultural growth; the economics of agrarian change under population pressure.* Chicago: Aldine.

Bourque, Bruce J., Kenneth Morris, and Arthur Speiss, 1978, Determining the seasons of death of mammal teeth from archeological sites: a new sectioning technique. *Science* 199: 530–531.

Boyd, William C., 1950, *Genetics and the races of man.* Boston: Little, Brown.

Braidwood, Robert J., 1959, Archeology and the evolutionary theory. In *Evolution and anthropology: a centennial appraisal.* Washington, D. C.: Anthropological Society of Washington, pp. 76–89.

Brennan, Louis A., 1973, *Beginner's guide to archaeology.* Harrisburg, Pa.: Stackpole Books.

Breternitz, David, A., 1966, An appraisal of tree-ring dated pottery in the Southwest. *Anthropological Papers of the University of Arizona* No. 10, Tucson: University of Arizona Press.

Brew, J. O., 1941, Preliminary report of the Peabody Museum Awatovi expedition of 1939. *Plateau* 13: 37–48.

Brose, David S., 1972, Comment on *Upper Paleolithic engraving* by Alexander Marshack. *Current Anthropology* 13: 462.

Brown, James A., 1976, The Southern Cult reconsidered. *Midcontinental Journal of Archaeology* 1: 115–135.

Brown, Peter Lancaster, 1976, *Megaliths, myths and men: an introduction to astro-archaeology.* New York: Harper & Row.

Brown, Robert, 1963, *Explanation in social science.* Chicago: Aldine.

Brown, Roger, 1965, *Social psychology.* New York: Free Press.

Buchler, I. R., and H. A. Selby, 1968, *Kinship and social organization.* New York: Macmillan.

Buckley, Theodore Alois, 1873, *The Iliad—Homer.* Bell and Daldy.

Buikstra, Jane E., 1976, Hopewell in the lower Illinois valley: a regional study of human biological variability and prehistoric mortuary behavior. *Northwestern Archeological Program Scientific Papers* 2.

———, 1977, Biocultural dimensions of archeological study: a regional perspective. In Biocultural adaptation in prehistoric America, Robert L. Blakely, ed., *Proceedings of the Southern Anthropological Society,* No. 11 Athens: University of Georgia Press, pp. 67–84.

Bullard, W. R. Jr., 1960, Maya settlement pattern in northeastern Petén, Guatemala. *American Antiquity* 25: 355–372.

Burgh, Robert F., 1950, Comment on Taylor's *A study of archeology. American Anthropologist* 52: 114–117.

C Caldwell, Joseph, 1959, The new American archaeology. *Science* 129: 303–307.

Cannon, Walter B., 1942, "Voodoo" death. *American Anthropologist* 44: 169–181.

Carneiro, Robert L., 1962, Scale analysis as an instrument for the study of cultural evolution. *Southwestern Journal of Anthropology* 18: 149–169.

———, 1968, Ascertaining, testing and interpreting sequences of cultural development. *Southwestern Journal of Anthropology* 24: 354–374.

———, 1970, A theory of the origin of the state. *Science* 169: 733–738.

———, 1972, From autonomous village to the state, a numerical estimation. In *Population growth: anthropological implications,* Brian Spooner, ed., Cambridge, Mass.: MIT Press, pp. 64–77.

———, 1973a, Classical evolution. In *Main currents in cultural anthropology,* Raoul Naroll and Frada Naroll, eds., Englewood Cliffs, N.J.: Prentice-Hall, pp. 57–121.

———, 1973b, The four faces of evolution: unilinear, universal, multilinear, and differential. In *Handbook of social and cultural anthropology,* John J. Honigmann, ed., Chicago: Rand McNally.

———, 1977, Comment. *Current Anthropology* 18: 222–223.

Casteel, Richard, W., 1970, Core and column sampling. *American Antiquity* 35: 465–467.

———, 1972a, Some archaeological uses of fish remains. *American Antiquity* 37: 404–419.

———, 1972b, Two static maximum population-density models for hunter-gatherers: a first approximation. *World Archaeology* 4: 19–40.

———, 1976a, Comparison of column with whole unit samples for recovering fish remains. *World Archaeology* 8: 192–196.

———, 1976b, *Fish remains in archaeology and paleo-environmental studies.* New York: Academic Press.

———, 1977, Characterization of faunal assemblages and the minimum number of individuals determined from paired elements: continuing problems in archaeology. *Journal of Archaeological Science* 4: 125–134.

Chamberlin, T. C., 1890, The method of multiple working hypotheses. *Science* (Old Series) XV: 92–96.

Chang, K. C., 1967, *Rethinking archaeology.* New York: Random House.

———, ed., 1968, *Settlement archaeology.* Palo Alto, Calif.: National Press.

Chaplin, R. E., 1971, *The study of animal bones from archaeological sites.* London: Seminar Press.

Childe, V. Gordon, 1951a, *Social evolution.* New York: Henry Schuman.

———, 1951b, *Man makes himself*. New York: New American Library.

Clark, Donovan L., 1964, Archaeological chronology in California and the obsidian hydration method: Part I. Los Angeles: *University of California Archaeological Survey Annual Report 1963–1964*, pp. 143–225.

Clark, George, 1979, Appendix: Seasonal growth variations in the shells of recent and prehistoric specimens of *Mercenaria mercenaria* from St. Catherines Island. In The anthropology of St. Catherines Island: The Refuge-Deptford mortuary complex, *Anthropological Papers of the American Museum of Natural History*.

Clark, J. D. G., 1954, *Excavations at Star Carr, an early Mesolithic site at Seamer, near Scarborough, England*. Cambridge: Cambridge University Press.

———, 1972, Star Carr: a case study in bioarchaeology. *Addison-Wesley Module in Anthropology*, No. 10.

Clarke, David L., 1968, *Analytical archaeology*. London: Metheun.

Cleator, P. E., 1976, *Archaeology in the making*. New York: St. Martin's Press.

Cochran, W. G., 1963, *Sampling techniques*. New York: Wiley.

Coe, Michael D., 1975, Native astronomy in Mesoamerica. In *Archaeoastronomy in Pre-Columbian America*, Anthony F. Aveni, ed., Austin: University of Texas Press, pp. 3–31.

Coggins, Clemens C. 1975, Painting and drawing styles at Tikal. Ph.D. diss., Harvard University, Cambridge, Mass.

Coghlan, H. H., 1940, Prehistoric copper and some experiments in smelting. *Transactions of the Newcomer Society* 20: 49–65.

Cohen, Mark Nathan, 1977, *The food crisis in prehistory*. New Haven: Yale University Press.

Coles, John M., 1967, Experimental archaeology. *Proceedings of the Society of Antiquaries of Scotland* 99: 1–120.

———, 1973, *Archaeology by experiment*. New York: Charles Scribner's Sons.

Collins, Paul W., 1965, Functional analysis in the symposium *Man, culture, and animals*. In Man culture and animals, Anthony Leeds and Andrew P. Vayda, eds., Washington, D.C.: *American Association for the Advancement of Science*, No. 78, pp. 271–282.

Cook, S. F., and Robert F. Heizer, 1965, Studies on the chemical analysis of archaeological sites. Berkeley: *University of California Publications in Anthropology* Vol. 2.

Cornwall, I. W., 1956, *Bones for the archaeologist*. London: Phoenix House.

———, 1969, Soil, stratification, and environment. In *Science in archaeology*, rev. ed., Don Brothwell and Eric Higgs, eds., London: Thames and Hudson, pp. 120–134.

Coutts, Peter J. F., 1970, Bivalve growth patterning as a method for seasonal dating in archaeology. *Nature* 226: 874.

———, 1975, The seasonal perspective of marine-oriented prehistoric hunter-gatherers. In *Growth rhythms and the history of the earth's rotation*, G. D. Rosenberg and S. K. Runcorn, eds., London: Wiley, pp. 243–252.

Coutts, Peter, and Charles Higham, 1971, The seasonal factor in prehistoric New Zealand. *World Archaeology* 2: 266–277.

Cowan, Richard A., 1967, Lake margin ecological exploitation in the Great Basin as demonstrated by an analysis of coprolites from Lovelock Cave, Nevada. Berkeley: *University of California Archaeological Survey Reports* 70: 21–35.

Cowgill, George L., 1968, Computer analysis of archeological data from Teoti-huacan, Mexico. In *New perspectives in archeology,* Sally R. Binford and Lewis R. Binford, eds., Chicago: Aldine, pp. 143–150.

————, 1975a, On the causes and consequences of ancient and modern population changes. *American Anthropologist* 77: 505–525.

————, 1975b, Population pressure as a non-explanation. In Population studies in archaeology and biological anthropology: a symposium, A. Swelund, ed., *Society of American Archaeology Memoir* No. 30, pp. 127–131.

Crabtree, Don E., 1966, A stoneworker's approach to analyzing and replicating the Lindenmeier Folsom. *Tebiwa* 9: 3–39.

————, 1968, Mesoamerican polyhedral cores and prismatic blades. *American Antiquity* 33: 446–478.

Cressman, Lurhur S., 1977, *Prehistory of the Far West: homes of the vanished peoples.* Salt Lake City: University of Utah Press.

Cronin, C., 1962, An analysis of pottery design elements, indicating possible relationships between three decorated types. In Chapters in the prehistory of eastern Arizona I, Paul S. Martin and others, eds., *Fieldiana Anthropology* 53: 105–114.

Crumley, Carole, 1976, Toward a locational definition of state systems of settlement. *American Anthropologist* 78: 59–73.

D Dancey, William S., 1976, Riverine period settlement and land use pattern in the Priest Rapids area, central Washington. *Northwest Anthropological Research Notes* 10: 147–160.

Daniel, Glyn E., 1950, *A hundred years of archaeology.* London: Duckworth.

————, 1962, *The idea of prehistory.* Baltimore: Penguin.

Dean, Jeffrey S., 1970, Aspects of Tsegi phase social organization: a trial reconstruction. In *Reconstructing prehistoric Pueblo societies,* William A. Long-acre, ed., Albuquerque: University of New Mexico Press, pp. 140–174.

Deetz, James, 1965, The dynamics of stylistic change in Arikara ceramics. Urbana, Illinois: *Illinois Studies in Anthropology* No. 4.

————, 1967, *Invitation to archaeology.* Garden City, N.Y.: Natural History Press.

————, 1968, The inference of residence and descent rules from archeological data. In *New perspectives in archeology,* Sally R. Binford and Lewis R. Binford, eds., Chicago: Aldine, pp. 41–48.

————, 1970, Archeology as a social science. Washington, D.C.: *Bulletins of the American Anthropological Society* 3: 115–125.

DePratter, Chester B., and James D. Howard, 1977, History of shoreline changes determined by archaeological dating: Georgia Coast, U.S.A. *Technical Papers and Abstracts, Gulf Coast Association of Geological Societies* XXVII: 252–258.

Deuel, Leo, 1977, *Memoirs of Heinrich Schliemann*. New York: Harper & Row.

DeVries, H. L., 1958, Variation in concentration of radiocarbon with time and location on earth. Koninkl. Nederl. Akademie van Wetenschappen, Amsterdam: *Proceedings,* Series B61: 1–9.

Díaz, Del Castillo, Bernal, 1956, *The conquest of new Spain*. Albert Idell, ed. and trans., Garden City, N.Y.: Dolphin Books.

Diener, Paul, and Eugene E. Robkin, 1978, Ecology, evolution and the search for cultural origins: the question of Islamic pig prohibition. *Current Anthropology* 19: 493–540.

Divale, William T., 1972, Systemic population control in the Middle and Upper Palaeolithic: inferences based on contemporary hunter-gatherers. *World Archaeology* 4: 222–243.

Dixon, Keith A., 1971, Archaeological site preservation: the neglected alternative to destruction. *Pacific Coast Archaeological Society Quarterly* 7: 51–70.

Donnan, Christopher B., 1971, Ancient Peruvian potter's marks and their interpretation through ethnographic analogy. *American Antiquity* 36: 460–466.

Dow, James W., 1967, Astronomical orientations at Teotihuacán: a case study in astroarchaeology. *American Antiquity* 32: 326–334.

Drennan, Robert D., 1976, A refinement of chronological seriation using nonmetric multidimensional scaling. *American Antiquity* 41: 290–302.

Dumond, Donald E., 1965, Population growth and cultural change. *Southwestern Journal of Anthropology* 21: 302–324.

———, 1977, Science in archaeology: the saints go marching in. *American Antiquity* 42: 330–349.

E   Eddy, J. A., 1974, Astronomical alignment of the Big Horn medicine wheel. *Science* 184: 1035–1043.

Ellis, Florence Hawley, 1975, A thousand years of the Pueblo sun-moon-star calendar. In *Archaeoastronomy in Pre-Columbian America,* Anthony F. Aveni, ed., Austin: University of Texas Press, pp. 59–88.

Emerson, J. N. 1973, Intuitive archaeology: the argellite carving. *The Midden, Archaeological Society of British Columbia,* 6.

———, 1974, Intuitive archaeology: a psychic approach. *New Horizons* 1: 14–18.

Erikson, J. E., 1975, New results in obsidian hydration dating. *World Archaeology* 7: 151–159.

Euler, Robert C., and George J. Gumerman, 1978, *Investigations of the Southwestern Anthropological Research Group: an experiment in archaeological cooperation*. Flagstaff: Museum of Northern Arizona.

Evans, J. A. S., 1977, Redating prehistory in Europe. *Archaeology* 30: 76–85.

F Faul, Henry, 1971, Potassium-argon dating. In *Dating techniques for the archaeologist,* Henry N. Michael and Elizabeth K. Ralph, eds. Cambridge, Mass.: MIT Press, pp. 157–163.

Feldman, Mark, 1977, *Archaeology for everyone.* New York: Quadrangle.

Fenton, William N., 1962, Introduction to *League of the Iroquois* by Lewis Henry Morgan. New York: Corinth Books, pp. v–xviii.

Fewkes, Jesse Walter, 1893, Tusayan katchinas. Washington, D.C.: *Fifteenth Annual Report of the Bureau of Ethnology 1893–1894,* pp. 251–313.

———, 1898, The winter solstice ceremony at Walpi. *American Anthropologist* 11: 65–87.

Findlow, Frank J., Victoria C. Bennett, Jonathan E. Erikson, and Suzanne P. De Atley, 1975, A new obsidian hydration rate for certain obsidians in the American Southwest. *American Antiquity* 40: 344–348.

Fitting, James, E., ed., 1973, *The development of North American archaeology.* Garden City, N.Y.: Anchor Press.

Flannery, Kent V., 1965, The ecology of early food production in Mesopotamia. *Science* 147: 1247–1255.

———, 1966, The postglacial "readaptation" as viewed from Mesoamerica. *American Antiquity* 31: 800–805.

———, 1967, Vertebrate fauna and hunting patterns. In *The prehistory of the Tehuacan Valley,* Vol. 1, Douglas S. Byers, ed., Austin: University of Texas Press, pp. 132–177.

———, 1968, Archeological systems theory and early Mesoamerica. In *Anthropological archeology in the Americas,* Betty J. Meggers, ed., Anthropological Society of Washington, pp. 67–87.

———, 1969, Origins and ecological effects of early domestication in Iran and the Near East. In *The domestication and exploitation of plants and animals,* P. J. Ucko and G. W. Dimbleby, eds., Chicago: Aldine, pp. 73–100.

———, 1972, The cultural evolution of civilizations. *Annual Review of Ecology and Systematics* 3: 399–426.

———, 1973, Archeology with a capital S. In *Research and theory in current archeology,* Charles L. Redman, ed., New York: Wiley, pp. 47–53.

———, 1976a, Empirical determination of site catchments in Oaxaca and Tehuacan. In *The early Mesoamerican village,* Kent V. Flannery, ed., New York: Academic Press, pp. 103–117.

———, 1976b, The trouble with regional sampling. In *The early Mesoamerican village,* Kent V. Flannery, ed., New York: Academic Press, pp. 159–160.

Flannery, Kent V., and Joyce Marcus, 1976, Formative Oaxaca. *American Scientist* 64: 374–383.

Flannery, Kent V., and Marcus C. Winter, 1976, Analyzing household activities. In *The early Mesoamerican village,* Kent V. Flannery, ed., New York: Academic Press, pp. 34–44.

Flenniken, J. Jeffrey, 1978, Reevaluation of the Lindenmeier Folsom: a replication experiment in lithic technology. *American Antiquity* 43: 473–480.

Fletcher, Roland, 1977, Settlement studies. In *Spatial archaeology,* David L. Clarke, ed., New York: Academic Press, pp. 47–162.

Ford, James A., 1952, Measurements of some prehistoric design developments in the Southeastern states. *Anthropological Papers of the American Museum of Natural History* 44.

———, 1957, Método cuantitativo para determinar la cronología arquelógica. *Divulgaciones Etnólogicas* 6, Columbia, S.A. pp. 9–22.

Ford, James A., and Clarence H. Webb, 1956, Poverty Point, a late Archaic site in Louisiana. *Anthropological Papers of the American Museum of Natural History* 46, pp. 5–136.

Forde, Daryll C., 1963, *Habitat, economy and society: a geographical introduction to ethnology.* New York: Dutton.

Fowler, Don D., 1977, Models and Great Basin prehistory—introductory remarks. In Models and Great Basin prehistory: a symposium, Don D. Fowler, ed., *Desert Research Institute Publications in the Social Sciences,* No. 12, pp. 3–10.

Fowler, Don D., and Catherine S. Fowler, eds., 1971, Anthropology of the Numa: John Wesley Powell's manuscripts on the Numic peoples of western North America, 1868–1880. Washington: *Smithsonian Contributions to Anthropology,* No. 14.

Fowler, Melvin L., and Richard S. MacNeish, 1972, Excavations in the Coxcatlan locality in the alluvial slopes. In *The prehistory of the Tehuacan Valley,* vol. 5, Richard S. MacNeish, Melvin L. Fowler, Angel Garcia Cook, Frederick A. Peterson, Antoinette Nelken-Terner, and James A. Neely, eds., Austin: University of Texas Press, pp. 219–340.

Freeman, Leslie G., Jr., 1962, Statistical analysis of painted pottery types from Upper Little Colorado drainage. In Chapters on the prehistory of eastern Arizona I, Paul J. Martin and others, eds., *Fieldiana Anthropology* vol. 53, pp. 87–104.

———, 1977, Paleolithic archeology and paleoanthropology in China. In Paleoanthropology in the People's Republic of China, W. W. Howells and Patricia Jones Tsuchitani, eds., *Committee on Scholarly Communication with the People's Republic of China,* Report No. 4, Washington, D.C.: National Academy of Sciences.

Freeman, Leslie G., Jr., and James A. Brown, 1964, Statistical analysis of Carter Ranch pottery. In Chapters in the prehistory of eastern Arizona II, Paul S. Martin and others, eds., *Fieldiana Anthropology,* vol. 55, pp. 126–154.

Fried, Morton H., 1967, *The evolution of political society.* New York: Random House.

Friedman, Irving, and R. L. Smith, 1960, A new dating method using obsidian, part I: the development of the method. *American Antiquity* 25: 476–493.

Friedman, Jonathan, 1974, Marxism, structuralism and vulgar materialism. *Man* 9: 444–469.

Friedrich, Margaret Hardin, 1970, Design structure and social interaction:

archaeological implications of an ethnographic analysis. *American Antiquity* 35: 332–343.

Fritts, H. C., 1976, *Tree rings and climate.* New York: Academic Press.

Fritz, John M., and Fred J. Plog, 1970, The nature of archaeological explanation. *American Antiquity* 35: 405–412.

Frolov, Boris A., 1970, Aspects mathematiques dans l'art préhistorique. *Valcamonica symposium: actes du symposium international d'art préhistorique,* E. Anati, ed. International Symposium on Prehistoric Art (Valcamonica), Capo di Ponte, pp. 475–478.

———, 1971, Die Magische Siebeh in der Altsteinzeit, *Bild der Wissenschaft,* pp. 258–261.

Fuson, R. H., 1969, The orientation of Mayan ceremonial centers. *Annals of the Association of American Geographers* 59: 494–511.

G Garn, Stanley M., and Walter D. Block, 1970, The limited nutritional value of cannibalism. *American Anthropologist* 72: 106.

Geertz, Clifford, 1966, Religion as a cultural system. In Anthropological approaches to the study of religion, Michael Banton, ed., *ASA Monographs,* No. 3, New York: Frederick A. Praeger, pp. 1–46.

———, 1973, *The interpretation of cultures.* New York: Basic Books.

Gentner, W., and H. J. Lippolt, 1969, The potassium-argon dating of Upper Tertiary and Pleistocene deposits. In *Science in archaeology,* Don Brothwell and Eric Higgs, eds., London: Thames and Hudson, pp. 88–100.

Giddings, J. L., 1961, Cultural continuities of Eskimos. *American Antiquity* 27: 155–173.

———, 1966, Cross-dating the archaeology of northwestern Alaska. *Science* 153: 127–135.

Gifford, James C., 1960, The type-variety method of ceramic classification as an indicator of cultural phenomena. *American Antiquity* 25: 341–347.

Goldschmidt, Walter, 1960, *Exploring the ways of mankind.* New York: Holt, Rinehart and Winston.

Goodenough, Ward H., 1957, Cultural anthropology and linguistics. In Report on the seventh annual round table meeting on linguistics and language study, P. Garvin, ed., Washington, D.C.: *Georgetown University Monograph Series in Language and Linguistics,* Vol. 9.

———, 1961, Comment on cultural evolution. *Daedalus* 90: 521–528.

———, 1965, Rethinking "status" and "role": toward a general model of the cultural organization of social relationships. In The relevance of models for social anthropology, Michael Banton, ed., *ASA Monographs,* No. 1, New York: Frederick A. Praeger, pp. 1–24.

———, 1970, *Description and comparison in cultural anthropology.* Chicago: Aldine.

———, 1971, Culture, language, and society. *Addison-Wesley Module in Anthropology* 7: 1–48.

Goodman, Jeffrey, 1977, *Psychic archaeology: time machine to the past.* New York: Putnam.

Gorenstein, Shirley, 1977, History of American archaeology. In Perspectives on anthropology, 1976, *Special Publication of the American Anthropological Association,* No. 10, pp. 86–100.

Gould, Richard A., 1966, Archaeology of the Point St. George site, and Tolowa prehistory. Berkeley: *University of California Publications in Anthropology,* Vol. 4.

Grayson, Donald K., 1973, On the methodology of faunal analysis. *American Antiquity* 38: 432–439.

Griffin, James B., 1959, The pursuit of archaeology in the United States. *American Anthropologist* 61: 379–389.

Gumerman, George J., ed., 1971, The distribution of prehistoric population aggregates. *Prescott College Anthropological Reports,* No. 1, Prescott College Press.

———, 1973, The reconciliation of theory and method in archeology. In *Research and theory in current archeology,* Charles L. Redman, ed., New York: Wiley, pp. 287–299.

Gumerman, George J., and David A. Phillips Jr., 1978, Archaeology beyond anthropology. *American Antiquity* 43: 184–191.

Gunn, Joel, 1975, Idiosyncratic behavior in chipping style: some hypotheses and preliminary analysis. In *Lithic technology: making and using stone tools,* Earl Swanson, ed., The Hague: Mouton, pp. 35–62.

H   Haag, William G., 1959, The status of evolutionary theory in American archeology. In *Evolution and anthropology: a centennial appraisal,* Anthropological Society of Washington, pp. 90–105.

Hall, Robert L., 1976, Ghosts, water barriers, corn, and sacred enclosures in the eastern Woodlands. *American Antiquity* 41: 360–364.

———, 1977, An anthropocentric perspective for eastern United States prehistory. *American Antiquity* 42: 499–518.

Hammond, Norman, 1976, "Introduction" in *Archaeology in northern Belize: 1974–1975 Interim Report of the British Report of the British Museum—Cambridge University Corozal Project,* Norman Hammond, ed., Cambridge: Cambridge University, Center of Latin American Studies.

Hardesty, Donald L., 1977, *Ecological anthropology.* New York: Wiley.

Hardin, Margaret Ann, 1977, Individual style in San José pottery painting: the role of deliberate choice. In *The individual in prehistory,* James N. Hill and Joel Gunn, eds., New York: Academic Press, pp. 109–136.

Harner, Michael, 1977a, The ecological basis for Aztec sacrifice. *American Ethnologist* 4: 117–135.

———, 1977b, The enigma of Aztec sacrifice. *Natural History* LXXXVI: 47–51.

Harper, K. T., and G. M. Alder, 1970, Appendix I: the microscopic plant remains of the deposits of Hogup Cave, Utah, and their paleoclimatic implications. In Hogup Cave, by C. Melvin Aikens, *University of Utah Anthropological Papers,* No. 93, pp. 215–240.

———, 1972, Paleoclimatic inferences concerning the last 10,000 years from a resampling of Danger Cave, Utah. In *Great Basin cultural ecology: a symposium,* Don D. Fowler, ed., Desert Research Institute Publications in the Social Sciences, No. 8, pp. 13–23.

Harris, D. R., 1972, The origins of agriculture in the tropics. *American Scientist* 60: 180–193.

Harris, Jack S., 1940, The White-Knife Shoshone of Nevada. In *Acculturation in seven American Indian tribes,* Ralph Linton, ed., New York: D. Appleton-Century, pp. 39–118.

Harris, Marvin, 1968a, *The rise of anthropological theory.* New York: Thomas Y. Crowell.

———, 1968b, Comments. In *New perspectives in archeology,* Sally R. Binford and Lewis R. Binford, eds., Chicago: Aldine, pp. 359–361.

———, 1974, *Cows, pigs, wars and witches: the riddles of culture.* New York: Random House.

———, 1975, *Culture, people, nature,* 2nd ed., New York: Thomas Y. Crowell.

Harrison, Peter D., and B. L. Turner II, 1978, *Pre-Hispanic Maya agriculture.* Albuquerque: University of New Mexico Press.

Hassan, F., 1974, Population growth and cultural evolution. *Reviews in Anthropology* 1: 205–212.

———, 1975, Determination of the size, density and growth rate of hunting-gathering populations. In *Population, ecology and social evolution,* S. Polgar, ed., The Hague: Mouton.

Haury, Emil W., 1950, *The stratigraphy and archaeology of Ventana Cave, Arizona.* Albuquerque: University of New Mexico Press and Tucson: University of Arizona Press.

Haury, Emil W., E. B. Sayles, and William W. Wasley, 1959, The Lehner mammoth site, southeastern Arizona, *American Antiquity* 25: 2–30.

Haviland, William A., 1965, Prehistoric settlement at Tikal, Guatemala. *Expedition* 7: 14–23.

———, 1969, A new population estimate for Tikal, Guatemala. *American Antiquity* 34: 429–433.

———, 1970, Tikal, Guatemala and Mesoamerican urbanism. *World Archaeology* 2: 186–198.

———, 1974, *Anthropology.* New York: Holt, Rinehart and Winston.

———, 1978, On Price's presentation of data from Tikal. *Current Anthropology* 19: 180–181.

Hawkes, Jaquetta, 1967, God in the machine. *Antiquity* 41: 174–180.

Hawkins, Gerald S., 1963, Stonehenge decoded. *Nature* 200: 306–308.

————, 1964, Stonehenge: a Neolithic computer, *Nature* 202: 1258–1261.

————, 1965, *Stonehenge decoded.* Garden City, N.Y.: Doubleday.

Hazard, Thomas, 1960, On the nature of Numaym and its counterparts elsewhere on the Northwest Coast. Paper presented to the 127th Annual Meeting of the American Association for the Advancement of Science, Denver, Colorado.

Heizer, Robert F., and M. A. Baumhoff, 1961, The archaeology of two sites at Eastgate, Churchill County, Nevada: Wagon Jack Shelter. Berkeley: *University of California Anthropological Records* 20: 119–149.

————, 1962, *Prehistoric rock art of Nevada and eastern California.* Berkeley: University of California Press.

Heizer, Robert F., and C. W. Clewlow, Jr., 1968, Projectile points from site NV-CH-15, Churchill County, Nevada. Berkeley: *University of California Archaeological Survey Reports,* No. 71: 59–88.

Heizer, Robert F., and John A. Graham, 1967, *A guide to field methods in archaeology: approaches to the anthropology of the dead.* Palo Alto, Calif.: National Press.

Hempel, Carl G., 1959, The logic of functional analysis. In *Symposium on sociological theory,* L. Gross, ed., Evanston, Ill.: Row, Peterson, pp. 271–307.

————, 1965, *Aspects of scientific explanation: other essays in the philosophy of science.* New York: Free Press.

Hester, James J., 1976, *Introduction to archaeology.* New York: Holt, Rinehart and Winston.

Heyerdahl, Thor, 1950, *The Kon-Tiki expedition: by raft across the South Seas.* London: George Allen and Unwin.

————, 1971, *The Ra expeditions.* Garden City, N.Y.: Doubleday.

Hill, James N., 1968, Broken K Pueblo: patterns of form and function. In *New perspectives in archeology,* Sally R. Binford and Lewis R. Binford, eds., Chicago: Aldine, pp. 103–142.

————, 1970a, Prehistoric social organization in the American Southwest: theory and method. In *Reconstructing prehistoric Pueblo societies,* William A. Longacre, ed., Albuquerque: University of New Mexico Press, pp. 11–58.

————, 1970b, Broken K Pueblo: prehistoric social organization in the American Southwest. Tucson: *Anthropological Papers of the University of Arizona,* No. 18.

————, 1977, Individual variability in ceramics and the study of prehistoric social organization. In *The individual in prehistory,* James N. Hill and Joel Gunn, eds., New York: Academic Press, pp. 55–108.

Hill, James N., and Joel Gunn, 1977, *The individual in prehistory: studies of variability in style in prehistoric technologies.* New York: Academic Press.

Hill, James N., and Richard H. Hevly, 1968, Pollen at Broken K Pueblo: some new interpretations. *American Antiquity* 33: 200–210.

Hole, Frank, Kent V. Flannery, and James A. Neely, 1969, Prehistory and human ecology of the Deh Luran Plain: an early village sequence from

Khuzistan, Iran. Ann Arbor: *Memoirs of the Museum of Anthropology, University of Michigan,* No. 1.

Hole, Frank, and Robert F. Heizer, 1973, *An introduction to prehistoric archeology,* 3rd ed., New York: Holt, Rinehart and Winston.

Hole, Frank, and Mary Shaw, 1967, Computer analysis of chronological seriation. Houston, Texas: *Rice University Studies,* Vol. 53.

Hosley, Edward, 1972, Comment on *Upper Paleolithic engraving* by Alexander Marshack. *Current Anthropology* 13: 465–466.

Howard, Hildegarde, 1929, The avifauna of Emeryville shellmound. Berkeley: *University of California Publications in Zoology,* 32: 301–394.

Hoyle, Fred, 1966a, Stonehenge—an eclipse predictor. *Nature* 211: 454–456.

——, 1966b, Speculations on Stonehenge. *Antiquity* 40: 262–276.

Huxley, Julian, ed., 1940, *The new systematics.* Oxford: Clarendon Press.

I Isaac, Glynn L., Richard E. Leakey, and Anna K. Behrensmeyer, 1971, Archaeological traces of early hominid activities, east of Lake Rudolph, Kenya. *Science,* 173: 1129–1133.

Iversen, J., 1956, Forest clearance in the Stone Age. *Scientific American* 194: 36–41.

J Jarman, H. N., A. J. Legge, and J. A. Charles, 1972. Retrieval of plant remains from archaeological sites by froth flotation. In *Papers in economic prehistory,* E. S. Higgs, ed., Cambridge: Cambridge University Press, pp. 39–48.

Jefferson, Thomas, 1787, *Notes on the State of Virginia.* London: John Stockdale (reprinted Chapel Hill: University of North Carolina Press, 1954).

Jennings, Jesse D., 1957, Danger Cave. Salt Lake City: *University of Utah Anthropological Papers,* No. 27.

Jeppson, Lawrence, 1970, *The fabulous frauds, fascinating tales of great art forgeries.* New York: Waybright and Talley.

Johnson, Gregory A., 1972, A test of the utility of central place theory in archaeology. In *Man, settlement and urbanism,* P. J. Ucko, R. Tringham, and G. W. Dimbleby, eds., London: Duckworth, pp. 769–785.

——, 1975, Locational analysis and Uruk local exchange systems. In *Ancient civilization and trade,* Jeremy A. Sabloff and C. C. Lamberg-Karlovsky, eds., Albuquerque: University of New Mexico Press, pp. 285–339.

Johnson, LeRoy, Jr., 1968, Item seriation as an aid for elementary scale and cluster analysis. Eugene: *University of Oregon Museum of Natural History Bulletin,* No. 15.

——, 1969, Obsidian hydration rate for the Klamath Basin of California and Oregon. *Science* 165: 1354–1356.

——, 1972, Problems in "avant-garde" archaeology, *American Anthropologist* 74: 366–377.

Jones, Olive, 1971, Glass bottle push-ups and pontil marks. *Historical Archaeology* 5: 62–73.

Judge, W. James, 1973, *Paleoindian occupation of the central Rio Grande Valley in New Mexico.* Albuquerque: University of New Mexico Press.

Judge, W. James, James I. Ebert, and Robert K. Hitchcock, 1975, Sampling in regional archaeological survey. In *Sampling in archaeology,* James W. Mueller, ed., Tucson: University of Arizona Press, pp. 82–123.

K Keeley, Lawrence H., 1974, Technique and methodology in microwear studies: a critical review. *World Archaeology* 5: 323–336.

Keesing, Roger M., 1974, Theories of culture. Palo Alto, Calif.: *Annual Review of Anthropology* 3: 73–97.

———, 1976, *Cultural anthropology: a contemporary perspective.* New York: Holt, Rinehart and Winston.

Kehoe, Alice B., and Thomas F. Kehoe, 1973, Cognitive models for archaeological interpretation. *American Antiquity* 38: 150–154.

Kelley, Jane Holden, 1977, Comment on Schiffer and House. *Current Anthropology* 18: 57.

Kemeny, John G., 1959, *A philosopher looks at science.* New York: Van Nostrand Reinhold.

Kessler, Evelyn S., 1972, Comment on *Upper Paleolithic engraving* by Alexander Marshack. *Current Anthropology* 13: 466.

Kidder, Alfred V., 1924, *An introduction to the study of Southwestern archaeology.* New Haven: Yale University Press.

———, 1928, *The present state of knowledge of American history and civilization prior to 1492.* Paris: International Congress of History, Oslo, 1928, Compte Rendu, pp. 749–753.

King, Thomas F., 1971, A conflict of values in American archaeology. *American Antiquity* 36: 255–262.

———, 1976, Review of *Public archaeology* by Charles McGimsey. *American Antiquity* 41: 236–238.

———, 1977, Issues on contract archaeology. *Archaeology* 30: 352–353.

King, Thomas F., Patricia Parker Hickman, and Gary Berg, 1977, *Anthropology in historic preservation: caring for culture's clutter.* New York: Academic Press.

Kish, Leslie, 1965, *Survey sampling.* New York: Wiley.

Kluckhohn, Clyde, 1942, Myths and rituals: a general theory. *Harvard Theological Review* 35: 45–79.

Koike, Hiroko, 1975, The use of daily and annual growth lines in the clam *Meretrix lusoria* in estimating seasons of Jomon period shell gathering. In *Quaternary studies,* R. P. Suggate and M. M. Cresswell, eds., Wellington: The Royal Society of New Zealand, pp. 189–193.

Kroeber, Alfred L., 1955, On human nature. *Southwestern Journal of Anthropology* 11: 195–204.

Kroeber, Alfred L., and Clyde Kluckhohn, 1952, Culture: a critical review of concepts and definitions. *Papers of the Peabody Museum of American Archaeology and Ethnology,* Vol. XLVII.

Kurtén, Bjorn, 1972, Comment on *Upper Paleolithic engraving* by Alexander Marshack. *Current Anthropology* 13: 466.

L Lane, Rebecca A., and Audrey J. Sublett, 1972, Osteology of social organization: residence pattern. *American Antiquity* 37: 186–201.

Lathrap, Donald W., 1973, Gifts of the Cayman: some thoughts on the subsistence basis of Chavin. In *Variation in anthropology,* Donald W. Lathrop and Jody Douglas, eds., Urbana: Illinois Archaeological Survey, pp. 91–105.

Layton, Thomas N., 1973, Temporal ordering of surface-collected obsidian artifacts by hydration measurement. *Archaeometry* 15: 129–132.

LeBlanc, Steven A., 1975, Micro-seriation: a method for fine chronologic differentiation. *American Antiquity* 40: 22–38.

LeBlanc, Steven A., and P. J. Watson, 1973, A comparative statistical analysis of painted pottery from seven Halafian sites. *Paleorient* I: 117–133.

Lee, Richard B., 1969, !Kung Bushman subsistence: an input-output analysis. In *Environment and cultural behavior,* A. P. Vayda, ed., Garden City, N.Y.: Natural History Press.

Lee, Richard B., and Irvin DeVore, 1968, *Man the hunter.* Chicago: Aldine.

Leone, Mark P., 1972, Issues in anthropological archaeology. In *Contemporary archaeology: a guide to theory and contributions,* Mark P. Leone, ed., Carbondale: Southern Illinois University Press, pp. 14–27.

Leroi-Gourhan, Arlette, 1975, The flowers found with Shanidar IV, a Neanderthal burial in Iraq. *Science* 190: 562–564.

Levi-Strauss, Claude, 1963a, *Structural anthropology,* New York: Basic Books, (reprinted 1967, New York: Anchor Books).

———, 1963b, Review of George G. Simpson's *Principles of animal taxonomy. L'homme* 3: 140.

———, 1969a, *The elementary structures of kinship,* 2nd ed., Boston: Beacon Press.

———, 1969b, *The raw and the cooked.* New York: Harper Torchbooks.

———, 1970, *Tristes tropiques: an anthropological study of primitive societies in Brazil.* New York: Atheneum.

Linton, Ralph, 1936, *The study of man: an introduction.* New York: D. Appleton-Century.

Lipe, William D., 1974, A conservation model for American archaeology. *Kiva* 39: 214–245.

Lipe, William D., and Alexander J. Lindsay, eds., 1974, Proceedings of the 1974 cultural resource management conference. *Museum of Northern Arizona Technical Series* 14.

Lipe, William D., and R. G. Matson, 1971, Human settlement and resources in the Cedar Mesa area, southeastern Utah. In *The distribution of prehistoric population aggregates,* George J. Gumerman, ed., Prescott College Press, pp. 126–151.

Loendorf, Lawrence L., 1973, Prehistoric settlement patterns in the Prior Mountains, Montana. Ph.D. diss., University of Missouri, Columbia, Mo.

Logan, Michael H., and William T. Sanders, 1976, The model. In *The Valley of Mexico,* Eric R. Wolf, ed. Albuquerque: University of New Mexico Press, pp. 31–58.

Lomax, Alan, and Conrad M. Arensberg, 1977, A worldwide evolutionary classification of cultures by subsistence systems. *Current Anthropology* 18: 659–708.

Longacre, William A., 1964, Archeology as anthropology: a case study. *Science* 144: 1454–1455.

———, 1968, Some aspects of prehistoric society in east-central Arizona. In *New perspectives in archeology,* Sally R. Binford and Lewis R. Binford, eds., Chicago: Aldine, pp. 89–102.

———, 1970, Archaeology as anthropology: a case study. Tucson: *University of Arizona Anthropological Papers,* No. 17.

Lorrain, Dessamae, 1968, An archaeologst's guide to nineteenth-century American glass. *Historical Archaeology,* II: 35–44.

Lowie, Robert H., 1948, *Social organization.* New York: Holt, Rinehart and Winston.

Lynch, Thomas F. 1972, Comment on *Upper Paleolithic engraving* by Alexander Marshack. *Current Anthropology* 13: 466–467.

M MacNeish, Richard S., 1964, Ancient Mesoamerican civilization. *Science* 143: 531–537.

———, 1967, A summary of the subsistence. In *The prehistory of the Tehuacan Valley,* vol. 1, Douglas S. Byers, ed., Austin: University of Texas Press, pp. 290–309.

———, 1972, Summary of the cultural sequence and its implications in the Tehuacan Valley. In *The prehistory of the Tehuacan Valley,* vol. 5, Richard S. MacNeish, Melvin L. Fowler, Angel Garcia Cook, Frederick A. Peterson, Antoinette Nelken-Terner, and James A. Neely, Austin: University of Texas Press, pp. 496–504.

———, 1978, *The science of archaeology?* North Scituate, Mass.: Duxbury Press.

MacNeish, Richard S., Frederick A. Peterson, and James A. Neely, 1972, The archaeological reconnaissance. In *The prehistory of the Tehuacan Valley,* vol. 5, Richard S. MacNeish, Melvin L. Fowler, Angel Garcia Cook, Frederick A. Peterson, Antoinette Nelken-Terner, and James A. Neely, Austin: University of Texas Press, pp. 341–495.

MacNeish, Richard S., Melvin L. Fowler, Angel Garcia Cook, Frederick A. Peterson, Antoinette Nelken-Terner, and James A. Neely, 1972, Excavations and reconnaissance. In *The prehistory of the Tehuacan Valley,* vol. 5 Austin: University of Texas Press.

Malinowski, Bronislaw, 1961 (original, 1922), *Argonauts of the Western Pacific.* New York: Dutton.

Marcus, Joyce, 1973, Territorial organization of the lowland Classic Maya. *Science* 180: 911–916.

————, 1976, *Emblem and state in the Classic Maya lowlands: an epigraphic approach to territorial organization.* Washington, D. C.: Dumbarton Oaks.

Marshack, Alexander, 1972a, *The roots of civilization.* New York: McGraw-Hill.

————, 1972b, Upper Paleolithic notation and symbol. *Science* 178: 817–828.

————, 1976, Implications of the Paleolithic symbolic evidence for the origin of language. *American Scientist* 64: 136–145.

Martin, Paul S., 1954, Comments on *Southwestern archaeology: its history and theory* by Walter W. Taylor. *American Anthropologist* 56: 570–572.

Matson, R. G., 1971, Adaption and environment in the Cerbat Mountains, Arizona, Ph.D. diss., University of California, Davis.

Mayer-Oakes, William J., 1955, Prehistory of the upper Ohio Valley. Pittsburgh: *Annals of the Carnegie Museum,* Vol. 34.

Mayer-Oakes, W. J., and R. J. Nash, 1965, Archeological research design—a critique. Department of Anthropology, University of Manitoba Mimeograph.

Mayes, P., 1962, The firing of a pottery kiln of Romano-British type at Boston, Lincs. *Archaeometry* 4: 4–18.

McDonald, William A., 1967, *Progress into the past: the rediscovery of Mycenean civilization.* New York: Macmillan.

McGimsey, Charles R., III, 1972, *Public archeology.* New York: Seminar Press.

McHargue, Georges, and Michael Roberts, 1977, *A field guide to conservation archaeology in North America.* Philadelphia: Lippincott.

Meggers, Betty J., 1955, The coming of age in American archeology. In *New interpretations of aboriginal American culture history,* Anthropological Society of Washington, pp. 116–129.

————, 1956, Functional and evolutionary implications of community patterning. In Seminars in archaeology, *Society for American Archaeology Memoir* No. 11, pp. 129–157.

————, ed., 1968, *Anthropological archeology in the Americas,* Anthropological Society of Washington.

————, 1971, *Amazonia: man and nature in a counterfeit paradise.* Chicago: Aldine.

Mehringer, Peter J., 1977, Great Basin late Quaternary environments and chronology. In Models and Great Basin prehistory: a symposium, Don D. Fowler, ed., *Desert Research Institute Publications in the Social Sciences,* No. 12, pp. 113–167.

Mehringer, Peter J., and Vance Haynes, 1965, The pollen evidence for the environment of early man and extinct mammals at the Lehner mammoth site, southeastern Arizona. *American Antiquity* 31: 17–23.

Meyers, J. T., 1971, The origins of agriculture: an evaluation of hypotheses. In *Prehistoric agriculture,* S. Struever, ed., Garden City, N.Y.: Natural History Press, pp. 101–121.

Michels, Joseph W., 1973, *Dating methods in archaeology.* New York: Seminar Press.

Michels, Joseph W., and Carl A. Bebrich, 1971, Obsidian hydration dating. In *Dating techniques for the archaeologist,* Henry N. Michael and Elizabeth K. Ralph, eds., Cambridge, Mass.: MIT Press, pp. 164–221.

Michener, James A., 1974, *Centennial.* New York: Random House.

Miller, J. A., 1969, Dating by the potassium-argon method—some advances in technique. In *Science in archaeology,* Don Brothwell and Eric Higgs, eds., London: Thames and Hudson, pp. 101–105.

Millon, René, 1973, *Urbanization at Teotihuacán, Mexico.,* Vol I., *The Teotihuacán map.* Austin: University of Texas Press.

Moore, Clarence B., 1905, Certain aboriginal remains of the Black Warrior River. *Journal of the Academy of Natural Sciences of Philadelphia,* second series, 13: 121–244.

———, 1907, Moundville revisited. *Journal of the Academy of Natural Sciences of Philadelphia,* second series, 13: 334–405.

———, 1913, Some aboriginal sites in Louisiana and Arkansas, *Journal of the Academy of Natural Sciences of Philadelphia,* second series, 16: 5–93.

Morgan, Lewis Henry, 1877, *Ancient society,* New York: World Publishers.

Morison, Samuel Eliot, 1974, *The European discovery of America: the southern voyages A.D. 1492–1616.* New York: Oxford University Press.

Morris, Ann Axtell, 1933, *Digging in the Southwest:* New York: Doubleday.

Morss, Noel, 1931, The ancient culture of the Fremont River in Utah. *Papers of the Peabody Museum of Archaeology and Ethnology* 12.

Mueller, James W., 1974, The use of sampling in archaeological survey. *Society for American Archaeology Memoir* No. 28.

———, ed., 1975, *Sampling in archaeology.* Tucson: University of Arizona Press.

Muller, Jon, 1977, Individual variations in art styles. In *The individual in prehistory,* James N. Hill and Joel Gunn, eds., New York: Academic Press, pp. 23–39.

Murdock, George Peter, 1949, *Social structure.* New York: Macmillan.

Murphy, Robert F., 1976, The quest for cultural reality: adventures in Irish social anthropology. *Michigan Discussions in Anthropology,* vol. 1, pp. 48–64.

N Napton, Lewis K., 1969, Archaeological and paleobiological investigations in Lovelock Cave, Nevada: further analysis of human coprolites. Berkeley: *The Kroeber Anthropological Society Papers, Special Publications,* No. 2.

Naroll, Raoul, 1956, A preliminary index of social development. *American Anthropologist* 58: 687–715.

Nelson, Nels. C., 1909, Shellmounds of the San Francisco Bay Region. *University of California Publications in American Archaeology and Ethnology* 7: 310–356.

———, 1916, Chronology of the Tano Ruins, New Mexico. *American Anthropologist* 18: 159–180.

Netting, Robert McC., 1977, Maya subsistence: mythologies, analogies, possibilities. In *The origins of Maya civilization,* Richard E. W. Adams, ed., Albuquerque: University of New Mexico Press, pp. 229–333.

Nuttall, Z., 1906, The astronomical methods of the ancient Mexicans. *In Boas Anniversary Volume,* Berthold Laufer, ed., New York: Stechert, pp. 290–298.

O Oakley, Kenneth P., 1964, The problem of man's antiquity: an historical survey. London: *Bulletin of the British Museum, Geology* 9: 83–155.

O'Connell, James F., 1975, The prehistory of Surprise Valley. *Ballena Press Anthropological Papers,* No. 4.

Odum, Eugene P., 1971, *Fundamentals of ecology,* 3rd ed., Philadelphia: Saunders.

Olsen, Stanley J., 1960, Post-cranial skeletal characters of bison and bos. *Papers of the Peabody Museum of Archaeology and Ethnology* 35: 4.

———, 1964, Mammal remains from archaeological sites, part 1, southeastern and southwestern United States. *Papers of the Peabody Museum of Archaeology and Ethnology* 61: 1.

———, 1968, Fish, amphibian, and reptile remains from archaeological sites, part 1, southeastern and southwestern United States. *Papers of the Peabody Museum of Archaeology and Ethnology* 61: 2.

Ortiz de Montellano, Bernard R., 1978, Aztec cannibalism: an ecological necessity? *Science* 200: 611–617.

P Parsons, Elsie Clews, 1925, A Pueblo Indian journal, 1920–1921. *Memoirs of the American Anthropological Association,* No. 32.

Parsons, Jeffrey, 1971, Prehistoric settlement patterns of the Texcoco region, Mexico. *Memoirs of the Museum of Anthropology,* University of Michigan, No. 3.

Peake, Harold, and Herbert John Fleure, 1927, *Peasants and potters.* London: Oxford University Press.

Peebles, Christopher S., 1971, Moundville and surrounding sites: some structural considerations of mortuary practices II. In Approaches to the social dimensions of mortuary practices, James A. Brown, ed., *Society of American Archaeology Memoir* No. 25, pp. 68–91.

———, 1974, Moundville: the organization of a prehistoric community and culture. Ph.D. diss., University of California, Santa Barbara.

———, 1977, Biocultural adaptation in prehistoric America: an archeologist's perspective. In Biocultural adaptation in prehistoric America, Robert L. Blakely, ed., *Southern Anthropological Society Proceedings,* No. 11, Athens: University of Georgia Press, pp. 115–130.

———, 1978, The determinants of settlement size and location in the Moundville phase. In *Mississippian settlement patterns,* Bruce Smith, ed., New York: Academic Press.

Peebles, Christopher S., and Susan M. Kus, 1977, Some archaeological correlates of ranked societies. *American Antiquity* 42: 421–448.

Perkins, Dexter, and Patricia Daly, 1968, A hunter's village in Neolithic Turkey. *Scientific American* 219: 96–106.

Petrie, W. M. F., 1899, Sequences in prehistoric remains. *Journal Royal Anthropological Institute* (new series) 29: 295–301.

Pfeiffer, John E., 1977, *The emergence of society: a prehistory of the establishment.*
New York: McGraw-Hill.

Phillips, E. D., 1964, The Greek vision of prehistory. *Antiquity* 38: 171–186.

Piddocke, Stuart, 1965, The potlatch system of the south Kwakiutl: a new
perspective. *Southwestern Journal of Anthropology* 21: 244–264.

Plog, Stephen, 1976, The inference of prehistoric social organization from
ceramic design variability. *Michigan Discussions in Anthropology* 1: 1–47.

Polgar, S., 1972, Population history and population policies from an anthropological perspective. *Current Anthropology* 13: 203–209.

Price, Barbara J., 1977, Shifts in production and organization: a cluster-interac-
tion model. *Current Anthropology* 18: 209–233.

Pyne, Nanette M., 1976, The fire-serpent and were-jaguar in Formative Oaxaca:
a contingency table analysis. In *The early Mesoamerican village,* Kent V.
Flannery, ed., New York: Academic Press, pp. 272–282.

R Ragir, Sonia, 1967, A review of techniques for archaeological sampling. In *A
guide to field methods in archaeology,* Robert F. Heizer and John A. Graham,
eds., Palo Alto, Calif.: National Press, pp. 181–197.

Rahtz, P. A., ed., 1974, Rescue archaeology. London: Penguin.

Ralph, Elizabeth K, 1971, Carbon-14 dating. In *Dating techniques for the
archaeologist,* Henry N. Michael and Elizabeth K. Ralph, eds., Cambridge,
Mass.: MIT Press, pp. 1–48.

Ralph, Elizabeth K., Henry N. Michael, and M. C. Han, 1973, Radiocarbon
dates and reality. *MASCA Newsletter* 9: 1–20.

Rapaport, Anatol, 1959, Uses and limitations of mathematical models in social
science. In *Symposium on sociological theory,* L. Gross, ed., Evanston, Ill.:
Row, Peterson, pp. 348–372.

Rappaport, Roy A., 1971a, Nature, culture, and ecological anthropology. In
Man, culture and society, Harry L. Shapiro, ed., New York: Oxford University Press, pp. 237–267.

———, 1971b, Ritual, sanctity and cybernetics. *American Anthropologist* 73: 59–
76.

Rathje, William L., 1971, The origin and development of lowland Classic Maya
civilization. *American Antiquity* 36: 275–285.

———, 1974, The garbage project: a new way of looking at the problems of
archaeology. *Archaeology* 27: 236–241.

———, 1975, Le projet du garbage 1975: historic trade-offs. Paper presented at
the annual meeting of the American Anthropological Association, San
Francisco.

Rathje, William L., and Wilson W. Hughes, 1975, The garbage project as a nonreactive approach: garbage in . . . garbage out. In Perspectives on attitude assessment, H. W. Sinaiko and L. A. Broedling, eds., *Manpower Research and Advisory Services, Smithsonian Institution, Technical Report* No. 2.

Rathje, William L., and Michael McCarthy, 1977, Regularity and variability in contemporary garbage. In *Research strategies in historic archeology,* Stanley South, ed., New York: Academic Press, pp. 261–286.

Read, Piers Paul, 1974, *Alive: the story of the Andes survivors.* Philadelphia: Lippincott.

Redman, Charles L., 1977, The "analytical individual" and prehistoric style variability. In *The individual in prehistory,* James N. Hill and Joel Gunn, eds., New York: Academic Press, pp. 41–53.

Reed, Charles A., 1963, Osteo-archaeology. In *Science in archaeology,* Don Brothwell and Eric Higgs, eds., New York: Basic Books, pp. 204–216.

Renfrew, Colin, 1971, Carbon-14 and the prehistory of Europe. *Scientific American* 225: 63–72.

———, 1973, *Before civilization: the radiocarbon revolution and prehistoric Europe.* New York: Alfred A. Knopf.

Riddell, Harry S., Jr., 1951, The archaeology of a Paiute village site in Owens Valley. Berkeley: *University of California Archaeological Survey Reports,* No. 12, pp. 14–28.

Rosenfeld, Andrée, 1972, Comment on Marshack. *Antiquity* 46: 65.

Rossman, David L., 1976, A site catchment analysis of San Lorenzo, Veracruz. In *The early Mesoamerican village,* Kent V. Flannery, ed., New York: Academic Press, pp. 95–103.

Rouse, Irving, 1960, The classification of artifacts in archaeology. *American Antiquity* 25: 313–323.

———, 1970, Classification for what? Comments on *Analytical archaeology. Norwegian Archaeological Review* (Oslo) 3: 4–34.

Rowe, John Howland, 1965, The renaissance foundations of anthropology. *American Anthropologist* 67: 1–20.

Rudner, Richard S., 1966, *Philosophy of social science.* Englewood Cliffs, N.J.: Prentice-Hall.

Ryder, M. L., 1969, *Animal bones in archaeology.* Oxford: Blackwell Scientific Publications.

S Sahlins, Marshall D., and Elman R. Service, 1960, *Evolution and culture.* Ann Arbor: University of Michigan Press.

Salmon, Merrilee H., 1975, Confirmation and explanation in archaeology. *American Antiquity* 40: 459–464.

———, 1976, "Deductive" versus "inductive" archaeology. *American Antiquity* 41: 276–381.

Sanders, William T., 1965, The cultural ecology of the Teotihuacán Valley: a preliminary report of the results of the Teotihuacán Valley project. Master's thesis, Department of Sociology and Anthropology, Pennsylvania State University.

———, 1972, Population, agriculture, history, and societal evolution in Mesoamerica. In *Population growth: anthropological implications,* Brian Spooner, ed., Cambridge, Mass.: MIT Press, pp. 101–153.

———, 1973, The cultural ecology of the lowland Maya: a reevaluation. In *The Classic Maya collapse,* T. Patrick Culbert, ed., Albuquerque: University of New Mexico Press, pp. 325–365.

———, 1977, Environmental heterogeneity and the evolution of lowland Maya civilization. In *The origins of Maya civilization,* Richard E. W. Adams, ed., Albuquerque: University of New Mexico Press, pp. 287–297.

Sanders, William T., and Barbara J. Price, 1968, *Mesoamerica: the evolution of a civilization.* New York: Random House.

Saraydar, S., and I. Shimada, 1971, A quantitative comparison of efficiency between a stone axe and a steel axe. *American Antiquity* 36: 216–217.

Schalk, Randall F., 1977, The structure of an anadromous fish resource. In *For theory building in archaeology,* Lewis R. Binford, ed., New York: Academic Press, pp. 207–249.

Schiffer, Michael B., 1972, Archaeological context and systemic context. *American Antiquity* 37: 156–165.

———, 1976, *Behavioral Archeology.* New York: Academic Press.

———, 1977, Toward a unified science of the cultural past. In *Research strategies in historical archeology,* Stanley South, ed., New York: Academic Press, pp. 13–40.

Schiffer, Michael B., and George J. Gumerman, 1977, *Conservation archaeology: a guide for cultural resource management studies.* New York: Academic Press.

Schiffer, Michael B., and James H. House, 1977, Cultural resource management and archaeological research: the cache project. *Current Anthropology* 18: 43–68.

Schliemann, Heinrich, 1875, *Troy and its remains.* New York: Scribner, Welford and Armstrong.

———, 1880, *Ilios: the city and country of the Trojans.* London: John Murray.

Scholte, Bob, 1973, The structural anthropology of Claude Levi-Strauss. In *Handbook of social and cultural anthropology,* John J. Honigmann, ed., Chicago: Rand McNally, pp. 637–716.

Schuchhardt, C., 1891, *Schliemann's excavations: an archaeological and historical study.* London: Macmillan.

Schwartz, Douglas W., 1968, North American archaeology in historical perspective. In *Actes du XIᵉ Congres International d'Historie de Sciences,* vol. 2, Warsaw and Cracow, pp. 311–315.

Service, Elman, 1962, *Primitive social organization.* New York: Random House.

———, 1968, Prime mover of cultural evolution. *Southwestern Journal of Anthropology* 24: 396–409.

———, 1971, *Primitive social organization: an evolutionary perspective,* 2nd ed., New York: Random House.

Shepard, Anna O., 1956, Ceramics for the archaeologist. Washington, D.C.: *Carnegie Institution of Washington Publication* 609.

Shotwell, J. Arnold, 1955, An approach to the paleoecology of mammals. *Ecology* 36: 327–337.

Sieveking, Ann, 1972, Review of *The roots of civilization* by Alexander Marshack. *Antiquity* 46: 329–330.

Silverberg, Robert, 1968, *Mound builders of ancient America.* Greenwich, Conn.: New York Graphic Society.

Solecki, Ralph S., 1971, *Shanidar: the first flower people.* New York: Alfred A. Knopf.

South, Stanley, 1977, *Method and theory in historica archeology.* New York: Academic Press.

Spencer, Herbert, 1887, *First principles.* London: Williams and Norgate.

Speth, John D., and Gregory A. Johnson, 1976, Problems in the use of correlation for the investigation of tool kits and activity areas. In *Cultural change and continuity: essays in honor of James Bennett Griffin,* Charles E. Cleland, ed., New York: Academic Press, pp. 35–57.

Spier, Leslie, 1931, N. C. Nelson's stratigraphic technique in the reconstruction of prehistoric sequences in southwestern America. In *Methods in social science,* S. A. Rice, ed., University of Chicago Press, pp. 275–283.

Spooner, B., ed., 1972, *Population growth: anthropological implications.* Cambridge, Mass.: MIT Press.

Stanislawski, Michael B., 1972, Review of *Archaeology as anthropology* by William A. Longacre. *American Antiquity* 38: 117–122.

Steponaitis, Vincas P., 1978, Locational theory and complex chiefdoms: a Mississippian example. In *Mississippian settlement patterns,* Bruce Smith, ed., New York: Academic Press.

Steward, Julian H., 1937a, Ecological aspects of southwestern society. *Anthropos* 32: 87–104.

———, 1937b, Ancient caves of the Great Salt Lake region. *Review of American Ethnology Bulletin* 116.

———, 1938, Basin-plateau aboriginal sociopolitical groups. Washington, D.C.: *Bureau of American Ethnology Bulletin* 120.

———, 1951, Levels of sociocultural integration: an operational concept. *Southwestern Journal of Anthropology* 7: 374–390.

———, 1953, Evolution and process. In *Anthropology today,* Alfred L. Kroeber, ed., University of Chicago Press, pp. 313–326.

———, 1954, Types of types. *American Anthropologist* 56: 54–57.

———, 1955, Theory of culture change. Urbana: University of Illinois Press.

Stewart, T. D., 1973, *The people of America.* New York: Charles Scribner's Sons.

Stoltman, James B., 1966, New radiocarbon dates for southeastern fiber-tempered pottery. *American Antiquity* 31: 872–874.

Stone, Irving, 1975, *The Greek treasure.* Garden City, N.Y.: Doubleday.

Struever, Stuart, 1964, The Hopewell interaction in riverine-western Great

Lakes cultural history. *Illinois State Museum Scientific Papers,* Vol. 12, pp. 85–106.

———, 1968a, Flotation techniques for the recovery of small-scale archaeological remains. *American Antiquity* 33: 353–362.

———, 1968b, Woodland subsistence settlement systems in the lower Illinois valley. In *New perspectives in archeology,* Sally R. Binford and Lewis R. Binford, eds., Chicago: Aldine, pp. 285–312.

Struever, Stuart, and John Carlson, 1977, Koster site: the new archaeology in action. *Archaeology* 30: 93–101.

Stuiver, Minze, Calvin J. Heusser, and In Che Yang, 1978, North American glacial history extended to 75,000 years ago. *Science* 200: 16–21.

Sturtevant, William, 1964, Studies in ethnoscience. *American Anthropologist* 66: 99–131.

Suttles, Wayne, 1960, Affinial ties, subsistence and prestige among the coast Salish. *American Anthropologist* 62: 296–305.

T Tatje, Terrance A., and Raoul Naroll, 1970, Two measures of societal complexity: an empirical cross-cultural comparison. In *A handbook of method in cultural anthropology,* Raoul Naroll and Ronald Cohen, eds., New York: Natural History Press, pp. 766–833.

Taylor, Walter W., 1948, A study of archeology. *American Anthropological Association, Memoir 69.*

———, 1972, Old wine and new skins: a contemporary parable. In *Contemporary archaeology,* Mark P. Leone, ed., Carbondale: Southern Illinois University Press, pp. 28–33.

Thom, Alexander, 1966, Megaliths and mathematics. *Antiquity* 40: 121–128.

———, 1967, *Megalithic sites in Britain.* London: Clarendon Press.

———, 1971, *Megalithic lunar observations.* Oxford: Clarendon Press.

Thomas, David Hurst, 1969, Great Basin hunting patterns: a quantitative method for treating faunal remains. *American Antiquity* 34: 392–401.

———, 1971, On the use of cumulative curves and numerical taxonomy. *American Antiquity* 36: 206–209.

———, 1972a, Western Shoshone ecology: settlement patterns and beyond. In Great Basin cultural ecology, a symposium, Don D. Fowler, ed., *Desert Research Institute Publications in the Social Sciences,* No. 8, pp. 135–153.

———, 1972b, A computer simulation model of Great Basin Shoshonean subsistence and settlement patterns. In *Models in archaeology,* David L. Clarke, ed., London: Methuen, pp. 671–704.

———, 1973, An empirical test for Steward's model of Great Basin settlement patterns. *American Antiquity* 38: 155–176.

———, 1974, *Predicting the past: an introduction to anthropological archaeology.* New York: Holt, Rinehart and Winston.

———, 1976, *Figuring anthropology: first principles of probability and statistics.* New York: Holt, Rinehart and Winston.

————, 1978, The awful truth about statistics in archaeology. *American Antiquity* 43: 231–244.

————, n.d., Archaeology of Gatecliff Shelter. *Anthropology Papers of the American Museum of Natural History* (in preparation).

Thomas, David Hurst, and Robert L. Bettinger, 1976, Prehistoric piñon ecotone settlements of the upper Reese River Valley, central Nevada. *Anthropological Papers of the American Museum of Natural History* 53: 263–366.

Thomas, David Hurst, and Clark Spencer Larsen, 1979, The anthropology of St. Catherines Island: II. The Refuge-Deptford mortuary complex. *Anthropological Papers of the American Museum of Natural History.*

Thompson, J. E. S., 1974, Maya astronomy. London: *Philosophical Transactions of the Royal Society* 276: 83–98.

Thompson, F. O. H., 1975, Rescue archaeology: research or rubbish collection? *Antiquity* 49: 43–45.

Titiev, Mischa, 1960, A fresh approach to the problem of magic and religion. *Southwestern Journal of Anthropology* 16: 292–298.

Trigger, Bruce G., 1971, Archaeology and ecology. *World Archaeology* 2: 321–336.

Tringham, Ruth, Glenn Cooper, George Odell, Barbara Voytek, and Anne Whitman, 1974, Experimentation in the formation of edge damage: a new approach to lithic analysis. *Journal of Field Archaeology* 1: 171–196.

Turner, Victor, 1967, *The forest of symbols: aspects of Ndembu Ritual.* Ithaca, New York: Cornell University Press.

————, 1968, Mukanda: the politics of a non-political ritual. In *Local level politics,* Marc J. Swartz, ed., Chicago: Aldine, pp. 135–150.

Tyler, Stephen A., 1969, *Cognitive anthropology.* New York: Holt, Rinehart and Winston.

Tylor, Edward Burnett, 1871, *Primitive culture,* Vols. I and II. New York: Henry Holt.

————, 1889, On a method of investigating the development of institutions, applied to laws of marriage and descent. *Journal of the Royal Anthropological Institute* 18: 245–272.

V Valliant, G. C., 1931, Excavations at Ticoman, *Anthropological Papers of the American Museum of Natural History* 32.

Vayda, Andrew P., and Bonnie J. McCay, 1975, New directions in ecology and ecological anthropology. *Annual Review of Anthropology* 4: 293–306.

Vita-Finzi, C., and E. S. Higgs, 1970, Prehistoric economy in the Mount Carmel area of Palestine: site catchment analysis. *Proceedings of the Prehistoric Society* 36: 1–37.

Vogt, Evon Z., 1952, Water witching: an interpretation of ritual pattern in a rural American community. *Scientific Monthly* 75: 175–186.

Von Däniken, Erich, 1969, *Chariots of the Gods?* New York: Bantam Books.

W   Wallace, Anthony F. C., 1966, *Religion: an anthropological view.* New York: Random House.

Waring, A. J., Jr., and Preston Holder, 1945, A prehistoric ceremonial complex in the Southeastern United States. *American Anthropologist* 47: 1–34.

Washburn, Dorothy K., 1976, Symmetry classification of Pueblo ceramic designs. In *The structure of Chacoan society in the northern Southwest; investigations at the Salmon site: 1974–1975,* Cynthia Irwin-Williams, ed., Eastern New Mexico University, pp. 91–120.

Washburn, Sherwood L., 1951, The new physical anthropology. *Transactions of the New York Academy of Sciences,* Series II, 13: 298–304.

Watson, Patty Jo, 1973, The future of archeology in anthropology: cultural history and social science. In *Research and theory in current archeology,* Charles L. Redman, ed., New York: Wiley, pp. 113–124.

———, 1974, Flotation procedures used on Salts Cave sediments. In *Archeology of the Mammoth Cave area,* Patty Jo Watson, ed., New York: Academic Press, pp. 107–108.

———, 1976, In pursuit of prehistoric subsistence: a comparative account of some contemporary flotation techniques. *Midcontinental Journal of Archaeology* 1: 77–100.

———, 1977, Design analysis of painted pottery. *American Antiquity* 42: 381–393.

Watson, Patty Jo, Steven A. LeBlanc, and Charles L. Redman, 1971, *Explanation in archeology: an explicitly scientific approach.* New York: Columbia University Press.

Watson, Richard A., 1972, The "new archaeology" of the 1960's. *Antiquity* 46: 210–215.

Wauchope, Robert, 1966, Archaeological survey of northern Georgia with a test of some cultural hypotheses. *Society for American Archaeology,* Memoir No. 21.

Weberman, A. J., 1971, The art of garbage analysis. *Esquire* 5: 113–117.

Webster, David L., 1977, Warfare and the evolution of Maya civilization. In *The origins of Maya civilization,* Richard E. W. Adams, ed., Albuquerque, University of New Mexico Press, pp. 335–372.

Wedel, Waldo R., 1967, The council circles of central Kansas: were they solstice registers? *American Antiquity* 32: 54–63.

Weide, Margaret L., 1969, Seasonality of Pismo clam collecting at Ora-82. Los Angeles: *University of California Archaeological Survey Annual Report, 1968–1969,* vol. 11: 127–141.

Wells, Philip V., and Rainer Berger, 1967, Late Pleistocene history of coniferous woodland in the Mohave Desert. *Science* 155: 1640–1647.

Werner, Oswald, 1973, Structural anthropology. In *Main currents in cultural anthropology,* Raoul Naroll and Freida Naroll, eds., Englewood Cliffs, N.J.: Prentice-Hall.

Whallon, Robert E., Jr., 1968, Investigations of late prehistoric social organization in New York State. In *New perspectives in archeology,* Sally R. Binford and Lewis R. Binford, eds., Chicago: Aldine, pp. 223–244.

———, 1973, Spatial analysis of occupation floors I: application of dimensional analysis of variance. *American Antiquity* 38: 266–278.

———, 1974a, Working with the "new paradigm." *Reviews in Anthropology* 1: 25–33.

———, 1974b, Spatial analysis of occupation floors II: the application of nearest neighbor analysis. *American Antiquity* 39: 16–34.

Wheat, Joe Ben, 1972, The Olsen-Chubbuck site: a Paleo-Indian bison kill. *Society for American Archaeology,* Memoir No. 26.

Wheat, Margaret M., 1967, *Survival arts of the primitive Paiutes.* Reno: University of Nevada Press.

Wheeler, Mortimer, 1954, *Archaeology from the earth.* Oxford: Clarendon Press.

White, J. P., and David Hurst Thomas, 1972, What mean these stones? Ethnotaxonomic models and archaeological interpretations in the New Guinea Highlands. In *Models in Archaeology,* David L. Clarke, ed., London: Methuen, pp. 275–308.

White, Leslie A., 1949, *The science of culture.* New York: Grove Press.

———, 1959, *The evolution of culture.* New York: McGraw-Hill.

———, 1975, *The concept of cultural systems.* New York: Columbia University Press.

White, T. A., 1953, A method of calculating the dietary percentage of various food animals utilized by aboriginal peoples. *American Antiquity* 18: 396–398.

Wilken, Gene C., 1971, Food-producing systems available to the ancient Maya. *American Antiquity* 36: 432–448.

Willey, Gordon R., 1953, Prehistoric settlement patterns in the Virú Valley, Peru. *Bureau of American Ethnology,* Bulletin 155.

———, ed., 1956, Prehistoric settlement patterns in the New World. *Viking Fund Publications in Anthropology,* No. 23.

———, 1967, Alfred Vincent Kidder. *National Academy of Sciences Biographical Memoirs,* Vol. 39, New York: Columbia University Press, pp. 292–322.

———, 1968, One hundred years of American archaeology. In *One hundred years of anthropology,* J. O. Brew, ed., Cambridge, Mass.: Harvard University Press, pp. 29–53.

———, 1969, (Obituary of) James Alfred Ford, 1911–1968. *American Antiquity* 34: 62–71.

———, 1974. The Virú Valley settlement pattern study. In *Archaeological researches in retrospect,* Gordon R. Willey, ed., Cambridge, Mass.: Winthrop, pp. 149–178.

———, 1976, Mesoamerican civilization and the idea of transcendence. *Antiquity* 50: 205–215.

———, 1977, The rise of Maya civilization: a summary view. In *The origins of*

Maya civilization, Richard E. W. Adams, ed., Albuquerque: University of New Mexico Press, pp. 383–423.

Willey, Gordon R., and Philip Phillips, 1958, *Method and theory in American archaeology.* Chicago: University of Chicago Press.

Willey, Gordon R., and Jeremy A. Sabloff, 1974, *A history of American archaeology.* San Francisco: W. H. Freeman.

Williams, Leonard, David Hurst Thomas, and Robert Bettinger, 1973, Notions to numbers: Great Basin settlements as polythetic sets. In *Research and theory in current archeology,* Charles L. Redman, ed., New York: Wiley, pp. 215–237.

Williamson, Ray A., Howard J. Fisher, and Donnel O' Flynn, 1977, Anasazi solar observations. In *Native American astronomy,* Anthony F. Aveni, ed., Austin: University of Texas Press, pp. 203–218.

Willis, E. H. 1969, Radiocarbon dating. In *Science in archaeology,* Don Brothwell and Eric Higgs, eds., London: Thames and Hudson, pp. 46–57.

Wilmsen, Edwin N., 1973, Interaction, spacing behavior, and the organization of hunting bands. *Journal of Anthropological Research* 29: 1–31.

Wilson, David, 1974, *The new archaeology.* New York: Alfred A. Knopf.

Winlock, H. E., 1942, *Excavations at Deir el Bahri,* 1911–1931. New York: Macmillan.

Wissler, Clark, 1917, The new archaeology. *The American Museum Journal* 17: 100–101.

Wittfogel, Karl A., 1957, *Oriental despotism: a comparative study of total power.* New Haven: Yale University Press.

Wobst, H. Martin, 1974, Boundary conditions for Paleolithic social systems: a simulation approach. *American Antiquity* 39: 147–178.

Wolf, Eric R., 1962, *Sons of the shaking earth.* Chicago: University of Chicago Press.

———, ed., 1976, *The valley of Mexico: studies in pre-Hispanic ecology and society.* Albuquerque: University of New Mexico Press.

Woodbury, Richard B., 1954, Review of *A study of archeology* by Walter W. Taylor. *American Antiquity* 19: 292–296.

———, 1960, Nels. C. Nelson and chronological archaeology. *American Antiquity* 25: 400–401.

Wright, Gary A., 1971, Origins of food production in southwestern Asia: a survey of ideas. *Current Anthropology* 12: 447–477.

Wright, Henry T., 1977, Toward an explanation of the origin of the state. In *Explanation of prehistoric change,* James N. Hill, ed., Albuquerque, University of New Mexico, pp. 215–230.

Wynne, E. J., and Tylecote, R. F., 1958, An experimental investigation with primitive iron-smelting techniques. *Journal of Iron and Steel Institute* 190: 339–348.

Y Yarnell, Richard A., 1974, Intestinal contents of the Salts Cave mummy and analysis of the initial Salts Cave flotation series. In *Archaeology of the*

Mammoth Cave area, Patty Jo Watson, ed., New York: Academic Press, pp. 109–112.

Yellen, John E., 1977, *Archaeological approaches to the present: models for reconstructing the past.* New York: Academic Press.

Z Zarky, Alan, 1976, Statistical analysis of catchments at Ocós, Guatemala. In *The early Mesoamerican village,* Kent V. Flannery, ed., New York: Academic Press, pp. 117–130.

Ziegler, Alan C., 1973, Inference from prehistoric faunal remains. *Addison-Wesley Module in Anthropology,* No. 43.

Zimmerman, Larry J., 1977, Prehistoric locational behavior: a computer simulation. *Office of the State Archaeologist,* Report 10, Iowa City: University of Iowa.

Zubrow, Ezra B. W., 1971, Carrying capacity and dynamic equilibrium in the prehistoric Southwest. *American Antiquity* 36: 127–138.

————, 1976, Demographic anthropology: an introductory analysis. In *Demographic anthropology: quantitative approaches,* Ezra B. W. Zubrow, ed., Albuquerque: University of New Mexico Press, pp. 1–25.

Index